Texts and Traditions

A Source Reader
for the Study of Second Temple and Rabbinic Judaism

Texts and Traditions

A Source Reader
for the Study of Second Temple and Rabbinic Judaism

COMPILED, EDITED, AND INTRODUCED BY

Lawrence H. Schiffman

KTAV PUBLISHING HOUSE, INC.
1998

Library of Congress Cataloging-in-Publication Data

Texts and traditions: a source reader for the study of Second Temple
and rabbinic Judaism / compiled, edited, and introduced by
Lawrence H. Schiffman.
    p.   cm.
    Includes bibliographical references.
    ISBN 0-88125-434-7 (hc) ISBN 0-88125-455-X (pbk)
    1. Judaism—History—Post-exilic period, 586 B.C.–210 A.D.—
Sources. 2. Judaism—History—Talmudic period, 10–425—
Sources. 3. Jews—History—586 B.C.–70 A.D.—Sources.
4. Jews—History—70–638—Sources. 5. Greek literature—Jewish
authors—Translations into English. 6. Rabbinical literature—
Translations into English. I. Schiffman, Lawrence H.
BM176.T49 1997
296'.09'014—dc21   97-35800
                                                            CIP

Manufactured in the United States of America
KTAV Publishing House, 900 Jefferson Street, Hoboken NJ, 07030

To my wife Marlene

חכמא שגיא עמהא, ודלידיהא יאא.

She possesses abundant wisdom, so that whatever she does is proper.

Genesis Apocryphon 20:7–8

Contents

6.1 THE HASMONEAN DYNASTY

6.2 PHARISEES AND SADDUCEES

6.3 APOCALYPTICS AND ASCETICS

10.2 WRITTEN AND ORAL TORAH

10.3 TANNAITIC ACADEMIES

10.4 MIDRASH AND MISHNAH

10.5 HALAKHAH AND AGGADAH

10.6 THE REDACTION OF THE MISHNAH

10.7 OTHER TANNAITIC TEXTS

11.1 DECLINE OF HELLENISTIC JUDAISM

11.2 UNDER BYZANTINE CHRISTIANITY

11.3 BY THE RIVERS OF BABYLON

Preface

This sourcebook owes its creation to the earlier publication of my volume, *From Text to Tradition: A History of Second Temple and Rabbinic Judaism* (Ktav, 1991). Since its publication, the book has been read widely and has become a popular book in the American academic setting. From the beginning, it was clear that it would be necessary to place before readers a collection of primary materials which would provide the evidence for the general picture presented there. Further, such a volume was needed in order to shift the emphasis from generalization to the detailed investigation of the texts and traditions which are the heritage of this important period in the history of Judaism.

Many people have contributed to this volume. Bernard Scharfstein's conviction of the need for such an anthology and his constant encouragement certainly helped to bring this project to fruition. Translations are drawn in many instances from the works of other scholars, as noted in each case. I am particularly proud of the assistance I received from a number of my students in the Skirball Department of Hebrew and Judaic Studies at New York University. The initial selection of sources was compiled with the help of Shani Berrin, who translated many passages for this book, and my daughter, Hadassah Schiffman Levy. Dr. Richard White provided scanned and machine-readable material, going way beyond the call of duty. Adam Oded entered corrections, edited selections, and also suggested some selections, even translating a few. Andrew Gross completed the process of gaining permission for the use of the translations by others and prepared an index of sources. Because of his efforts, the references and bibliography are complete and accurate. Professor Yaakov Elman made helpful suggestions in the course of publication. Professor Erik Larson of Florida International University provided helpful advice regarding a few texts.

My work is consistently enriched by my colleagues at New York University, who help to provide the fertile environment in which I work. Professor Robert Chazan, Chairman of the Skirball Department for the past ten years, has always been totally supportive of the needs of my research. Professors Baruch A. Levine, Jeffrey Rubenstein, Daniel Fleming, Elliot Wolfson, and Frank Peters continue to influence my thinking in many ways and have never stinted with their advice. Dean Matthew Santirocco, Director of the Center for Ancient Studies at New York University, has been an inspiration for the interdisciplinary study of antiquity, and this perspective has surely contributed to this volume.

I have learned over more than a quarter of a century that no book can be completed by me without the conceptual and editorial assistance of my wife, Marlene, who dedicated so many nights and weekends to this project. This book, the difficulties of which I had not realized when I started, would never have been completed without her.

Acknowledgments

Excerpts from *Literature of the Synagogue,* eds. J. Heinemann, J. J. Petuchowski, copyright 1975 by Behrman, used by permission.

Excerpts from *A Manual of Palestinian Aramaic Texts* by J. A. Fitzmyer and D. J. Harrington, copyright 1978 by the Biblical Institute Press, used by permission.

Excerpts from *Rabbinic Instruction in Sasanian Babylonia* by D. M. Goodblatt, copyright 1975 by E. J. Brill, used by permission.

Excerpts from *The Dead Sea Scrolls Translated* by F. García Martínez, (trans. W. G. E. Watson), copyright 1994 by E. J. Brill, used by permission.

Excerpts from *Aphrahat and Judaism* by J. Neusner, copyright 1975 by E. J. Brill, used by permission.

Excerpts from *A History of the Jews in Babylonia* by J. Neusner, copyright 1975 by E. J. Brill, used by permission.

Excerpts from *The Elephantine Papyri in English* by B. Porten, copyright 1975 by E. J. Brill, used by permission.

Excerpts from *Jewish Inscriptions of Graeco-Roman Egypt* by W. Horbury and D. Noy, copyright 1992 by Cambridge University Press, used by permission.

Excerpts from *Writings of St. Justin Martyr* by T. B. Falls, copyright 1948 by The Catholic University Press of America, used by permission.

Excerpts from *The Old Testament Pseudepigrapha* by J. C. Charlesworth, copyright 1983, 1985 by James H. Charlesworth. Used by permission of Doubleday, a division of Bantam Doubleday Dell Publishing Group, Inc.

Excerpts from *Sefer ha-Qabbalah by Abraham ibn Daud* by G. D. Cohen, copyright 1967 by the Jewish Publication Society, used by permission.

Excerpts from *Post-Biblical Hebrew Literature, An Anthology* by B. Halper, copyright 1921 by the Jewish Publication Society, used by permission.

Excerpts from *Mekhilta de-Rabbi Ishmael* by J. Z. Lauterbach, copyright 1976 by the Jewish Publication Society, used by permission.

Excerpts from *Three Jewish Philosophers* by H. Lewy, et al., copyright 1965 by the Jewish Publication Society, used by permission.

Excerpts from *The Passover Haggadah* by N. Goldberg, copyright 1973 by Ktav Publishing Company, used by permission.

Excerpts from *The Tosefta* by J. Neusner, copyright 1977-80 by Ktav Publishing Company, used by permission.

Excerpts from *Chronicon Paschale 284-628 AD* translated with notes and introduction by M. Whitby and M. Whitby, copyright 1989 by Liverpool University Press, used by permission.

Excerpts from *Amulets and Magic Bowls* by J. Naveh and S. Shaked, copyright 1985 by Magnes Press, used by permission.

Excerpts from *Nazarene Jewish Christianity* by R. A. Pritz, copyright 1988 by Magnes Press, used by permission.

Excerpts from *Mystical Prayer in Ancient Judaism* by M. D. Swartz, copyright 1992 by J. C. B. Mohr, used by permission.

All New Testament excerpts from the Revised Standard Version of the Bible, copyright 1946, 1952, 1971 by the Division of Christian Education of the National Council of the Churches of Christ in the USA. Used by permission.

All Apocrypha excerpts from the Revised Standard Version Apocrypha, copyright 1957 by the Division of Christian Education of the National Council of the Churches of Christ in the USA. Used by permission.

Excerpts from the Mishnah from *The Mishnah* translated by H. Danby, copyright 1933 by Oxford University Press, used by permission.

Excerpts from *From Politics to Piety: The Emergence of Pharisaic Judaism* by J. Neusner, copyright 1973 by Jacob Neusner, used by permission.

1

Introduction

The study of Judaism in any period of its history is to a great extent the discovery of the unfolding of a written tradition through which Jewish thought and history were passed from one generation to the next. Accordingly, the historian of Judaism faces a special challenge in that the very sources which must be used to trace the complex history of Jewish civilization are, at the same time, not only witnesses to that history but reflections of it. This means that sources that might be looked upon as primary documents for the study of the history of the Jews and their civilization must be studied also as if they were secondary sources, analyzing and processing earlier material.

This is certainly the case concerning the sequence of documents which Jewish tradition regards as canonical—Bible, Mishnah, Midrash, and Talmud. But it is also the case with other non-canonical sources on which our study is based. Second Temple works, whether they be historiographical texts like Josephus and 1 and 2 Maccabees, or whether they be religious texts like the Dead Sea Scrolls, are themselves dependent and interconnected with the earlier biblical texts. Even inscriptions, usually assumed to reflect elements of the population not at the center of the development of the Jewish tradition, often reflect the same kind of intertextuality.

Any attempt to study the history and civilization of the Jews in Late Antiquity must therefore operate on a number of planes. It must investigate the various source materials available to us, determining for each the date, provenance (origin), purpose, and the prejudices of the author. Such an approach will allow the careful sifting of the vast array of source material available to us for our study.

In the volume that follows, we have assembled a large sampling of the primary sources which make possible an inquiry into the history of Judaism in Second Temple and Rabbinic times. These selections have been chosen so as to provide readers with the most important Jewish and non-Jewish sources for this period. The sources are arranged in an order that conforms to the discussion in *From Text to Tradition: A History of Second Temple and Rabbinic Judaism* (Ktav, 1991) and are to be read along with it. Each chapter (chapters 2–14) has been provided with a general introduction explaining the significance of each source within the context of the general study of the period. Short introductory remarks before each selection provide necessary background information or indicate the main points to be gathered from it. Explanatory notes have been provided to clarify difficult passages.

The process of selecting and preparing the texts involved numerous difficulties. In many cases new translations had to be prepared especially for this volume. In other cases minor revisions were introduced into existing English translations, used with permission, in order to provide consistency of style and presentation. Many were further edited in order to make the English less archaic, less dependent on the original language, or more intelligible to the average reader. Readers may encounter some inconsistencies of style between various selections included in this anthology, especially regarding matters of capitalization. This is because of the need to respect the decisions of the translators and copyright holders whose work has been included.

A particular problem was encountered in regard to translations from the Greek text of Josephus. In order to provide readable translations, a decision was made to revise, correct, and update the translation of William Whiston in light of the translations of H. St. J. Thackeray, Ralph Marcus, Allen Wikgren, and L. H. Feldman in the Loeb Classical Library. Our revisions did not involve a complete examination of the Greek text except where it seemed necessary in the course of our work. We therefore view the texts of Josephus presented here as a faithful representation of the contents of Josephus' work but make no claim to have produced a new translation.

While in some ways these sources, as they are here arranged, tell a story, they have really been gathered for an entirely different purpose. The main challenge to the student of the history of Judaism is to be able to assess the reliability of sources and to extract significant historical data from them. Here there will, of course, be differences of opinion regarding historicity and significance, but without the direct study of the primary sources, no original conclusions can ever be drawn. Indeed, the writing of history is an exercise, to a great extent, in textual study, and training students in the methods and approaches to reading these texts is therefore essential.

Investigation of the complex history of a group so diverse and variegated as the Jews of Late Antiquity cannot be undertaken without casting the widest possible net in order to collect a wide variety of literary, documentary, and archaeological sources. Since these sources are called upon to illuminate so many questions, each will have to be evaluated with methods appropriate to its linguistic character, literary genre, and reliability. Our quest will take us through the literary and archaeological remains of many centuries, ranging over a wide geographical area as well. Texts dating back to the First Temple period will be read, as will texts dating as late as the early Middle Ages. Texts will come from the great geographic centers of Jewish population in the Land of Israel or in the Diaspora and from smaller, outlying communities. Numerous original languages will also be featured. While Hebrew and Aramaic are the languages of biblical and Rabbinic literature and of the Dead Sea Scrolls, we will encounter Hellenistic Jewish literature in Greek, non-Jewish historical narratives in Latin, Greek, and Aramaic, and even some texts in Ethiopic or Slavonic. Among the materials which have been mined for this collection are biblical texts, Second Temple literature consisting of apocrypha, pseudepigrapha and Dead Sea Scrolls, Jewish historiographers such as Josephus and the authors of 1 and 2 Maccabees, Hellenistic authors like Philo Judeus, documentary texts from archaeological finds, for example, the Bar Kokhba letters, Rabbinic literature, that is, Mishnah, Talmud, and Midrash, liturgy, descriptions of the ancient world and histories written by Greco-Roman historians and early Church fathers, inscriptions in synagogues, dedicatory inscriptions, epitaphs on gravestones, Byzantine law codes, magical amulets and protective spells, even anti-Semitic literature of the Hellenistic world.

In many of these categories, we can compare how closely the writing of Jewish history parallels the Greek notion of history, the closest concept among the ancient philosophies of history to our own. And we will learn that, in spite of the great differences between ancient literature and our concept of history, much historical evidence can still be extracted from the ancient authors. The non-Jewish source material puts into larger context the Jewish nation as a political entity, and, with the destruction of the Jewish state, the Jews as a minority group living all over the ancient world. Evidence from Jewish inscriptions and dedicatory plaques gives an idea of the continuity of religious life even after the two revolts against the Romans. The final stage in this study explains the establishment of two principal centers of Jewry in Palestine and Babylonia where, even under difficult circumstances, the creativity of Jewish religious life and Torah study continued. We conclude by outlining the nature of the Judaism that emerged from this process and present a brief collection of sources regarding the continuity of Rabbinic tradition into the early Middle Ages.

Some may raise serious objections to the method used in this volume. We will be told that it is not legitimate to consider together such disparate materials as we have assembled here. Instead, it will be argued that each corpus of Jewish materials from Late Antiquity, perhaps each document, must be considered on its own, and that the conclusions of one may not be utilized to illumine the significance of another. We totally reject this nihilistic approach to the reconstruction of Jewish history, whether it be in ancient times or any other period. The claim that the various approaches to Judaism can only be understood by negating the complex interactions and interconnections between them amounts to a plea for oversimplification and a refusal to undertake the difficult task of reconstructing complex phenomena. Each and every source must be weighed and evaluated; each and every detail must be made to tell its own part of the story. The painstaking work of assembling an overall picture from these variegated materials will indeed justify itself if the final product recognizes that Jewish civilization in antiquity was itself a complicated and variegated phenomenon. In other words, the use of sources of differing dates, languages, and provenance to reconstruct an overarching picture of Second Temple and Rabbinic Judaism is a legitimate, in fact, compelling process provided that the final picture does not artificially harmonize the various stages in the chronology of ancient Judaism or the various religious manifestations of the Jewish people.

Perhaps the greatest accomplishment of the collective enterprise in which ancient Jewish authors and sages were involved was the ability to create a unified but diverse whole out of the many texts and traditions of Second Temple and Rabbinic Judaism. It will be our job, as critical and historical readers, to examine each in context in order to understand its place in the reconstruction of the history of Judaism in this formative period.

2

The Biblical Heritage

There is certainly no possibility of understanding the history of Judaism in postbiblical times without a firm grounding in the biblical heritage which has played so formative a role in shaping Jewish self-understanding for millennia. In Second Temple and talmudic times, the impact of the Bible was felt in virtually every area of Jewish life, thought, and literature. For this reason we must begin our study of Judaism in Late Antiquity with an examination of those aspects of the biblical past which had the greatest influence on the later history of Judaism. In this spirit we present here numerous relevant selections from the Hebrew Bible.

The selections in this chapter are intended to provide background for the study of the subsequent history of Judaism. Accordingly, the ancient Near Eastern materials which are so valuable for the study of the Hebrew Bible in context do not concern us here, since they were not part of the biblical heritage which later Judaism received, and which shaped all subsequent Jewish thought.

We first look at passages presenting the biblical view of the history of civilization and the rise of the Jewish people (text 2.1.1). Genesis 1 and 2 provide two different approaches to creation, both sharing the avoidance of mythological approaches familiar from the ancient Near Eastern creation myths. Genesis 1 makes man and woman full equals who are created together in one divine act. Genesis 3, the Garden of Eden story, sets out basic Jewish ideas of sin and forgiveness.

It is not long, in the biblical view, before the sin of Eve in the Garden is duplicated by humanity in general, so that the flood comes to destroy the earth, as described in Genesis 6–9 (text 2.2.1). Here we see further the biblical view on sin and its punishment, while at the same time being taught that humanity is all descended from the postdiluvian (after the flood) spread of people throughout the world. The Bible believed that civilization had started in one place and, therefore, that civilized man had common roots, hence, the brotherhood of humanity. This point is underscored in the Tower of Babel story in Genesis 11 (text 2.2.2).

Before leaving these accounts of the early history of humanity, it needs to be emphasized that the Bible here seeks to teach us principles of theology—good and evil, sin and atonement, and the brotherhood of humanity—not the material history or anthropology of the human race. The lessons of the Bible would become the fundamental points of later Jewish teaching on these areas, spun out in a variety of Second Temple texts, such as Jubilees and the *Genesis Apocryphon,* and later in such Rabbinic aggadic works as *Genesis Rabbah.*

Beginning with Abraham, the patriarch, we see the development of the Jewish people based on the covenant with God. God commands Abraham to leave his father's house and journey to the land of Canaan, where he is promised that he will become a great nation. In Genesis 22 (text 2.2.3), Abraham is tested as to his willingness to give his only son as a sacrifice for that covenant, a story which would become a fulcrum for later justifications of Jewish martyrdom and self-sacrifice. In its biblical context, however, it seeks to make the point that the God of Israel is unalterably opposed to human sacrifice. The rivalry of Jacob and Esau, depicted here in the extract from Genesis 27 (text 2.2.4), would serve for later Jews as the paradigm for that of the Jews and Rome, and, later, that of the Jews and Christendom.

These selections give us a sense of how Israel saw itself in its infancy, as a nation which had emerged out of the divine covenant and commitment of the patriarchs. In the next section, dealing with revelation and law, we see the Jewish people moving from existence as a group of wandering shepherds toward the national destiny of the Jewish people. It is the view of the Bible, and of later Judaism, that their destiny is fully carved out only with the acceptance of the Torah as binding and of the covenant as spelled out in God's revelation.

The passage from Exodus 1 (text 2.3.1) sets the stage, explaining how the children of Israel, the sons of Jacob and their clans, went down to Egypt where they were eventually enslaved. They were later to be redeemed after a series of divinely caused plagues, of which the last, the destruction of the firstborn sons of Egypt, is depicted in Exodus 12 (text 2.3.2). Exodus 13 and 14 (text 2.3 3) describe the Exodus itself, which is the basis for the festival of Passover celebrated from biblical times on.

Exodus 19–20 (text 2.3.4) describes the formative event in the history of Israel, the revelation at Sinai. Whatever may have actually happened there, the traditions passed on in the Bible and in later Jewish texts make the point that Israel as a people committed itself to the commandments of God, and God appeared to them in a theophany, declaring his commitment to them. This treaty, as it were, sealed the future of the Jewish people and served as the basis for the later development of Judaism. This event was celebrated by later Jews on the holiday of Shavuot. Part of this revelation, the Bible tells us, was Exodus 21–22 (text 2.3.5), primarily a code of civil law, with great similarity to the laws of the ancient Near East. Here scholars have noted the tendency of biblical law toward fairness and equality, features not part of the Mesopotamian parallels.

The biblical codes also set out the basics of the sacrificial system, as we find in Leviticus 1 (text 2.4.1). The manner in which the system of ritual purity and purification rituals fits into the daily life of the Jew, sanctifying even the physical aspects, is illustrated by Leviticus 13 dealing with the nexus of medicine and spiritual purity relating to skin diseases (text 2.4.2).

Chapters 28–29 of Numbers (text 2.4.3) constitute the sacrificial festival calendar of the Torah, specifying the festivals that continued to be the basic cycle of the year in Second Temple and Rabbinic Jewish practice. This remains the system of Jewish holidays observed until modern times.

We then present a few passages further elaborating on aspects of sacrifice and priesthood, and the rules pertaining to their qualifications and conduct in Leviticus 21 (text 2.4.4). In particular, these passages illustrate the sense of sanctity of the priests who were understood to represent Israel before God. With the destruction of the Second Temple in 70 C.E. this role would effectively be eclipsed, but it certainly was basic to Judaism up to that time.

The rise of prophecy was crucial to the development of Judaism, and it is in the Prophets that much of the theology and ethics inherent in the Torah is put forth and developed. Joshua may be seen as the first to take over for Moses, the prophet par excellence, and this succession is effectively the theme of Joshua 1 (text 2.5.1). Chapter 6 of Joshua (text 2.5.2) illustrates the military exploits of this soldier-prophet which themselves were conducted, in the biblical view, under God's direct influence. Indeed, the conquest is pictured here, as in the Torah, as a divinely inspired act.

Joshua was succeeded by the judges, also leaders combining prophecy with military exploits and political leadership. We select from Judges 4 the examples of Deborah and Jael, the women who aided Israel in battle against its enemies (text 2.5.3), and from 13 and 15 that of Samson, the enigmatic lone protector of the Israelites from Philistine depredations (text 2.5.4). The story of his complicated relationship with Delilah later became a popular theme in Western literature.

Following the judges, there comes the figure of Samuel (text 2.5.5), who was in a sense the last of the judges, making way for the monarchy. He anoints King Saul, who was chosen by God, though the notion of monarchy was not seen by the Book of Samuel as God's preferred form of government, although monarchy was mandated by Deuteronomy.

The mantle of prophecy is taken up in the period of the monarchy by Elijah about whose career we read in 1 Kings 18 (text 2.5.6). Thereafter we enter the period of the literary prophets, those who have left us books. Isaiah may be seen as the crown of literary prophecy, and so we examine several passages: chapter 1 is the basic statement of the book and its ideology (text 2.5.7), although it is in chapter 6 (text 2.5.8) that Isaiah receives his call to prophecy while at the Temple in Jerusalem. Isaiah 10–11 (text 2.5.9), which presents his view of the restoration of the Israelite monarchy, was later understood to foretell the messianic era.

Ezekiel 1 (text 2.5.10) presents the prophet's initial encounter with God, a prophecy which greatly influenced the rise of mystical speculation in Judaism. In chapter 37 (text 2.5.11), the prophet sees the resurrection of the dead as symbolizing the resurrection of the people of Israel after its destruction. This passage has become important for the later doctrine of resurrection at the end of the messianic era.

We turn finally to wisdom literature and psalmody. Proverbs 8 (text 2.6.1) is the *locus classicus* for the biblical understanding of wisdom, later identified as Torah, which influenced the conception of wisdom in later Judaism. The excerpts from Job 38 (text 2.6.2) give an indication of the debate over the existence of evil which takes place in this book. Ecclesiastes 3 (text 2.6.3) essentially poses the same question.

From the Psalms we present Psalm 1 (text 2.6.4), a wisdom type of psalm calling for righteousness. Psalm 130 (text 2.6.5) is a request for God's help in a time of distress. Finally, Psalm 150 sounds the clarion call of the book of Psalms (text 2.6.6), the obligation to praise God, which falls on all humanity.

In reading these selections for the purpose of studying Judaism in the Second Temple and Rabbinic periods, we need to look ahead to the many developments in Judaism which take their cue from the biblical heritage. We will see that the Bible was and remains the foundation stone of Judaism in all its manifestations. Biblical interpretation has always been one of the major sources of development of the Jewish tradition. Yet it is the interpretation of the Bible which separates the various Jewish groups we will encounter in Second Temple times, and which will eventually lie at the root of the Jewish-Christian schism.

2.1 HISTORICAL SKETCH

2.1.1 Genesis 1–3: The Creation[1]

In the biblical creation story, as opposed to the mythological accounts of the ancient Near East, there is no description of the birth of God; God is

---

1. All Hebrew Bible texts are from *Tanakh: A New Translation of the Holy Scriptures* (Philadelphia: The Jewish Publication Society, 1985).

assumed to have preexisted all creation. The earth with its sequence of days and seasons, as well as all plant and animal life, were created for the use of humankind with the one exception of the tree of life which was prohibited to Adam and Eve. By violating its prohibition, humans changed their destiny forever. This passage, with which the Torah begins, teaches the fundamental theology of the religion of Israel.

๛

1:1 When God began to create heaven and earth 2 the earth being unformed and void, with darkness over the surface of the deep and a wind from God sweeping over the water 3 God said, "Let there be light;" and there was light. 4 God saw that the light was good, and God separated the light from the darkness. 5 God called the light Day, and the darkness He called Night. And there was evening and there was morning, a first day.

6 God said, "Let there be an expanse in the midst of the water, that it may separate water from water." 7 God made the expanse, and it separated the water which was below the expanse from the water which was above the expanse. And it was so. 8 God called the expanse Sky. And there was evening and there was morning, a second day.

9 God said, "Let the water below the sky be gathered into one area, that the dry land may appear." And it was so. 10 God called the dry land Earth, and the gathering of waters He called Seas. And God saw that this was good. 11 And God said, "Let the earth sprout vegetation: seed-bearing plants, fruit trees of every kind on earth that bear fruit with the seed in it." And it was so. 12 The earth brought forth vegetation: seed-bearing plants of every kind, and trees of every kind bearing fruit with the seed in it. And God saw that this was good. 13 And there was evening and there was morning, a third day.

14 God said, "Let there be lights in the expanse of the sky to separate day from night; they shall serve as signs for the set times—the days and the years; 15 and they shall serve as lights in the expanse of the sky to shine upon the earth." And it was so. 16 God made the two great lights, the greater light to dominate the day and the lesser light to dominate the night, and the stars. 17 And God set them in the expanse of the sky to shine upon the earth, 18 to dominate the day and the night, and to separate light from darkness. And God saw that this was good. 19 And there was evening and there was morning, a fourth day.

20 God said, "Let the waters bring forth swarms of living creatures, and birds that fly above the earth across the expanse of the sky." 21 God created the great sea monsters, and all the living creatures of every kind that

creep, which the waters brought forth in swarms, and all the winged birds of every kind. And God saw that this was good. 22 God blessed them, saying, "Be fertile and increase, fill the waters in the seas, and let the birds increase on the earth." 23 And there was evening and there was morning, a fifth day.

24 God said, "Let the earth bring forth every kind of living creature: cattle, creeping things, and wild beasts of every kind." And it was so. 25 God made wild beasts of every kind and cattle of every kind, and all kinds of creeping things of the earth. And God saw that this was good. 26 And God said, "Let us make man in our image, after our likeness. They shall rule the fish of the sea, the birds of the sky, the cattle, the whole earth, and all the creeping things that creep on earth." 27 And God created man in His image, in the image of God He created him; male and female He created them. 28 God blessed them and God said to them, "Be fertile and increase, fill the earth and master it; and rule the fish of the sea, the birds of the sky, and all the living things that creep on earth."

29 God said, "See, I give you every seed-bearing plant that is upon all the earth, and every tree that has seed-bearing fruit; they shall be yours for food. 30 And to all the animals on land, to all the birds of the sky, and to everything that creeps on earth, in which there is the breath of life, [I give] all the green plants for food." And it was so. 31 And God saw all that He had made, and found it very good. And there was evening and there was morning, the sixth day.

2:1 The heaven and the earth were finished, and all their array. 2 On the seventh day[2] God finished the work that He had been doing, and He ceased[3] on the seventh day from all the work that He had done. 3 And God blessed the seventh day and declared it holy, because on it God ceased from all the work of creation that He had done.[4] 4 Such is the story of heaven and earth when they were created.

When the Lord God made earth and heaven 5 when no shrub of the field was yet on earth and no grasses of the field had yet sprouted, because the Lord God had not sent rain upon the earth and there was no man to till the soil, 6 but a flow would well up from the ground and water the whole surface of the earth, 7 the Lord God formed man from the dust

---

2. The Sabbath.

3. Or "rested."

4. Modern biblical scholars have understood this as the end of the first version of the creation story and have seen the verses that follow as presenting a second creation account. They have accordingly suggested that the text is a composite. Jewish tradition, however, saw Gen. 1:1–2:7 as representing a literary unity teaching diverse concepts of the nature of humanity and its relationship to God.

of the earth. He blew into his nostrils the breath of life, and man became a living being.

8 The Lord God planted a garden in Eden, in the east, and placed there the man whom He had formed. 9 And from the ground the Lord God caused to grow every tree that was pleasing to the sight and good for food, with the tree of life in the middle of the garden, and the tree of knowledge of good and bad. . . .

15 The Lord God took the man and placed him in the garden of Eden, to till it and tend it. 16 And the Lord God commanded the man, saying, "Of every tree of the garden you are free to eat; 17 but as for the tree of knowledge of good and bad, you must not eat of it; for as soon as you eat of it, you shall die."

18 The Lord God said, "It is not good for man to be alone; I will make a fitting helper for him." 19 And the Lord God formed out of the earth all the wild beasts and all the birds of the sky, and brought them to the man to see what he would call them; and whatever the man called each living creature, that would be its name. 20 And the man gave names to all the cattle and to the birds of the sky and to all the wild beasts; but for Adam no fitting helper was found. 21 So the Lord God cast a deep sleep upon the man; and, while he slept, He took one of his ribs and closed up the flesh at that spot. 22 And the Lord God fashioned the rib that He had taken from the man into a woman; and He brought her to the man. 23 Then the man said,

"This one at last
Is bone of my bones
And flesh of my flesh.
This one shall be called Woman,
For from man was she taken."

24 Hence a man leaves his father and mother and clings to his wife, so that they become one flesh.

25 The two of them were naked, the man and his wife, yet they felt no shame.

3:1 Now the serpent was the shrewdest of all the wild beasts that the Lord God had made. He said to the woman, "Did God really say: You shall not eat of any tree of the garden?" 2 The woman replied to the serpent, "We may eat of the fruit of the other trees of the garden. 3 It is only about fruit of the tree in the middle of the garden that God said: 'You shall not eat of it or touch it, lest you die.'" 4 And the serpent said to the woman, "You are not going to die, 5 but God knows that as soon as you eat of it your eyes will be opened and you will be like divine beings who know good and bad." 6 When the woman saw that the tree was good for eating and a delight to the eyes, and that the tree was desirable as a source of wisdom, she took of its fruit and ate. She also gave some to her husband, and he ate. 7 Then the eyes of both of them were opened and they perceived that they were naked; and they sewed together fig leaves and made themselves loincloths.

8 They heard the sound of the Lord God moving about in the garden at the breezy time of day; and the man and his wife hid from the Lord God among the trees of the garden. 9 The Lord God called out to the man and said to him, "Where are you?" 10 He replied, "I heard the sound of You in the garden, and I was afraid because I was naked, so I hid." 11 Then He asked, "Who told you that you were naked? Did you eat of the tree from which I had forbidden you to eat?" 12 The man said, "The woman You put at my side—she gave me of the tree, and I ate." 13 And the Lord God said to the woman, "What is this you have done!" The woman replied, "The serpent duped me, and I ate." 14 Then the Lord God said to the serpent,

> "Because you did this,
> More cursed shall you be
> Than all cattle
> And all the wild beasts:
> On your belly shall you crawl
> And dirt shall you eat
> All the days of your life.
> 15 I will put enmity
> Between you and the woman,
> And between your offspring and hers;
> They shall strike at your head,
> And you shall strike at their heel."

16 And to the woman He said,

> "I will make most severe
> Your pangs in childbearing;
> In pain shall you bear children.
> Yet your urge shall be for your husband,
> And he shall rule over you."

17 To Adam He said, "Because you did as your wife said and ate of the tree about which I commanded you, 'You shall not eat of it,'

> Cursed be the ground because of you;
> By toil shall you eat of it

All the days of your life:
18 Thorns and thistles shall it sprout for you.
But your food shall be the grasses of the field;
19 By the sweat of your brow
Shall you get bread to eat,
Until you return to the ground—
For from it you were taken.
For dust you are,
And to dust you shall return."

20 The man named his wife Eve, because she was the mother of all the living.[5] 21 And the Lord God made garments of skins for Adam and his wife, and clothed them.

22 And the Lord God said, "Now that the man has become like one of us, knowing good and bad, what if he should stretch out his hand and take also from the tree of life and eat, and live forever!" 23 So the Lord God banished him from the garden of Eden, to till the soil from which he was taken. 24 He drove the man out, and stationed east of the garden of Eden the cherubim and the fiery ever-turning sword, to guard the way to the tree of life.

2.2 A HISTORIOGRAPHY OF CIVILIZATION

2.2.1 Genesis 6–9: Noah and the Flood

In the flood narrative, God effectively creates the world over again from a small remnant of surviving people and animals, wiping out all the evil that had come to engulf the earth. When the flood waters recede, God promises never to destroy the earth in like manner again but establishes his covenant with Noah. The biblical flood story explains the flood as resulting from God's displeasure at human immorality, whereas the ancient Near Eastern versions saw the gods as capriciously annoyed at humanity.

᛭

6:5 The Lord saw how great was man's wickedness on earth, and how every plan devised by his mind was nothing but evil all the time. 6 And the Lord regretted that He had made man on earth, and His heart was saddened. 7 The Lord said, "I will blot out from the earth the men whom I created—men together with beasts, creeping things, and birds of the sky; for I regret that I made them." 8 But Noah found favor with the Lord.

---

5. Eve in Hebrew is *Ḥavvah*, and "living" is *ḥay*, both from the same Hebrew verbal root meaning "live."

9 This is the line of Noah—Noah was a righteous man; he was blameless in his age; Noah walked with God. 10 Noah begot three sons: Shem, Ham, and Japheth.

11 The earth became corrupt before God; the earth was filled with lawlessness. 12 When God saw how corrupt the earth was, for all flesh had corrupted its ways on earth, 13 God said to Noah, "I have decided to put an end to all flesh, for the earth is filled with lawlessness because of them: I am about to destroy them with the earth. 14 Make yourself an ark of gopher wood; make it an ark with compartments, and cover it inside and out with pitch. 15 This is how you shall make it: the length of the ark shall be three hundred cubits,[6] its width fifty cubits, and its height thirty cubits. 16 Make an opening for daylight in the ark, and terminate it within a cubit of the top. Put the entrance to the ark in its side; make it with bottom, second, and third decks.

17 "For My part, I am about to bring the Flood-waters upon the earth—to destroy all flesh under the sky in which there is breath of life; everything on earth shall perish. 18 But I will establish My covenant with you, and you shall enter the ark, with your sons, your wife, and your sons' wives. 19 And of all that lives, of all flesh, you shall take two of each into the ark to keep alive with you; they shall be male and female. 20 From birds of every kind, cattle of every kind, every kind of creeping thing on earth, two of each shall come to you to stay alive. 21 For your part, take of everything that is eaten and store it away, to serve as food for you and for them." 22 Noah did so; just as God commanded him, so he did.

7:1 Then the Lord said to Noah, "Go into the ark, with all your household, for you alone have I found righteous before Me in this generation. 2 Of every clean animal you shall take seven pairs, males and their mates, and of every animal that is not clean, two, a male and its mate; 3 of the birds of the sky also, seven pairs, male and female, to keep seed alive upon all the earth. 4 For in seven days' time I will make it rain upon the earth, forty days and forty nights, and I will blot out from the earth all existence that I created." 5 And Noah did just as the Lord commanded him.

6 Noah was six hundred years old when the Flood came, waters upon the earth. 7 Noah, with his sons, his wife, and his sons' wives, went into the ark because of the waters of the Flood. 8 Of the clean animals, of the animals that are not clean, of the birds, and of everything that creeps on the ground, 9 two of each, male and female, came to Noah into the ark, as God had commanded Noah. 10 And on the seventh day the waters of the Flood came upon the earth.

---

6. A cubit is about 18 inches.

11 In the six hundredth year of Noah's life, in the second month, on the seventeenth day of the month, on that day

All the fountains of the great deep burst apart,
And the floodgates of the sky broke open.

(12 The rain fell on the earth forty days and forty nights.) 13 That same day Noah and Noah's sons, Shem, Ham, and Japheth, went into the ark, with Noah's wife and the three wives of his sons—14 they and all beasts of every kind, all cattle of every kind, all creatures of every kind that creep on the earth, and all birds of every kind, every bird, every winged thing. 15 They came to Noah into the ark, two each of all flesh in which there was breath of life. 16 Thus they that entered comprised male and female of all flesh, as God had commanded him. And the Lord shut him in.

17 The Flood continued forty days on the earth, and the waters increased and raised the ark so that it rose above the earth. 18 The waters swelled and increased greatly upon the earth, and the ark drifted upon the waters. 19 When the waters had swelled much more upon the earth, all the highest mountains everywhere under the sky were covered. 20 Fifteen cubits higher did the waters swell, as the mountains were covered. 21 And all flesh that stirred on earth perished—birds, cattle, beasts, and all the things that swarmed upon the earth, and all mankind. 22 All in whose nostrils was the merest breath of life, all that was on dry land, died. 23 All existence on earth was blotted out—man, cattle, creeping things, and birds of the sky; they were blotted out from the earth. Only Noah was left, and those with him in the ark.

24 And when the waters had swelled on the earth one hundred and fifty days, 8:1 God remembered Noah and all the beasts and all the cattle that were with him in the ark, and God caused a wind to blow across the earth, and the waters subsided. 2 The fountains of the deep and the flood gates of the sky were stopped up, and the rain from the sky was held back; 3 the waters then receded steadily from the earth. At the end of one hundred and fifty days the waters diminished, 4 so that in the seventh month, on the seventeenth day of the month, the ark came to rest on the mountains of Ararat. 5 The waters went on diminishing until the tenth month; in the tenth month, on the first of the month, the tops of the mountains became visible.

6 At the end of forty days, Noah opened the window of the ark that he had made 7 and sent out the raven; it went to and fro until the waters had dried up from the earth. 8 Then he sent out the dove to see whether the waters had decreased from the surface of the ground. 9 But the dove could not find a resting place for its foot, and returned to him to the ark,

for there was water over all the earth. So putting out his hand, he took it into the ark with him. 10 He waited another seven days, and again sent out the dove from the ark. 11 The dove came back to him toward evening, and there in its bill was a plucked-off olive leaf! Then Noah knew that the waters had decreased on the earth. 12 He waited still another seven days and sent the dove forth; and it did not return to him any more.

13 In the six hundred and first year, in the first month,[7] on the first of the month, the waters began to dry from the earth; and when Noah removed the covering of the ark, he saw that the surface of the ground was drying. 14 And in the second month, on the twenty-seventh day of the month, the earth was dry.

15 God spoke to Noah, saying, 16 "Come out of the ark, together with your wife, your sons, and your sons' wives. 17 Bring out with you every living thing of all flesh that is with you: birds, animals, and everything that creeps on earth; and let them swarm on the earth and be fertile and increase on earth." 18 So Noah came out, together with his sons, his wife, and his sons' wives. 19 Every animal, every creeping thing, and every bird, everything that stirs on earth came out of the ark by families.

20 Then Noah built an altar to the Lord and, taking of every clean animal and of every clean bird, he offered burnt offerings on the altar. 21 The Lord smelled the pleasing odor, and the Lord said to Himself: "Never again will I doom the earth because of man, since the devisings of man's mind are evil from his youth; nor will I ever again destroy every living being, as I have done.

> 22 So long as the earth endures,
> Seedtime and harvest,
> Cold and heat,
> Summer and winter,
> Day and night
> Shall not cease."

9:1 God blessed Noah and his sons, and said to them, "Be fertile and increase, and fill the earth. 2 The fear and the dread of you shall be upon all the beasts of the earth and upon all the birds of the sky—everything with which the earth is astir—and upon all the fish of the sea; they are given into your hand. 3 Every creature that lives shall be yours to eat; as with the green grasses, I give you all these. 4 You must not, however, eat

---

7. Following a calendar in which the first lunar month, later known as Nisan, begins on about April 15.

flesh with its life-blood in it. 5 But for your own life-blood I will require a reckoning: I will require it of every beast; of man, too, will I require a reckoning for human life, of every man for that of his fellow man!

6 Whoever sheds the blood of man,
By man shall his blood be shed;
For in His image
Did God make man.

7 Be fertile, then, and increase; abound on the earth and increase on it."

8 And God said to Noah and to his sons with him, 9 "I now establish My covenant with you and your offspring to come, 10 and with every living thing that is with you—birds, cattle, and every wild beast as well—all that have come out of the ark, every living thing on earth. 11 I will maintain My covenant with you: never again shall all flesh be cut off by the waters of a flood, and never again shall there be a flood to destroy the earth."

12 God further said, "This is the sign that I set for the covenant between Me and you, and every living creature with you, for all ages to come. 13 I have set My bow in the clouds, and it shall serve as a sign of the covenant between Me and the earth. 14 When I bring clouds over the earth, and the bow appears in the clouds, 15 I will remember My covenant between Me and you and every living creature among all flesh, so that the waters shall never again become a flood to destroy all flesh.

2.2.2 Genesis 11: The Tower of Babel

Building the Tower of Babel represents an attempt by humanity to rebel against God's sovereignty. In answer to man's presumptuousness, God scattered the builders of the tower and generated the many different tongues spoken all over the earth. Nevertheless, this story assumes that humanity was at one time all united. This is in accord with the biblical view that all civilization had arisen in the Fertile crescent from which it had later been spread to the rest of the world.

꿎

11:1 Everyone on earth had the same language and the same words. 2 And as they migrated from the east, they came upon a valley in the land of Shinar and settled there. 3 They said to one another, "Come, let us make bricks and burn them hard."—Brick served them as stone, and bitumen served them as mortar. 4 And they said, "Come, let us build us a city, and a tower with its top in the sky, to make a name for ourselves; else we shall be scattered all over the world." 5 The Lord came down to look at the city and tower that man had built, 6 and the Lord said, "If, as one people with one language for all, this is how they have begun to act, then nothing that they may propose to do will be out of their reach. 7 Let us, then, go down and confound their speech there, so that they shall not understand one another's speech." 8 Thus the Lord scattered them from there over the face of the whole earth; and they stopped building the city. 9 That is why it was called Babel, because there the Lord confounded the speech of the whole earth; and from there the Lord scattered them over the face of the whole earth.

2.2.3 Genesis 22: The Sacrifice of Isaac

The focus of the Bible now narrows to the patriarch, Abraham, who by his devotion and obedience to God, merits the founding of a great nation. God's command to Abraham to sacrifice his son Isaac was a major test of his faith. For the Bible and later Jewish tradition, it was also the classic condemnation of human sacrifice.

1 Some time afterward, God put Abraham to the test. He said to him, "Abraham," and he answered, "Here I am." 2 And He said, "Take your son, your favored one, Isaac, whom you love, and go to the land of Moriah, and offer him there as a burnt offering on one of the heights that I will point out to you." 3 So early the next morning, Abraham saddled his ass and took with him two of his servants and his son Isaac. He split the wood for the burnt offering, and he set out for the place of which God had told him. 4 On the third day Abraham looked up and saw the place from afar. 5 Then Abraham said to his servants, "you stay here with the ass. The boy and I will go up there; we will worship and we will return to you."

6 Abraham took the wood for the burnt offering and put it on his son Isaac. He himself took the firestone and the knife; and the two walked off together. 7 Then Isaac said to his father Abraham, "Father!" And he answered, "Yes, my son." And he said, "Here are the firestone and the wood; but where is the sheep for the burnt offering?" 8 And Abraham said, "God will see to the sheep for His burnt offering, my son." And the two of them walked on together.

9 They arrived at the place of which God had told him. Abraham built an altar there; he laid out the wood; he bound his son Isaac; he laid him on the altar, on top of the wood. 10 And Abraham picked up the knife to

slay his son. 11 Then an angel of the Lord called to him from heaven: "Abraham! Abraham!" And he answered, "Here I am." 12 And he said, "Do not raise your hand against the boy, or do anything to him. For now I know that you fear God, since you have not withheld your son, your favored one, from Me." 13 When Abraham looked up, his eye fell upon a ram, caught in the thicket by its horns. So Abraham went and took the ram and offered it up as a burnt offering in place of his son. 14 And Abraham named that site Adonai-yireh,[8] whence the present saying, "On the mount of the Lord there is vision."

15 The angel of the Lord called to Abraham a second time from heaven, 16 and said, "By Myself I swear, the Lord declares: Because you have done this and have not withheld your son, your favored one, 17 I will bestow my blessing upon you and make your descendants as numerous as the stars of heaven and the sands on the seashore; and your descendants shall seize the gates of their foes. 18 All the nations of the earth shall bless themselves by your descendants, because you have obeyed My command." 19 Abraham then returned to his servants, and they departed together for Beer-sheba; and Abraham stayed in Beer-sheba.

2.2.4 Genesis 27: The Rivalry of Jacob and Esau

Central to the biblical account is a process of elimination in which one child in each patriarchal generation is to carry on the developing Israelite tradition. The rivalry of Jacob and Esau sets the stage for Jacob's emerging as that bearer of tradition. For later Judaism, Esau (Edom) would symbolize Rome and then Christianity, not just rivals but often bitter enemies of the Jewish people.

ﭏ

27:1 When Isaac was old and his eyes were too dim to see, he called his older son Esau and said to him, "My son." He answered, "Here I am." 2 And he said, "I am old now, and I do not know how soon I may die. 3 Take your gear, your quiver and bow, and go out into the open and hunt me some game. 4 Then prepare a dish for me such as I like, and bring it to me to eat, so that I may give you my innermost blessing before I die."

5 Rebekah had been listening as Isaac spoke to his son Esau. When Esau had gone out into the open to hunt game to bring home, 6 Rebekah said to her son Jacob, "I overheard your father speaking to your brother Esau, saying, 7 'Bring me some game and prepare a dish for me to eat, that I may bless you, with the Lord's approval, before I die.' 8 Now, my son,

---

8. "The Lord will see;" cf. v. 8.

listen carefully as I instruct you. 9 Go to the flock and fetch me two choice kids, and I will make of them a dish for your father, such as he likes. 10 Then take it to your father to eat, in order that he may bless you before he dies." 11 Jacob answered his mother Rebekah, "But my brother Esau is a hairy man and I am smooth-skinned. 12 If my father touches me, I shall appear to him as a trickster and bring upon myself a curse, not a blessing." 13 But his mother said to him, "Your curse, my son, be upon me! Just do as I say and go fetch them for me."

14 He got them and brought them to his mother, and his mother prepared a dish such as his father liked. 15 Rebekah then took the best clothes of her older son Esau, which were there in the house, and had her younger son Jacob put them on; 16 and she covered his hands and the hairless part of his neck with the skins of the kids. 17 Then she put in the hands of her son Jacob the dish and the bread that she had prepared.

18 He went to his father and said, "Father." And he said, "Yes, which of my sons are you?" 19 Jacob said to his father, "I am Esau, your first-born; I have done as you told me. Pray sit up and eat of my game, that you may give me your innermost blessing." 20 Isaac said to his son, "How did you succeed so quickly, my son?" And he said, "Because the Lord your God granted me good fortune." 21 Isaac said to Jacob, "Come closer that I may feel you, my son—whether you are really my son Esau or not." 22 So Jacob drew close to his father Isaac, who felt him and wondered. "The voice is the voice of Jacob, yet the hands are the hands of Esau." 23 He did not recognize him, because his hands were hairy like those of his brother Esau; and so he blessed him.

24 He asked, "Are you really my son Esau?" And when he said, "I am," 25 he said, "Serve me and let me eat of my son's game that I may give you my innermost blessing." So he served him and he ate, and he brought him wine and he drank. 26 Then his father Isaac said to him, "Come close and kiss me, my son"; 27 and he went up and kissed him. And he smelled his clothes and he blessed him, saying, "Ah, the smell of my son is like the smell of the fields that the Lord has blessed.

28 "May God give you
Of the dew of heaven and the fat of the earth,
Abundance of new grain and wine.
29 Let peoples serve you,
And nations bow to you;
Be master over your brothers,
And let your mother's sons bow to you.
Cursed be they who curse you,
Blessed they who bless you."

30 No sooner had Jacob left the presence of his father Isaac—after Isaac had finished blessing Jacob—than his brother Esau came back from his hunt. 31 He too prepared a dish and brought it to his father. And he said to his father, "Let my father sit up and eat of his son's game, so that you may give me your innermost blessing." 32 His father Isaac said to him, "Who are you?" And he said, "I am your son, Esau, your first-born!" 33 Isaac was seized with very violent trembling. "Who was it then," he demanded, "that hunted game and brought it to me? Moreover, I ate of it before you came, and I blessed him; now he must remain blessed!" 34 When Esau heard his father's words, he burst into wild and bitter sobbing, and said to his father, "Bless me too, Father!" 35 But he answered, "Your brother came with guile and took away your blessing." 36 [Esau] said, "Was he, then, named Jacob that he might supplant me these two times? First he took away my birthright and now he has taken away my blessing!" And he added, "Have you not reserved a blessing for me?" 37 Isaac answered, saying to Esau, "But I have made him master over you: I have given him all his brothers for servants, and sustained him with grain and wine. What, then, can I still do for you, my son?" 38 And Esau said to his father, "Have you but one blessing, Father? Bless me too, Father!" And Esau wept aloud. 39 And his father Isaac answered, saying to him,

"See, your abode shall enjoy the fat of the earth
And the dew of heaven above.
40 Yet by your sword you shall live,
And you shall serve your brother;
But when you grow restive,
You shall break his yoke from your neck."

41 Now Esau harbored a grudge against Jacob because of the blessing which his father had given him, and Esau said to himself, "Let but the mourning period of my father come, and I will kill my brother Jacob." 42 When the words of her older son Esau were reported to Rebekah, she sent for her younger son Jacob and said to him, "Your brother Esau is consoling himself by planning to kill you. 43 Now, my son, listen to me. Flee at once to Haran, to my brother Laban. 44 Stay with him a while, until your brother's fury subsides—45 until your brother's anger against you subsides—and he forgets what you have done to him. Then I will fetch you from there. Let me not lose you both in one day!"

2.3 REVELATION AND LAW

2.3.1 Exodus 1: Descent of Israel to Egypt

The sons of Jacob came to Egypt during a famine in Canaan and remained until they became a numerous element in the population. The king of Egypt, afraid of their might, enslaved them and set them to work building two cities. The Bible often urges sympathy for the downtrodden by reminding the people: "You yourselves were slaves in the land of Egypt."

༃

1: 1 These are the names of the sons of Israel who came to Egypt with Jacob, each coming with his household: 2 Reuben, Simeon, Levi, and Judah; 3 Issachar, Zebulun, and Benjamin; 4 Dan and Naphtali, Gad and Asher. 5 The total number of persons that were of Jacob's issue came to seventy, Joseph being already in Egypt. 6 Joseph died, and all his brothers, and all that generation. 7 But the Israelites were fertile and prolific; they multiplied and increased very greatly, so that the land was filled with them. 8 A new king arose over Egypt who did not know Joseph. 9 And he said to his people, "Look, the Israelite people are much too numerous for us. 10 Let us deal shrewdly with them, so that they may not increase; otherwise in the event of war they may join our enemies in fighting against us." 11 So they set taskmasters over them to oppress them with forced labor; and they built garrison cities[9] for Pharaoh: Pithom and Raamses. 12 But the more they were oppressed, the more they increased and spread out, so that the [Egyptians] came to dread the Israelites.

13 The Egyptians ruthlessly imposed upon the Israelites the various labors that they made them perform. Ruthlessly they made life bitter for them with harsh labor at mortar and bricks and with all sorts of tasks in the field.

2.3.2 Exodus 12: The Night of the Exodus

Moses was chosen by God to plead before Pharaoh for the release of the slaves, first for a short period to worship God in the wilderness, then to be freed altogether. God sent Moses and Aaron, his brother, to announce nine plagues which attacked the Egyptian people and their animals, but even these plagues, designed to demonstrate the power of the God of Israel, did not persuade Pharaoh to let the Israelites go. The final plague was so harsh that it

---

9. Others "store cities."

caused Pharaoh to order the Israelite departure in great haste. The departure of
the Israelites was celebrated in the holiday of Passover.

🌾

29 In the middle of the night the Lord struck down all the first-born in
the land of Egypt, from the first-born of Pharaoh who sat on the throne
to the first-born of the captive who was in the dungeon, and all the first
born of the cattle. 30 And Pharaoh arose in the night, with all his courtiers and all the Egyptians—because there was a loud cry in Egypt; for
there was no house where there was not someone dead. 31 He summoned
Moses and Aaron in the night and said, "Up, depart from among my people, you and the Israelites with you! Go, worship the Lord as you said!
32 Take also your flocks and your herds, as you said, and begone! And
may you bring a blessing upon me also!"

33 The Egyptians urged the people on, impatient to have them leave
the country, for they said, "We shall all be dead." 34 So the people took
their dough before it was leavened, their kneading bowls wrapped in
their cloaks upon their shoulders. 35 The Israelites had done Moses' bidding and borrowed from the Egyptians objects of silver and gold, and
clothing. 36 And the Lord had disposed the Egyptians favorably toward
the people, and they let them have their request; thus they stripped the
Egyptians.

37 The Israelites journeyed from Rameses to Succoth, about six hundred thousand men on foot, aside from children. 38 Moreover, a mixed
multitude went up with them, and very much livestock, both flocks and
herds. 39 And they baked unleavened cakes[10] of the dough that they had
taken out of Egypt, for it was not leavened, since they had been driven
out of Egypt and could not delay; nor had they prepared any provisions
for themselves.

40 The length of time that the Israelites lived in Egypt was four hundred and thirty years; 41 at the end of the four hundred and thirtieth
year, to the very day, all the ranks of the Lord departed from the land of
Egypt. 42 That was for the Lord a night of vigil to bring them out of the
land of Egypt; that same night is the Lord's, one of vigil for all the children of Israel throughout the ages.

2.3.3 Exodus 13–14: The Splitting of the Sea

God continued to watch over Israel, pursued by the Egyptian king who had
a change of heart over his allowing the slaves to leave. His forces overtook the

---

10. Matzah.

Israelites at the Sea of Reeds where they were trapped between the Egyptian army and the Sea. Only a miracle was able to save them. Thus, they learned the lesson of reliance on God.

❧

13:17 Now when Pharaoh let the people go, God did not lead them by way of the land of the Philistines,[11] although it was nearer; for God said, "The people may have a change of heart when they see war, and return to Egypt." 18 So God led the people roundabout, by way of the wilderness at the Sea of Reeds.

Now the Israelites went up armed out of the land of Egypt. 19 And Moses took with him the bones of Joseph, who had exacted an oath from the children of Israel, saying, "God will be sure to take notice of you: then you shall carry up my bones from here with you."

20 They set out from Succoth, and encamped at Etham, at the edge of the wilderness. 21 The Lord went before them in a pillar of cloud by day, to guide them along the way, and in a pillar of fire by night, to give them light, that they might travel day and night. 22 The pillar of cloud by day and the pillar of fire by night did not depart from before the people.

14:1 The Lord said to Moses: 2 Tell the Israelites to turn back and encamp before Pi-hahiroth, between Migdol and the sea, before Baal Zephon; you shall encamp facing it, by the sea. 3 Pharaoh will say of the Israelites, "They are astray in the land; the wilderness has closed in on them." 4 Then I will stiffen Pharaoh's heart and he will pursue them, that I may gain glory through Pharaoh and all his host; and the Egyptians shall know that I am the Lord.

And they did so.

5 When the king of Egypt was told that the people had fled, Pharaoh and his courtiers had a change of heart about the people and said, "What is this we have done, releasing Israel from our service?" 6 He ordered his chariot and took his men with him; 7 he took six hundred of his picked chariots, and the rest of the chariots of Egypt, with officers in all of them. 8 The Lord stiffened the heart of Pharaoh king of Egypt, and he gave chase to the Israelites. As the Israelites were departing defiantly, boldly, 9 the Egyptians gave chase to them, and all the chariot horses of Pharaoh, his horsemen, and his warriors overtook them encamped by the sea, near Pi-hahiroth, before Baal-zephon.

10 As Pharaoh drew near, the Israelites caught sight of the Egyptians advancing upon them. Greatly frightened, the Israelites cried out to the

---

11. The present-day Gaza Strip.

Lord. 11 And they said to Moses, "Was it for want of graves in Egypt that you brought us to die in the wilderness? What have you done to us, taking us out of Egypt? 12 Is this not the very thing we told you in Egypt, saying, 'Let us be, and we will serve the Egyptians, for it is better for us to serve the Egyptians than to die in the wilderness'?" 13 But Moses said to the people, "Have no fear! Stand by, and witness the deliverance which the Lord will work for you today; for the Egyptians whom you see today you will never see again. 14 The Lord will battle for you; you hold your peace!"

15 Then the Lord said to Moses, "Why do you cry out to Me? Tell the Israelites to go forward. 16 And you lift up your rod and hold out your arm over the sea and split it, so that the Israelites may march into the sea on dry ground. 17 And I will stiffen the hearts of the Egyptians so that they go in after them; and I will gain glory through Pharaoh and all his warriors, his chariots and his horsemen. 18 Let the Egyptians know that I am Lord, when I gain glory through Pharaoh, his chariots, and his horsemen."

19 The angel of God, who had been going ahead of the Israelite army, now moved and followed behind them; and the pillar of cloud shifted from in front of them and took up a place behind them, 20 and it came between the army of the Egyptians and the army of Israel. Thus there was the cloud with the darkness, and it cast a spell upon the night, so that the one could not come near the other all through the night.

21 Then Moses held out his arm over the sea and the Lord drove back the sea with a strong east wind all that night, and turned the sea into dry ground. The waters were split, 22 and the Israelites went into the sea on dry ground, the waters forming a wall for them on their right and on their left. 23 The Egyptians came in pursuit after them into the sea, all of Pharaoh's horses, chariots, and horsemen. 24 At the morning watch, the Lord looked down upon the Egyptian army from a pillar of fire and cloud, and threw the Egyptian army into panic. 25 He locked the wheels of their chariots so that they moved forward with difficulty. And the Egyptians said, "Let us flee from the Israelites, for the Lord is fighting for them against Egypt."

26 Then the Lord said to Moses, "Hold out your arm over the sea, that the waters may come back upon the Egyptians and upon their chariots and upon their horsemen." 27 Moses held out his arm over the sea, and at daybreak the sea returned to its normal state, and the Egyptians fled at its approach. But the Lord hurled the Egyptians into the sea. 28 The waters turned back and covered the chariots and the horsemen—Pha-

raoh's entire army that followed them into the sea; not one of them remained. 29 But the Israelites had marched through the sea on dry ground, the waters forming a wall for them on their right and on their left.

30 Thus the Lord delivered Israel that day from the Egyptians. Israel saw the Egyptians dead on the shore of the sea. 31 And when Israel saw the wondrous power which the Lord had wielded against the Egyptians, the people feared the Lord; they had faith in the Lord and His servant Moses.

2.3.4 Exodus 19–20: The Revelation at Sinai

The great deliverance from Egypt forged the numerous descendants of the sons of Jacob into a unified nation. Their national destiny was revealed during the revelation of the Torah which contained the moral, ethical, and ritual codes that would sustain them in the desert and guide them once they reached the Promised Land. Later Jewish tradition understood the Sinai revelation as including the entire Torah. Chapter 20 contains the Ten Commandments which the Rabbis noted were divided into the first five (verses 1–11) which deal with the relationship between humanity and God, and the second five (verses 12–14) which deal with human interrelationships.

19:18 Now Mount Sinai was all in smoke, for the Lord had come down upon it in fire; the smoke rose like the smoke of a kiln, and the whole mountain trembled violently. 19 The blare of the horn grew louder and louder. As Moses spoke, God answered him in thunder. 20 The Lord came down upon Mount Sinai, on the top of the mountain, and the Lord called Moses to the top of the mountain and Moses went up. 21 The Lord said to Moses, "Go down, warn the people not to break through to the Lord to gaze, lest many of them perish. 22 The priests also, who come near the Lord, must stay pure, lest the Lord break out against them." 23 But Moses said to the Lord, "The people cannot come up to Mount Sinai, for You warned us saying, 'Set bounds about the mountain and sanctify it.'" 24 So the Lord said to him, "Go down, and come back together with Aaron; but let not the priests or the people break through to come up to the Lord, lest He break out against them." 25 And Moses went down to the people and spoke to them.

20:1 God spoke all these words, saying:

2 I the Lord am your God who brought you out of the land of Egypt, the house of bondage: 3 You shall have no other gods besides Me.

4 You shall not make for yourself a sculptured image, or any likeness of what is in the heavens above, or on the earth below, or in the waters under the earth. 5 You shall not bow down to them or serve them. For I the Lord Your God am an impassioned God, visiting the guilt of the parents upon the children, upon the third and upon the fourth generations of those who reject Me, 6 but showing kindness to the thousandth generation of those who love Me and keep My commandments.

7 You shall not swear falsely by the name of the Lord your God; for the Lord will not clear one who swears falsely by His name.

8 Remember the sabbath day and keep it holy. 9 Six days you shall labor and do all your work, 10 but the seventh day is a sabbath of the Lord your God: you shall not do any work—you, your son or daughter, your male or female slave, or your cattle, or the stranger who is within your settlements. 11 For in six days the Lord made heaven and earth and sea, and all that is in them, and He rested on the seventh day; therefore the Lord blessed the sabbath day and hallowed it.

12 Honor your father and your mother, that you may long endure on the land that the Lord Your God is assigning to you.

13 You shall not murder.

You shall not commit adultery.

You shall not steal.

You shall not bear false witness against your neighbor.

14 You shall not covet your neighbor's house: you shall not covet your neighbor's wife, or his male or female slave, or his ox or his ass, or anything that is your neighbor's.

15 All the people witnessed the thunder and lightning, the blare of the horn and the mountain smoking; and when the people saw it, they fell back and stood at a distance. 16 "You speak to us," they said to Moses, "and we will obey; but let not God speak to us, lest we die." 17 Moses answered the people, "Be not afraid; for God has come only in order to test you, and in order that the fear of Him may be ever with you, so that you do not go astray." 18 So the people remained at a distance, while Moses approached the thick cloud where God was.

2.3.5 Exodus 21–22: The Code of Civil Law

The Bible does not distinguish between civil and religious law—all are God's commandments. In this section, laws applying to the orderly functioning of society are set forth. For the most heinous crimes of murder and kidnapping, a person may be put to death. But for personal injury, destruction of property, or theft, monetary compensation is mandated. Similar laws area also found in ancient Mesopotamian codes of law like the Code of Hammurabi, but biblical law greatly mitigates the degree of punishment and, in the view of most commentators, substitutes financial penalties for corporal punishment in cases of injury.

꘠

21:1 These are the rules that you shall set before them:

12 He who fatally strikes a man shall be put to death. 13 If he did not do it by design, but it came about by an act of God, I will assign you a place to which he can flee.

14 When a man schemes against another and kills him treacherously, you shall take him from My very altar[12] to be put to death.

15 He who strikes his father or his mother shall be put to death.

16 He who kidnaps a man—whether he has sold him or is still holding him—shall be put to death.

17 He who insults[13] his father or his mother shall be put to death.

18 When men quarrel and one strikes the other with stone or fist, and he does not die but has to take to his bed—19 if he then gets up and walks outdoors upon his staff, the assailant shall go unpunished, except that he must pay for his idleness and his cure.

20 When a man strikes his slave, male or female, with a rod, and he dies there and then, he must be avenged. 21 But if he survives a day or two, he is not to be avenged, since he is the other's property.

22 When men fight, and one of them pushes a pregnant woman and a miscarriage results, but no other damage ensues, the one responsible shall be fined according as the woman's husband may exact from him, the payment to be based on reckoning. 23 But if other damage ensues, the penalty shall be life for life, 24 eye for eye, tooth for tooth, hand for hand, foot for foot, 25 burn for burn, wound for wound, bruise for bruise.[14]

26 When a man strikes the eye of his slave, male or female, and destroys it, he shall let him go free on account of his eye. 27 If he knocks out the tooth of his slave, male or female, he shall let him go free on account of his tooth. . . .

22:6 When a man gives money or goods to another for safekeeping, and they are stolen from the man's house—if the thief is caught, he shall

---

12. Even if he seeks sanctuary in the Temple.

13. Others, "curses."

14. Most commentators take this to refer to monetary compensation in accord with the value of the injury. Some modern scholars, however, believe that biblical law, like ancient Near Eastern codes, required the physical application of equivalent punishments, in accord with the literal meaning of the text.

pay double; 7 if the thief is not caught, the owner of the house shall depose before God[15] that he has not laid hands on the other's property. 8 In all charges of misappropriation—pertaining to an ox, an ass, a sheep, a garment, or any other loss, whereof one party alleges, "This is it"[16]—the case of both parties shall come before God: he whom God declares guilty shall pay double to the other.

9 When a man gives to another an ass, an ox, a sheep or any other animal to guard, and it dies or is injured or is carried off, with no witness about, 10 an oath before the Lord shall decide between the two of them that the one has not laid hands on the property of the other; the owner must acquiesce, and no restitution shall be made. 11 But if [the animal] was stolen from him, he shall make restitution to its owner. 12 If it was torn by beasts, he shall bring it as evidence; he need not replace what has been torn by beasts.

13 When a man borrows [an animal] from another and it dies or is injured, its owner not being with it, he must make restitution. 14 If its owner was with it, no restitution need be made; but if it was hired, he is entitled to the hire. . . .

19 Whoever sacrifices to a god other than the Lord alone shall be proscribed.

20 You shall not wrong a stranger or oppress him, for you were strangers in the land of Egypt.

21 You shall not ill-treat any widow or orphan. 22 If you do mistreat them, I will heed their outcry as soon as they cry out to Me, 23 and My anger shall blaze forth and I will put you to the sword, and your own wives shall become widows and your children orphans. . . .

2.4 SACRIFICE AND PRIESTHOOD

2.4.1 Leviticus 1: The Sacrificial System

Biblical law prescribed a variety of sacrifices for different purposes: festivals, atonement rituals, family celebrations. Leviticus systematically set out the specific procedures for the offering of each kind of sacrifice in its various forms. These complex rituals were later practiced in both the First and Second Temples in Jerusalem.

---

15. Or, "the judges."
16. Claiming that he is not responsible for the damage or loss.

꽃

1:1 The Lord called to Moses and spoke to him from the Tent of Meeting,[17] saying: 2 Speak to the Israelite people, and say to them:

When any of you presents an offering of cattle to the Lord, he shall choose his offering from the herd or from the flock. 3 If his offering is a burnt offering from the herd, he shall make his offering a male without blemish. He shall bring it to the entrance of the Tent of Meeting, for acceptance in his behalf before the Lord. 4 He shall lay his hand upon the head of the burnt offering, that it may be acceptable in his behalf, in expiation for him. 5 The bull shall be slaughtered before the Lord; and Aaron's sons, the priests, shall offer the blood, dashing the blood against all sides of the altar which is at the entrance of the Tent of Meeting. 6 The burnt offering shall be flayed and cut up into sections. 7 The sons of Aaron the priest shall put fire on the altar and lay out wood upon the fire; 8 and Aaron's sons, the priests, shall lay out the sections, with the head and the suet, on the wood that is on the fire upon the altar. 9 Its entrails and legs shall be washed with water, and the priest shall turn the whole into smoke on the altar as a burnt offering, an offering by fire of pleasing odor to the Lord.

10 If his offering for a burnt offering is from the flock, of sheep or of goats, he shall make his offering a male without blemish. 11 It shall be slaughtered before the Lord on the north side of the altar, and Aaron's sons, the priests, shall dash its blood against all sides of the altar. 12 When it has been cut up into sections, the priest shall lay them out, with the head and the suet, on the wood that is on the fire upon the altar. 13 The entrails and the legs shall be washed with water; the priest shall offer up and turn the whole into smoke on the altar. It is a burnt offering, an offering by fire, of pleasing odor to the Lord.

14 If his offering to the Lord is a burnt offering of birds, he shall choose his offering from turtledoves or pigeons. 15 The priest shall bring it to the altar, pinch off its head, and turn it into smoke on the altar; and its blood shall be drained out against the side of the altar. 16 He shall remove its crop with its contents, and cast it into the place of the ashes, at the east side of the altar. 17 The priest shall tear it open by its wings, without severing it, and turn it into smoke on the altar, upon the wood that is on the fire. It is a burnt offering, an offering by fire, of pleasing odor to the Lord.

---

17. The Tabernacle, the tent-like desert shrine.

2.4.2 Leviticus 13: The Law of Skin Diseases

In addition to tending to the sacrificial offerings, priests also had a medical function. They were entrusted with the examination of persons and objects for the possibility of infection with ẓara'at, a contagious disease here translated "leprosy," which could infect people, leather, fabrics, and plaster or mud-covered bricks. Those affected were declared "impure" and had to be quarantined until the disease healed, or, if it never did, the person so affected had to live outside the camp permanently.

ҁ

13:1 The Lord spoke to Moses and Aaron, saying:

2 When a person has on the skin of his body a swelling, a rash, or a discoloration, and it develops into a scaly affection on the skin of his body, it shall be reported to Aaron the priest or to one of his sons, the priests. 3 The priest shall examine the affection on the skin of his body: if hair in the affected patch has turned white and the affection appears to be deeper than the skin of his body, it is a leprous affection; when the priest sees it, he shall pronounce him unclean. 4 But if it is a white discoloration on the skin of his body which does not appear to be deeper than the skin and the hair in it has not turned white, the priest shall isolate the affected person for seven days. 5 On the seventh day the priest shall examine him, and if the affection has remained unchanged in color and the disease has not spread on the skin, the priest shall isolate him for another seven days. 6 On the seventh day the priest shall examine him again: if the affection has faded and has not spread on the skin, the priest shall pronounce him clean. It is a rash; he shall wash his clothes, and he shall be clean. 7 But if the rash should spread on the skin after he has presented himself to the priest and been pronounced clean, he shall present himself again to the priest. 8 And if the priest sees that the rash has spread on the skin, the priest shall pronounce him unclean; it is leprosy. . . .

45 As for the person with a leprous affection, his clothes shall be rent, his head shall be left bare, and he shall cover over his upper lip; and he shall call out, "Unclean! Unclean!" 46 He shall be unclean as long as the disease is on him. Being unclean, he shall dwell apart; his dwelling shall be outside the camp. . . .

2.4.3 Numbers 28–30: The Festival Offerings

This section sets forth the biblical festivals of the Jewish ritual calendar which were celebrated with sacrifices. After the destruction of the Second Temple in 70 C.E., the daily offerings were replaced by morning and afternoon prayer services, and the Sabbath and festival offerings became the source for the additional services. The biblical requirement to abstain from ordinary work is still observed.

ᘛ

28:1 The Lord spoke to Moses, saying: 2 Command the Israelite people and say to them: Be punctilious in presenting to Me at stated times the offerings of food due Me, as offerings by fire of pleasing odor to Me. 3 Say to them: These are the offerings by fire that you are to present to the Lord:

As a regular burnt offering every day, two yearling lambs without blemish. 4 You shall offer one lamb in the morning, and the other lamb you shall offer at twilight.[18] 5 And as a meal offering, there shall be a tenth of an ephah[19] of choice flour with a quarter of a hin[20] of beaten oil mixed in, 6 the regular burnt offering instituted at Mount Sinai, an offering by fire of pleasing odor to the Lord.

7 The libation with it shall be a quarter of a hin for each lamb, to be poured in the sacred precinct as an offering of fermented drink to the Lord. 8 The other lamb you shall offer at twilight, preparing the same meal offering and libation as in the morning, an offering by fire of pleasing odor to the Lord.

9 On the sabbath day: two yearling lambs without blemish, together with two-tenths of a measure of choice flour with oil mixed in as a meal offering, and with the proper libation 10 a burnt offering for every sabbath,[21] in addition to the regular burnt offering and its libation.

11 On your new moons[22] you shall present a burnt offering to the Lord: two bulls of the herd, one ram, and seven yearling lambs, without blemish. 12 As meal offering for each bull: three-tenths of a measure of choice flour with oil mixed in. As meal offering for each ram: two-tenths of a measure of choice flour with oil mixed in. 13 As meal offering for each lamb: a tenth of a measure of fine flour with oil mixed in. Such shall be the burnt offering of pleasing odor, an offering by fire to the Lord. 14 Their libations shall be: half a hin of wine for a bull, a third of a hin for

---

18. This twice-daily offering, known as the *tamid,* was conducted in the Temple as long as it stood.

19. About 3/8 to 2/3 of a U.S. bushel.

20. About 1 quart.

21. The Sabbath and all holidays required a *musaf,* or "additional" offering besides the daily *tamid* sacrifice.

22. The New Moon was a semi-holiday on which special rites were performed but which did not require cessation of all normal occupations.

a ram, and a quarter of a hin for a lamb. That shall be the monthly burnt offering for each new moon of the year. 15 And there shall be one goat as a sin offering to the Lord, to be offered in addition to the regular burnt offering and its libation.

16 In the first month, on the fourteenth day of the month, there shall be a passover sacrifice to the Lord, 17 and on the fifteenth day of that month a festival. Unleavened bread shall be eaten for seven days.[23] 18 The first day shall be a sacred occasion: you shall not work at your occupations. 19 You shall present an offering by fire, a burnt offering, to the Lord: two bulls of the herd, one ram, and seven yearling lambs: see that they are without blemish. 20 The meal offering with them shall be of choice flour with oil mixed in: prepare three-tenths of a measure for a bull, two-tenths for a ram; 21 and for each of the seven lambs prepare one-tenth of a measure. 22 And there shall be one goat for a sin offering, to make expiation in your behalf. 23 You shall present these in addition to the morning portion of the regular burnt offering. 24 You shall offer the like daily for seven days as food, an offering by fire of pleasing odor to the Lord; they shall be offered, with their libations, in addition to the regular burnt offering. 25 And the seventh day shall be a sacred occasion for you: you shall not work at your occupations.

26 On the day of the first fruits, your Feast of Weeks, when you bring an offering of new grain to the Lord, you shall observe a sacred occasion: you shall not work at your occupations.[24] 27 You shall present a burnt offering of pleasing odor to the Lord: two bulls of the herd, one ram, seven yearling lambs. 28 The meal offering with them shall be of choice flour with oil mixed in, three-tenths of a measure for a bull, two-tenths for a ram, 29 and one-tenth for each of the seven lambs. 30 And there shall be one goat for expiation in your behalf. 31 You shall present them: see that they are without blemish, with their libations, in addition to the regular burnt offering and its meal offering.

---

23. The Passover holiday, known as the Feast of Unleavened Bread, took place in the spring. Only unleavened bread, called matzah, was to be eaten on this holiday which commemorates the Exodus from Egypt.

24. According to the Rabbinic calendar, the Feast of Weeks, also called Shavuot, falls exactly seven weeks after Passover. The date of the festival of Shavuot was later a matter of debate in Second Temple times. According to some views, the festival was held seven weeks after the first Sunday following the week-long observance of Passover. The Pharisees, followed by the Rabbinic tradition, fixed Shavuot as seven weeks from the second night of Passover. Shavuot is a day which simultaneously celebrates the revelation at Mt. Sinai and is also a harvest festival of "new grain." The first of the spring harvest was brought to the Temple as an offering and was distributed to the priests.

29:1 In the seventh month, on the first day of the month, you shall observe a sacred occasion: you shall not work at your occupations. You shall observe it as a day when the horn is sounded.[25] 2 You shall present a burnt offering of pleasing odor to the Lord: one bull of the herd, one ram, and seven yearling lambs, without blemish. 3 The meal offering with them, choice flour with oil mixed in, shall be: three-tenths of a measure for a bull, two-tenths for a ram, 4 and one-tenth for each of the seven lambs. 5 And there shall be one goat for a sin offering, to make expiation in your behalf 6 in addition to the burnt offering of the new moon with its meal offering and the regular burnt offering with its meal offering, each with its libation as prescribed, offerings by fire of pleasing odor to the Lord.

7 On the tenth day of the same seventh month you shall observe a sacred occasion when you shall practice self-denial.[26] You shall do no work. 8 You shall present to the Lord a burnt offering of pleasing odor: one bull of the herd, one ram, seven yearling lambs; see that they are without blemish. 9 The meal offering with them, of choice flour with oil mixed in, shall be: three-tenths of a measure for a bull, two-tenths for the one ram, 10 one-tenth for each of the seven lambs. 11 And there shall be one goat for a sin offering, in addition to the sin offering of expiation and the regular burnt offering with its meal offering, each with its libation.

12 On the fifteenth day of the seventh month, you shall observe a sacred occasion: you shall not work at your occupations. Seven days you shall observe a festival of the Lord.[27] 13 You shall present a burnt offering, an offering by fire of pleasing odor to the Lord: Thirteen bulls of the herd, two rams, fourteen yearling lambs; they shall be without blemish. 14 The meal offerings with them, of choice flour with oil mixed in, shall be: three-tenths of a measure for each of the thirteen bulls, two-tenths for each of the two rams, 15 and one-tenth for each of the fourteen lambs. 16 And there shall be one goat for a sin offering, in addition to the regular burnt offering, its meal offering and libation.

---

25. The horn to be sounded was the Shofar, and the holiday was called Rosh ha-Shanah or New Year's in Rabbinic tradition. This "new year" occurs in the seventh month because it is the beginning of the year for counting years, but the Torah regards the first month, in which the Exodus and Passover occur, as the first month. This ambivalence reflects the alternation of spring and fall regnal years in the ancient Near Eastern civilizations and, most probably, in ancient Israel as well.

26. By fasting on the Day of Atonement.

27. This is the festival termed Sukkot, or Tabernacles, a harvest festival as well as a national celebration commemorating the tabernacles or booths erected in the desert wandering period.

17 Second day: Twelve bulls of the herd, two rams, fourteen yearling lambs, without blemish; 18 the meal offerings and libations for the bulls, rams, and lambs, in the quantities prescribed; 19 and one goat for a sin offering in addition to the regular burnt offering, its meal offering and libations.

20 Third day: Eleven bulls, two rams, fourteen yearling lambs, without blemish; 21 the meal offerings and libations for the bulls, rams, and lambs, in the quantities prescribed; 22 and one goat for a sin offering in addition to the regular burnt offering, its meal offering and libation.

23 Fourth day: Ten bulls, two rams, fourteen yearling lambs, without blemish; 24 the meal offerings and libations for the bulls, rams, and lambs, in the quantities prescribed; 25 and one goat for a sin offering in addition to the regular burnt offering, its meal offering and libation.

26 Fifth day: Nine bulls, two rams, fourteen yearling lambs, without blemish; 27 the meal offerings and libations for the bulls, rams, and lambs, in the quantities prescribed; 28 and one goat for a sin offering in addition to the regular burnt offering, its meal offering and libation.

29 Sixth day: Eight bulls, two rams, fourteen yearling lambs, without blemish; 30 the meal offerings and libations for the bulls, rams, and lambs, in the quantities prescribed; 31 and one goat for a sin offering in addition to the regular burnt offering, its meal offering and libations.

32 Seventh day: Seven bulls, two rams, fourteen yearling lambs, without blemish; 33 the meal offerings and libations for the bulls, rams, and lambs, in the quantities prescribed; 34 and one goat for a sin offering in addition to the regular burnt offering, its meal offering and libation.

35 On the eighth day you shall hold a solemn gathering;[28] you shall not work at your occupations. 36 You shall present a burnt offering, an offering by fire of pleasing odor to the Lord; one bull, one ram, seven yearling lambs, without blemish; 37 the meal offerings and libations for the bull, the ram, and the lambs, in the quantities prescribed; 38 and one goat for a sin offering in addition to the regular burnt offering, its meal offering and libation.

39 All these you shall offer to the Lord at the stated times, in addition to your votive and freewill offerings, be they burnt offerings, meal offerings, libations, or offerings of well-being. 30:1 So Moses spoke to the Israelites just as the Lord had commanded Moses.

---

28. Understood by the Rabbis to be a separate festival of Shemini Aẓeret (the Eighth Day of Solemn Assembly).

2.4.4 Leviticus 21: Laws of Purity for Priests

The laws of purity for priests emphasize the high standards which must be observed by those who serve in the holiest place, God's Temple. These laws especially sought to distance the priests from impurity, contact with the dead, and pagan rituals such as shaving the head or making gashes in the skin.

ﺲﻌ

21:1 The Lord said to Moses: Speak to the priests, the sons of Aaron, and say to them:

None shall defile himself for any [dead] person among his kin, 2 except for the relatives that are closest to him: his mother, his father, his son, his daughter, and his brother; 3 also for a virgin sister, close to him because she has not married, for her he may defile himself. 4 But he shall not defile himself as a kinsman by marriage, and so profane himself.

5 They shall not shave smooth any part of their heads, or cut the side growth of their beards, or make gashes in their flesh. 6 They shall be holy to their God and not profane the name of their God; for they offer the Lord's offerings by fire, the food of their God, and so must be holy.

7 They shall not marry a woman defiled by harlotry, nor shall they marry one divorced from her husband. For they are holy to their God 8 and you must treat them as holy, since they offer the food of your God; they shall be holy to you, for I the Lord who sanctify you am holy.

2.5 PROPHECY

2.5.1 Joshua 1: Joshua Succeeds Moses

In this passage, Joshua is charged with the task of succeeding Moses, leading the Israelites into the land across the Jordan, and promulgating the "Book of the Teaching," the Torah of Moses. Accordingly, Joshua was seen by later tradition as the second of the prophets of Israel.

ﺲﻌ

1:1 After the death of Moses the servant of the Lord, the Lord said to Joshua son of Nun, Moses' attendant: 2 "My servant Moses is dead. Prepare to cross the Jordan, together with all this people, into the land that I am giving to the Israelites. 3 Every spot on which your foot treads I give to you, as I promised Moses. 4 Your territory shall extend from the wilderness and the Lebanon to the Great River, the River Euphrates [on the east]—the whole Hittite country—and up to the Mediterranean Sea on the west. 5 No one shall be able to resist you as long as you live. As I was with Moses, so I will be with you; I will not fail you or forsake you.

6 "Be strong and resolute, for you shall apportion to this people the land that I swore to their fathers to assign to them. 7 But you must be very strong and resolute to observe faithfully all the Teaching that My servant Moses enjoined upon you. Do not deviate from it to the right or to the left, that you may be successful wherever you go. 8 Let not this Book of the Teaching cease from your lips, but recite it day and night, so that you may observe faithfully all that is written in it. Only then will you prosper in your undertakings and only then will you be successful.

9 "I charge you: Be strong and resolute; do not be terrified or dismayed, for the Lord your God is with you wherever you go."

2.5.2 Joshua 6: The Conquest of Jericho

God here instructs Joshua as to how to conquer the city of Jericho. Priests were to precede the warriors; their weapons were rams' horns and the Ark of the Covenant. This unconventional form of warfare emphasized the nature of the conquest of the Land of Israel as a form of divine commandment, and its accomplishment as a result of divine aid.

૬૭

6:1 Now Jericho was shut up tight because of the Israelites; no one could leave or enter. 2 The Lord said to Joshua, "See, I will deliver Jericho and her king [and her] warriors into your hands. 3 Let all your troops march around the city and complete one circuit of the city. Do this six days, 4 with seven priests carrying seven ram's horns preceding the Ark. On the seventh day, march around the city seven times, with the priests blowing the horns. 5 And when a long blast is sounded on the horn—as soon as you hear that sound of the horn—all the people shall give a mighty shout. Thereupon the city wall will collapse, and the people shall advance, every man straight ahead."

6 Joshua son of Nun summoned the priests and said to them, "Take up the Ark of the Covenant, and let seven priests carrying seven ram's horns precede the Ark of the Lord." 7 And he instructed the people, "Go forward, march around the city, with the vanguard marching in front of the Ark of the Lord." 8 When Joshua had instructed the people, the seven priests carrying seven ram's horns advanced before the Lord, blowing their horns; and the Ark of the Lord's Covenant followed them. 9 The vanguard marched in front of the priests who were blowing the horns, and the rear guard marched behind the Ark, with the horns sounding all the

time. 10 But Joshua's orders to the rest of the people were, "Do not shout, do not let your voices be heard, and do not let a sound issue from your lips until the moment that I command you, 'Shout!' Then you shall shout."

11 So he had the Ark of the Lord go around the city and complete one circuit; then they returned to camp and spent the night in camp. 12 Joshua rose early the next day; and the priests took up the Ark of the Lord, 13 while the seven priests bearing the seven ram's horns marched in front of the Ark of the Lord, blowing the horns as they marched. The vanguard marched in front of them, and the rear guard marched behind the Ark of the Lord, with the horns sounding all the time. 14 And so they marched around the city once on the second day and returned to the camp. They did this six days.

15 On the seventh day, they rose at daybreak and marched around the city, in the same manner, seven times; that was the only day that they marched around the city seven times. 16 On the seventh round, as the priests blew the horns, Joshua commanded the people, "Shout! For the Lord has given you the city. 17 The city and everything in it are to be proscribed for the Lord; only Rahab the harlot is to be spared, and all who are with her in the house, because she hid the messengers we sent. 18 But you must beware of that which is proscribed, or else you will be proscribed. If you take anything from that which is proscribed, you will cause the camp of Israel to be proscribed; you will bring calamity upon it. 19 All the silver and gold and objects of copper and iron are consecrated to the Lord; they must go into the treasury of the Lord."

20 So the people shouted when the horns were sounded. When the people heard the sound of the horns, the people raised a mighty shout and the wall collapsed. The people rushed into the city, every man straight in front of him, and they captured the city. 21 They exterminated everything in the city with the sword: man and woman, young and old, ox and sheep and ass.

2.5.3 Judges 4: The Battle against Sisera

After Joshua, the leadership mantle passed to a series of charismatic leaders, termed "judges." Throughout the period of the judges, the Israelites repeatedly offended God, and His response was to take away their sovereignty over the land and subject them to foreign and oppressive rule. In this narrative, the Israelites responded by throwing off this rule through the initiatives of two women, Deborah, the prophetess and military leader, and Jael, who delivered the enemy general into the hands of Israel.

᧔

4:1 The Israelites again did what was offensive to the Lord—Ehud now being dead. 2 And the Lord surrendered them to King Jabin of Canaan, who reigned in Hazor.[29] His army commander was Sisera, whose base was Harosheth-goiim. 3 The Israelites cried out to the Lord; for he had nine hundred iron chariots, and he had oppressed Israel ruthlessly for twenty years.

4 Deborah, wife of Lappidoth, was a prophetess; she led Israel at that time. 5 She used to sit under the Palm of Deborah, between Ramah and Bethel in the hill country of Ephraim, and the Israelites would come to her for decisions.

6 She summoned Barak son of Abinoam, of Kedesh in Naphtali, and said to him, "The Lord, the God of Israel, has commanded: Go, march up to Mount Tabor, and take with you ten thousand men of Naphtali and Zebulun. 7 And I will draw Sisera, Jabin's army commander, with his chariots and his troops, toward you up to the Wadi Kishon; and I will deliver him into your hands." 8 But Barak said to her, "If you will go with me, I will go; if not, I will not go." 9 "Very well, I will go with you," she answered. "However, there will be no glory for you in the course you are taking, for then the Lord will deliver Sisera into the hands of a woman." So Deborah went with Barak to Kedesh. 10 Barak then mustered Zebulun and Naphtali at Kedesh; ten thousand men marched after him, and Deborah also went up with him.

11 Now Heber the Kenite had separated from the other Kenites, descendants of Hobab, father-in-law of Moses, and had pitched his tent at Elon-bezaanannim, which is near Kedesh.

12 Sisera was informed that Barak son of Abinoam had gone up to Mount Tabor. 13 So Sisera ordered all his chariots—nine hundred iron chariots—and all the troops he had to move from Harosheth-goiim to the Wadi Kishon. 14 Then Deborah said to Barak, "Up! This is the day on which the Lord will deliver Sisera into your hands: the Lord is marching before you." Barak charged down Mount Tabor, followed by the ten thousand men, 15 and the Lord threw Sisera and all his chariots and army into a panic before the onslaught of Barak. Sisera leaped from his chariot and fled on foot 16 as Barak pursued the chariots and the soldiers as far as Harosheth-goiim. All of Sisera's soldiers fell by the sword; not a man was left.

---

29. A city in northern Israel.

17 Sisera, meanwhile, had fled on foot to the tent of Jael, wife of Heber the Kenite; for there was friendship between King Jabin of Hazor and the family of Heber the Kenite. 18 Jael came out to greet Sisera and said to him, "Come in, my lord, come in here, do not be afraid." So he entered her tent, and she covered him with a blanket. 19 He said to her, "Please let me have some water; I am thirsty." She opened a skin of milk and gave him some to drink; and she covered him again. 20 He said to her, "Stand at the entrance of the tent. If anybody comes and asks you if there is anybody here, say 'No.'" 21 Then Jael wife of Heber took a tent pin and grasped the mallet. When he was fast asleep from exhaustion, she approached him stealthily and drove the pin through his temple till it went down to the ground. Thus he died.

22 Now Barak appeared in pursuit of Sisera. Jael went out to greet him and said, "Come, I will show you the man you are looking for." He went inside with her, and there Sisera was lying dead, with the pin in his temple.

23 On that day God subdued King Jabin of Hazor before the Israelites. 24 The hand of the Israelites bore harder and harder on King Jabin of Canaan, until they destroyed King Jabin of Canaan.

2.5.4 Judges 13, 15–16: The Story of Samson

The charismatic, heroic nature of the so-called "judges" is best illustrated by the rustic character of Samson, perhaps most famous of these leaders, but also the most violent. Once again God was displeased with the behavior of the Israelites and caused them to be conquered, this time by the Philistines. And once again a leader arose in Israel who, with divine aid, vanquished the enemy. This time it was Samson, born in miraculous circumstances and especially consecrated to God from birth in order to fulfill his destiny. Although he is unusually strong, his downfall comes with his involvement with Philistine women, especially his wife Delilah, who gets him to reveal the secret of his strength and turns this information over to the Philistines.

🦊

13:1 The Israelites again did what was offensive to the Lord, and the Lord delivered them into the hands of the Philistines for forty years.

2 There was a certain man from Zorah, of the stock of Dan, whose name was Manoah. His wife was barren and had borne no children. 3 An angel of the Lord appeared to the woman and said to her, "You are barren and have borne no children; but you shall conceive and bear a son. 4 Now

be careful not to drink wine or other intoxicant, or to eat anything unclean. 5 For you are going to conceive and bear a son; let no razor touch his head, for the boy is to be a nazirite[30] to God from the womb on. He shall be the first to deliver Israel from the Philistines."

6 The woman went and told her husband, "A man of God came to me; he looked like an angel of God, very frightening. I did not ask him where he was from, nor did he tell me his name. 7 He said to me, 'You are going to conceive and bear a son. Drink no wine or other intoxicant, and eat nothing unclean, for the boy is to be a nazirite to God from the womb to the day of his death!'" . . .

24 The woman bore a son, and she named him Samson. The boy grew up, and the Lord blessed him. 25 The spirit of the Lord first moved him in the encampment of Dan, between Zorah and Eshtaol. . . .

15:1 Some time later, in the season of the wheat harvest, Samson came to visit his wife, bringing a kid as a gift. He said, "Let me go into the chamber to my wife." But her father would not let him go in. 2 "I was sure," said her father, "that you had taken a dislike to her, so I gave her to your wedding companion. But her younger sister is more beautiful than she; let her become your wife instead." 3 Thereupon Samson declared, "Now the Philistines can have no claim against me for the harm I shall do them."

4 Samson went and caught three hundred foxes. He took torches and, turning [the foxes] tail to tail, he placed a torch between each pair of tails. 5 He lit the torches and turned [the foxes] loose among the standing grain of the Philistines, setting fire to stacked grain, standing grain, vineyards, [and] olive trees.

6 The Philistines asked, "Who did this?" And they were told, "It was Samson, the son-in-law of the Timnite, who took Samson's wife and gave her to his wedding companion." Thereupon the Philistines came up and put her and her father to the fire. 7 Samson said to them, "If that is how you act, I will not rest until I have taken revenge on you." 8 He gave them a sound and thorough thrashing. Then he went down and stayed in the cave of the rock of Etam.

9 The Philistines came up, pitched camp in Judah and spread out over Lehi. 10 The men of Judah asked, "Why have you come up against us?" They answered, "We have come to take Samson prisoner, and to do to him as he did to us." 11 Thereupon three thousand men of Judah went down to the cave of the rock of Etam, and they said to Samson, "You knew that the Philistines rule over us; why have you done this to us?" He

---

30. One who abstains from wine and from cutting his hair.

replied, "As they did to me, so I did to them." 12 "We have come down," they told him, "to take you prisoner and to hand you over to the Philistines." "But swear to me," said Samson to them, "that you yourselves will not attack me." 13 "We won't," they replied. "We will only take you prisoner and hand you over to them; we will not slay you." So they bound him with two new ropes and brought him up from the rock.

14 When he reached Lehi, the Philistines came shouting to meet him. Thereupon the spirit of the Lord gripped him, and the ropes on his arms became like flax that catches fire; the bonds melted off his hands. 15 He came upon a fresh jawbone of an ass and he picked it up; and with it he killed a thousand men. 16 Then Samson said:

> "With the jaw of an ass,
> Mass upon mass!
> With the jaw of an ass
> I have slain a thousand men."

17 As he finished speaking, he threw the jawbone away; hence that place was called Ramath-lehi. . . .[31]

20 He led Israel in the days of the Philistines for twenty years.

16:1 Once Samson went to Gaza; there he met a whore and slept with her. 2 The Gazites [learned] that Samson had come there, so they gathered and lay in ambush for him in the town gate the whole night; and all night long they kept whispering to each other, "When daylight comes, we'll kill him." 3 But Samson lay in bed only till midnight. At midnight he got up, grasped the doors of the town gate together with the two gateposts, and pulled them out along with the bar. He placed them on his shoulders and carried them off to the top of the hill that is near Hebron.

4 After that, he fell in love with a woman in the Wadi Sorek, named Delilah. 5 The lords of the Philistines went up to her and said, "Coax him and find out what makes him so strong, and how we can overpower him, tie him up, and make him helpless; and we'll each give you eleven hundred shekels of silver."

6 So Delilah said to Samson, "Tell me, what makes you so strong? And how could you be tied up and made helpless?" 7 Samson replied, "If I were to be tied with seven fresh tendons that had not been dried, I should become as weak as an ordinary man." 8 So the lords of the Philistines brought up to her seven fresh tendons that had not been dried. She bound him with them, 9 while an ambush was waiting in her room. Then she called out to him, "Samson, the Philistines are upon you!" Whereat he

---

31. Hebrew for "the Height of the Jawbone."

pulled the tendons apart, as a strand of tow comes apart at the touch of fire. So the secret of his strength remained unknown.

10 Then Delilah said to Samson, "Oh, you deceived me; you lied to me! Do tell me now how you could be tied up." 11 He said, "If I were to be bound with new ropes that had never been used, I would become as weak as an ordinary man." 12 So Delilah took new ropes and bound him with them, while an ambush was waiting in a room. And she cried, "Samson, the Philistines are upon you!" But he tore them off his arms like a thread. 13 Then Delilah said to Samson, "You have been deceiving me all along; you have been lying to me! Tell me, how could you be tied up?" He answered her, "If you weave seven locks of my head into the web." 14 And she pinned it with a peg and cried to him, "Samson, the Philistines are upon you!" Awaking from his sleep, he pulled out the peg, the loom, and the web.

15 Then she said to him, "How can you say you love me, when you don't confide in me? This makes three times that you've deceived me and haven't told me what makes you so strong." 16 Finally, after she had nagged him and pressed him constantly, he was wearied to death 17 and he confided everything to her. He said to her, "No razor has ever touched my head, for I have been a nazirite to God since I was in my mother's womb. If my hair were cut, my strength would leave me and I should become as weak as an ordinary man."

18 Sensing that he had confided everything to her, Delilah sent for the lords of the Philistines, with this message: "Come up once more, for he has confided everything to me." And the lords of the Philistines came up and brought the money with them. 19 She lulled him to sleep on her lap. Then she called in a man, and she had him cut off the seven locks of his head; thus she weakened him and made him helpless: his strength slipped away from him. 20 She cried, "Samson, the Philistines are upon you!" And he awoke from his sleep, thinking he would break loose and shake himself free as he had the other times. For he did not know that the Lord had departed from him. 21 The Philistines seized him and gouged out his eyes. They brought him down to Gaza and shackled him in bronze fetters, and he became a mill slave in the prison. 22 After his hair was cut off, it began to grow back.

23 Now the lords of the Philistines gathered to offer a great sacrifice to their god Dagon and to make merry. They chanted,

"Our god has delivered into our hands
Our enemy Samson."

24 When the people saw him, they sang praises to their god, chanting,

"Our god has delivered into our hands
The enemy who devastated our land,
And who slew so many of us."

25 As their spirits rose, they said, "Call Samson here and let him dance for us." Samson was fetched from the prison, and he danced for them. Then they put him between the pillars. 26 And Samson said to the boy who was leading him by the hand, "Let go of me and let me feel the pillars that the temple rests upon, that I may lean on them." 27 Now the temple was full of men and women; all the lords of the Philistines were there, and there were some three thousand men and women on the roof watching Samson dance. 28 Then Samson called to the Lord, "O Lord God! Please remember me, and give me strength just this once, O God, to take revenge of the Philistines, if only for one of my two eyes." 29 He embraced the two middle pillars that the temple rested upon, one with his right arm and one with his left, and leaned against them; 30 Samson cried, "Let me die with the Philistines!" and he pulled with all his might. The temple came crashing down on the lords and on all the people in it. Those who were slain by him as he died outnumbered those who had been slain by him when he lived.

31 His brothers and all his father's household came down and carried him up and buried him in the tomb of his father Manoah, between Zorah and Eshtaol. He had led Israel for twenty years.

2.5.5 1 Samuel 8: The Desire for a King over Israel

Samuel can be seen as the last of the judges, yet with his career, biblical leadership takes a decided turn toward the prophetic. So long as Samuel, the righteous judge, made his rounds throughout the land, there was justice in Israel, and the Philistines did not attack. But with the appointment of Samuel's sons as judges, corruption and injustice again appeared, and Israel had once again exposed itself to God's wrath. The people came to Samuel with the request that he anoint a king over them as the solution to this leadership crisis.

ℜ

8:4 All the elders of Israel assembled and came to Samuel at Ramah, 5 and they said to him, "You have grown old, and your sons have not followed your ways. Therefore appoint a king for us, to govern us like all other nations." 6 Samuel was displeased that they said "Give us a king to govern us." Samuel prayed to the Lord, 7 and the Lord replied to Samuel, "Heed the demand of the people in everything they say to you. For it is not you that they have rejected; it is Me they have rejected as their king. 8 Like everything else they have done ever since I brought them out of Egypt to this day—forsaking Me and worshipping other gods—so they are doing to you. 9 Heed their demand; but warn them solemnly, and tell them about the practices of any king who will rule over them."

10 Samuel reported all the words of the Lord to the people, who were asking him for a king. 11 He said, "This will be the practice of the king who will rule over you: He will take your sons and appoint them as his charioteers and horsemen, and they will serve as outrunners for his chariots. 12 He will appoint them as his chiefs of thousands and of fifties; or they will have to plow his fields, reap his harvest, and make his weapons and the equipment for his chariots. 13 He will take your daughters as perfumers, cooks, and bakers. 14 He will seize your choice fields, vineyards, and olive groves, and give them to his courtiers. 15 He will take a tenth part of your grain and vintage and give it to his eunuchs and courtiers. 16 He will take your male and female slaves, your choice young men, and your asses, and put them to work for him. 17 He will take a tenth part of your flocks, and you shall become his slaves. 18 The day will come when you cry out because of the king whom you yourselves have chosen; and the Lord will not answer you on that day."

19 But the people would not listen to Samuel's warning. "No," they said. "We must have a king over us, 20 that we may be like all the other nations: Let our king rule over us and go out at our head and fight our battles." 21 When Samuel heard all that the people said, he reported it to the Lord. 22 And the Lord said to Samuel, "Heed their demands and appoint a king for them." Samuel then said to the men of Israel, "All of you go home."

2.5.6 1 Kings 18: Elijah Challenges Baal on Mt. Carmel

With the career of Elijah prophecy continued to grow in importance in Israelite society and religion. Elijah played a major role in the fight against foreign worship. Elijah had to make a public demonstration to lure the people away from worship of the cult of Baal which King Ahab and Queen Jezebel nurtured. While the prophets of Baal and Asherah were eating at her table, Jezebel killed the prophets of the God of Israel and forced the remainder to flee for their lives and conceal themselves in caves. At the same time there was a severe drought.

18:2 ... The famine was severe in Samaria...

16 ... and Ahab went to meet Elijah. 17 When Ahab caught sight of Elijah, Ahab said to him, "Is that you, you troubler of Israel?" 18 He retorted, "It is not I who have brought trouble on Israel, but you and your father's House, by forsaking the commandments of the Lord and going after the Baalim. 19 Now summon all Israel to join me at Mount Carmel, together with the four hundred and fifty prophets of Baal and the four hundred prophets of Asherah who eat at Jezebel's table."

20 Ahab sent orders to all the Israelites and gathered the prophets at Mount Carmel. 21 Elijah approached all the people and said, "How long will you keep hopping between two opinions? If the Lord is God, follow Him; and if Baal, follow him!" But the people answered him not a word. 22 Then Elijah said to the people, "I am the only prophet of the Lord left, while the prophets of Baal are four hundred and fifty men. 23 Let two young bulls be given to us. Let them choose one bull, cut it up, and lay it on the wood, but let them not apply fire; I will prepare the other bull, and lay it on the wood, and will not apply fire. 24 You will then invoke your god by name, and I will invoke the Lord by name; and let us agree: the god who responds with fire, that one is God." And all the people answered, "Very good!"

25 Elijah said to the prophets of Baal, "Choose one bull and prepare it first, for you are the majority; invoke your god by name, but apply no fire." 26 They took the bull that was given them; they prepared it, and invoked Baal by name from morning until noon, shouting, "O Baal, answer us!" But there was no sound, and none who responded; so they performed a hopping dance about the altar that had been set up. 27 When noon came, Elijah mocked them, saying, "Shout louder! After all, he is a god. But he may be in conversation, he may be detained, or he may be on a journey,[32] or perhaps he is asleep and will wake up." 28 So they shouted louder, and gashed themselves with knives and spears, according to their practice, until the blood streamed over them. 29 When noon passed they kept raving until the hour of presenting the meal offering. Still there was no sound, and none who responded or heeded.

30 Then Elijah said to all the people, "Come closer to me"; and all the people came closer to him. He repaired the damaged altar of the Lord. 31 Then Elijah took twelve stones, corresponding to the number of the

---

32. Others translate, "he may be relieving himself."

tribes of the sons of Jacob to whom the word of the Lord had come: "Israel shall be your name" 32 and with the stones he built an altar in the name of the Lord. Around the altar he made a trench large enough for two seahs of seed. 33 He laid out the wood, and he cut up the bull and laid it on the wood. 34 And he said, "Fill four jars with water and pour it over the burnt offering and the wood." Then he said, "Do it a second time"; and they did it a second time. "Do it a third time," he said; and they did it a third time. 35 The water ran down around the altar, and even the trench was filled with water.

36 When it was time to present the meal offering, the prophet Elijah came forward and said, "O Lord, God of Abraham, Isaac, and Israel! Let it be known today that You are God in Israel and that I am Your servant, and that I have done all these things at Your bidding. 37 Answer me, O Lord, answer me, that this people may know that You, O Lord, are God; for You have turned their hearts backward."

38 Then fire from the Lord descended and consumed the burnt offering, the wood, the stones, and the earth; and it licked up the water that was in the trench. 39 When they saw this, all the people flung themselves on their faces and cried out: "The Lord alone is God, The Lord alone is God!"

40 "Then Elijah said to them, "Seize the prophets of Baal, let not a single one of them get away." They seized them, and Elijah took them down to the Wadi Kishon and slaughtered them there.

41 Elijah said to Ahab, "Go up, eat and drink, for there is a rumbling of [approaching] rain," 42 and Ahab went up to eat and drink. Elijah meanwhile climbed to the top of Mount Carmel, crouched on the ground, and put his face between his knees. 43 And he said to his servant, "Go up and look toward the Sea." He went up and looked and reported, "There is nothing." Seven times [Elijah] said, "Go back," 44 and the seventh time, [the servant] reported, "A cloud as small as a man's hand is rising in the west." Then [Elijah] said, "Go say to Ahab, 'Hitch up [your chariot] and go down before the rain stops you.' " 45 Meanwhile the sky grew black with clouds; there was wind, and a heavy downpour fell; Ahab mounted his chariot and drove off to Jezreel. 46 The hand of the Lord had come on Elijah. He tied up his skirts and ran in front of Ahab all the way to Jezreel.

2.5.7 Isaiah 1: The Lord Chastises His Rebellious People

By Isaiah's time, literary prophecy was fully established. Isaiah prophesied in Judah between 740 and 701 B.C.E. and refers to events which took place prior to the fall of the Northern Kingdom in 722/21 B.C.E. He castigates the

elite of Judah for their moral failings. Some of his words have been incorpo-
rated into the liturgy for the Day of Atonement.

༚

1:1 The prophecies of Isaiah son of Amoz, who prophesied concerning Judah and Jerusalem in the reigns of Uzziah, Jotham, Ahaz, and Hezekiah, kings of Judah.

2 Hear, O heavens, and give ear, O earth,
For the Lord has spoken:
"I reared children and brought them up
And they have rebelled against Me!
3 An ox knows its owner,
An ass its master's crib:
Israel does not know,
My people takes no thought."
4 Ah, sinful nation!
People laden with iniquity!
Brood of evildoers!
Depraved children!
They have forsaken the Lord,
Spurned the Holy One of Israel,
Turned their backs [on Him].
5 Why do you seek further beatings,
That you continue to offend?
Every head is ailing,
And every heart is sick.
6 From head to foot
No spot is sound:
All bruises, and welts,
And festering sores—
Not pressed out, not bound up, Not softened with oil.
7 Your land is a waste,
Your cities burnt down;
Before your eyes, the yield of your soil
Is consumed by strangers—
A wasteland as overthrown by strangers!. . .
10 Hear the word of the Lord,
You chieftains of Sodom;
Give ear to our God's instruction,
You folk of Gomorrah!
11 "What need have I of all your sacrifices?"
Says the Lord.

"I am sated with burnt offerings of rams,
And suet of fatlings,
And blood of bulls;
And I have no delight
In lambs and he-goats.
12 That you come to appear before Me—
Who asked that of you?
Trample My courts 13 no more;
Bringing oblations is futile,
Incense is offensive to Me.
New moon and sabbath,
Proclaiming of solemnities,
Assemblies with iniquity,
I cannot abide.
14 Your new moons and fixed seasons
Fill Me with loathing;
They are become a burden to Me,
I cannot endure them.
15 And when you lift up your hands,
I will turn My eyes away from you;
Though you pray at length,
I will not listen.
Your hands are stained with crime—
16 Wash yourselves clean;
Put your evil doings
Away from My sight.
Cease to do evil;
17 Learn to do good.
Devote yourselves to justice;
Aid the wronged.
Uphold the rights of the orphan;
Defend the cause of the widow.
18 "Come, let us reach an understanding,"
—says the Lord
"Be your sins like crimson,
They can turn snow-white;
Be they red as dyed wool,
They can become like fleece."
19 If, then, you agree and give heed,
You will eat the good things of the earth;
20 But if you refuse and disobey,
You will be devoured [by] the sword.
For it was the Lord who spoke.

21 Alas, she has become a harlot,
The faithful city
That was filled with justice,
Where righteousness dwelt—
But now murderers.
22 Your silver has turned to dross;
Your wine is cut with water.
23 Your rulers are rogues
And cronies of thieves,
Every one avid for presents
And greedy for gifts;
They do not judge the case of the orphan,
And the widow's cause never reaches them.
24 Assuredly, this is the declaration
Of the Sovereign, the Lord of Hosts,
The Mighty One of Israel:
"Ah, I will get satisfaction from My foes;
I will wreak vengeance on My enemies!
25 I will turn My hand against you,
And smelt out your dross as with lye,
And remove all your slag:
26 I will restore your magistrates as of old,
And your counselors as of yore.
After that you shall be called
City of Righteousness, Faithful City."
27 Zion shall be saved in the judgment;
Her repentant ones, in the retribution.
28 But rebels and sinners shall all be crushed,
And those who forsake the Lord shall perish.

2.5.8 Isaiah 6: The Heavenly Vision

This vision is thought by most scholars to be Isaiah's first prophetic experience. In it he sees a vision of the heavenly throne and God's angelic retinue. This description of the angelic praise of God would become a basic ingredient of the Jewish daily liturgy.

ॐ

6:1 In the year that King Uzziah died, I beheld my Lord seated on a high and lofty throne; and the skirts of His robe filled the Temple. 2 Seraphs stood in attendance on Him. Each of them had six wings: with two he covered his face, with two he covered his legs, and with two he would fly.

3 And one would call to the other,
"Holy, holy, holy!
The Lord of Hosts!
His presence fills all the earth!"

4 The doorposts would shake at the sound of the one who called, and the House kept filling with smoke. 5 I cried,

"Woe is me; I am lost!
For I am a man of unclean lips
And I live among a people
Of unclean lips;
Yet my own eyes have beheld
The King Lord of Hosts."

6 Then one of the seraphs flew over to me with a live coal, which he had taken from the altar with a pair of tongs. 7 He touched it to my lips and declared,

"Now that this has touched your lips,
Your guilt shall depart
And your sin be purged away."

8 Then I heard the voice of my Lord saying, "Whom shall I send? Who will go for us?" And I said, "Here am I; send me." 9 And He said, "Go, say to that people:

'Hear, indeed, but do not understand;
See, indeed, but do not grasp.'
10 Dull that people's mind,
Stop its ears,
And seal its eyes—
Lest, seeing with its eyes
And hearing with its ears,
It also grasp with its mind,
And repent and save itself."
11 I asked, "How long, my Lord?" And He replied:
"Till towns lie waste without inhabitants
And houses without people,
And the ground lies waste and desolate—
12 For the Lord will banish the population—
And deserted sites are many
In the midst of the land.

13 "But while a tenth part yet remains in it, it shall repent. It shall be ravaged like the terebinth and the oak, of which stumps are left even when they are felled: its stump shall be a holy seed."

2.5.9 Isaiah 10–11: A Glimpse of the Messianic Era

Isaiah was keenly aware of the imperfections of the world and yearned for an era of peace and prosperity for Israel and all the nations. His vision was ultimately understood in Second Temple texts and in the Rabbinic tradition as a prototype for the end of days which would be led, in his view, by a Davidic king.

༄

10:32 . . . O mount of Fair Zion!
O hill of Jerusalem!
33 Lo! The Sovereign Lord of Hosts
Will hew off the tree-crowns with an ax:
The tall ones shall be felled,
The lofty ones cut down:
34 The thickets of the forest shall be hacked away with iron,
And the Lebanon trees shall fall in their majesty.
11:1 But a shoot shall grow out of the stump of Jesse,
A twig shall sprout from his stock.
2 The spirit of the Lord shall alight upon him:
A spirit of wisdom and insight,
A spirit of counsel and valor,
A spirit of devotion and reverence for the Lord.
3 He shall sense the truth by his reverence for the Lord:
He shall not judge by what his eyes behold,
Nor decide by what his ears perceive.
4 Thus he shall judge the poor with equity
And decide with justice for the lowly of the land.
He shall strike down a land with the rod of his mouth
And slay the wicked with the breath of his lips.
5 Justice shall be the girdle of his loins,
And faithfulness the girdle of his waist.
6 The wolf shall dwell with the lamb,
The leopard lie down with the kid;
The calf, the beast of prey, and the fatling together,
With a little boy to herd them.
7 The cow and the bear shall graze,
Their young shall lie down together;

And the lion, like the ox, shall eat straw.
8 A babe shall play
Over a viper's hole,
And an infant passed his hand
Over an adder's den.
9 In all of My sacred mount
Nothing evil or vile shall be done;
For the land shall be filled with devotion to the Lord
As water covers the sea.
10 In that day,
The stock of Jesse that has remained standing
Shall become a standard to peoples—
Nations shall seek his counsel
And his abode shall be honored.

2.5.10 Ezekiel 1: The Four Winged Creatures

The prophet Ezekiel was exiled from Jerusalem in 597 B.C.E. and experienced the destruction of the Temple from afar in Babylonia. There he had a vision of the divine throne and the surrounding angels which has served as a paradigm for much of later Jewish mysticism.

1:1 In the thirtieth year, on the fifth day of the fourth month, when I was in the community of exiles by the Chebar Canal, the heavens opened and I saw visions of God. 2 On the fifth day of the month—it was the fifth year of the exile of King Jehoiachin—3 the word of the Lord came to the priest Ezekiel son of Buzi, by the Chebar Canal, in the land of the Chaldeans. And the hand of the Lord came upon him there.

4 I looked, and lo, a stormy wind came sweeping out of the north—a huge cloud and flashing fire, surrounded by a radiance; and in the center of it, in the center of the fire, a gleam as of amber. 5 In the center of it were also the figures of four creatures. And this was their appearance:

They had the figures of human beings. 6 However, each had four faces, and each of them had four wings; 7 the legs of each were [fused into] a single rigid leg, and the feet of each were like a single calf's hoof; and their sparkle was like the luster of burnished bronze. 8 They had human hands below their wings. The four of them had their faces and their wings on their tour sides. 9 Each one's wings touched those of the other. They did not turn when they moved; each could move in the direction of any of its faces.

10 Each of them had a human face [at the front]; each of the four had the face of a lion on the right; each of the four had the face of an ox on the left; and each of the four had the face of an eagle [at the back].11 Such were their faces. As for their wings, they were separated: above, each had two touching those of the others, while the other two covered its body. 12 And each could move in the direction of any of its faces; they went wherever the spirit impelled them to go, without turning when they moved.

13 Such then was the appearance of the creatures. With them was something that looked like burning coals of fire. This fire, suggestive of torches, kept moving about among the creatures; the fire had a radiance, and lightning issued from the fire. 14 Dashing to and fro [among] the creatures was something that looked like flares.

15 As I gazed on the creatures, I saw one wheel on the ground next to each of the four-faced creatures. 16 As for the appearance and structure of the wheels, they gleamed like beryl.[33] All four had the same form; the appearance and structure of each was as of two wheels cutting through each other. 17 And when they moved, each could move in the direction of any of its four quarters; they did not veer when they moved. 18 Their rims were tall and frightening, for the rims of all four were covered all over with eyes. 19 And when the creatures moved forward, the wheels moved at their sides; and when the creatures were borne above the earth, the wheels were borne too. 20 Wherever the spirit impelled them to go, they went—wherever the spirit impelled them—and the wheels were borne alongside them; for the spirit of the creatures was in the wheels. 21 When those moved, these moved; and when those stood still, these stood still; and when those were borne above the earth, the wheels were borne alongside them—for the spirit of the creatures was in the wheels.

22 Above the heads of the creatures was a form: an expanse, with an awe-inspiring gleam as of crystal, was spread out above their heads. 23 Under the expanse, each had one pair of wings extended toward those of the others; and each had another pair covering its body. 24 When they moved, I could hear the sound of their wings like the sound of mighty waters, like the sound of Shaddai,[34] a tumult like the din of an army. When they stood still, they would let their wings droop. 25 From above the expanse over their heads came a sound. When they stood still, they would let their wings droop.

---

33. A colored mineral.
34. A name for God, often translated "the Mighty One."

26 Above the expanse over their heads was the semblance of a throne, in appearance like sapphire; and on top, upon this semblance of a throne, there was the semblance of a human form. 27 From what appeared as his loins up, I saw a gleam as of amber—what looked like a fire encased in a frame; and from what appeared as his loins down, I saw what look like fire. There was a radiance all about him. 28 Like the appearance of the bow which shines in the clouds on a day of rain, such was the appearance of the surrounding radiance. That was the appearance of the semblance of the Presence of the Lord. When I beheld it, I flung myself down on my face. And I heard the voice of someone speaking.

2.5.11 Ezekiel 37: The Valley of the Dry Bones

Writing after the destruction of Jerusalem, Ezekiel prophesied that the nation would be rebuilt. His prophesy took the form of a metaphor in which he pictured the nation as dry bones strewn upon a valley. These bones are seen as coming together and coming back to life, symbolizing the destiny of the Jewish nation.

37:1 The hand of the Lord came upon me. He took me out by the Spirit of the Lord and set me down in the valley. It was full of bones. 2 He led me all around them; there were very many of them spread over the valley, and they were very dry. 3 He said to me, "O mortal, can these bones live again?" I replied, "O Lord God, only You know." 4 And He said to me, " Prophesy over these bones and say to them: O dry bones, hear the word of the Lord! 5 Thus said the Lord God to these bones: I will cause breath to enter you and you shall live again. 6 I will lay sinews upon you, and cover you with flesh, and form skin over you. And I will put breath into you, and you shall live again. And you shall know that I am the Lord!"

7 I prophesied as I had been commanded. And while I was prophesying, suddenly there was a sound of rattling, and the bones came together, bone to matching bone. 8 I looked, and there were sinews on them, and flesh had grown, and skin had formed over them; but there was no breath in them. 9 Then He said to me, "Prophesy to the breath, prophesy, O mortal! Say to the breath: Thus said the Lord God: Come, O breath, from the four winds, and breathe into these slain, that they may live again." 10 I prophesied as He commanded me. The breath entered them, and they came to life and stood up on their feet, a vast multitude.

11 And He said to me, "O mortal, these bones are the whole House of Israel. They say, 'Our bones are dried up, our hope is gone; we are doomed.' 12 Prophesy, therefore, and say to them: Thus said the Lord God: I am going to open your graves and lift you out of the graves, O My people, and bring you to the land of Israel. 13 You shall know, O My people, that I am the Lord, when I have opened your graves and lifted you out of your graves. 14 I will put My breath into you and you shall live again and I will set you upon your own soil. Then you shall know that I the Lord have spoken and have acted"—declares the Lord.

2.6 WISDOM LITERATURE

2.6.1 Proverbs 8: The Character of Wisdom

The Book of Proverbs draws much of its inspiration from the ancient Near Eastern wisdom tradition. Whereas wisdom was understood in the ancient Near East in a universalistic manner, Jewish tradition came to understand it as an equivalent to Torah, itself perceived as a reflection of the divine intellect. This passage, like many others, personifies wisdom as a woman and speaks of the happiness and riches of those who achieve wisdom. Later Jewish interpretators identified wisdom with Torah in its wider sense—the wisdom of God.

🌿

8:1 It is Wisdom calling,
Understanding raising her voice.
2 She takes her stand at the topmost heights,
by the wayside, at the crossroads,
3 Near the gates at the city entrance;
At the entryways, she shouts,
4 "O men, I call to you;
My cry is to all mankind.
5 O simple ones, learn shrewdness;
O dullards, instruct your minds.
6 Listen, for I speak noble things;
Uprightness comes from my lips;
7 My mouth utters truth;
Wickedness is abhorrent to my lips.
8 All my words are just,
None of them perverse or crooked;
9 All are straightforward to the intelligent man,
And right to those who have attained knowledge.

10 Accept my discipline rather than silver,
Knowledge rather than choice gold.
11 For wisdom is better than rubies;
No goods can equal her.
12 I, Wisdom, live with Prudence;
I attain knowledge and foresight.
13 To fear the Lord is to hate evil;
I hate pride, arrogance, the evil way,
And duplicity in speech.
14 Mine are counsel and resourcefulness;
I am understanding; courage is mine.
15 Through me kings reign
And rulers decree just laws;
16 Through me princes rule,
Great men and all the righteous judges.
17 Those who love me I love,
And those who seek me will find me.
18 Riches and honor belong to me,
Enduring wealth and success.
19 My fruit is better than gold, fine gold,
And my produce better than choice silver.
20 I walk on the way of righteousness,
On the paths of justice.
21 I endow those who love me with substance;
I will fill their treasuries. . . .
32 . . . Now, sons, listen to me;
Happy are they who keep my ways.
33 Heed discipline and become wise;
Do not spurn it.
34 Happy is the man who listens to me,
Coming early to my gates each day,
Waiting outside my doors.
35 For he who finds me finds life
And obtains favor from the Lord.
36 But he who misses me destroys himself;
All who hate me love death."

2.6.2 Job 38: God's Infinite Powers

Another wisdom tract is the Book of Job. Set in the mythical land of Oz, it pictures a pious man tried at the hands of a divine adversary sent by God to test his righteous follower. After all of Job's protestations, and the attempts of his friends to comfort him in his time of grief, God finally enters the debate on the reasons for the existence of evil in the world and responds that human beings cannot possibly understand the infinite wisdom of God, the nature of the world, and the divine plan. Trust in the wisdom of God, such as Job had, is the only option for humanity. This excerpt accents the ultimate wisdom of God when compared with that of humans.

ೋ

38:1 Then the Lord replied to Job out of the tempest and said:

2 Who is this who darkens counsel,
Speaking without knowledge?
3 Gird your loins like a man;
I will ask and you will inform Me.
4 Where were you when I laid the earth's foundations?
Speak if you have understanding.
5 Do you know who fixed its dimensions
Or who measured it with a line?
6 Onto what were its bases sunk?
Who set its cornerstone
7 When the morning stars sang together
And all the divine beings shouted for joy?
8 Who closed the sea behind doors
When it gushed forth out of the womb,
9 When I clothed it in clouds,
Swaddled it in dense clouds,
10 When I made breakers My limit for it,
And set up its bar and doors,
11 And said, "You may come so far and no farther;
Here your surging waves will stop"?
12 Have you ever commanded the day to break,
Assigned the dawn its place,
13 So that it seizes the corners of the earth
And shakes the wicked out of it?. . .
16 Have you penetrated to the sources of the sea,
Or walked in the recesses of the deep?
17 Have the gates of death been disclosed to you?
Have you seen the gates of deep darkness?
18 Have you surveyed the expanses of the earth?
If you know of these—tell Me.
19 Which path leads to where light dwells,

And where is the place of darkness,
20 That you may take it to its domain
And know the way to its home?
21 Surely you know, for you were born then,
And the number of your years is many!

2.6.3 Ecclesiastes 3: The Nature of Man in Time

The Book of Ecclesiastes, Hebrew Kohelet, like Job and Proverbs, is a wisdom text. Ecclesiastes and Proverbs were taken by later Rabbinic tradition to have been composed by King Solomon. Modern scholars, however, see Hellenistic influence on this book. In the passage that follows, often quoted in Western literature, the author muses upon the meaning of time and the finite nature of human existence.

꙳

3: 1 A season is set for everything, a time for every experience under heaven:
2 A time for being born and a time for dying,
A time for planting and a time for uprooting the planted;
3 A time for slaying and a time for healing,
A time for tearing down and a time for building up;
4 A time for weeping and a time for laughing,
A time for wailing and a time for dancing;
5 A time for throwing stones and a time for gathering stones,
A time for embracing and a time for shunning embraces;
6 A time for seeking and a time for losing,
A time for keeping and a time for discarding;
7 A time for ripping and a time for sewing,
A time for silence and a time for speaking;
8 A time for loving and a time for hating;
A time for war and a time for peace.
9 What value, then, can the man of affairs get from what he earns?. . .

17 I mused: "God will doom both righteous and wicked, for there is a time for every experience and for every happening." 18 So I decided, as regards men, to dissociate them [from] the divine beings and to face the fact that they are beasts. 19 For in respect of the fate of man and the fate of beast, they have one and the same fate: as the one dies so dies the other, and both have the same lifebreath; man has no superiority over beast, since both amount to nothing. 20 Both go to the same place; both came from dust and both return to dust. 21 Who knows if a man's lifebreath does rise upward and if a beast's breath does sink down into the earth?

22 I saw that there is nothing better for man than to enjoy his possessions, since that is his portion. For who can enable him to see what will happen afterward?

2.6.4 Psalm 1: The Wages of Righteousness and Sin

The book of Psalms begins with the wisdom-like assertion that transgression brings with it its own punishment while following the way of the Lord brings happiness and stability. God's love of the righteous and punishment of the wicked are the main motifs of this psalm.

჻

1:1 Happy is the man who has not followed the counsel of the wicked,
or taken the path of sinners,
or joined the company of the insolent;
2 rather, the teaching of the Lord is his delight,
and he studies that teaching day and night.
3 He is like a tree planted beside streams of water,
which yields its fruit in season,
whose foliage never fades,
and whatever it produces thrives.
4 Not so the wicked;
rather, they are like chaff that wind blows away.
5 Therefore the wicked will not survive judgment,
nor will sinners, in the assembly of the righteous.
6 For the Lord cherishes the way of the righteous,
but the way of the wicked is doomed.

2.6.5 Psalm 130: Sin and Forgiveness

Many chapters of the book of Psalms are written in the style of individual plaints, calling upon God to give help to the worshipper in a time of dire need. This psalm, which continued to fulfill this purpose throughout Jewish history, calls on God to be merciful and forgiving and to grant aid, for it is God alone Who is capable of forgiving and saving His people.

჻

130:1 A song of ascents.[35]
Out of the depths I call You, O Lord.
2 O Lord, listen to my cry;

---

35. This prefix refers to psalms that were sung on the stairs of the Temple.

let Your ears be attentive
to my plea for mercy.
3 If You keep account of sins, O Lord,
Lord, who will survive?
4 Yours is the power to forgive
so that You may be held in awe.
5 I look to the Lord;
I look to Him;
I await His word.
6 I am more eager for the Lord
than watchmen for the morning,
watchmen for the morning.
7 O Israel, wait for the Lord;
for with the Lord is steadfast love
and great power to redeem.
8 It is He who will redeem Israel from all their iniquities.

2.6.6 Psalm 150: Musical Praise of God

The Book of Psalms concludes with a stirring poem calling on all people to join in praise of God with all manner of musical instruments. These instruments were used in the worship of the Jerusalem Temple where this text was recited.

꿏

150:1 Hallellujah.
Praise God in His sanctuary;
praise Him in the sky, His stronghold.
2 Praise Him for His mighty acts;
praise Him for His exceeding greatness.
3 Praise Him with blasts of the horn;
praise Him with harp and lyre.
4 Praise Him with timbrel and dance;
praise Him with lute and pipe.
5 Praise Him with resounding cymbals;
praise Him with loud-clashing cymbals.
6 Let all that breathes praise the Lord.
Hallelujah.

3

Judaism in the Persian Period

The Persian period was inaugurated with the conquest of Babylon by Cyrus the Great in 539 B.C.E. For the Jews, however, much more significant was the proclamation of Cyrus the Great (538 B.C.E.) permitting them to return to the Land of Israel and rebuild their homeland, at least in the area of Jerusalem and the surrounding countryside of Judea. The text of this decree, as handed down by the biblical tradition, is found in Ezra 1 (text 3.1.1) as well as at the very end of 2 Chronicles. But there has also been preserved a Declaration of Cyrus, presented here (text 3.1.2), which was issued at the time of his accession. This document is a general one, indicating that all exiled peoples are to be permitted to return and to reinstitute worship in the manner of their local religions. There are two possible interpretations of the biblical decree. It may preserve a version of the decree made specifically for the Jews, if, indeed, there were specific decrees issued by Cyrus to put the general decree into effect. Alternatively, it may represent a version of the original decree adapted by Jews who understood the decree of Cyrus primarily for its relevance to the Jewish community. In the biblical account, even the Temple vessels were returned to the Jews by the Persians (text 3.1.3).

While the rise of the Persian Empire brought about an amelioration of the status of the Jews in Judea, this was not the only Jewish community which existed. Thanks to the documents from Elephantine (also called Yev or Assuan), we know of the colony of Jewish soldiers who lived in this Egyptian town. Among the various legal and historical documents left by this community, known as the Elephantine papyri, a number are of special interest. The so-called Passover Papyrus (text 3.2.1) is an exhortation from the governor of Judea to the people of Elephantine to observe Passover. In the course of giving these laws, the text makes direct reference to the biblical commands and indicates the widespread observance of Passover at that time. Another letter, the Temple Papyrus (text 3.2.2), actually preserved in two copies, indicates that there was a Jewish temple at Elephantine which had been destroyed. In this document, the Jewish authorities request permission to rebuild the temple. We learn that certain sacrificial rites were performed in this temple. Indeed, we will see that sacrifices were later to be offered in Egypt at the Temple of Leontopolis in the Hellenistic period. Whereas that temple resulted from the disaffection of a claimant to the post of high priest, we are dealing in the papyrus with a community which has not yet been affected by the notion that exiled Jews may not sacrifice outside of Jerusalem. Further, this community had syncretistically adopted elements of paganism. At least for these Jews, sacrifice was considered permissible. This community carried on extensive legal activity in numerous spheres, as exemplified here by the marriage contract (text 3.2.3) and by a contract regarding a loan of grain (3.2.4).

Meanwhile, in Judea, the Temple was being rebuilt and sacrifices reinstated in Jerusalem. The first item in the stabilization of the renewed Jewish settlement in Jerusalem was the building of the city walls and gate as described in Nehemiah (text 3.2.5) The beginning of sacrifice, alluded to in Ezra 3 (text 3.2.6), was regarded as a major occasion. The arrival of Ezra heralded a revolution. Henceforth, the Torah would become the constitution of the returned exiles and that new elements would join in the efforts to rebuild (text 3.2.7). Nehemiah 8 (text 3.2.8) relates the public reading of the Torah (later taken as paradigmatic for the synagogue service in Rabbinic tradition) in which the people entered into a covenant to observe the law of the Torah, the fundamental constitution of the Jewish nation in the Persian period.

Fundamental issues of Jewish status and identity came up early, and these are discussed in Ezra 9–10 (text 3.2.9) dealing with the problem of foreign, that is, non-Jewish, wives. It was decided by

Ezra, according to the biblical account, to require that those married to such women separate from them. This passage is taken as an important step in affirming the prohibition on intermarriage which has typified Judaism throughout its history. Furthermore, in our view, this text indicates that Jewish descent was already determined through the status of the mother at this time.

Scholars have debated the chronology of Ezra and Nehemiah, although the biblical account understands them to overlap. After the days of Ezra and Nehemiah, Judea began to be ruled by priests. Their line of succession is discussed, apparently based on some traditional sources, by Josephus in *Antiquities* (text 3.2.10). In this excerpt we learn about the darker side of some of the political maneuvering in the Persian period in Judea. The passage also discusses the tensions between the Jews (Judeans) and the Samaritans who inhabited the northern part of Israel, also called Cutheans. We learn here of an alliance by marriage between the high priest's brother and the daughter of the Samaritan Sanballat.

Central to the Judean community in this period, and indeed, to Judaism for the entire Second Temple period was the Temple and its worship. Even before the Temple was actually built, sacrifices began where the First Temple had stood (3.3.1). Permission to rebuild the Temple was secured from the Persian authorities, as explained in Ezra 6 (text 3.3.2). In accord with the Edict of Cyrus, discussed above, the Judeans were given help by the Persian authorities for this project. Yet early in the project, the Samaritans, as described in Ezra 4 (text 3.4.1), wanted to join in. They were a mixed people, descended from the North Israelites and the foreigners brought in by the Assyrians after they destroyed the north in 722 B.C.E. Samaritan opposition to the Temple-building project is narrated in detail in 1 Esdras (text 3.4.2), an alternative version of Ezra and Nehemiah with some later expansions. To understand the background of the Samaritans we present here 2 Kings 17 (text 3.4.3), from which some information about their origins can be derived. We date this sect to this early date, although many scholars believe that it did not come into being until much later.

The story of the building of the Temple and the Samaritan interference is told in detail by Josephus in *Antiquities* (text 3.4.4). Here we see in detail the flurry of political machinations which sur-

rounded the attempt of the Samaritans to block its construction after
their offer to help build the Temple had been rebuffed by the
Judeans. Yet the Edict of Cyrus prevailed, and as a result the building was permitted. With the building of the Temple and adoption of
the Torah as the community's constitution, Jewish life in the Second
Commonwealth was off to a firm start.

One of the most important products of the last years of the biblical period was the rise of midrashic interpretation, a method of
interpreting the Bible in which one verse was to be understood in
light of another. This form of interpretation was used in Nehemiah
8, as part of the covenant-renewal ceremony, to derive the details for
the building of the Sukkah, the booth for the festival of Sukkot (text
3.5.1). In Nehemiah 10 (text 3.5.2) an entire series of regulations
was undertaken by the people of Judea which scholarly investigation
shows to have resulted from midrashic interpretation of the Bible. In
this respect, the exegetical basis for the development of postbiblical
Judaism was already set out in the later biblical books. The influence
of this kind of interpretation is seen in the Apocrypha, Pseudepigrapha, Dead Sea Scrolls, and Rabbinic literature.

The late biblical books, stemming primarily from the Persian
period, present a rich literature which tells us of the religious aspirations as well as the historical accounts of the period. At this time the
books of Chronicles were edited from ancient sources, including the
books of Samuel and Kings. Chronicles, closely related to Ezra and
Nehemiah in style, stresses the centrality of David and his dynasty to
Jewish history and ideology. For this reason, we present selections
dealing with David and Solomon from 1 Chronicles 28–29 (text
3.6.1). In this passage David is pictured as delivering a religious message; he is also depicted as setting up the sacrificial system even
before the construction of the Temple.

One of the ongoing struggles in the early period of Persian rule
was the slow pace of the rebuilding of the Temple. In our excerpt
from Haggai 1 (text 3.6.2) the prophet calls upon the people to
complete the House of God quickly. The prophet rallied the support of the leaders even as they seemed to waver (text 3.6.3).

From the book of Zechariah we present the vision of the cleansing of the priest Joshua and the promise that if he discharges his
tasks in an upright manner, the Branch—the messiah son of

David—will be brought by God (text 3.6.4). Clearly, the text means to legitimate priestly rule as temporary, and as a means of bringing about the restoration of the Davidic house. In chapter 4, the message is delivered to Zerubbabel, governor of Judea and a Davidic scion, that he shall succeed in building the Temple. Zechariah 8 includes a vision of the rebuilt Jerusalem, speaking of the completion of the building of the Temple, as well as a time in which the traditional fast days will be abolished and turned into days of rejoicing. We hear of the participation of the nations in this universalistic day of triumph. These passages were taken by later tradition to refer to the messianic era. Chapter 14 includes a vision of the coming destruction of the wicked, and helped to influence the rise of the catastrophic trend in Jewish messianism, which takes its cue from the biblical Day of the Lord.

Malachi 2 (text 3.6.5) is a prophecy against injustice on the part of the priests, who are called upon to be righteous. Such an appeal to the covenant with Levi would have been extremely important in Second Temple times since the priests played such an important role in both political and religious affairs. Here God's relation to Israel is likened to that of a husband to his wife, a familiar theme in First Temple prophecy as well. Chapter 3 speaks of those who had doubts about the need to observe Jewish practice, and assures them that the day of the destruction of the wicked is coming. The passage, which concludes the prophets as a corpus, ends with an appeal to the Torah of Moses and with mention of the vision that Elijah the prophet would speedily come as the harbinger of the messianic redeemer.

We turn finally to investigate the collection of holy scriptures, the biblical canon. The authenticity of Jewish Scripture, as opposed to the texts of the Greco-Roman world, was argued strongly by Josephus (3.7.1). The list of books and their order is found in a passage in Babylonian Talmud Bava Batra (text 3.7.2). This passage gives us a sense of the final notion of canon in Rabbinic tradition, even though its order is different from that which became traditional for Jews in the Middle Ages. Josephus, *Against Apion* I (text 3.7.1) asserts the consistency and unanimity of the biblical corpus and the authenticity of the biblical texts.

Mishnah Yadayim (text 3.7.3) takes up the inclusion of a few books still in question in Rabbinic times, Song of Songs and Ecclesiastes. This discussion is framed in terms of whether the books defile the hands, and it is assumed that for some reason the holy books included in the canon render the hands impure, whereas those outside this collection do not. Tosefta Yadayim (text 3.7.4) expands upon this theme. In any case, these sources demonstrate that the content of the collection of biblical books was agreed upon by Rabbinic times. Yet we should note that the New Testament and the Dead Sea Scrolls indicate that such agreement was for the most part reached much earlier.

The documents we have presented here open up to us a formative period in the history of Judaism in which Judaism moved from the biblical era toward the development of its postbiblical manifestations. Already in these sources we see tendencies toward sectarianism and schism, yet at the same time the priesthood, Temple, and biblical canon were asserting themselves as the basic organizing principles of Jewish life and religion in Late Antiquity.

3.1 HISTORICAL AND ARCHAEOLOGICAL BACKGROUND

3.1.1 Ezra 1: Inaugurating the Return[1]

According to the biblical account, soon after Cyrus the Great conquered Babylon in 539/8 B.C.E., he decreed that the Jews could return from exile in Babylonia and rebuild their city and Temple. This declaration may be said to have inaugurated the Second Temple period.

🕎

1:1 In the first year of King Cyrus of Persia, when the word of the Lord spoken by Jeremiah was fulfilled, 2 the Lord roused the spirit of King Cyrus of Persia to issue a proclamation throughout his realm by word of mouth and in writing as follows:

2 "Thus said King Cyrus of Persia: The Lord God of Heaven has given me all the kingdoms of the earth and has charged me with building Him a house in Jerusalem, which is in Judah. 3 Anyone of you of all his people— may his God be with him, and let him go up to Jerusalem that is in Judah and build the house of the Lord God of Israel, the God that is in Jerusalem; 4 and all who stay behind, wherever he may be living, let the people

---

1. All biblical texts are from *Tanakh: A New Translation of the Holy Scriptures* (Philadelphia: The Jewish Publication Society, 1985).

of his place assist him with silver, gold, goods, and livestock, besides the freewill offering to the House of God that is in Jerusalem."

3.1.2 The Declaration of Cyrus: The Rebuilding of Ancient Shrines[2]

Cyrus conquered Babylonia in 539 B.C.E., and, with his ascendance to the throne, he published this edict of 538 B.C.E. Its purpose was to allow the rebuilding of local temples and the reinstitution of worship in them by the peoples who had previously been exiled. This edict was the basis for the Jewish effort to return to the province of Yahud (Judea) and rebuild the Jerusalem Temple.

$\mathcal{K}$

. . . an inferior man has been appointed enu[3] of his land . . . he commanded that copies be set upon them. A model of the temple of Esagila[4] . . . for Ur[5] and for the remaining holy cities improper rites (he) . . . daily he babbled, yet blasphemously he discontinued the regular offerings. He revealed(?) . . . he set up in the holy cities. The worship of Marduk,[6] the king of the gods, he [changed] into abomination, daily he used to do evil against (Marduk's) city. [He tortured its inhabitants] with a yoke without relief; he ruined them all. Upon their protestations, the lord of the gods was enraged and [. . .] their region, and the other gods living among them abandoned their houses, angered that he had brought them into Babylon. May(?) Marduk . . . return his favor to all the settlements whose dwellings have lain in ruins!

Further, he showed mercy to and had pity on the people of Sumer and Akkad[7] who had become like dead men. He searched and looked through all the countries, seeking a just king of his own choosing, whom he took by the hand. He named Cyrus, king of Anshan; he appointed him to rule all the world. He made the Guti-country and all the Manda-host prostrate themselves before (Cyrus') feet. And (Cyrus) always undertook to administer fairly and justly the black-haired[8] people whom (Marduk) made him

---

2. Trans. S. Berrin with the assistance of D. Fleming from F. H. Weissbach, *Die Keilschriften der Achmeniden* (Vorderasiatische Bibliothek 3; Leipzig: J.C. Hidrichs, 1911), 2ff.

3. An Old Sumerian title for leader.

4. The temple precinct of Babylon.

5. One of the oldest cities in southern Mesopotamia, the biblical "Ur of the Chaldees."

6. The chief god of Babylon.

7. An expression denoting Babylonia in terms of the two major ethnic groups which dominated it in the second millenium B.C.E.

8. Literally, "black-headed."

conquer. The great lord Marduk, guardian of his people, observed with approval (Cyrus') good deeds and his upright heart and ordered him to march against his city Babylon. He had him start upon the way to Babylon, accompanying him like a friend and companion. His outspread host, whose number was as indistinguishable as the water drops of a river, marched at his side with girded weapons. He allowed him to enter his city Babylon without battle or conflict, averting any harm to Babylon. He delivered into his hands Nabonidus,[9] the king who did not worship him. All the inhabitants of Babylon as well as the entire country of Sumer and Akkad, officers and governors, knelt low to (Cyrus) and kissed his feet, elated at his kingship and radiant. They hailed him joyously as a master whose aid had returned them to life from death, and had saved them from tragedy and ruin, and they worshipped his name.

I am Cyrus, king of the world, great king, legitimate king, king of Babylon, king of Sumer and Akkad, king of the four ends (of the earth), son of Cambyses, great king, king of Anshan, grandson of Cyrus, great king, king of Anshan, descendant of Teispes, great king, king of Anshan, of a family of eternal kingship, whose rule Bel and Nebo[10] love, whose kingship they require for their satisfaction. When I entered Babylon peaceably, I took up a lordly residence in the royal palace amid joy and celebration, and the great lord Marduk aroused the love of the . . . citizens of Babylon to me, and I worshipped him daily. My outspread hosts marched within Babylon peacefully, and I prohibited anybody from oppressing [Sumer] and Akkad. I pursued peace in Babylon and in all his holy cities. As for the Babylonians, who against the will of the gods were subjected to a yoke not proper for their status . . . , I relieved their weariness, I released their. . . . The great lord Marduk was well pleased with my deeds and sent generous blessings to myself, Cyrus, the king who worships him, to Cambyses, my son, the offspring of my loins, as well as to all my host, so we shall live happily in his presence, in peace.

All the kings of the entire world from the Upper to the Lower Sea, those who sit on a throne dais, those who live in other buildings, and all the kings of the West Land living in tents, brought their heavy tributes and kissed my feet in Babylon. From . . . as far as Ashur and Susa, Agade, Eshnunna, the towns Zamban, Me-Turnu, Der, as far as the Gutian territory and the settlements on the other side of the Tigris, where their temples have long lain in ruin, I returned the gods who lived therein to their places and provided them with permanent temples. I gathered all their

---

9. The last king of Babylon (556–539 B.C.E.).
10. Mesopotamian deities.

inhabitants and returned them to their homes. Furthermore, upon the command of the great lord Marduk, the gods of Sumer and Akkad whom Nabonidus had brought to Babylon, so enraging the lord of the gods, I ensconced securely in their abodes, the places which make them happy.

Daily, may all the gods whom I have brought back to their holy sites speak on my behalf for long life and plead my favor before Bel and Nebo. To my lord Marduk may they say thus: Cyrus the king who worships you, and Cambyses his son . . . all of them I settled in a peaceful place. . . .

3.1.3 Ezra 1: The Vessels of the Temple

The biblical account sees the support for the return as coming both from the Jewish community in Babylonia as well as from the Persian ruler who returned the sacred vessels taken by the Babylonians when they sacked the Jerusalem Temple in 586 B.C.E.

$\mathfrak{S}$

1: 5 So the chiefs of the clans of Judah and Benjamin, and the priests and Levites, all whose spirit had been roused by God, got ready to go up to build the House of the Lord that is in Jerusalem. 6 All their neighbors supported them with silver vessels, with gold, with goods, with livestock, and with precious objects, besides what had been given as a freewill offering. 7 King Cyrus of Persia released the vessels of the Lord's house which Nebuchadnezzar had taken away from Jerusalem and had put in the house of his god. 8 These King Cyrus of Persia released through the office of Mithredath the treasurer, who gave an inventory of them to Sheshbazzar the prince of Judah. 9 This is the inventory: 30 gold basins, 1,000 silver basins, 29 knives, 10 30 gold bowls, 410 silver double bowls, 1,000 other vessels; 11 in all, 5,400 gold and silver vessels. Sheshbazzar brought all these back when the exiles came back from Babylon to Jerusalem.

3.2 POLITICAL AFFAIRS

3.2.1 Elephantine Passover Papyrus: The Observance of Passover[11]

The celebration of Passover at Elephantine in the fifth century B.C.E. already included many of the observances we recognize today—the eating of unleavened bread (matzah), the abstention from work, as well as the putting

---

11. Trans. S. Berrin from the Aramaic in B. Porten and A. Yardeni, *Textbook of Aramaic Documents from Ancient Egypt* (Jerusalem: The Hebrew University, Department of the History of the Jewish People, Texts and Studies for Students, 1986), p. 54 (Cowley 21).

away of all leaven and fermented substances such as beer. The second para-graph is for the most part a pastiche of biblical commands.

❧

[To my brothers Je]daniah and his colleagues, the garrison of the Jews, (from) your brother Hananiah. May God [be concerned about] the welfare of my brothers [at all times.] And now, this year, year 5 of Darius the King (419 B.C.E.), from the king it has been sent to Arsa[mes. . .].[12]

And now, you shall count fou[rteen days in Nisan, and on the 14th day at twilight, observe the Passover.] And from the 15th day until the 21st day of [Nisan observe the holiday of unleavened bread. Seven days eat unleavened bread. Now,] be pure and be careful that you do no work [on the 15th day and on the 21st day of Nisan. All beer] you shall not drink and all matter of leaven you shall not [eat, and it may not be seen in your houses from the 14th day of Nisan] at sundown until the 21st day of Nisa[n at sundown. All leaven which you have in your houses] lock inside your storage rooms and seal it up between [these] days.

3.2.2 Elephantine Temple Papyrus:
The Destruction of the Temple at Elephantine[13]

This papyrus indicates that the Jewish military colony of Elephantine, established in the 6th century B.C.E., had a Temple at which they worshipped. When this Temple was violently destroyed, they appealed for the right to rebuild it, indicating in their letter that they had performed sacrifices there.

❧

To our lord Bagoas, governor of Judea, from your servants Jedaniah and his colleagues the priests who are in Elephantine the fortress. May the God of Heaven be concerned about the welfare of our lord greatly at all times, and grant you favor before Darius the King and the members of his household a thousand times more than now, and give you long life. May you be happy and strong at all times. And now, your servant Jedaniah and his colleagues say thus:

In the month of Tammuz, year 14 of Darius the King,[14] when Arsames had left and gone to the king, at that time the priests of Khnub the god,

---

12. A high official in the Persian Empire directly responsible to the king.

13. Trans. S. Berrin from the Aramaic in B. Porten and A. Yardeni, *Textbook of Aramaic Documents from Ancient Egypt*, p. 72 (Cowley 31, 32).

14. 410 B.C.E. Darius II ruled from 423–404 B.C.E.

who are in Elephantine the fortress, gave silver and goods to Vidrang who was fratarak[15] here, saying: "The temple of YHW the God,[16] which is in Elephantine the fortress, let them remove from there." Then that Vidrang, the accursed, sent a letter to his son Nafyan who was garrison commander in Syene the fortress, saying: "The temple of the God YHW which is in Elephantine the fortress, let them demolish." Then, that Nafyan led Egyptians with the other troops. They came to the Elephantine fortress with their arms, entered the temple and demolished it to the ground. And the pillars of stone which were there, they smashed. They even demolished the five great gateways, built of stone sculpture, which were in that temple. And the upright doors and the bronze hinges of those doors and the roof of that temple, all of it cedarwood, with the rest of the temple and the other things which were there, all these they burned with fire. As for the basins of gold and silver and the things which were in that Temple—all these they took and made their own.

And in the days of the kings of Egypt, our fathers had built that temple in Elephantine the fortress. And when Cambyses entered Egypt,[17] he found that temple built. And the temples of the gods of the Egyptians—all of them they overthrew, but none damaged anything in that temple. And when this had been done, we with our wives and children were wearing sackcloth and fasting and praying to YHW, Lord of the Heaven, who has let us see the punishment of that Vidrang. The dogs removed the fetters from his legs and all the possessions which he had acquired were lost. And every man who had sought evil to that temple, all were killed and we watched their punishment.

Moreover, before this, when this evil was done to us, we sent a letter regarding this. We sent to our lord, even to Yoḥanan the High Priest, and his colleagues the priests who are in Jerusalem, and to Ostanes the brother of Anani and the nobles of Judea. Not one letter did they send us. Moreover, from the month of Tammuz, year 14 of Darius the king, and until this day, we have been wearing sackcloth and fasting. Our wives are made as widows. We do not annoint ourselves with oil and do not drink wine.[18] Moreover, from that time and until this day, the year 17 of Darius the king, meal-offering, incense, and burnt-offering are not made in that temple.

---

15. A term for governor.
16. A designation for the God of Israel.
17. 525 B.C.E. Cambyses was the eldest son of Cyrus and succeeded him after his death in 530 B.C.E.
18. They abstained from sexual relations, oil, and wine as a sign of mourning.

And now, your servants Jedaniah and his colleagues the priests, and the Jews, all of them, the citizens of Elephantine say thus: If it please our lord, take thought of that temple to build it, as they do not allow us to build it. Look to your benefactors and friends who are here in Egypt. Let a letter be sent to them from you about the temple of YHW the God to build it in Elephantine the fortress as it was built before. And meal-offering, incense, and burnt-offering we will sacrifice on the altar of YHW in your name, and we will pray for you at all times, we and our wives and our children, and all the Jews who are here, if you will do so without fail, so that that temple will be built. And you will have merit before YHW the God of Heaven more than a man who sacrifices to Him burnt-offerings and sacrifices worth 1000 talents of silver. Regarding this we have sent to inform our lord. . . . Moreover, all this which was done to us, Arsames did not know.

On the 20th of Marheshvan, the 17th year of Darius the king.[19]

3.2.3 Marriage Contract from the Ananiah Archive: Document of Wifehood[20]

This record of the marriage of a free man to a handmaiden presents a unique opportunity to reconstruct the haggling that went on between the groom and master regarding the status of the bride and the rights of the parties to the contract. Tamet's status may be described as comparable to that of the biblical "slave woman designated for a man" for the purpose of marriage (Lev. 19:20). In Rabbinic terms she was "part slave and part free."

ᔑᔑ

RECTO:

[On] the 18th of [A]b, [that is day 30] of the month of Pharmouthi, year 16 of Artaxer(xes) the king,[21] said Ananiah son of Azariah,[22] a servitor of YHH[23] the God who is in Elephantine the fortress,[24] to Meshullam son of Zaccur, an Aramean of Syene[25] of the detachment of Varyazata, saying:

---

19. 408 B.C.E.

20. Trans. B. Porten, *The Elephantine Papyri in English* (Leiden; New York: E. J. Brill, 1996), pp. 208–11.

21. August 9, 449 B.C.E.

22. Ananiah son of Azariah was a temple official of unknown status whose archives were found at Elephantine.

23. An alternate spelling of the divine name.

24. The God of Israel whose temple stood at Elephantine (see text 3.2.2), an island in the Nile which was set up as a fortress to guard the southern border of Egypt.

25. A fort on the mainland opposite Elephantine.

I came to you (and asked you) to give me Tamet by name, who is your handmaiden,[26] for wifehood.

She is my wife and I am her husband from this day and forever.

Tamet brought into me in her hand:[27]

1 garment of wool,[28] worth (in) silver 7 shekels;[29]
1 mirror, worth (in) silver 7 (and a) half hallurs;
1 pair of sandals;
(ERASURE: 1 handful of)[30] one-half handful of balsam oil;
6 handfuls of castor oil;[31]
1 tray.
All the silver and the
value of the goods: (in) silver, 7 shekels,
7 (and a) half hallurs.

Tomorrow or (the) next day,[32] should Anani stand up in an assembly and say: "I hated Tamet my wife," silver of hatre(d) is on his head. He shall give Tamet silver, 7 shekels <2 q(uarters)>[33] and all that she brought in in her hand she shall take out, from straw to string.

Tomorrow or (the) next day, should Tamet stand up and say: "I hated my husband Anani," 2 q(uarters) silver of hatre(d) is on her head. She shall give to Anani silver, 7 shekels[34] and all that she brought in in her hand she shall take out, from straw to string.[35]

Tomorrow or (the) next day, should Ananiah die (ERASURE: [It is Meshullam son of Zaccur (who)] has right to half),[36] it is Tamet (who) has right to all goods which will be between Anani and Tamet.

---

26. In a document of manumission dated 427 B.C.E. (Porten, pp. 220–22), Meshullam emancipated Tamet.

27. This is the formula that introduces the enumeration of the items of the dowry.

28. Tamet's dowry consisted of little more than the dress on her back and some toilet articles.

29. Originally, the value of the garment was set at 5 shekels, but presumably at the insistence of Meshullam, the scribe was instructed to add two more strokes to the number, raising it to 7 shekels.

30. One of the parties must have prevailed upon the other to change the quantity of balsam oil from one handful to one-half a handful.

31. A regular component of the Elephantine bride's dowry.

32. Meaning "any time in the future."

33. The signs <-> indicate material written above the lines as an addition.

34. Originally 5 shekels, the amount was raised by haggling to 7 1/2 shekels.

35. Note that Tamet has the right to initiate divorce.

36. Initially Meshullam was given property rights in the event that Anani died before Tamet, but the document was revised to allocate the marital property solely between husband and wife, thereby eliminating Meshullam's benefits.

Tomorrow or (the) next day, should Tamet die, it is Anani, he (who) has right (ERASURE: to half) to all goods which will be between (ERASURE: between) Tamet and between Anani.

And I, Meshullam, tomorrow or (the) next day, shall not be able to reclaim Pilti[37] from under your heart unless you expel his mother Tamet. <And if I do reclaim him from you I shall give Anani silver 5 karsh. >

Wrote Nathan son of Ananiah this document.[38]

And the witnesses herein:

witness Nathan son of Gaddul;

Menahem son of Zaccur;

Gemariah son of Mahseiah.

VERSO:

Tamet brought in to Anani in her hand silver, 1 karsh, 5 shekels.[39]

Document (*sealing*) of wi[fehood which Anani wrote for Ta]met.

3.2.4 Contract from the Ananiah Archive: Loan of Grain[40]

In the middle of December, Anani went to Syene to borrow from the Egyptian-named Aramean, Pakhnum son of Besa, a certain amount of emmer, a type of wheat widely cultivated in Egypt in the Persian period. The amount was the equivalent of a double ration for a month which Anani promised to pay back as soon as he received his ration.

༃

(In the) month of Thoth, year 4 of Artaxerxes the king,[41] then in Syene the fortress, said Anani son of Haggai son of Meshullam, a Jew of the detachment of Nabukudurri, to Pakhnum son of Besa, an Aramean of Syene of that detachment likewise, saying:

I came to you in your house in Syene the fortress and borrowed from you and you gave me emmer, 2 *peras*, 3 seahs.

---

37. Pilti was Tamet's son born of a free man and a slave mother, and so he was a slave. Meshullam's ultimate control of him was also his check on Anani's behavior should he decide to expel Tamet. If he did so, Anani would lose this child to Meshullam. The clause added above the line actually served to elevate Pilti's status from mere chattel, easily recoverable and reverting to bondage, to that of a son with protected rights and the prospects of attaining complete freedom.

38. This line serves as the identification of the scribe who wrote the contract.

39. This was an addition of cash to Tamet's dowry written on the verso after the document had been all but tied and sealed.

40. Porten, *The Elephantine Papyri in English,* pp. 252–4.

41. Between December 2 and 31, 402 B.C.E.

Afterwards, I, Anani son of Haggai, shall pay and give you that emmer, e(mmer), 2 p(eras),[42] 3 seahs from the ration which will be given me from the treasury of the king.[43]

And if I do not pay and give you that emmer which above is written when the ration is given me from the (store-)house of the king, afterwards I, Anani, shall be obligated and shall give you silver, a penalty of one, 1, karsh pure silver. Afterwards, I, Anani, shall pay and give you the penalty which is above written within 20, that is twenty, days, without suit.[44]

And if I die and have not yet paid[45] and given you the silver of yours which is above written, afterwards my children or my guarantors shall pay you your silver which is above written.

And if my children or my guarantors not pay you this silver which is above written, afterwards you, Pakhnum, have right to my security to seize (it) and you may take for yourself from (among) a house of bricks, slave or handmaiden, bronze or iron utensils, raiment or grain <which you will find of mine in Elephantine or in Syene or in the province> until you are paid your silver which above is written without suit.[46]

Wrote Shaweram son of Eshemram son of Eshemshezib[47] this document in Syene the fortress at the instruction of Anani son of (ERASURE: Meshullam) Haggai son of Meshullam.

The witnesses herein:[48]

(2nd hand) witness Menahem son of Shallum;
(3rd hand) witness Haggai;
(4th hand) witness Nahum the houseborn;
(5th hand) witness Haggai son of Mardu.

VERSO:
[Do]cument of grain [which Anani son of Haggai] son of Meshuallam [wrote] for Pakhnum son of Besa.

---

42. The value of the *peras* is uncertain.

43. The loan was interest free if repaid within a month, i.e. at the time of the monthly distribution of rations.

44. The fine was to be paid within twenty days of the receipt of rations.

45. A provision typical of loan contracts.

46. The right to seize personal property as security to enforce the payment of debts was commonly granted in contracts.

47. The Aramean scribe.

48. All the witnesses to this document were Jewish.

3.2.5 Nehemiah 1–6:
Rebuilding the Wall and Gates of Jerusalem

Nehemiah, cupbearer to King Artaxerxes, hearing about the destruction of Jerusalem and the dire conditions there, takes it upon himself to go personally and implement the rebuilding of the walls of Jerusalem. Each section was built privately by a group or family despite local opposition which caused the builders to have to arm themselves. Nehemiah also causes the well-to-do to forgive the debts of the poor, and he rescinds the heavy taxes they once had to pay.

✦

1:1 The narrative of Nehemiah son of Hacaliah:

In the month of Kislev of the twentieth year,[49] when I was in the fortress of Shushan, 2 Hanani, one of my brothers, together with some men of Judah, arrived, and I asked them about the Jews, the remnant who had survived the captivity, and about Jerusalem. 3 They replied, "The survivors who have survived the captivity there in the province are in dire trouble and disgrace; Jerusalem's wall is full of breaches, and its gates have been destroyed by fire."

4 When I heard that, I sat and wept, and was in mourning for days, fasting and praying to the God of Heaven. 5 I said, "O Lord, God of Heaven, great and awesome God, who stays faithful to His covenant with those who love Him and keep His commandments! 6 Let Your ear be attentive and Your eyes open to receive the prayer of Your servant that I am praying to You now, day and night, on behalf of the Israelites, Your servants, confessing the sins that we Israelites have committed against You, sins that I and my father's house have committed. 7 We have offended You by not keeping the commandments, the laws, and the rules that You gave to Your servant Moses. 8 Be mindful of the promise You gave to Your servant Moses: 'If you are unfaithful, I will scatter you among the peoples; 9 but if you turn back to Me, faithfully keep My commandments, even if your dispersed are at the ends of the earth, I will gather them from there and bring them to the place where I have chosen to establish My name.' 10 For they are Your servants and Your people whom You redeemed by Your great power and Your mighty hand. 11 O Lord! Let Your ear be attentive to the prayer of Your servant, and to the prayer of Your servants who desire to hold Your name in awe. Grant Your servant success today, and dispose that man to be compassionate toward him!"

I was the king's cupbearer at the time.

---

49. I.e., of King Artaxerxes; cf. Neh. 2.1.

2:1 In the month of Nisan, in the twentieth year of King Artaxerxes, wine was set before him; I took the wine and gave it to the king—I had never been out of sorts in his presence. 2 The king said to me, "How is it that you look bad, though you are not ill? It must be bad thoughts." I was very frightened, 3 but I answered the king, "May the king live forever! How should I not look bad when the city of the graveyard of my ancestors lies in ruins, and its gates have been consumed by fire?" 4 The king said to me, "What is your request?" With a prayer to the God of Heaven, 5 I answered the king, "If it please the king, and if your servant has found favor with you, send me to Judah, to the city of my ancestors' graves, to rebuild it." 6 With the consort seated at his side, the king said to me, "How long will you be gone and when will you return?" So it was agreeable to the king to send me, and I gave him a date. 7 Then I said to the king, "If it please the king, let me have letters to the governors of the province of Beyond the River, directing them to grant me passage until I reach Judah; 8 likewise, a letter to Asaph, the keeper of the King's Park, directing him to give me timber for roofing the gatehouses of the temple fortress and the city walls and for the house I shall occupy." The king gave me these, thanks to my God's benevolent care for me. 9 When I came to the governors of the province of Beyond the River I gave them the king's letters. The king also sent army officers and cavalry with me.

10 When Sanballat the Horonite and Tobiah the Ammonite servant heard, it displeased them greatly that someone had come, intent on improving the condition of the Israelites.

11 I arrived in Jerusalem. After I was there three days 12 I got up at night, I and a few men with me, and telling no one what my God had put into my mind to do for Jerusalem, and taking no other beast than the one on which I was riding, 13 I went out by the Valley Gate, at night, toward the Jackals' Spring and the Dung Gate; and I surveyed the walls of Jerusalem that were breached, and its gates, consumed by fire. 14 I proceeded to the Fountain Gate and to the King's Pool, where there was no room for the beast under me to continue. 15 So I went up the wadi by night, surveying the wall, and, entering again by the Valley Gate, I returned. 16 The prefects knew nothing of where I had gone or what I had done, since I had not yet divulged it to the Jews—the priests, the nobles, the prefects, or the rest of the officials.

17 Then I said to them, "You see the bad state we are in—Jerusalem lying in ruins and its gates destroyed by fire. Come, let us rebuild the wall of Jerusalem and suffer no more disgrace." 18 I told them of my God's benevolent care for me, also of the things that the king had said to me,

and they said, "Let us start building!" They were encouraged by [His] benevolence.

19 When Sanballat the Horonite and Tobiah the Ammonite servant and Geshem the Arab heard, they mocked us and held us in contempt and said, "What is this that you are doing? Are you rebelling against the king?" 20 I said to them in reply, "The God of Heaven will grant us success, and we, His servants, will start building. But you have no share or claim or stake in Jerusalem!"

3:1 Then Eliashib the high priest and his fellow priests set to and rebuilt the Sheep Gate; they consecrated it and set up its doors, consecrating it as far as the Hundred's Tower, as far as the Tower of Hananel. 2 Next to him, the men of Jericho built. Next to them, Zaccur son of Imri. 3 The sons of Hassenaah rebuilt the Fish Gate; they roofed it and set up its doors, locks, and bars. 4 Next to them, Meremoth son of Uriah son of Hakkoz repaired; and next to him, Meshullam son of Berechiah son of Meshezabel. Next to him, Zadok son of Baana repaired. 5 Next to him, the Tekoites repaired, though their nobles would not take upon their shoulders the work of their lord. 6 Joiada son of Paseah and Meshullam son of Besodeiah repaired the Jeshanah Gate; they roofed it and set up its doors, locks, and bars. 7 Next to them, Melatiah the Gibeonite and Jadon the Meronothite repaired, [with] the men of Gibeon and Mizpah, under the jurisdiction of the governor of the province of Beyond the River. 8 Next to them, Uzziel son of Harhaiah, [of the] smiths, repaired. Next to him, Hananiah, of the perfumers.[50] They restored Jerusalem as far as the Broad Wall. 9 Next to them, Rephaiah son of Hur, chief of half the district of Jerusalem, repaired. 10 Next to him, Jedaiah son of Harumaph repaired in front of his house. Next to him, Hattush son of Hashabneiah repaired. 11 Malchijah son of Harim and Hasshub son of Pahath-moab repaired a second stretch, including the Tower of Ovens. 12 Next to them, Shallum son of Hallohesh, chief of half the district of Jerusalem, repaired—he and his daughters.

33 When Sanballat heard that we were rebuilding the wall, it angered him, and he was extremely vexed. He mocked the Jews, 34 saying in the presence of his brothers and the Samarian force, "What are the miserable Jews doing? Will they restore, offer sacrifice, and finish one day? Can they revive those stones out of the dust heaps, burned as they are?" 35 Tobiah the Ammonite, alongside him, said, "That stone wall they are building—if a fox climbed it he would breach it!"

---

50. I.e., member of the guild of perfumers.

36 Hear, our God, how we have become a mockery, and return their taunts upon their heads! Let them be taken as spoil to a land of captivity! 37 Do not cover up their iniquity or let their sin be blotted out before You, for they hurled provocations at the builders.

38 We rebuilt the wall till it was continuous all around to half its height; for the people's heart was in the work.

4:1 When Sanballat and Tobiah, and the Arabs, the Ammonites, and the Ashdodites heard that healing had come to the walls of Jerusalem, that the breached parts had begun to be filled, it angered them very much, 2 and they all conspired together to come and fight against Jerusalem and to throw it into confusion. 3 Because of them we prayed to our God, and set up a watch over them[51] day and night. . . . 7 I stationed, on the lower levels of the place, behind the walls, on the bare rock—I stationed the people by families with their swords, their lances, and their bows. 8 Then I decided to exhort the nobles, the prefects, and the rest of the people, "Do not be afraid of them! Think of the great and awesome Lord, and fight for your brothers, your sons and daughters, your wives and homes!"

9 When our enemies learned that it had become known to us, since God had thus frustrated their plan, we could all return to the wall, each to his work. 10 From that day on, half my servants did work and half held lances and shields, bows and armor. And the officers stood behind the whole house of Judah 11 who were rebuilding the wall. The basket-carriers were burdened, doing work with one hand while the other held a weapon. 12 As for the builders, each had his sword girded at his side as he was building. The trumpeter stood beside me. 13 I said to the nobles, the prefects, and the rest of the people, "There is much work and it is spread out; we are scattered over the wall, far from one another. 14 When you hear a trumpet call, gather yourselves to me at that place; our God will fight for us!" 15 And so we worked on, while half were holding lances, from the break of day until the stars appeared. . . .

5:1 There was a great outcry by the common folk and their wives against their brother Jews. 2 Some said, "Our sons and daughters are numerous; we must get grain to eat in order that we may live!" 3 Others said, "We must pawn our fields, our vineyards, and our homes to get grain to stave off hunger." 4 Yet others said, "We have borrowed money against our fields and vineyards to pay the king's tax. 5 Now we are as good as our brothers, and our children as good as theirs; yet here we are subjecting our sons and daughters to slavery—some of our daughters are already sub-

---

51. I.e., the workers on the walls.

jected—and we are powerless, while our fields and vineyards belong to others."

6 It angered me very much to hear their outcry and these complaints. 7 After pondering the matter carefully, I censured the nobles and the prefects, saying, "Are you pressing claims on loans made to your brothers?" Then I raised a large crowd against them 8 and said to them, "We have done our best to buy back our Jewish brothers who were sold to the nations; will you now sell your brothers so that they must be sold [back] to us?" They kept silent, for they found nothing to answer. 9 So I continued, "What you are doing is not right. You ought to act in a God-fearing way so as not to give our enemies, the nations, room to reproach us. 10 I, my brothers, and my servants also have claims of money and grain against them; let us now abandon those claims! 11 Give back at once their fields, their vineyards, their olive trees, and their homes, and [abandon] the claims for the hundred pieces of silver, the grain, the wine, and the oil that you have been pressing against them!" 12 They replied, "We shall give them back, and not demand anything of them; we shall do just as you say." Summoning the priests, I put them under oath to keep this promise. 13 I also shook out the bosom of my garment and said, "So may God shake free of his household and property any man who fails to keep this promise; may he be thus shaken out and stripped." All the assembled answered, "Amen," and praised the Lord.

The people kept this promise.

14 Furthermore, from the day I was commissioned to be governor in the land of Judah—from the twentieth year of King Artaxerxes until his thirty-second year, twelve years in all—neither I nor my brothers ever ate of the governor's food allowance. 15 The former governors who preceded me laid heavy burdens on the people, and took from them for bread and wine more than forty shekels of silver. Their servants also tyrannized over the people. But I, out of the fear of God, did not do so. 16 I also supported the work on this wall; we did not buy any land, and all my servants were gathered there at the work. 17 Although there were at my table, between Jews and prefects, one hundred and fifty men in all, beside those who came to us from surrounding nations; 18 and although what was prepared for each day came to one ox, six select sheep, and fowl, all prepared for me, and at ten-day intervals all sorts of wine in abundance— yet I did not resort to the governor's food allowance, for the [king's] service lay heavily on the people.

19 O my God, remember to my credit all that I have done for this people!

6:1 When word reached Sanballat, Tobiah, Geshem the Arab, and the rest of our enemies that I had rebuilt the wall and not a breach remained in it—though at that time I had not yet set up doors in the gateways—2 Sanballat and Geshem sent a message to me, saying, "Come, let us get together in Kephirim in the Ono valley"; they planned to do me harm. 3 I sent them messengers, saying, "I am engaged in a great work and cannot come down, for the work will stop if I leave it in order to come down to you." 4 They sent me the same message four times, and I gave them the same answer. 5 Sanballat sent me the same message a fifth time by his servant, who had an open letter with him. 6 Its text was: "Word has reached the nations, and Geshem too says that you and the Jews are planning to rebel—for which reason you are building the wall—and that you are to be their king. Such is the word. 7 You have also set up prophets in Jerusalem to proclaim about you, 'There is a king in Judah!' Word of these things will surely reach the king; so come, let us confer together."

8 I sent back a message to him, saying, "None of these things you mention has occurred; they are figments of your imagination"—9 for they all wished to intimidate us, thinking, "They will desist from the work, and it will not get done." Now strengthen my hands!...

14 "O my God, remember against Tobiah and Sanballat these deeds of theirs, and against Noadiah the prophetess, and against the other prophets that they wished to intimidate me!"

15 The wall was finished on the twenty-fifth of Elul, after fifty-two days. 16 When all our enemies heard it, all the nations round about us were intimidated, and fell very low in their own estimation; they realized that this work had been accomplished by the help of our God.

3.2.6 Ezra 3: The Beginning of Sacrifice

By 520 B.C.E., despite the fact that the Temple had still not been rebuilt, sacrifice began, as explained in this excerpt from the book of Ezra.

3:1 When the seventh month arrived—the Israelites being settled in their towns—the entire people assembled as one man in Jerusalem. 2 Then Jeshua son of Jozadak[52] and his brother priests, and Zerubbabel son of Shealtiel and his brothers set to and built the altar of the God of Israel to offer burnt offerings upon it as is written in the Teaching of Moses (Torah), the man of God. 3 They set up the altar on its site because they were in fear of the peoples of the land, and they offered burnt offerings

---

52. The high priest.

each morning and evening. 4 Then they celebrated the festival of Tabernacles as is written, with its daily burnt offerings in the proper quantities, on each day as is prescribed for it, 5 followed by the regular burnt offering and the offerings of the new moons and for all the sacred fixed times of the Lord, and whatever freewill offerings were made to the Lord. 6 From the first day of the seventh month they began to make burnt offerings to the Lord, though the foundation of the Temple of the Lord had not been laid. 7 They paid the hewers and craftsmen with money, and the Sidonians and Tyrians with food, drink, and oil to bring cedarwood from Lebanon by sea to Joppa, in accord with the authorization granted them by King Cyrus of Persia.

3.2.7 Ezra 7–8: The Arrival of Ezra

Ezra arrived in Jerusalem to furnish the Temple, gather the Levites to minister there, and allow the returning exiles to sacrifice for the first time in the Temple.

ﷺ

7:1 After these events,[53] during the reign of King Artaxerxes of Persia, Ezra son of Seraiah son of Azariah son of Hilkiah . . . 6 that Ezra came up from Babylon, a scribe expert in the Teaching of Moses which the Lord God of Israel had given, whose request the king had granted in its entirety, thanks to the benevolence of the Lord toward him.

(7 Some of the Israelites, the priests and Levites, the singers, the gatekeepers, and the temple servants set out for Jerusalem in the seventh year of King Artaxerxes, 8 arriving in Jerusalem in the fifth month in the seventh year of the king.) 9 On the first day of the first month the journey up from Babylon was started, and on the first day of the fifth month he arrived in Jerusalem, thanks to the benevolent care of his God for him. 10 For Ezra had dedicated himself to study the Teaching of the Lord so as to observe it, and to teach laws and rules to Israel.

11 The following is the text of the letter which King Artaxerxes gave Ezra the priest-scribe, a scholar in matters concerning the commandments of the Lord and His laws to Israel:

12 "Artaxerxes king of kings, to Ezra the priest, scholar in the law of the God of heaven, and so forth. And now, 13 I hereby issue an order that anyone in my kingdom who is of the people of Israel and its priests and Levites who feels impelled to go to Jerusalem may go with you.

---

53. The dedication of the House of God and the celebration of the Passover by the returned exiles in the Land of Israel.

14 For you are commissioned by the king and his seven advisers to regulate Judah and Jerusalem according to the law of your God, which is in your care, 15 and to bring the freewill offering of silver and gold, which the king and his advisers made to the God of Israel, whose dwelling is in Jerusalem, 16 and whatever silver and gold that you find throughout the province of Babylon, together with the freewill offerings that the people and the priests will give for the House of their God, which is in Jerusalem. 17 You shall, therefore, with dispatch acquire with this money bulls, rams, and lambs, with their meal offerings and libations, and offer them on the altar of the House of your God in Jerusalem. 18 And whatever you wish to do with the leftover silver and gold, you and your kinsmen may do, in accord with the will of your God. 19 The vessels for the service of the House of your God that are given to you, deliver to God in Jerusalem, 20 and any other needs of the House of your God that it falls to you to supply, do so from the royal treasury. 21 I, King Artaxerxes, for my part, hereby issue an order to all the treasurers in the province of Beyond the River that whatever request Ezra the priest, scholar in the law of the God of Heaven, makes of you is to be fulfilled with dispatch 22 up to the sum of one hundred talents of silver, one hundred kor of wheat, one hundred bath of oil, and salt without limit. 23 Whatever is by order of the God of Heaven must be carried out diligently for the House of the God of Heaven, else wrath will come upon the king and his sons. 24 We further advise you that it is not permissible to impose tribute, poll tax, or land tax on any priest, Levite, singer, gatekeeper, temple servant, or other servant of this House of God. 25 And you, Ezra, by the divine wisdom you possess, appoint magistrates and judges to judge all the people in the province of Beyond the River who know the laws of your God, and to teach those who do not know them. 26 Let anyone who does not obey the law of your God and the law of the king be punished with dispatch, whether by death, corporal punishment, confiscation of possessions, or imprisonment."

27 Blessed is the Lord God of our fathers, who put it into the mind of the king to glorify the House of the Lord in Jerusalem, 28 and who inclined the king and his counselors and the king's military officers to be favorably disposed toward me. For my part, thanks to the care of the Lord for me, I summoned up courage and assembled leading men in Israel to go with me.

8:1 These—the chiefs of the clans and the register of the genealogy of those who came up with me from Babylon in the reign of King Artaxerxes ... 15 These I assembled by the river that enters Ahava, and we encamped there for three days. I reviewed the people and the priests, but I did not find any Levites there. 16 I sent for Eliezer, Ariel, Shemaiah, Elnathan, Jarib, Elnathan, Nathan, Zechariah, and Meshullam, the leading men, and also for Joiarib and Elnathan, the instructors, 17 and I gave them an order for Iddo, the leader at the place [called] Casiphia. I gave them a message to convey to Iddo [and] his brother, temple-servants at the place [called] Casiphia, that they should bring us attendants for the House of our God. 18 Thanks to the benevolent care of our God for us, they brought us a capable man of the family of Mahli son of Levi son of Israel, and Sherebiah and his sons and brothers, eighteen in all, 19 and Hashabiah, and with him Jeshaiah of the family of Merari, his brothers and their sons, twenty in all; 20 and of the temple servants whom David and the officers had appointed for the service of the Levites—220 temple servants, all of them listed by name.

21 I proclaimed a fast there by the Ahava River to afflict ourselves before our God to beseech Him for a smooth journey for us and for our children and for all our possessions; 22 for I was ashamed to ask the king for soldiers and horsemen to protect us against any enemy on the way, since we had told the king, "The benevolent care of our God is for all who seek Him, while His fierce anger is against all who forsake Him." 23 So we fasted and besought our God for this, and He responded to our plea. 24 Then I selected twelve of the chiefs of the priests, namely Sherebiah and Hashabiah with ten of their brothers, 25 and I weighed out to them the silver, the gold, and the vessels, the contribution to the House of our God which the king, his counselors and officers, and all Israel who were present had made. 26 I entrusted to their safekeeping the weight of six hundred and fifty talents of silver, one hundred silver vessels of one talent each, one hundred talents of gold; 27 also, twenty gold bowls worth one thousand darics and two vessels of good, shining bronze, as precious as gold. 28 I said to them, "You are consecrated to the Lord, and the vessels are consecrated, and the silver and gold are a freewill offering to the Lord God of your fathers. 29 Guard them diligently until such time as you weigh them out in the presence of the officers of the priests and the Levites and the officers of the clans of Israel in Jerusalem in the chambers of the House of the Lord."

30 So the priests and the Levites received the cargo of silver and gold and vessels by weight, to bring them to Jerusalem to the House of our God. 31 We set out for Jerusalem from the Ahava River on the twelfth of the first month. We enjoyed the care of our God, who saved us from enemy ambush on the journey.

32 We arrived in Jerusalem and stayed there three days. 33 On the fourth day the silver, gold, and vessels were weighed out in the House of our God. . . . 34 Everything accorded as to number and weight, the entire cargo being recorded at that time.

35 The returning exiles who arrived from captivity made burnt offerings to the God of Israel: twelve bulls for all Israel, ninety-six rams, seventy-seven lambs and twelve he-goats as a purification offering, all this a burnt offering to the Lord. 36 They handed the royal orders to the king's satraps and the governors of the province of Beyond the River who gave support to the people and the House of God.

3.2.8 Nehemiah 7–8: The Reading of the Torah

Soon after the arrival of Ezra in Judea in the middle of the fifth century B.C.E., the Judeans entered into a pact to observe the laws of the Torah. As part of this covenant renewal ceremony, the Torah was read aloud and explained.

🙚

7:73 When the seventh month arrived—the Israelites being [settled] in their towns—8:1 the entire people assembled as one man in the square before the Water Gate, and they asked Ezra the scribe to bring the scroll of the Teaching of Moses (Torah) with which the Lord had charged Israel. 2 On the first day of the seventh month, Ezra the priest brought the Teaching before the congregation, men and women and all who could listen with understanding. 3 He read from it, facing the square before the Water Gate, from the first light until midday, to the men and the women and those who could understand; the ears of all the people were given to the scroll of the Teaching.

4 Ezra the scribe stood upon a wooden tower made for the purpose, and beside him stood Mattithiah, Shema, Ananiah, Uriah, Hilkiah, and Maaseiah at his right, and at his left Pedaiah, Mishael, Malchijah, Hashum, Hashbaddanah, Zechariah, Meshullam.[54] 5 Ezra opened the scroll in the sight of all the people, for he was above all the people; as he opened it, all the people stood up. 6 Ezra blessed the Lord, the great God, and all the people answered, "Amen, Amen," with hands upraised. Then they bowed their heads and prostrated themselves before the Lord with their faces

---

54. There is a mixture of Hebrew and Persian names in this list, showing the influence of the Babylonian exile.

to the ground. 7 Jeshua, Bani, Sherebiah, Jamin, Akkub, Shabbethai, Hodiah, Maaseiah, Kelita, Azariah, Jozabad, Hanan, Pelaiah, and the Levites explained the Teaching to the people, while the people stood in their places. 8 They read from the scroll of the Teaching of God, translating it and giving it the sense; so they understood the reading.

3.2.9 Ezra 9–10: Expulsion of Foreign Wives

Ezra was soon confronted with the problem of intermarriage of some Judeans with women from the neighboring nations. Reasoning that the Torah forbade such unions, Ezra forced these men to divorce their wives.

🙚

9:1 When this was over, the officers approached me, saying, "The people of Israel and the priests and the Levites have not separated themselves from the peoples of the land whose abhorrent practices are like those of the Canaanites, the Hittites, the Perizzites, the Jebusites, the Ammonites, the Moabites,[55] the Egyptians,[56] and the Amorites. 2 They have taken their daughters as wives for themselves and for their sons, so that the holy seed has become intermingled with the peoples of the land;[57] and it is the officers and prefects who have taken the lead in the trespass."

3 When I heard this, I rent my garment and robe,[58] I tore hair out of my head and beard, and I sat desolate. 4 Around me gathered all who were concerned over the words of the God of Israel because of the returning exiles' trespass, while I sat desolate until the evening offering. 5 At the time of the evening offering I ended my self-affliction; still in my torn garment and robe, I got down on my knees and spread out my hands to the Lord my God, 6 and said, "O my God, I am too ashamed and mortified to lift my face to You, O my God, for our iniquities are overwhelming and our guilt has grown as high as heaven. 7 From the time of our fathers to this very day we have been handed over to foreign kings, to the sword, to captivity, to pillage, and to humiliation, as is now the case.

---

55. The people who were displaced by the Israelites when they entered the Land of Israel.

56. The Egyptians were representative of their former overlords, and their practices, such as the cult of the dead, polytheism, immorality, etc. were to be shunned.

57. This passage indicates that Jewish descent was already traced through the mother in this period.

58. As a sign of mourning.

8 "But now, for a short while, there has been a reprieve from the Lord our God, who has granted us a surviving remnant and given us a stake in His holy place; our God has restored the luster to our eyes and furnished us with a little sustenance in our bondage. 9 For bondsmen we are, though even in our bondage God has not forsaken us, but has disposed the king of Persia favorably toward us, to furnish us with sustanance and to raise again the House of our God, repairing its ruins and giving us a hold in Judah and Jerusalem.

10 "Now, what can we say in the face of this, O our God, for we have forsaken Your commandments, 11 which You gave us through Your servants the prophets when You said, 'The land that you are about to possess is a land unclean through the uncleanliness of the peoples of the land, through their abhorrent practices with which they, in their impurity, have filled it from one end to the other.[59] 12 Now then, do not give your daughters in marriage to their sons or let their daughters marry your sons;[60] do nothing for their well being or advantage, then you will be strong and enjoy the bounty of the land and bequeath it to your children forever.' 13 After all that has happened to us because of our evil deeds and our deep guilt—though You, our God, have been forebearing, [punishing us] less than our iniquity [deserves] in that You have granted us such a remnant as this—14 shall we once again violate Your commandments by intermarrying with these peoples who follow such abhorrent practices? Will You not rage against us till we are destroyed without remnant or survivor? 15 O Lord, God of Israel, You are benevolent, for we have survived as a remnant, as is now the case. We stand before You in all our guilt, for we cannot face You on this account."

10:1 While Ezra was praying and making confession, weeping and prostrating himself before the House of God, a very great crowd of Israelites gathered about him, men, women, and children; the people were weeping bitterly. 2 Then Shecaniah son of Jehiel of the family of Elam spoke up and said to Ezra, "We have trespassed against our God by bringing into our homes foreign women from the peoples of the land; but there is still hope for Israel despite this. 3 Now then, let us make a covenant with our God to expel all these women and those who have been born to them, in accordance with the bidding of the Lord and of all who are concerned over the commandment of our God, and let the Teaching be

59. Cf. Lev. 18:24–30.
60. Cf. Deut. 7:1–3.

obeyed. 4 Take action, for the responsibility is yours and we are with you. Act with resolve!"

3.2.10 Josephus, *Antiquities* XI, 297–303:
The High Priesthood and the Samaritans[61]

Josephus, based on sources not known to us, supplies information about the relations of the leaders of the priesthood of Judea and the Samaritans in the later Persian Period. We see that by this time the families had entered into relationships cemented by marriage. He also makes clear the violent conflicts that divided the priesthood at this time. Some have taken this passage to indicate a date for the Samaritan schism ca. 330 B.C.E., on the eve of the coming of Alexander the Great.

༚

(297) When Eliashib the high priest died, his son Judas succeeded in the high priesthood. When he died, his son John took that office. Because of him, Bagoses,[62] the general of Artaxerxes II's[63] army, polluted the temple and imposed tributes on the Jews so that before they offered the daily sacrifices, they had to pay fifty *drachmae* for every lamb out of the public treasury. (298) Now Jesus was the brother of John, a friend of Bagoses who had promised to procure for him the high priesthood. (299) With this assurance, Jesus quarreled with John in the temple and provoked his brother so that in his anger his brother killed him. Now it was a horrible thing for John, when he was high priest, to perpetrate so great a crime, and so much the more horrible since there never was so cruel and impious a thing done, neither by the Greeks nor barbarians. (300) However, God did not neglect its punishment for the people were for that very reason enslaved, and the temple was polluted by the Persians. Now when Bagoses, the general of Artaxerxes' army, knew that John, the high priest of the Jews, had killed his own brother Jesus in the temple, he came upon the Jews immediately, and began in anger to say to them, "Have you had the impudence to perpetrate a murder in your temple?" (301) And as he was aiming to go into the temple, they forbade him so to do. But he said

---

61. All passages from Josephus are from W. Whiston, trans. *The Works of Josephus* (Peabody, MA: Hendrickson, 1987), revised by L. H. Schiffman in consultation with H. St. J. Thackeray, Ralph Marcus, Allen Wikgren, and L. H. Feldman, trans., *Josephus: in Nine Volumes* (Loeb Classical Library; Cambridge: Harvard University Press, 1976–79).

62. Probably the Bagoas mentioned in the Elephantine Papyri.

63. Artaxerxes II, 404–359 B.C.E.

to them, "Am I not purer than he who was killed in the temple?" When he had said these words, he went into the temple. Accordingly, Bagoses made use of this pretense, and punished the Jews seven years for the murder of Jesus.

(302) Now when John had departed this life, his son Jaddua succeeded in the high priesthood. He had a brother whose name was Manasseh. Now there was one Sanballat who was sent by Darius, the last king [of Persia], into Samaria. He was a Cuthean by birth, of which stock were the Samaritans also. (303) This man [Sanballat] knew that the city Jerusalem was a famous city and that their kings had given a great deal of trouble to the Assyrians and to the people of Celesyria. So he willingly gave his daughter, whose name was Nikaso, in marriage to Manasseh, thinking that this alliance by marriage would be a pledge and security that the nation of the Jews should continue their good will to him.

3.3 THE SECOND TEMPLE

3.3.1 Ezra 3: The Renewal of Sacrifices

Soon after the return of the first exiles, sacrifices were renewed, even before the Temple was rebuilt.

꽃

3:1 When the seventh month arrived—the Israelites being settled in their towns—the entire people assembled as one man in Jerusalem. 2 Then Jeshua son of Jozadak and his brother priests, and Zerubbabel son of Shealtiel and his brothers set to and built the altar of the God of Israel to offer burnt offerings upon it as is written in the Teaching of Moses, the man of God. 3 They set up the altar on its site because they were in fear of the peoples of the land, and they offered burnt offerings on it to the Lord, burnt offerings each morning and evening. 4 Then they celebrated the festival of Tabernacles as is written, with its daily burnt offerings in the proper quantities, on each day as is prescribed for it, 5 followed by the regular burnt offering and the offerings for the new moons and for all the sacred fixed times of the Lord, and whatever freewill offerings were made to the Lord. 6 From the first day of the seventh month they began to make burnt offerings to the Lord, though the foundation of the Temple of the Lord had not been laid. 7 They paid the hewers and craftsmen with money, and the Sidonians and Tyrians with food, drink, and oil to bring cedarwood from Lebanon by sea to Joppa, in accord with the authorization granted them by King Cyrus of Persia.

8 In the second year after their arrival at the House of God, at Jerusalem, in the second month, Zerubbabel son of Shealtiel and Jeshua son of Jozadak, and the rest of their brother priests and Levites, and all who had come from the captivity to Jerusalem, as their first step appointed Levites from the age of twenty and upward to supervise the work of the House of the Lord. 9 Jeshua, his sons and brothers, Kadmiel and his sons, the sons of Judah, together were appointed in charge of those who did the work in the House of God; also the sons of Henadad, their sons and brother Levites.

10 When the builders had laid the foundation of the Temple of the Lord, priests in their vestments with trumpets, and Levites sons of Asaph with cymbals were stationed to give praise to the Lord, as King David of Israel had ordained. 11 They sang songs extolling and praising the Lord, "For He is good, His steadfast love for Israel is eternal."[64] All the people raised a great shout extolling the Lord because the foundation of the House of the Lord had been laid. 12 Many of the priests and Levites and the chiefs of the clans, the old men who had seen the first house, wept loudly at the sight of the founding of this house. Many others shouted joyously at the top of their voices. 13 The people could not distinguish the shouts of joy from the people's weeping, for the people raised a great shout, the sound of which could be heard from afar.

3.3.2 Ezra 6: The Order to Rebuild

Biblical sources assert that after sacrifices were quickly restarted after the Return, the building of the Temple was delayed. Eventually, permission was obtained from the Persian officials, as well as financial support, for the rebuilding of the Temple in Jerusalem. The book of Ezra reproduces an edict to this effect said to originate in the Persian chancellery.

๕๗

6:1 Thereupon, at the order of King Darius,[65] they searched the archives where the treasures were stored in Babylon. 2 But it was in the citadel of Ecbatana, in the province of Media, that a scroll was found in which the following was written: "Memorandum: 3 In the first year of King Cyrus,[66] King Cyrus issued an order concerning the House of God in Jerusalem: 'Let the house be rebuilt, a place for offering sacrifices, with

---

64. Cf. Ps. 106.1; 136.
65. Darius I, King of Persia, ruled 521–486 B.C.E.
66. 540 B.C.E.

a base built up high. Let it be sixty cubits high and sixty cubits wide, 4 with a course of unused timber for each three courses of hewn stone. The expenses shall be paid by the palace. 5 And the gold and silver vessels of the House of God which Nebuchadnezzar had taken away from the temple in Jerusalem and transported to Babylon shall be returned, and let each go back to the temple in Jerusalem where it belongs; you shall deposit it in the House of God.'

6 "Now you, Tattenai, governor of the province of Beyond the River,[67] Shethar-bozenai and colleagues, the officials of the province of Beyond the River, stay away from that place. 7 Allow the work of this House of God to go on; let the governor of the Jews and the elders of the Jews rebuild this House of God on its site. 8 And I hereby issue an order concerning what you must do to help these elders of the Jews rebuild this House of God: the expenses are to be paid to these men with dispatch out of the resources of the king, derived from the taxes of the province of Beyond the River, so that the work not be stopped. 9 They are to be given daily, without fail, whatever they need of young bulls, rams, or lambs as burnt offerings for the God of Heaven, and wheat, salt, wine, and oil, at the order of the priests in Jerusalem, 10 so that they may offer pleasing sacrifices to the God of heaven and pray for the life of the king and his sons. 11 I also issue an order that whoever alters this decree shall have a beam removed from his house, and he shall be impaled on it and his house confiscated. 12 And may the God who established His name there cause the downfall of any king or nation that undertakes to alter or damage that House of God in Jerusalem. I, Darius, have issued the decree; let it be carried out with dispatch."

13 Then Tattenai, governor of the province of Beyond the River, Shethar-bozenai, and their colleagues carried out with dispatch what King Darius had written. 14 So the elders of the Jews progressed in the building, urged on by the prophesying of Haggai the prophet and Zechariah son of Iddo,[68] and they brought the building to completion under the aegis of the God of Israel and by the order of Cyrus and Darius and King Artaxerxes of Persia. 15 The house was finished on the third of the month of Adar in the sixth year of the reign of King Darius.[69] 16 The Israelites, the priests, and the Levites, and all the other exiles celebrated

---

67. The area on the west side of the Euphrates River which was a province in the Assyrian and Persian Empires.

68. The biblical prophet Zechariah.

69. 516 B.C.E.

the dedication of the House of God with joy. 17 And they sacrificed for the dedication of this House of God one hundred bulls, two hundred rams, four hundred lambs, and twelve goats as a purification offering for all of Israel, according to the number of the tribes of Israel. 18 They appointed the priests in their courses and the Levites in their divisions for the service of God in Jerusalem, according to the prescription in the Book of Moses.

3.4 THE SAMARITAN SCHISM

3.4.1 Ezra 4: The Samaritans and the Temple

Already before the rebuilding of the Temple commenced, the Samaritans, a mixed people made up of descendants of the North Israelites who were left in the land after the exile by Assyria in 722 B.C.E. and foreigners brought in by the Assyrians, asked to participate. Because of their questionable lineage, they were rebuffed by the Judeans. As a result, they tried all kinds of machinations to stop the rebuilding of the Temple. In our view, this was the start of the Samaritan schism, the gradual separation of this group from the Jewish people.

🕉

4:1 When the adversaries of Judah and Benjamin heard that the returned exiles were building a temple to the Lord God of Israel, 2 they approached Zerubbabel[70] and the chiefs of the clans and said to them, "Let us build with you, since we too worship your God, having offered sacrifices to Him since the time of King Esarhaddon of Assyria,[71] who brought us here." 3 Zerubbabel, Jeshua,[72] and the rest of the chiefs of the clans of Israel answered them, "It is not for you and us to build a House to our God, but we alone will build it to the Lord God of Israel, in accord with the charge that the king, King Cyrus of Persia, laid upon us." 4 Thereupon the people of the land undermined the resolve of the people of Judah, and made them afraid to build. 5 They bribed ministers in order to thwart their plans all the years of King Cyrus of Persia and until the reign of King Darius of Persia.

---

70. A Davidic scion who served as governor of Judea under King Darius I.

71. Ruled ca. 681–669 B.C.E.

72. Jeshua son of Jehozadak, high priest who was instrumental in the building of the Second Temple in 516 B.C.E.

3.4.2 1 Esdras 2: Opposition to the Temple[73]

The Greek text of 1 Esdras provides an alternative or expanded version of
Ezra 4:7–24. This text relates the attempt of the Samaritans to stop the
Judeans from building the Temple and the city walls.

ᛊᛊ

2:16 But in the time of Artaxerxes king of the Persians, Bishlam, Mithridates, Tabeel, Rehum, Beltethmus, Shimshai the scribe, and the rest of
their associates, living in Samaria and other places, wrote him the following letter, against those who were living in Judea and Jerusalem:

17 "To King Artaxerxes our lord, your servants Rehum the recorder
and Shimshai the scribe and the other judges of their council in Coele-
syria and Phoenicia: 18 Now be it known to our lord the king that the
Jews who came up from you to us have gone to Jerusalem and are building that rebellious and wicked city, repairing its market places and walls
and laying the foundations for a temple. 19 Now if this city is built and
the walls finished, they will not only refuse to pay tribute but will even
resist kings. 20 And since the building of the temple is now going on, we
think it best not to neglect such a matter, 21 but to speak to our lord the
king, in order that, if it seems good to you, search may be made in the
records of your fathers. 22 You will find in the chronicles what has been
written about them, and will learn that this city was rebellious, troubling
both kings and other cities, 23 and that the Jews were rebels and kept setting up blockades in it from of old. That is why this city was laid waste.
24 Therefore we now make known to you, O lord and king, that if this
city is built and its walls finished, you will no longer have access to Coele-
syria and Phoenicia."

25 Then the king, in reply to Rehum the recorder and Beltethmus and
Shimshai the scribe and the others associated with them and living in
Samaria and Syria and Phoenicia, wrote as follows:

26 "I have read the letter which you sent me. So I ordered search to be
made, and it has been found that this city from of old has fought against
kings, 27 and that the men in it were given to rebellion and war, and that
mighty and cruel kings ruled in Jerusalem and exacted tribute from Coelesyria and Phoenicia. 28 Therefore I have now issued orders to prevent
these men from building the city and to take care that nothing more be

---

73. The Revised Standard Version (New York: Oxford University Press, Inc.), 1973,
1977.

done 29 and that such wicked proceedings go no further to the annoyance of kings."

30 Then, when the letter from King Artaxerxes was read, Rehum and Shimshai the scribe and their associates went in haste to Jerusalem, with horsemen and a multitude in battle array, and began to hinder the builders. And the building of the temple in Jerusalem ceased until the second year of the reign of Darius king of the Persians.

3.4.3 2 Kings 17: Samaritan Origins

Samaritan origins were described in 2 Kings. Later Rabbis would call them "lion converts," that is, converts against their will, and further argue against their Jewish status based on this account.

ૐ

17:24 The king of Assyria brought (people) from Babylon, Cuthah, Avva, Hamath and Sepharvaim,[74] and he settled them in the towns of Samaria[75] in place of the Israelites; they took possession of Samaria and dwelt in its towns. 25 When they first settled there, they did not worship the Lord; so the Lord sent lions against them which killed some of them. 26 They said to the king of Assyria: "The nations which you deported and resettled in the towns of Samaria do not know the rules of the God of the land; therefore He has let lions loose against them which are killing them—for they do not know the rules of the God of the land."

27 The king of Assyria gave an order: "Send there one of the priests whom you have deported; let him go and dwell there, and let him teach them the practices of the God of the land." 28 So one of the priests whom they had exiled from Samaria came and settled in Bethel; he taught them how to worship the Lord. 29 However, each nation continued to make its own gods and to set them up in the cult places which had been made by the people of Samaria, each nation (set them up) in the towns in which it lived. 30 The Babylonians made Succoth-benoth and the men of Cuth made Nergal, and the men of Hamath made Ashima, 31 and the Avvites made Nibhaz and Tartak ; and the Sepharvites burned their children (as offerings) to Adrammelech and Anamelech, the gods of Sepharvaim. 32 They worshipped the Lord, but they also appointed from their own ranks priests of the shrines, who officiated for them in the cult places. 33 They worshipped the Lord, while serving their own gods according to the practices of the nations from which they had been

---

74. Various cities in Babylonia and Syria.
75. A region in the central portion of the Land of Israel.

deported. 34 To this day, they follow their former practices. They do not worship the Lord (properly). They do not follow the laws and practices, the Teaching and Instruction that the Lord enjoined upon the descendants of Jacob—who was given the name Israel—35 with whom He made a covenant and whom He commanded: "You shall worship no other gods; you shall not bow down to them nor serve them nor sacrifice to them. 36 You must worship only the Lord your God, who brought you out of the land of Egypt with great might and with an outstretched arm; to Him alone shall you bow down and to Him alone shall you sacrifice. 37 You shall observe faithfully, all your days, the laws and practices; the Teaching and Instruction that I wrote down for you; do not worship other gods. 38 Do not forget the covenant that I made with you; do not worship other gods. 39 Worship only the Lord your God, and He will save you from the hands of all your enemies." 40 But they did not obey, they continued their former practices. 41 Those nations worshipped the Lord, but they also served their idols. To this day their children and their children's children do as their ancestors did.

3.4.4 Josephus, *Antiquities* XI, 75–108:
The Restoration of the Temple

Josephus provides an account of the building of the Temple which supplements that in Ezra. However, it clearly draws on 1 Esdras while at the same time including other traditions which expand the narrative. Aspects of his account must therefore be seen as independent of that preserved in the Bible, and with careful evaluation certain of the details he presents may be accepted as historical.

(75) In the seventh month after they had departed from Babylon, both Jeshua the high priest, and Zerubbabel the governor sent messengers all around and showed no lack of zeal in gathering those who were in the country together as a group at Jerusalem. (76) They then built the altar on the same place it had formerly been built so that they might offer the appointed sacrifices upon it to God according to the laws of Moses. But in doing this, they did not please the neighboring nations, all of whom bore ill will towards them. (77) They also celebrated the Feast of Tabernacles [Sukkot] at that time as the legislator [Moses] had ordained concerning it. After that they offered sacrifices and what were called the daily sacrifices, and the offerings proper for the Sabbaths and for all the holy festivals. Those also who had made vows fulfilled them and offered their sacrifices

from the first day of the seventh month.[76] (78) They also began to build the temple, and gave a great deal of money to the masons and to the carpenters and what was necessary for the maintenance of the workmen. The Sidonians also were very willing and ready to bring the cedar trees from Lebanon, to bind them together, and to make a united float of them, and to bring them to the port of Joppa. This was what Cyrus had commanded at first, and now it was being done at the command of Darius.

(79) In the second year after the return of the Jews to Jerusalem, in the second month, the building of the temple was undertaken. When they had laid its foundations on the first day of the second month of that second year, they appointed as overseers of the work, Levites who were at least twenty years old, and Jeshua and his sons and brothers, and Zodmiel, the brother of Judas, the son of Aminadab, with his sons. (80) The temple, by the great diligence of those who were in charge of it, was finished sooner than anyone would have expected. When the temple was finished, the priests, adorned with their customary garments, stood with their trumpets, while the Levites and the sons of Asaph stood and sang hymns to God, as David had first shown them to bless God.

(81) The priests and Levites, and the elders of the families, recollecting how much greater and more sumptuous the old temple had been, seeing that the one now constructed was much inferior to the old one, on account of their poverty, considered how far their prosperity had sunk below what it had been of old, as well as their temple. Thereupon they were disconsolate and not able to contain their grief, and were moved to lament and shed tears at this thought. (82) But the people in general were content with their present condition because they were allowed to build themselves a temple. They desired no more and neither regarded nor remembered, nor indeed at all tormented themselves with the comparison of this one and the former temple, as if this were below their expectations. (83) But the wailing of the old men and of the priests on account of the deficiency of this temple, in their opinion, if compared with that which had been demolished, overcame the sounds of the trumpets and the rejoicing of the people.

(84) But when the Samaritans, who were still enemies of the tribes of Judah and Benjamin, heard the sound of the trumpets, they came running together and desired to know what was the occasion of this tumult. When they perceived that it was from the Jews who had been carried captive to Babylon who were rebuilding their temple, they came to Zerubbabel and to Jeshua, and to the heads of the families, and requested that

---

76. The fall New Year, called Rosh ha-Shanah by the Rabbis.

they give them permission to build the temple with them and to be partners with them in building it. For they said, (85) "We worship their God, and pray fervently to Him, and have been zealous in His service ever since Shalmanezer, the king of Assyria, transplanted us out of Cuthah and Media, to this place." (86) When they said this, Zerubbabel and Jeshua the high priest, and the heads of the families of the Israelites, replied to them that it was impossible for them to permit them to be their partners since they [only] had been appointed to build that temple, at first by Cyrus and now by Darius. (87) They said that it was indeed lawful for them to come and worship there if they pleased, but that they could allow them nothing in common with them except that which was common to them with all other men, to come to their temple and worship God there.

(88) When the Cutheans heard this, for the Samaritans have that appellation, they were indignant at it and persuaded the nations of Syria to request of the governors, in the same manner as they had done formerly in the days of Cyrus and again in the days of Cambyses afterwards, to put a stop to the building of the temple and to endeavor to delay and protract the Jews in their zeal about it. (89) At this time Sisinnes,[77] the governor of Syria and Phoenicia, and Sathrabuzanes[78] with certain others came up to Jerusalem. He asked the rulers of the Jews, by whose grant it was that they built the temple in this manner since it was more like a citadel than a temple. And for what reason it was that they built porticoes and strong walls around the city? (90) To this Zerubbabel and Jeshua the high priest replied, that they were the servants of God Almighty; that this temple was built for him by a king of theirs who lived in great prosperity, and one that exceeded all men in virtue; and that it had stood for a long time. (91) Because of their fathers' impiety towards God, Nebuchadnezzar, king of the Babylonians and Chaldeans, took their city by force, destroyed it, pillaged the temple, burned it down, transplanted the people whom he had made captives, and removed them to Babylon. (92) Cyrus, who, after him was king of Babylonia and Persia, wrote to them to build the temple and committed the gifts and vessels and whatever Nebuchadnezzar had taken from it, to Zerubbabel and Mithridates the treasurer, and ordered them to be carried to Jerusalem and restored to their own temple when it was built. (93) He had sent to them to have this done speedily and commanded Sanabassar[79] to go up to Jerusalem and to take care of the building of the temple. Upon receiving that epistle from Cyrus, he came and

---

77. Tattenai in the biblical account.
78. Biblical Shethar-boznai.
79. Biblical Sheshbazzar.

immediately laid its foundations, and although it had been in construction from that time on, it had not yet been finished, because of the malice of their enemies. (94) "If therefore you have a mind, and think it proper, write this account to Darius so that when he has consulted the records of the kings, he may find that we have told you nothing that is false about this matter."

(95) When Zerubbabel and the high priest had given this answer, Sisinnes and those who were with him decided not to hinder the building until they had informed King Darius of all this. So they immediately wrote to him about these affairs. (96) Since the Jews were now in terror, and afraid lest the king should change his mind about the building of Jerusalem and of the temple, there were two prophets at that time among them, Haggai and Zechariah, who encouraged them, and bade them to be of good cheer and to suspect no discouragement from the Persians, for God had foretold this to them. So in dependence on those prophets, they applied themselves earnestly to building and did not interrupt one day.

(97) But the Samaritans wrote to Darius, and in their epistle accused the Jews of fortifying the city and building the temple more like a citadel than a temple, and that what was being done was not to the king's advantage. Besides they cited the epistle of Cambyses, wherein he forbade them to build the temple. (98) When Darius thereby understood that the restoration of Jerusalem was not safe for his government, and when he had read the epistle that was brought to him from Sisinnes and those that were with him, he ordered that what concerned these matters should be searched for among the royal records. (99) Thereupon a book was found at Ecbatana,[80] a fortress in Media, wherein was written as follows:

"In the first year of his reign, Cyrus the king commanded that the temple should be built in Jerusalem with its altar sixty cubits high and its width the same, its wall to be made three courses of polished stone, and one course of wood of their own country. (100) He ordained that the expenses for this should be paid out of the king's revenue. He also commanded that the vessels which Nebuchadnezzar had pillaged [from the temple] and had carried to Babylon should be restored to the people of Jerusalem (101) and that the supervision of these matters should belong to Sanabassar, the eparch and governor of Syria and Phoenicia, and to his associates, and that they may not meddle with that place, but should permit the servants of God, the Jews and their rulers, to build the temple. (102) He also ordained that they should assist them in the work, and that they should pay out of the tribute of the country of which they were gov-

---

80. The summer residence of the Persian kings.

ernors the expenses of the Jews for sacrifices of bulls, rams, sheep, kids of the goats, fine flour, oil and wine and all other things that the priests should suggest to them so that they should pray for the preservation of the king and of the Persians. (103) Whoever transgresses any of these orders thus sent to them, he commanded that they should be caught, hung upon a cross, and their property confiscated to the royal treasury. He also prayed to God that if anyone attempted to hinder the building of the temple, God would strike him dead and thereby restrain his wickedness."

(104) When Darius found this book among the records of Cyrus, he wrote an answer to Sisinnes and his associates, whose contents were these:—"King Darius to Sisinnes the governor, and to Sathrabuzanes, sends greeting. Having found a copy of this epistle among the records of Cyrus, I have sent it to you. It is my will that all things be done as therein written. Farewell." (105) So when Sisinnes, and those that were with him, understood the intention of the king, they resolved to follow his directions entirely for the time to come. So they helped to advance the sacred works and assisted the elders of the Jews and the chiefs of the senate.[81] (106) The construction of the temple was brought to a conclusion with great diligence by the prophecies of Haggai and Zechariah according to God's commands and by the injunctions of Cyrus and Darius the kings. The temple was built in seven years' time. (107) In the ninth year of the reign of Darius, on the twenty-third day of the twelfth month, which is by us called Adar,[82] but by the Macedonians Dystrus, the priests and Levites, and the rest of the Israelite people, offered sacrifices to celebrate the restoration of their former prosperity after their captivity and because they now had the rebuilt temple: a hundred bulls, two hundred rams, four hundred lambs, and twelve kids of the goats, according to the number of their tribes (for this is the number of the tribes of the Israelites), to atone for the sins of each tribe. (108) The priests and the Levites set the porters at every gate according to the laws of Moses. The Jews also built the porticoes around the temple within the sacred precincts.

3.5 MIDRASH AND THE FOUNDATIONS OF JEWISH LAW

3.5.1 Nehemiah 8: The Building of the Booths

One of the earliest examples of midrashic exegesis was in the manner in which Lev. 23:40–42 was interpreted by the book of Ezra. The interpreta-

---

81. The council of elders, later termed Gerousia.
82. March.

tion proposed here was rejected by Jewish tradition which saw Lev. 23:40 as referring to the taking of the lulav and etrog, not to the building of the sukkah.

৭১৭

8:13 On the second day,[83] the heads of the clans of all the people and the priests and Levites gathered to Ezra the scribe to study the words of the Teaching.[84] 14 They found written in the Teaching that the Lord had commanded Moses that the Israelites must dwell in booths during the festival of the seventh month,[85] 15 and that they must announce and proclaim throughout all their towns and Jerusalem as follows, "Go out to the mountains and bring leafy branches of olive trees, pine trees, myrtles, palms and [other] leafy trees to make booths, as it is written."[86] 16 So the people went out and brought them, and made themselves booths on their roofs, in their courtyards, in the courtyards of the House of God, in the square of the Water Gate and in the square of the Ephraim Gate. 17 The whole community that returned from the captivity made booths and dwelt in the booths—the Israelites had not done so from the days of Joshua son of Nun to that day—and there was very great rejoicing. 18 He read from the scroll of the Teaching of God each day, from the first to the last day. They celebrated the festival seven days, and there was a solemn gathering on the eighth, as prescribed.[87]

3.5.2 Nehemiah 10: The Oath of the Covenant

After the public reading of the Torah, the people entered into a pact to fulfill its commands. The specific details of the obligations of this covenant indicate by their formulation that they are based on halakhic (legal) midrash, mostly intended to harmonize various prescriptions in the Torah. The most prominent aspect of this pact is the effort to set the Temple and its sacrificial service on sound footing.

৭১৭

10:29 "And the rest of the people, the priests, the Levites, the gatekeepers, the singers, the temple servants, and all who separated themselves

---

83. The day after the public Torah reading and covenant renewal ceremony.
84. Hebrew, " Torah."
85. The festival of Sukkot.
86. Cf. Lev. 23:40–42 of which this is clearly an interpretation.
87. Lev. 23:33–36.

from the peoples of the lands to [follow] the Teaching of God, their wives, sons and daughters, all who know enough to understand, 30 join with their noble brothers, and take an oath with sanctions to follow the Teaching of God, given through Moses the servant of God, and to observe carefully all the commandments of the Lord our Lord, His rules and laws.

31 "Namely: We will not give our daughters in marriage to the peoples of the land, or take their daughters for our sons.

32 "The peoples of the land who bring their wares and all sorts of food stuff for sale on the sabbath day—we will not buy from them on the sabbath or a holy day.

"We will forgo [the produce of] the seventh year, and every outstanding debt.

33 "We have laid upon ourselves obligations: To charge ourselves one-third of a shekel yearly for the service of the House of our God—34 for the rows of bread (showbread), for the regular meal offering and for the regular burnt offering, [for those of the] sabbaths, new moons, festivals, for consecrations, for sin offerings to atone for Israel, and for all the work in the House of our God.

35 "We have cast lots [among] the priests, the Levites, and the people, to bring the wood offering to the House of our God by clans annually at set times in order to provide fuel for the altar of the Lord our God, as is written in the Teaching.

36 "And [we undertake] to bring to the House of the Lord annually the first fruits of our soil, and of every fruit of every tree; 37 also, the first born of our sons and our beasts, as is written in the Teaching; and to bring the firstlings of our cattle and flocks to the House of our God for the priests who minister in the House of our God.

38 "We will bring to the storerooms of the House of our God the first part of our dough, and our gifts [of grain], and of the fruit of every tree, wine and oil for the priests, and the tithes of our land for the Levites—the Levites who collect the tithe in all our towns subject to royal service. 39 An Aaronite priest must be with the Levites when they collect the tithe, and the Levites must bring up a tithe of the tithe to the House of our God, to the storerooms of the treasury. 40 For it is to the storerooms that the Israelites and the Levites must bring the gifts of grain, wine, and oil. The equipment of the sanctuary and of the ministering priests and the gatekeepers and the singers is also there.

"We will not neglect the House of our God."

3.6 THE LITERATURE OF THE PERIOD

3.6.1 1 Chronicles 28–9:
The Kingdom of David and Solomon

During the Persian period, the Book of Chronicles was edited from a variety of earlier sources. A major theme of Chronicles is King David and his dynasty. The Davidic Dynasty represented the ideal era of peace and security in the Land of Israel. Its promise of perfection has led the restoration of the Davidic House to be equated with the messianic era. David's blessing included here is a sample of the psalmodic literature attributed to him. Many of the psalms are still recited in the Jewish liturgy, prefaced by "A psalm of David."

28:1 David assembled all the officers of Israel—the tribal officers, the divisional officers who served the king, the captains of thousands and the captains of hundreds, and the stewards of all the property and cattle of the king and his sons, with the eunuchs and the warriors, all the men of substance—to Jerusalem. 2 King David rose to his feet and said, "Hear me, my brothers, my people! I wanted to build a resting-place for the Ark of the Covenant of the Lord, for the footstool of our God, and I laid aside material for building. 3 But God said to me, 'You will not build a house for My name, for you are a man of battles and have shed blood.' 4 The Lord God of Israel chose me of all my father's house to be king over Israel forever. For He chose Judah to be ruler, and of the family of Judah, my father's house; and of my father's sons, He preferred to make me king over all Israel; 5 and of all my sons—for many are the sons the Lord gave me—He chose my son Solomon to sit on the throne of the kingdom of the Lord over Israel. 6 He said to me, 'It will be your son Solomon who will build My House and My courts, for I have chosen him to be a son to Me, and I will be a father to him. 7 I will establish his kingdom forever, if he keeps firmly to the observance of My commandments and rules as he does now.' 8 And now, in the sight of all Israel, the congregation of the Lord, and in the hearing of our God, [I say:] Observe and apply yourselves to all the commandments of the Lord your God in order that you may possess this good land and bequeath it to your children after you forever.

9 "And you, my son Solomon, know the God of your father, and serve Him with single mind and fervent heart, for the Lord searches all minds and discerns the design of every thought; if you seek Him He will be available to you, but if you forsake Him He will abandon you forever. 10 See then, the Lord chose you to build a house as the sanctuary; be strong and do it."

11 David gave his son Solomon the plan of the porch and its houses, its storerooms and its upper chambers and inner chambers; and of the place of the Ark-cover; 12 and the plan of all that he had by the spirit: of the courts of the House of the Lord and all its surrounding chambers, and of the treasuries of the House of God and of the treasuries of the holy things; 13 the divisions of priests and Levites for all the work of the service of the House of the Lord and all the vessels of the service of the House of the Lord; 14 and gold, the weight of gold for vessels of every sort of use; silver for all the vessels of silver by weight, for all the vessels of every kind of service, 15 the weight of the gold lampstands and their gold lamps, and the weight of the silver lampstands, each lampstand and its silver lamps, according to the use of every lampstand; 16 and the weight of gold for the tables of the rows of bread, for each table, and of silver for the silver tables; 17 and of the pure gold for the forks and the basins and the jars; and the weight of the gold bowls, every bowl; and the weight of the silver bowls, each and every bowl; 18 the weight of refined gold for the incense altar and the gold for the figure of the chariot, the cherubs, those with outspread wings screening the Ark of the Covenant of the Lord. 19 "All this that the Lord made me understand by His hand on me, I give you in writing—the plan of all the works."[88]

20 David said to his son Solomon, "Be strong and of good courage and do it; do not be afraid or dismayed, for the Lord God my God is with you; He will not fail you or forsake you till all the work on the House of the Lord is done. 21 Here are the divisions of the priests and Levites for all kinds of service of the House of God, and with you in all the work are willing men, skilled in all sorts of tasks; also the officers and all the people are at your command."

29:1 King David said to the entire assemblage, "God has chosen my son Solomon alone, an untried lad, although the work to be done is vast—for the temple is not for a man but for the Lord God. 2 I have spared no effort to lay up for the House of my God gold for golden objects, silver for silver, copper for copper, iron for iron, wood for wooden, onyx-stone and inlay-stone, stone of antimony and variegated colors—every kind of precious stone and much marble. 3 Besides, out of my solicitude for the House of my God, I gave over my private hoard of gold and silver to the House of my God in addition to all that I laid aside for the holy House: 4 3,000 gold talents of Ophir[89] gold, and 7,000 talents of refined silver

---

88. This passage asserts that the plan of the Solomonic Temple was given by God to David, who passed it on to his son Solomon.

89. Ophir, a place whose location is disputed, was the source of gold for Solomon's kingdom.

for covering the walls of the houses 5 (gold for golden objects, silver for silver for all the work)—into the hands of craftsmen. Now who is going to make a freewill offering and devote himself today to the Lord?"

6 The officers of the clans and the officers of the tribes of Israel and the captains of thousands and hundreds and the supervisors of the king's work made freewill offerings, 7 giving for the work of the House of God: 5,000 talents of gold, 10,000 darics,[90] 10,000 talents of silver, 18,000 talents of copper, 100,000 talents of iron. 8 Whoever had stones in his possession gave them to the treasury of the House of the Lord in the charge of Jehiel the Gershonite. 9 The people rejoiced over the freewill offerings they made, for with a whole heart they made freewill offerings to the Lord; King David also rejoiced very much.

10 David blessed the Lord in front of all the assemblage; David said, "Blessed are You, Lord, God of Israel our father, from eternity to eternity. 11 Yours, Lord, are greatness, might, splendor, triumph, and majesty—yes, all that is in heaven and on earth; to You, Lord, belong kingship and preeminence above all. 12 Riches and honor are Yours to dispense; You have dominion over all; with You are strength and might, and it is in Your power to make anyone great and strong. 13 Now, God, we praise You and extol Your glorious name. 14 Who am I and who are my people, that we should have the means to make such a freewill offering; but all is from You, and it is Your gift that we have given to You. 15 For we are sojourners with You, mere transients like our fathers; our days on earth are like a shadow, with nothing in prospect. 16 O Lord our God, all this great mass that we have laid aside to build You a House for Your holy name is from You, and it is all Yours. 17 I know, God, that You search the heart and desire uprightness; I, with upright heart, freely offered all these things; now Your people, who are present here—I saw them joyously making freewill offerings. 18 O Lord God of Abraham, Isaac, and Israel, our fathers, remember this to the eternal credit of the thoughts of Your people's hearts, and make their hearts constant toward You. 19 As to my son Solomon, give him a whole heart to observe Your commandments, Your admonitions, and Your laws, and to fulfill them all, and to build this temple for which I have made provision."

20 David said to the whole assemblage, "Now bless the Lord your God." All the assemblage blessed the Lord God of their fathers, and bowed their heads low to the Lord and the king. 21 They offered sacrifices to the Lord and made burnt offerings to the Lord on the morrow of that

---

90. A Persian monetary unit.

day: 1,000 bulls, 1,000 rams, 1,000 lambs, with their libations; [they made] sacrifices in great number for all Israel, 22 and they ate and drank in the presence of the Lord on that day with great joy. They again proclaimed Solomon son of David king, and they anointed him as ruler before the Lord, and Zadok as high priest. 23 Solomon successfully took over the throne of the Lord as king instead of his father David, and all went well with him. All Israel accepted him; 24 all the officials and the warriors, and the sons of King David as well, gave their hand in support of King Solomon. 25 The Lord made Solomon exceedingly great in the eyes of all Israel, and endowed him with a regal majesty that no king of Israel before him ever had.

26 Thus David son of Jesse reigned over all Israel; 27 the length of his reign over Israel was forty years: he reigned seven years in Hebron and thirty-three years in Jerusalem. 28 He died at a ripe old age, having enjoyed long life, riches and honor, and his son Solomon reigned in his stead. 29 The acts of King David, early and late, are recorded in the history of Samuel the seer, the history of Nathan the prophet, and the history of Gad the seer,[91] 30 together with all the mighty deeds of his kingship and the events that befell him and Israel and all the kingdoms of the earth.

3.6.2 Haggai 1: Rebuilding the House of the Lord

Haggai, prophesying around 520 B.C.E., yearned for the restoration of the Temple to be completed and called upon the nation to devote itself to this project. He attributed all unprofitable activities to the desire of people to build their own homes while neglecting the House of God.

৶৻

1:1 In the second year of King Darius,[92] on the first day of the sixth month, this word of the Lord came through the prophet Haggai to Zerubbabel son of Shealtiel, the governor of Judah, and to Joshua son of Jehozadak, the high priest:

2 Thus said the Lord of Hosts: These people say, "The time has not yet come for rebuilding the House of the Lord"....

4 Is it a time for you to dwell in your paneled houses, while this House is lying in ruins? 5 Now thus said the Lord of Hosts: Consider how you have been faring! 6 You have sowed much and brought in little, you

---

91. These three sources, used by the Chronicler, were not preserved.
92. 520 B.C.E.

eat without being satisfied; you drink without getting your fill; you clothe yourselves, but no one gets warm; and he who earns anything earns it for a leaky purse.

7 Thus said the Lord of Hosts: Consider how you have fared: 8 Go up to the hills and get timber, and rebuild the House; then I will look on it with favor and I will be glorified—said the Lord.

9 You have been expecting much and getting little; and when you brought it home, I would blow on it![93] Because of what?—says the Lord of Hosts. Because of My House which lies in ruins, while you all hurry to your own houses! 10 That is why the skies above you have withheld (their) moisture and the earth has withheld its yield, 11 and I have summoned fierce heat upon the land—upon the hills, upon the new grain and wine and oil, upon all that the ground produces, upon man and beast, and upon all the fruits of labor.

3.6.3 Haggai 2: Recalling the Splendor of the First Temple

Haggai encourages those who remembered the greater glory of the First Temple, proclaiming that the Second Temple would eventually surpass it.

೩

2:1 On the twenty-first day of the seventh month, the word of the Lord came through the prophet Haggai:

2 Speak to Zerubbabel son of Shealtiel, the governor of Judah, and to the high priest Joshua son of Jehozadak, and to the rest of the people: 3 Who is there left among you who saw this House in its former splendor? How does it look to you now? It must seem like nothing to you. 4 But be strong, O Zerubbabel—says the Lord—be strong, O high priest Joshua son of Jehozadak; be strong, all you people of the land—says the Lord—and act! For I am with you—says the Lord of Hosts. 5 So I promised you when you came out of Egypt, and My spirit is still in your midst. Fear not!

6 For thus said the Lord of Hosts: In just a little while longer I will shake the heavens and the earth, the sea and the dry land; 7 I will shake all the nations. And the precious things of all the nations shall come [here], and I will fill this House with glory, said the Lord of Hosts. 8 Silver is Mine and gold is Mine—says the Lord of Hosts. 9 The glory of this latter House shall be greater than that of the former one, said the Lord of Hosts; and in this place I will grant prosperity—declares the Lord of Hosts.

---

93. That is, I sent a plague against it.

3.6.4 Zechariah 3–14: The Prophecy of Restoration

The prophecies of Zechariah date from 520–518 B.C.E. The prophet called for the rebuilding of the Temple and its ritual, as we see in the excerpts from chapters 3–4. The prophecies in the second half of the book, represented here by chapters 8 and 14, are taken by most modern scholars to be the work of later followers of Zechariah, most probably in the Persian period. These prophecies tell of the coming renewal of the Jewish people in their land which was expected to be inaugurated by a cataclysmic destruction of the evildoers. These visions were very influential in the later apocalyptic messianic movements.

🙟

3:1 He further showed me Joshua,[94] the high priest, standing before the angel of the Lord, and the Accuser standing at his right to accuse him. 2 But [the angel of] the Lord said to the Accuser, "The Lord rebuke you, O Accuser; may the Lord who has chosen Jerusalem rebuke you! For this is a brand plucked from the fire." 3 Now Joshua was clothed in filthy garments when he stood before the angel. 4 The latter spoke up and said to his attendants, "Take the filthy garments off him!" And he said to him, "See, I have removed your guilt from you, and you shall be clothed in [priestly] robes." 5 Then he gave the order, "Let a pure diadem be placed on his head." And they placed the pure diadem on his head and clothed him in [priestly] garments, as the angel of the Lord stood by.

6 And the angel of the Lord charged Joshua as follows: 7 "Thus said the Lord of Hosts: If you walk in My paths and keep My charge, you in turn will rule My House and guard My courts, and I will permit you to move about among these attendants. 8 Hearken well, O High Priest Joshua, you and your fellow priests sitting before you! For those men are a sign that I am going to bring My servant the Branch. 9 For mark well this stone which I place before Joshua, a single stone with seven eyes. I will execute its engraving—declares the Lord of Hosts—and I will remove that country's guilt in a single day. 10 On that day—declares the the Lord of Hosts—you will be inviting each other to the shade of vines and fig trees. . . .

4:1 The angel who talked with me came back and woke me as a man is wakened from sleep. 2 He said to me, "What do you see?" And I answered, "I see a lampstand all of gold, with a bowl above it. The lamps on it are seven in number, and the lamps above it have seven pipes; 3 and

---

94. Son of Jehozadak.

by it are two olive trees, one on the right of the bowl and one on its left."
4 I, in turn, asked the angel who talked with me, "What do those things
mean, my lord?" 5 "Do you not know what those things mean?" asked
the angel who talked with me; and I said, "No, my lord." 6 Then he
explained to me as follows:

"This is the word of the Lord to Zerubbabel: Not by might, nor by
power, but by My spirit—said the Lord of Hosts. 7 Whoever you are, O
great mountain in the path of Zerubbabel, turn into level ground! For he
shall produce that excellent stone; it shall be greeted with shouts of 'Beautiful! Beautiful!'"

8 And the word of the Lord came to me: 9 "Zerubbabel's hands have
founded this House and Zerubbabel's hands shall complete it. Then you
shall know that it was the Lord of Hosts who sent me to you. 10 Does
anyone scorn a day of small beginnings? When they see the stone of distinction in the hand of Zerubbabel, they shall rejoice. "Those are the
seven eyes of the Lord ranging over the whole earth. . . ."

8:1 The word of the Lord of Hosts came [to me]: 2 Thus said the Lord
of Hosts: I am very jealous for Zion, I am fiercely jealous for her. 3 Thus
said the Lord: I have returned to Zion, and I will dwell in Jerusalem.
Jerusalem will be called the City of Faithfulness, and the mount of the
Lord of Hosts the Holy Mount.

4 Thus said the Lord of Hosts: There shall yet be old men and women
in the squares of Jerusalem, each with staff in hand because of their great
age. 5 And the squares of the city shall be crowded with boys and girls
playing in the squares. 6 Thus said the Lord of Hosts: Though it will seem
impossible to the remnant of this people in those days, shall it also be
impossible to Me?—declares the Lord of Hosts. 7 Thus said the Lord of
Hosts: I will rescue My people from the lands of the east and from the
lands of the west, 8 and I will bring them home to dwell in Jerusalem.
They shall be My people, and I will be their God in truth and sincerity.

9 Thus said the Lord of Hosts: Take courage you who now hear these
words which the prophets spoke when the foundations were laid for the
rebuilding of the Temple, the House of the Lord of Hosts.

10 For before that time, the earnings of men were nil, and profits from
beasts were nothing. It was not safe to go about one's business on account
of enemies; and I set all men against one another. 11 But now I will not
treat the remnant of this people as before—declares the Lord of Hosts,
12 but what it sows shall prosper: the vine shall produce its fruit, the
ground shall produce its yield, and the skies shall provide their moisture. I
will bestow all these things upon the remnant of this people. 13 And just

as you were a curse among the nations, O House of Judah and House of Israel, so, when I vindicate you, you shall become a blessing. Have no fear; take courage!

14 For thus said the Lord of Hosts: Just as I planned to afflict you and did not relent when your fathers provoked Me to anger—said the Lord of Hosts—15 so, at this time, I have turned and planned to do good to Jerusalem and to the House of Judah. Have no fear! 16 These are the things you are to do: Speak the truth to one another, render true and perfect justice in your gates. 17 And do not contrive evil against one and other, and do not love perjury, because all those are things that I hate—declares the Lord.

18 And the word of the Lord of Hosts came to me, saying, 19 Thus said the Lord of Hosts: the fast of the fourth month, the fast of the fifth month, the fast of the seventh month, and the fast of the tenth month shall become occasions for joy and gladness, happy festivals for the house of Judah; but you must love honesty and integrity. 20 Thus said the Lord of Hosts: Peoples and the inhabitants of many cities shall yet come— 21 the inhabitants of one shall go to the other and say, "Let us go and entreat the favor of the Lord, let us seek the Lord of Hosts; I will go, too." 22 The many peoples and the multitude of nations shall come to seek the Lord of Hosts in Jerusalem and to entreat the favor of the Lord. 23 Thus said the Lord of Hosts: In those days, ten men from nations of every tongue will take hold—they will take hold of every Jew by the corner of his cloak and say, "Let us go with you, for we have heard that God is with you."

14:1 Lo, a day of the Lord is coming when your spoil shall be divided in your very midst! 2 For I will gather all the nations to Jerusalem for war. The city shall be captured, the houses plundered, and the women violated and a part of the city shall go into exile. But the rest of the population shall not be uprooted from the city.

3 Then the Lord will come forth and make war on those nations as He is wont to make war on a day of battle. 4 On that day, He will set His feet on the Mount of Olives, near Jerusalem on the east, and the Mount of Olives shall split across from east to west, and one part of the Mount shall shift to the north and the other to the south, a huge gorge. 5 And the Valley in the Hills shall be stopped up, for the Valley of the Hills shall reach only to Azal; it shall be stopped up as it was stopped up as a result of the earthquake in the days of King Uzziah of Judah.[95]—And the Lord my God, with all the holy beings, will come to you.

---

95. Ruled ca. 783–742 B.C.E.

6 In that day, there shall be neither sunlight nor cold moonlight, 7 but there shall be a continuous day—only the Lord knows when—of neither day nor night, and there shall be light at eventide.

8 In that day, fresh water shall flow from Jerusalem, part of it to the Eastern Sea and part to the Western Sea, throughout the summer and winter.

9 And the Lord shall be king over all the earth; in that day there shall be one Lord with one name.

10 Then the whole country shall become like the Arabah, from Geba to Rimmon south of Jerusalem. The latter, however, shall perch high up where it is, and shall be inhabited from the Gate of Benjamin to the site of the Old Gate, down to the Corner Gate, and from the Tower of Hananel to the king's winepresses.[96] 11 Never again shall destruction be decreed, and Jerusalem shall dwell secure.

12 As for those peoples that warred against Jerusalem, the Lord will smite them with this plague: Their flesh shall rot away, while they stand on their feet; their eyes shall rot away in their sockets; and their tongues shall rot away in their mouths.

13 In that day, a great panic from the Lord shall fall upon them, and everyone shall snatch at the hand of another, and everyone shall raise his hand against everyone else's hand. 14 Judah shall join the fighting in Jerusalem, and the wealth of all the nations roundabout—vast quantities of gold, silver, and clothing—shall be gathered in.

15 The same plague shall strike the horses, the mules, the camels, and the asses; the plague shall affect all the animals in those camps.

16 All who survive of all those nations that came up against Jerusalem shall make a pilgrimage year by year to bow low to the King Lord of Hosts and to observe the Feast of Booths.[97] 17 Any of the earth's communities that does not make the pilgrimage to Jerusalem to bow low to the King Lord of Hosts shall receive no rain. . . .

20 In that day, even the bells on the horses shall be inscribed "Holy to the Lord." The metal pots in the House of the Lord shall be like the basins before the altar, 21 indeed every metal pot in Jerusalem and in Judah shall be holy to the Lord of Hosts. And all those who sacrifice shall come and take of these to boil [their sacrificial meat] in; in that day there shall be no more traders in the House of the Lord of Hosts.

---

96. All places in Jerusalem.
97. The festival of Sukkot in the fall.

3.6.5 Malachi 2–3: The Last of the Prophets

Malachi's prophetic career is probably to be dated to 500–450 B.C.E. He calls for morality and fidelity to God's teachings, as well as emphasizing the role of the priests as teachers of Torah. Malachi looks forward to the Day of the Lord when the wicked will be destroyed and the righteous will be victorious.

❧

2:1 And now, O priests, this charge is for you: 2 Unless you obey and unless you lay it to heart, and do honor to My name—said the Lord of Hosts—I will send a curse and turn your blessings into curses. (Indeed, I have turned them into curses, because you do not lay it to heart). 3 I will put your seed under a ban, and I will strew dung upon your faces, the dung of your festal sacrifices, and you shall be carried out to its (heap).

4 Know, then, that I have sent this charge to you that My covenant with Levi may endure—said the Lord of Hosts. 5 I had with him a covenant of life and well-being, which I gave to him, and of reverence, which he showed Me. For he stood in awe of My name.

> 6 Proper rulings were in his mouth,
> And nothing perverse was on his lips;
> He served Me with complete loyalty
> And held the many back from iniquity.
> 7 For the lips of a priest guard knowledge,
> And men seek rulings from his mouth;
> For he is a messenger of the Lord of Hosts.

8 But you have turned away from that course: You have made the many stumble through your rulings; you have corrupted the covenant of the Levites—said the Lord of Hosts. 9 And I, in turn, have made you despicable and vile in the eyes of the people, because you disregard My ways and show partiality in your rulings.

10 Have we not all one Father? Did not one God create us? Why do we break faith with one another, profaning the covenant of our ancestors? 11 Judah has broken faith; abhorrent things have been done in Israel and in Jerusalem. For Judah has profaned what is holy to the Lord—what He desires—and espoused daughters of alien gods. 12 May the Lord leave to him who does this no descendants dwelling in the tents of Jacob and presenting offerings to the Lord of Hosts. 13 And this you do as well. You cover the altar of the Lord with tears, weeping, and moaning, so that He refuses to regard the obligation any more and to accept what you offer.

14 But you ask, "Because of what?" Because the Lord is a witness between you and the wife of your youth with whom you have broken faith, though she is your partner and covenanted spouse. 15 Did not the One make [all], so that all remaining life-breath is His? And what does that One seek but godly folk? So be careful of your life-breath, and let no one break faith with the wife of his youth. 16 For I detest divorce—said the Lord, the God of Israel—and covering oneself with lawlessness as with a garment—said the Lord of Hosts. So be careful of your life-breath and do not act treacherously.

17 You have wearied the Lord with your talk. But you ask, "By what have we wearied [Him]?" By saying, "All who do evil are good in the sight of the Lord, and in them He delights," or else, "Where is the God of justice?"

3:13 You have spoken hard words against Me—said the Lord. But you ask, "What have we been saying among ourselves against You?" 14 You have said, "It is useless to serve God. What have we gained by keeping His charge and walking in abject awe of the Lord of Hosts? 15 And so, we account the arrogant happy: they have indeed done evil and endured, they have indeed dared God and escaped." 16 In this vein have those who revere the Lord been talking to one another. The Lord has heard and noted it, and a scroll of remembrance has been written at His behest concerning those who revere the Lord and esteem His name. 17 And on the day that I am preparing, said the Lord of Hosts, they shall be my treasured possession; I will be tender toward them as a man is tender toward a son who ministers to him. 18 And you shall come to see the difference between the righteous and the wicked, between him who has served the Lord and him who has not served Him.

19 For lo! That day is at hand, burning like an oven. All the arrogant and all the doers of evil shall be straw, and the day that is coming—said the Lord of Hosts—shall burn them to ashes and leave of them neither stock nor boughs. 20 But for you who revere My name a sun of victory shall rise to bring healing. You shall go forth and stamp like stall-fed calves, 21 and you shall trample the wicked to a pulp, for they shall be dust beneath your feet on that day that I am preparing—said the Lord of Hosts.

22 Be mindful of the Teaching of My servant Moses, whom I charged at Horeb with laws and rules for all Israel.[98]

23 Lo, I will send the prophet Elijah to you before the coming of the awesome, fearful day of the Lord. 24 He shall reconcile parents with children and children with parents, so that when I come I do not strike the whole land with utter destruction.

3.7 THE CANONIZATION
OF THE HEBREW SCRIPTURES

3.7.1 Josephus, *Against Apion* I, 37–43:
Authenticity of the Scripture

The historian, Josephus, argues the authenticity of the Jewish tradition by referring to the antiquity, accuracy, and divine inspiration of the Jewish scriptures. In the process, he obliquely refers to all the books of the Bible. He also testifies to Jewish loyalty to their holy texts.

ξ

(37) . . . Everyone is not permitted of his own accord to be a writer, nor is there any disagreement in what is written; they being only prophets that have written the original and earliest accounts of things as they learned them from God himself by inspiration; and writing down what happened in their own times in a very exact manner also.

(38) For we do not have an innumerable multitude of books among us, disagreeing from and contradicting one another [as the Greeks have], but only twenty-two books, which contain the records of all the past times which are justly believed to be divine. (39) Five of them belong to Moses, which contain his laws and the traditions of the origin of mankind till his death. This interval of time was a little short of three thousand years. (40) But as to the time from the death of Moses till the reign of Artaxerxes, king of Persia, who reigned after Xerxes,[99] the prophets, who came after Moses, wrote down the history of their times in thirteen books. The remaining four books contain hymns to God and precepts for the conduct of human life. (41) Our history has been written since Artaxerxes very thoroughly, but it has not been considered of equal authority with the earlier records by our forefathers, because there has not been an exact succession of prophets since that time. (42) How firmly we have given credit to those books of our own nation is evident by what we do. For although so many ages have already passed, no one has been so bold as either to add anything to them, to take anything from them, or to make any change in them. But it becomes natural to all Jews, immediately and

---

98. This mention of Moses and his Torah comes at the end of the prophets as if to conclude this canonical section with an appeal to the dependence of the prophets on the Torah—a central concept in Judaism. Some scholars, therefore, take this to be an addition by those who fixed the canon of the Prophets.

99. Artaxerxes I succeeded Xerxes in 465 B.C.E. Josephus considered him to be the King Ahasueras of the Book of Esther.

from their very birth, to regard those books as containing divine doctrines, and to abide by them, and, if need be, willingly to die for them.

(43) Our captives, many of them in number, and frequently in time, have been seen to endure torture and deaths of all kinds in the theaters so that they may not be forced to utter one word against our laws and the records that contain them.

3.7.2 Babylonian Talmud Bava Batra 14b-15a: The Order of Scripture[100]

The Rabbis of the Talmud, in a baraita, listed the order of the biblical books in a way different even from the later Jewish Bibles. This passage shows that the tri-partite canon was the norm. The Rabbis also dealt with the question of who had actually committed the various books to writing.

☙

Our Rabbis taught:

The order of the Prophets (Nevi'im) is: Joshua, Judges, Samuel, Kings, Jeremiah, Ezekiel, Isaiah, and the Twelve Minor Prophets. Now, Hosea came first, as it is written, "God first spoke to Hosea" (Hos. 1:2). But did He first speak to Hosea? Were there not a number of prophets from Moses to Hosea? However, Rabbi Yoḥanan said that he was the first of four prophets who prophesied at that time, and these are they: Hosea, and Isaiah, Amos, and Micah. Then Hosea should have been placed first? Since his prophesies are written (in the collection together) with Haggai, Zechariah and Malachi, and Haggai, Zechariah, and Malachi were the last of the prophets, Hosea is considered together with them. Then it should have been written separately and placed earlier? Since it is small, it might have gotten lost. Now, Isaiah is before Jeremiah and Ezekiel, so Isaiah should have been placed first? Kings ends with an account of destruction, and Jeremiah is entirely an account of destruction, and Ezekiel begins with destruction and concludes with consolation, and Isaiah is entirely consolation. Thus, we adjoin destruction to destruction and consolation to consolation.

The order of the Writings (*Ketuvim*) is: Ruth, and the Book of Psalms, and Job, and Proverbs, Ecclesiastes, Song of Songs, and Lamentations, Daniel, and the Scroll of Esther, Ezra, and Chronicles. According to the view that Job lived in the days of Moses, Job should have been placed first? It is not proper to begin with calamity. But Ruth also deals with

---

100. Trans. S. Berrin.

calamity? It is calamity which has a good end, as Rabbi Yoḥanan said: "Why was she called Ruth? (Hebrew: *rwt*) Because from her descended David who delighted (Hebrew: *rywhw*) God with songs and hymns."[101]

And who recorded [the biblical books]? Moses recorded his book, including the portion of Balaam, and Job. Joshua recorded his book and eight verses of the Pentateuch. Samuel recorded his book and Judges and Ruth. David recorded the Book of Psalms with the help of ten elders: Adam, Melchizedek, Abraham, Moses, Heman, Yeduthan, Asaph, and the three sons of Korah. Jeremiah recorded his book and the Book of Kings and Lamentations. Hezekiah and his assistants recorded Isaiah, Proverbs, Song of Songs, and Ecclesiastes. The Men of the Great Assembly recorded Ezekiel, and the Twelve Minor Prophets, Daniel, and the Scroll of Esther. Ezra recorded his book and the genealogies of Chronicles up to his own time.[102] This supports Rav, as Rabbi Judah said, "Rav said: 'Ezra did not go up from Babylonia until he recorded his genealogy, and then he went up.'" And who concluded [the Book of Chronicles]? Nehemiah the son of Hachaliah.

3.7.3 Mishnah Yadayim 3:5:
The Debate over the Biblical Canon[103]

In the time of the Mishnah the Rabbis debated the contents of the canon, that is, which books would be considered part of the Bible and which were not accorded this holy status. The Song of Songs, with its explicit sexual imagery, and Ecclesiastes, which could be understood to present a rather cynical view of the world, were the most hotly contested.

❦

All Holy Scriptures defile the hands.[104] Song of Songs and Ecclesiastes defile the hands. Rabbi Judah says, "Song of Songs defiles the hands but there is a dispute regarding Ecclesiastes." Rabbi Jose says, "Ecclesiastes does not defile the hands, and there is a dispute about Song of Songs."

---

101. Although the story of Job precedes the other works of the *Ketuvim* chronologically, it is not placed first in the collection because it consists entirely of afflictions. Ruth is the first book, according to the order proposed here, despite the fact that it begins with affliction because it ends well.

102. Modern scholars have also accepted the notion that Ezra, Nehemiah, and Chronicles are by the same author.

103. Trans. S. Berrin.

104. All books which are included in the biblical canon transmit defilement to those who touch them.

Rabbi Simeon says, "[The status of] Ecclesiastes is one of the lenient rulings of the School of Shammai, and one of the strict rulings of the School of Hillel."[105]

Rabbi Simeon ben Azzai said, "I have a tradition from the seventy-two elders (of the Sanhedrin) that on the day when Rabbi Eleazar ben Azariah was appointed head of the Academy, it was decided that Song of Songs and Ecclesiastes defile the hands."

Rabbi Akiva said, "God forbid! No one in Israel disputed about Song of Songs, saying that it does not defile the hands. For all of eternity in its entirety is not as worthy as the day on which Song of Songs was given to Israel, for all the Writings are holy, but Song of Songs is the Holy of Holies. And if they disputed at all, they disputed only regarding Ecclesiastes."

Rabbi Yoḥanan ben Joshua the son of Rabbi Akiba's father-in-law said, "As according to Ben Azzai, so did they dispute and so did they determine [that both Song of Songs and Ecclesiastes are included in the canon]."

3.7.4 Tosefta Yadayim 2:14:
The Biblical Canon and Divine Inspiration[106]

In the debate concerning the biblical canon, Rabbi Simeon explains canonical status as dependent on divine inspiration. In spite of his ruling that Ecclesiastes in only wisdom, both the Song of Songs and Ecclesiastes are considered part of the twenty-four books of the Hebrew Bible.

ﭫ

Rabbi Simeon ben Menasya says, "Song of Songs defiles the hands since it was written with divine inspiration. Ecclesiastes does not defile the hands since it is only the wisdom of Solomon."

They said to him, "And did he (Solomon) write only this? Is it not stated, 'He wrote three thousand proverbs and his songs numbered one thousand and five' (1 Kings 5:12)?"[107] It is stated, "Do not add to his words" (Prov. 30:6).[108]

---

105. The School of Shammai takes the view that Ecclesiastes does not defile the hands, which is to say that it is not canonical. The School of Hillel rules that Ecclesiastes does defile the hands and is part of the canon.

106. Trans. S. Berrin.

107. This verse is cited to demonstrate that Solomon also wrote Proverbs and Song of Songs, books the canonical status of which is universally accepted. Since these books of wisdom which were written by Solomon indisputably defile the hands, so too Ecclesiastes which was written by Solomon must also defile the hands.

108. This verse is cited to counter the previous argument. Despite the undeniably canonical status of Proverbs and Song of Songs, the book of Ecclesiastes cannot be added to the corpus of books which defile the hands.

4

The Hellenistic Age

Hellenism was a widespread cultural phenomenon which was to a great extent spread and fostered by the growth of Greek cities (*poleis*; singular, *polis*) throughout the Mediterranean world. Certainly, this was the case in the Land of Israel. To understand this phenomenon we begin with a series of excerpts from Pausanias (text 4.1.1), a second century C.E. author from Asia Minor, who describes the city of Athens, to a great extent the mother of the type of culture which, when merged with the native Near Eastern, came to be known as Hellenism. From these passages one gets a sense of the all-pervasive character of culture and religion in these cities.

The Hellenistic period begins technically with the coming of Alexander to the Near East. Two sources say that he actually visited the Land of Israel. Josephus's *Antiquities of the Jews* contains one such account (text 4.2.1). It begins with the attempt of Sanballat to advance the interests of the Samaritans, still rivals of the Judeans. According to the almost miraculous, legendary account of Josephus, the high priest was Jaddua, and he met Alexander at Jerusalem. The account preserved in the Babylonian Talmud Yoma 69a (text 4.2.2), however, identifies the high priest as the more famous Simon the Just and the place of the meeting as Antipatris, present-day Rosh Ha-Ayin near the Mediterranean coast. Because there is no earlier record of this meeting, it is a subject of considerable controversy. Those historians who accept the report as historical believe that it was Jaddua who met Alexander, as in Josephus, but that the meeting took place at Antipatris, as stated in the talmudic account.

121

After the death of Alexander in 323 B.C.E., the Land of Israel entered a period of warfare in which the Ptolemies and Seleucids vied for control over it. Josephus describes this period in detail. In *Antiquities* (text 4.2.3) he discusses the manner in which Ptolemy I Soter (301 B.C.E.) gained control of Jerusalem. Ptolemaic control finally gave way to Seleucid rule under Antiochus III the Great (201 B.C.E.), and this transfer of power is chronicled by Josephus (text 4.2.4), who also preserves earlier documentary evidence that he was able to use. The conquest of the Land of Israel by the Seleucids set the stage for the Hellenistic reform and the Maccabean Revolt which would soon occur.

There is much to be learned from documentary evidence regarding life in the Ptolemaic period. The excerpts from the Zenon Papyri (text 4.2.5) tell us about economic conditions. Papyrus 1 indicates that the Ptolemaic aristocracy bought Sidonian slaves, male and female, for import into Egypt. More importantly, the guarantor to this transaction was a Jew, son of a certain Ananias, who was part of a troop settled in a cleruchy (military colony) in service to the Tobiads, who were important Jewish fiscal agents and tax farmers in Palestine and in Ptolemaic Egypt, and whose activities would help to precipitate the Hellenistic reform. Clearly there was a developed Jewish Diaspora in Egypt, continuing the Elephantine tradition. Papyrus 4 testifies to the importance of circumcision already at this time, yet we cannot be certain that the circumcised slaves were Jewish. Papyrus 5 concerns gifts which Tobiah, head of a Jewish military unit, provided to the king. Papyrus 6, besides indicating the complexity of a transaction between Ptolemaic Palestine and Egypt, gives a sense of the occasional violence which broke out against Ptolemaic rule in Palestine. Vienna Papyrus 68 (text 4.2.6) gives an indication of the complex system of taxation in the Ptolemaic Empire. Specifically, it refers to military colonists in Syria and Phoenicia. These colonists helped to spread Hellenism throughout the Near East, and their settlements were constituted as cleruchies.

From these various documents we see that in the Ptolemaic age the external trappings of Hellenism did indeed spread in the Land of Israel. But little if any cultural or religious Hellenism can be documented for this period.

The Temple and the priesthood continued to stand at the center of religious life for the Jews of the Land of Israel. Among the more interesting descriptions of the Temple in the Hellenistic period is that of the Greek historian and ethnographer, Hecateus of Abdera, who wrote ca. 300 B.C.E. His description is quoted by Josephus (text 4.3.1). Hecateus was struck by the centrality of the Temple in the city, by the absence of pagan symbols and images, and by the prohibition against the priests' drinking liquor before or during the services. From ca. 180 B.C.E. we have the description of the grandeur of the high priest Simon the Just, son of Onias, in the book of Ben Sira (text 4.3.2). This work reflects the pride of the people in their high priest, known for his piety and his concern for his people. It was the decline of the priesthood which to a great extent touched off the Hellenistic reform. One of the important institutions in this period, which was connected to other, later institutions of Jewish self-government is the Gerousia, the council of elders. The early Seleucid rulers recognized its authority (text 4.4.1), and it continued into the Hasmonean period (text 4.4.2). It was recognized by foreign cities entering into relationships with Judea (text 4.4.3).

The process of Hellenization was helped along by the Tobiad family. Josephus relates the interesting story of the founder of this "dynasty," Joseph son of Tobiah, in *Antiquities* (text 4.5.1). This court tale, clearly embellished with legendary elements in Josephus' source, gives a sense of the extent to which wealthy aristocratic Jews were involved in non-Jewish society.

The influence of Hellenistic culture eventually intensified to bring about the Hellenistic reform. Because of the importance of these events, we present extensive material from 1 and 2 Maccabees. It is important to remember that these are two separate books which differ in authorship and outlook and, therefore, that their accounts are often at variance in matters of detail.

2 Maccabees 3–6 (text 4.6.1) provides the background, explaining how the high priesthood deteriorated in the Seleucid period, becoming an object of purchase, and how members of the priestly families fought among themselves. It also stresses the Hellenistic reform, the attempt to make the Jewish people like the other peoples of the Hellenistic world, which was first undertaken by Jews. It was only after internal struggles broke out between extremely Hel-

lenized Jews and what we might call traditionalists (themselves probably moderately Hellenized also) that King Antiochus IV issued his
famous decrees forbidding the practice of Judaism.

The narrative of the revolt presented here is from 1 Maccabees
(text 4.6.2). Suprisingly, the author does not seem to know about
the events which led up to it. In chapter 1 we read of the persecutions and of the bringing of idolatrous worship into the Temple.
Chapter 2 tells of the early period of the revolt under Mattathias,
until his death and Judah's rise to leadership. As seen in chapter 3,
the Maccabees, Judah's followers, engaged in full-scale battles against
the Seleucid forces, against whom they were victorious, as seen in
the selection from chapter 4.

The Maccabees fought on until the conquest of Jerusalem, as
described in 1 Maccabees 4–6 (text 4.6.3). Their successes were
great enough for the Seleucids to seek a compromise with Judah
and his men, as shown in the letter preserved in 2 Maccabees 11
(text 4.6.4). It was this victory and the cleansing of the Temple
which are celebrated in the Jewish holiday of Hanukkah.

But contrary to the popular conception, the rededication of the
Temple was not the end of the story. As a result of continuing con-
quests by Judah, as described in 2 Maccabees chapter 5, the Seleucids attempted to regain control after the death of Antiochus IV, but
soon had to arrive at a settlement with the Jews. In this arrangement
they attempted to support a moderate Hellenizer, Alcimus, as high
priest. Once again, under his influence, attempts were made to dislodge the Maccabees, as presented in 1 Maccabees 7–10 (text 4.6.5).
A series of armies were sent against Judah and his army by the
Seleucids in order to install Alcimus as high priest, and each was
defeated. In a battle described in chapter 9, Judah fell. The Seleucids
now succeeded in installing Alcimus. This state of affairs changed
only in 152 B.C.E., when the succession to the Seleucid throne was
in contention, and the pretenders each sought the help of Jonathan,
Judah's brother and successor; accordingly, as described in chapter
10, he was appointed high priest and returned to Jerusalem. This
date marks the official founding of the Hasmonean dynasty. This
event, not the rededication of the Temple in 164 B.C.E., marks the
real end of the Maccabean Revolt.

Extensive sources allow us to trace the rise of Hellenism in Palestine and its influence on the people. Further, these sources allow us to understand the Maccabean revolt as resulting from inner Jewish turmoil over the extent to which to adapt to the new culture of Hellenism while retaining at the same time the tradition and culture of Judaism.

4.1 HELLENISM AS A CULTURAL PHENOMENON

4.1.1 Pausanias, *Description of Greece,* Book I: The Greek Cultural Institutions[1]

Pausanias, the second century C.E. traveler from Asia Minor, described at length the physical character of the city of Athens, the ideal prototype for the Hellenistic cities (poleis) that spread throughout the Near East. This description provides a sense of how the city itself was a source of cultural influence. The many elipses are due to the elaborate historical information which Pausanias inserts into his physical description.

꽃

On entering the city there is a building for the preparation of the processions, which are held in some cases every year, in others at longer intervals. Hard by is a temple of Demeter[2] with images of the goddess herself and of her daughter,[3] and of Iacchus[4] holding a torch. . . . From the gate to the Cerameicus[5] there are porticoes, and in front of them brazen statues of such as had some title to fame, both men and women. One of the porticoes contains shrines of gods, and a gymnasium called that of

---

1. Trans. W. H. S. Jones, *Pausanias, Description of Greece I* (Loeb Classical Library; Cambridge: Harvard University Press, 1979), pp. 11–16.

2. Greek goddess of corn who controlled all crops and therefore sustained life. She was worshipped at agricultural festivals throughout the year which corresponded to the seasonal activities of farmers.

3. The goddess Persephone, also called Kore, was the daughter of Demeter and Zeus. She spent half a year in the Underworld as queen of the dead and, when she resumed her life above ground each spring, she brought the flowers and the fertility of the fields. Demeter and Kore were closely identified with one another and often called the Two Goddesses.

4. In the annual festival of the mysteries held in Eleusis, a section of Athens, Iacchus was the patron god of those initiated into the mysteries. Since he was to lead their procession, he is often pictured as holding a torch aloft.

5. A large district in northwest Athens containing the potters' quarter and especially famous for its public cemetery.

Hermes.[6] In it is the house of Pulytion, at which it is said that a mystic rite was performed by the most notable Athenians, parodying the Eleusinian mysteries.[7] But in my time it was devoted to the worship of Dionysus. . . .[8]

Here is built also a sanctuary of the Mother of the gods; the image is by Pheidias. Hard by is the council chamber of those called the Five Hundred, who are the Athenian councillors for a year. In it are a wooden figure of Zeus Counsellor and an Apollo, the work of Peisias, and a Demos by Lyson. . . .[9]

Near to the Council Chamber of the Five Hundred is what is called Tholos (Round House); here the Presidents sacrifice, and there are a few small statues made of silver. Farther up stand statues of heroes, from whom afterwards the Athenian tribes received their names. Who the man was who established ten tribes instead of four, and changed their old names to new ones—all this is told by Herodotus.[10] The *eponymoi*—this is the name given to them. . . .[11]

Near the statue of Demosthenes is a sanctuary of Ares, where are placed two images of Aphrodite, one of Ares made by Alcamenes, and one of Athena made by a Parian of the name of Locrus. About the temple stand images of Heracles, Theseus, Apollo binding his hair with a fillet, and statues of Calades, who it is said framed laws for the Athenians, and of Pindar,[12] the statue being one of the rewards Athenians gave him for praising them in an ode. . . .

---

6. The god Hermes was the son of Zeus and the nymph Maia. He was the swiftly traveling messenger of Zeus, and, in one of his many functions, also the god of athletes pictured as a charming youth. In this role he was often associated with the gymnasium and the school.

7. The Eleusinian mysteries were a civic cult in Athens from the late 6th century B.C.E. In the early autumn festival, initiates were privileged to be inducted into the secrets of the cult, attain collective purification, and witness the dramatic presentation of myths.

8. The god of wine and intoxication, ecstasy, impersonation and the theater, and the afterlife, Dionysus was the son of Zeus and Semele. A powerful deity and often linked with opposing traits, such as the god of both tragedy and comedy, Dionysus was the most represented god in ancient art.

9. The dates of these artists are unknown.

10. Historian of the 5th century B.C.E., born in present day Turkey. His most famous account is that of the Persian Wars which details those events through a combination of narrative and interviews of informants.

11. That is, those after whom others are named.

12. Lyric poet, born ca. 518 B.C.E. He was often commissioned to compose victory odes for athletic events.

Before the entrance of the theatre which they call the Odeum (*Music Hall*) are statues of Egyptian kings. They are all alike called Ptolemy, but each has his own surname. For they call one Philometor, and the other Philadelphus, while the son of Lagus is called Soter, a name given him by the Rhodians. . . .

When you have entered the Odeum at Athens you meet, among other objects, a figure of Dionysus worth seeing. Hard by is a spring called Enneacrunos (*Nine Jets*), embellished as you see it by Pisistratus.[13] There are cisterns all over the city, but this is the only fountain. Above the springs are two temples, one to Demeter and the Maid, while in that of Triptolemus[14] is a statue of him. . . .

As you go to the portico which they call Painted, because of its pictures, there is a bronze statue of Hermes of the Market-place, and near it a gate. On it is a trophy erected by the Athenians, who in a cavalry action overcame Pleistarchus, to whose command his brother Cassander had entrusted his cavalry and mercenaries. . . .

Here are placed bronze statues, one, in front of the Portico, of Solon,[15] who composed the laws for the Athenians, and, a little farther away, one of Seleucus. . . .[16]

In the Athenian market-place among the objects not generally known is an altar to Mercy, of all divinities the most useful in the life of mortals and in the vicissitudes of fortune, but honored by the Athenians alone among the Greeks. And they are conspicuous not only for their humanity but also for their devotion to religion. They have an altar to Shamefastness, one to Rumor and one to Effort. It is quite obvious that those who excel in piety are correspondingly rewarded by good fortune. In the gym-

---

13. Tyrant of Athens of the 6th century B.C.E., he ruled for 36 years during which there was peace and an ambitious building program. He constructed several cult sites dedicated to Apollo, the fountain house mentioned by Pausanius, and enhanced the Agora, the civic center of Athens.

14. A prince of Eleusis, he was given the arts of agriculture by Demeter. He is also a lawgiver who became a judge in the Underworld.

15. Athenian politician and poet who lived in the 6th century B.C.E. His legislation was aimed at expanding the rights of citizens and the peasantry and strengthening the power of the assembly and judicial system at the expense of the aristocracy.

16. Founder of the Seleucid dynasty, he was born in ca. 358 B.C.E. and served as a general in the army of Alexander the Great. After Alexander's death, he campaigned all over the Near East until his empire stretched from Anatolia to Syria, Babylonia, Iran and Central Asia. His dream of reuniting Alexander's kingdom was cut short when he was assassinated in 281 B.C.E.

nasium not far from the Market-place, called Ptolemy's from the founder, are stone Hermae[17] well worth seeing and a likeness in bronze of Ptolemy. Here also is Juba the Lybian and Chrysippus of Soli.[18]

Hard by the gymnasium is a sanctuary of Theseus,[19] where are pictures of Athenians fighting Amazons. This war they have also represented on the shield of their Athena and upon the pedestal of the Olympian Zeus. In the sanctuary of Theseus is also a painting of the battle between the Centaurs and the Lapithae....[20]

There is also a gymnasium named after Hadrian; of this too the pillars are a hundred in number from the Lybian quarries....

There is but one entry to the Acropolis.[21] It affords no other, being precipitous throughout and having a strong wall. The gateway has a roof of white marble, and down to the present day it is unrivalled for the beauty and size of its stones....

Hard by is a sanctuary of the goddesses which the Athenians call the August, but Hesiod[22] in the *Theogony* calls them Erinyes.[23] It was Aeschylus who first represented them with snakes in their hair. But on the images neither of these nor of any of the under-world deities is there anything

---

17. Marble or bronze four-cornered pillars topped by a bust. As representations of the god Hermes, they were placed at crossroads, in doorways as protectors of the house, and at the gates of sanctuaries.

18. Ca. 280–207 B.C.E. He became head of the Stoa, center of the philosophical movement of Stoicism, in 232 and wrote extensively on Stoicism, formulating its standard positions and defending it.

19. The legendary king of Athens who embodied the ideals of the Greeks in his heroism. In one of his exploits he initiated the campaign against the Amazons and eventually defeated them.

20. Pirithous, king of the Lapiths, was at war with the Centaurs, creatures who were half man and half horse. These wild forest dwellers lived on the edges of civilization and threatened society with their savagery, lust, and drunkenness. Theseus joined the battle against the Centaurs.

21. A fortress on a hill of rock, enclosed with a wall, which contained the main sanctuary dedicated to Athena, the patron goddess of Athens, and dozens of smaller temples. It was destroyed in 480 B.C.E. by the Persians and rebuilt about fifty years later by Phidias, chief engineer under Pericles. At the time of Pausanius it had four major buildings, including the Parthenon, the marble temple dedicated to the virgin Athena (constructed between 447 and 432 B.C.E.) which still stands.

22. An epic poet who lived ca. 700 B.C.E. The *Theogony* describes the birth and genealogy of the gods in which the Titans, the former gods, are succeeded by the Olympians.

23. The Erinyes were female powers of the Underworld who controlled the souls of the dead, arranged retribution for wrongs, and carried out curses. Aeschylus, the tragedian (born ca. 525 B.C.E.) dramatized them as dressed in black with snakes in their hair.

terrible. There are images of Pluto, Hermes, and Earth, by which sacrifice those who have received an acquittal on the Hill of Ares; sacrifices are also offered on other occasions by both citizens and aliens. . . .

The Athenians have other law courts as well, which are not so famous. We have the Parabystum (*Thrust aside*) and the Triangle; the former is in an obscure part of the city, and in it the most trivial cases are tried; the latter is named from its shape. The names of Green Court and Red Court, due to their colors, have lasted down to the present day. The largest court, to which the greatest number come, is called Heliaea. One of the other courts that deal with bloodshed is called "At Palladium," into which are brought cases of involuntary homicide. . . .

Outside the city, too, in the parishes and on the roads, the Athenians have sanctuaries of the gods, and graves of heroes and of men. The nearest is the Academy,[24] once the property of a private individual, but in my time a gymnasium. As you go down to it you come to a precinct of Artemis,[25] and wooden images of Ariste (*Best*) and Calliste (*Fairest*). In my opinion, which is supported by the poems of Pamphos,[26] these are the surnames of Artemis. . . .

In the Academy is an altar to Prometheus,[27] and from it they run to the city carrying burning torches. The contest is while running to keep the torch still alight; if the torch of the first runner goes out, he has no longer any claim to victory, but the second runner has. If his torch also goes out, no one is left to be winner. There is an altar to the Muses,[28] and another to Hermes, and one within to Athena, and they have built one to Heracles.[29]

---

24. The public gymnasium of Athens named after the hero Academus. The Academy gave its name to the school founded there by Plato in the 4th century B.C.E.

25. Daughter of Zeus and Leto, Artemis was goddess of the hunt and war and of transitional aspects of the life cycle, particularly for women. There were numerous cults dedicated to her throughout Greece. Artemis was often identified with other goddesses whose name was added to hers as an epithet.

26. A Hellenistic poet whose works have for the most part not survived.

27. Prometheus is the figure associated with the theft of fire from the gods and its bestowal on man, and was worshipped by potters and in the Academy. A torch race was held in his honor in Athens.

28. The nine goddesses of Olympus who controlled artistic expression and were worshipped by poets, artists, dancers, musicians, actors, etc.

29. The greatest Greek hero, said to have performed the twelve superhuman labors. Throughout his adventures, Heracles was aided by Athena who transported him to Olympus after his death. His cult was associated with military training and gymnasia, and Pisistratus claimed special divine protection by Heracles.

4.2 UNDER PTOLEMIES AND SELEUCIDS

4.2.1 Josephus, *Antiquities* XI, 321–47: Alexander and the Jews[30]

Josephus transmits what must have been an old tradition regarding early contacts between the Jews and Alexander the Great. This legendary account portrays the rivalry of the Jews and the Samaritans while claiming that Alexander paid homage to the Jewish high priest to whose intercession he credited his military victories.

꽃

(321) But Sanballat thought he had now gotten a proper opportunity to make his attempt, so he abandoned Darius and, taking with him eight thousand of his own subjects, he came to Alexander. Finding him beginning the siege of Tyre, he said to him that he was delivering up to him the places under his dominion, and that he gladly accepted him as his lord instead of Darius. (322) So when Alexander had received him kindly, Sanballat thereupon took courage and spoke to him about that subject. He told him that he had a son-in-law, Manasseh, who was brother to the high priest Jaddua; and that there were many others of his own nation now with him who were desirous to have a temple in the places subject to him. (323) It would be to the king's advantage, he said, to have the strength of the Jews divided into two parts lest, if the nation were of one mind and united, upon any attempt of revolution, it would prove troublesome for the kings, as it had formerly proven to the kings of Assyria. (324) When Alexander gave Sanballat permission to do so, he used the utmost diligence and built the temple, made Manasseh the high priest, and deemed it a great reward that his daughter's children should have that office.

(325) But when the seven months of the siege of Tyre were over, and after two months of the siege of Gaza, Sanballat died. Now Alexander, when he had taken Gaza, made haste to go up to Jerusalem. (326) Jaddua the high priest, when he heard that, was in agony and terror, not knowing how he could meet the Macedonians since the king was displeased at his former disobedience. He therefore ordained that the people should make supplications and should join with him in offering sacrifices to God, whom he besought to protect that nation and to deliver them from the

---

30. Trans. W. Whiston, *The Works of Josephus* (Peabody, MA: Hendrickson, 1987), revised by L. H. Schiffman in consultation with H. St. J. Thackeray, Ralph Marcus, Allen Wikgren, and L. H. Feldman, trans., *Josephus: in Nine Volumes* (Loeb Classical Library; Cambridge: Harvard University Press, 1976–79).

perils that were coming upon them. (327) Then God warned him in a dream, which came upon him after he had offered sacrifice, telling him that he should take courage, adorn the city, and open the gates; that the people should appear in white garments, but that he and the priests should meet the king in the garments proper to their order, without the dread of any ill consequences, which the providence of God would prevent. (328) Thereupon, he rose from his sleep greatly rejoicing and declared to all the revelation he had received from God, according to which he acted entirely and so waited for the coming of the king.

(329) When he understood that Alexander was not far from the city, he went out in procession, with the priests and the multitude of the citizens. The procession was venerable, and the manner of it different from that of other nations. It reached a place called Sapha;[31] which name, translated into Greek, signifies a "lookout" for you have a view from there both of Jerusalem and of the temple. (330) The Phoenicians and Chaldeans who followed him thought that the king in his anger would naturally permit them to plunder the city and torment the high priest to death, but the very reverse of it happened. (331) For Alexander, when he saw the multitude at a distance, in white garments, while the priests stood clothed with fine linen and the high priest in purple and scarlet clothing, with his mitre on his head with the golden plate on which the name of God was engraved, he approached by himself and bowed down before the name [of God], and first saluted the high priest. (332) The Jews also all together, with one voice, saluted Alexander, and surrounded him, whereupon the kings of Syria and the others were surprised at what Alexander had done and supposed him disordered in his mind. (333) However, Parmenio[32] alone went up to him and asked him how it came to pass that when all others bowed before him, he should bow before the high priest of the Jews? He replied to him, "I did not bow before him, but before that God who has honored him with the high priesthood; (334) for I saw this very person in a dream, in this very apparel[33] when I was at Dios, in Macedonia. When I was considering how I might obtain dominion over Asia, he exhorted me to make no delay but boldly to pass over the sea for he would lead my army and would give me the dominion over the Persians. (335) Since then, having seen no other in that clothing, and now seeing this person in it, and remembering that vision and the exhortation

---

31. Mount Scopus on the north side of Jerusalem where the Hebrew University is located today.

32. Macedonian general, second in command to Alexander.

33. A reference to the priestly garments.

which I had in my dream, I believe that I bring this army under divine guidance and shall therewith conquer Darius and destroy the power of the Persians, and that all things will succeed according to what is in my own mind." (336) And when he had said this to Parmenio, and had given the high priest his right hand, the priests ran alongside him and he came into the city. When he went up into the temple, he offered sacrifice to God, according to the high priest's direction, and magnificently treated both the high priest and the priests.

(337) When the book of Daniel was shown him, wherein Daniel declared that one of the Greeks should destroy the empire of the Persians,[34] he supposed that he himself was the person intended. As he was then glad, he dismissed the multitude for the present, but the next day he called them to him and bade them ask what favors they wished of him, (338) whereupon the high priest requested that they might observe the laws of their forefathers and might pay no tribute on the seventh year.[35] He granted all they requested. And when they entreated him that he should permit the Jews in Babylon and Media to enjoy their own laws also, he willingly promised to do what they requested. (339) When he said to the multitude that if any of them would enlist themselves in his army on condition that they would continue to adhere to the laws of their forefathers and live according to them, he was willing to take them with him, many were ready to accompany him in his wars.

(340) So when Alexander had thus settled matters at Jerusalem, he led his army against the neighboring cities. But all the inhabitants to whom he came received him with great kindness. Then the Samaritans, who had then had Shechem for their metropolis (a city situated at Mount Gerizim and inhabited by apostates of the Jewish nation), seeing that Alexander had so greatly honored the Jews, determined to profess themselves Jews. (341) For such is the disposition of the Samaritans, as we have already elsewhere declared,[36] that when the Jews are in adversity they deny their kinship to them, thus confessing the truth. But when they perceive that some good fortune has befallen them, they immediately pretend to have a connection with them, saying that they belong to them and derive their genealogy from the posterity of Joseph, Ephraim, and Manasseh. (342) Accordingly, they made their address to the king with splendor, and showed great alacrity in meeting him a short distance from Jerusalem. When Alexander had commended them, the Shechemites

---

34. Cf. Dan. 8:20–21.
35. The Sabbatical year in which tilling the land is forbidden.
36. *Ant.* IX, 291.

approached him, taking with them the troops that Sanballat had sent him, and they requested that he come to their city and do honor to their temple also. (343) He promised them that when he returned he would come to them, but when they petitioned that he would remit the tribute of the [seventh] year to them because they did not now sow thereon, he asked who they were that they made such a petition. (344) When they said that they were Hebrews, but had the name of Sidonians living at Shechem, he asked them again whether they were Jews. When they said that they were not Jews, "It was to the Jews," said he, "that I granted that privilege; however, when I return and am thoroughly informed by you of this matter, I will do what I shall think proper." And in this manner he took leave of the Shechemites. (345) But he ordered that the troops of Sanballat should follow him into Egypt because there he designed to give them lands, which he did a little after in Thebais, when he ordered them to guard that country.

(346) When Alexander died, the government was divided among his successors (the Diadochi). The temple upon Mount Gerizim remained; and if anyone were accused by the people of Jerusalem of having eaten unclean food, or of having broken the Sabbath, or of any other such crime, (347) he fled to the Shechemites and said that he was accused unjustly. About this time it was that Jaddua the high priest died, and Onias his son succeeded to the high priesthood. This was the state of the affairs of the people of Jerusalem at this time.

4.2.2 Babylonian Talmud Yoma 69a: The Meeting of Alexander and the High Priest[37]

The Talmudic version of the meeting of the Jews and Alexander is preserved in a baraita which correctly identifies the place of the meeting as Antipatris. This version also points to the Jewish-Samaritan conflict and to Alexander's recognition of the Jews and rejection of the Samaritans.

❧

It is taught in a *baraita*:[38] "On the twenty-fifth of Tevet,[39] which is the 'day of Mount Gerizim,'[40] the mourning eulogy is not permitted." On this day, the Samaritans petitioned Alexander the Great of Macedon for

---

37. Trans. S. Berrin.

38. A Rabbinic tradition contemporary with those compiled in the Mishnah (edited ca. 200 C.E.), but not included in that work.

39. January.

40. The site of the Samaritan temple.

permission to destroy the House of our God (the Jerusalem Temple), and he granted it to them. [Some people] came and informed Simon the Just.[41] What did he do? He dressed himself in priestly garments and wrapped himself in priestly garments and some of the nobles of Israel [went] with him, bearing torches of light in their hands. All night this group was walking from one direction and the other (Alexander's) group was walking from the other direction.

At dawn [Alexander] said to them, "Who are those [people approaching]?"

They told him, "Jews, who rebelled against you."

When he arrived at Antipatris, the sun was shining, and the groups met each other. When [Alexander] saw Simon the Just he descended from his chariot and bowed down before him.

[The Samaritans] said to him, "A great king like yourself bows down to this Jew?!"

He said to them, "The image of this man appears before me always in my command post." He said to [the Jews], "Why did you come?"

They said, "Is it possible that non-Jews should mislead you to destroy the House in which people pray for you and for your kingdom not to be destroyed?"

He said to them, "Who are they?"

They said to him, "These Samaritans who are standing before you."

He said to them, "Here, they are given into your hands."

At once, they pierced their heels, tied them to their horses' tails and dragged them over thorns and thistles until they arrived at Mount Gerizim. When they arrived at Mount Gerizim, they ploughed it and planted it with vetch as [the Samaritans] had planned to do to the House of God. And that day they made into a festival.

4.2.3 Josephus, *Antiquities* XII, 1–9: Alexander's Successors

In 301 B.C.E., after the death of Alexander and the division of his empire, Ptolemy I Soter, who had ruled over Egypt since 323 B.C.E., conquered Palestine. According to Josephus, this was the origin of the substantial community of Hellenized Jews in Egypt.

ॐ

(1) Now when Alexander, king of Macedon, had put an end to the dominion of the Persians and had settled the affairs of Judea in the manner

---

41. High priest, ca. 200 B.C.E. Josephus' identification of the high priest must be accepted as accurate.

described above, he died.[42] (2) His government fell among many: Antigonus obtained Asia, Seleucus Babylon, and of the other nations which were there, Lysimachus governed the Hellespont, and Cassander possessed Macedonia; and Ptolemy, the son of Lagus, seized Egypt. (3) While these princes ambitiously strove one against the other, every one for his own principality, it came to pass that there were continual and prolonged wars. The cities were the sufferers and lost a great many of their inhabitants in these times of distress, so that all Syria because of Ptolemy, the son of Lagus, underwent the reverse of his name, for he was called Soter (Savior). (4) He also seized Jerusalem and for that purpose made use of deceit and treachery. For he came into the city on a Sabbath day, as if he would offer a sacrifice, and, without any trouble, gained the city; for the Jews did not oppose him as they did not suspect him to be their enemy. He gained it thus because they were free from suspicion of him, and because on that day they were at rest and idle. When he had gained it, he reigned over it in a cruel manner. (5) Indeed, Agatharchides of Cnidus,[43] who wrote the acts of Alexander's successors, reproaches us with superstition, as if because of it, we had lost our liberty, when he says thus: (6) "There is a nation called the nation of the Jews who inhabit a city strong and great, named Jerusalem. These men let it come into the hands of Ptolemy by their unwillingness to take arms; they thereby submitted to be under a hard master because of their untimely superstition." (7) This is what Agatharchides relates of our nation.

But when Ptolemy had taken a great many captives, both from the mountainous parts of Judea and from the places around Jerusalem and Samaria, and the places near Mount Gerizim, he led them all into Egypt and settled them there. (8) Since he knew that the people of Jerusalem were most faithful in the keeping of oaths and covenants, as shown by the answer they gave to Alexander when he sent an embassy to them after he had beaten Darius in battle, he distributed many of them into garrisons. At Alexandria he gave them equal privileges as citizens with the Macedonians themselves, and he required them to take oaths that they would keep faith with the posterity of those who committed these places to their care. (9) Indeed, there were not a few other Jews who, of their own accord, came to Egypt, attracted by the goodness of the soil, and by the liberality of Ptolemy.

---

42. In Babylon in June, 323 B.C.E.

43. Lived ca. 215 to after 145 B.C.E., Greek historian and geographer whose works are preserved only in fragmentary form. One of his books is *Asian Affairs* which includes the period of the Diadochi, the successors of Alexander the Great.

4.2.4 Josephus, *Antiquities* XII, 129–46:
Antiochus III Conquers Jerusalem

By 201 B.C.E. the Seleucid ruler Antiochus III the Great conquered the Land of Israel. He immediately restored to Jews the rights of living under their laws and practicing their religion as well as providing for the enforcement of their laws regarding entry to the temple of forbidden animals and the maintenance of ritual purity.

೩೪

(129) In the reign of Antiochus the Great[44] who ruled over all Asia, the Jews as well as the inhabitants of Celesyria, suffered greatly, and their land was greatly devastated. (130) For while he was at war with Ptolemy Philopater[45] and with his son, who was called Epiphanes,[46] it turned out that these nations suffered equally, both when he was defeated and when he was victorious. They were very much like a ship in a storm which is tossed by the waves on both sides, for they found themselves in the middle between Antiochus's successes and the change to adversity. (131) But at length, when Antiochus had beaten Ptolemy, he seized Judea. When Philopater was dead,[47] his son sent out a great army under Scopas, the general of his forces, against the inhabitants of Celesyria. He took many of their cities, and in particular our nation, (132) which, when he attacked it, went over to him. Yet was it not long afterward that Antiochus overcame Scopas, in a battle fought at the sources of the Jordan (River), and destroyed a great part of his army. (133) But afterward, when Antiochus subdued those cities of Celesyria which Scopas had gotten into his possession, including Samaria, the Jews, of their own accord, went over to him and received him into the city [Jerusalem], and gave plentiful provision to all his army and to his elephants, and readily assisted him when he besieged the garrison which was in the citadel of Jerusalem. (134) For this reason, Antiochus thought it but just to reward the Jews' diligence and zeal in his service. So he wrote to the generals of his armies and to his friends, gave testimony to the good behavior of the Jews towards him, and informed them what rewards he had resolved to bestow on them for their behavior.

(135) I will set down presently the epistles themselves which he wrote to the generals concerning them, but will first produce the testimony of

---

44. 223–187 B.C.E.
45. Ptolemy IV Philopater, 221–203 B.C.E.
46. Ptolemy V Epiphanes, 203–181 B.C.E.
47. 203 B.C.E.

Polybius of Megalopolis[48] for thus does he speak, in the sixteenth book of his history: "Now Scopas, the general of Ptolemy's army, went in haste to the upper parts of the country,[49] and in the wintertime overthrew the nation of the Jews." (136) In the same book, he also says that "when Scopas was defeated by Antiochus, Antiochus received Batanea, Samaria, Abila, and Gadara.[50] A short time afterwards, there came over to him those Jews who lived near the temple called Jerusalem,[51] concerning which, although I have more to say, particularly concerning the presence of God connected with that temple, yet I put off that account until another opportunity." (137) This it is which Polybius relates. But we will return to the main subject of the narrative after we have first produced the epistles of king Antiochus.

King Antiochus to Ptolemy,[52] Sends Greeting.

(138) "Since the Jews, upon our first entrance into their country demonstrated their friendship towards us, . . . (140) . . . we have determined, on account of their piety towards God, to bestow on them a pension for their sacrifices of animals that are fit for sacrifice, for wine, oil, and frankincense, the value of twenty thousand pieces of silver, and sacred *artabae*[53] of fine flour, with one thousand four hundred and sixty *medimni*[54] of wheat and three hundred and seventy-five *medimni* of salt. (141) These payments I order to be fully paid to them, as I have sent orders to you. I also order the work on the temple and the porticoes finished and anything else that ought to be rebuilt. For the materials of wood, let them be brought out of Judea itself and out of the other countries and out of Lebanon tax free, and the same shall be done regarding those other materials which will be necessary in order to render the temple more glorious. (142) Let all of that nation live according to the laws of their own country. And let the senate, the priests, the scribes of the temple, and the sacred singers be relieved from the poll tax, the crown tax, and other taxes also. (143) So that the city may recover its inhabitants sooner, I grant an exemption from taxes for three years to its present inhabitants and to who-

---

48. Greek historian, ca. 200–ca. 118 B.C.E., who chronicled the rise of the Roman Empire and its effects on the various nations it enveloped.

49. Northern Palestine.

50. Areas in northern Transjordan.

51. Because of the prominence of the Temple in the city, Polybius refers to the Temple as if it were named Jerusalem.

52. Probably Ptolemy, son of Thraseas, governor of Coele-Syria and Phoenicia under Antiochus III.

53. The *artaba* was an Egyptian measure equal to about 40 litres.

54. The *medimnus* was equal to about 50 liters.

ever shall come to it until the month of Hyperberetus.[55] (144) We also exempt them for the future from a third part of their taxes so that the losses they have sustained may be repaired. As for all those citizens who have been carried away and have become slaves, we grant them and their children their freedom and order that their property be restored to them."

(145) And these were the contents of this epistle. He also published a decree through all his kingdom in honor of the temple which contained what follows: "It shall be unlawful for any foreigner to come within the enclosure of the temple which is forbidden also to the Jews, except to those who, according to the laws of the country, have purified themselves.[56] (146) Nor let any flesh of horses, mules, or asses, be brought into the city, whether they be wild or tame, nor that of leopards, foxes, or hares; and, in general, that of any animal which is forbidden for the Jews to eat. Nor let their skins be brought into it; nor let any such animal be bred in this city. Let them only be permitted to use the sacrificial animals known to their forefathers with which they have been obligated to make acceptable atonements to God. And the person who transgresses any of these orders shall pay the priests three thousand drachmae of silver."

4.2.5 Zenon Papyri: Jews in Hellenistic Egypt[57]

The Zenon Papyri are the archives of a third century B.C.E. agent of the finance minister of Ptolemaic Egypt. He visited the Land of Israel on an economic mission and accompanied his master on trips in Egypt. His archives are an important source for Jewish social history.

§℧

Papyrus 1[58]

In the 27th year of the reign of Ptolemy, son of Ptolemy,[59] and of his son Ptolemy, the priest of Alexander and of the gods Adelphoi and the kanephoros[60] of Arsinoe Philadelphos being those in office in Alexandria, in the month Xandikos,[61] at Birta of the Ammanitis.[62] Nikanor son of

---

55. Corresponding to Hebrew Tishre, a month falling in September and October.

56. The same regulation was found on an inscription which was part of the wall of the Temple courtyard.

57. Trans. from *Corpus Papyrum Judaicorum*, ed. V. A. Tcherikover with A. Fuks (Cambridge: For Magnes Press, Hebrew University by Harvard University Press, 1957), vol. 1.

58. Tcherikover and Fuks, p. 120.

59. The 27th year of Ptolemy Philadelphus was 256 B.C.E.

60. A female cultic official.

61. April-May.

62. In Transjordan.

Xenokles, Knidian, in the service of Toubias, sold to Zenon son of Agreophon, Kaunian, in the service of Apollonios the dioiketes,[63] a Sidonian girl named Sphragis, about seven years of age, for fifty drachmai. Guarantor . . . son of Ananias, Persian, of the troop of Toubias, kleruch.[64] Witnesses: . . . judge; [[. . . son of Agathon, Persian]][65] (cancelled) Polemon son of Straton, Macedonian, of the cavalrymen of Toubias, kleruch; Timopolis son of Botes, Milesian, Herakleitos son of Philippos, Athenian, Zenon son of Timarchos, Kolophonian, Demostratos, son of Dionysios, Aspendian, all four in the service of Apollonios the dioiketes.

[Endorsed] Deed of sale of a girl.

Papyrus 4[66]

Toubias to Apollonios greeting. If you and all your affairs are flourishing, and everything else is as you wish it, many thanks to the gods! I too have been well, and have thought of you at all times, as was right.

I have sent to you Aineias bringing a eunuch and four boys, houseslaves and of good stock, two of whom are uncircumcised.[67] I append descriptions of the boys for your information. Goodbye. Year 29, Xandikos 10.[68]

Haimos. About 10
Dark skin
Curly hair
Black eyes
Rather big jaws
with moles on the right jaw
Uncircumcised.
Atikos. About 8
Light skin
Curly hair
Nose somewhat flat
Black eyes, scar
below the
right eye
Uncircumcised.
Audomos. About 10

---

63. Chief financial officer in Ptolemaic Egypt.

64. The Jewish head of the military cleruchy in Transjordan.

65. The words in double square brackets were marked for erasure ("cancelled") by the scribe.

66. Tcherikover and Fuks, pp. 126–7.

67. Circumcision does not mean that they were Jews, as other Near Eastern peoples practiced circumcision as well. It was just a physical description of the slave boys.

68. May 12, 257 B.C.E.

Black eyes
Curly hair. Nose flat
Protruding lips
Scar near the right
eyebrow
Circumcised.
Okaimos. About 7
Round face. Nose
flat.
Gray eyes
Fiery complexion
Long straight hair
Scar on forehead
above the right
eyebrow
Circumcised.

(Addressed) To Apollonios

(Docketed) Toubias, about a eunuch and 4 boys he has sent. Year 29, Artemision 16,[69] at Alexandria.

Papyrus 5[70]

Toubias to Apollonios greeting. On the tenth of Xandikos I sent Aineias our servant, bringing the gifts for the king which you wrote and asked me to send in the month of Xandikos: two horses, six dogs, one wild mule out of an ass,[71] two white Arab donkeys, two wild mules' foals, one wild ass's foal. They are all tame. I have also sent you the letter which I have written to the king about the gifts, together with a copy for your information.

Goodbye. Year 29, Xandikos 10.

To King Ptolemy from Toubias, greeting. I have sent you two horses, six dogs, one wild mule out of an ass, two white Arab donkeys, two wild mules' foals and one wild ass's foal.

Farewell.

(Addressed) To Apollonios

---

69. June 17, 257 B.C.E. The letter took 36 days to travel from Transjordan to Alexandria.

70. Tcherikover and Fuks, pp. 128–9.

71. A mule is normally the offspring of a male donkey and a mare. This rare animal was born to a horse and a female donkey.

(Docketed)[72] Toubias, about his consignment to the king, and the copy of his letter to the king. Year 29, 16 Artemision, at Alexandria.

Papyrus 6[73]

[Alexan]dros to Oryas, greeting. I have received your letter, to which you added a copy of the letter written by Zenon to Jeddous[74] saying that unless he gave the money to Straton, Zenon's man, we were to hand over his pledge to him (Straton). I happened to be unwell as a result of taking some medicine, so I sent a lad, a servant of mine, with Straton, and wrote a letter to Jeddous. When they returned they said that he had taken no notice of my letter, but had attacked them and thrown them out of the village. So I am writing to you (for your information).

Goodbye. Year 27, Peritios intercalary 20.[75]

(Addressed) To Oryas.

4.2.6 Vienna Papyrus:
Jewish Military Settlers in Ptolemaic Palestine[76]

This papyrus is an important source for our understanding of the Land of Israel in Ptolemaic times. Especially noteworthy are the technical administrative terms. The document contains two royal edicts pertaining to registration of cattle and slaves. It is dated to the twenty-fifth year of an Egyptian king, generally accepted to be Ptolemy II Philadelphus, whose twenty-fifth year was 261 B.C.E. Note especially the explicit mention of soldiers and colonists in Syria and Palestine who had married native women.

🜲

. . . and those tax collectors,[77] having leased villages, and the heads of the villages are to register at the same time the cattle in the villages, and their fathers' names and their home district and by whom it is pastured, and likewise also as much (cattle) as they know is unregistered and (in the village), until Dustron[78] of the twenty-fifth year as per the written com-

---

72. That is, filed in the archives.

73. Tcherikover and Fuks, p. 130.

74. No doubt a Jew, most probably a landowner in Palestine.

75. April 5, 258 B.C.E.

76. Trans. S. Berrin from the Greek text in *Sammelbuch griechischer Urkunden aus Agypten*, ed. F. Preisigke, F. Bilabel, E. Kiessling (=SB-8008), (Heidelberg and Wiesbaden: vol. 5), pp. 156–8. The translation of this difficult text must be considered tentative.

77. Probably tax farmers.

78. Dystrus, the Macedonian name for the month of March.

mand of the king. And they will make registrations annually at the same times, and they will pay dues, just as it has been made clear in the letter from the king in the appropriate months according to the decree.

Those who do not comply with some aspect of the public notices, such as those who register their own cattle by another name, will be liable to the penalties thereof. Whoever is willing to inform will receive of the penalties being exacted according to the decree, just as it has been declared in the decree, (he will receive) one-third of the property which is confiscated to the royal treasury.

By order of the king: If some of those in Syria and Phoenicia have bought a free native person, or have kidnapped or detained (him) or acquired one by any another means . . . person . . . someone . . . before the administrator who is appointed in each district, within twenty days from the time that the order has been displayed in public. If someone does not register or does not pay taxes for a slave, the slave will be confiscated and payment of 6000 drachmae per slave will be exacted for the royal treasury, and the king will judge him. If they prove that they have bought, as for actual slaves, any of the persons registered and taken . . . [they] will be returned to them.

But those who had been sold in the royal auctions, if somebody alleges them to be free, the purchasers are (nevertheless) entitled to their possessions. Those of the soldiers and of the other colonists in Syria and Phoenicia who cohabit with native women they have taken up with, shall not register (these). Hereafter, it will not be lawful to buy or mortgage free native people, or under any pretense except by approaching those given up in a bankruptcy sale by the economic manager of Syria and Phoenicia, and submitting an application, as per established practice, according to the manner recorded in the law concerning lease. Otherwise, they will be liable to the same penalties, and likewise also those selling and mortgaging. But to the informers, 300 drachmae ought to be given from the money collected for each person.

4.3 THE JERUSALEM TEMPLE AND PRIESTHOOD

4.3.1 Josephus, *Against Apion* I, 195–99: Hecateus of Abdera on Jerusalem

Hecateus of Abdera, ca. 360–290 B.C.E., was a historian and ethnographer. Josephus quotes this description of the city of Jerusalem and its Temple from him. Some scholars, however, believe that this description was written by another author who wrote under the name of Hecateus in the first half of the second century B.C.E. *The selection contrasts the religion of Israel to that of* *paganism in singling out the lack of images and the prohibition of alcohol to* *the priests of the Jewish Temple.*

⚞

(195) The same person[79] takes notice in his history of how large the country is which we inhabit as well as of its excellent character and says that "the land which the Jews inhabit contains three million *arourae*[80] and is generally of a most excellent and most fertile soil. Such is the extent of Judea." (196) The same man describes our city Jerusalem itself also as of a most excellent structure and very large, and inhabited from most ancient times. He also discourses about the multitude of people in it and of the construction of our temple in the following manner: (197) "There are many strong places and villages in the country of Judea, but there is one strong city, about fifty furlongs in circumference, which is inhabited by a hundred and twenty thousand people or thereabouts; they call it Jerusalem. (198) There is in the middle of the city a wall of stone, the length of which is five hundred feet and the breadth a hundred cubits,[81] approached by a pair of gates. Inside there is a square altar, not made of hewn stone,[82] but composed of stones gathered together, each side of which is twenty cubits long, and its height is ten cubits. Beside it is a large edifice within which is an altar and a lampstand, both of gold, weighing two talents. (199) Upon these there is a light that is never extinguished, neither by night nor by day. There is no image, nor statue, nor votive offering therein; nothing at all is planted there, neither a grove nor anything of that sort. The priests abide therein both nights and days, performing certain purification rites, and drinking not the least drop of wine while they are in the temple."[83]

4.3.2 Ben Sira 50: The Glory of the High Priest[84]

Writing in 180 B.C.E., Simeon ben Sira, the Jerusalemite sage, described *the glory of the high priest in his service to his people and to God. Praises like* *this would be echoed later in the mishnaic description of the high priest as he*

---

79. Hecateus of Abdera.

80. An Egyptian measure of land, approximately half an acre.

81. A cubit is approximately 18 inches.

82. Cf. Ex. 20:22–23.

83. Cf. Lev. 10:9 and Ezek. 44:21 which state that the priests are forbidden to drink wine.

84. All texts from the Apocrypha taken from the *Revised Standard Version Apocrypha* (New York: National Council of Churches, 1957).

exited the Holy of Holies on the Day of Atonement, repeated in the liturgy for that day composed in medieval times.

꩜

1 The leader of his brethren
and the pride of his people
was Simon the high priest, son of Onias, [85]
who in his life repaired the house,
and in his time fortified the temple.
2 He laid the foundations for the high double walls,
the high retaining walls for the temple enclosure.
3 In his days a cistern for water was quarried out,
a reservoir like the sea in circumference.
4 He considered how to save his people from ruin,
and fortified the city to withstand a siege.
5 How glorious he was when the people gathered round him
as he came out of the inner sanctuary!
6 Like the morning star among the clouds,
like the moon when it is full;
7 like the sun shining upon the temple of the Most High,
and like the rainbow gleaming in glorious clouds;
8 like roses in the days of the first fruits,
like lilies by a spring of water.
like a green shoot on Lebanon on a summer day
9 like fire and incense in the censer,
like a vessel of hammered gold
adorned with all kinds of precious stones;
10 like an olive tree putting forth its fruit,
and like a cypress towering in the clouds.
11 When he put on his glorious robe
and clothed himself with superb perfection
and went up to the holy altar,
he made the court of the sanctuary glorious.
12 And when he received the portions
from the hands of the priests,
as he stood by the hearth of the altar
with a garland of brethren around him,
he was like a young cedar on Lebanon;
and they surrounded him like the trunks of palm trees,
13 all the sons of Aaron in their splendor
with the Lord's offering in their hands,

---

85. Simon II, son of Onias, was high priest in about 219–196 B.C.E.

before the whole congregation of Israel.
14 Finishing the service at the altars
and arranging the offering to the Most High, the Almighty,
15 he reached out his hand to the cup
and poured a libation of the blood of the grape;
he poured it out at the foot of the altar,
a pleasing odor to the Most High, the King of all.
16 Then the sons of Aaron shouted,
they sounded the trumpets of hammered work,
they made a great noise to be heard
for remembrance before the Most High.
17 Then all the people together made haste
and fell to the ground upon their faces
to worship their Lord,
the Almighty, God Most High.
18 And the singers praised him with their voices
in sweet and full-toned melody.
19 And the people besought the Lord Most High
in prayer before him who is merciful,
till the order of worship of the Lord was ended:
so they completed his service.
20 Then Simon came down, and lifted up his hands
over the whole congregation of the sons of Israel,
to pronounce the blessing of the Lord with his lips,[86]
and to glory in his name;
21 and they bowed down in worship a second time,
to receive the blessing from the Most High.

4.4 THE GEROUSIA

4.4.1 Josephus, *Antiquities* XII, 138–9: King Antiochus' Favorable Attitude to the Jews

The first mention of the Jewish Gerousia (literally, "Council of Elders"), here termed the "senate," occurs in this passage from Josephus speaking of the time of Antiochus the Great (223–187 B.C.E.).

᧞

(138) "King Antiochus to Ptolemy, sends greeting. Since the Jews, upon our first entrance into their country demonstrated their friendship towards us, and when we came to their city [Jerusalem], received us in a

---

86. The priestly blessing, Num. 6:24–25.

splendid manner and came to meet us with their senate, and gave abundance of provisions to our soldiers, and to the elephants and joined with us in ejecting the garrison of the Egyptians who were in the citadel, (139) we have thought it fit to reward them and to retrieve the condition of their city which has been greatly depopulated by such accidents as have befallen its inhabitants and to bring those who have been scattered abroad back to the city. . . ."

4.4.2 1 Maccabees 12: Letter to the Spartans

The intent of this letter was to renew an alliance with the Spartans. It mentions the "senate" (Gerousia) of the Jewish nation as distinct from the high priest, the priests, and the rest of the people.

🕮

5 This is a copy of the letter which Jonathan wrote to the Spartans: 6 "Jonathan the high priest, the senate of the nation, the priests, and the rest of the Jewish people to their brethren the Spartans, greeting. 7 Already in time past a letter was sent to Onias the high priest from Arius, who was king among you, stating that you are our brethren, as the appended copy shows. 8 Onias welcomed the envoy with honor and received the letter which contained a clear declaration of alliance and friendship. 9 Therefore, though we have no need of these things, since we have as encouragement the holy books which are in our hands, 10 we have undertaken to send to renew our brotherhood and friendship with you so that we may not become estranged from you, for considerable time has passed since you sent your letter to us. 11 We therefore remember you constantly on every occasion, both in our feasts and on other appropriate days, at the sacrifices which we offer and in our prayers, as it is right and proper to remember brethren. . . ."

4.4.3 1 Maccabees 14: Letter from the Spartans

After the death of Jonathan in 143 B.C.E., the rulers of Sparta felt it necessary to renew their alliance with the new high priest, Simon. Although the "elders" are mentioned as a separate entity, the letter clearly refers to Simon as the chief authority.

🕮

20 This is a copy of the letter which the Spartans sent: "The rulers and the city of the Spartans to Simon the high priest and to the elders and the priests and the rest of the Jewish people, our brethren, greeting. 21 The

envoys who were sent to our people have told us about your glory and honor, and we rejoiced at their coming. 22 And what they said we have recorded in our public decrees as follows: 'Numenius the son of Antiochus and Antipater the son of Jason, envoys of the Jews, have come to us to renew their friendship with us. 23 It has pleased our people to receive these men with honor and to put a copy of their words in the public archives, so that the people of the Spartans may have a record of them. And they have sent a copy of this to Simon the high priest.' "

4.5 HELLENISTIC TRENDS IN PALESTINIAN JUDAISM

4.5.1 Josephus, *Antiquities* XII, 156–85: The Ascendancy of the Tobiads

The story of the ascension of Joseph, the Tobiad, as a tax farmer in the Ptolemaic period, illustrates the rise of a new Hellenistic Jewish elite which gained power through Hellenization and which, in turn, fostered further Hellenization of the society. It is probable that this romantic account was taken over by Josephus from an earlier source.

🕊

This happened when Onias was high priest.[87] (157) After Eleazar's death,[88] his uncle Manasseh took over the high priesthood, and after he died, Onias received that office. He was the son of Simon, who was called the Just. (158) This Simon was the brother of Eleazar, as I said before.[89] This Onias was small-minded and a great lover of money, and for that reason, he did not pay that tax of twenty talents of silver which his forefathers paid to these kings (the Ptolemies) out of their own estates, and this provoked King Ptolemy Euergetes,[90] the father of Philopater,[91] to anger. (159) The king sent an ambassador to Jerusalem and complained that Onias did not pay his taxes and threatened that if he did not receive them, he would seize their land and send soldiers to live upon it. When the Jews heard this message of the king, they were dismayed, but so sordidly covetous was Onias, that nothing of this nature made him ashamed.

---

87. Onias II, second half of the third century B.C.E.

88. Eleazar was a brother of Simon the Just who succeeded him because Onias II was too young to assume the priesthood.

89. *Ant.* XII, 44.

90. Ptolemy III Euergetes, 246–221 B.C.E.

91. An alternative reading omits "Euergetes, the father of Philopater" thus making the text refer to Ptolemy V Epiphanes, 203–181 B.C.E.

(160) Now there was a certain Joseph, young in age but of great reputation among the people of Jerusalem for dignity, prudence, and justice. His father's name was Tobias, and his mother was the sister of Onias the high priest. She informed him of the coming of the ambassador for he was then away at a village named Phicol, where he was born.[92]

(161) Then he came to the city (Jerusalem) and reproved Onias for not taking care of the safety of his countrymen but bringing the nation into danger by not paying this money. He told him that it was for their safety that he had received authority over them and had been made high priest. (162) But in case he was so great a lover of money as to endure to see his country in danger on that account and his countrymen suffer the greatest damages, he advised him to go to the king and petition him to remit either the whole or a part of the sum demanded. (163) Onias's answer was this: that he did not care for his authority, and that he was ready, if it were practicable, to lay down his high priesthood, and that he would not go to the king because he did not trouble himself at all about such matters. Joseph then asked him if he would give him permission to go to Ptolemy as ambassador on behalf of the nation. (164) He replied that he would give him permission.

Then Joseph went up into the temple and called the multitude together to an assembly and exhorted them not to be disturbed nor frightened because of his uncle Onias's carelessness, but he begged them to be at rest and not terrify themselves about it; for he promised them that he would be their ambassador to the king and persuade him that they had done him no wrong. (165) When the multitude heard this, they thanked Joseph. So he went down from the temple and treated Ptolemy's ambassador in an hospitable manner. He also presented him with rich gifts, feasted him magnificently for many days, and then sent him to the king before him, and told him that he would soon follow. (166) For he was now more willing to go to the king because of the encouragement of the ambassador who earnestly persuaded him to come to Egypt, and who promised him that he would take care that he should obtain everything that he desired of Ptolemy. For he was highly pleased with his frank and liberal temperament, and with the dignity of his deportment.

(167) When Ptolemy's ambassador came to Egypt, he told the king of the thoughtless behavior of Onias, and he informed him of the goodness of the disposition of Joseph and that he was coming to him to ask forgiveness for the multitude for he was their protector. In short, he was so

---

92. Tobias was most probably born in Transjordan, but the site has not been identified.

extravagant in his praise of the young man that he disposed both the king and his wife Cleopatra to have affection for him before he came. (168) So Joseph sent to his friends at Samaria and borrowed money from them and got ready what was necessary for his journey—garments, drinking vessels, and beasts of burden, which amounted to about twenty thousand drachmae—and went to Alexandria. (169) Now it happened that at this time all the principal men and rulers went up from the cities of Syria and Phoenicia to bid for their tax-farming rights, [93] for every year the king sold them to the wealthy men in every city. (170) So these men saw Joseph journeying on the road and laughed at him for his poverty and threadbare appearance.

But when he came to Alexandria, he heard that King Ptolemy was at Memphis, and so he went there to meet with him. (171) The king was sitting in his chariot with his wife and with his friend Athenion who was the very person who had been ambassador at Jerusalem and had been entertained by Joseph. Therefore, as soon as Athenion saw him, he immediately introduced him to the king, making known to him how good and generous a young man he was. (172) So Ptolemy greeted him first and asked him to come up into his chariot. As Joseph sat there, he began to complain of the actions of Onias. To this he (Joseph) answered, "Forgive him on account of his age; for you certainly cannot be unaware that old men and infants have similar minds. But you shall have from us, who are young men, everything you desire, and shall have no cause to complain." (173) The king was so delighted with this good humor and pleasantry of the young man, that he began already, as though he were an old and tried friend, to have still a greater affection for him. He therefore bade him take up residence in the king's palace and be a guest at his own table every day. (174) So when the king came to Alexandria, the principal men of Syria saw Joseph sitting with the king and were very much offended by it.

(175) When the day came on which the king was to sell the taxes of the cities to farm, the principal men of rank in their several countries were to bid for them. When the sum of the taxes together of Celesyria and Phoenicia and of Judea with Samaria came to eight thousand talents, (176) then Joseph accused the bidders of having agreed together to estimate the value of the taxes at too low a rate. He promised that he would himself give twice as much for them, and that for those who did not pay, he would send the king home their property, for this privilege was sold

---

93. Kings rented out the privilege of collecting taxes, a process called tax farming.

together with the taxes themselves. (177) The king was pleased to hear that offer and, because it augmented his revenues, he said that he would confirm the sale of the tax-farming rights to him. But when he asked him whether he had any persons to provide surety for the payment of the money, he answered very cleverly, "I will give such security of persons good and responsible and which you shall have no reason to distrust." (178) When he asked him to tell him who they were, he replied, "I give you no other persons, O King, for my guarantors except yourself and your wife, and you shall each be security for the other's share." So Ptolemy laughed at the proposal and granted him the farming of the taxes without any guarantors. (179) This act gave great pain to those who came from the cities into Egypt, for they were utterly disappointed and returned, every one to his own country, with discomfort.

(180) Then Joseph took with him two thousand foot soldiers from the king for he asked that he might have some assistance in order to force any in the cities who were contemptuous to pay. And borrowing five hundred talents from the king's friends at Alexandria, he made haste back to Syria. (181) When he arrived at Askelon, he demanded the taxes of the people of Askelon, but they refused to pay anything and insulted him also. Therefore, he seized about twenty of the principal men, killed them, and gathered what they had together and sent it all to the king, informing him what he had done. (182) Ptolemy admired the prudent conduct of the man, commended him for what he had done, and gave him permission to do as he pleased. When the Syrians heard of this, they were astonished. Having before them the sad example of the men of Askelon who were killed, they opened their gates, willingly admitted Joseph, and paid their taxes. (183) And when the inhabitants of Scythopolis[94] attempted to insult him and would not pay him those taxes which they formerly used to pay without dispute, he also killed the principal men of that city and sent their property to the king. (184) By this means he gathered great wealth and made vast profits by the farming of taxes. He made use of what estate he had thus acquired in order to support his authority, thinking it prudent to preserve what had been the source and foundation of his present good fortune. This he did by the assistance of what he already possessed (185) for he privately sent many presents to the king, to Cleopatra, to their friends, and to all that were powerful around the court, thereby purchasing their good-will for himself.

---

94. Modern Beth Shean south of Lake Tiberias.

4.6 HELLENISTIC REFORM AND THE MACCABEAN REVOLT

4.6.1 2 Maccabees 3–6:
The Hellenistic Reform and the Onset of Persecution

2 Maccabees was written in Greek sometime in the first century B.C.E., itself condensed from the five-volume work of Jason of Cyrene in North Africa. It relates in detail the account of the events leading up to the Maccabean Revolt (168–64 B.C.E.), showing that the revolt and the resulting persecutions had their roots in an inner Jewish struggle.

ᘓᗗ

3:1 While the holy city was inhabited in unbroken peace and the laws were very well observed because of the piety of the high priest, Onias, and his hatred of wickedness, 2 it came about that the kings themselves honored the place and glorified the temple with the finest presents, 3 so that even Seleucus, the king of Asia, defrayed from his own revenues all the expenses connected with the service of the sacrifices. 4 But a man named Simon, of the tribe of Benjamin, who had been made captain of the temple, had a disagreement with the high priest about the administration of the city market; 5 and when he could not prevail over Onias he went to Apollonius of Tarsus, who at that time was governor of Coelesyria and Phoenicia. 6 He reported to him that the treasury in Jerusalem was full of untold sums of money, so that the amount of the funds could not be reckoned, and that they did not belong to the account of the sacrifices, but that it was possible for them to fall under the control of the king. 7 When Apollonius met the king, he told him of the money about which he had been informed. The king chose Heliodorus, who was in charge of his affairs, and sent him with commands to effect the removal of the aforesaid money. . . .

24 But when he arrived at the treasury with his bodyguard, then and there the Sovereign of spirits and of all authority caused so great a manifestation that all who had been so bold as to accompany him were astounded by the power of God, and became faint with terror.

4:1 The previously mentioned Simon, who had informed about the money against his own country, slandered Onias, saying that it was he who had incited Heliodorus and had been the real cause of the misfortune. 2 He dared to designate as a plotter against the government the man who was the benefactor of the city, the protector of his fellow countrymen, and a zealot for the laws. 3 When his hatred progressed to such a degree that even murders were committed by one of Simon's approved agents, 4 Onias recognized that the rivalry was serious and that Apollonius, the son of Menestheus and governor of Coelesyria and Phoenicia, was intensifying the malice of Simon. 5 So he betook himself to the king, not accusing his fellow citizens but having in view the welfare, both public and private, of all the people. 6 For he saw that without the king's attention, public affairs could not again reach a peaceful settlement, and that Simon would not stop his folly.

7 When Seleucus died and Antiochus who was called Epiphanes succeeded to the kingdom, Jason the brother of Onias obtained the high priesthood by corruption, 8 promising the king at an interview three hundred and sixty talents of silver and, from another source of revenue, eighty talents. 9 In addition to this he promised to pay one hundred and fifty more if permission were given to establish by his authority a gymnasium and a body of youth for it, and to enroll the men of Jerusalem as citizens of Antioch. 10 When the king assented and Jason came to office, he at once shifted his countrymen over to the Greek way of life. 11 He set aside the existing royal concessions to the Jews, secured through John the father of Eupolemus, who went on the mission to establish friendship and alliance with the Romans; and he destroyed the lawful ways of living and introduced new customs contrary to the law. 12 For with alacrity he founded a gymnasium right under the citadel, and he induced the noblest of the young men to wear the Greek hat. 13 There was such an extreme of Hellenization and increase in the adoption of foreign ways because of the surpassing wickedness of Jason, who was ungodly and no high priest, 14 that the priests were no longer intent upon their service at the altar. Despising the sanctuary and neglecting the sacrifices, they hastened to take part in the unlawful proceedings in the wrestling arena after the call to the discus, 15 disdaining the honors prized by their fathers and putting the highest value upon Greek forms of prestige. 16 For this reason heavy disaster overtook them, and those whose ways of living they admired and wished to imitate completely became their enemies and punished them. 17 For it is no light thing to show irreverence to the divine laws, a fact which later events will make clear.

18 When the quadrennial games were being held at Tyre and the king was present, 19 the vile Jason sent envoys, chosen as being Antiochian citizens from Jerusalem, to carry three hundred silver drachmas for the sacrifice to Hercules. Those who carried the money, however, thought best not to use it for sacrifice, because that was inappropriate, but to expend it for another purpose. 20 So this money was intended by the sender for the

sacrifice to Hercules, but by the decision of its carriers it was applied to the construction of triremes.[95]

21 When Apollonius the son of Menestheus was sent to Egypt for the coronation of Philometor as king, Antiochus learned that Philometor had become hostile to his government, and he took measures for his own security. Therefore upon arriving at Joppa he proceeded to Jerusalem. 22 He was welcomed magnificently by Jason and the city, and ushered in with a blaze of torches and with shouts. Then he marched into Phoenicia.

23 After a period of three years Jason sent Menelaus, the brother of the previously mentioned Simon, to carry the money to the king and to complete the records of essential business. 24 But he, when presented to the king, extolled him with an air of authority, and secured the high priesthood for himself, outbidding Jason by three hundred talents of silver. 25 After receiving the king's orders he returned, possessing no qualification for the high priesthood, but having the hot temper of a cruel tyrant and the rage of a savage wild beast. 26 So Jason, who after supplanting his own brother was supplanted by another man and was driven as a fugitive into the land of Ammon. 27 And Menelaus held the office, but he did not pay regularly any of the money promised to the king. 28 When Sostratus the captain of the citadel kept requesting payment, for the collection of the revenue was his responsibility, the two of them were summoned by the king on account of this issue. 29 Menelaus left his own brother Lysimachus as deputy in the high priesthood, while Sostratus left Crates, the commander of the Cyprian troops.

30 While such was the state of affairs, it happened that the people of Tarsus and of Mallus revolted because their cities had been given as a present to Antiochis, the king's concubine. 31 So the king went hastily to settle the trouble, leaving Andronicus, a man of high rank, to act as his deputy. 32 But Menelaus, thinking he had obtained a suitable opportunity, stole some of the gold vessels of the temple and gave them to Andronicus; other vessels, as it happened, he had sold to Tyre and the neighboring cities. 33 When Onias became fully aware of these acts he publicly exposed them, having first withdrawn to a place of sanctuary at Daphne near Antioch. 34 Therefore Menelaus, taking Andronicus aside, urged him to kill Onias. Andronicus came to Onias, and resorting to treachery offered him sworn pledges and gave him his right hand, and in spite of his suspicion persuaded Onias to come out from the place of sanctuary; then, with no regard for justice, he immediately put him out of the way. 35 For this reason not only Jews, but many also of other nations, were grieved and dis-

---

95. War vessels manned by three benches of rowers.

pleased at the unjust murder of the man. 36 When the king returned from the region of Cilicia, the Jews in the city appealed to him with regard to the unreasonable murder of Onias, and the Greeks shared their hatred of the crime. 37 Therefore Antiochus was grieved at heart and filled with pity, and wept because of the moderation and good conduct of the deceased; 38 and inflamed with anger, he immediately stripped off the purple robe from Andronicus, tore off his garments, and led him about the whole city to that very place where he had committed the outrage against Onias, and there he dispatched the bloodthirsty fellow. The Lord thus repaid him with the punishment he deserved.

39 When many acts of sacrilege had been committed in the city by Lysimachus with the connivance of Menelaus, and when report of them had spread abroad, the populace gathered against Lysimachus, because many of the gold vessels had already been stolen. 40 And since the crowds were becoming aroused and filled with anger, Lysimachus armed about three thousand men and launched an unjust attack under the leadership of a certain Auranus, a man advanced in years and no less advanced in folly. 41 But when the Jews became aware of Lysimachus' attack, some picked up stones, some blocks of wood, and others took handfuls of the ashes that were lying about, and threw them in wild confusion at Lysimachus and his men. 42 As a result, they wounded many of them and killed some, and put them all to flight; and the temple robber himself they killed close by the treasury. . . . 50 But Menelaus, because of the cupidity of those in power, remained in office, growing in wickedness, having become the chief plotter against his fellow citizens.

5:1 About this time Antiochus made his second invasion of Egypt. . . . 5 When a false rumor arose that Antiochus was dead, Jason took no less than a thousand men and suddenly made an assault upon the city. When the troops upon the wall had been forced back and at last the city was being taken, Menelaus took refuge in the citadel. 6 But Jason kept relentlessly slaughtering his fellow citizens, not realizing that success at the cost of one's kindred is the greatest misfortune, but imagining that he was setting up trophies of victory over enemies and not over fellow countrymen. 7 He did not gain control of the government, however; and in the end got only disgrace from his conspiracy, and fled again into the country of the Ammonites. 8 Finally he met a miserable end. . . . 10 He who had cast out many to lie unburied had no one to mourn for him; he had no funeral of any sort and no place in the tomb of his fathers.

11 When news of what had happened reached the king, he took it to mean that Judea was in revolt. So, raging inwardly, he left Egypt and took the city[96] by storm. 12 And he commanded his soldiers to cut down

relentlessly every one they met and to slay those who went into the houses. 13 Then there was killing of young and old, destruction of boys, women, and children, and slaughter of virgins and infants. 14 Within the total of three days eighty thousand were destroyed, forty thousand in hand-to-hand fighting; and as many were sold into slavery as were slain.

15 Not content with this, Antiochus dared to enter the most holy temple in all the world, guided by Menelaus, who had become a traitor both to the laws and to his country. 16 He took the holy vessels with his polluted hands, and swept away with profane hands the votive offerings which other kings had made to enhance the glory and honor of the place. . . .

21 So Antiochus carried off eighteen hundred talents from the temple, and hurried away to Antioch, thinking in his arrogance that he could sail on the land and walk on the sea, because his mind was elated. 22 And he left governors to afflict the people: at Jerusalem, Philip, by birth a Phrygian and in character more barbarous than the man who appointed him; 23 and at Gerizim, Andronicus; and besides these Menelaus, who lorded it over his fellow citizens worse than the others did. In his malice toward the Jewish citizens, 24 Antiochus sent Apollonius, the captain of the Mysians, with an army of twenty-two thousand, and commanded him to slay all the grown men and to sell the women and boys as slaves. 25 When this man arrived in Jerusalem, he pretended to be peaceably disposed and waited until the holy sabbath day; then, finding the Jews not at work, he ordered his men to parade under arms. 26 He put to the sword all those who came out to see them, then rushed into the city with his armed men and killed great numbers of people.

27 But Judas Maccabeus, with about nine others, got away to the wilderness, and kept himself and his companions alive in the mountains as wild animals do; they continued to live on what grew wild, so that they might not share in the defilement.

6:1 Not long after this, the king sent an Athenian senator to compel the Jews to forsake the laws of their fathers[97] and cease to live by the laws of God, 2 and also to pollute the temple in Jerusalem and call it the temple of Olympian Zeus, and to call the one in Gerizim the temple of Zeus the Friend of Strangers, as did the people who dwelt in that place.

3 Harsh and utterly grievous was the onslaught of evil. 4 For the temple was filled with debauchery and reveling by the Gentiles who dallied with harlots and had intercourse with women within the sacred precincts,

---

96. Jerusalem.
97. What had been voluntary was now enforced.

and besides brought in things for sacrifice that were unfit. 5 The altar was covered with abominable offerings which were forbidden by the laws. 6 A man could neither keep the sabbath, nor observe the feasts of his fathers, nor so much as confess himself to be a Jew.

4.6.2 1 Maccabees 1–4: The Maccabean Uprising

The account of 1 Maccabees, composed in Hebrew as an official court history for the Hasmonean House in ca. 100 B.C.E., portrays the course of the persecutions and the battle that led to Jewish victory. The leadership of the Hasmonean House is a central theme of the book.

ॐ

1:43 All the Gentiles accepted the command of the king. Many even from Israel gladly adopted his religion; they sacrificed to idols and profaned the sabbath. 44 And the king sent letters by messengers to Jerusalem and the cities of Judah; he directed them to follow customs strange to the land, 45 to forbid burnt offerings and sacrifices and drink offerings in the sanctuary, to profane sabbaths and feasts, 46 to defile the sanctuary and the priests, 47 to build altars and sacred precincts and shrines for idols, to sacrifice swine and unclean animals, 48 and to leave their sons uncircumcised. They were to make themselves abominable by everything unclean and profane, 49 so that they should forget the law and change all the ordinances. 50 "And whoever does not obey the command of the king shall die."

51 In such words he wrote to his whole kingdom. And he appointed inspectors over all the people and commanded the cities of Judah to offer sacrifice, city by city. 52 Many of the people, everyone who forsook the law, joined them, and they did evil in the land; 53 they drove Israel into hiding in every place of refuge they had.

54 Now on the fifteenth day of Chislev, in the one hundred and forty fifth year,[98] they erected a desolating sacrilege[99] upon the altar of burnt offering. They also built altars in the surrounding cities of Judah, 55 and burned incense at the doors of the houses and in the streets. 56 The books of the law which they found they tore to pieces and burned with fire. 57 Where the book of the covenant (the Torah) was found in the possession of anyone, or if anyone adhered to the law, the decree of the king condemned him to death. 58 They kept using violence against Israel,

---

98. December, 167 B.C.E.

99. An altar to Zeus Olympius and perhaps a statue of him as well in the Jerusalem Temple.

against those found month after month in the cities. 59 And on the twenty-fifth day of the month[100] they offered sacrifice on the altar which was upon the altar of burnt offering. 60 According to the decree, they put to death the women who had their children circumcised 61 and their families and those who circumcised them; and they hung the infants from their mothers' necks.

62 But many in Israel stood firm and were resolved in their hearts not to eat unclean food. 63 They chose to die rather than to be defiled by food or to profane the holy covenant; and they did die. 64 And very great wrath came upon Israel.

2:1 In those days Mattathias the son of John, son of Simeon, a priest of the sons of Joarib, moved from Jerusalem and settled in Modein.[101] 2 He had five sons, John surnamed Gaddi, 3 Simon called Thassi, 4 Judas called Maccabeus, 5 Eleazar called Avaran, and Jonathan called Apphus. 6 He saw the blasphemies being committed in Judah and Jerusalem. . . . 14 And Mattathias and his sons rent their clothes, put on sackcloth, and mourned greatly.

15 Then the king's officers who were enforcing the apostasy came to the city of Modein to make them offer sacrifice. 16 Many from Israel came to them; and Mattathias and his sons were assembled. 17 Then the king's officers spoke to Mattathias as follows: "You are a leader, honored and great in this city, and supported by sons and brothers. 18 Now be the first to come and do what the king commands, as all the Gentiles and the men of Judah and those that are left in Jerusalem have done. Then you and your sons will be numbered among the friends of the king, and you and your sons will be honored with silver and gold and many gifts."

19 But Mattathias answered and said in a loud voice: "Even if all the nations that live under the rule of the king obey him, and have chosen to do his commandments, departing each one from the religion of his fathers, 20 yet I and my sons and my brothers will live by the covenant of our fathers. 21 Far be it from us to desert the law and the ordinances. 22 We will not obey the king's words by turning aside from our religion to the right hand or to the left."

23 When he had finished speaking these words, a Jew came forward in the sight of all to offer sacrifice upon the altar in Modein, according to the king's command. 24 When Mattathias saw it, he burned with zeal and his heart was stirred. He gave vent to righteous anger; he ran and killed

---

100. The 25th of Kislev would also be the day of the rededication of the Temple in 164 B.C.E.

101. About 17 miles northwest of Jerusalem.

him upon the altar. 25 At the same time he killed the king's officer who was forcing them to sacrifice, and he tore down the altar. . . .

27 Then Mattathias cried out in the city with a loud voice, saying: "Let every one who is zealous for the law and supports the covenant come out with me!" 28 And he and his sons fled to the hills and left all that they had in the city. 29 Then many who were seeking righteousness and justice went down to the wilderness to dwell there, 30 they, their sons, their wives, and their cattle, because evils pressed heavily upon them. . . .

42 Then there united with them a company of Hasideans,[102] mighty warriors of Israel, every one who offered himself willingly for the law. 43 And all who became fugitives to escape their troubles joined them and reinforced them. 44 They organized an army, and struck down sinners in their anger and lawless men in their wrath; the survivors fled to the Gentiles for safety. 45 And Mattathias and his friends went about and tore down the altars; 46 they forcibly circumcised all the uncircumcised boys that they found within the borders of Israel. 47 They hunted down the arrogant men, and the work prospered in their hands. 48 They rescued the law out of the hands of the Gentiles and kings, and they never let the sinner gain the upper hand.

49 Now the days drew near for Mattathias to die, and he said to his sons: "Arrogance and reproach have now become strong; it is a time of ruin and furious anger. 50 Now, my children, show zeal for the law, and give your lives for the covenant of our fathers. . . ."

70 He died in the one hundred and forty-sixth year[103] and was buried in the tomb of his fathers at Modein. And all Israel mourned for him with great lamentation.

3:1 Then Judas his son, who was called Maccabeus, took command in his place. . . .

38 Lysias[104] chose Ptolemy the son of Dorymenes, and Nicanor and Gorgias, mighty men among the friends of the king, 39 and sent with them forty thousand infantry and seven thousand cavalry to go into the land of Judah and destroy it, as the king had commanded. 40 So they departed with their entire force, and when they arrived they encamped near Emmaus[105] in the plain. 41 When the traders of the region heard what was said of them, they took silver and gold in immense amounts,

---

102. Literally, "pious ones."

103. 166 B.C.E.

104. Lysias is identified in 2 Macc. 11:1 as "the king's guardian and kinsman who was in charge of the government."

105. Located about 25 miles northwest of Jerusalem.

and fetters, and went to the camp to get the sons of Israel for slaves. And forces from Syria and the land of the Philistines joined with them.

42 Now Judas and his brothers saw that misfortunes had increased and that the forces were encamped in their territory. They also learned what the king had commanded to do to the people to cause their final destruction. 43 But they said to one another, "Let us repair the destruction of our people, and fight for our people and the sanctuary." 44 And the congregation assembled to be ready for battle, and to pray and ask for mercy and compassion.

45 Jerusalem was uninhabited like a wilderness;
not one of her children went in or out.
The sanctuary was trampled down,
and the sons of aliens held the citadel;
it was a lodging place for the Gentiles.
Joy was taken from Jacob;
the flute and the harp ceased to play.

46 So they assembled and went to Mizpah, opposite Jerusalem,[106] because Israel formerly had a place of prayer in Mizpah. 47 They fasted that day, put on sackcloth and sprinkled ashes on their heads, and rent their clothes. 48 And they opened the book of the law to inquire into those matters about which the Gentiles were consulting the images of their idols.[107] 49 They also brought the garments of the priesthood and the first fruits and the tithes, and they stirred up the Nazirites who had completed their days;[108] 50 and they cried aloud to Heaven, saying,

"What shall we do with these?
Where shall we take them?
51 Thy sanctuary is trampled down and profaned,
and thy priests mourn in humiliation.
52 And behold, the Gentiles are assembled against us to destroy us;
thou knowest what they plot against us.
53 How will we be able to withstand them,
if thou dost not help us?"

54 Then they sounded the trumpets and gave a loud shout. 55 After this Judas appointed leaders of the people, in charge of thousands and hundreds and fifties and tens. 56 And he said to those who were building

---

106. North of the city.

107. The Jews consulted the Bible, whereas the non-Jews were accustomed to seeking oracles from their gods.

108. Cf. Num. 6:1–21.

houses, or were betrothed, or were planting vineyards, or were faint-hearted, that each should return to his home, according to the law.[109] 57 Then the army marched out and encamped to the south of Emmaus.

58 And Judas said, "Gird yourselves and be valiant. Be ready early in the morning to fight with these Gentiles who have assembled against us to destroy us and our sanctuary. 59 It is better for us to die in battle than to see the misfortunes of our nation and of the sanctuary. 60 But as his will in heaven may be, so he will do. . . ."

4:12 When the foreigners looked up and saw them[110] coming against them, 13 they went forth from their camp to battle. Then the men with Judas blew their trumpets 14 and engaged in battle. The Gentiles were crushed and fled into the plain, 15 and all those in the rear fell by the sword. They pursued them to Gazara,[111] and to the plains of Idumea,[112] and to Azotus[113] and Jamnia;[114] and three thousand of them fell.

4.6.3 1 Maccabees 4–6: The Rededication of the Temple

1 Maccabees describes the rededication of the Temple, which took place after Judah (Judas) the Maccabee and his men conquered Jerusalem, and the institution of the holiday of Hanukkah. Thereafter, Judah undertook a policy of fighting against Israel's neighbors who had supported the Hellenists and the Seleucids. But after the death of Antiochus IV in 164 B.C.E., the Seleucids again turned their attention to Judea.

༄

4:36 Then said Judas and his brothers, "Behold, our enemies are crushed; let us go up to cleanse the sanctuary and dedicate it." 37 So all the army assembled and they went up to Mount Zion. 38 And they saw the sanctuary desolate, the altar profaned, and the gates burned. In the courts they saw bushes sprung up as in a thicket, or as on one of the mountains. They saw also the chambers of the priests in ruins. 39 Then they rent their clothes, and mourned with great lamentation, and sprinkled themselves with ashes. 40 They fell face down on the ground, and sounded the signal on the trumpets, and cried out to Heaven. 41 Then

---

109. Deut. 20:5–8 details the laws of conscription and exemption from military service.
110. Judas and his forces.
111. Modern Gezer in the foothillls of the Judean Mountains.
112. In the Negev region in the south.
113. Modern Ashdod on the Mediterranean coast.
114. Modern Yavneh on the Mediterranean coast.

Judas detailed men to fight against those in the citadel[115] until he had cleansed the sanctuary.

42 He chose blameless priests devoted to the law, 43 and they cleansed the sanctuary and removed the defiled stones to an unclean place. 44 They deliberated what to do about the altar of burnt offering, which had been profaned. 45 And they thought it best to tear it down, lest it bring reproach upon them, for the Gentiles had defiled it. So they tore down the altar, 46 and stored the stones in a convenient place on the temple hill until there should come a prophet to tell what to do with them. 47 Then they took unhewn stones, as the law directs,[116] and built a new altar like the former one. 48 They also rebuilt the sanctuary and the interior of the temple, and consecrated the courts. 49 They made new holy vessels, and brought the lampstand, the altar of incense, and the table into the temple. 50 Then they burned incense on the altar and lighted the lamps on the lampstand, and these gave light in the temple. 51 They placed the bread on the table and hung up the curtains. Thus they finished all the work they had undertaken.

52 Early in the morning on the twenty-fifth day of the ninth month which is the month of Chislev, in the one hundred and forty-eighth year,[117] 53 they rose and offered sacrifice, as the law directs, on the new altar of burnt offering which they had built. 54 At the very season and on the very day that the Gentiles had profaned it,[118] it was dedicated with songs and harps and lutes and cymbals. 55 All the people fell on their faces and worshipped and blessed Heaven, who had prospered them. 56 So they celebrated the dedication of the altar for eight days, and offered burnt offerings with gladness; they offered a sacrifice of deliverance and praise. 57 They decorated the front of the temple with golden crowns and small shields, they restored the gates and the chambers for the priests, and furnished them with doors. 58 There was very great gladness among the people, and the reproach of the Gentiles was removed.

59 Then Judas and his brothers and all the assembly of Israel determined that every year at that season the days of the dedication of the altar should be observed with gladness and joy for eight days, beginning with the twenty-fifth day of the month of Chislev. 60 At that time they fortified Mount Zion with high walls and strong towers round about, to keep

---

115. The *akra*, "citadel," remained throughout a garrison of Seleucids and Hellenized Jews within Jerusalem.

116. According to Ex. 20:23 and Deut. 27:5–6, the stones of the Temple altar had to be unhewn.

117. December, 164 B.C.E.

118. 25 Kislev; see 1 Macc. 1:59.

the Gentiles from coming and trampling them down as they had done before. 61 And he stationed a garrison there to hold it. He also fortified Beth-zur,[119] so that the people might have a stronghold that faced Idumea.

5:1 When the Gentiles round about heard that the altar had been built and the sanctuary dedicated as it was before, they became very angry, 2 and they determined to destroy the descendants of Jacob who lived among them. So they began to kill and destroy among the people. 3 But Judas made war on the sons of Esau in Idumea, at Akrabattene,[120] because they kept lying in wait for Israel. He dealt them a heavy blow and humbled them and despoiled them. 4 He also remembered the wickedness of the sons of Baean,[121] who were a trap and a snare to the people and ambushed them on the highways. 5 They were shut up by him in their towers; and he encamped against them, vowed their complete destruction, and burned with fire their towers and all who were in them. 6 Then he crossed over to attack the Ammonites[122] where he found a strong band and many people with Timothy as their leader. 7 He engaged in many battles with them and they were crushed before him; he struck them down. 8 He also took Jazer[123] and its villages; then he returned to Judea. . . .

20 Then three thousand men were assigned to Simon to go to Galilee, and eight thousand to Judas for Gilead.

21 So Simon went to Galilee and fought many battles against the Gentiles, and the Gentiles were crushed before him. 22 He pursued them to the gate of Ptolemais,[124] and as many as three thousand of the Gentiles fell, and he despoiled them. 23 Then he took the Jews of Galilee and Arbatta[125] with their wives and children, and all they possessed, and led them to Judea with great rejoicing.

6:14 Then he (Antiochus IV) called for Philip, one of his friends, and made him ruler over all his kingdom. 15 He gave him the crown and his robe and the signet, that he might guide Antiochus (V) his son and bring him up to be king. 16 Thus Antiochus the king died there in the one hundred and forty-ninth year.[126] 17 And when Lysias learned that the

---

119. Four and a half miles north of Hebron.
120. Perhaps on the border of Judea and Idumaea, in the Negev.
121. Probably in Transjordan.
122. In Transjordan.
123. West of Amman.
124. Modern Akko, north of Haifa.
125. Either near the Sea of Galilee or south of the Dead Sea.

king was dead, he set up Antiochus the king's son to reign. Lysias had brought him up as a boy, and he named him Eupator.[127]

18 Now the men in the citadel kept hemming Israel in around the sanctuary. They were trying in every way to harm them and strengthen the Gentiles. 19 So Judas decided to destroy them, and assembled all the people to besiege them. 20 They gathered together and besieged the citadel in the one hundred and fiftieth year;[128] and he built siege towers and other engines of war. 21 But some of the garrison escaped from the siege and some of the ungodly Israelites joined them. 22 They went to the king and said, "How long will you fail to do justice and to avenge our brethren?. . . "

28 The king was enraged when he heard this. He assembled all his friends, the commanders of his forces and those in authority. 29 And mercenary forces came to him from other kingdoms and from islands of the seas. 30 The number of his forces was a hundred thousand foot soldiers, twenty thousand horsemen, and thirty-two elephants accustomed to war. 31 They came through Idumea and encamped against Beth-zur, and for many days they fought and built engines of war; but the Jews sallied out and burned these with fire, and fought manfully.

4.6.4 2 Maccabees 11: Letters of Antiochus

In 164 B.C.E. the Seleucids succeeded in convincing many Jews, including the Hasideans, to accept a truce and amnesty. The Hasmoneans, seeking not only religious freedom but political independence, refused to accept the amnesty. Judah seems to have lost power in this period.

෯

11:22 The king's letter ran thus:

"King Antiochus[129] to his brother Lysias, greeting. 23 Now that our father[130] has gone on to the gods, we desire that the subjects of the kingdom be undisturbed in caring for their own affairs. 24 We have heard that the Jews do not consent to our father's change to Greek customs but prefer their own way of living and ask that their own customs be allowed them. 25 Accordingly, since we choose that this nation also be free from disturbance, our decision is that their temple be restored to them and that

---

127. Literally, "of a good father."
128. 162 B.C.E.
129. Antiochus V Eupator, ruled 164–163 B.C.E.
130. Antiochus IV.

they live according to the customs of their ancestors. 26 You will do well, therefore, to send word to them and give them pledges of friendship, so that they may know our policy and be of good cheer and go on happily in the conduct of their own affairs."

27 To the nation the king's letter was as follows:

"King Antiochus to the senate of the Jews and to the other Jews, greeting. 28 If you are well, it is as we desire. We also are in good health. 29 Menelaus has informed us that you wish to return home and look after your own affairs. 30 Therefore those who go home by the thirtieth day of Xanthicus[131] will have our pledge of friendship and full permission 31 for the Jews to enjoy their own food and laws, just as formerly, and none of them shall be molested in any way for what he may have done in ignorance. 32 And I have also sent Menelaus to encourage you. 33 Farewell. The one hundred and forty-eighth year,[132] Xanthicus fifteenth."

4.6.5 1 Maccabees 7–10: The Final Hasmonean Victory

The Seleucids attempted to neutralize Judah by appointing Alcimus as high priest. Together with the Seleucid commanders, he fought against the Hasmonean forces. Ultimately, Judah himself fell in battle. Once again, the Hellenizers and their Seleucid supporters controlled Judea for a time, until Jonathan began to retake the countryside. The Seleucids were forced to recognize Jonathan as ruler and high priest. The battle had finally been won.

7:1 In the one hundred and fifty-first year Demetrius the son of Seleucus[133] set forth from Rome, sailed with a few men to a city by the sea,[134] and there began to reign. . . . 5 Then there came to him all the lawless and ungodly men of Israel; they were led by Alcimus who wanted to be high priest.[135] 6 And they brought to the king this accusation against the people: "Judas and his brothers have destroyed all your friends, and have driven us out of our land. 7 Now then send a man whom you trust; let him go and see all the ruin which Judas has brought upon us and upon the land of the king, and let him punish them and all who help them."

---

131. March–April.

132. 164 B.C.E.

133. Demetrius I Soter (reigned 162–150 B.C.E.) was the son of Seleucus IV Philopater and the brother of Antiochus IV.

134. 2 Macc. 14:1 identifies this city as Tripolis.

135. Alcimus was not a member of the high priestly family and so had no legitimate claim to that position. He was an extreme Hellenizer and allied himself with the Seleucids.

8 So the king chose Bacchides, one of the king's friends, governor of the province Beyond the River;[136] he was a great man in the kingdom and was faithful to the king. 9 And he sent him, and with him the ungodly Alcimus, whom he made high priest; and he commanded him to take vengeance on the sons of Israel. 10 So they marched away and came with a large force into the land of Judah; and he sent messengers to Judas and his brothers with peaceable but treacherous words. 11 But they paid no attention to their words, for they saw that they had come with a large force.

12 Then a group of scribes appeared in a body before Alcimus and Bacchides to ask for just terms. 13 The Hasideans were the first among the sons of Israel to seek peace from them, 14 for they said, "A priest of the line of Aaron has come with the army, and he will not harm us." 15 And he spoke peaceable words to them and swore this oath to them, "We will not seek to injure you or your friends." 16 So they trusted him; but he seized sixty of them and killed them in one day, in accordance with the word which was written.

17 "The flesh of thy saints and their blood
they poured out round about Jerusalem,
and there was none to bury them.'"[137]

18 Then the fear and dread of them fell upon all the people, for they said, "There is no truth or justice in them, for they have violated the agreement and the oath which they swore."

19 Then Bacchides departed from Jerusalem and encamped in Bethzaith.[138] And he sent and seized many of the men who had deserted to him, and some of the people, and killed them and threw them into the great pit. 20 He placed Alcimus in charge of the country and left with him a force to help him; then Bacchides went back to the king.

21 Alcimus strove for the high priesthood 22 and all who were troubling their people joined him. They gained control of the land of Judah and did great damage in Israel. 23 And Judas saw all the evil that Alcimus and those with him had done among the sons of Israel; it was more than the Gentiles had done. 24 So Judas went out into all the surrounding parts of Judea, and took vengeance on the men who had deserted and he prevented those in the city from going out into the country. 25 When Alci-

---

136. The province west of the Euphrates River.
137. Ps. 79:2–3.
138. South of Jerusalem.

mus saw that Judas and those with him had grown strong, and realized that he could not withstand them, he returned to the king and brought wicked charges against them.

26 Then the king sent Nicanor, one of his honored princes, who hated and detested Israel, and he commanded him to destroy the people. . . .

43 So the armies met in battle on the thirteenth day of the month of Adar.[139] The army of Nicanor was crushed, and he himself was the first to fall in the battle. 44 When his army saw that Nicanor had fallen, they threw down their arms and fled. 45 The Jews pursued them a day's journey, from Adasa[140] as far as Gazara, and as they followed kept sounding the battle call on the trumpets. 46 And men came out of all the villages of Judea round about, and they out-flanked the enemy and drove them back to their pursuers, so that they all fell by the sword; not even one of them was left. 47 Then the Jews seized the spoils and the plunder, and they cut off Nicanor's head and the right hand which he had so arrogantly stretched out, and brought them and displayed them just outside of Jerusalem. 48 The people rejoiced greatly and celebrated that day as a day of great gladness. 49 And they decreed that this day should be celebrated each year on the thirteenth day of Adar. 50 So the land of Judah had rest for a few days. . . .

9:1 When Demetrius heard that Nicanor and his army had fallen in battle, he sent Bacchides and Alcimus into the land of Judah a second time, and with them the right wing of the army. 2 They went by the road which leads to Gilgal and encamped against Mesaloth in Arbela,[141] and they took it and killed many people. 3 In the first month of the one hundred and fifty second year[142] they encamped against Jerusalem. . . .

11 Then the army of Bacchides marched out from the camp and took its stand for the encounter. . . .

17 The battle became desperate, and many on both sides were wounded and fell. 18 Judas also fell, and the rest fled.

19 Then Jonathan and Simon took Judas their brother and buried him in the tomb of their fathers at Modein, 20 and wept for him. And all Israel made great lamentation for him; they mourned many days and said,

---

139. March, 161 B.C.E.

140. Five and a half miles north of Jerusalem.

141. Northwest of Tiberias in the Galilee, Hebrew Arbel. Mesaloth literally means "steps."

142. April 160 B.C.E.

21 "How is the mighty fallen,
the savior of Israel!"[143]

22 Now the rest of the acts of Judas, and his wars and the brave deeds that he did, and his greatness, have not been recorded, for they were very many.

23 After the death of Judas, the lawless emerged in all parts of Israel; all the doers of injustice appeared. 24 In those days a very great famine occurred, and the country deserted with them to the enemy. 25 And Bacchides chose the ungodly and put them in charge of the country. 26 They sought and searched for the friends of Judas, and brought them to Bacchides, and he took vengeance on them and made sport of them. 27 Thus there was great distress in Israel, such as had not been since the time that prophets ceased to appear among them.

28 Then all the friends of Judas assembled and said to Jonathan, 29 "Since the death of your brother Judas there has been no one like him to go against our enemies and Bacchides, and to deal with those of our nation who hate us. 30 So now we have chosen you today to take his place as our ruler and leader, to fight our battle." 31 And Jonathan at that time accepted the leadership and took the place of Judas his brother. . . .

50 Bacchides then returned to Jerusalem and built strong cities in Judea: the fortress in Jericho, and Emmaus, and Beth-horon, and Bethel, and Timnath, and Pharathon, and Tephon, with high walls and gates and bars. 51 And he placed garrisons in them to harass Israel. 52 He also fortified the city of Beth-zur, and Gazara, and the citadel, and in them he put troops and stores of food. 53 And he took the sons of the leading men of the land as hostages and put them under guard in the citadel at Jerusalem.

54 In the one hundred and fifty-third year, in the second month,[144] Alcimus gave orders to tear down the wall of the inner court of the sanctuary. He tore down the work of the prophets! 55 But he only began to tear it down, for at that time Alcimus was stricken and his work was hindered; his mouth was stopped and he was paralyzed, so that he could no longer say a word or give commands concerning his house.

56 And Alcimus died at that time in great agony. 57 When Bacchides saw that Alcimus was dead, he returned to the king, and the land of Judah had rest for two years.

58 Then all the lawless plotted and said, "See! Jonathan and his men are living in quiet and confidence. So now let us bring Bacchides back,

---

143. Cf. 2 Sam. 1:19.
144. April–May of 159 B.C.E.

and he will capture them all in one night." 59 And they went and consulted with him. 60 He started to come with a large force, and secretly sent letters to all his allies in Judea, telling them to seize Jonathan and his men; but they were unable to do it, because their plan became known. 61 And Jonathan's men seized about fifty of the men of the country who were leaders in this treachery, and killed them. . . .

68 They fought with Bacchides, and he was crushed by them. They distressed him greatly, for his plan and his expedition had been in vain. 69 So he was greatly enraged at the lawless men who had counseled him to come into the country, and he killed many of them. Then he decided to depart to his own land.

70 When Jonathan learned of this, he sent ambassadors to him to make peace with him and obtain release of the captives. 71 He agreed, and did as he said, and he swore to Jonathan that he would not try to harm him as long as he lived. 72 He restored to him the captives whom he had formerly taken from the land of Judah, then he turned and departed to his own land, and came no more into their territory. 73 Thus the sword ceased from Israel. And Jonathan dwelt in Michmash.[145] And Jonathan began to judge the people, and he destroyed the ungodly out of Israel.

10:1 In the one hundred and sixtieth year[146] Alexander Epiphanes, the son of Antiochus,[147] landed and occupied Ptolemais. They welcomed him, and there he began to reign. 2 When Demetrius the king heard of it, he assembled a very large army and marched out to meet him in battle. 3 And Demetrius sent Jonathan a letter in peaceable words to honor him; 4 for he said, "Let us act first to make peace with him before he makes peace with Alexander against us, 5 for he will remember all the wrongs which we did to him and to his brothers and his nation." 6 So Demetrius gave him authority to recruit troops, to equip them with arms, and to become his ally; and he commanded that the hostages in the citadel should be released to him.

7 Then Jonathan came to Jerusalem and read the letter in the hearing of all the people and of the men in the citadel. 8 They were greatly alarmed when they heard that the king had given him authority to recruit troops. 9 But the men in the citadel released the hostages to Jonathan, and he returned them to their parents.

---

145. Eight miles northeast of Jerusalem.

146. 152 B.C.E.

147. Alexander Balas, who ruled 152–145 B.C.E., claimed to be the son of Antiochus IV.

10 And Jonathan dwelt in Jerusalem and began to rebuild and restore the city. 11 He directed those who were doing the work to build the walls and encircle Mount Zion with squared stones, for better fortification; and they did so. . . .

15 Now Alexander the king heard of all the promises which Demetrius had sent to Jonathan, and men told him of the battles that Jonathan and his brothers had fought, of the brave deeds that they had done, and of the troubles that they had endured. 16 So he said, "Shall we find another such man? Come now, we will make him our friend and ally." 17 And he wrote a letter and sent it to him, in the following words:

18 "King Alexander to his brother Jonathan, greeting. 19 We have heard about you, that you are a mighty warrior and worthy to be our friend. 20 And so we have appointed you today to be the high priest of your nation; you are to be called the king's friend" (and he sent him a purple robe and a golden crown) "and you are to take our side and keep friendship with us."

21 So Jonathan put on the holy garments in the seventh month of the one hundred and sixtieth year, at the feast of tabernacles,[148] and he recruited troops and equipped them with arms in abundance.

---

148. The festival of Sukkot in September–October of 152 B.C.E.

5

Judaism in the Hellenistic Diaspora

Eventually, as Jewish history developed, the communities of the Diaspora, those outside of Israel, would carry the burden of Jewish survival and cultural development for almost two millennia. These Diaspora communities came into existence in Antiquity, beginning with the Babylonian exile, and somewhat later there developed the Greek-speaking Hellenistic Diaspora.

While we have no extensive historical documents regarding the Babylonian Diaspora in this early period, before the age of the Babylonian Talmud, Josephus, in *Antiquities* (text 5.1.1) does give us a glimpse of this community in relating the story of the royal house of Adiabene, a principality in the upper Tigris region. The story shows us that Jews and Judaism were spreading slowly throughout Syria and Mesopotamia, and that non-Jews were attracted to Judaism, as they were in the Hellenistic world. This story, no doubt, was a source of pride to Josephus's Jewish readers.

At this early date, the rising Hellenistic Diaspora left us much more historical evidence, and we concentrate on it in the rest of this chapter. We have already encountered the Jewish Temple in Egypt at Elephantine, in the days of the Persian Empire, and we now look at the story of the Temple of Onias, as related by Josephus in *Antiquities* (text 5.2.1). This Temple was built at Leontopolis, as a result of the displacement of Onias IV as high priest in Jerusalem after the death of the usurper Menelaus. Onias preferred to minister in Egypt rather than to be passed over in Jerusalem.

Onias was later involved in the political intrigues of the Hellenistic world, and he supported Cleopatra II against Ptolemy VII Physcon. Josephus (text 5.2.2) describes the resulting pogrom, the first recorded outbreak of large scale anti-Semitic violence. Hilkiah (Chelkia) and Hananiah (Ananias), sons of Onias, were sufficiently powerful in the army of Cleopatra to influence her not to attack Alexander Janneus, the Hasmonean ruler of Judea, as discussed by Josephus (text 5.2.3). All this testifies to a high level of integration of the Egyptian Jewish community into the affairs of state in their adopted Diaspora homeland, a trend which would typify Jewish communities throughout the world.

Evidence for similar integration is available from Seleucid Syria where Jews were granted citizenship, according to Josephus (text 5.3.1), and attempts to limit their rights by the natives were unsuccessful. They clearly were held in high respect as loyal citizens by Antiochus III, the Great, who depended on them to give stability to his empire (text 5.3.2). Further, Josephus (text 5.3.3) quotes a long series of legal documents extending privileges to the Jews, in order to prove their favored status in the Roman Empire. Among these documents is Julius Caesar's official recognition of the Hasmonean priesthood and of the high priest as ethnarch of the Jews, a status that did not last for too long, however. Repeatedly, the various decrees stress the right of the Jews to follow their religious laws and customs, especially emphasizing the laws of the Sabbath and kosher food. Josephus concludes with the claim that he has produced more than sufficient evidence and, therefore, has decided to omit the many other examples of such documents that were available to him.

Many scholars have doubted that Jewish observance was widespread among the Jews of the Greco-Roman Diaspora. To be sure, this observance was not the same as that of the Hebrew-speaking Jews of Palestine, soon to come under the influence of the Rabbinic tradition. Some evidence for religious life can be gleaned from inscriptions on tombs (text 5.4.1) and dedications (text 5.4.2) in the Diaspora. The Aphrodisias Inscription (text 5.4.3), one of the most significant inscriptions, has settled a long-standing debate. There can no longer be any question of the existence of semi-proselytes, non-Jews who adopted Jewish practices, in the Greco-Roman world. Even when deriding the Jews, authors like the Roman historian

Tacitus (text 5.5.1) who lived ca. 56–118 C.E., indicate that ritual observance was indeed common. On the other hand, his description of Jewish life is typical of much of the anti-Semitism that circulated in this period. To say the least, these descriptions are full of gross errors of fact. We should note that the attachment of the Diaspora to the Land of Israel is also mentioned here.

Indeed, anti-Semitism was quite common in the Hellenistic world, as we demonstrate by including passages from a number of otherwise refined authors. Plutarch (text 5.5.2), a Greek biographer and antiquarian (ca. 46–120 C.E.), preserves all kinds of strange ideas regarding why the Jews do not eat pork, basing himself ultimately on the myth that Jews worshipped an ass which they supposedly believed had taken them out of Egypt. The stoic philosopher Seneca (ca. 5 B.C.E. –65 C.E.) also has unkind things to say about the Jews (text 5.5.3). At the same time he testifies to the widespread influence of the Jews in the Roman world. Extremely interesting is his comment that many Jews observed the customs without knowing their meaning. Juvenal, the Roman satirist and rhetorician (ca. 50-ca. 127 C.E.), sees Judaism as a mystery religion, the rules of which were only made known to initiates (text 5.5.4). Again, anti-Semitic stereotypes were very common in Late Antiquity. Sabbath observance is regarded by him as a waste of time.

Philo's embassy to Gaius, from which we present some excerpts (text 5.6.1), describes the contemptuous reception which the emperor Gaius Caligula gave to the Alexandrian Jewish delegation, of which Philo was a member, who came to him in 38 or 39 B.C.E. to protest the anti-Jewish riots that had recently taken place in Alexandria. Our first excerpt presents a description of some of the rioting as it was directed against the Jews, and the second discusses the ill-fated embassy to Rome. This passage again shows that the Romans did not understand Judaism, were perplexed by the Jewish food laws, and felt no obligation to protect the Jews from persecution. We have come a long way from the pro-Jewish decrees quoted by Josephus.

Anti-Semitism was so widespread in the Greco-Roman world that Josephus devoted an entire treatise to refuting its arguments. In *Against Apion*, he argues against the myth that the Jews were originally a group of lepers expelled from Egypt (text 5.6.2). He also had to argue against the very common myth, encountered by us already above, that Jews worshipped an ass's head in the Jerusalem Temple (text 5.6.3). This notion was intimately connected up with the earliest blood libel, the notion that Jews killed a non-Jew as part of their ritual. Further, Josephus argues that many of the things of which the Jews are accused are in direct contradiction to the laws of the Torah which Jews faithfully observe.

Certainly, the Greek translation of the Bible, loosely termed the Septuagint, a term which actually refers only to the translation of the Torah, was one of the most important classics of Hellenistic Jewish literature. It is actually evidence of the process of cultural symbiosis that led to the requirement of a translation both for Greek-speaking Jews and for Hellenistic pagans who wanted to be acquainted with the great classic of Jewish literature, the Pentateuch. Two versions of the story of the Torah's translation into Greek were current in Antiquity, one being in the Letter of Aristeas (text 5.6.4), a fascinating document testifying to the nature of Hellenistic Jewish life in Egypt in the third century B.C.E. We present those parts of this document which testify to the history of the translation. Along the way, and indeed even more so in the entire text of the Letter of Aristeas, we learn a lot about the Jewish religious practices of the time and about Jerusalem and its Temple.

We include the talmudic account of the translation of the Torah into Greek (text 5.6.5), which shows that a story circulated among the Rabbis similar to that which appeared in the Letter of Aristeas. The examples of altered translations given here indicate the Rabbinic sensitivity to the manner in which the words of the Torah would be received in the Hellenistic world, yet they do not accord for the most part with the preserved Septuagint texts.

Important evidence for Hellenistic Judaism also comes from Philo Judaeus. His works are so extensive that only a small part of his religious teachings can be presented. For this reason we include an anthology of passages from his works which illustrate the main ideas he put forward (text 5.6.6). One can gauge from them the extensive contribution which he made to Jewish philosophy and biblical interpretation in the Hellenistic context, a contribution which was quickly lost to the Jewish people, only to be recovered in the Renaissance when Jews began to read classical languages again.

These materials give us just a glimpse of the tremendously rich culture of the Jewish people in the Hellenistic Diaspora. Much of this great culture did not survive in the living Jewish communities which carried on the tradition, but it remains testimony to the ability of Judaism to interact with a variety of cultures and environments throughout history.

5.1 THE EARLY HISTORY OF BABYLONIAN JEWRY

5.1.1 Josephus, *Antiquities* XX, 17–95: The Conversion of the House of Adiabene[1]

Large numbers of non-Jews were interested in Jewish practices in the Greco-Roman world. Yet to the Jews, a particular source of pride was the decision of the royal house of Adiabene, a minor kingdom in Northern Syria, to convert to Judaism. Josephus' account, probably taken from an earlier source, indicates the requirements of circumcision, study of the Torah and sacrifice as symbols of the transition to membership in the Jewish community.

ॐ

(17) About this time it was that Helena, queen of Adiabene, and her son Izates, changed their course of life, and embraced the Jewish customs, and this on the following occasion: (18) Monobazus, the king of Adiabene, who also had the name of Bazeus, fell in love with his sister Helena, took her to be his wife, and conceived a child with her. But as he was in bed with her one night, he laid his hands upon his wife's belly and fell asleep, and seemed to hear a voice which bade him take his hands off his wife's belly, and not to hurt the infant that was therein which, by God's providence, would be safely born, and have a happy end. (19) This voice put him into disorder, so he awakened immediately and told the story to his wife. When his son was born, he called him Izates.[2] (20) He had indeed Monobazus, his elder brother, by Helena also, as he had other sons by other wives besides. Yet he openly placed all his affections on Izates as if he were his only begotten son. (21) This was the origin of that envy which his other brothers, by the same father, bore to him, for they hated him more and more and were all under great affliction that their

---

1. Trans. by W. Whiston, *The Works of Josephus* (Peabody, MA: Hendrickson, 1987), revised by L. H. Schiffman in consultation with H. St. J. Thackeray, Ralph Marcus, Allen Wikgren, and L. H. Feldman, trans., *Josephus: in Nine Volumes* (Loeb Classical Library; Cambridge, MA: Harvard University, 1976–79).
2. An Iranian name meaning "genius, divine being."

father should prefer Izates to them all. (22) Now although their father was very sensible of their passions, yet he forgave them, as not indulging those passions out of an ill disposition, but out of a desire each of them had to be beloved by their father. However, he sent Izates, with many presents, to Abennerigus,[3] the king of Charax-Spasini,[4] because of the great fear he was in about him, lest he should come to some misfortune by the hatred his brothers bore him; and he committed his son's preservation to him. (23) Abennerigus gladly received the young man, and had such great affection for him that he married him to his own daughter, whose name was Samacha. He also bestowed a territory upon him, from which he received large revenues.

(24) But when Monobazus had grown old, and saw that he had but a little time to live, he wanted to see his son before he died. So he sent for him and embraced him in the most affectionate manner, and bestowed on him the country called Carrae. (25) It was a soil that bore amomum[5] in great plenty. There are also in it the remains of that ark, wherein it is related that Noah escaped the deluge, and where they are still shown to whoever wants to see them. (26) Accordingly Izates stayed in that land until his father's death. But the very day that Monobazus died, Queen Helena sent for all the grandees and governors of the kingdom and for those that had the armies committed to their command. (27) When they came, she made the following speech to them: "I believe you are not unaware that my husband was desirous that Izates should succeed him in the government and thought him worthy to do so. However, I await your determination for happy is he who receives a kingdom not from a single person only, but from the willing consent of a great many." (28) This she said in order to test those who were invited and to discover their sentiments. Upon hearing this, they first of all paid their homage to the queen, as their custom was, and then they said that they confirmed the king's determination and would submit to it. They rejoiced that Izates's father had preferred him before the rest of his brothers, as being agreeable to all their wishes. (29) But they were desirous first of all to kill his brothers and kinsmen, that so the government might come securely to Izates because if they were once destroyed, all that fear would be over which might arise from their hatred and envy of him. (30) Helena replied to this that she appreciated their kindness to herself and to Izates but desired that

---

3. From 5–21 C.E.

4. Capital of the kingdom of Charakene located between the mouths of the Tigris and Euphrates Rivers in southern Mesopotamia.

5. An aromatic plant of the ginger family.

they should, however, defer the execution of this slaughter of Izates's brothers until he should be there himself and give his approval to it. (31) So since these men did not prevail with her when they advised her to kill them, they exhorted her at least to keep them in bonds until he should come for their own security. They also gave her counsel to set up someone in whom she could put the greatest trust as governor of the kingdom in the meantime. (32) So Queen Helena complied with this counsel of theirs and set up Monobazus, the eldest son, to be king, and put the diadem upon his head, and gave him his father's ring, with its signet as well as the ornament which they called Sampser, and exhorted him to administer the affairs of the kingdom until his brother came. (33) He came suddenly upon hearing that his father was dead and succeeded his brother Monobazus, who surrendered the government to him.

(34) Now, during the time Izates abode at Charax-Spasini, a certain Jewish merchant, whose name was Ananias, visited the king's wives and taught them to worship God according to the Jewish religion. (35) Moreover, through them he became known to Izates: and persuaded him, in like manner, to embrace that religion. He also, at the earnest entreaty of Izates, accompanied him when he was sent for by his father to come to Adiabene. It also happened that Helena, about the same time, was instructed by a certain other Jew and went over to their laws. (36) But when Izates had taken the kingdom and had come to Adiabene, and there saw his brothers and other kinsmen in bonds, he was displeased by it. (37) He thought it an instance of impiety either to kill or imprison them, but still thought it a hazardous thing to let them have their liberty, with the remembrance of the injuries that had been offered to them. He sent some of them and their children as hostages to Rome, to Claudius Caesar, and sent the others to Artabanus, the king of Parthia, with like intentions.

(38) And when he perceived that his mother was highly pleased with the Jewish customs, he made haste to convert and to embrace them entirely. As he supposed that he could not be thoroughly a Jew unless he were circumcised, he was ready to have it done. (39) But when his mother understood his intention, she endeavored to hinder him from doing it. She said to him that it would bring him into danger; and that since he was a king, he would thereby bring about great disaffection among his subjects when they would find out that he was so devoted to rites that were to them strange and foreign, and that they would never bear to be ruled over by a Jew. (40) This it what she said to him, and for the present she persuaded him to forbear. When he had related what she had said to Ananias, he confirmed what his mother had said. He also threatened to leave him and to leave the land unless he complied with him. (41) He said that

he was afraid lest if such an action became public, he should himself be in danger of punishment for having been the cause of it, having been the king's instructor in actions that were unseemly. He said that Izates might worship God without being circumcised, if he had resolved to be a devoted adherent of Judaism and that such worship of God was of a superior nature to circumcision. (42) He added that God would forgive him, though he did not perform the operation, since it was omitted out of necessity and for fear of his subjects. So the king at that time complied with these persuasions of Ananias.

(43) But afterwards, as he had not given up his desire of doing this, a certain other Jew from Galilee, whose name was Eleazer, and who was esteemed very skillful in the learning of his country, persuaded him to do it. (44) For as he entered into his palace to pay him respects and found him reading the law of Moses, he said to him, "You do not consider, O king! that you unjustly break what is commanded in those laws and transgress against God himself for you ought not only to read them, but even more to practice what they enjoin you. (45) How long will you continue to be uncircumcised? If you have not yet read the law about circumcision, and do not know how great an impiety you art guilty of by neglecting it, read it now." (46) When the king had heard what he said, he delayed the thing no longer, but retired to another room and sent for a surgeon, and did what he was commanded to do. He then sent for his mother, and Ananias his tutor, and informed them that he had done this. (47) They were immediately struck with astonishment and fear beyond measure lest the thing should be openly discovered and censured, and the king should risk the loss of his kingdom since his subjects would not bear to be governed by a man who was so zealous for another religion and lest they should themselves run some risk because they would be supposed the cause of his so doing. (48) But it was God himself who prevented what they feared from taking effect. For He preserved both Izates himself and his sons when they fell into many dangers and procured their deliverance when it seemed to be impossible, and demonstrated thereby that the reward for piety does not perish for those who have regard to Him and fix their faith upon Him only, but these events we shall relate below.[6]

(49) But as to Helena, the king's mother, when she saw that the affairs of Izates's kingdom were in peace, and that her son was a happy man, and admired among all men and even among foreigners, by means of God's providence over him, she had a mind to go to the city of Jerusalem, in

---

6. Cf. 69–91, but since this promise is largely unfulfilled, it may be that Josephus copied this account from elsewhere.

order to worship at that temple of God which was so very famous among all men and to offer her thank offerings there. So she asked her son to give her permission to go there. (50) He gave his consent to what she desired very willingly, and made great preparations for her departure, and gave her a great deal of money. She set out for the city of Jerusalem, her son accompanying her on her journey a great way. (51) Now her arrival was of very great advantage to the people of Jerusalem since a famine oppressed them at that time, and many people died for lack of money with which to procure food. Queen Helena sent some of her servants to Alexandria with money to buy a great quantity of corn, and others of them to Cyprus to bring a cargo of dried figs. (52) As soon as they came back and brought those provisions, which was done very quickly, she distributed food to those who were in need of it, and left a most excellent memorial behind her of this benefaction, which she bestowed on our whole nation. (53) When her son Izates was informed of this famine, he sent great sums of money to the principal men in Jerusalem. However, the favors that this queen and king conferred upon our city Jerusalem shall be further related below.[7]

(75) Now when the king's brother, Monobazus, and his other relatives saw how Izates, by his piety to God, had become greatly esteemed by all men, they also had a desire to leave the religion of their land and to embrace the customs of the Jews. (76) But that act of theirs was discovered by Izates's subjects. Whereupon the nobles were much displeased, and could not contain their anger at them, but had an intention, when they should find a proper opportunity, to inflict a punishment upon them. (77) Accordingly, they wrote to Abia, king of the Arabians, and promised him great sums of money if he would make an expedition against their king. They further promised him that on the first engagement, they would desert their king because they were desirous to punish him because of the hatred he had for their religious worship. Then they obligated themselves by oaths to be faithful to each other, and requested that he make haste in his design. (78) The king of Arabia complied with their requests, brought a great army into the field, and marched against Izates. At the beginning of the first engagement and before they came to a close fight, those nobles, as if they were stricken by panic, all deserted Izates, as they had agreed to do, and, turning their backs upon their enemies, ran away. (79) Yet Izates was not dismayed at this. But when he understood that the nobles had betrayed him, he also retired into his camp and made inquiry

---

7. Again, this promise is not fulfilled, indicating that this was copied by Josephus from a source.

into the matter. As soon as he knew who they were who had made this conspiracy with the king of Arabia, he cut off those who were found guilty. Renewing the fight on the next day, he killed the greatest part of his enemies, (80) and so forced all the rest to flee. He also pursued their king, and drove him into a fortress called Arsamus, and, following on the siege vigorously, he took that fortress. When he had plundered it of all the prey that was in it, which was not small, he returned to Adiabene. But he did not take Abia alive because when he had found himself encompassed upon every side, he killed himself.[8]

(92) It was not long before Izates died after he had completed fifty-five years of life and had ruled his kingdom for twenty-four years. He left behind him twenty-four sons and twenty-four daughters. (93) However, he gave an order that his brother Monobazus should succeed to the king-ship thereby rewarding him since, while he was himself absent after their father's death, he had faithfully preserved the government for him. (94) But when Helena, his mother, heard of her son's death, she was greatly distressed, as was but natural, upon her loss of such a most dutiful son. Yet it was a comfort to her that she heard that the succession came to her eldest son. Accordingly she went to him in haste, and after she arrived in Adiabene, she did not long outlive her son Izates. (95) But Monobazus sent her bones, as well as those of Izates, his brother, to Jerusalem, and gave an order that they should be buried at the tombs which their mother had erected. They were three in number, and distant no more than three furlongs from the city of Jerusalem.[9]

5.2 JEWS IN THE HELLENISTIC WORLD

5.2.1 Josephus, *Antiquities* XIII, 62–73: The Temple of Onias

Already in the sixth century B.C.E. at Elephantine, Egypt there stood a temple at which some Jews worshipped. This may have set the pattern for the later establishment of the Temple of Onias which Onias IV received permis-sion to build in 154 B.C.E. It was a local center of worship, probably for the Jewish military settlement in Leontopolis, six miles north of Cairo. The priests in Jerusalem regarded the Temple of Onias and its rituals as invalid. The temple was destroyed by Vespasian in 73 C.E., lest it serve as a center for further Jewish rebelliousness.

---

8. Josephus then relates an account of a similar attempt by the nobles to use the king of Parthia to dislodge Izates.

9. These tombs can be seen today on Nablus Road in East Jerusalem.

꧁

(62) But then the son of Onias the high priest, who was of the same name as his father and who fled to King Ptolemy, who was called Philometor,[10] lived now at Alexandria, as we have said already.[11] When this Onias saw that Judea was oppressed by the Macedonians and their kings, (63) out of a desire to purchase to himself a memorial and eternal fame, he resolved to ask permission of King Ptolemy and Queen Cleopatra to build a temple in Egypt like the one in Jerusalem and to ordain Levites and priests of his own stock. (64) His chief reason for doing so was that he relied upon the prophet Isaiah, who lived about six hundred years before and foretold that there certainly was to be a temple built to Almighty God in Egypt by a man who was a Jew.[12]

Onias was excited by this prediction and wrote the following epistle to Ptolemy and Cleopatra: (65) "Having done many and great things for you in the affairs of war by the assistance of God in Celesyria[13] and Phoenicia, I came at length with the Jews to Leontopolis in the nome of Heliopolis[14] and to other places where our nation is settled. (66) I found that most of them had temples in an improper manner, and that for this reason they bore ill will to one another which happens to the Egyptians also because of the multitude of their temples and the difference of opinions about divine worship. Now I found a very fit place in a fortress that has its name Bubastis of the Fields which is full of trees of several sorts and full of sacred animals. (67) I request, therefore, that you grant me permission to cleanse this holy place which belongs to no master and is in ruins, and to build there a temple to Almighty God after the pattern of the one in Jerusalem and of the same dimensions, for your benefit, and for your wife and children, so that those Jews who dwell in Egypt may have a place where they may come and meet together in mutual harmony with one another and serve your interests to your advantage. (68) For the prophet Isaiah foretold that 'there shall be an altar in Egypt to the Lord God,'[15] and many other such things did he prophesy relating to that place."

(69) And this was what Onias wrote to King Ptolemy. Now anyone may observe his piety and that of his sister and wife Cleopatra by that

---

10. Ruled 181–146 B.C.E.

11. *Ant.*, XII, 386–388.

12. Cf. Is. 19:18–25.

13. The region between the Lebanon and Anti-Lebanon mountains, known today as the Bekaa Valley. At times this term designated the entirety of Palestine and Phoenicia (present-day Lebanon). Also called Coele-Syria.

14. About 30 miles northeast of Memphis.

15. Is. 19:19

epistle which they wrote in answer to it. For they laid the blame and the transgression of the law upon the head of Onias. And this was their reply: (70) "King Ptolemy and Queen Cleopatra to Onias send greeting. We have read your petition wherein you request permission to be given to you to cleanse that temple which fell down at Leontopolis in the nome of Heliopolis and which is named Bubastis of the Fields. Therefore, we cannot but wonder how it should be pleasing to God to have a temple erected in a place so unclean and so full of sacred animals.[16] (71) But since you say that Isaiah the prophet foretold this long ago, we give you permission to do it, if it may be done according to your law, and so that we may not appear to have at all offended God herein."

(72) So Onias took the place and built a temple and an altar to God, similar indeed to the one in Jerusalem but smaller and less elaborate. I do not think it proper for me now to describe its dimensions or its vessels which have been already described in my seventh book of the *War of the Jews*.[17] (73) However, Onias found other Jews like himself, together with priests and Levites, who performed divine service there. But we have said enough about this temple.

5.2.2 Josephus, *Against Apion* II, 51–5: An Anti-Semitic Pogrom

In 146 B.C.E., at the death of Ptolemy Philometer, there was a struggle over the throne between Ptolemy Physcon, his brother, and his son, Ptolemy VIII, a boy put forward by the king's widow, Cleopatra. Because the Jews supported the queen, Ptolemy Physcon unleashed an anti-Semitic pogrom, the first such event recorded in history. Ptolemy Physcon subsequently killed the boy and married Cleopatra to consolidate his power.

🜋

(51) . . . Ptolemy, who was called Physcon, upon the death of his brother Ptolemy Philometor, came from Cyrene[18] and intended to eject Cleopatra and her sons from their kingdom (52) so that he might unjustly obtain it for himself. For this reason, then, Onias undertook a war against him on Cleopatra's behalf, refusing to desert during the crisis the trust placed in him by the royal family. (53) Accordingly, God gave a remarkable attestation to his righteous action. For when Ptolemy Physcon had the presumption to fight against Onias's army, and had arrested all the Jews

---

16. Full of animals sacred to the Egyptians.
17. *War* VII, 426–32.
18. In North Africa, present-day Tunisia.

in the city [Alexandria] with their children and wives, and exposed them naked and in bonds to his elephants so that they might be trampled to death, and when he had made those elephants drunk for that purpose, the event proved contrary to his intentions. (54) For these elephants left the Jews who were exposed to them, fell violently upon Physcon's friends, and killed a great number of them. Indeed, after this, Ptolemy saw a terrible apparition which prohibited his hurting those men. (55) His concubine whom he loved so well (some call her Ithaca and others Irene) made supplication to him not to perpetrate such great wickedness. So he complied with her request and repented of what he either had already done or was about to do. It is well known that the Alexandrian Jews do with good reason celebrate this day because on it they were granted such an evident deliverance by God.[19]

5.2.3 Josephus, *Antiquities* XIII, 348–55: Cleopatra's Jewish Generals

Jews were active in every walk of life in Hellenistic Egypt. As generals in Cleopatra's army, they were also able to protect their brothers in the Land of Israel, then under Ptolemaic rule. Ananias, her Jewish general, persuaded Cleopatra to conclude an agreement with the Hasmonean ruler, Alexander Janneus, rather than attack him.

༄

(348) When Cleopatra[20] saw that her son[21] had grown great and laid Judea waste without disturbance, and had gotten the city of Gaza under his power, she resolved no longer to overlook what he did.[22] Since he was almost at her gates, she concluded that now he was so much stronger than before, and he would be very desirous of dominion over the Egyptians. (349) So she immediately marched against him, with a fleet at sea and an army of infantry on land, and made the Jews, Chelcias and Ananias, generals of her entire army, while she sent the greatest part of her riches, her grandchildren, and her testament to Cos[23] for safe keeping.

---

19. Cf. 3 Macc. 5–6 where a similar story is told about Ptolemy IV Philopater (222–205 B.C.E.). Both accounts, no doubt, reflect the same historical event.

20. Cleopatra III ruled Egypt from 116–101 B.C.E.

21. Ptolemy VIII Lathyros (Soter II) who ruled with her from 116–108 B.C.E. and again from 88–80.

22. Cleopatra III had ruled jointly with her son, Ptolemy Lathyros, until 108 B.C.E. when she drove him out. After fleeing to Cyprus, he attacked Judea. From there he intended to attack Egypt.

23. An island in the southeast Aegean.

(350) Cleopatra also ordered her son Alexander to sail with a great fleet to Phoenicia. She herself came to Ptolemais, and because the people of Ptolemais did not receive her, she besieged the city. (351) But Ptolemy left Syria and hastened to Egypt, supposing that he would find it left without an army and soon take it, but his hopes were disappointed. At this time Chelcias, one of Cleopatra's generals, died in Celesyria, while he was in pursuit of Ptolemy.

(352) When Cleopatra heard of her son's attempt, and that his Egyptian expedition did not succeed according to his expectations, she sent part of her army there and drove him out of that country. So when he returned from Egypt again, he stayed during the winter at Gaza (353) while Cleopatra took the garrison that was in Ptolemais by siege as well as the city. When Alexander[24] came to her, he gave her presents and such marks of respect as were but proper, since, after the miseries he endured at the hands of Ptolemy, he had no other refuge but her. Now some of her friends advised her to seize Alexander and to overrun and take possession of his country [Judea], and not to sit still and see such an abundance of resources belong to one man, a Jew. (354) But Ananias's counsel was contrary to theirs saying that she would commit an injustice if she deprived a man who was her ally of that authority which belonged to him, especially when this man is related to us. "For (he said) I would not have you ignorant of this, that whatever injustice you do to him will cause all of us Jews to be your enemies." (355) Cleopatra complied with this request of Ananias, and she did no harm to Alexander but made a league of mutual assistance with him at Scythopolis,[25] a city of Celesyria.

5.3 POLITICAL, SOCIAL, AND ECONOMIC DEVELOPMENTS

5.3.1 Josephus, *Antiquities* XII, 119–21: Jews as Seleucid Soldier Citizens

Josephus reports that Jews served in military units of the Seleucid Empire in such locations as Alexandria and Antioch. No doubt these soldiers served as the nucleus of the Jewish communities which developed in these areas. In addition, Jews were granted equal rights of citizenship in the Seleucid Empire.

---

24. Alexander Janneus (103–76 B.C.E.), the Hasmonean ruler
25. Modern Beit Shean where archeologists have found extensive evidence of occupation in the Greco-Roman period.

꩜

(119) The Jews also obtained honors from the kings of Asia when they became their auxiliaries. For Seleucus Nicator[26] made them citizens in those cities which he built in Asia, in Lower Syria and in the capital itself, Antioch. And he gave them privileges equal to those of the Macedonians and Greeks who were the inhabitants, so that this citizenship privilege continues to this very day. (120) Proof of this is the fact that those Jews who do not make use of oil prepared by foreigners receive a certain sum of money from the gymnasiarchs[27] equivalent to the value of that oil. When the people of Antioch proposed to deprive them of this privilege, Mucianus,[28] who was then governor of Syria, preserved it for them. (121) After that, when the people of Alexandria and of Antioch, during the time in which Vespasian[29] and Titus[30] his son governed the habitable earth, asked that these privileges of citizenship might be taken away, they did not obtain their request.

5.3.2 Josephus, *Antiquities* XII, 147–53: Antiochus and the Jews

In order to quell a revolt in Lydia and Phrygia in Asia Minor, King Antiochus III, the Great (223–187 B.C.E.), proposed to use two thousand Jewish families from Babylonia as a stabilizing factor. Josephus sees this as a proof of the high regard in which the king held the Jews.

꩜

(147) Moreover, Antiochus bore testimony to our piety and fidelity in his epistle written when he was informed of revolts in Phrygia and Lydia while he was in the upper provinces, wherein he commanded Zeuxis,[31] the general of his forces and his most intimate friend, to send some of our nation out of Babylon into Phrygia. The epistle was as follows:

(148) "King Antiochus to Zeuxis, His Father,[32] sends Greeting.

---

26. The founder of the Seleucid dynasty, ruled 312–280 B.C.E.

27. In the Hellenistic period, the supervisor of the gymnasium was a central figure in the *polis*. He distributed olive oil since in athletic training and competition, athletes covered their bodies with it to keep off dust.

28. Licinius Mucianus, Roman governor of Syria, 67–69 C.E.

29. 69–79 C.E.

30. 79–81 C.E.

31. Governor of Babylonia.

32. A title of honor.

"If you are in good health, it is well. I am also in good health. (149) Having been informed that a revolt has arisen in Lydia and Phrygia, I thought that matter required great care. Upon talking with my friends[33] as to what was to be done, it has been thought proper to remove two thousand families of Jews with their property out of Mesopotamia and Babylon into the fortresses and places that are most important. (150) For I am persuaded that they will be loyal guardians of our possessions because of their piety towards God and because I know that my predecessors have borne witness regarding them that they are faithful and that they do what they are asked to do with alacrity. It is my will, therefore, though it be a laborious job, that you remove these Jews under a promise that they shall be permitted to observe their own laws.

(151) You shall give every one of their families a place for building their houses and a portion of land for their husbandry and for the plantation of their vines, and you shall exempt them from paying taxes on the produce of the earth for ten years. (152) Let them have a proper quantity of wheat for the maintenance of their servants until they get produce out of the earth. Also let a sufficient share be given to those engaged in public service so that by enjoying our kind treatment, they may show themselves the more willing and ready about our affairs. (153) Take care likewise of that nation, as far as you are able, that they may not have any disturbance caused them by anyone."

Now these testimonials, which I have produced, are sufficient to declare the friendship that Antiochus the Great bore to the Jews.

5.3.3 Josephus, *Antiquities* XIV, 185–267: Jewish Legal Status in the Roman World

Josephus emphasizes the positive regard that the rulers of the ancient world had for the Jews while they maintained a kingdom of their own. This positive outlook even extended to the Diaspora which by now was established in all the major cities of the Roman Empire. Josephus here reproduces the official documents testifying to the privileges extended to the Jews in these various places. The authenticity of some of these decrees has been questioned by scholars as it was common in ancient times for such documents to be forged for obvious political reasons.

---

33. The "friends" of the king constituted his council of advisors.

❧

(185) Now when (Julius) Caesar came to Rome,[34] he was ready to sail into Africa to fight against Scipio and Cato when Hyrcanus[35] sent ambassadors to him, and through them requested that he continue the league of friendship and mutual alliance between them. (186) It seems to me to be necessary here to give an account of all the honors that the Romans and their emperors paid to our nation, and of the alliances of mutual assistance they have made with it, so that all the rest of humanity may know what regard the kings of Asia and Europe have had for us, and that they have been abundantly satisfied by our courage and fidelity. (187) For whereas many will not believe what has been written about us by the Persians and Macedonians because those writings are not everywhere to be found, nor are they deposited in public places but among us ourselves and certain other barbarous nations,[36] (188) there is no contradiction to be raised against the decrees of the Romans, for they are kept in the public places of the cities and are extant still in the capitol, and engraved upon pillars of brass. Indeed, besides this, Julius Caesar made a pillar of brass for the Jews at Alexandria and declared publicly that they were citizens of Alexandria. (189) From these documents I will demonstrate what I say and will now set down the decrees made both by the senate and by Julius Caesar which relate to Hyrcanus and to our nation.

(190) "Gaius Julius Caesar, imperator[37] and high priest, and dictator the second time, to the magistrates, senate, and people of Sidon, sends greeting. If you are in good health, it is well. I and the army are also well. (191) I have sent you a copy of that decree, inscribed on a tablet, which concerns Hyrcanus, the son of Alexander,[38] the high priest and ethnarch of the Jews, so that it may be deposited among the public records, and it is my will that it be openly set up on a tablet of brass both in Greek and in Latin.

(192) "It is as follows: 'I, Julius Caesar, imperator the second time and high priest, have made this decree with the approbation of the senate: Whereas Hyrcanus, the son of Alexander the Jew, has demonstrated his

---

34. Summer, 47 B.C.E.

35. Hyrcanus II, high priest after the Roman conquest of 63 B.C.E.

36. I.e., non-Greek-speaking nations.

37. Originally a generic term for a Roman commander, Imperator came to denote the autocratic supreme ruler of the Roman empire, similar in meaning to its English cognate "Emperor."

38. Hyrcanus II was the son of Alexander Janneus.

fidelity and diligence about our affairs both now and in former times, both in peace and in war, as many of our generals have borne witness, (193) and came to our assistance in the last Alexandrian war with fifteen hundred soldiers; and when he was sent by me to Mithridates[39] showed himself superior in valor to all the rest of that army; (194) for these reasons it is my will that Hyrcanus, the son of Alexander, and his children, be ethnarchs of the Jews and hold the office of high priest of the Jews forever according to the customs of their forefathers, and that he and his son be our allies; and that besides this, every one of them be reckoned among our particular friends. (195) I also ordain that he and his children retain whatever privileges belong to the office of high priest, or whatever favors have been hitherto granted them. If at any time hereafter there arise any questions about the Jewish customs, it is my will that he determine the same. And I think it not proper that they should be obligated to find us winter quarters or that any money should be required from them.'"

(196) "The decrees of Gaius Caesar, consul, containing what has been granted and determined, are as follows: That Hyrcanus and his children should rule over the nation of the Jews and have the profits of the places bequeathed to them; and that he, as himself the high priest and ethnarch of the Jews, should defend those Jews who are unjustly treated; (197) and that ambassadors be sent to Hyrcanus, the son of Alexander the high priest of the Jews, who may discuss with him an alliance of friendship and mutual assistance; and that a tablet of brass, containing these decrees, be openly set up in the capitol, and at Sidon, Tyre, and Askelon, and in the temple, engraved in Latin and Greek letters; (198) that this decree may also be communicated to the quaestors[40] and praetors[41] of the several cities and to the friends of the Jews; and that the ambassadors should have hospitality shown to them, and that these decrees should be sent everywhere."

(200) "Gaius Caesar, consul the fifth time,[42] has decreed that the Jews shall possess Jerusalem and may encompass that city with walls; and that Hyrcanus, the son of Alexander, the high priest and ethnarch of the Jews, retain it in the manner he himself chooses. (201) And the Jews may be allowed to deduct out of their tribute, in the second year of the rent period [of the seven-year Sabbatical cycle], one kor[43] of that tribute. . . ."

---

39. Mithridates of Pergamum (in Asia Minor) came to the aid of Caesar in Egypt in 47 B.C.E. and he in turn received support from Hyrcanus and Antipater.

40. Roman magistrates of low rank who often had financial responsibilities.

41. Roman magistrates or military officials who often became governors of provinces or legates of legions.

42. 44 B.C.E.

43. Approximately 370 litres or 11 bushels.

(202) "Gaius Caesar, imperator the second time,[44] has ordained that all the country of the Jews, except Joppa,[45] pay a tribute yearly for the city Jerusalem, excepting the seventh, which they call the Sabbatical Year, because thereon they neither take the fruits from their trees nor do they sow their land; (203) and that they pay their tribute in Sidon[46] on the second year [of that Sabbatical period] consisting of a quarter of what was sown. Besides this, they are to pay the same tithes to Hyrcanus and his sons which they paid to their forefathers. (204) And no one, neither magistrate, nor praetor, nor legate, may raise auxiliaries within the bounds of Judea, nor may soldiers exact money from them for winter quarters or under any other pretense, but they shall be free from all sorts of molestation. (205) Whatever they shall hereafter have, are in possession of, or have bought, they shall retain. It is also our pleasure that the city of Joppa, which the Jews had originally when they made an alliance of friendship with the Romans, shall belong to them as it formerly did; (206) and that Hyrcanus, the son of Alexander, and his sons have as tribute of that city from those who occupy the land, for the country and for what they export every year to Sidon, twenty thousand six hundred and seventy-five modii[47] every year, the seventh year, which they call the Sabbatical Year, excepted, whereon they neither plow nor receive the product of their trees.

(207) "It is also the pleasure of the senate that, as to the villages which are in the great plain[48] which Hyrcanus and his forefathers formerly possessed, Hyrcanus and the Jews shall have them with the same privileges with which they formerly had them; (208) and that the same original ordinances still remain in force concerning the Jews with regard to their high priests; and that they enjoy the same benefits which they have had formerly by the vote of the people and of the senate; and let them enjoy the privileges in Lydda[49] also. (209) It is the pleasure also of the senate that Hyrcanus the ethnarch and the Jews retain those places, countries, and villages which belonged to the kings of Syria and Phoenicia as allies of the Romans and which they had bestowed on them as their free gifts. (210) It is also granted to Hyrcanus and to his sons, and to the ambassadors sent to us by them, that in the fights between single gladiators and in those with beasts, they shall sit among the senators to see those shows; and that when

---

44. 47 B.C.E.

45. Modern-day Jaffa, south of Tel Aviv on the Mediterranean coast.

46. A city on the coast of Lebanon.

47. A measure of grain.

48. The plain of Esdraelon, the Jezreel valley in northern Israel.

49. Hebrew Lod, a town on the coastal plain of Israel, 10 miles southeast of present day Tel Aviv.

they desire an audience, they shall be introduced into the senate by the dictator or by the general of the horse; and when they have introduced them, their answers shall be returned to them in ten days at the most, after the decree of the senate is made about their affairs. . . ."

(213) "Julius Gaius, praetor, consul of the Romans, to the magistrates, senate, and people of Parium,[50] sends greeting. The Jews of Delos[51] and some other Jews who sojourn there in the presence of your ambassadors, signified to us that, by a decree of yours, you forbid them from observing the customs of their forefathers and their way of sacred worship. (214) Now it does not please me that such decrees should be made against our friends and allies whereby they are forbidden to live according to their own customs or to contribute money for common meals and holy festivals, for they are not forbidden to do so even in Rome itself. (215) For even Gaius[52] Caesar, our imperator and consul, in that decree wherein he forbade the religious societies to meet in the city, did yet permit these Jews and these only, both to collect contributions and to hold their common meals. (216) Accordingly, when I forbid other religious societies, I permit these Jews to gather together and feast according to the customs and laws of their forefathers. It will therefore be good for you that if you have made any decree against these our friends and allies, to abrogate the same by reason of their virtue and good will towards us. . . ."

(256) The decree of the people of Halicarnassus.[53] "When Memnon, the son of Orestidas by descent, but by adoption (the son) of Euonymus, was priest, on the [. . .] day of the month Anthasterion,[54] the decree of the people upon the motion of Marcus Alexander was this: (257) 'Since we have ever a great regard to piety towards God and to holiness; and since we aim to follow the people of the Romans who are the benefactors of all men, and what they have written to us about an alliance of friendship and mutual assistance between the Jews and our city to the effect that their sacred services and accustomed festivals and assemblies may be observed by them; (258) we have decreed that as many men and women of the Jews as are willing to do so may celebrate their Sabbaths and perform their sacred rites according to the Jewish laws; and may make their places of prayer at the seaside,[55] according to the customs of their forefa-

---

50. On the coast of the Troad, east of the Hellespont. This may also refer to the island of Paros about 10 miles south of Delos.

51. An island in the Aegean Sea.

52. Julius Caesar whose first name was Gaius.

53. A Greek city in southwestern Asia Minor.

54. February/March. The day of the month is missing in the text.

55. It was customary in the Hellenistic world to build synagogues at the seashore.

thers. If anyone, whether he be a magistrate or a private person, hinders them from so doing, he shall be liable to a fine to be applied to the uses of the city.'"

(259) The decree of the people of Sardis:[56] "This decree was made by the senate and people upon the representation of the praetors: 'Whereas those Jews who are our fellow citizens and live with us in this city have always had great privileges bestowed upon them by the people, and have come now before the senate (260) and the people, and have requested that, upon the restitution of their law and their liberty by the senate and people of Rome, they may assemble together according to their ancient legal custom and adjudicate suits among themselves,[57] and that a place may be given them where they may have their congregations with their wives and children, and that they may offer, as did their forefathers, their prayers and offerings to God; (261) now the senate and people have decreed to permit them to assemble together on the days formerly appointed according to their own laws;[58] and that a place be set apart for them by the praetors for them to build and inhabit[59] as they shall deem fit for that purpose; and that the market officials of the city shall take care that such sorts of food as they esteem fit for their eating[60] may be imported into the city.'"

(262) The decree of the people of Ephesus:[61] "When Menophilus was president, on the first day of the month Artemision,[62] this decree was made by the people, and Nicanor, the son of Euphemus, pronounced it upon the representation of the praetors. (263) 'Since the Jews that dwell in this city have petitioned Marcus Julius Pomperus, the son of Brutus, the proconsul,[63] that they might be allowed to observe their Sabbaths and to act in all things according to the customs of their forefathers without impediment from anyone, the praetor (proconsul) has granted their petition. (264) Accordingly, it was decreed by the senate and people that since this affair concerns the Romans, none of them should be hindered

---

56. A city in western Asia Minor where a synagogue was found closely integrated with other city institutions, showing that the Jewish community was well integrated with their neighbors.

57. The Jews had independent courts to judge their disputes according to Jewish practice.

58. The Sabbath and festivals.

59. That is, for a synagogue and community facilities.

60. In accordance with the laws pertaining to kosher food.

61. A city on the west coast of Asia Minor. A Jewish community thrived there, and the apostle Paul accordingly visited this city to establish Christianity there.

62. March 24 on the Roman calendar.

63. Probably Marcus Brutus who was in Asia in 42 B.C.E.

from keeping the Sabbath day nor be fined for so doing; but that they may be allowed to do all things according to their own laws.'"

(265) There are many other such decrees of the senate and imperators of the Romans which have been made in favor of Hyrcanus and of our nation. Also there have been more decrees of the cities and rescripts of the provincial governors to such epistles as concerned our rights and privileges. Certainly all who are not ill-disposed to what we write may believe on faith that they are all to this purpose, based on the specimens which we have included. (266) For since we have produced clear proofs that may still be seen of the friendship we have had with the Romans, and demonstrated that those decrees are engraved upon columns and tablets of brass in the capitol that are still preserved to this day, we have refrained from setting them all down since it is both needless and disagreeable. (267) For I cannot suppose anyone so perverse as not to believe the friendship we have had with the Romans since they have demonstrated the same by such a great number of their decrees relating to us. Nor will they doubt our fidelity as to the rest of these decrees since we have shown the same on the basis of the examples we have produced. And thus we have sufficiently explained the friendship and alliance we had with the Romans at those times.

5.4 RELIGIOUS LIFE

5.4.1 Inscriptions from the Catacombs: Evidence of Jewish Religious Life in Rome[64]

The Jewish catacombs are underground cemeteries dating from the first to the fourth century C.E., rediscovered at the beginning of the 16th century and continuously excavated and published through the 20th century. The inscriptions found there are representative of a Diaspora Jewish community which was established in the first century B.C.E. and became a large element in the population of the city. There was a more or less tolerant attitude by the rulers of the Roman Empire to the Jews in Rome. This positive attitude flourished as long as Rome itself was the prosperous capital of the Empire.

---

64. Trans. H. J. Leon, *The Jews of Ancient Rome*, updated edition, with appendix by C. Osiek (Peabody, MA: Hendrickson, 1995, originally published 1960), Appendix of Inscriptions, pp. 263–346.

৵৻

The presence of proselytes in the community is evident from the following tomb-stone carved on marble, written in Greek:

Irene, foster child, proselyte, her father and mother Jewish, an Israelite, lived 3 years, 7 months, 1 day.[65]

Here is a stone erected by a gerusiarch, head of a local Jewish council of elders:

To the virgin, Dulcitia, bride-to-be. Pancharius, the Gerusiarch, set up (this stone) to his daughter. In peace your sleep.[66]

This inscription is accompanied by a menorah carved into the stone:

Alexander, a butcher from the market, who lived 30 years, a good soul, friend of everyone. Your sleep among the righteous.[67]

This funerary inscription also features a menorah and another unidentified object.

Marcia, a good Jewess. Your sleep among the just.[68]

This inscription indicates the respect accorded to those who observe the commandments and supported the poor:

[...] lover of his people, lover of the Commandments (?), lover of the poor. [In peace] the sleep of the [...].[69]

The presence of a synagogue is indicated in this inscription:

[...] of the Synagogue of Elea,[70] lived 80 years. Sleep well among the just.[71]

The Synagogue of the Augustesians cannot be definitely located, but reference to it has been found in six inscriptions which mention a scribe and archon-designate of the congregation, Annius, the gerusiarch, an archon, a life archon, and a Mother of the Synagogue. The congregation might have been named for the Emperor Augustus, a friend of the Jews and perhaps patron of the community.

---

65. Leon, p. 267.
66. Leon, p. 279.
67. Leon, pp. 293–4.
68. Leon, p. 300.
69. Leon, p. 292.
70. It is uncertain whether this is a place name or an allusion to the prophet Elijah.
71. Leon, p. 305.

Here lies Annius, the Gerusiarch of the Synagogue of the Auguste-sians. In peace his sleep.[72]

This inscription appears in Aramaic and Greek and mentions an annually elected synagogue official, termed the archon. This was a common designation in the catacombs although scholars cannot determine what the duties of this official were.

Isidora, daughter of the Archon of the Hebrews.[73]

"The memory of the righteous is for a blessing" is a biblical formula quoted from Prov. 10:7.

Here lies Macedonius, the Hebrew, a Caesarean of Palestine, son of Alexander. The memory of the righteous is for a blessing. In peace your sleep.[74]

In this inscription featuring the Jewish symbols shofar, lulav, and menorah, "Peace on Israel" is written in Hebrew:

Here lies Sabbatius, twice Archon. He lived 35 years. In peace his sleep. Peace on Israel.[75]

The epitaph of Regina, composed by her sorrowing husband, is the most elabo-rate of all the inscriptions found in the Jewish catacombs. It was composed in Latin in the poetic form of dactylic hexameter.

Here lies Regina, covered by this tomb,
Which, to reveal his love, her husband raised.
A score of years plus one, four months, and eight
Days more she spent in wedlock by his side.
Again she'll live, again will see the light;
For she may hope that she will rise aloft
To that eternal life which is ordained,
As our true faith doth teach, for all the worthy
And all the pious.[76] She has merited
To find a home in that most hallowed land.[77]
This is assured thee by thy piety,
Thy life so chaste, the love of all thy people,
Observance of our Law, and faithfulness
Unto our marriage bond, which thou didst strive

---

72. Leon, p. 308.
73. Leon, p. 307.
74. Leon, p. 319.
75. Leon, p. 325.
76. This text reveals faith in immortal life for the virtuous and pious.
77. Paradise.

Ever to glorify. For all these deeds
Thy future bliss is certain. In this faith
Thy sorrowing husband finds his only comfort.[78]

Carved on a sarcophagus, this epitaph includes "Mother of the Synagogue,"
either an honorary title given to a woman or the designation of a female official of
the community. This woman, after converting to Judaism sixteen years before her
death, took the biblical name Sara, as was later customary in Jewish tradition.

Veturia Paulla F (?), consigned to her eternal home, who lived 86 years,
6 months, a proselyte of 16 years, named Sara, Mother of the Synagogues
of Campus and Volumnius. In peace her sleep.[79]

5.4.2 Dedicatory Inscriptions:
Evidence of Jewish Religious Life in Hellenistic Egypt[80]

Another place in which the Jews lived in large numbers in Late Antiquity
was Egypt. These inscriptions show evidence of integration into the fabric of
Egyptian society and the existence of particularly Jewish institutions such as
synagogues.

§

The following inscription was written on a marble dedication plaque at Athribis,
Egypt in the 2nd or 1st century B.C.E:

On behalf of King Ptolemy and Queen Cleopatra, Ptolemy son of
Epikydes, chief of police, and the Jews in Athribis (dedicated) the proseuche[81] to the Most High God.[82]

This inscription was carved into a limestone stele in Arsinoe-Crocodilopolis,
present-day Medinet el-Fayum, sometime between 246 and 221 B.C.E. Along
with Jewish names on tax lists, contracts, and a land survey mentioning a proseuche,
it is evidence that Arsinoe-Crocodilopolis had a significant Jewish population.

On behalf of King Ptolemy, son of Ptolemy, and Queen Berenice his
wife and sister and their children, the Jews in Crocodilopolis (dedicated)
the proseuche. . . .[83]

---

78. Leon, pp. 248–9; 334–5.
79. Leon, p. 341.
80. Trans. W. Horbury and D. Noy, *Jewish Inscriptions of Graeco-Roman Egypt* (Cambridge: Cambridge University Press, 1992).
81. Prayer hall.
82. Horbury and Noy, p. 45.
83. Horbury and Noy, p. 201.

Two thanksgiving dedications were found on rocks at the Temple of Pan at El-Kanais in the desert east of Apollinopolis Magna, present-day Edfu in Upper (Southern) Egypt. They date from either the 2nd or 1st century B.C.E. It is curious that Jews offered dedications at the Temple of Pan. Perhaps this practice was a result of syncretism, or it is possible that they were required to make contributions to pagan temples.

Bless God. Theodotus son of Dorion, the Jew, returned safely from overseas [*or* saved from the sea].[84]

Praise God. Ptolemy, son of Dionysios, the Jew.[85]

This inscription from a marble stele dates from approximately 79 B.C.E. and was found in Hermopolis Magna, present day El-Ashmunein. This is another example of the appearance of Jewish names in pagan inscriptions:

On behalf of King Ptolemy and Queen Cleopatra also called Tryphaina, the Father-loving and Brother-loving Gods, the foreign soldiers of Apollonia (?) on guard in Hermopolis and their fellow-citizens, the founders, whose names are listed below, (dedicated) to Apollo and Zeus and the associated gods the shrine and the precinct and all the appurtenances. In the second year. . . .

. . . Hyrcanus son of Ptolemy . . . Chabas[86] son of Herophon . . . Apollodorus son of Zabbdelos[87] . . . Ptolemy son of Dositheus[88] . . .

This inscription describes the honoring of a woman benefactor to the synagogue of Phocaea in Asia Minor (Turkey). Here the term "synagogue" refers not to a building but to a congregation of Jews.

Tation, daughter of Straton, son of Empedon, having erected the assembly hall and the enclosure of the open courtyard with her own funds, gave them as a gift to the Jews. The synagogue of the Jews honored Tation, daughter of Straton, Son of Empedon, with a golden crown and the privilege of sitting in the seat of honor.[89]

This inscription from Apamea, Syria dates from the year 391 C.E:

Under the three most honored *archisynagogi*,[90] Eusebios, Nemeos, and Phineas, the gerousiarch Theodorus and the three most honored elders,

---

84. Horbury and Noy, p. 207.

85. Horbury and Noy, p. 209.

86. Possibly a Jewish name.

87. A name of non-Hebrew origin much used by Jews.

88. Horbury and Noy, p. 247. Dositheus was an almost exclusively Jewish name in Ptolemaic Egypt.

89. Trans. L. H. Feldman, "Diaspora Synagogues," in *Sacred Realm*, ed. S. Fine (Oxford: Oxford University Press; New York: Yeshiva University Museum, 1996), p. 54.

90. A term for the head of the synagogue or perhaps benefactor.

Isakios, Saulos, and others, Ilasios, the *archisynagogos* of Antioch, made the mosaic of the entrance [of the synagogue], 150 feet; the year 703, the 7th day of Audunaios. Blessing to all.[91]

An inscription from Smyrna, modern Izmir on the western coast of Asia Minor, attests to a wealthy woman who, acting alone and in her own name, built a tomb for her ex-slaves:

Rufina, a Jewess, head of the synagogue, built the tomb for her freed slaves and the slaves raised in her house. No one else has the right to bury anyone [here]. If someone should dare to, he will pay 1,500 denarii to the sacred treasury and 1,000 denarii to the Jewish people. A copy of this inscription has been placed in the [public] archives.[92]

5.4.3 The Aphrodisias Inscription: Evidence for God-Fearers[93]

This inscription, found at Aphrodisias in Asia Minor, dates most probably to the third century C.E. It shows without any doubt that semi-proselytes, also termed God-fearers, non-Jews attracted to Jewish rituals, existed in the Greco-Roman world, and that they were among its aristocracy. The text clearly differentiates "sympathizers" from both Jews and proselytes, full converts to Judaism.

꽃

FACE A: God our help. Building [?] for the soup kitchen [?].[94] Below [are] listed the [members] of the decany[95] of the disciples of the law, also known as those who fervently praise God, [who] erected, for the relief of suffering for the community, at their personal expense, [this] memorial [building]:

Jael,[96] president, with son Joshua, magistrate [in margin: Samuel, elder, from Perge];[97] Theodotus, employee of the [emperor's] court, with son Ilarianos; Samuel leader of the decany [?], a proselyte; Ioses [i.e. Joseph] son of Iesseos; Benjamin psalm-singer [?]; Judas good-tempered; Ioses

---

91. Feldman, "Diaspora Synagogues," p. 53.

92. Feldman, "Diaspora Synagogues," p. 56.

93. Trans. L. H. Feldman, *Jewish Life and Thought among Greeks and Romans*, ed. L. H. Feldman and M. Reinhold (Minneapolis: Fortress Press, 1996), pp. 142–3.

94. Apparently the reference is to a dish used for the daily collection of cooked food for the poor. The word here translated "soup kitchen" may stand for the distribution station for charity food.

95. The decany is apparently ten men who insure that a quorum will always be on hand for prayer and other ritual purposes. It may also refer to a benevolent society.

96. Maybe a woman's name as women were given titles of high synagogue office.

97. A city in Pamphylia in Asia Minor.

[i.e. Joseph] a proselyte; Sabbatios son of Amachios; Emmonios 'God-fearer'; Antoninos 'God-fearer'; Samuel son of Politianos; Joseph a prose-lyte son of Eusebios; and Judas son of Theodoros; and Antipeos son of Hermes; and Sabathios fragrant;[98] and Samuel old priest.

FACE B: . . . son of Serapion; Joseph son of Zenon; Zenon Jacob; Manasseh Job [?]; Judas son of Eusebios; Eortasios son of Kallikarpos; Biotikos; Judas son of Amphianos; Eugenios goldsmith; Praoilios; Judas son of Praoilios; Rufus; Oxucholios an old man; Amantios son of Chari-nos; Murtilos Jacob shepherd [?]; Seberos; Euodos; Jason son of Euodos; Eusabbathios greengrocer [?]; Anusios Eusabbathios an immigrant; Milon Oxucholios the younger; Diogenes; Eusabbathios son of Diogenes; Judas son of Paulos; Theophilos; Jacob and Apellion; Zacharias retailer [?]; Leontios son of Leontios; Gemellos; Judas son of Acholios; Damonikos; Eutarkios son of Judas; Joseph son of Philer [?]; Eusabbathios son of Euge-nios; Kurillos; Eutuchios bronze-smith [?]; Joseph confectioner [?]; Rouben confectioner [?]; Judas son of Ortasios; Eutuchios poulterer [?]; Judas and Zosi [?]; Zenon rag-dealer [?]; Ammianos dealer in horse-fod-der[99] [?]; Ailianos son of Ailianos; Ailianos and Samuel Philanthos; Gor-gionos son of Oxucholios; Eortasios son of Achilleus; Eusabbathios son of Oxucholios; Pareforios; Eortasios son of Aotikos; Simon Zen [?] . . . ; and as many as are God-fearers: Zenon councillor; Tertullos councillor; Diogenes councillor; Onesimos councillor; Zenon son of Longianos [?] councillor; Antipeos councillor; Antiochos councillor; Romanos council-lor; Aponerios councillor; Eupithios purple-dyer; Strategios; Xanthos; Xanthos son of Xanthos; Aponerios son of Aponerios; Hupsikles ink-maker [?]; Poluchronios son of Xanthos; Athenion son of Ailianos [?]; Kallimorphos son of Kallimorphos [?]; Iounbalos; Tuchikos son of Tuchi-kos; Glegorios son of Tuchikos; Poluchronios missile-maker [?]; Chrusip-pos; Gorgonios bronze-smith [?]; Tatianos son of Oxucholios [?]; Apellas son of Hegemoneus [?]; Balerianos maker of wooden tablets [?]; Eusab-bathios son of Heduchrous [?]; Manikos [?] son of Attalos [?]; Ortasios stone-cutter [?]; Brabeus; Klaudianos son of Kallimorphos [?]; Alexandros boxer [?]; Appianos marble-worker [?]; Adolios maker of mincemeat; Zotikos armlet-maker [?]; Zotikos Grullos [?]; Eupithios son of Eupi-thios; Patrikios bronze-smith; Elpidianos athlete [?]; Heduchrous; Eutro-pios son of Heduchrous [?]; Kallinikos; Balerianos treasurer [?]; Euretos son of Athenagoras; Paranomos image-painter [?]; Eutuchianos fuller; Prokopios money-changer [?]; Pounikios fuller; Stratonikos fuller; Ath-enagoras carpenter; Meliton son of Amazonios. . . .

---

98. This may be a second name or a descriptive adjective.
99. Or perhaps stitcher, braider, plaiter.

5.5 ANTI-SEMITISM IN THE HELLENISTIC WORLD

5.5.1 Tacitus, *Historiae* V, 4–5: Jewish Origins and Rituals[100]

Roman writers continually wondered about the nature of Judaism which seemed so strange to them, the origins of the Jewish people and the role of Moses. They often combined a hatred of the Jews as a minority group with misinformation about their rites, and the claim that they were xenophobic, resulting in a grotesque presentation of Jewish customs. Typical of this trend is Tacitus, a Latin historian who lived between 56 and 118 C.E., and who held government posts in Rome and various places in the empire.

꽃

4:1 To establish his influence over this people for all time, Moses introduced new religious practices, quite opposed to those of all other religions. The Jews regard as profane all that we hold sacred; on the other hand, they permit all that we abhor. 2 They dedicated, in a shrine, a statue of that creature whose guidance enabled them to put an end to their wandering and thirst, sacrificing a ram, apparently in derision of Ammon.[101] They likewise offer the ox, because the Egyptians worship Apis.[102] They abstain from pork, in recollection of a plague, for the scab to which this animal is subject once afflicted them. 3 By frequent fasts, even now they bear witness to the long hunger with which they were once distressed, and the unleavened Jewish bread is still employed in memory of the haste with which they seized the grain. They say that they first chose to rest on the seventh day because that day they ended their toils; but after a time they were led by the charms of indolence to give over the seventh year as well to inactivity. 4 Others say that this is done in honor of Saturn, whether it be that the primitive elements of their religion were given by the Idaeans,[103] who, according to tradition, were expelled with Saturn and became the founders of the Jewish race, or is due to the fact that, of the seven planets that rule the fortunes of mankind, Saturn moves in the highest orbit and has the greatest potency; and that many of the heavenly bodies traverse their paths and courses in multiples of seven.

---

100. Trans. C. H. Moore, *Tacitus III: Histories 4–5 and Annals 1–3* (Loeb Classical Library; Cambridge: Harvard University Press, 1931), pp. 179–85.

101. The ancient Egyptian god Amun, pictured as a ram.

102. A sacred bull in ancient Egyptian religion.

103. Ida was the name of a mountain in Crete, and it was falsely believed by some that the term Iudaeus, "Judean," was derived from this name.

5:1 Whatever their origin, these rites are maintained by their antiquity: the other customs of the Jews are base and abominable, and owe their persistence to their depravity. For the worst rascals among other peoples, renouncing their ancestral religions, always kept sending tribute and contributions to Jerusalem, thereby increasing the wealth of the Jews; again, the Jews are extremely loyal toward one another, and always ready to show compassion, but toward every other people they feel only hate and enmity. 2 They sit apart at meals, and they sleep apart, and although as a race they are prone to lust, they abstain from intercourse with foreign women; yet among themselves, nothing is unlawful. They adopted circumcision to distinguish themselves from other peoples by this difference. Those who are converted to their ways follow the same practice, and the earliest lesson they receive is to despise the gods, to disown their country, and to regard their parents, children and brothers as of little account. 3 However, they take thought to increase their numbers; for they regard it as a crime to kill any late-born child, and they believe that the souls of those who are killed in battle or by the executioner are immortal: hence comes their passion for begetting children, and their scorn of death. They bury the body rather than burn it, thus following the Egyptians' custom; they likewise bestow the same care on the dead, and hold the same belief about the world below; but their ideas of heavenly things are quite the opposite. 4 The Egyptians worship many animals and monstrous images; the Jews conceive of one god only, and that with the mind alone: they regard as impious those who make from perishable materials representations of gods in man's image; that supreme and eternal being is to them incapable of representation and without end. Therefore they set up no statues in their cities, still less in their temples; this flattery is not paid their kings, nor this honor given to the Caesars.[104] 5 But since their priests used to chant to the accompaniment of pipes and cymbals and to wear garlands of ivy, and because a golden vine was found in their temple, some thought that they were devotees of Father Liber,[105] the conqueror of the East, in spite of the incongruity of their customs. For Liber established festive rites of a joyous nature, while the ways of the Jews are preposterous and mean.

---

104. They do not make statues of rulers.

105. An Italian god of fertility, especially of wine, later commonly identified with Dionysus.

5.5.2 Plutarch, *Questiones Convivales* IV, Question 5: The Jewish Abstention from Pork[106]

Plutarch, ca. 46-ca. 120 C.E., was a philosopher, biographer, and priest at Delphi, Greece who traveled extensively in the Roman Empire. He was most interested in ancient religions.

ॐ

Whether the Jews abstain from eating pork because of reverence or aversion for the pig.

1. When he had finished, and some of those present would have made an extended reply to his arguments, Callistratus headed them off by saying, "What do you think of the assertion that it is precisely the most proper type of meat that the Jews avoid eating?"

"I heartily agree with it," replied Polycrates, "but I have another question: do they abstain from eating pork by reason of some special respect for hogs of from abhorrence of the creature? Their own accounts sound like pure myth, but perhaps they have some serious reasons which they do not publish."

2. "My impression," said Callistratus, "is that the beast enjoys a certain respect among that folk; granted he is ugly and dirty, still he is no more absurd in appearance or crude in disposition than dung-beetle, field mouse, crocodile, or cat, each of which is treated as sacred by a different group of Egyptian priests. . . .

So I think the Jews would kill pigs if they hated them, as the Magi kill water mice; but in fact it is just as unlawful for Jews to destroy pigs as to eat them. Perhaps it is consistent that they should revere the pig who taught them sowing and plowing, inasmuch as they honor the ass who first led them to a spring of water. Otherwise, so help me, someone will say that the Jews abstain from the hare because they can't stomach anything so filthy and unclean."

3 . . . "The Jews apparently abominate pork because barbarians especially abhor skin diseases like lepra[107] and white scale, and believe that human beings are ravaged by such maladies through contagion. Now we observe that every pig is covered on the underside by lepra and scaly eruptions, which, if there is a general weakness and emaciation, are thought to

---

106. Trans. H. B. Hoffleit, *Plutarch's Moralia VIII* (Loeb Classical Library; Cambridge: Harvard University Press, 1969), pp. 351–9.

107. Leprosy.

spread rapidly over the body. What is more, the very filthiness of their habits produces an inferior quality of meat. We observe no other creature so fond of mud and of dirty, unclean places, if we leave out of account those animals that have their origin and natural habitat there.

5.5.3 Seneca, *De Superstitione*: Popularity of Jewish Ethics[108]

Seneca, the Younger, ca. 5 B.C.E.–65 C.E., Stoic philosopher and advisor to the emperor Nero, testifies to the widespread influence of Judaism in the Roman world.

இ

But when speaking of the Jews he says: "Meanwhile the customs of this accursed race have gained such influence that they are now received throughout all the world. The vanquished have given laws to their victors." He shows his surprise as he says this, not knowing what was being wrought by the providence of God. But he adds a statement that shows what he thought of their system of sacred institutions: "The Jews, however, are aware of the origin and meaning of their rites. The greater part of the people go through a ritual not knowing why they do so."

5.5.4 Juvenal, *Satires* XIV, 96–106: Judaism as a Mystery Religion[109]

Juvenal was a Roman satirist who lived ca. 60–130 C.E., and wrote at about the same time as Tacitus, but details of his private life are unknown. This passage shows the widespread observance of Jewish rituals in the Greco-Roman world even by non-Jews.

இ

Some who have had a father who reveres the Sabbath, worship nothing but the clouds, and the divinity of the heavens, and see no difference between eating swine's flesh, from which their father abstained, and that of man; and in time they take to circumcision. Having been wont to flout the laws of Rome, they learn and practice and revere the Jewish law, and all that Moses handed down in his secret tome forbidding to point out

---

108. This selection is quoted by Augustine, trans. W. M. Green, *Saint Augustine: The City of God Against the Pagans* II (Loeb Classical Library; Cambridge: Harvard University Press, 1963), p. 361.

109. Trans. G. G. Ramsey, *Juvenal and Persius* (Loeb Classical Library; Cambridge, Harvard University Press, 1940), pp. 271–3.

the way to any not worshipping the same rites, and conducting none but the circumcised to the desired fountain. For all which the father was to blame, who gave up every seventh day to idleness, keeping it apart from all the concerns of life.

5.6 THE LITERATURE OF THE HELLENISTIC DIASPORA

5.6.1 Philo, *Embassy to Gaius* 132–4, 349–67: The Attitude of Gaius toward the Jews[110]

After an anti-Semitic pogrom, a delegation of Jews visited Gaius, emperor from 37–41 C.E., but his hostile attitude was immediately apparent, and the Jews were unable to secure any protection from him. Gaius demanded exceptional homage and was savage if his superiority was not recognized. The refusal of the Jews to consider him a god must have been highly irritating to him.

🕊

(132) But as the governor of the country, who by himself could, if he had chosen to do so, have put down the violence of the multitude in a single hour, pretended not to see what he did see and not to hear what he did hear, but allowed the mob to carry on the war against our people without any restraint and to throw our former state of tranquillity into confusion, the populace, being excited still more, proceeded onwards to still more shameless and more audacious designs and treachery. Collecting very large companies of men, they attacked some of the synagogues (and there are a great many in every section of the city). Some they razed to the very foundations, and into some they threw fire and burned them in their insane madness and frenzy, without caring for the neighboring houses. For there is nothing more rapid than fire when it gets hold of fuel.

(133) I omit to mention the ornaments in honor of the emperor which were destroyed and burnt with these synagogues, such as gilded shields, gilded crowns, pillars, and inscriptions, for the sake of which they ought even to have spared the other things. But they were full of confidence, inasmuch as they did not fear any chastisement at the hand of Gaius, as they well knew that he cherished an indescribable hatred against the Jews. Accordingly, their opinion was that no one could do him a more acceptable service than by inflicting every description of injury on the nation which he hated. (134) And as they wished to curry favor with him

---

110. Trans. C. D. Yonge, *The Works of Philo* (Peabody, MA: Hendrickson, 1993), pp. 769, 788–90.

by a novel kind of flattery, so as to secure complete immunity for every sort of ill treatment of us without ever being called to account, what did they proceed to do? All the synagogues that they were unable to destroy by burning and razing to the ground, because a great number of Jews lived in a dense mass in the neighborhood, they outraged and defaced in another manner, simultaneously totally overthrowing our laws and customs. For they set up in every one of them images of Gaius, and in the greatest, most conspicuous, and most celebrated of them they erected a brazen statue of him borne on a four-horse chariot. . . .

(349) It is worthwhile to make mention of what we both saw and heard when we were sent for to take part in a debate about our citizenship. The moment we entered into the presence of the emperor, we perceived from his looks and from his state of agitation, that we had come not before a judge but before an accuser, more hostile than those arrayed against us. . . . (353) For, said he, "You are haters of god, inasmuch as you do not think that I am a god, I who am already acknowledged to be a god by every other nation, but who is refused that appellation by you." And then, stretching up his hands to heaven, he uttered a remark which it was impious to hear, much more would it be so to repeat it literally.

(354) And immediately all the ambassadors of the opposite side were filled with all imaginable joy, thinking that their embassy was already successful, on account of the first words uttered by Gaius. So they clapped their hands and danced for joy, and called him by every title which is applicable to any one of the gods.

(355) And while he (Gaius) was triumphing in these super-human appellations, the sycophant Isidorus, seeing the mood in which he was, said, "O master, you would hate with still greater vehemence these men whom you see before you and their fellow countrymen, if you would be acquainted with their disaffection and disloyalty towards yourself. For when all other men were offering up sacrifices of thanksgiving for your safety, these men alone refused to offer any sacrifice at all; and when I say, 'these men,' I include all the rest of the Jews." (356) Then we all cried out with one accord, "O Lord Gaius, we are falsely accused; for we did sacrifice, and we offered up entire hecatombs,[111] the blood of which we poured in a libation upon the altar. And the flesh we did not carry to our homes to make a feast and banquet upon it, as is the custom of some people to do, but we committed the animals entirely to the sacred flame as a burnt offering. And we have done this three times already, and not only once; on the first occasion when you succeeded to the empire, and the

---

111. A public sacrifice of one hundred oxen.

second time when you recovered from that terrible disease with which all the habitable world was afflicted at the same time, and the third time we sacrificed in hope of your victory over the Germans."

(357) "Grant," said he, "that all this is true, and that you did sacrifice. Nevertheless you sacrificed to another god and not to me; and then what good did you do me, even if it was to me?" Immediately a profound shuddering came upon us the first moment that we heard this statement, similar to that which overwhelmed us when we first came into his presence. (358) And while he was saying this, he entered into the outer buildings, examining the chambers of the men and the chambers of the women, and the rooms on the ground floor, and all the apartments in the upper story, and criticizing some points of their structure as defective, and planning alterations and suggesting designs, and giving orders himself to make them more costly. (359) Then we, being driven about in this way, followed him up and down through the entire place, being mocked and ridiculed by our adversaries like people at a play in the theatre. For indeed the whole matter was a kind of farce: the judge assumed the part of an accuser, and the accusers the part of an unjust judge, looking upon the defendants with an eye of hostility and acting not in accordance with the nature of truth. . . .

(361) But when he had given some of his orders about the buildings, he then asked a very important and solemn question; "Why is it that you abstain from eating pig's flesh?" Again at this question such a violent laughter was raised by our adversaries, partly because they were really delighted and partly as they wished to court the emperor out of flattery and, therefore, wished to make it appear that this question was dictated by wit and uttered with grace. The laughter was so great that some of the servants who were following him were indignant at their appearing to treat the emperor with so little respect, since it was not safe for his most intimate friends to do so much as smile at his words. (362) And when we gave the answer that, "Different nations have different laws, and there are some things of which use is forbidden both to us and to our adversaries"; and when someone said, "There are also many people who do not eat lamb's flesh which is the most tender of all meat," he laughed and said, "They are quite right, for it is not nice." (363) Being joked with, trifled with, and ridiculed in this manner, we were in great perplexity; and at last he said in a rapid and peremptory manner, " I desire to know what principles of justice you recognize with regard to your constitution."

(364) When we began to reply to him and to explain it, as soon as he had a taste of our pleading on the principles of justice, and as soon as he perceived that our arguments were not contemptible, before we could

bring forward the more important things which we had to say, he cut us short, ran forward, and burst into the large room of the house. As soon as he had entered it, he commanded that the windows which were around it be filled up with transparent pebbles very much resembling white crystal which do not hinder the light, but which keep out the wind and the heat of the sun. (365) Then proceeding on deliberately he asked in a more moderate tone, "What are you saying?" When we began to connect our reply with what we had said before, he again ran on and went into another room in which he had commanded some ancient and admirable pictures to be placed.

(366) But when our pleadings on behalf of justice were thus broken up, cut short, interrupted, and crushed as one may almost say, we, being wearied and exhausted and having no strength left in us, but being in continual expectation of nothing else but death, could no longer keep our hearts as they had been, but in our agony we took refuge in supplications to the one true God, praying to him to check the wrath of this falsely called god. (367) He had compassion on us, and turned his (the emperor's) mind to mercy. And he, becoming pacified, merely said, "These men do not appear to me to be wicked so much as unfortunate and foolish in not believing that I have been endowed with the nature of God." So he dismissed us, and commanded us to depart.

5.6.2 Josephus, *Against Apion* I, 223–311:
The Origins of the Jewish People

In this selection, Josephus deems Jewish superiority in divine worship and Egyptian envy the causes of anti-Semitism. Josephus refutes the nonsensical stories of Egyptian historians who gave an account of the ancient presence of Jews in Egypt and the Exodus which was, in effect, an anti-Semitic myth.

૱

(223) The Egyptians were the first who cast reproaches upon us. In order to please that nation, some others undertook to pervert the truth, so that they would neither admit that our forefathers came into Egypt from another country, as the fact was, nor give a true account of our departure from there. (224) Indeed, the Egyptians took many occasions to hate us and envy us, in the first place because our ancestors had had dominion over their country and because of their prosperity when they were delivered from [the Egyptians] and returned to their own country. Further, the difference of our religion from theirs has occasioned great enmity between us since our way of divine worship is as distant from that which their laws

appointed as is the nature of God from that of brute beasts. (225) For they all agree throughout the entire country to esteem such animals as gods although they differ from one another in the particular worship they pay to them. Certainly these men are entirely of vain and foolish minds, and have thus accustomed themselves from the beginning to have such incorrect notions concerning their gods, and could not think of imitating that decent form of divine worship which we practiced. However, when they saw our institutions approved of by many others, they could not but envy us on that account. (226) For some of them have proceeded to such a degree of folly and meanness in their conduct as not to hesitate to contradict their own ancient records, indeed, to contradict themselves also in their writings, and yet they were so blinded by their passions as not to discern it.

(227) And now I will turn my discourse to one of their principal writers whom I have a little earlier made use of as a witness to our antiquity; (228) I mean Manetho.[112] He promised to interpret Egyptian history from their sacred writings, and began by stating that our people came into Egypt, many ten thousands in number, and subdued its inhabitants. Then he further confessed that we went out of that country afterward, settled in the country which is now called Judea, and there built Jerusalem and its Temple. Now thus far he followed his ancient records. (229) But after this he permits himself, claiming to have written what rumors and reports circulated about the Jews, to introduce incredible tales, wishing to present us as mixed with the Egyptian multitude who had leprosy and other diseases and who were condemned to flee Egypt. (230) He mentions Amenophis, a fictitious king's name, though for that reason he would not set down the number of years of his reign which he had accurately done for the other kings he mentions. He then ascribes certain fabulous stories to this king, having presumably forgotten how he had already related that the departure of the shepherds for Jerusalem had been five hundred and eighteen years before. . . .

(304) I shall now add to these accounts something about Lysimachus[113] who has taken up the same topic as those previously mentioned—the false story of the lepers and cripples—but has gone far beyond them in the incredible nature of his forgeries which plainly demonstrates that he contrived them out of his virulent hatred of our nation. (305) His words are these: "The people of the Jews being leprous and scabby and subject to

---

112. Egyptian high priest, ca. 280 B.C.E., who wrote a history of Egypt from mythical times to 342 B.C.E.

113. An Alexandrian writer of uncertain date, but later than the 2nd century B.C.E.

certain other kinds of diseases in the days of Bocchoris, king of Egypt,[114] fled to the temples, and got their food there by begging. As the numbers of those who had been afflicted with these diseases were very great, there arose a scarcity in Egypt. (306) Thereupon Bocchoris, the king of Egypt, sent some to consult the oracle of Ammon[115] about this scarcity.

"The god's answer was this, that he must purge his temples of impure and impious men by expelling them out of those temples into desert places. But as to the scabby and leprous people, he must drown them and purge his temples, the sun being indignant that these men were allowed to live; and by this means the land will bring forth its fruits. (307) Upon Bocchoris's having received these oracles, he called for their priests and the attendants upon their altars and ordered them to make a collection of the impure people and to deliver them to the soldiers, to carry them away into the desert, but to take the leprous people, wrap them in sheets of lead, and let them down into the sea. (308) Thereupon, the scabby and leprous people were drowned, and the rest were collected and sent into the desert in order to be exposed to destruction. There they assembled together, took counsel as to what they should do, and determined that, as the night was coming on, they should kindle fires and lamps and keep watch; that they also should fast the next night and propitiate the gods in order to obtain deliverance from them.

(309) On the next day, there was one, Moses, who advised them that they should venture upon a journey and go along one road till they should come to places fit for habitation. He charged them to have no kind regards for any man, nor to give good counsel to any, but always to advise them for the worst, and to overturn all those temples and altars of the gods they should meet with. (310) The rest agreed with what he had said and did what they had resolved to do, and so crossed the desert. The difficulties of the journey being over, they came to an inhabited country, and there they abused the population and plundered and burned their temples, and then came into that land which is called Judea where they built a city and dwelled therein. (311) That city was named Hierosyla,[116] because of their robbing of the temples. After the success they had, they through the course of time changed its name, that it might not be a reproach to them, and called the city Hierosolyma (Jerusalem) and themselves Hierosolymites (Jerusalemites)."

---

114. Bocchoris is mentioned by Manetho as ruling in the 8th century B.C.E., and this is the date Apion gives to the Exodus, according to Josephus, *Against Apion* II, 17. Josephus dates Bocchoris much earlier, however, in *Against Apion* II, 16.

115. The Egyptian god Amun.

116. "(Town) of Temple Robbers."

5.6.3 Josephus, *Against Apion* II, 80–111:
Jewish Worship Defended

Josephus repeats the "calumnies" and "fables" that he asserts were perpe-trated for political reasons. In this selection, he disputes what appears to be the earliest evidence for the blood libel—the false accusation that Jewish ritual requires the killing of a Gentile.

శ్రీ

(80) For Apion has the impudence to pretend that "the Jews placed an ass's head in their holy place," and he affirms that this was discovered when Antiochus Epiphanes[117] despoiled our temple[118] and found that ass's head there made of gold, and worth a great deal of money. . . . (89) He adds another fable of Greek origin in order to reproach us. In reply to which, it would be enough to say that they who presume to speak about divine worship ought not to be ignorant of this plain truth, that it is a lesser degree of impurity to pass through the temple precincts than to forge wicked calumnies about its priests. (90) Now, such men as he are more zealous to justify a sacrilegious king than to write what is just and what is true about us and about our Temple. For when they are desirous of grati-fying Antiochus, and of concealing that perfidiousness and sacrilege of which he was guilty with regard to our nation, when he wanted money, they endeavor to disgrace us and tell fictitious lies as follows:

(91) Apion becomes other men's spokesman on this occasion, and says that "Antiochus found in our temple a bed and a man lying upon it with a small table before him, full of delicacies from the [fishes of the] sea and the fowls of the dry land. This man was amazed at these delicacies thus set before him. (92) He immediately adored the king upon his coming in, hoping that he would afford him all possible assistance. Falling down upon his knees, he stretched his right hand out to him and begged to be released. When the king bade him sit down and tell him who he was, why he dwelled there, and what was the meaning of those various sorts of food that were set before him, the man made a lamentable complaint, and with sighs and tears in his eyes, gave him this account of the distress he was in.

(93) "He said that he was a Greek, and that as he traveled through this province in order to make his living, he was suddenly seized by foreigners, brought to this temple, and shut up therein, and was seen by nobody, but was fattened by these curious provisions thus set before him. (94) At first

---

117. Antiochus IV Epiphanes, ruled 175–164 B.C.E., was the Seleucid king against whom the Maccabees revolted.
118. Ca. 170 B.C.E., cf. *Ant.* XII, 248–50, where there is no mention of an ass's head.

such unexpected advantages seemed to him a matter of great joy. But after a while they led him to suspicion and at length astonishment as to what their meaning might be. At last he inquired of the servants who came to him, and was informed by them that it was in order to fulfill a law of the Jews, which they must not tell him, that he was thus fed. They did the same at a set time every year. (95) They used to catch a Greek foreigner and fatten him up thus every year, then lead him to a certain forest, kill him, sacrifice with their customary rituals, taste of his entrails, and take an oath upon sacrificing this Greek that they would always be in enmity with the Greeks; and that then they threw the remaining parts of the miserable wretch into a certain pit." (96) Apion adds further, "The man said that there were but a few days to come until he was to be killed, and he implored Antiochus that, out of the reverence he bore to the Greek gods, he would disappoint the snares the Jews had laid for his blood and would deliver him from his miserable predicament."

(97) Now this is a most tragic fable and is full of nothing but cruelty and impudence. Yet it does not excuse Antiochus for his sacrilegious attempts, as those who wrote to vindicate him are willing to suppose. (98) For he could not presume beforehand that he would meet with any such thing in coming to the Temple but must have found it unexpectedly. He was therefore still an impious person who was given to unlawful pleasures and had no regard for God in his actions. But [as for Apion], he did whatever his extravagant love of lying dictated to him, as it is most easy to discover by a consideration of his writings. (99) The conflict of our laws is known not to concern the Greeks alone, but they are principally against the Egyptians and some other nations also. While it so happens that men of all countries come sometimes and sojourn among us, how would it come about that we take an oath and conspire only against the Greeks by the shedding of their blood? (100) Again, how is it possible that all the Jews should get together to partake of these sacrifices, and the entrails of one man should be sufficient for so many thousands, as Apion pretends? Further, why did the king not carry this man, whoever he was and whatever his name was (which is not set down in Apion's book), (101) with great pomp back to his own country; when he might thereby have been esteemed a religions person himself and a great lover of the Greeks, and might thereby have procured himself great assistance from all men against that hatred the Jews bore to him. (102) But I leave this matter, for the proper way of confuting fools in not to use just words, but to appeal to the facts themselves. . . .

(109) . . . What then can we say of Apion, except that he examined nothing that concerned these things, while he still uttered incredible

words about them! But it is a great shame for a grammarian not to be able to write true history. (110) Now he knew the purity of our Temple, yet he entirely failed to take notice of it; but he forged a story about the seizing of a Greek; an unmentionable banquet of the richest and most sumptuous foods; and pretends that strangers could go into a place into which the noblest men among the Jews are not allowed to enter unless they are priests. (111) This, therefore, is the utmost degree of impiety and a lie in order to mislead those who will not investigate the facts. For the one purpose of the inventors of the unspeakable horrors to which I have referred is to raise calumny against us.

5.6.4 The Letter of Aristeas: How the Jewish Law was Translated from Hebrew into Greek[119]

The Letter of Aristeas is an ancient source which details the process by which the Torah was translated into Greek, producing the version known as the Septuagint. Aristeas must have been composed by an Alexandrinian Jew, between 170 and 100 B.C.E.

꙰

(1) A trustworthy narrative has been compiled, Philocrates,[120] of the meeting which we had with Eleazar, high priest of the Jews, arising out of your attaching great importance to hearing a personal account of our mission, its content and purpose. . . .

(9) On his appointment as keeper of the king's library, Demetrius of Phalerum[121] undertook many different negotiations aimed at collecting, if possible, all the books in the world. By purchase and translation he brought to a successful conclusion, as far as lay in his power, the king's plan. (10) We were present when the question was put to him, "How many thousand books are there (in the royal library)?" His reply was, "Over two hundred thousand, O King. I shall take urgent steps to increase in a short time the total to five hundred thousand. Information has reached me that the lawbooks of the Jews are worth translation and inclusion in your royal library."

(11) "What is there to prevent you from doing this?" he said. "Everything for your needs has been put at your disposal."

---

119. Trans. R. J. H. Shutt, in *The Old Testament Pseudepigrapha*, ed. J. H. Charlesworth (Garden City, N.Y.: Doubleday, 1985), vol. 2, pp. 12–34.

120. The brother of the author to whom the letter is addressed.

121. Demetrius of Phalerum served Ptolemy I Soter and died c. 283 B.C.E. He could not, therefore have served Ptolemy II Philopater (283–246 B.C.E.) who is credited with arranging the translation of the Torah into Greek.

Demetrius replied, "Translation is needed. They use letters characteristic of the language of the Jews, just as Egyptians use the formation of their letters in accordance with their own language. The Jews are supposed to use Syrian language, but this is not so, for it is another form (of language)."

The king, in answer to each point, gave orders that a letter be written to the high priest of the Jews that the aforementioned project might be carried out....

(28) When this had been completed, he commanded Demetrius to report on the copying of the Jewish books. All measures were taken by these kings[122] by means of edicts and in complete safety, with no trace of negligence or carelessness. For this reason I have set down the copies of the report and of the letters, as well as the number of those returned and the state of each, because each of them was outstanding in magnificence and skill. (29) The copy of the memorandum is as follows: "To the great king from Demetrius. Your command, O King, concerned the collection of missing volumes needed to complete the library, and of items which accidentally fell short of the requisite condition. I gave highest priority and attention to these matters, and now make the following further report: (30) Scrolls of the Law of the Jews, together with a few others, are missing (from the library), for these (works) are written in Hebrew characters and language. But they have been transcribed somewhat carelessly and not as they should be, according to the report of the experts because they have not received royal patronage. (31) These (books) also must be in your library in an accurate version, because this legislation, as could be expected from its divine nature, is very philosophical and genuine. Writers therefore and poets and the whole army of historians have been reluctant to refer to the aforementioned books, and to the men past (and present) who featured largely in them, because the consideration of them is sacred and hallowed, as Hecateus of Abdera says.[123] (32) If you approve, O King, a letter shall be written to the high priest at Jerusalem, asking him to dispatch men of the most exemplary lives and mature experience, skilled in matters pertaining to their Law, six in number from each tribe, in order that after the examination of the text agreed by the majority, and the achievement of accuracy in the translation, we may produce an outstand-

---

122. Referring to the Ptolemaic kings of Egypt.

123. Probably a reference to his lost "History of Egypt" which must have contained extensive material on the Jews. Hecateus was a contemporary of Alexander the Great and Ptolemy I. (Cf. above text 4.3.1.)

ing version in a manner worthy both of the contents and of your purpose. Farewell always."

(33) On receiving this report, the king ordered a letter to be written to Eleazar regarding these matters, announcing also the actual release of the prisoners.[124] He made them a gift also for the provision of cups and goblets and a table and libation vessels weighing fifty talents of gold, seventy talents of silver, and a goodly number of (precious) stones—he commanded the treasurers to allow the craftsmen to select whatever they might prefer—and of currency for sacrifices and other requirements one hundred talents. (34) We will show you details of the provisions after we have given the copies of the letters.

The letter of the king was of the following pattern. (35) "King Ptolemy to Eleazar the high priest, hearty greetings. It is a fact that a large number of the Jews settled in our country after being uprooted from Jerusalem by the Persians during the time of their ascendancy,[125] and also came with our father into Egypt as prisoners.[126] (36) He put many of them into the military forces on generous pay, and in the same way, having judged the veterans to be trustworthy, he set up establishments which he handed over to them, to prevent the Egyptian people from feeling any apprehension on their account. Having now inherited the throne, we adopt a more liberal attitude to all our subjects, and more especially to your citizens.

(37) We have freed more than a hundred thousand prisoners, paying to their captors the price in silver proportionate to their rank. We also make amends for any damage caused by mob violence. We decided to do this as a religious obligation, making of it a thank offering to the Most High God, who has preserved the kingdom for us in peace and highest renown throughout the whole world. Those at the peak of their youth we have appointed to the army, and those who are able to be at our court, being worthy of confidence in our household, we have put in charge of (some) ministries. (38) It is our wish to grant favors to them and to all the Jews throughout the world, including future generations.[127] We have accordingly decided that your Law shall be translated into Greek letters from

---

124. No doubt a reference to Jewish prisoners.

125. Referring to the Jewish military units established by the Persians after their ascendancy in 540 B.C.E.

126. As a result of the military campaigns of Ptolemy I Soter (ruled 323–283 B.C.E.) in Judea.

127. The author no doubt exaggerates the status of the Jews and the concern of Ptolemy for them.

what you call the Hebrew letters, in order that they too should take their place with us in our library with the other royal books. (39) You will therefore act well, and in a manner worthy of our zeal, by selecting elders of exemplary lives, with experience of the Law and ability to translate it, six from each tribe, so that an agreed version may be found from the large majority, in view of the great importance of the matters under consideration. We believe that the completion of this project will win (us) high reputation. (40) We have dispatched on this business Andreas of the chief bodyguards and Aristeas,[128] men held in high esteem by you, to confer with you; they bring with them first fruits of offerings for the Temple and one hundred talents of silver for sacrifices and the other requirements. Write to us on any matters you wish, and your requests will be gratified; you will be performing also an act worthy of friendship for what you choose will be carried out with all dispatch. Farewell."

(41) In reply to this letter Eleazar wrote in acceptance as follows: "Eleazar the high priest to King Ptolemy, dear friend, greeting. Good health to you and to Queen Arsinoe, your sister,[129] and to your children; if that is so, it would be well, and as we wish. We too are in good health. (42) On receipt of your letter we rejoiced greatly because of your purpose and noble plan; we therefore collected together the whole multitude and read it to them, that they might know your piety toward our God. We also showed them the vessels which you sent, twenty of silver and thirty of gold, five cups, and a table for offering, and for the performance of the sacrifices and the furnishing of the Temple requirements one hundred talents of silver, (43) brought by two men highly esteemed by you, Andreas and Aristeas, gentlemen of integrity, outstanding in education, worthy in every respect of your conduct and justice. . . .

(45) . . . The whole multitude made supplication that it should come to pass for you entirely as you desire, and that God the ruler of all should preserve your kingdom in peace and glory, and that the translation of the sacred Law should come to pass in a manner expedient to you and in safety. (46) In the presence of the whole assembly we selected elders, honorable men and true, six from each tribe, whom we have sent with the Law in their possession. It will be a noble deed, O righteous King, if you command that once the translation of the books is complete these men be restored to us again in safety. Farewell. . . ."

---

128. The purported author of the text.

129. Arsinoe married her brother, Ptolemy II Philadelphus, in ca. 278 B.C.E. Such marriages were normal among Egyptian royalty.

Eleazar offered sacrifice, selected the men, and made ready an abundance of gifts for the king. He then sent us forth on our journey with a large escort. (173) When we reached Alexandria, news of our arrival was given to the king. Andreas and I were introduced to the court, we paid our warm respects to the king, and presented the letters from Eleazar. (174) The king was anxious to meet the members of the deputation, so he gave orders to dismiss all the other court officials, and to summon these delegates. (175) The unprecedented nature of this step was very clear to all, because it was an established procedure that important bona fide visitors should be granted an audience with the king only four days after arrival, while representatives of kings or important cities are rarely admitted to the court within thirty days. However, he deemed the present arrivals to be deserving of greater honor, having regard to the preeminence of him who had sent them. So he dismissed all the officials whom he considered superfluous and remained walking among the delegates until he had greeted the whole delegation. (176) So they arrived with the gifts which had been sent at their hands and with the fine skins on which the Law had been written in letters of gold in Jewish characters; the parchment had been excellently worked, and the joining together of the letters[130] was imperceptible. When the king saw the delegates, he proceeded to ask questions about the books, (177) and when they had shown what had been covered and unrolled the parchments, he paused for a long time, did obeisance about seven times, and said, "I offer to you my thanks, gentlemen, and to him who sent you even more, and most of all to the God whose oracles these are." (178) They all, visitors and the court present alike, said together and with one voice, "It is well, O King." At this the king was moved to tears, so deeply was he filled with joy. . . .

(179) The king commanded the parcels to be returned in order,[131] and then immediately greeted the delegates with these words: "It is (meet and) right, O men of God, first to render homage to the documents for the sake of which I have sent for you, and after that to extend to you the right hand of greeting. This explains my first action. (180) I regard this day of your arrival as of great importance, and it shall be specially marked year by year throughout the time of our life, for by a happy chance it coincides with our victory at sea against Antigonus.[132] It will therefore be

---

130. Most probably a reference to the stitching together of the sheets of parchment.

131. The scrolls were again placed in their wrappings.

132. Actually, Ptolemy II Philadelphus was defeated by Antigonus Gonatas, king of Macedonia (ruled ca. 277–239 B.C.E.) at the naval battle of Cos (ca. 254 B.C.E.).

my wish to dine with you this day." (181) Everything of which you partake," he said, "will be served in compliance with your habits;[133] it will be served to me as well as to you." They expressed their pleasure and the king ordered the finest apartments to be given them near the citadel, and the preparations for the banquet to be made.

(182) The chief steward Nicanor summoned Dorotheus, who was appointed in charge of these matters, and bade him complete preparations for each guest. . . . (184) When they had taken their places, he ordered Dorotheus to carry everything out in accordance with the customs practiced by all his visitors from Judea. So Dorotheus passed over the sacred heralds, the sacrificial ministers and the rest, whose habitual role was to offer the prayers. Instead, he invited Eleazar, "the oldest of the priests, our guests," to offer a prayer. He stood and spoke these memorable words: (185) "May the almighty God fill you, O King, with all the blessings which he has created and may he grant you, your wife, and children, and those of the same mind to enjoy all blessings without end all the days of your life." (186) At these words from this man thunderous applause broke out with cries and rapturous joy, lasting a long time. Then they straightway turned to the enjoyment provided by the foods which had been made ready, all the service being carried out through the organization of Dorotheus, including the royal pages and the king's honored guests. . . .

(301) Three days afterward, Demetrius took the men with him, traversed the mile-long jetty into the sea toward the island, crossed the bridge, and went in the direction of the north. There he assembled them in a house which had been duly furnished near the shore—a magnificent building in a very quiet situation—and invited the men to carry out the work of translation, all that they would require being handsomely provided. (302) They set to completing their several tasks, reaching agreement among themselves on each by comparing versions.

The result of their agreement thus was made into a fair copy by Demetrius. (303) The business of their meeting occupied them until the ninth hour,[134] after which they were free for bodily rest and relaxation, everything which they desired being furnished on a lavish scale. (304) Apart from all this, Dorotheus also provided for them all that was prepared for the king—this was the order which he had received from the king. At the first hour of the day they attended the court daily, and after offering salutations to the king, retired to their own quarters.

---

133. It will be prepared according to Jewish dietary laws.
134. 3:00 pm.

(305) Following the custom of all the Jews, they washed their hands in the sea in the course of their prayers to God, and then proceeded to the reading and explication of each point. (306) I asked this question: "What is their purpose in washing their hands while saying their prayers?" They explained that it is evidence that they have done no evil, for all activity takes place by means of righteousness and truth. (307) In this way, as we said previously, each day they assembled in their quarters, which were pleasantly situated for quiet and light, and proceeded to fulfill their prescribed task. The outcome was such that in seventy-two days the business of translation was completed, just as if such a result was achieved by some deliberate design.

(308) When it was completed, Demetrius assembled the company of the Jews in the place where the task of the translation had been finished, and read it to all, in the presence of the translators, who received a great ovation from the crowded audience for being responsible for great blessings. (309) Likewise also they gave an ovation to Demetrius and asked him, now that he had transcribed the whole Law, to give a copy to their leaders. (310) As the books were read, the priests stood up, with the elders from among the translators and from the representatives of the "Community,"[135] and with the leaders of the people, and said, "Since this version has been made rightly and reverently, and in every respect accurately, it is good that this should remain exactly so, and that there should be no revision." (311) There was general approval of what they said, and they commanded that a curse should be laid, as was their custom, on anyone who should alter the version by any addition or change to any part of the written text, or any deletion either. This was a good step taken, to insure that the words were preserved completely and permanently in perpetuity.

When the king received messages about these events, he rejoiced greatly, because it seemed that the purpose which he shared had been safely accomplished. All of the version was read by him, and he marveled profoundly at the genius of the lawgiver. . . . (317) When the king had received, as I previously mentioned, Demetrius' account on these matters, he bowed and gave orders for great care to be taken of the books and for their hallowed preservation. (318) He invited the translators to visit him often after their return to Judea. It was, he said, only fair for their departure to take place, but when they returned he would, as was right, treat them as friends, and they would receive the most liberal hospitality at

---

135. The Jewish community.

his hands. (319) He ordered preparations to be made for their departure, and treated the men magnificently, presenting to each one three robes of the finest materials, two talents of gold, a cup worth a talent, and complete furnishing for a dining room. (320) He also sent to Eleazar, along with their luggage, ten silver-footed couches, with all accessories to go with them, a cup worth thirty talents, ten robes, purple cloth, a magnificent crown, one hundred lengths of finest linen, vessels, bowls, and two golden goblets for a dedication.

5.6.5 Babylonian Talmud Megillah 9a–b: Translation of the Torah into Greek[136]

The Rabbis also preserved a tradition according to which seventy-two elders had translated the Torah into Greek. This Talmudic account, however, stressed the intentional changes introduced unanimously by the translators into the text in order to prevent misunderstandings or embarrassment to the Jewish religion.

శ్రీ

It is taught in a *baraita*:[137] It happened that Ptolemy the king assembled seventy-two Elders and placed them in seventy-two rooms, and did not reveal to them for what purpose he had assembled them. He went into each one and said to them, "Translate for me the Torah of Moses your teacher." God gave counsel to the heart of each one, and they all agreed as one mind. They all wrote:

"*God created in the beginning*";[138]

"*I* will make a man in an image and a form";[139]

"And He completed on the *sixth* day. . . and He rested on the seventh day,"[140]

"male and female He created *him*," and they did not write "he created *them*";[141]

---

136. Trans. S. Berrin.

137. A tradition of the mishnaic teachers which was not included in the Mishnah.

138. Instead of "in the beginning God created," Gen. 1:1, which might be taken to mean that another deity named "in the beginning" created God.

139. Gen. 1:26, instead of "Let us make man in our image and in our likeness" which could imply a multiplicity of deities.

140. Gen. 2:2, instead of "And He completed on the seventh day . . . and He rested on the seventh day" which might seem to indicate work being done on the seventh day.

141. Gen. 5:2, since the plural may be taken to imply that God created two humans, each comprised of male and female, rather than one single hermaphrodite body.

"Let *me* descend and *I* will confuse their language there";[142]

"And Sarah laughed *among her relatives*";[143]

"for in their wrath they slew an *ox* and at their will they uprooted a manger";[144]

"and Moses took his wife and his sons and he mounted them upon *bearers of men*";[145]

"and the dwelling of the Israelites which they dwelled in Egypt *and in other lands* was four hundred [and thirty] years. . . ";[146]

"and he sent the *za'atute* of Israel";[147]

"and against the *za'atute* of Israel He did not stretch forth his hand";[148]

"not one *valuable item* of theirs have I taken";[149]

"which the Lord your God has apportioned *to give light* to all the nations";[150]

"And he went and served other gods which I have not commanded *to worship them*."[151]

---

142. Gen. 11:7, instead of "Let us descend and we will confuse their language there."

143. Gen. 18:12, "among her relatives" (*biqroveha*) instead of "to herself" (*be-qirbah*), which describes Sarah as publicly doubting God's promise of her bearing a child in her old age. The translators would have been prompted to make this alteration to differentiate between Sarah, who was rebuked for laughing, and Abraham, who was not.

144. Gen. 49:6 reads, "in their anger they slew a man and at their will they maimed an ox." The verse is Jacob's rebuke of Levi and Simeon for slaying the men of Shechem, an action here mitigated to reckless animal slaughter and vandalism.

145. Ex. 4:20 specifies "donkey," presumably too undignified an animal to be named. In view of the anti-Semitic claims that Jews worshipped an ass, there may have been other reasons to choose this translation.

146. Ex. 12:40. The italicized words were added to the verse, since biblical accounts make clear that the period of slavery in Egypt was less than four hundred thirty years.

147. Ex. 24:5, using an unusual, and perhaps ambiguous, word instead of "youths." Since the Greek word for youths may also denote "slave" or "servant," the translators refrained from applying it to these young men chosen to sacrifice at Mount Sinai.

148. Ex. 24:11. Instead of translating "nobles," the translators repeated the odd word from verse 11 to clarify that the reference was to the same men.

149. Num. 16:15. Instead of "not one donkey;" *ḥmd* replaces *ḥmr*, presumably to insure the understanding that Moses took nothing at all from the people, lest a reader understand "donkey" literally rather than paradigmatically. Avoidance of the mention of a "donkey" may also be connected with the Hellenistic myth that Jews worshipped an ass.

150. Deut. 4:19. This verse warns the Israelites against worshipping the sun, moon, and stars, "which the Lord your God has apportioned unto all the nations." The translators stress that these luminaries were given, even to all the other nations, only for light and not for worship.

151. Deut. 17:3. The italicized words are added, as without them the verse may be understood to imply that God did not command the other gods to exist, and their existence would be viewed as proof against God's omnipotence.

Further, they wrote for his (Ptolemy's) benefit, "the short-legged creature," and they did not write for him, "and the hare,"[152] since the wife of Ptolemy was named "Hare," so that he would not say, "The Jews mocked me and placed my wife's name in the Torah (among the unclean animals)."[153]

5.6.6 The Works of Philo: A Survey of his Ideas[154]

An Alexandrian Jew, ca. 20 B.C.E.–50 C.E., Philo Judaeus wrote extensively on matters of Jewish philosophy and biblical interpretation in an attempt to fuse the tradition of the Torah with that of Greek philosophy. He was an observant Jew, and also was deeply involved in the leadership of the Jewish community of Egypt. Because of the vastness of his work, we present here only a small sample of his teachings.

ᛩᛪ

On the Creation of the World, 3: The Creation of the World in Accordance with the Law of Nature[155]

[Moses'] exordium[156] (Gen. 1), as I have said, is one that excites our admiration in the highest degree. It consists of an account of the creation of the world, implying that the world is in harmony with the Law, and the Law with the world, and that the man who observes the law is constituted thereby a loyal citizen of the world, regulating his doings by the purpose and will of Nature, in accordance with which the entire world itself also is administered.

The Confusion of Tongues, 136–7: God's Ubiquity[157]

God fills all things; He contains but is not contained. To be everywhere and nowhere is His Property and His alone. He is nowhere, because He Himself created space and place. . . coincident with material things, and it is against all right principle to say that the maker is contained in anything that He has made. He is everywhere, because He has made His powers extend through earth and water, air and heaven, and left no part of the universe without His presence, and uniting all with all

---

152. Lev. 11:16, Deut. 14:17.

153. Actually, Ptolemy I Soter's father was named "hare" (Lagos in Greek).

154. Trans. H. Lewy, *Three Jewish Philosophers, Philo: Selections* (New York: Harper & Row with Jewish Publication Society, 1965), pp. 27–106.

155. Lewy, p. 27.

156. Opening speech.

157. Lewy, pp. 27–8.

has bound them fast with invisible bonds, that they should never be loosed. . . .

The Unchangeableness of God, 47–9: On the Liberty of Men[158]

For the other living creatures in whose souls the mind, the element set apart for liberty, has no place, have been committed under yoke and bridle to the service of men, as slaves to a master. But man, possessed of a spontaneous and self-determined will, whose activities for the most part rest on deliberate choice, is with reason blamed for what he does wrong with intent, praised when he acts rightly of his own will. In the others, the plants and animals, no praise is due if they bear well, nor blame if they fare ill: for their movements and changes in either direction come to them from no deliberate choice or volition of their own. But the soul of man alone has received from God the faculty of voluntary movement, and in this way especially is made like to Him, and thus being liberated, as far as might be, from that hard and ruthless mistress, necessity, may justly be charged with guilt, in that it does not honor its Liberator. . . . For God had made man free and unfettered, to employ his powers of action with voluntary and deliberate choice for this purpose, that, knowing good and ill and receiving the conception of the noble and the base, and setting himself in sincerity to apprehend just and unjust and in general what belongs to virtue and what to vice, he might practice to choose the better and eschew the opposite.

On the Giants, 60–1: Three Kinds of Men[159]

Some men are earth-born, some heaven-born, and some God-born. The earth-born are those who take the pleasures of the body for their quarry, who make it their practice to indulge in them and enjoy them and provide the means by which each of them may be promoted. The heaven-born are the votaries of the arts and of knowledge, the lovers of learning. For the heavenly element in us is the mind, as the heavenly beings are each of them a mind. And it is the mind which pursues the learning of the schools and the other arts one and all, which sharpens and whets itself, aye, and trains and drills itself solid in the contemplation of what is intelligible by mind. But the men of God are priests and prophets who have refused to accept membership in the commonwealth of the world and to become citizens therein, but have risen wholly above the sphere of sense-perception and have been translated into the world of the

---

158. Lewy, pp. 29–30.
159. Lewy, p. 36.

intelligible and dwell there registered as freemen of the commonwealth of Ideas, which are imperishable and incorporeal.

On the Migration of Abraham, 89–93: Soul and Body of the Divine Laws[160]

There are some who, regarding laws in their literal sense in the light of symbols of matters belonging to the intellect, are over punctilious about the latter, while treating the former with easy-going neglect. Such men I for my part should blame for handling the matter in too easy and off-hand a manner: they ought to have given careful attention to both aims, to a more full and exact investigation of what is not seen and in what is seen, to be stewards without reproach. As it is, as though they were living alone by themselves in a wilderness, or as though they had become disembodied souls, and knew neither city nor village nor household nor any company of human beings at all, overlooking all that the mass of men regard, they explore reality in its naked absoluteness. These men are taught by the sacred word to have thought for good repute, and to let go nothing that is part of the customs fixed by divinely empowered men greater than those of our time.

It is quite true that the Seventh Day is meant to teach the power of the Unoriginate[161] and the non-action of created beings.[162] But let us not for this reason abrogate the laws laid down for its observance, and light fires or till the ground or carry loads or institute proceedings in court or act as jurors or demand the restoration of deposits or recover loans, or do all else that we are permitted to do as well on days that are not festival seasons. It is true also that keeping of festivals is a symbol of gladness of soul and of thankfulness to God, but we should not for this reason turn our backs on the general gatherings of the year's seasons. It is true that receiving circumcision does indeed portray the excision of pleasure and all passions, and the putting away of the impious conceit, under which the mind supposed that it was capable of begetting by its own power: but let us not on this account repeal the law laid down for circumcising. Why, we shall be ignoring the sanctity of the Temple and a thousand other things, if we are going to pay heed to nothing except what is shown us by the inner meaning of things. Nay, we should look on all these outward observances as resembling the body, and their inner meaning as resembling the soul. It follows that, exactly as we have to take thought for the body, because it is

---

160. Lewy, pp. 40–41.

161. God Who was not created but exists for eternity.

162. The Sabbath rest reminds us that all our laboring is ineffectual compared with the eternal activity of God.

the abode of the soul, so we must pay heed to the letter of the laws. If we keep and observe these, we shall gain a clearer conception of those things of which these are the symbols; and besides that we shall not incur the censure of the many and the charges they are sure to bring against us.

On the Unchangeableness of God, 143: The Way of Wisdom[163]

Wisdom is a straight high road, and it is when the mind's course is guided along that road that it reaches the goal which is the recognition and knowledge of God. Every comrade of the flesh hates and rejects this path and seeks to corrupt it. For there are no two things so utterly opposed as knowledge and pleasure of the flesh.

On the Creation of the World, 45–7: Why Heaven was Created after Earth[164]

On the fourth day, the earth being now finished, God ordered the heaven in varied beauty. Not that He put the heaven in a lower rank than the earth, giving precedence to the inferior creation, and accounting the higher and more divine worthy only of the second place; but to make clear beyond all doubt the mighty sway of His sovereign power. For being aware beforehand of the ways of thinking that would mark the men of future ages, how they would be intent on what looked probable and plausible, with much in it that could be supported by argument, but would not aim at sheer truth; and how they would trust phenomena rather than God, admiring sophistry more than wisdom; and how they would observe in time to come the circuits of sun and moon, on which depend summer and winter and the changes of spring and autumn, and would suppose that the regular movements of the heavenly bodies are the causes of all things that year by year come forth and are produced out of the earth; that there might be none who owing either to shameless audacity or to overwhelming ignorance should venture to ascribe the first place to any created thing, "let them," said He, "go back in thought to the original creation of the universe, when, before sun or moon existed, the earth bore plants of all sorts and fruits of all sorts; and having contemplated this let them form in their minds the expectation that hereafter too shall it bear these at the Father's bidding, whensoever it may please Him." For He has no need of His heavenly offspring on which He bestowed powers but not independence: for, like a charioteer grasping the reins or a pilot the tiller, He guides all things in what direction He pleases as law and right demand, standing in need of no one besides: for all things are possible to God. This

---

163. Lewy, p. 52.
164. Lewy, pp. 52–3.

is the reason why the earth put forth plants and bore herbs before the heaven was furnished.

The Special Laws I, 32–51: On the Apprehension of God[165]

Doubtless hard to unriddle and hard to apprehend is the Father and Ruler of all, but that is no reason why we should shrink from searching for Him. But in such searching two principal questions arise which demand the consideration of the genuine philosopher. One is whether the Deity exists, a question necessitated by those who practice atheism, the worst form of wickedness, the other is what the Deity is in essence. Now to answer the first question does not need much labor, but the second is not only difficult but perhaps impossible to solve. Still, both must be examined. We see then, that any piece of work always involves the knowledge of a workman. Who can look upon statues or painting without thinking at once of a sculptor or painter? Who can see clothes or ships or houses without getting the idea of a weaver and a shipwright and a housebuilder? And when one enters a well-ordered city in which the arrangements for civil life are very admirably managed, what else will he suppose but that this city is directed by good rulers? So then he who comes to the truly Great City, this world, and beholds hills and plains teeming with animals and plants, the rivers, spring-fed or winter torrents, streaming along the seas with their expanses, the air with its happily tempered phases, the yearly seasons passing into each other, and then the sun and moon ruling the day and night, and the other heavenly bodies fixed or planetary and the whole firmament revolving in rhythmic order, must he not naturally or rather necessarily gain the conception of the Maker and Father and Ruler also? For none of the works of human art is self made, and the highest art and knowledge is shown in this universe, so that purely it has been wrought by one of excellent knowledge and absolute perfection. In this way we have gained the conception of the existence of God.

As for the divine essence, though in fact it is hard to track and hard to apprehend, it still calls for all the inquiry possible. For nothing is better than to search for the true God, even if the discovery of Him eludes human capacity, since the very wish to learn, if earnestly entertained, produces untold joys and pleasures. We have the testimony of those who have not taken a mere sip of philosophy but have feasted abundantly on its reasonings and conclusions. For with them the reason soars away from earth into the heights, travels through the upper air and accompanies the revolutions of the sun and moon and the whole heaven and in its desire to

---

165. Lewy, pp. 58–62.

see all that is there finds its powers of sight blurred, for so pure and vast is the radiance that pours therefrom that the soul's eye is dizzied by the flashing of the rays. Yet it does not therefore faintheartedly give up the task, but with purpose unsubdued presses onwards to such contemplation as is possible, like the athlete who strives for the second prize since he has been disappointed of the first. Now second to the true vision stands conjecture and theorizing and all that can be brought into the category of reasonable probability. So then just as, though we do not know and cannot with certainty determine what each of the stars is in the purity of its essence, we eagerly persist in the search because our natural love of learning makes us delight in what seems probable, so too, though the clear vision of God as He really is is denied us, we ought not to relinquish the quest. For the very seeking, even without finding, is felicity in itself, just as no one blames the eyes of the body because when unable to see the sun itself they see the emanation of its rays as it reaches the earth, which is but the extremity of the brightness which the beams of the sun give forth.

It was this which Moses, the sacred guide, most dearly beloved of God, had before his eyes when he besought God with the words, "Reveal Yourself to me" (Ex. 33:13). In these words we may almost hear plainly the inspired cry: "This universe has been my teacher, to bring me to the knowledge that You are and do subsist. As Your son, it has told me of its Father, as Your work, of its contriver. But what You are in Your essence I desire to understand, yet find in no part of the All any to guide me to this knowledge. Therefore I pray and beseech You to accept the supplication of a suppliant, a lover of God, one whose mind is set to serve You alone; for as knowledge of the light does not come by any other source but what itself supplies, so too You alone can tell me of Yourself. Wherefore I crave pardon, if, for lack of a teacher, I venture to appeal to You in my desire to learn of You."

He replies, "Your zeal I approve as praiseworthy, but the request cannot fitly be granted to any that are brought into being by creation. I freely bestow (cf. Ex. 33:19) what is in accordance with the recipient; for not all that I can give with ease is within man's power to take, and therefore to him that is worthy of My grace I extend all the boons which he is capable of receiving. But the apprehension of Me is something more than human nature, yea even the whole heaven and universe will be able to contain. Know yourself, then, and do not be led away by impulses and desires beyond your capacity, nor let yearning for the unattainable uplift and carry you off your feet, for of the obtainable nothing shall be denied you."

When Moses heard this, he addressed to Him a second petition and said, "I bow before Your admonitions, that I never could have received the vision of You clearly manifested, but I beseech You that I may at least see the glory that surrounds You (cf. Ex. 33:18), and by Your glory understand the powers that keep guard around You, of whom I would fain gain apprehension, for though hitherto that has escaped me, the thought of it creates in me a mighty longing to have knowledge of them."

To this He answers, "The powers which you seek to know are discerned not by sight but by mind even as I Whose they are, am discerned by mind and not by sight, and when I say "they are discerned by mind" I do not mean that they are now discerned by mind, but mean that if these other powers could be apprehended it would not be by sense but by mind at its purest. But while in their essence they are beyond your apprehension, they nevertheless present to your sight a sort of impress and copy of their active working. You men have for your use seals which when brought into contact with wax or similar material stamp on them any number of impressions while they themselves are not docked in any part thereby but remain as they were. Such you must conceive My powers to be, supplying quality and shape to things which lack either and yet changing or lessening nothing of their eternal nature. Some among you call them not inaptly "forms" or "ideas," since they bring form into everything that is, giving order to the disordered, limit to the unlimited, bounds to the unbounded, shape to the shapeless, and in general changing the worse to something better. Do not, then, hope to be ever able to apprehend Me or any of My powers in Our essence. But I readily and with right goodwill will admit you to a share of what is attainable. That means that I bid you come and contemplate the universe and its contents, a spectacle apprehended not by the eye of the body but by the unsleeping eyes of the mind. Only let there be the constant and profound longing for wisdom which fills its scholars and disciples with verities glorious in their exceeding loveliness."

When Moses heard this, he did not cease from his desire but kept the yearning for the invisible aflame in his heart. All of like sort to him, all who spurn idle fables and embrace truth in its purity, whether they have been such from the first or through conversion to the better side have reached that higher state, obtain His approval, the former because they were not false to the nobility of their birth, the latter because their judgment led them to make the passage to piety. These last he calls "proselytes," or newly-joined, because they have joined the new and godly commonwealth.

On Flight and Finding, 161–5: The Symbol of the Burning Bush[166]

The prophet (Moses), led on by his love of acquiring knowledge, was seeking after the causes by which the most essential occurrences in the universe are brought about; for observing all created things wasting away and coming to the birth, perishing and yet remaining, he is smitten with amazement and cries out saying, "Why is it that the bush is burning and not being consumed?" (Ex. 3:2ff.), for his thoughts are busy over the untrodden place, familiar only to Divine natures. But when now on the point of engaging in an endless and futile labor, he is relieved of it by the kindness and providence of God the Savior of all men, who from out of the hallowed spot warned him "Draw not nigh hither" (ibid. 5), as much as to say "Enter not on such an inquiry"; for the task argues a busy, restless curiosity too great for human ability; marvel at all that has come into being, but as for the reasons for which they have either come into being or are decaying, cease to busy yourself with them. For "the place on which you stand is holy ground," it says (ibid. 5). What kind of place or topic is meant? Evidently that of causation, a subject which He has assigned to Divine natures only, deeming no human being capable of dealing with the study of causation. But the prophet owing to desire of knowledge lifts his eyes above the whole universe and becomes a seeker regarding its Creator, asking of what sort this Being is so difficult to see, so difficult to conjecture. . . . Nevertheless he did not succeed in finding anything by search respecting the essence of Him that Is. For he is told "What is behind Me you shall see, but my face you shall by no means see" (Ex. 33:23). For it amply suffices the wise man to come to a knowledge of all that follows on after God and in His wake, but the man that wishes to set his gaze upon the Supreme Essence, before he sees Him will be blinded by the rays that beam forth all round Him.

Allegorical Interpretation, III, 47: The Withdrawal of the Mind[167]

But whether you will find God when you seek is uncertain, for to many He has not manifested Himself, but their zeal has been without success all along. And yet the mere seeking by itself is sufficient to make us partakers of good things, for it always is the case that endeavors after noble things, even if they fail to attain their object, gladden in their very course those who make them.

---

166. Lewy, pp. 65–6.
167. Lewy, p. 72.

On the Decalogue, 44–7: The Theophany on Sinai[168]

It was natural that the place should be the scene of all that was wonderful, claps of thunder louder than the ears could hold, flashes of lightning of surpassing brightness, the sound of an invisible trumpet reaching to the greatest distance, the descent of a cloud which like a pillar stood with its foot planted on the earth, while the rest of its body extended to the height of the upper air, the rush of heaven-sent fire which shrouded all around in dense smoke. For when the power of God arrives, needs must be that no part of the world should remain inactive, but all move together to do Him service. Nearby stood the people. . . . Then from the midst of the fire that streamed from heaven there sounded forth to their utter amazement a voice, for the flame became articulate speech in the language familiar to the audience, and so clearly and distinctly were the words formed by it that they seemed to see rather than hear them. What I say is vouched for by the law in which it is written, "All the people saw the voice" (Ex. 20:18), a phrase fraught with much meaning, for it is the case that the voice of men is audible, but the voice of God truly visible. Why so? Because whatever God says is not words but deeds, which are judged by the eyes rather than the ears.

On the Sacrifices of Abel, 55: On Man's Nothingness[169]

"And forget the Lord your God" (Deut. 8:12–14). When then will you not forget God? Only when you do not forget yourself. For if you remember your own nothingness in all things, you will also remember the transcendence of God in all things.

The Special Laws, II, 163–7: The Legacy of Israel[170]

The Jewish nation is to the whole inhabited world what the priest is to the State. For the holy office in very truth belongs to the nation because it carries out all the rites of purification and both in body and soul obeys the injunctions of the Divine laws. . . setting reason to guide the irrational senses, and also check and rein in the wild and extravagant impulses of the soul, sometimes through gentler remonstrances and philosophical admonitions, sometimes through severer and more forcible condemnations and the fear of punishment which they hold over it as a deterrent. But not only is the legislation in a sense a lesson on the sacred office, not only does a life led in conformity with the laws necessarily confer priesthood or rather high priesthood in the judgment of truth, but there is

---

168. Lewy, pp. 77–8.
169. Lewy, p. 87.
170. Lewy, pp. 101–2.

another point of special importance. There is no bound or limit to the number of deities, male and female, honored in different cities, the vain inventions of the tribe of poets and of the great multitude of men to whom the quest for truth is a task of difficulty and beyond their powers of research. Yet instead of all peoples having the same gods, we find different nations venerating and honoring different gods. The gods of the foreigner they do not regard as gods at all. They treat their acceptance by the others as a jest and a laughingstock and denounce the extreme folly of those who honor them and the failure to think soundly shown thereby. But if He exists Whom all Greeks and barbarians unanimously acknowledge, the supreme Father of gods and men and the Maker of the whole universe, Whose nature is invisible and inscrutable not only by the eye, but by the mind, yet is a matter into which every student of astronomical science and other philosophy desires to make research and leaves nothing untried which would help him to discern it and do it service—then it was the duty of all men to cleave to Him and not introduce new gods. . . to receive the same honors.

When they went wrong in what was the most vital matter of all, it is the literal truth that the error which the rest committed was corrected by the Jewish nation which passed over all created objects because they were created and naturally liable to destruction and chose the service only of the Uncreated and Eternal, first because of its excellence, secondly because it is profitable to dedicate and attach ourselves to the elder rather than to the younger, to the ruler rather than to the subject, to the maker rather than to the thing created. And therefore it astonishes me to see that some people venture to accuse of inhumanity the nation which has shown so profound a sense of fellowship and goodwill to all men everywhere, by using its prayers and festivals and first-fruit offerings as a means of supplication for the human race in general and of making its homage to the truly existent God in the name of those who have evaded the service which it was their duty to give, as well as of itself.

On the Virtues, 119–20: The Scope of the Mosaic Law[171]

What our most holy prophet through all his regulations especially desires to create is unanimity, neighborliness, fellowship, reciprocity of feeling, whereby houses and cities and nations and countries and the whole human race may advance to supreme happiness. Hitherto, indeed, these things live only in our prayers, but they will, I am convinced, become facts beyond all dispute, if God, even as He gives us the yearly

---

171. Lewy, p. 102.

fruits, grants that the virtues should bear abundantly. And may some share in them be given to us, who from well-nigh our earliest days have carried with us the yearning to possess them.

On the Special Laws, **IV, 177–80: Israel the Orphan among the Nations**[172]

When Moses has hymned the excellence of the Self-existent in this manner (Deut. 10:17, 18): "God the great and powerful, Who has no respect to persons, will receive no gifts and executes judgment" he proceeds to say for whom the judgment is executed—not for satraps and despots and men invested with power by land and sea, but for the "incomer (stranger), for the orphan and widow." For the incomer, because he has turned his kinsfolk, who in the ordinary course of things would be his sole confederates, into mortal enemies, by coming as a pilgrim to truth and the honoring of One who alone is worthy of honor, and by leaving the mythical fables and multiplicity of sovereigns, so highly honored by the parents and grandparents and ancestors and blood relations of this immigrant to a better home. For the orphan, because he has been bereft of his father and mother, his natural helpers and champions, deserted by the sole force which was bound to take up his cause. For the widow because she has been deprived of her husband who took over from the parents the charge of guarding and watching over her, since for the purpose of giving protection the husband is to the wife what the parents are to the maiden.

One may say that the whole Jewish race is in the position of an orphan compared with all the nations on every side. They when misfortunes fall upon them which are not by the direct intervention of heaven are never, owing to international intercourse, unprovided with helpers who join sides with them. But the Jewish nation has none to take its part, as it lives under exceptional laws which are necessarily grave and severe, because they inculcate the highest standard of virtue. But gravity is austere, and austerity is held in aversion by the great mass of men because they favor pleasure. Nevertheless, as Moses tells us, the orphan-like desolate state of his people is always an object of pity and compassion to the Ruler of the Universe whose portion it is, because it has been set apart out of the whole human race as a kind of first fruits to the Maker and Father.

---

172. Lewy, p. 106.

6

Sectarianism in the
Second Commonwealth

From the point of view of the history of Judaism, the years of the Hasmonean dynasty, in which an independent Jewish state existed in the Land of Israel, were most significant for the rise of Jewish sectarianism. The various sects each had their own approaches to fundamental religious questions, and these seem to have come to the fore in the aftermath of the Maccabean Revolt. But, of course, to understand these developments one has to begin with the political history of the Hasmonean kingdom.

For this reason we begin by presenting Josephus' account of the end of the career of Jonathan (text 6.1.1), the first truly independent Hasmonean ruler. The details of his death as a result of treachery and the affairs of his successor, his brother Simon, are related in detail in 1 Maccabees (text 6.1.12). It was under Simon that the constitution of the Hasmonean state was formally adopted, and he received full recognition from the Seleucid Empire. His death is related by Josephus in *Antiquities* (text 6.1.3). He was followed by the illustrious John Hyrcanus whose entire career is related at length in *Antiquities* (text 6.1.4). While his reign was a period of expansion and prosperity for the Hasmonean state, it was also a period in which sectarian strife became much more prominent, affecting both religious and political affairs.

Simon's rule was followed by the short reign of Aristobulus, as is described by Josephus (text 6.1.5). After one year as king, he was in turn succeeded by another great Hasmonean, Alexander Janneus, whose reign is also narrated by Josephus (text 6.1.6). He greatly expanded the kingdom but came into conflict with the Pharisees, who opposed him to the point of fomenting an armed struggle against him with the aid of the Seleucids. He was succeeded by his wife Salome Alexandra, the first and only Hasmonean queen, and her reign is described in *Antiquities* (text 6.1.7). Following her husband's deathbed advice, she allied herself with the Pharisees, and in consequence her reign was a peaceful one.

However, she was not able to properly arrange for the succession after her death, and her sons Aristobulus and Hyrcanus ended up warring against each other for rule over the kingdom. Their struggle is discussed by Josephus (text 6.1.8). It ended with the dissolution of the Hasmonean kingdom at the hands of the Romans. In his account Josephus was aided by the works of Roman historians, and also by the work of Nicolaus of Damascus, King Herod's non-Jewish secretary of state who was a historian. The Babylonian Talmud likewise preserves a narrative of this internecine struggle and of the manner in which it led to interruption of the normal Temple rituals (text 6.1.9).

It was amidst these political developments that sectarianism as we know it developed in the Jewish community. In *Antiquities* Josephus pictures the sects, Pharisees, Sadducees and Essenes, as arguing over theological matters, most importantly in regard to the role of God in human affairs (text 6.2.1). Additional matters are taken up in his account in *War* (text 6.2.2). Here we hear about the approaches of the Pharisees and Sadducees to Jewish law and revelation, about the soul, and also about the general behavior of the members of these groups. A parallel account is also presented in *Antiquities* (text 6.2.3), where the popularity of the Pharisees is also stressed. The theological differences between Pharisees and Sadducees are confirmed by the New Testament (text 6.2.4).

The halakhic debates between the Pharisees and Sadducees, about which no details are provided in Josephus, are discussed in a number of Rabbinic sources. Many of these parallel disagreements are documented in the Dead Sea Scrolls as well. Extremely significant in this respect is the collection of such debates found in Mishnah Yadayim (text 6.2.5). These primarily concern issues of ritual purity. Other sources discuss similar issues, such as Mishnah Ḥagigah (text 6.2.6), in which we learn about the common people, termed the *'am ha-arez*, "people of the land," who in Rabbinic sources were distinguished from the Pharisees because they did not observe the laws of ritual impurity and tithing properly. A negative view of at least some Pharisees is presented in Mishnah Sotah (text 6.2.7). The stringency of the Sadducees regarding the prohibition of carrying on the Sabbath is highlighted in Mishnah Eruvin (text 6.2.8). They did not accept the use of the Eruv to permit carrying from one domain to another. Their strict interpretation of the law of false witnesses was stressed in Mishnah Makkot (text 6.2.9). Mishnah Parah presents an extremely important aspect of Sadducean law (text 6.2.10). They did not accept the notion that even before sunset a person could be considered pure for most purposes on the last day of his purification ritual. Such people, termed *tevul yom*, were considered still impure in the Saducean view. The final example from Mishnah Niddah (text 6.2.11) indicates the difficulties of a Pharisee's marrying a woman who observed Sadducean purity laws.

The Babylonian Talmud Qiddushin (text 6.2.12) relates a parallel story to one which is told by Josephus. According to this story, a confrontation occurred at a banquet hosted by a Hasmonean ruler, and it resulted in a break with the Pharisees who had previously supported him. In this account it is asserted that sectarian issues in the Hasmonean period were primarily dominated by halakhic matters, a view to a great extent supported by the Dead Sea Scrolls, which testify to the significance of Jewish law in the sectarian arguments of this period. But this text says more, since it deals also with the political ramifications of such strife and with the violence that sometimes ensued.

We now turn to the more separatist groups of apocalyptic sectarians. We begin by examining Josephus' description of the Essenes in *Antiquities* (text 6.3.1). Most scholars assume the Essenes to be identical with the sect of the Dead Sea Scrolls. Much more detail is available in his discussion in *War* (text 6.3.2). The special initiation and purification rites of the sect are described, as well as its communal way of life and theological tenets. This group was widely known and admired in the Greco-Roman world as is clear from Pliny (text 6.3.3), who is the one source to locate this group on the shore of the Dead Sea. This text has been an extremely important support for the view of those who identify the Essenes with the Dead Sea sect, since the latter lived at Qumran on the western shore of the Dead Sea. A more Hellenistic description of the Essenes is given by Philo (text 6.3.4). If this description and aspects of the reports of Josephus are accurate, they argue against the parallel with the Qumran scrolls since the scrolls sect was not in any way influenced by Hellenism.

For comparison, we next present the central Qumran text outlining the nature of the sect and its basic theology. The *Rule of the Community* (text 6.3.5) provides information on the initiation rites, beliefs, and system of penalties of the sectarians. These pietists separated themselves from the larger community by locating at Qumran and other sectarian centers, where they practiced their particular way of communal life and ritual, refusing to participate in the Temple ritual, which they regarded as conducted in an illegitimate manner. Another exceedingly important sectarian text is the *Damascus Document*, also known as the *Zadokite Fragments* (text 6.3.6). This text describes the sectarians' sense of their own history as well as quite a number of laws representing their view of Jewish law. This text, which was known well before the scrolls were found, helped to shape our entire sense of the sect, even though the Qumran manuscripts of this work were only published recently.

This material taken as a whole testifies to a period in which political life should have allowed the unification of the people and the consolidation of the renewed Jewish kingdom. Yet sectarian strife and disagreements about essentially religious matters spilled over, at times violently, into political life. The result was a lost opportunity for independence, and the sowing of the seeds of instability which would later lead to the Roman conquest in 63 B.C.E. and the eventual destruction of the Temple in 70 C.E.

6.1 THE HASMONEAN DYNASTY

6.1.1 Josephus, *Antiquities* XIII, 179–83: The Ascendancy of Jonathan[1]

After receiving Seleucid recognition in 152 B.C.E., Jonathan began to do battle with the Nabatean Arabs and then turned to fortifying Jerusalem.

૱

(179) Jonathan went into Arabia and fought against the Nabateans. He drove away many of their cattle, took [many] captives, and came to Damascus, where he sold off what he had taken.

(180) About the same time Simon, his brother, went through all Judea and Palestine, as far as Askelon, and fortified the strongholds. When he had made them very strong, both in the edifices erected and in the garrisons placed in them, he came to Joppa. When he had taken it, he brought a great garrison into it, for he heard that the people of Joppa were disposed to deliver up the city to Demetrius'[2] generals.

(181) When Simon and Jonathan had finished these affairs, they returned to Jerusalem where Jonathan gathered all the people together in the temple, and took counsel to restore the walls of Jerusalem, to rebuild the wall that encompassed the temple which had been thrown down, and to make the temple precincts stronger by very high towers; (182) and besides that, to build another wall in the midst of the city in order to keep the garrison which was in the citadel[3] from reaching the city and by that means to cut them off from the supply of provisions; and moreover, to make the fortresses that were in the country much stronger and more defensible than they were before. (183) When these things were approved by the people as proposed, Jonathan himself took care of the building that belonged to the city and sent Simon away to make the fortresses in the country more secure than formerly.

---

1. All passages from Josephus trans. W. Whiston, *The Works of Josephus* (Peabody, MA: Hendrickson, 1987), revised by L. H. Schiffman in consultation with H. St. J. Thackeray, Ralph Marcus, Allen Wikgren, and L. H. Feldman, trans., *Josephus: in Nine Volumes* (Loeb Classical Library; Cambridge: Harvard University Press, 1976–79).

2. Demetrius II Nicator, who ruled 145–138 B.C.E.

3. The Seleucid garrison that remained as a symbol of Seleucid rule. It was expelled by Simon in 142 B.C.E.

6.1.2 1 Maccabees 12–15:
Jonathan's Death and the Reign of Simon[4]

After the death of Jonathan in 143 B.C.E., the Hasmonean state was ruled by Simon. He succeeded in expelling the Seleucids from the citadel and in gaining an official charter from the Seleucid ruler, making Judea truly independent. Especially important are the royal documents of Seleucid provenance confirming this status which were preserved in 1 Maccabees.

꽃

12:39 Then Trypho attempted to become king of Asia[5] and put on the crown, and to raise his hand against Antiochus the king.[6] 40 He feared that Jonathan might not permit him to do so, but might make war on him, so he kept asking to seize and kill him, and he marched forth and came to Beth-Shan.[7] 41 Jonathan went out to meet him with forty thousand picked fighting men, and he came to Beth-Shan. 42 When Trypho saw that he had come with a large army, he was afraid to raise his hand against him. 43 So he received him with honor and commended him to all his friends, and he gave him gifts and commanded his friends and his troops to obey him as they would himself. 44 Then he said to Jonathan, "Why have you wearied all these people when we are not at war? 45 Dismiss them now to their homes and choose for yourself a few men to stay with you, and come with me to Ptolemais. I will hand it over to you as well as the other strongholds and the remaining troops and all the officials and will turn around and go home. For that is why I am here."

46 Jonathan trusted him and did as he said; he sent away his troops, and they returned to the land of Judah. 47 He kept with himself three thousand men, two thousand of whom he left in Galilee, while a thousand accompanied him. 48 But when Jonathan entered Ptolemais, the men of Ptolemais closed the gates and seized him, and all who had entered with him they killed with the sword.[8]

49 Then Trypho sent troops and cavalry into Galilee and the Great Plain to destroy all of Jonathan's soldiers. 50 But they realized that Jonathan had been seized and had perished along with his men, and they encouraged one another and kept marching in close formation, ready for

---

4. All texts from the Apocrypha taken from the *Revised Standard Version Apocrypha* (New York: National Council of Churches, 1957).

5. That is, to take control of the Seleucid Empire.

6. Antiochus VI.

7. Beth Shean, south of Lake Tiberias in northern Israel.

8. Jonathan was killed shortly afterwards, late in 143 B.C.E. or early in 142.

battle. 51 When their pursuers saw that they would fight for their lives, they turned back. 52 So they all reached the land of Judah safely, and they mourned for Jonathan and his companions and were in great fear; and all Israel mourned deeply. 53 And all the nations round about them tried to destroy them, for they said, "They have no leader or helper. Now therefore let us make war on them and blot out the memory of them from among men."

13:25 And Simon sent and took the bones of Jonathan his brother, and buried him in Modein, the city of his fathers. 26 All Israel bewailed him with great lamentation, and mourned for him many days. 27 And Simon built a monument over the tomb of his father and his brothers; he made it high that it might be seen, with polished stone in front and back. 28 He also erected seven pyramids, opposite one another, for his father and mother and four brothers. 29 And for the pyramids he devised an elaborate setting, erecting about them great columns, and upon the columns he put suits of armor for a permanent memorial, and beside the suits of armor carved ships, so that they could be seen by all who sail the sea. 30 This is the tomb which he built in Modein; it remains to this day. 31 Trypho dealt treacherously with the young king Antiochus;[9] he killed him 32 and became king in his place, putting on the crown of Asia; and he brought great calamity upon the land. 33 But Simon built up the strongholds of Judea and walled them all around with high towers and great walls and gates and bolts, and he stored food in the strongholds.

14:16 It was heard in Rome, and as far away as Sparta, that Jonathan had died, and they were deeply grieved. 17 When they heard that Simon his brother had become high priest in his place, and that he was ruling over the country and the cities in it, 18 they wrote to him on bronze tablets to renew with him the friendship and alliance which they had established with Judas and Jonathan his brothers. . . .

25 When the people heard these things they said, "How shall we thank Simon and his sons? 26 For he and his brothers and the house of his father have stood firm; they have fought and repulsed Israel's enemies and established its freedom." 27 So they made a record on bronze tablets and put it upon pillars on Mount Zion.

This is a copy of what they wrote: "On the eighteenth day of Elul, in the one hundred and seventy-second year, which is the third year of Simon the great high priest, 28 in Asaramel, in the great assembly of the priests and the people and the rulers of the nation and the elders of the country, the following was proclaimed to us: . . .

---

9. Antiochus VI was killed at age seven in 142 B.C.E. after ruling from 145 B.C.E.

35 "The people saw Simon's faithfulness and the glory which he had resolved to win for his nation, and they made him their leader and high priest, because he had done all these things and because of the justice and loyalty which he had maintained toward his nation. He sought in every way to exalt his people. 36 And in his days things prospered in his hands, so that the Gentiles were put out of the country, as were also the men in the city of David in Jerusalem, who had built themselves a citadel from which they used to sally forth and defile the environs of the sanctuary and do great damage to its purity. 37 He settled Jews in it, and fortified it for the safety of the country and of the city and built the walls of Jerusalem higher.

38 "In view of these things King Demetrius confirmed him in the high priesthood, 39 and he made him one of the king's friends and paid him high honors. 40 For he had heard that the Jews were addressed by the Romans as friends and allies and brethren, and that the Romans had received the envoys of Simon with honor.

41 "And the Jews and their priests decided that Simon should be their leader and high priest for ever, until a trustworthy prophet should arise, 42 and that he should be governor over them and that he should take charge of the sanctuary and appoint men over its tasks and over the country and the weapons and the strongholds, and that he should take charge of the sanctuary 43 and that he should be obeyed by all, and that all contracts in the country should be written in his name, and that he should be clothed in purple and wear gold. . . ."

46 And all the people agreed to grant Simon the right to act in accord with these decisions. 47 So Simon accepted and agreed to be high priest, to be commander and ethnarch of the Jews and priests, and to be protector of them all. 48 And they gave orders to inscribe this decree upon bronze tablets, to put them up in a conspicuous place in the precincts of the sanctuary, 49 and to deposit copies of them in the treasury, so that Simon and his sons might have them.

15:1 Antiochus, the son of Demetrius the king,[10] sent a letter from the islands of the sea to Simon, the priest and ethnarch of the Jews, and to all the nation; 2 its contents were as follows: "King Antiochus to Simon the high priest and ethnarch and to the nation of the Jews, greeting. 3 Whereas certain pestilent men have gained control of the kingdom of our fathers, and I intend to lay claim to the kingdom so that I may restore it as it formerly was, and have recruited a host of mercenary troops and have equipped warships, 4 and intend to make a landing in the country

---

10. Antiochus VII Sidetes, younger brother of Demetrius II, reigned 138–129 B.C.E.

so that I may proceed against those who have destroyed our country and those who have devastated many cities in my kingdom, 5 now therefore I confirm to you all the tax remissions that the kings before me have granted you, and release from all the other payments from which they have released you. 6 I permit you to mint your own coinage as money for your country, 7 and I grant freedom to Jerusalem and the sanctuary. All the weapons which you have prepared and the strongholds which you have built and now hold shall remain yours. 8 Every debt you owe to the royal treasury and any such future debts shall be canceled for you from henceforth and for all time. 9 When we gain control of our kingdom, we will bestow great honor upon you and your nation and the temple, so that your glory will become manifest in all the earth."

6.1.3 Josephus, *Antiquities* XIII, 225–9: The Death of Simon

Simon, who ruled from 142 to 134 B.C.E., successfully defended the Jews against Seleucid incursions later in his reign, only to fall victim to internecine strife in his own court. His son, John Hyrcanus, survived and became the next Hasmonean ruler.

⁂

(225) However, Antiochus forgot the kind assistance that Simon had afforded him in his necessity, and committed an army of soldiers to his friend Cendebeus, and sent him at once to ravage Judea, and to seize Simon. (226) When Simon heard of Antiochus' breaking his alliance with him, although he was now advanced in years, yet provoked by the unjust treatment he had met with from Antiochus, and showing resolution greater than his age could well bear, he went like a young man to act as general of his army. (227) He also sent his sons ahead among the most hardy of his soldiers, and he himself marched on with his army another way and laid many of his men in ambushes in the narrow valleys between the mountains. Nor did he fail in any one of his engagements but was too strong for his enemies in every one of them. So he passed the rest of his life in peace, and also made an alliance with the Romans. (228) Now he was ruler of the Jews in all for eight years,[11] but at a feast came to his end. It was caused by the treachery of his son-in-law Ptolemy, who also captured his wife and two of his sons and kept them in bonds. He also sent some men to kill John the third son, whose name was Hyrcanus. (229) But the young man, perceiving them coming, avoided the danger he was

---

11. 142–135 B.C.E.

in from them and made haste into the city [Jerusalem], relying on the good will of the multitude because of the benefits they had received from his father and because of the hatred the same multitude had for Ptolemy. When Ptolemy tried to enter the city by another gate, they drove him away, having already admitted Hyrcanus.

6.1.4 Josephus, *Antiquities* XIII, 230–300: The Reign of John Hyrcanus

John Hyrcanus (ruled 134–104 B.C.E.) established himself quickly as ruler and successfully negotiated his relationship with the Seleucids. He also maintained close ties with Rome which was increasingly interested in Judea as a bridge to Syria.

⟡

(230) So Ptolemy retired to one of the fortresses above Jericho which was called Dagon. But Hyrcanus, having taken the high priesthood that had been his father's before,[12] immediately propitiated God by sacrifices and then made an expedition against Ptolemy. When he made his attacks upon the place, in all other respects he was stronger than Ptolemy, but was rendered weaker only by the feeling of pity he had for his mother and his brothers. (231) For Ptolemy brought them to the wall and tormented them in the sight of all, and threatened that he would throw them down headlong unless Hyrcanus would give up the siege. Since he thought that to the extent that he relaxed the siege and capture of the place, the greater was the favor that he showed those who were dearest to him by preventing their misery, his zeal about it was cooled.

(232) However, his mother spread out her hands and begged of him that he would not grow remiss on her account, but indulge his indignation so much the more, and that he would do his utmost to take the place quickly in order to get their enemy under his power, and then to avenge upon him what he had done to those that were dearest to himself. For death would be to her sweet, though with torment, if that enemy of theirs might but be brought to punishment for his wicked dealings against them. (233) Now when his mother said this, he resolved to take the fortress immediately, but when he saw her beaten and torn to pieces, his courage failed him, and he could not but sympathize with what his mother suffered, and was thereby overcome. (234) As the siege was drawn out by this means, the year on which the Jews are accustomed to rest

---

12. John Hyrcanus was high priest and ruler from 134–104 B.C.E.

came on,[13] for the Jews observe this rest every seventh year, as they do every seventh day. (235) So Ptolemy, being for this reason released from the war, killed the brothers of Hyrcanus and his mother. When he had so done, he fled to Zeno, who was called Cotylas, who was then the tyrant of the city Philadelphia.[14]

(236) But Antiochus, being very resentful of the injuries that Simon had brought upon him, invaded Judea in the fourth year of his reign and the first year of the principality of Hyrcanus, in the hundred and sixty-second Olympiad.[15] (237) And when he had burnt the country, he shut up Hyrcanus in the city (Jerusalem) which he surrounded with seven encampments. But he did nothing at first because of the strength of the walls and because of the valor of the besieged, and also because they were in need of water, although they were delivered by a large shower of rain which fell at the setting of the Pleiades. (238) However, on the north part of the wall, where it happened that the city was on the same level as the outward ground, the king (Antiochus) raised a hundred towers each three stories high, and placed companies of soldiers upon them. (239) He made his attacks every day, and he cut a double ditch, deep and broad, and confined the inhabitants within it as within a wall. But the besieged contrived to make frequent sallies out; and if the enemy were anywhere not on their guard, they fell upon them and did them a great deal of harm. But if they perceived them, they then returned to the city with ease.

(240) Because Hyrcanus discerned the inconvenience caused by so great a number of men in the city since the provisions were the sooner used up by them, and yet, as it is natural to suppose, those great numbers did nothing, he separated the useless part and expelled them from the city and retained only that part who were in the flower of their age and fit for war. (241) However, Antiochus would not let those that were expelled leave. They, therefore, wandered about between the walls, and were consumed by famine and almost died miserably. But when the feast of Tabernacles[16] was at hand, those that were within took pity on their condition and admitted them again. (242) And when Hyrcanus sent to Antiochus, and desired that there might be a truce for seven days because of the festival, he gave way to this piety towards God and made that truce accordingly. Besides that, he sent in a magnificent sacrifice, bulls with their

---

13. The Sabbatical year extended from October 135 to October 134 B.C.E.
14. Amman in Transjordan.
15. The war seems to have lasted from 134–132 B.C.E.
16. The fall festival of Sukkot.

horns gilded, with all sorts of sweet spices, and with cups of gold and silver. . . .

(245) Accordingly, Hyrcanus took this moderation of his kindly, and when he understood how religious he was towards the Deity, he sent envoys to him, and requested that he restore to the Jews their native form of government. So he (Antiochus) rejected the counsel of those who would have had him utterly destroy the nation because of the separateness of their way of living and paid no attention to what they said. (246) But being persuaded that all they did was out of a pious frame of mind, he answered the envoys that if the besieged would deliver up their arms, pay tribute for Joppa and the other cities which bordered upon Judea, and admit a garrison of his, on these terms he would no longer make war against them. (247) But the Jews, although they were content with the other conditions, did not agree to admit the garrison because they could not associate with other people because of their separateness. Yet they were willing, instead of the admission of the garrison, to give him hostages and five hundred talents of silver, of which they paid down three hundred and handed over the hostages immediately which King Antiochus accepted. One of those hostages was Hyrcanus' brother. But still he broke down the fortifications that surrounded the city. (248) Upon these conditions Antiochus broke off the siege and departed.

(249) Hyrcanus also opened the sepulcher of David, who excelled all other kings in riches, and took out of it three thousand talents. He was also the first of the Jews who, relying on this wealth, maintained foreign troops. There was also an alliance of friendship and mutual assistance made with Antiochus upon which Hyrcanus admitted him into the city and furnished him with whatever his army wanted in great plenty and with great generosity. (250) He marched along with him when he made an expedition against the Parthians,[17] of which Nicolaus of Damascus[18] is a witness for us. In his history, he writes: (251) "When Antiochus had erected a trophy at the river Lycus,[19] upon the conquest of Indates, the general of the Parthians, he stayed there for two days. It was at the request of Hyrcanus the Jew because it was such a festival derived from their forefathers, on which the law of the Jews did not allow them to travel." (252) And truly he did not speak falsely in saying so, for the festival, which we call Pentecost,[20] did then occur on the day following the Sabbath, and is it not law-

---

17. In 130 B.C.E.
18. A high non-Jewish official of Herod's kingdom who was a historian as well.
19. The Greater Zab River in Assyria.
20. The holiday of Shavuot in May/June.

ful for us to travel, either on the Sabbath day or on a festival day. (253) But when Antiochus joined battle with Arsaces, the king of Parthia, he lost a great part of his army, and was himself killed. His brother Demetrius (II) succeeded to the kingdom of Syria, by the permission of Arsaces, who freed him from his captivity at the same time that Antiochus attacked Parthia, as we have formerly related elsewhere.[21] (254) When Hyrcanus heard of the death of Antiochus,[22] he immediately made an expedition against the cities of Syria, hoping to find them empty of fighting men, and of such as were able to defend them. (255) However, it was not until the sixth month that he took Medaba,[23] and that not without the greatest hardship to his army. After this he took Samega[24] and the neighboring places; and besides these, Shechem and Gerizim, and the nation of the Cutheans,[25] (256) who dwelled near the temple, which resembled the temple at Jerusalem and which Alexander permitted Sanballat, the general of his army, to build for the sake of Manasseh, who was son-in-law to Jadua the high priest, as we have formerly related.[26] This temple was now destroyed two hundred years after it was built. (257) Hyrcanus also took Adora and Marissa, cities of Idumea, and subdued all the Idumeans. He permitted them to stay in their country if they would circumcise themselves and observe the laws of the Jews. (258) They were so desirous of living in the country of their forefathers, that they submitted to the practice of circumcision and the rest of the Jewish way of life, and since the time in which this happened to them, they thereafter continued to be Jews.

(259) But Hyrcanus the high priest was desirous of renewing the alliance of friendship they had with the Romans. Accordingly, he sent an embassy to them. When the senate received their epistle, they made an alliance of friendship with them according to the following terms:

(260) "Fanius, the son of Marcus, the praetor, gathered the senate together on the eighth day before the Ides of February, in the senate house, when Lucius Manlius, the son of Lucius, of the Mentine tribe, and Gaius Sempronius, the son of Gaius, of the Falernian tribe, were present.[27] The occasion was that the ambassadors sent by the people of the Jews, Simon, the son of Dositheus, Apollonius, the son of Alexander, and

---

21. There is no such passage in Josephus, but this cross-reference was taken from his source.

22. 129 B.C.E.

23. An ancient Moabite city, now in Jordan, then ruled by the Nabateans.

24. Probably to be located about eight miles northeast of Medaba.

25. "Cutheans" is an alternative term for Samaritans.

26. *Ant.* XI, 322–4.

27. These two men served as praetors in 132 B.C.E.

Diodorus, the son of Jason, who were good and virtuous men, (261) had something to propose about that alliance of friendship and mutual assistance which existed between them and the Romans, and about other public affairs. They requested that Joppa and its ports and Gazara, and the Pegae[28] and the several other cities and countries of theirs, which Antiochus had taken from them in the war contrary to the decree of the senate, might be restored to them; (262) and that it might not be lawful for the king's troops to pass through their country and the countries of those that are subject to them; and that the laws Antiochus had made during that war, without the decree of the senate, might be made void; (263) and that the Romans would send ambassadors who should take care that restitution be made to them for what Antiochus had taken from them, and that they should make an estimate of the value of the country that had been laid waste in the war; and that they would grant the envoys letters of protection to the kings and free cities in order to assure their safe return home. (264) It was therefore decreed concerning these points that they should renew their alliance of friendship and mutual assistance with these good men who were sent by a good and friendly people." (265) But as to the letters requested, their answer was that the senate would consult about that matter when their own affairs would allow them and that they would endeavor, for the time to come, to prevent similar injury to them; and that the praetor Fanius should give them money out of the public treasury to bear their expenses home.

(266) And thus did Fanius dismiss the Jewish ambassadors. He gave them money out of the public treasury and gave the decree of the senate to those that were to conduct them on their way and to take care that they should return home in safety. . . .

(275) So Hyrcanus made an expedition against Samaria which was a very strong city. About its present name, Sebaste, and its rebuilding by Herod we shall speak at a proper time.[29] But he made his attack against it and besieged it vigorously, for he was greatly displeased with the Samaritans for the injuries they had done to the people of Marissa, who were colonists and allies of the Jews, in compliance with the kings of Syria. . . .

(281) And when Hyrcanus had taken the city after a year's siege, he was not contented with doing that only, but he demolished it entirely, and left it to be swept away by the mountain-torrents, for he dug such hollows as might let the waters run under it. Indeed, he took away the very evidence that there had ever been such a city there. (282) A very surprising

---

28. About ten miles north of Joppa.
29. *Ant.* XV, 296–8.

thing is related of this high priest Hyrcanus, how God came to discourse with him. For they say that on the very same day on which his sons fought with Antiochus Cyzicenus, he was alone in the temple as high priest offering incense, and he heard a voice saying that his sons had just then overcome Antiochus. (283) He openly declared this before all the multitude as he came out of the temple, and it accordingly proved true.[30] This was the situation of the affairs of Hyrcanus.

(284) At this time not only those Jews who were at Jerusalem and in Judea were prosperous but also those of them who were at Alexandria, and in Egypt and Cyprus. (285) For Cleopatra, the queen, was at war with her son Ptolemy, who was called Lathyrus, and she appointed for her generals Chelcias and Ananias, the sons of that Onias who built the temple in the nome of Heliopolis, like that at Jerusalem, as we have elsewhere related.[31] (286) Cleopatra entrusted these men with her army and did nothing without their advice, as Strabo of Cappadocia[32] attests, when he says thus: (287) "Now the greater part, both those that came to Cyprus with us and those that were sent there afterward, revolted with Ptolemy immediately. Only the Jews who were called Onias' party continued to be faithful because their countrymen Chelcias and Ananias were in special favor with the queen." These are the words of Strabo.

(288) However, this prosperous state of affairs moved the Jews to envy Hyrcanus. They who were the worst disposed to him were the Pharisees, who are one of the sects of the Jews, as we have informed you already. These have so great a power over the multitude that when they say anything against the king or against the high priest, they are immediately believed. (289) Now Hyrcanus was a disciple of theirs and greatly beloved by them.[33] When he once invited them to a feast and entertained them very kindly, and when he saw them in a good humor, he began to say to them that they knew he was desirous to be a righteous man and to do all things whereby he might please God, which was the profession of the Pharisees also. (290) However, he requested, that if they observed him offending in any point and straying from the right way, they should call him back and correct him. On that occasion they attested to his being entirely virtuous, and with this commendation he was very pleased. But

---

30. This revelation is also mentioned in Tosefta Sotah13:5.

31. *Ant.* XIII, 62–73.

32. Strabo of Amaseia (ca. 64-the 20's of the first century C.E.) was a geographer and historian from Cappadocia in Asia Minor, modern Turkey. This passage is quoted from the lost work, *Historia Hypomnemata*.

33. The following story appears in the Babylonian Talmud Qiddushin 66a, regarding Alexander Janneus.

there was one of his guests there whose name was Eleazar, (291) a man of evil nature, who delighted in seditious practices. This man said, "Since you desire to know the truth, if you are righteous in earnest, give up the high priesthood and content yourself with the civil government of the people." (292) And when he desired to know why he ought to give up the high priesthood, he replied, "We have heard it from the elders that your mother had been a captive during the reign of Antiochus Epiphanes."[34] This story was false, and Hyrcanus was furious with him, and all the Pharisees were very indignant against him.

(293) Now there was one Jonathan, a very great friend of Hyrcanus, but of the sect of the Sadducees whose notions are quite contrary to those of the Pharisees. He told Hyrcanus that Eleazar had cast such a reproach upon him with the general approval of all the Pharisees, and that this would be made manifest if he would only ask them the question of what punishment they thought this man deserved. (294) He might be sure that the reproach was not laid on him with their approbation if they were for punishing him as his crime deserved. So the Pharisees gave an answer that he deserved lashes and chains, but that it did not seem right to punish reproaches with death; and indeed the Pharisees, even upon other occasions, are not apt to be severe in punishments. (295) At this gentle sentence Hyrcanus was very angry, and he thought that this man reproached him with their approval. It was this Jonathan who chiefly aggravated him and influenced him so that he joined the Sadducean party, (296) made him leave the party of the Pharisees, and abolish the decrees they had imposed on the people, and punish those who observed them. From this source arose that hatred which he and his sons met with from the multitude.

(297) But of these matters we shall speak later.[35] What I would now explain is this: that the Pharisees have delivered to the people a great many observances handed down by their fathers, which are not written in the law of Moses. For that reason the Sadducees reject them and say that we are to consider obligatory only those observances which are in the written word, but are not to observe those that are derived from the tradition of our forefathers. (298) Concerning these things, great disputes and differences have arisen among them. The Sadducees are able to persuade none but the rich and have no following among the populace, but the Phari-

---

34. The accusation meant that his mother could not be depended on to have been a virgin at marriage, and so he was not a legitimate priest. Cf. Lev. 21:13–14.

35. *Ant.* XIII, 301 ff., 320 ff.

sees have the masses on their side. But these two sects and that of the Essenes, I have treated in detail in the second book of Jewish affairs.[36]

(299) When Hyrcanus had put an end to this sedition, he lived happily thereafter and administered the government in the best manner for thirty-one years[37] and then died, leaving behind him five sons. He was considered by God to be worthy of the three privileges: the government of his nation, the office of the high priesthood, and prophecy. (300) For God was with him and enabled him to know the future and to foretell this in particular, that his two eldest sons would not long continue as masters of the state. Their unhappy catastrophe will be worth our description so that we may thence learn how far they were from having their father's good fortune.

6.1.5 Josephus, *Antiquities* XIII, 301–23: The Reign of Aristobulus

Aristobulus, who succeeded his father John Hyrcanus, reigned from 104 to 103 B.C.E. He was a tragic figure destroyed by his jealousy and suspicion. He serves as little more than a transitional figure between John Hyrcanus and Alexander Janneus. He was, however, the first Hasmonean to take the title of King.

🕮

(301) Now when their father Hyrcanus was dead, the eldest son Aristobulus, intending to change the government into a kingdom, for so he resolved to do, first of all put a diadem on his head, four hundred and eighty-one years and three months after the people had been delivered from the Babylonian captivity and were returned to their own country again.[38] (302) This Aristobulus loved his next brother Antigonus and treated him as his equal, but the others he held in bonds. He also threw his mother into prison because she disputed the government with him, for Hyrcanus had left her to be mistress of all. He went so far in his barbarity as to kill her in prison by starvation. (303) To the death of his mother he added that of Antigonus from whom he was alienated by calumnies even though he had seemed to have an affection for him, and he had made him above the rest a partner with him in the kingdom. At first he did not give

---

36. *War* II, 119–66.

37. 135–104 B.C.E.

38. Actually, it was about 481 years since the destruction of Jerusalem by the Babylonians in 586 B.C.E.

credence to those calumnies, partly because he loved him, and so he paid no attention to what was said against him, and partly because he thought the reproaches were caused by the envy of those who related them.

(304) But when Antigonus once returned from a military campaign, and that feast was then at hand when they make tabernacles [to the honor of] God,[39] it happened that Aristobulus had fallen sick, and Antigonus went up most splendidly adorned with his soldiers about him in their armor to the temple to celebrate the feast and to pray earnestly for the recovery of his brother. (305) Some wicked persons, who had a great desire to create a dispute between the brothers, made use of the opportunity of the pompous appearance of Antigonus and of the successes which he had achieved. They went to the king and spitefully exaggerated his pompous appearance at the feast, (306) and pretended that all these actions were not like those of a private person but indications of an affectation of royal authority; and that his coming with a strong body of men must indicate the intention to kill Aristobulus; and that his way of reasoning was this: that it was a silly thing, while it was in his power to reign himself, to look upon it as a great favor that he was honored with a lower office by his brother.

(307) Aristobulus began to believe these charges, but took care both that his brother should not suspect him and that he himself might not risk his own safety. So he stationed his guards in a dark, underground passage (he himself was then lying sick in the tower which was called Antonia), and he commanded them that in case Antigonus came in to him unarmed, they should not touch anybody, but if armed, they should kill him. (308) Moreover, he sent to Antigonus and requested that he come unarmed. But the queen, and those that joined with her in the plot against Antigonus, persuaded the messenger to tell him the direct opposite, how his brother had heard that he had made himself a fine suit of armor for war and invited him to come to him in that armor so that he might see how fine it was. (309) So Antigonus, suspecting no treachery but depending on the good will of his brother, came to Aristobulus armed, as he used to be, with his entire armor, in order to show it to him. But when he had come to a place which was called Strato's Tower, where the passage happened to be exceedingly dark, the guards killed him. (310) Now his death demonstrates that nothing is stronger than envy and calumny, and that nothing does more certainly divide the good will and natural affection of men than those passions.

---

39. The fall festival of Sukkot.

(311) But here one may take occasion to wonder at one Judas, who was of the sect of the Essenes, and who never missed the truth in his predictions. For this man, when he saw Antigonus passing by the temple, cried to his companions and friends, who stayed with him as his students in order to learn the art of foretelling things to come, (312) that it was good for him (Judas himself) to die now, since he had spoken falsely about Antigonus, since Antigonus was still alive and was passing by, although he had foretold that he would die at the place called Strato's Tower that very day. For the place is six hundred stades away from where he had foretold that he would be slain; and the greater part of the day had already passed so that he was in danger of proving a false prophet. (313) As he was saying this in a melancholy mood, the news came that Antigonus had been slain in the underground passage which was also called Strato's Tower, by the same name as Caesarea which is located at the sea. This fact had confused the prophet.

(314) Aristobulus repented immediately of the slaughter of his brother. But because of it, disease came upon him, and he was disturbed in his mind from the guilt of such wickedness, so that his entrails were corrupted by intolerable pain, and he vomited blood.... (317) He died, having reigned a year.

(318) He was called a lover of the Greeks, and had conferred many benefits on his own country. He made war against Iturea,[40] added a great part of it to Judea, and compelled the inhabitants, if they would remain in that country, to be circumcised and to live according to the Jewish laws. (319) He was naturally a man of candor and of great modesty, as Strabo bears witness in the name of Timagenes[41] who says thus: "This man was a person of candor and very serviceable to the Jews, for he added a territory to them and obtained a part of the nation of the Itureans for them and bound them to them by the bond of circumcision."

When Aristobulus died, his wife Salome,[42] who was called Alexandra by the Greeks, let his brothers out of prison (for Aristobulus had kept them in chains, as we have said already[43]) and made Alexander Janneus king for he was the superior in age and in moderation.... (323) ...He killed one of his brothers who had designs on the kingdom, and the other, who chose to live a private and quiet life, he held in honor.

---

40. The Bekaa Valley in Southern Lebanon.
41. A first century B.C.E. historian who wrote in Rome.
42. Hebrew, Shelomzion, literally, "peace of Zion."
43. *Ant.* XIII, 302.

6.1.6 Josephus, _Antiquities_ XIII, 356–83:
The Reign of Alexander Janneus

Alexander Janneus (103–76 B.C.E.) cruelly defeated his enemies and expanded the boundaries of the Hasmonean state. But his people revolted against him in a violent revolt which he cruelly suppressed.

🏵

(356) When Alexander was delivered from his fear of Ptolemy,[44] he immediately made an expedition against Celesyria.[45] He also took Gadara after a siege of ten months. He then took Amathus, a very strong fortress belonging to the inhabitants beyond the Jordan where Theodorus, the son of Zeno,[46] kept his chief and most precious treasures. This man fell unexpectedly upon the Jews and killed ten thousand of them and seized Alexander's baggage. (357) Yet this misfortune did not terrify Alexander. Instead he made an expedition against the maritime parts of the country, Raphia and Anthedon (the name of which king Herod afterwards changed to Agrippas), and took even that by force. (358) But when Alexander saw that Ptolemy had returned from Gaza to Cyprus, and his mother Cleopatra had returned to Egypt, he grew angry at the people of Gaza because they had invited Ptolemy to assist them. Therefore, he besieged their city and ravaged their country. (359) But Apollodotus, the general of the army of Gaza, fell upon the camp of the Jews by night with two thousand foreign and ten thousand of his own forces. While the night lasted, the Gazans prevailed because the enemy was made to believe that it was Ptolemy who had attacked them. But when daylight appeared and that mistake was corrected, and the Jews knew the truth of the matter, they came back again and fell upon the Gazans and killed about a thousand of them.

(360) But since the Gazans stoutly resisted them and would not yield for either their lack of supplies nor because of the great multitude that were killed (for they would rather suffer any hardship whatever than come under the power of their enemies), Aretas, king of the Arabians, a

---

44. Ptolemy Lathyrus, ruler of Cyprus, who had been driven from Egypt by his mother, Cleopatra. He invaded Palestine at the beginning of Alexander Janneus' reign. Cleopatra, however, was persuaded by her Jewish generals to come to Hyrcanus' aid.

45. Transjordan, in this context.

46. One of a number of tyrants who ruled small territories or cities as the Seleucid Empire was declining.

person then very illustrious, encouraged them to go on with alacrity, and promised them that he would come to their assistance. (361) However, before he arrived, Apollodotus was killed. For his brother Lysimachus, envying him for the great reputation he had gained among the citizens, killed him and got the army together and delivered the city to Alexander. (362) When he came in, at first he acted peaceably, but afterwards set his army upon the inhabitants of Gaza and let them punish them. . . . Yet the Gazans were not of cowardly heart but opposed those who came to kill them, and killed as many of the Jews. (363) Some of them, when they saw themselves deserted, burned their own houses so that the enemy might get none of their spoils. Indeed, some of them, with their own hands, killed their children and their wives, having no other way but this of avoiding slavery for them. (364) The senators, who were in all five hundred, fled to Apollo's temple (for this attack happened to be made as they were sitting in council), but Alexander killed them. When he had totally overthrown their city, he returned to Jerusalem, having spent a year on that siege.

(372) As to Alexander, his own people revolted against him. For at a festival which was then celebrated, when he stood upon the altar and was going to sacrifice, the nation rose up against him and pelted him with citrons[47] [which they then had in their hands, because] the laws of the Jews required that at the feast of Tabernacles[48] everyone should have branches of the palm tree and citron fruits which we have elsewhere related.[49] They also reviled him as descended from a captive and therefore unworthy of his office and of sacrificing. (373) At this he flew into a rage and killed about six thousand of them. He also built a partition wall of wood around the altar and the temple. Beyond that partition it was lawful only for the priests to enter, and by this means he obstructed the people from coming to him. (374) He also maintained foreign troops of Pisidians and Cilicians, for he was at war with the Syrians and so made no use of them. He also overcame the Arabs of Moab and Gilead, and made them pay tribute. Moreover, he demolished Amathus since Theodorus dared not fight with him. (375) Then he joined battle with Obedas, king of the Arabians, and falling into an ambush in a rugged region where it was quite difficult to

---

47. A similar event is mentioned in M. Sukkah 4:9 where the name of the priest is not given.

48. The fall festival of Sukkot.

49. *Ant.* III, 245. This practice was based on traditional interpretation of Lev. 23:40. The palm and citron are known in Hebrew as *lulav* and *etrog*.

travel, he was thrown down into a deep valley by a multitude of camels at Gadara,[50] a village of Gilead, and hardly escaped with his life. From there he fled to Jerusalem (376) where, because of his misfortunes, the nation insulted him. He fought against them for six years and killed no fewer than fifty thousand of them. When he requested that they desist from their ill will toward him, they only hated him much more on account of what had already happened. And when he asked them what he ought to do, they all cried out that he ought to kill himself. They also sent to Demetrius Eukairos,[51] and asked him to make a league of mutual defense with them.

So Demetrius came with an army, took those who invited him, and pitched his camp near the city Shechem. Alexander, with his six thousand two hundred mercenaries and about twenty thousand Jews who were of his party, went out to meet Demetrius, who had three thousand horsemen and forty thousand footmen. (378) Now there was great activity on both sides—Demetrius trying to cause the mercenaries who were with Alexander to desert because they were Greeks, and Alexander trying to cause the Jews who were with Demetrius to desert. However, when neither of them could persuade them to do so, they engaged in battle, and Demetrius was the conqueror. All Alexander's mercenaries were killed after they had given proof of their fidelity and courage. A great number of Demetrius' soldiers were also killed.

Then as Alexander fled to the mountains, six thousand Jews then came to his side out of pity at the change of his fortune. Then Demetrius was afraid and withdrew from the country. Afterwards the Jews fought against Alexander and were defeated, and many died in the battles. (380) When he had shut up the most powerful of them in the city of Bethome,[52] he besieged them there. When he had taken the city and gotten the men into his power, he brought them to Jerusalem and did one of the most barbarous actions in the world to them. For as he was feasting with his concubines, in the sight of all the city, he ordered about eight hundred of them to be crucified. And while they were still alive, he ordered the throats of their children and wives to be cut before their eyes. . . . (383) However, this barbarity seems to have been without any necessity, for which reason he bore the nickname "Thracian" ("Cossack") among the Jews. Then the soldiers who had fought against him, being about eight thousand, ran

---

50. An alternate reading has Garada.
51. Seleucid ruler, who ruled from 96–88 B.C.E.
52. A village probably to be located in Samaria, about 10 miles northeast of Sebaste.

away by night and remained fugitives the entire time that Alexander lived. Then he, being freed now from any further disturbance from them, reigned for the rest of his time in the utmost tranquility.

6.1.7 Josephus, *Antiquities* XIII, 398–432: Queen Salome Alexandra

Alexander Janneus was soon succeeded by his wife, Salome Alexandra (76–67 B.C.E.) whose reign brought the Pharisees back to power. But the Queen's rule sowed the seeds of the eventual decline of the Hasmonean House after her death.

৯৫

(398) After this, King Alexander[53] fell ill because of hard drinking and had a quartan fever for three years, but he would not give up going out with his army until he was quite exhausted from the labors he had undergone, and died while besieging Ragaba, a fortress beyond the Jordan. (399) But when his queen saw that he was ready to die, and no longer had any hopes of surviving, she came to him weeping and lamenting, and bewailed the desolate condition in which she and her sons would be left. And she said to him, "To whom do you thus leave me and my children who are without any other support, and this when you know how much ill will your nation bears you?"

(400) So he gave her the following advice, which, if she would but follow his suggestions, would allow her to retain the kingdom securely for her children: that she should conceal his death from the soldiers until she captured that fortress. (401) After this, she should go triumphantly and victoriously to Jerusalem and put some of her authority into the hands of the Pharisees. For they would commend her for the honor she had done them and would reconcile the nation to her. For he told her they had great authority among the Jews, both to do harm to whomever they hated and to bring advantage to those to whom they were friendly. (402) For they are believed best of all by the multitude when they speak harshly against others, even though it be only out of envy at them. And he said that it was by their means that he had incurred the displeasure of the nation whom indeed he had injured. (403) "Therefore," said he, "when you come to Jerusalem, send for the leading men among them and show them my body, and with great appearance of sincerity give them permission to treat it as they themselves please, whether they will dishonor the

---

53. Alexander Janneus, who ruled between 103–76 B.C.E.

dead body by refusing it burial for having severely suffered by my hands, or whether in their anger they will offer any other injury to that body. Promise them also that you will do nothing without them in the affairs of the kingdom. (404) If you do but say this to them, I shall have the honor of a more glorious funeral from them than you could have made for me; and when it is in their power to abuse my dead body, they will do it no injury at all, and you will rule in safety."

When he had given his wife this advice, he died, after he had reigned twenty-seven years and lived forty-nine years.

(405) So Alexandra, when she had taken the fortress, acted as her husband had suggested to her, and spoke to the Pharisees, and put all things into their power, both as to the dead body and as to the affairs of the kingdom. Thereby she pacified their anger against Alexander and made them bear good will and friendship to him. (406) They then went to the people and made speeches to them, laid before them the actions of Alexander, and told them that they had lost a righteous king. By the commendation they gave him, they brought them to grieve and to lament for him, so that he had a funeral more splendid than had any of the kings before him. (407) Alexander left two sons, Hyrcanus and Aristobulus, but committed the kingdom to Alexandra. Of these two sons, Hyrcanus was indeed unable to manage public affairs and delighted rather in a quiet life, but the younger one, Aristobulus, was an active and a bold man. As for this woman herself, Alexandra, she was loved by the multitude because she seemed displeased at the offenses of which her husband had been guilty.

(408) So she made Hyrcanus high priest because he was the elder, but much more because he did not care to meddle with politics and permitted the Pharisees to do everything. She also ordered the multitude to be obedient to the Pharisees. She then restored those practices which the Pharisees had introduced according to the traditions of their forefathers which her father-in-law, Hyrcanus, had abrogated. (409) So she had indeed the name of the sovereign, but the Pharisees had the authority for it was they who allowed many who had been banished to return and set prisoners free, and, in a word, they differed in nothing from absolute rulers. However, the queen also took care of the affairs of the kingdom, got together a great body of mercenary soldiers, and increased her own army to such a degree that she struck terror in the neighboring tyrants and took hostages from them.

(410) The country was entirely at peace, except the Pharisees, for they pestered the queen desiring that she should kill those who persuaded Alexander to slay the eight hundred men. After this they cut the throat of one of them, Diogenes. After him they did the same to several, one after another, (411) until the men who were the most powerful came into the palace, and Aristobulus was with them, for he seemed to be displeased at what was done. It appeared openly that, if he had an opportunity, he would not permit his mother to go on so. They reminded the queen of the great dangers they had gone through and the great things they had done, whereby they had demonstrated the firmness of their fidelity to their master, as a result of which they had received the greatest honors from him. (412) They begged of her that she would not utterly destroy their hopes, for when they had escaped the hazards that arose from their [open] enemies, they were now to be slaughtered at home by their [private] enemies, like brute beasts, without any help whatsoever. (413) They said also that if their adversaries would be satisfied with those that had been slain already, they would take what had been done patiently, on account of their natural devotion to their masters. But if they must expect the same for the future also, they requested of her to be dismissed from her service, for they could not bear to think of attempting any method for their deliverance without her, but would rather die willingly before the palace gate if she would not forgive them. (414) It was a great shame, they added, both for themselves and for the queen, that when they were abandoned by her, they should be given shelter by her husband's enemies. For Aretas, the Arabian king, and other monarchs would give any reward if they could get such men as foreign auxiliaries, to whom their very names, before their voices were heard, caused them to shudder. (415) But if they could not obtain this second request, and if she had determined to prefer the Pharisees over them, they still insisted that she should place each one of them in her fortresses. For if some evil genius were angry with Alexander's house, they would be willing to bear their part, and to live in humble circumstances there.

(416) After these men had spoken so and called upon Alexander's spirit to take pity on those already slain and those in danger of it, all the bystanders broke out into tears. But Aristobulus chiefly made manifest what his sentiments were, and used many reproachful expressions to his mother [saying], (417) "But, indeed, the case is this, that they have been themselves the causes of their own calamities for permitting a woman who, against reason, was mad with ambition, to reign over them, when

her sons were in the prime of life." So Alexandra, not knowing what to do with any decency, committed the fortresses to them, all but Hyrcania,[54] Alexandrium,[55] and Machaerus,[56] where her principal treasures were. (418) After a little while also, she sent her son Aristobulus with an army to Damas-cus against Ptolemy, who was called Menneus, who was such a bad neighbor to the city. But he did nothing considerable there, and so returned home. . . .

(422) After this, when the queen suffered with a dangerous disease, Aristobulus resolved to attempt to seize the government. So he stole away secretly by night with only one of his servants, and went to the fortresses, where his friends from the days of his father were settled. (423) For although he had been for a long time displeased at his mother's conduct, he was now much more afraid lest, upon her death, their whole family should be under the power of the Pharisees, for he saw the inability of his brother who would then succeed to the government. (424) No one was conscious of what he was doing except his wife whom he left in Jerusalem with their children. He first of all came to Agaba[57] where Palestes was, one of the powerful men mentioned before, and was received by him. (425) On the next day, the queen perceived that Aristobulus had fled, but for some time she supposed that his departure was not in order to start a revolt. But when messengers came one after another with the news that he had secured the first fortress, the second fortress, and all the fortresses, for as soon as one had begun, they all submitted to his will, then it was that the queen and the nation were in the greatest disorder, (426) for they were aware that it would not be long before Aristobulus would be able to establish himself firmly in the government. What they were principally afraid of was that he would inflict punishment upon them for the excesses his house had suffered from them, so they decided to take his wife and children into custody and to keep them in the fortress that overlooked the temple.

(427) Now there was a mighty conflux of people that came to Aristobulus from all parts so that he had a kind of royal entourage around him. For in little more than fifteen days, he took twenty-two fortresses which gave him the opportunity of raising an army from Lebanon and Trachoni-

---

54. Khirbet Mird, about eight miles southeast of Jerusalem.
55. About three miles southwest of the confluence of the Jabok and Jordan Rivers.
56. About five miles east of the Dead Sea.
57. Perhaps emend to "Ragaba," a fortress in Transjordan.

tis,[58] and the local princes; for men are easily drawn to the stronger side and easily submit to it. And, besides this, by affording him their assistance when he could not expect it, they, as well as he, should have the advantages that would come by his being king because they had been the means of his gaining the kingdom. (428) Then the elders of the Jews, and Hyrcanus with them, went in to the queen and requested that she give them her counsel about the present state of affairs, for Aristobulus was in effect ruler of almost all the kingdom by possessing so many strongholds, and it was absurd for them to take any counsel by themselves, however ill she was, while she was alive; and yet the danger was not at all far off. (429) But she bade them do what they thought proper to be done, saying that they had many circumstances in their favor still remaining—a nation in good condition, an army, and money in their various treasuries; for she had little concern about public affairs now when the strength of her body was failing her.

(430) A little while after she had said this to them she died, after reigning nine years,[59] and she had lived in all seventy-three. She was a woman who showed no signs of the weakness of her sex, for she was sagacious to the greatest degree in her ambition of governing, and demonstrated by her deeds at once that her mind was fit for action, and that sometimes men themselves show the little understanding they have by the frequent mistakes they make in government. (431) For she always preferred the present to the future and preferred the power of absolute dominion above all things, and on account of that had no regard to what was good or what was right. However, she brought the affairs of her house to such an unfortunate condition that she was the reason for the removal of that authority from it not so long afterward. She had obtained it by a vast number of dangers and misfortunes out of a desire for what does not belong to a woman, and all by compliance in her sentiments with those who bore ill will to their family, and by leaving the administration lacking the proper support of great men. (432) Indeed, her management during her administration, while she was alive, was such as filled the palace after her death with calamities and disturbance. However, although this had been her way of governing, she had preserved the nation in peace, and this is the conclusion of the affairs of Alexandra.

---

58. A province of the area of Bashan east of the Jordan River and north of the Yarmuk River, today in the Golan Heights.

59. 76–67 B.C.E.

6.1.8 Josephus, *Antiquities* XIV, 4–79:
Hyrcanus II and Aristobulus

The coming of the Romans led, in turn, to the rise of the Idumean Anti-
pater who manipulated Hyrcanus II to advance his own interests. The infight-
ing of the last Hasmoneans made it possible for the Romans to side with
Antipater and Hyrcanus, thus gaining power over Judea in 63 B.C.E.

§

(4) Hyrcanus then began his rule on the third year of the hundred and
seventy-seventh olympiad when Quintus Hortensius and Quintus Metellus, who was called Metellus of Crete, were consuls at Rome.[60] Immediately, Aristobulus began to make war against him, and in battle with
Hyrcanus at Jericho, many of his soldiers deserted him and went over to
his brother.[61] (5) Then Hyrcanus fled into the citadel where Aristobulus'
wife and children had been imprisoned by his mother, as we have said
already,[62] and attacked and overcame his adversaries who had fled there
and taken refuge within the walls of the temple. (6) So after he had sent a
message to his brother about coming to an agreement regarding the matters between them, he laid aside his enmity to him on these conditions:
that Aristobulus should be king, and that he (Hyrcanus) should live without meddling in public affairs and quietly enjoy the estate he had
acquired.[63] (7) When they had agreed upon these terms in the temple and
had confirmed the agreement with oaths and giving one another their
right hands and embracing one another in the sight of the whole multitude, they departed, the one, Aristobulus, to the palace, and Hyrcanus, as
a private man, to the former house of Aristobulus.

(8) But there was a certain friend of Hyrcanus, an Idumean called Antipater, who was very rich, and in his nature an active and a seditious man,
who was an enemy of Aristobulus and had differences with him
on account of his good will to Hyrcanus. (9) It is true that Nicolaus of
Damascus[64] says that Antipater was of the stock of the principal Jews who
came from Babylon into Judea; but that assertion of his was to gratify
Herod, who was his (Antipater's) son, and who, by certain revolutions of
fortune, came afterwards to be king of the Jews, whose history we shall

---

60. 70–69 B.C.E.

61. Hyrcanus' soldiers deserted to his brother, Aristobulus.

62. *Ant.* XIII, 426.

63. Apparently, he gave up the high priesthood.

64. Herod's non-Jewish secretary of state whose historical works served as a principal
source for Josephus.

give you in its proper place.[65] (10) However, this Antipater was at first called Antipas, and that was his father's name also, of whom they relate this: That king Alexander and his wife made him general of all Idumea, and that he made a league of friendship with those Arabs, Gazans, and Ascalonites who were of his own party, and by many and large presents made them his loyal friends. (11) But now this young Antipater was suspicious of the power of Aristobulus and was afraid of some harm he might do him because of his hatred of him. So he stirred up the most powerful of the Jews and talked against him to them privately, and said that it was unjust to overlook the conduct of Aristobulus who had gotten the government unrighteously and had driven his brother who was the elder from the throne, who ought to retain what belonged to him by prerogative of his birth. (12) He perpetually made the same speeches to Hyrcanus and told him that his own life would be in danger unless he guarded himself and got rid of Aristobulus. For he said that the friends of Aristobulus lost no opportunity to advise him to kill him, as then, and not before, he was sure to retain his power. (13) Hyrcanus gave no credit to these words of his, being of a gentle disposition and one that did not easily admit of calumnies against other men. This temperament of his, not disposing him to meddle in public affairs, and his lack of spirit, made him appear to observers to be degenerate and unmanly, while Aristobulus was of a contrary temperament, an active man, and an alert spirit.

(14) Since, therefore, Antipater saw that Hyrcanus did not listen to what he said, he never ceased, day by day, to charge feigned crimes to Aristobulus and to slander him before Hyrcanus, saying that Aristobulus had a mind to kill him. So by urging him perpetually, he advised him and persuaded him to flee to Aretas, the king of Arabia, and promised that if he would comply with his advice, he would also assist him himself. (15) When Hyrcanus heard this, he said that it was to his advantage to flee to Aretas, the Arab king. (Arabia is a country that borders upon Judea.) However, Hyrcanus sent Antipater first to the Arab king in order to receive assurances from him that when he would come as a supplicant to him, he would not deliver him up to his enemies. (16) So Antipater, having received such assurances, returned to Hyrcanus in Jerusalem. A while afterward he took Hyrcanus and stole out of the city by night, traveled a great distance, and came and brought him to the city called Petra where the palace of Aretas was. (17) As he was a very familiar friend of that king, he urged him to bring back Hyrcanus into Judea, and this persuasion he continued every day without any intermission. He also proposed

---

65. *Antiquites* 15.

to make him presents on that account. At length he finally persuaded Aretas. (18) Moreover, Hyrcanus promised him that when he had been brought there and had received his kingdom, he would restore that territory and those twelve cities which his father Alexander had taken from the Arabians. . . .

(19) After these promises had been given to Aretas, he made an expedition against Aristobulus with an army of fifty thousand horsemen and foot soldiers and beat him in battle. When after that victory many went over to Hyrcanus as deserters, Aristobulus was left desolate and fled to Jerusalem. (20) Then the king of Arabia took his entire army and made an assault upon the temple, and besieged Aristobulus therein. The people still supported Hyrcanus and assisted him in the siege, while none but the priests continued to be loyal to Aristobulus. (21) So Aretas united the forces of the Arabians and of the Jews together and pressed on vigorously with the siege. As this happened at the time when the feast of unleavened bread was celebrated, which we call the Passover, the principal men among the Jews left the country and fled into Egypt.

(22) There was one, whose name was Onias, a righteous man, beloved of God, who, in a certain drought, had prayed to God to put an end to the intense heat, and whose prayers God had heard, and had sent them rain.[66] This man had hidden himself because he saw that this revolt would last a great while. However, they brought him to the Jewish camp and desired that just as by his prayers he had once put an end to the drought, so he would in like manner make imprecations against Aristobulus and those of his faction. (23) And when, upon his refusal, and the excuses that he made, he was still compelled to speak by the multitude, he stood up in the midst of them and said, (24) "O God, the King of the whole world! since those that stand now with me are Your people, and those that are besieged are also Your priests, I beseech You that You will neither hearken to the prayers of those against these, nor bring to effect what these pray against those." Whereupon those wicked Jews who stood about him, as soon as he had uttered this prayer, stoned him to death.

(25) But God punished them immediately for their barbarity and took vengeance on them for the murder of Onias in the following manner: While the priests and Aristobulus were besieged, it happened that the feast called the Passover occurred, at which it is our custom to offer a great number of sacrifices to God. (26) But those that were with Aristobulus

---

66. In Rabbinic tradition, this man was known as Ḥoni, the Circle-drawer. This story appears in Mishnah Ta'anit 3:8, cf. Babylonian Talmud Ta'anit 23a, Jerusalem Talmud 3:10–12 (66d).

wanted sacrifices, and desired that their countrymen outside would furnish them with such sacrifices, and assured them they should have as
much money for them as they should desire. And when they required
them to pay a thousand drachmae for each head of cattle, Aristobulus and
the priests willingly undertook to pay for them accordingly; and those
within let down the money over the walls and gave it to them. (27) But
when the others had received it they did not deliver the sacrifices, but
arrived at the height of wickedness as to break the assurances they had
given and to be guilty of impiety towards God by not furnishing those
that wanted them with sacrifices. (28) And when the priests found that
they had been cheated and that the agreements they had made were violated, they prayed to God that He would exact satisfaction on their behalf
from their countrymen. Nor did He delay their punishment, but sent a
strong and vehement storm of wind that destroyed the fruits of the whole
country until a modius[67] of wheat was then bought for eleven drachmae.

(29) In the meantime, Pompey sent Scaurus[68] into Syria,[69] while he
was himself in Armenia and making war with Tigranes. But when Scaurus
came to Damascus and found that Lollius and Metellus had newly taken
the city, he hurried to Judea. (30) When he arrived there, ambassadors
came to him, both from Aristobulus and Hyrcanus, and both desired that
he assist them. When both of them promised to give him money, Aristobulus four hundred talents and Hyrcanus no less, he accepted Aristobulus'
promise, (31) for he (Aristobulus) was rich, and had a great soul, and
desired to obtain nothing but what was moderate; whereas the other
(Hyrcanus) was poor and tenacious, and made incredible promises in
hope of greater advantages. . . . (32) He therefore made an agreement
with Aristobulus for the reason mentioned before, took his money, raised
the siege, and ordered Aretas to depart, or else he should be declared an
enemy of the Romans. (33) So Scaurus returned to Damascus again. Then
Aristobulus, with a great army, made war with Aretas and Hyrcanus and
fought them at a place called Papyron,[70] beat them in battle, and killed
about six thousand of the enemy, among them Phalion, the brother of
Antipater.

(34) A little later Pompey came to Damascus and marched into Celesyria. At that time ambassadors came to him from all of Syria and Egypt,
and from Judea also, for Aristobulus had sent him a great present which

---

67. A modius equals about one-quarter of a bushel.

68. M. Aemilius Scaurus, Roman governor of Syria, 65–63 B.C.E. He is one of a few
historical characters mentioned in the Dead Sea Scrolls.

69. Ca. 65 B.C.E.

70. Probably someplace near Jericho.

was a golden vine of the value of five hundred talents. (35) Now Strabo of Cappadocia mentions this present in these words: "There came also an embassy from Egypt, and a crown of the value of four thousand pieces of gold. And from Judea there came another, whether you call it a vine or a garden; they call the thing *Terpole*, 'Delight.' (36) However, we ourselves saw that present deposited at Rome in the temple of Jupiter Capitolinus with this inscription: 'The Gift of Alexander, the king of the Jews.' It was valued at five hundred talents, and the report is that Aristobulus, the ruler of the Jews, sent it."

(37) Not long afterward, ambassadors came again to him, Antipater from Hyrcanus, and Nicodemus from Aristobulus. The latter also accused first Gabinius and then Scaurus of having taken bribes, the one three hundred talents, and the other four hundred. By this accusation he made these two his enemies besides those he had before. (38) When Pompey had ordered those that had controversies with one another to come to him at the beginning of the spring, he brought his army out of their winter quarters and marched into the country of Damascus. . . . (41) It was there that he heard the causes of the Jews and of their leaders Hyrcanus and Aristobulus who had differences with one another. But the nation had complaints against them both and did not desire to be governed by a king because the form of government they received from their forefathers was that of subjection to the priests of God whom they worshiped. And [they complained] that though these two were of the posterity of priests, yet they sought to change the government of their nation to another form in order to enslave them. (42) Hyrcanus complained that although he was the elder brother, he was deprived of the prerogative of his birth by Aristobulus and that he had but a small part of the country under him, Aristobulus having taken away the rest from him by force. (43) He also charged that the incursions which had been made into their neighbors' countries and the piracies that had taken place at sea, were owing to him, and that the nation would not have revolted unless Aristobulus had been a man given to violence and disorder. There were no fewer than a thousand Jews, the most reputable among them provided by Antipater, who confirmed this accusation. (44) But Aristobulus alleged against him that it was Hyrcanus' own temperament which was inactive, and on that account contemptible, which caused him to be deprived of the government; and that for himself he was required to take it upon himself lest it be transferred to others; and that as to his title [of king], it was no other than what his father had taken [before him]. (45) He also called witnesses to what he had said, some persons who were both young and insolent, whose purple garments, fine heads of hair, and other ornaments, were

detested [by the court], and which they appeared in, not as though they were to plead their cause in a court of justice, but as if they were marching in a pompous procession.

(46) When Pompey had heard the claims of these two, he condemned Aristobulus for his violent procedure. He then spoke civilly to them and sent them away, and told them that when he came again into their country, he would settle all their affairs after he had first taken a view of the affairs of the Nabateans. In the meantime, he ordered them to keep the peace, and treated Aristobulus civilly lest he should make the nation revolt and hinder his return. (47) This Aristobulus did, for without waiting for any further determination which Pompey had promised them, he went to the city Delius[71] and then marched into Judea. . . .

(52) But when Pompey commanded Aristobulus to deliver up the fortresses he held and to send an order to their commanders under his own hand for that purpose, for they had been forbidden to deliver them up upon any other commands, he indeed agreed to do so, but still he retired in displeasure to Jerusalem and made preparation for war. (54) Now when Pompey had pitched his camp at Jericho (where the palm tree grows and that balsam which is the most precious of all ointments, which, upon any incision made in the wood with a sharp stone, oozes out like sap), he marched in the morning to Jerusalem. (55) Thereupon Aristobulus repented of what he was doing and came to Pompey, [promised to] give him money and admit him into Jerusalem, and begged that he should stop the war and do what he pleased peaceably. So Pompey, upon his entreaty, forgave him and sent Gabinius and soldiers with him to receive the money and the city. (56) Yet no part of this was performed, but Gabinius came back, both being excluded from the city and receiving none of the money promised because Aristobulus' soldiers would not permit the agreements to be executed. (57) At this Pompey was very angry, so he put Aristobulus into prison and came himself to the city which was strong on every side except the north which was not so well fortified. For there was a broad and deep ditch that encompassed the city and included within it the temple which was itself surrounded by a very strong stone wall.

(58) Now there was dissension among the men who were within the city, for they did not agree as to what was to be done in their present circumstances. While some thought it best to deliver up the city to Pompey, Aristobulus' party exhorted them to shut the gates because he was kept in

---

71. Probably to be corrected to "Dium," a city in the Decapolis, a group of Hellenistic cities in Transjordan.

prison. Now these prevented the others and seized the temple, cut off the bridge which extended from it to the city, and prepared themselves for a siege. (59) But the others admitted Pompey's army and delivered up both the city and the king's palace to him. So Pompey sent his legate Piso with an army, and placed garrisons both in the city and in the palace to secure them, and fortified the houses that were adjacent to the temple as well as all those which were more distant and outside it. . . .

(64) Because the Romans understood this,[72] on those days which we call Sabbaths, they shot nothing at the Jews, nor met them in any pitched battle, but raised up their earthen banks, and brought up their siege-engines so that they might be put to work on the next day. (65) Anyone may hence learn what very great piety we exercise towards God and the observance of His laws since the priests were not at all hindered from their sacred ministrations by their fear during this siege, but still twice each day, in the morning and about the ninth hour (3:00 P.M.), they offered their sacrifices on the altar. Nor did they omit those sacrifices if any misfortune happened by the stones that were being thrown at them. (66) For although the city was taken in the third month, on the day of the fast,[73] upon the hundred and seventy-ninth olympiad, when Gaius Antonius and Marcus Tullius Cicero were consuls,[74] and the enemy then fell upon them and cut the throats of those that were in the temple, (67) yet those that offered the sacrifices could not be compelled to run away, neither by the fear they were in for their own lives nor by the number that were already killed, thinking it better to suffer whatever came upon them at their very altars than to omit anything that their laws required of them. (68) That this is not a mere boast to manifest a degree of our piety that was false but is the real truth, is attested by those that have written of the acts of Pompey; and, among them Strabo and Nicolaus [of Damascus]; and besides these Titus Livius, the writer of the Roman history.

(69) But when the battering-engine was brought near, the greatest of the towers was shaken by it and fell down, and broke down a part of the fortifications, so that the enemy poured in . . . (70) Some of the Jews were killed by the Romans and some by one another. Indeed, there were some who threw themselves down the precipices or set fire to their houses and burned them for they were not able to bear the miseries they were under.

---

72. That the Jews would defend themselves on the Sabbath but not try to stop the Romans from raising seige works.

73. An incorrect designation of the Jewish Sabbath common among classical writers, apparently borrowed by Josephus from his source.

74. July, 63 B.C.E.

(71) Of the Jews there fell twelve thousand, but of the Romans very few. Absalom, who was at once both uncle and father-in-law to Aristobulus, was taken captive. No small sins were committed about the temple itself which in former ages had been inaccessible and seen by none. (72) For Pompey and some of those who were with him also went into it and saw all that which it was unlawful for any other men to see except for the high priests. There were in that temple the golden table, the holy candlestick, and the libation vessels, and a great quantity of spices, and besides these there were among the treasures two thousand talents of sacred money. Yet Pompey touched nothing of all this on account of his regard for religion, and in this point also he acted in a manner that was worthy of his virtue. (73) The next day he gave an order to those who had charge of the temple to cleanse it and to bring what offerings the law required to God, and restored the high priesthood to Hyrcanus, both because he had been useful to him in other respects and because he hindered the Jews in the country from giving Aristobulus any assistance in his war against him. He also beheaded those who had been the authors of that war, and bestowed proper rewards on Faustus and on those others who had mounted the wall with such alacrity. (74) He made Jerusalem tributary to the Romans, and took away those cities of Celesyria which the inhabitants of Judea had subdued,[75] and put them under the rule of the Roman governor, and confined the whole nation, which had elevated itself so high before, within its own boundaries. . . .

(77) The causes of this misery which came upon Jerusalem were Hyrcanus and Aristobulus by raising dissension one against the other. For now we lost our liberty and became subject to the Romans, and that territory which we had gained by our arms from the Syrians we were compelled to restore to the Syrians. (78) Moreover, the Romans exacted of us, in a short time, more than ten thousand talents; and the royal authority, which was an office formerly bestowed on those who were high priests by the right of their family, became the property of private men. But we shall treat these matters in their proper places. (79) Now Pompey committed Celesyria, as far as the river Euphrates and Egypt, to Scaurus, with two Roman legions, and then went away to Cilicia and made haste to Rome. He also carried bound along with him Aristobulus and his children; for he had two daughters and as many sons, one of whom ran away. But the younger, Antigonus, was carried to Rome together with his sisters.

---

75. This refers to the Hasmonean conquest. Cf. the list of cities conquered by Alexander Janneus in *Ant.* XIII, 393.

6.1.9 Babylonian Talmud Sotah 49b:
Hyrcanus and Aristobulus at War[76]

Rabbinic tradition also preserves a tannaitic report of the siege of Jerusalem by Hyrcanus against Aristobulus. The Rabbis used the story to learn a lesson, but their account indicates awareness of the basic events.

꙰

Our Rabbis taught: when the kings of the Hasmonean House laid siege one to another, Hyrcanus was outside and Aristobulus inside.[77] Every day they would lower down *dinarii* in a basket and raise up (animals for) daily sacrifices. There was one elder who knew the Greek language. He spoke to them in Greek. He said to them, "As long as they busy themselves with (divine) worship, they will not be given over into your hands." On the next day, they lowered down to them the *denarii* in the basket, and they sent up to them a pig. When it reached halfway up the wall, it dug its hooves into the wall. The Land of Israel shook for four hundred Persian miles. (And regarding) that time they (the sages) said, "Cursed is the man who raises pigs, and cursed is the man who teaches his son the Greek language." And regarding that year we have learned it happened that the omer sacrifice came from Gagot Tserifim[78] and the two loaves from the Valley of Ein Sokher.[79]

6.2 PHARISEES AND SADDUCEES

6.2.1 Josephus, *Antiquities* XIII, 171–3:
The Sects and God's Role in Human Affairs

Josephus portrays the Jewish sects as three schools of philosophy, each with different tenets about the role of God in human affairs. He explains that they subscribe in different degrees to the doctrine of predestination.

꙰

(171) At this time there were three schools of thought among the Jews, each of which had different opinions concerning human actions. One

---

76. Also found in Bava Qamma 82b, Menahot 64b.

77. Of the walls of Jerusalem.

78. Because the Roman soldiers despoiled the countryside, the omer grain had to be brought from this area which was far away from Jerusalem.

79. The first fruits offering of wheat for the holiday of Shavuot also had to be brought from afar because of the destruction of the land.

was called the Pharisees, another the Sadducees, and the other the Essenes. (172) Now for the Pharisees, they say that some actions, but not all, are the work of fate, [80] and some of them are in our own power and that they are liable to fate but are not caused by fate. But the sect of the Essenes affirms that fate governs all things, and that nothing befalls men except that which is according to its determination. (173) And as for the Sadducees, they exclude fate and say that there is no such thing, and that the events of human affairs are not at its disposal. But they suppose that all our actions are in our own power, so that we are ourselves the cause of what is good, and we suffer what is evil as a result of our own folly.

6.2.2 Josephus, *War* II, 119–66: Three Philosophical Schools

Here Josephus elaborates on the three sects which he identifies amongst the Jews. We include here only the material on the Pharisees and the Sadducees, reserving his extensive discussion of the Essenes to be discussed below. In regard to the Pharisees and Sadducees, he notes their attitudes toward the immortality of the soul, life after death, and their behavior to one another. Josephus ascribes the popularity of the Pharisees to their friendly disposition.

🕉

(119) For there are three philosophical schools among the Jews. The followers of the first are the Pharisees, the second the Sadducees, and the third, who pretend to a more severe discipline, are called Essenes. . . .

(162) Of the two first-named schools, the Pharisees are those who are considered most skillful in the exact explication of their laws, and are the leading school. They ascribe all to fate and to God, (163) and yet allow that to do what is right, or the contrary, is principally in the power of men, although fate does cooperate in every action. They say that all souls are imperishable, but that the souls of good men only pass into other bodies while the souls of evil men are subject to eternal punishment.

(164) But the Sadducees are those that compose the second order and exclude fate entirely, and suppose that God is not concerned with our doing or not doing what is evil. (165) They say that to do what is good or what is evil is men's own choice, and that the (choice of) one or the other belongs to each person who may act as he pleases. They also

---

80. Josephus means providence, but he uses a term familiar to his Greek readers.

exclude the belief in the immortality of the soul and the punishments and rewards in the underworld.

(166) Moreover, the Pharisees are friendly to one another and cultivate harmonious relations with the community. But the behavior of the Sadducees towards one another is in some degree boorish; and their conversation with those that are of their own party is as barbarous as if they were strangers to them. And this is what I have to say concerning the philosophic schools among the Jews.

6.2.3 Josephus, *Antiquities* XVIII, 11–17: More about the Pharisees and Sadducees

In this selection, Josephus gives us an idea of the numerical strength of the Pharisees and Sadducees. He asserts that the Pharisees had the greatest support among the multitude, and especially in the cities, so that the Sadducees had to bow to their wishes in order to hold positions of leadership. Here he attributes the popularity of the Pharisees to their doctrines.

꙳

(11) The Jews had for a great while three schools of philosophy peculiar to themselves: the Essenes, the Sadducees, and the third was that of those called Pharisees. . . .

(12) Now, for the Pharisees, they live simply, and despise delicacies in diet. And they follow the conduct of reason;[81] and what that prescribes to them as good for them, they do. They think they ought earnestly to strive to observe those commandments which it has seen fit to dictate to them. They also pay respect to those who are advanced in years, nor are they so bold as to contradict them in anything which they have introduced. (13) Though they determine that all things are done by fate, they do not exclude the freedom from men of acting as they think fit, since their notion is that it has pleased God to make a temperament whereby what he wills is done, but so that the will of men can act virtuously or viciously. (14) They also believe that souls have an immortal power in them, and that under the earth there will be rewards or punishments, depending on whether they have lived virtuously or viciously in this life. The latter are to be detained in an everlasting prison, but the former shall have power to revive and live again. (15) On account of these doctrines, they are very influential among the body of the people, and whatever they do about

---

81. Feldman translates, "the guidance of that which their doctrine has selected."

divine worship, prayers, and sacrifices, they perform them according to their direction. In this way, the inhabitants of the cities gave great tribute to the Pharisees by conducting themselves virtuously, both in their way of life and their discourses as well.

(16) But the doctrine of the Sadducees is that souls die with the bodies. Nor do they regard as obligatory the observance of anything besides what the law enjoins them. For they think it an instance of virtue to dispute with those teachers of philosophy whom they frequent. (17) This doctrine is accepted only by a few, yet by those still of the greatest standing.[82] But they are able to do almost nothing by themselves, for when they become magistrates, as they are unwillingly and by force sometimes obliged to be, they submit themselves to the notions of the Pharisees because the multitude would not otherwise tolerate them.

6.2.4 Acts 23:
The Pharisees and Sadducees on Resurrection[83]

Testimony from the New Testament affirms the beliefs of the Sadducees and Pharisees on resurrection of the dead.

ड़ॢ

6 But when Paul perceived that one part were Sadducees and the other Pharisees, he cried out in the council, "Brethren, I am a Pharisee, a son of Pharisees; with respect to the hope and the resurrection of the dead I am on trial." 7 And when he had said this, a dissension arose between the Pharisees and the Sadducees; and the assembly was divided. 8 For the Sadducees say that there is no resurrection, nor angel, nor spirit; but the Pharisees acknowledge them all. 9 Then a great clamor arose; and some of the scribes of the Pharisees' party stood up and contended, "We find nothing wrong in this man. What if a spirit or an angel spoke to him?"

6.2.5 Mishnah Yadayim 4:6–8:
The Pharisee-Sadducee Debate[84]

The Mishnah records some of the points of law on which the Sadducees differed from the Pharisees. More than the philosophic issues which Josephus identifies, these halakhic standards defined and set one sect apart from the other.

---

82. Among the Sadducees were representatives of the aristocracy.

83. *Revised Standard Version of the Bible* (New York: National Council of Churches, 1971).

84. Trans. S. Berrin.

4:6 The Sadducees say: "We complain against you, Pharisees, for you say that the Holy Scriptures defile the hands,[85] but the writings of Homer do not defile the hands."

Rabban Yoḥanan ben Zakai said: "And do we hold only this against the Pharisees? Behold they say: 'The bones of an ass are pure and the bones of Yoḥanan the high priest are impure.'"[86]

[The Sadducees] said to him: "Their impurity is according to (our) love for them; so that no one should make the bones of his mother and father into spoons."

He said to them: "So too, regarding the Holy Scriptures, their impurity is according to (our) love for them. But the books of Homer, which are not beloved, do not defile the hands."

7 The Sadducees say: "We complain against you, Pharisees, for you declare the liquid stream (being poured from a pure vessel to an impure vessel) to be pure."[87]

The Pharisees say: "We accuse you, Sadducees, for you declare the aquaduct which flows from a cemetery is pure."

The Sadducees say: "We complain against you, Pharisees, for you say that [for] my ox and my ass which have caused damage [I am] culpable, but [for] my slave and my maid-servant who have caused damage [I am] exempt. If for my ox and my ass, for whom I am not responsible for their fulfillment of commandments, I am responsible for the damage caused by them, then for my slave and maid-servant regarding whom I am responsible for their fulfillment of the commandments—is it not a logical conclusion that I should be responsible for damage caused by them?"

The [Pharisees] said to [the Sadducees]: "No! Shall we say that [it is the same for] my ox and my ass which have no understanding as for my slave and my maid-servant who have understanding? [If so, then] if I will anger [the slave or maid-servant], they will go and set fire to the grain of another and I will be obligated to pay."

---

85. It was required for priests to wash their hands after contact with those Holy Scriptures considered part of the biblical canon.

86. How can animal bones not carry defilement when those of the purest of people are considered to defile?

87. The Pharisees maintained that a liquid stream being poured from a pure vessel into an impure one did not connect the two vessels so as to render the upper one impure. The Sadducees, however, saw the stream as conducting the impurity upwards from the lower vessel to the upper and rendering it impure.

8 A Galilean Sadducee said: "I complain against you, Pharisees, for you write the name of the [gentile] ruler[88] with that of Moses on a writ of divorce."

The Pharisees say: "We complain against you, Galilean Sadducee, for you write the name of the ruler with the name of God on the [same] page. And furthermore, you write the name of the ruler above and the name of God below, as it is written, 'And Pharoah said, "Who is God that I should listen to his voice and let Israel go?"'" (Ex. 5:2).[89]

6.2.6 Mishnah Ḥagigah 2:7:
The Pharisees and Ritual Purity[90]

This Mishnaic passage indicates that the Pharisees observed purity laws at a level which placed them between the common people and the priestly families who ate of the terumah offerings.

The clothing of an *'am ha-'arez*[91] is the source of the highest level of defilement for the Pharisees. The clothing of Pharisees is the source of the highest level of defilement for those who eat the priestly portion. The clothing of those who eat the priestly portion is the source of the highest level of defilement to those who eat sacrifices. The clothing of those who eat sacrifices is a source of the highest level of defilement to [those priests who sprinkle the water of] the sin-offering.[92]

6.2.7 Mishnah Sotah 3:4:
A Negative View of the Pharisees[93]

The following passage shows that for some, Pharisaic extremism, or perhaps even hypocrisy, would be an object of ridicule.

---

88. A reference to dating by consular year as found in the Jewish documents from the first and second centuries.

89. This is a sort of tongue-in-cheek response, for the Pharisees are not actually accusing the Sadducee of a deviant or objectionable action, but rather pointing out that their own action is unobjectionable, as the Bible itself has recorded the name of a gentile ruler above that, not only of Moses, but of God.

90. Trans. S. Berrin.

91. One of the common people who were not strict in the observance of the laws of ritual purity or the tithing of produce.

92. Cf. Num. 19:9. This refers to the preparation of the water of purification from impurity of the dead after the sacrifice of a red heifer.

93. Trans. S. Berrin.

꽃

[Rabbi Joshua] used to say: A foolish pietist, a cunning wicked person, an ascetic woman,[94] and the plagues of the Pharisees, these destroy the world.

6.2.8 Mishnah Eruvin 6:2:
The Sadducees and the Law of Eruv[95]

This passage indicates that although the Sadducees strictly observed the prohibition of carrying from domain to domain on the Sabbath, they did not accept the Pharisaic device of Eruv designed to make possible the joining of domains and thus permit carrying in a common alleyway.

꽃

Rabban Gamliel said: Once a Sadducee lived with us adjoining the same alley in Jerusalem and my father told us: "Hurry and take all the vessels out to the alley before he takes things there and makes it forbidden to you."[96] Rabbi Judah says this in different words: "Hurry and do all you have to do in the alley so that he does not take something there and make it unlawful to you."

6.2.9 Mishnah Makkot 1:6:
The Debate over the Punishment of False Witnesses[97]

This Mishnaic passage records a debate between the Sadducees and Pharisees on the treatment of men who gave false testimony in a capital case. Different interpretations of the biblical law resulted in different judicial rulings.

꽃

Scheming witnesses[98] are not executed until a verdict [for death] has been rendered [against the accused]. For the Sadducees say: until [the

---

94. Hebrew *perushah*, "ascetic," can also be rendered "Pharisee."

95. Trans. S. Berrin.

96. If a Sadducee who did not accept the law of Eruv lived in the alleyway, his refusal to participate made impossible the creation of a common domain to allow carrying in the common alleyway. But if the Saducee did not make use of the alley on the Sabbath, then the others were permitted to carry in the common domain.

97. Trans. S. Berrin.

98. The term used refers to a particular type of perjured witnesses. Their testimony has been invalidated since a second pair of witnesses testifies that the first pair of witnesses could not have been present at the scene of the alleged crime because the first witnesses were, in fact, in the presence of these second witnesses elsewhere at that particular time. In a capital case, the punishment of these false witnesses is execution.

accused] has been executed, as it is written, "life for life" (Deut.19:21). The Sages said to them: But it is already written, "you shall do to him as he *schemed* to do to his fellow" (Deut.19:19). Thus the accused is still alive! If so, then why is it written, "life for life?" One might have thought that they may be killed from the time that their testimony was heard. [To teach otherwise,] the Torah writes, "life for life" from which one can derive that they may not be executed until a verdict has been rendered.

6.2.10 Mishnah Parah 3:7:
Purification at Sunset[99]

The Mishnah asserts that the Pharisees were able to compel the Sadducees to follow their rulings, even in the Temple, a matter of controversy among modern scholars. In this case, they insisted that the preparation of the ashes of the red heifer (Num. 19) be done by one whom they regarded as fully pure but whom the Sadducees regarded as still being impure until sunset on the final day of his purification.

🙢

[The Elders of Israel] used to defile the priest who was to burn the red heifer because of the Sadducees, so that they would not say: [the burning] was done by one upon whom the sun had set.

6.2.11 Mishnah Niddah 4:2:
The Pharisaic Ruling on Sadducee Women[100]

The Mishnah rules that if Sadducee women do not fulfill the laws of menstrual impurity as understood by the Pharisaic-Rabbinic tradition, it is forbidden to marry them, as it is with Samaritan women. Rabbi Yose rules that it can be generally assumed that they do follow Pharisaic practice, further evidence that the Rabbis believed that the Sadducees accepted their authority.

🙢

The daughters of the Sadducees, when they are accustomed to follow the ways of their fathers, are like Samaritan women.[101] If they separated

---

99. Trans. S. Berrin.
100. Trans. S. Berrin.
101. For purposes of marriage. Cf. the parallel in *Ant.* XIII, 288–96 (Text 6.1.4 in this volume). They are always considered to be menstrually impure.

themselves to follow the paths of Israel, they are like Israelites. Rabbi
Yose says: "They are always considered like Israel unless they separate
themselves so as to follow the paths of their fathers."

6.2.12 Babylonian Talmud Qiddushin 66a: King Alexander Janneus and the Pharisees[102]

*This passage presents a story which is also told by Josephus (text 6.1.4) in
reference to John Hyrcanus. In the Talmudic version, however, the Rabbinic
understanding of the oral law is emphasized, and it is assumed that the Pharisees and even initially the Hasmonean king shared these beliefs.*

స్ట్

It is taught in a *baraita:*[103] It once happened that King Yannai[104] went to
Koḥalit in the desert and captured sixty cities there. Upon his return he
rejoiced with great joy and called all the sages of Israel. He said to them:
"Our fathers ate salted plants at the time that they were occupied with the
construction of the Temple; so too let us eat salted food in remembrance
of our fathers."

They served salted plants on golden tables and they ate. There was one
man there, a wicked mocker with an evil heart, a worthless man, and
Eleazar ben Poʻeirah was his name. Eleazar ben Poʻeirah said to King Yannai: "King Yannai, the hearts of the Pharisees are against you."

"And what shall I do?" [said Yannai].

"Make them swear an oath by the high-priestly front-plate[105] which is
between your eyes," [said Eleazar ben Poʻeirah]. He made them swear by
the front-plate between his eyes. There was one elder there, and Judah ben
Gedidyah was his name.

Judah ben Gedidyah said to King Yannai: "King Yannai, the crown of
kingship is ample for you; leave the crown of priesthood to the descendants of Aaron," for they had said that Yannai's mother had been taken
captive in Modiin.[106] The matter was investigated and it was not validated.
The sages departed in anger.

---

102. Trans. S. Berrin.

103. A teaching from the Mishnaic period not included in the Mishnah.

104. Alexander Janneus.

105. The metal plate on the priests' miter which had the words "Holy to the Lord"
written upon it.

106. If this were the case, his suspect lineage would invalidate him for the high priesthood.

Eleazar ben Po'eirah said to King Yannai: "King Yannai, this would be the law for an ordinary man, but you—a king and high priest—should this be your law!"

"And what shall I do?"

"If you take my advice, trample them."

"And what will happen to the Torah?"

"Here it is, rolled up in the corner. Whoever wants to may come and learn."

Said Rav Naḥman, son of Isaac, "Immediately heresy was cast into him, for he should have said, 'Granted that that is the case for the written Torah, but what about the oral Torah?'"[107]

Immediately, misfortune broke out because of Eleazar ben Po'eirah, for they killed all the sages of Israel, and the world was desolate[108] until Shimon ben Shetaḥ came and restored the Torah to its previous status.[109]

6.3 APOCALYPTICS AND ASCETICS

6.3.1 Josephus, *Antiquities* XVIII, 18–22: The Doctrines of the Essenes

Josephus provides the most expansive contemporary description of the Essenes. He presents them as an agricultural, virtuous people worthy of admiration for their pious, peaceful ways, their communal economic life, and celibacy.

۩

(18) The doctrine of the Essenes is that all things are best ascribed to God. They teach the immortality of the soul and believe that the rewards of righteousness are to be earnestly striven for. (19) When they send what they have dedicated to God to the temple, they do not offer sacrifices because they have more purification rituals of their own, because of which they are excluded from the common court of the temple, but offer their sacrifices themselves. Yet their course of life is better than that of other men, and they entirely devote themselves to agricultural labor. (20) It also deserves our admiration how much they exceed all other men who claim to be virtuous, and indeed to such a degree as has never appeared among any other people, neither Greeks nor barbarians, no, not even

---

107. While the written Torah can be studied from the scroll, the oral law must be transmitted by teachers.

108. Since there were no sages to teach the oral law.

109. During the time of Shimon ben Shetaḥ, the Pharisees were returned to power under Queen Salome Alexandra (text 6.1.7).

briefly. But it has endured for so long among them and has never been interrupted since they adopted them from of old. This is demonstrated by that institution of theirs in which all things are held in common; so that a rich man enjoys no more of his own wealth than he who has nothing at all. There are about four thousand men that live in this way.

(21) Neither do they marry wives nor are they desirous to keep servants, thinking that the latter tempts men to be unjust and the former opens the way to domestic quarrels; but as they live by themselves, they minister one to another. (22) They also appoint certain stewards to receive the incomes of their revenues and of the fruits of the ground, those who are good men and priests, who are to get their grain and their food ready for them.

6.3.2 Josephus, *War* II, 119–61: The Life of the Essenes

The much more detailed description given here of a closed fraternity of Essenes living a simple, pious life has led scholars to identify Josephus' Essenes with the Dead Sea sect. Josephus sought to picture the Essenes as a Greek philosophic school and therefore emphasized their closeness to Hellenistic ways of thought.

(119) The Essenes are Jews by birth and seem to have a greater affection for one another than the other schools have. (120) These Essenes reject pleasures as an evil, but consider continence and the conquest over our passions to be virtue. They disdain marriage but seek other persons' children, while they are pliable and fit for learning, and regard them to be of their kind and form them according to their own principles. (121) They do not absolutely deny the fitness of marriage and the succession of mankind thereby continued, but they guard against the lascivious behavior of women and are persuaded that none of them preserves her fidelity to one man.[110] (122) These men are despisers of riches, and so their community of goods raises our admiration. Nor is there anyone to be found among them who has more than another, for it is a law among them that those who join them must let what they have be common to the whole order. For among them all there is no appearance of poverty or excess of riches, but everyone's possessions are intermingled with every other's possessions, and so there is, as it were, one patrimony among all the fellows. (123) They think that oil is a defilement, and if any one of them be anointed without his approval, it is wiped off his body. For they think that to have a

---

110. See below, sections 160–61, on those Essenes who practiced marriage.

dry skin is a good thing, as they do also to be clothed in white garments. They also have stewards appointed to take care of their common affairs, every one of whom performs special services as determined by the entire group.

(124) They have no one city, but many of them dwell in every city. And if any of their school come from other places, their resources are available to them, just as if it were their own, and they go into the homes of those whom they never knew before as if they had been ever so long acquainted with them. (125) For this reason they carry nothing with them when they travel into remote parts, though still they take their weapons with them for fear of thieves. Accordingly there is, in every city where they live, one appointed particularly to take care of strangers and to provide garments and other necessities for them. (126) But the dress and behavior is such as children practice who are in fear of their masters. Nor do they allow the change of garments or of shoes until they are first entirely torn to pieces or worn out by time. (127) Neither do they either buy or sell anything to one another, but every one of them gives what he has to him that needs it and receives from him again in lieu of it what may be convenient for himself. Although there is no repayment made, they are fully allowed to take what they want from whomsoever they please.

(128) And as for their piety towards God, it is very extraordinary. For before sunrise they speak not a word about mundane matters, but offer certain prayers which they have received from their forefathers, as if they made a supplication for its rising. (129) After this every one of them is sent away by their superiors to exercise some of those crafts wherein they are skilled, in which they labor with great diligence until the fifth hour. After that, they assemble together again in one place, and when they have clothed themselves in linen garments, they then bathe their bodies in cold water. After this purification is over, they all meet together in an apartment of their own, into which it is not permitted to any of another school to enter. They go, after a pure manner, into the dining room as into some holy temple. (130) They quietly sit down. Then the baker places loaves before them in order; the cook also brings a single portion of one sort of food and sets it before every one of them. (131) A priest says grace before meat, and it is unlawful for anyone to taste the food before grace is said. The same priest, after he has dined, says grace again after meat, and when they begin and when they end, they praise God as the One Who bestows their food upon them. After this, they lay aside their [white] garments, and return to their labors again until the evening.

(132) Then they return home to supper in the same manner, and if there are any strangers there, they sit down with them. Nor is there ever

any clamor or disturbance to pollute their house, but they give every one permission to speak in his turn. (133) The silence thus kept in their house appears to foreigners like some tremendous mystery. In fact, the cause of it is that perpetual sobriety that they exercise and the limitation of meat and drink that is allotted to them to that which is abundantly sufficient for them.

(134) And truly, as for other things, they do nothing but according to the injunctions of their superiors. Only these two things are done among them at everyone's own free will, namely, to assist those in need and to show mercy. For they are permitted of their own accord to afford succor to such as deserve it when they stand in need of it and to bestow food on those in distress, but they cannot give anything to their relatives without permission from the managers. (135) They hold their anger in reserve in a just manner and restrain their passion. They are famous for fidelity and are the ministers of peace. Also whatever they say is firmer than an oath, but swearing is avoided by them, and they consider it worse than perjury. For they say that he who cannot be believed without [swearing by] God is already condemned. (136) They also take great pains in studying the writings of the ancients, and choose from them that which is most to the advantage of their soul and body. And they inquire after such roots and medicinal stones as may cure diseases.

(137) But now, if anyone has a mind to join their school,[111] he is not immediately admitted, but he is prescribed the same way of life which they practice for a year, while he continues to be excluded; and they give him a small hatchet, the aforementioned loin-cloth,[112] and the white garment. (138) And when he has given evidence during that time that he can observe their way of life, he approaches nearer to their way of living and is allowed to partake of the waters of purification. Yet he is not even now admitted to live with them, for after this demonstration of his fortitude, his character is tested for two more years. If he appears to be worthy, they then admit him into their society. (139) Before he is allowed to touch their common food, he is obligated to take tremendous oaths: that, in the first place, he will exercise piety towards God; and then that he will observe justice towards men; and that he will do no harm to anyone, either of his own accord or by the command of others; that he will always hate the wicked and fight the battle of the righteous; (140) that he will

---

111. The admission process described here has certain parallels in the Dead Sea Scrolls which has led scholars to identify the Essenes with the scrolls sect. Note, however, that the Pharisees had similar initiatory practices for the *ḥavurah*, the fellowship of those who practiced purity laws and tithing with stringency.

112. The linen garment mentioned in (129).

always show fidelity to all men, especially to those in authority, because no one obtains office without God's assistance; and that if he is in authority, he will at no time whatever abuse his authority nor endeavor to outshine his subjects, either in his garments or any other finery; (141) that he will perpetually be a lover of truth and expose those that tell lies; that he will keep his hands from theft and his soul from unlawful gains; and that he will neither conceal anything from those of his own school nor reveal any of their doctrines to others, no, not even if any one should compel him to do so at the hazard of his life. (142) Moreover, he swears to communicate their doctrines exactly as he received them himself, to abstain from robbery, and to carefully preserve the books belonging to their school and the names of the angels. These are the oaths by which they secure their proselytes.

(143) But those that are caught in any heinous sins, they cast out of their society. He who is thus separated from them often dies in a miserable manner, for as he is bound by the oath he has taken and by the customs he has been engaged in, he is not at liberty to partake of that food which he finds elsewhere, but is forced to eat grass and to starve his body with hunger until he perishes. (144) For this reason they receive many of them again when they are at their last gasp, out of compassion for them, considering the miseries they have endured until they come to the very brink of death to be a sufficient punishment for the sins of which they had been guilty. (145) But in the judgments they exercise they are most accurate and just, nor do they pass sentence by the votes of a court that is fewer than a hundred. And as to what is once decided by that number, it is unalterable. What they most of all honor, after God himself, is the name of their legislator [Moses], for if any one blasphemes Moses, he is capitally punished.

(146) They also think it a good thing to obey their elders and a majority. Accordingly, if ten of them are sitting together, no one of them will speak if the other nine are against it. (147) They also avoid spitting in their midst or on the right side. Moreover, they are stricter than any other Jews in resting from their labors on the seventh day, for they not only get their food ready the day before so that they may not be obliged to kindle a fire on that day, but they will not remove any vessel out of its place nor relieve themselves. (148) Rather, on the other days they dig a small pit a foot deep with a mattock (a kind of hatchet which is given them when they are first admitted among them), and covering themselves round about with their garment, so that they may not affront the divine rays of light, they ease themselves into that pit, (149) after which they put the earth that was dug out again into the pit. This they do only in the more

lonely places which they choose out for this purpose; and although this easement of the body is natural, yet it is a rule with them to wash themselves after it as if it were a defilement to them.

(150) Now according to the duration of their discipline, they are divided into four classes; and so far are the juniors inferior to the seniors that if the seniors should be touched by the juniors, they must wash themselves, as if they had had contact with a foreigner. (151) They are long-lived also, as many of them live more than a hundred years by means of the simplicity of their diet; indeed, I think, by means of the regular course of life they observe also. They make light of the miseries of life and are above pain by their resolute will. And as for death, if it will be for their glory, they consider it better than immortality. (152) Indeed our war with the Romans gave abundant evidence of what great souls they had in their trials, wherein, although they were tortured and distorted, burnt and torn to pieces, and went through all kinds of instruments of torment so that they might be forced either to blaspheme their legislator or to eat what was forbidden to them, yet they could not be made to do either of these things, no, nor once to flatter their tormentors or to shed a tear. (153) But they smiled in their pains and laughed in scorn at those who inflicted the torments upon them, and resigned their souls cheerfully, expecting to receive them again.

(154) For their doctrine is that bodies are corruptible, and that the matter they are made of it not permanent. But the souls are immortal and continue forever, and they come out of the most subtle air and are united to their bodies as in prisons into which they are drawn by a certain natural enticement. (155) But when they are set free from the bonds of the flesh, they then, as if released from a long bondage, rejoice and mount upward. And this is like the opinion of the Greeks, that good souls have their habitations beyond the ocean in a region that is neither oppressed with storms of rain or snow, or with intense heat, but that this place is refreshed by the gentle breathing of a west wind perpetually blowing from the ocean; while they allot to bad souls a dark and tempestuous dungeon full of never-ceasing punishments. (156) And indeed the Greeks seem to me to have followed the same notion, when they allot the islands of the blessed to their brave men whom they call heroes and demigods; and to the souls of the wicked, the region of the ungodly, in Hades, where their fables relate that certain persons, such as Sisyphus, Tantalus, Ixion, and Tityus, are punished. Their view was first to establish that souls are immortal, and second to promote virtue and deter wickedness. (157) For good men are bettered in the conduct of their life by the hope they have of reward after their death, and the vehement inclinations of bad men to vice are

restrained by the fear and expectation they are in, that although they should lie concealed in this life, they should suffer immortal punishment after their death. (158) These are the divine doctrines of the Essenes about the soul by which they irresistably attract all who have once had a taste of their philosophy. (159) There are also those among them who undertake to foretell things to come by reading the holy books, using several sorts of purifications, and being perpetually conversant in the discourses of the prophets. And it is but seldom that they miss in their predictions.

(160) Moreover, there is another order of Essenes who agree with the rest as to their way of life, customs, and laws, but differ from them in the point of marriage, thinking that by not marrying they cut off the principal part of human life which is the prospect of succession. Indeed, if all men should be of the same opinion, the whole race of mankind would die out. (161) However, they test their spouses for three years. If they find that they have their natural periods thrice as evidence that they are likely to be fruitful, they then actually marry them. But they do not have relations with their wives when they are pregnant as a demonstration that they do not marry out of regard for pleasure but only for the sake of posterity. The women go into the baths with some of their garments on as the men do with a loin-cloth. These are the customs of this order of Essenes.

6.3.3 Pliny, *Natural History* V, xv: The Solitary Essenes[113]

In contrast to Josephus' Essenes who marry for purposes of propagation, Pliny's Essenes never marry. While Josephus says that this sect is found in every city, Pliny locates them on the western coast of the Dead Sea. This account has been a major linchpin in the identification of Qumran on the shore of the Dead Sea as an Essene center.

꽃

On the west side of the Dead Sea, but out of range of the noxious exhalations of the coast, is the solitary tribe of the Essenes which is remarkable beyond all the other tribes of the whole world as it has no women and has renounced all sexual desire, has no money, and has only palm trees for company. Day by day the throng of refugees is recruited to an equal number by numerous accessions of persons tired of life and driven there by the waves of fortune to adopt their manners. Thus,

---

113. Trans. H. Rackham, *Pliny: Natural History II* (Loeb Classical Library; Cambridge: Harvard University Press, 1942), p. 277.

through thousands of ages (incredible to relate) a race in which no one is born lives on forever: so prolific for their advantage is other men's weariness of life!

Lying below[114] the Essenes was formerly the town of Engedi, second only to Jerusalem in the fertility of its land and in its groves of palm trees, but now like Jerusalem a heap of ashes. Next comes Masada, a fortress on a rock, itself also not far from the Dead Sea. This is the limit of Judaea.

6.3.4 Philo, *Every Good Man is Free* XII, 75–87: Description of the Essenes[115]

Another ancient source, Philo, who lived in Alexandria, Egypt between ca. 20 B.C.E. and 50 C.E., also describes the Essenes. Philo tells of a group of pious individuals who live in villages, and, like the Essenes of Josephus, practice communal ownership of goods and services, adhere to regulations of purity, and maintain an agricultural way of life.

꿏

(75) Moreover, Palestine and Syria are not barren of exemplary wisdom and virtue. In these countries lives no small portion of that most populous nation of the Jews. There is a portion of those people called Essenes, in number something more than four thousand in my opinion, who derive their name from their piety, though not according to an accurate form of the Greek language,[116] because they are above all especially devoted to the service of God, not sacrificing living animals, but studying rather to preserve their own minds in a state of holiness and purity. (76) These men, in the first place, live in villages, avoiding all cities on account of the habitual lawlessness of those who inhabit them, knowing that such a moral disease is contracted from associations with wicked men, just as a real disease might be from an unhealthy atmosphere, and that this would have a deadly effect on their souls. Of these men, some cultivating the earth and others devoting themselves to those arts which are the result of peace, benefit both themselves and all those who come in contact with them, not storing up treasures of silver and gold, nor acquiring vast sections of land out of a desire for ample revenues, but providing all things which are requisite for the natural purposes of life. (77) For they

---

114. To the south of the Essene settlement.

115. Revised from *The Works of Philo*, trans. C. D. Yonge (Peabody, MA: Hendrickson, 1993), pp. 689–70, in consultation with *Philo*, trans. F. H. Colson, vol. 9 (Loeb Classical Library; Cambridge: Harvard University Press, 1941), pp. 53–61.

116. The exact derivation of "Essene" is still a matter of dispute.

alone of almost all men have become poor and destitute by deliberate action rather than by any real deficiency of good fortune, but are nevertheless accounted very rich, judging contentment and frugality to be great abundance, as in truth they are.

(78) Among those men you will find no makers of arrows, javelins, swords, helmets, breastplates, shields; no makers of arms or of military engines; no one, in short, attending to any employment whatever connected with war, or even to any of those occupations even in peace which are easily perverted to wicked purposes. For they are utterly ignorant of all business and of all commercial dealings, and of all sea trade, but they repudiate and keep aloof from everything which can possibly afford any inducement to covetousness. (79) There is not a single slave among them, but they are all free, aiding one another with a reciprocal interchange of services. They condemn the owner of slaves not only as unjust, inasmuch as they corrupt the very principles of equality, but likewise as impious, because they annul the ordinances of nature which created them all equally and brought them up like a mother, as if they were all legitimate brethren, not in name only, but in reality and truth.

But in their view this natural relationship of all men to one another has been thrown into disorder by scheming covetousness, continually wishing to surpass others in good fortune, which has therefore engendered alienation instead of affection, and hatred instead of friendship. (80) Leaving the logical part of philosophy, as in no respect necessary for the acquisition of virtue, to the word-catchers, and the natural part, as being too sublime for human nature to master, to those who love to converse about high objects (except indeed so far as such a study takes in the contemplation of the existence of God and the creation of the universe), they devote all their attention to the moral part of philosophy, using as instructors the laws of their fathers which it would have been impossible for the human mind to devise without divine inspiration.

(81) Now these laws they are taught at other times, indeed, but most especially on the seventh day, for the seventh day is accounted sacred, on which they abstain from all other work and frequent the sacred places which are called synagogues. There they sit according to their age in classes, the younger sitting below the elder and listening with eager attention. (82) Then one, indeed, takes up the books and reads them, and another of the men of the greatest experience comes forward and explains what is not very intelligible, for a great many precepts are delivered in enigmatic modes of expression, and allegorically, as the old fashion was. (83) Thus the people are taught piety, holiness, justice, economy, the science of regulating the state, and the knowledge of such things as are

naturally good, bad, or indifferent, and to choose what is right and to avoid what is wrong, using a threefold variety of definitions, rules, and criteria, namely, the love of God, the love of virtue, and the love of mankind.

(84) Accordingly, they present a multitude of proofs of their love of God, and of a continued and uninterrupted purity throughout the whole of life, of a careful avoidance of oaths and of falsehood, and of a strict adherence to the principle of looking on the Deity as the cause of everything which is good and of nothing which is evil. They also furnish us with many proofs of a love of virtue, such as abstinence from all covetousness of money, from ambition, from indulgence in pleasures, temperance, endurance, and also moderation, simplicity, good temper, the absence of pride, obedience to the laws, steadiness, and everything of that kind. Lastly, they bring forward as proofs of the love of mankind good-will, equality beyond all power of description, and fellowship, about which it is not unreasonable to say a few words.

(85) In the first place, then, there is no one who has a house so absolutely his own private property that it does not in some sense also belong to everyone. For besides the fact that they all dwell together in communities, the house is open to all those of the same convictions who come to them from elsewhere. (86) Then there is one treasury among them all, and their expenses are all in common. Their garments belong to them all in common, and their food is common through the institution of public meals. For there is no other people among which you can find common use of the same house, common adoption of one mode of living, and common use of the same table more thoroughly established in fact than among this tribe. And is this not very natural? For whatever they receive for their wages after having been working during the day, they do not retain as their own, but bring it into the common stock and give any advantage that is to be derived from it to all who desire to avail themselves of it. (87) Those who are sick are not neglected because they are unable to contribute to the common stock, inasmuch as the tribe has in their public stock the means for supplying their necessities and treating their weakness, so that from their ample means they support them liberally and abundantly. They give respect to their elders, honor them and care for them, just as parents are honored and cared for by their lawful children, being supported by them in all abundance both by their personal efforts and by generous maintenance.

6.3.5 Rule of the Community I–VII:
The Teachings and Structure of the Dead Sea Sect[117]

In addition to Bible and other religious literature, the Dead Sea Scrolls include documents authored by the sectarians themselves. One of these, the Rule of the Community, outlines the goals of the sect to seek communion with God through purity, communal rituals, and interpretation of the law according to the sectarian understanding. This scroll of regulations also explains how a person who wishes to enter the sectarian covenant and follow the sectarian way of life may come into full membership and take his place among the ranks of the order.

𝕾

I 1 For [the Instructor ... the book of the Rul]e of the Community: in order to 2 seek God [with all (one's) heart and with all (one's) soul; in order] to do what is good and just in his presence, as 3 commanded through Moses and his servants the Prophets; in order to love everything 4 which he has chosen and to hate everything that he has rejected; in order to keep oneself at a distance from all evil, 5 and to become attached to all good works; to bring about truth, justice and uprightness 6 on earth and not to walk in the stubbornness of a guilty heart and of lecherous eyes 7 performing every evil; in order to welcome into the covenant of kindness all those who freely volunteer to carry out God's decrees, 8 so as to be united in the counsel of God and walk before him in perfection in his sight, complying with all 9 revealed things concerning the regulated times of their stipulations; in order to love all the sons of light, each one 10 according to his lot in God's plan, and to detest all the sons of darkness, each one in accordance with his blame 11 in God's vindication.

All those who submit freely to his truth will convey all their knowledge, their energies, 12 and their riches to the Community of God in order to refine their knowledge in the truth of God's decrees and marshal their energies 13 in accordance with his perfect paths and all their riches in accordance with his just counsel. They shall not stray from any one 14 of all God's orders concerning their appointed times; they shall not advance their appointed times nor shall they retard 15 any one of their feasts. They shall not veer from his reliable precepts in order to go either

---

117. F. García Martínez, *The Dead Sea Scrolls Translated* (New York; Leiden: E. J. Brill, 1994), pp. 3–11.

to the right or to the left. 16 And all those who enter in the Rule of the Community shall establish a covenant before God in order to carry out 17 all that he commands and in order not to stray from following him for any fear, dread or grief 18 that might occur during the dominion of Belial.[118]

When they enter the covenant, the priests 19 and the Levites shall bless the God of salvation and all the works of his faithfulness, and all 20 those who enter the covenant shall repeat after them: "Amen, Amen." 21 The priests shall recite the just deeds of God in his mighty works, 22 and they shall proclaim all his merciful favors towards Israel. And the Levites shall recite 23 the sins of the children of Israel, all their blameworthy transgressions and their sins during the dominion of 24 Belial.

[And all] those who enter the covenant shall confess after them and they shall say:

> "We have acted sinfully,
> 25 [we have transgressed,
> we have si]nned, we have acted irreverently,
> we and our fathers before us,
> inasmuch as we walk
> 26 [in the opposite direction to the precepts] of truth and justice
> [...] his judgment upon us and upon our fathers;
> II 1 but he has showered on us his merciful favour
> for ever and ever."

And the priests shall bless all 2 the men of God's lot who walk unblemished in all his paths and they shall say:

> "May he bless you with everything good,
> 3 and may he protect you from everything bad.
> May he illuminate your heart with the discernment of life
> and grace you with eternal knowledge.
> 4 May he lift upon you the countenance of his favour
> for eternal peace."

And the Levites shall curse all the men 5 of the lot of Belial. They shall begin to speak and shall say:

> "Accursed are you for all your wicked, blameworthy deeds.
> May he (God) hand you over to dread
> 6 into the hands of all those carrying out acts of vengeance.

---

118. Belial is a term used in sectarian literature to denote the leader of the forces of evil in the ongoing cosmic struggle.

7 Accursed, without mercy,
for the darkness of your deeds,
and sentenced
8 to the gloom of everlasting fire.
May God not be merciful when you entreat him,
nor pardon you when you do penance for your faults.
9 May he lift the countenance of his anger to avenge himself on you,
and may there be no peace for you
in the mouth of those who intercede."

10 And all those who enter the covenant shall say, after those who pronounce blessings and those who pronounce curses: "Amen, Amen."
11 And the priests and the Levites shall continue, saying:

"Cursed by the idols which his heart reveres be
12 whoever enters this covenant
leaving the obstacle of his transgression in front of himself so as to fall over it.
13 When he hears the words of this covenant,
he will congratulate himself in his heart, saying:
'I will have peace,
14 in spite of my walking in the stubbornness of my heart.'
However, his spirit will be obliterated,
the dry with the moist, with no forgiveness.
15 May God's anger and the wrath of his verdicts
consume him for everlasting destruction.
16 May all the curses of this covenant
stick fast to him.
May God segregate him for evil,
and may he be cut off from the midst of all the sons of light
because of his straying from following God
17 on account of his idols and his blameworthy obstacle.
May he assign his lot with the cursed ones for ever."

18 And all those who enter the covenant shall begin speaking and shall say after them: "Amen, Amen."
19 They shall act in this way year after year, all the days of Belial's dominion. The priests shall pass 20 muster first, one behind the other, according to their spirits. And the Levites shall enter after them. 21 In third place all the people shall pass muster, one after another, in thousands, hundreds, 22 fifties and tens, so that all the children of Israel may know their standing in God's Community 23 in conformity with the eternal plan. And no one shall move down from his rank nor move up from the place of his lot. 24 For all shall be in a single Community of truth, of proper humility, of compassionate love and upright purpose, 25 towards

each other in the holy council, associates of an everlasting society. And anyone who declines to enter the covenant of God in order to walk in the stubbornness of his heart shall not [enter the Com]munity of his truth, since III 1 his soul loathes the restraints of knowledge of just judgment. He has not remained constant in the transformation of his life and shall not be counted with the upright. 2 His knowledge, his energy and his wealth shall not enter the council of the Community because he ploughs in the slime of irreverence and there are stains 3 on his conversion. . . .

13 For the wise man, that he may inform and teach all the sons of light about the history of all the sons of man, 14 concerning all the ranks of their spirits, in accordance with their signs, concerning their deeds and their generations, and concerning the visitation of their punishment and 15 the moment of their reward. From the God of knowledge stems all there is and all there shall be. Before they existed he made all their plans,[119] 16 and when they come into being they will execute all their works in compliance with his instructions, according to his glorious design, without altering anything. In his hand are 17 the laws of all things and he supports them in all their needs. He created man to rule 18 the world and placed within him two spirits so that he would walk with them until the moment of his visitation: 19 they are the spirits of truth and of deceit.

20 In the hand of the Prince of Lights is dominion over all the sons of justice; they walk in paths of light. And in the hand of the Angel 21 of Darkness is total dominion over the sons of deceit; they walk in paths of darkness.[120] Due to the Angel of Darkness 22 all the sons of justice stray, and all their sins, their iniquities, their failings and their mutinous deeds are under his dominion 23 in compliance with the mysteries of God, until his moment; and all their punishments and their periods of grief are caused by the dominion of his enmity; 24 and all the spirits of their lot cause the sons of light to fall. However, the God of Israel and the angel of his truth assist all 25 the sons of light. He created the spirits of light and of darkness and on them established all his deeds 26 [on their p]aths.

V 7 These are the regulations of behavior concerning all these decrees when they are enrolled in the Community. Whoever enters the council of the Community 8 enters the covenant of God in the presence of all

---

119. The Dead Sea sect believed in predestination, meaning that God had predetermined the course of the history of the world as well as the lot, good or evil, to which each person was assigned.

120. The scroll sect understood light and darkness as symbolic of the duality of both heavenly and earthly beings, which they saw as divided into camps of good and evil. Until the final eschatological battle, these groups would compete with one another for dominion.

who freely volunteer. He shall swear with a binding oath to revert to the Law of Moses with all that it decrees, with whole 9 heart and whole soul, in compliance with all that has been revealed concerning it to the sons of Zadok, the priests who keep the covenant and interpret his will, and to the multitude of the men of their covenant 10 who freely volunteer together for this truth and to walk according to his will. He should swear by the covenant to be segregated from all the men of sin who walk 11 along paths of irreverence. For they are not included in his covenant since they have neither sought nor examined his decrees in order to learn the hidden matters in which they err 12 by their own fault, and because they treated revealed matters with disrespect; this is why wrath will rise up for judgment in order to effect revenge by the curses of the covenant, in order to administer fierce 13 punishments for everlasting annihilation without there being any remnant. . . . 17 . . . For 18 all those not numbered in his covenant will be segregated, they and all that belongs to them. No holy man should support himself on any deed of 19 futility, for futile are all those who do not know the covenant. And all those who scorn his word he shall cause to vanish from the world; all his deeds are uncleanness 20 before him and there is uncleanness in all his possessions.

VI 2 They shall eat together, 3 together they shall bless and together they shall take counsel. In every place where there are ten men of the Community council, there should not be a priest missing amongst them. 4 And when they prepare the table to dine or the new wine 5 for drinking, the priest shall stretch out his hand as the first to bless the first fruits of the bread 6 and of the new wine. And in the place in which the Ten assemble there should not be missing a man to interpret the law day and night, 7 always, each man relieving his fellow. And the Many shall be on watch together for a third of each night of the year in order to read the book, explain the regulation, 8 and bless together.

This is the Rule for the session of the Many. Each one by his rank: the priests will sit down first, the elders next and the remainder of 9 all the people will sit down in order of rank. And following the same system they shall be questioned with regard to the judgment, the counsel and any matter referred to the Many, so that each can impart his wisdom 10 to the council of the Community. No one should talk during the speech of his fellow before his brother has finished speaking. And neither should he speak before one whose rank is listed 11 before his own. Whoever is questioned should speak in his turn. And in the session of the Many no one should utter anything without the consent of the Many. And if the 12 Examiner of the Many prevents someone having something to say to the Many but he is not in the position of one who is asking questions to the

Community council, 13 that man should stand up and say: "I have something to say to the Many." If they tell him to, he should speak.

And 95 to any in Israel who freely volunteers 14 to enroll in the council of the Community, the Instructor who is at the head of the Many shall test him with regard to his insight and his deeds. If he suits the discipline, he shall introduce him 15 into the covenant so that he can revert to the truth and shun all sin, and he shall teach him all the precepts of the Community. And then, when he comes in to stand in front of the Many, they shall be questioned, 16 all of them, concerning his affairs. And depending on the outcome of the lot in the council of the Many he shall be included or excluded. If he is included in the Community council, he must not touch the pure food of 17 the Many while they test him about his spirit and about his deeds until he has completed a full year; neither should he share in the possessions of the Many. 18 When he has completed a year within the Community, the Many will be questioned about his affairs, concerning his insight and his deeds in connection with the law. And if the lot results in his 19 joining the foundations of the Community according to the priests and the majority of the men of the covenant, his wealth and his belongings will also be included at the hands of the 20 Inspector of the belongings of the Many. And they shall be entered into the ledger in his hand, but they shall not use them for the Many. He must not touch the drink of the Many until 21 he completes a second year among the men of the Community. And when this second year is complete, he will be examined by command of the Many. And if 22 the lot results in his joining the Community, they shall enter him in the Rule according to his rank among his brothers for the law, for the judgment, for purity and for the placing of his possessions in common. And his advice will be 23 for the Community as will his judgment.

24 And these are the regulations by which they shall judge him in the scrutiny of the Community depending on the case. If one is found among them who has lied 25 knowingly concerning goods, he shall be excluded from the pure food of the Many for a year and shall be sentenced to a quarter of his bread.[121] And whoever retorts to 26 his fellow with stubbornness and speaks with brusqueness, ignoring the discipline of his fellow, defying the authority of his fellow who is enrolled ahead of him, 27 he has taken the law into his own hands; he will be punished for a year. . . . Whoever enunciates the Name (which is) honored above all

---

121. His rations are reduced by one-fourth.

[...] VII 1 whether blaspheming, or overwhelmed by misfortune or for any other reason, . . . or reading a book, or blessing, will be excluded 2 and shall not go back to the Community council. And if he has spoken angrily against one of the priests enrolled in the book, he will be punished 3 for a year and shall be excluded from the pure food of the Many. However, if he had spoken unintentionally, he will be punished for six months. And whoever lies knowingly 4 shall be punished for six months. Whoever knowingly and for no reason insults his fellow will be punished for a year 5 and will be excluded. And whoever speaks to his fellow with deception or knowingly deceives him, will be punished for six months. And if 6 he is negligent to his fellow, he will be punished for three months. However, if he is negligent with the possessions of the Community achieving a loss, he shall replace them. . . 7 in full. . . . 10 And if he does not manage to replace them, he will be punished for sixty days. And whoever feels animosity towards his fellow for no cause will be punished for [six months] a year.[122] 11 And likewise for anyone retaliating for any reason. Whoever utters with his mouth futile words, three months; and for talking in the middle of the words of his fellow, 12 ten days. And whoever lies down and goes to sleep in the session of the Many, thirty days. And the same applies to whoever leaves the session of the Many 13 without cause, or falls asleep up to three times during a session shall be punished ten days; however, if . . . 14 and he withdraws, he shall be punished for thirty days. And whoever walks about naked in front of his fellow, without needing to, shall be punished for three months. 15 And the person who spits in the course of a meeting of the Many shall be punished thirty days. And whoever takes out his hand from under his clothes, or if these are rags 16 which allow his nakedness to be seen, he will be punished thirty days. And whoever giggles inanely causing his voice to be heard shall be sentenced to thirty 17 days. And whoever takes out his left hand to gesticulate with it shall be punished ten days. And whoever goes around defaming his fellow 18 shall be excluded for one year from the pure food of the Many and shall be punished; however, whoever goes around defaming the Many shall be expelled from their midst 19 and will never return. And whoever complains against the foundation of the Community they shall expel and he will never return; however, if he complains against his fellow 20 without cause, he will be punished six months.

---

122. The text originally read "six months" but was then revised to read "a year."

6.3.6 Damascus Document I–XII:
The History and Self-image of the Dead Sea Sectarians[123]

This Dead Sea Scroll, also known as the Zadokite Fragments, originally found in the Cairo Genizah about a century ago, is addressed to the people of the covenant. It begins with a schematized history, explaining the role of the leader of the sect, the Teacher of Righteousness. The text then continues with a doctrine of reward and punishment followed by a series of collections of regulations with an emphasis on purity and the distancing of oneself from impure persons or things.

I 1 And now, listen, all those who know justice, and understand the actions of 2 God; for he has a dispute with all flesh and will carry out judgment on all those who spurn him. 3 For when they were unfaithful in forsaking him, he hid his face from Israel and from his sanctuary 4 and delivered them up to the sword. However, when he remembered the covenant of the very first, he saved a remnant 5 for Israel and did not deliver them up to destruction. And at the moment of wrath, three hundred and 6 ninety years after having delivered them up into the hands of Nebuchadnezzar, king of Babylon, 7 he visited them and caused to sprout from Israel and from Aaron a shoot of the planting, in order to possess 8 his land and to become fat with the good things of his soil. And they realized their sin and knew that 9 they were guilty men; but they were like blind persons and like those who grope for the path 10 over twenty years. And God appraised their deeds, because they sought him with a perfect heart 11 and raised up for them a Teacher of Righteousness, in order to direct them in the path of his heart.

And he made known 12 to the last generations what he had done for the last generation, the congregation of traitors. 13 These are the ones who stray from the path. This is the time about which it has been written (Hos. 4:16), "Like a stray heifer 14 so has Israel strayed," when "the scoffer" arose, who scattered 15 the waters of lies over Israel and made them veer off into a wilderness without path, flattening the everlasting heights, diverging 16 from tracks of justice and removing the boundary with which the very first had marked their inheritance, so that 17 the curses of his covenant would adhere to them, to deliver them up to the sword carrying out the vengeance 18 of the covenant. For they sought easy interpretations, chose illusions, scrutinized 19 loopholes, chose the

123. García Martínez, *The Dead Sea Scrolls Translated*, pp. 33–43.

handsome neck,[124] acquitted the guilty and sentenced the just, 20 violated the covenant, broke the precept, colluded together against the life of the just man; their soul abominated all those who walk 21 in perfection, they hunted them down with the sword and provoked the dispute of the people. And kindled was the wrath II 1 of God against his congregation, laying waste all its great number, for their deeds were unclean in front of him.

2 And now, listen to me, all entering the covenant, and I will open your ears to the paths of 3 the wicked. God loves knowledge; he has established wisdom and counsel before him; 4 discernment and knowledge are at his service; patience is his and abundance of pardon, 5 to atone for persons who repent from wickedness. However, strength and power and a great anger with flames of fire 6 by the [hand] of all the angels of destruction are against persons turning aside from the path and abominating the precept, without there being for them either a remnant 7 or survivor. For God did not choose them at the beginning of the world, and before they were established he knew 8 their deeds, and abominated the generations on account of blood and hid his face from the country, 9 from [Israel], until their extinction. And he knew the years of their existence, and the number and detail of their ages, of all 10 those who exist over the centuries, and of those who will exist, until it occurs in their ages throughout all the everlasting years. 11 And in all of them he raised up men of renown for himself to leave a remnant for the country and in order to fill 12 the surface of the earth with their offspring. And he taught them by the hand of the anointed ones through his holy spirit and through seers of the 13 truth, and their names were established with precision. But those he hates, he causes to stray.

14 And now, my sons, listen to me and I shall open your eyes so that you can see and understand the deeds of 15 God, so that you can choose what he is pleased with and repudiate what he hates, so that you can walk perfectly 16 on all his paths and not follow after the thoughts of a guilty inclination and lascivious eyes. For many 17 wandered off on account of these matters; brave heroes yielded on account of them, from ancient times until now. III 1 Through it, the sons of Noah and their families strayed, through it, they were cut off. 2 Abraham did not walk in it, and was counted as a friend for keeping God's precepts and not following 3 the desire of his spirit. And he passed (them) on to Isaac and to Jacob, and they kept (them) and were written up as friends 4 of God and as members of the covenant for ever. Jacob's sons strayed because of them and

---

124. The way of luxury.

were punished in accordance with 5 their mistakes. And in Egypt their sons walked in the stubbornness of their hearts, plotting against 6 God's precepts and each one doing what was right in his own eyes; and they ate blood, 7 and their males were cut off in the wilderness. He [spoke] to them in Kadesh (Deut. 9:23), "Go and possess the land." But they preferred the desire of their hearts, and did not listen to 8 the voice of their creator, to the precepts he had taught them, and murmured in their tents. And the wrath of God flared up 9 against their congregation. And their sons died through it, and through it their kings were cut off and through it their warriors 10 perished and through it their land was laid waste. Through it, the very first to enter the covenant made themselves guilty and were delivered up 11 to the sword, for having deserted God's covenant and having chosen their whims, and having followed the stubbornness 12 of their heart, each one doing (what was) his desire. But with those who remained steadfast in God's precepts, 13 with those who were left from among them, God established his covenant with Israel for ever, revealing to them 14 hidden matters in which all Israel had gone astray: his holy Sabbaths and his 15 glorious feasts, his just stipulations and his truthful paths, and the wishes of his will which 16 man must do in order to live by them. He disclosed (these matters) to them and they dug a well of plentiful water. . . .

20 Those who remained steadfast in it will acquire eternal life, and all the glory of Adam is for them. As 21 God established for them by means of Ezekiel the prophet, saying (Ezek. 44:15): "The priests and the Levites and the sons of IV 1 Zadok, who maintained the service of my temple when the children of Israel strayed 2 far away from me, shall offer the fat and the blood." The priests are the converts of Israel 3 who left the land of Judah; and [the Levites] are those who joined them; and the sons of Zadok are the chosen of 4 Israel, "those called by name" who arose at the end of days. . . . VI 14 [If] they are careful to act in accordance with the exact interpretation of the law for the age of wickedness: to separate themselves 15 from the sons of the pit; to abstain from wicked wealth which defiles, either by promise or by vow, 16 and from the wealth of the temple and from stealing from the poor of the people, from making their widows their spoils 17 and from murdering orphans; to separate unclean from clean and differentiate between 18 the holy and the common; to keep the Sabbath day according to the exact interpretation, and the festivals 19 and the day of fasting according to what those who entered the new covenant in the land of Damascus had discovered; 20 to set apart holy portions according to their exact interpretation; for each to love his brother 21 as himself; to strengthen the hand of the poor, the needy and

the foreigner; for each to seek the peace VII 1 of his brother and not commit sin against his blood relation; to refrain from fornication 2 in accordance with the regulation; for each to reprove his brother in accordance with the precept, and not to bear resentment 3 from one day to the next; to keep apart from every uncleanness according to their regulations, without 4 anyone defiling his holy spirit, according to what God kept apart for them; for all those who walk 5 according to these matters in perfect holiness, in accordance with his teaching, God's covenant is a guarantee for them 6 that they shall live a thousand generations.

And if they reside in the camps in accordance with the rule of the land, and marry 7 women and beget children, they shall walk in accordance with the law and according to the regulation 8 of the teachings, according to the rule of the law which says (Num. 30:17), "Between a man and his wife, and between a father 9 and his son." But all those who despise [...] when God visits the earth in order to empty over them the punishment of the wicked, 10 when there comes the word which is written in the words of Isaiah, son of Amoz, the prophet, 11 which says (Is. 7:17), "There shall come upon you, upon your people and upon your father's house, days such as 12 have [not] come since the day Ephraim departed from Judah." When the two houses of Israel separated, 13 Ephraim detached itself from Judah, and all the renegades were delivered up to the sword; but those who remained steadfast 14 escaped to the land of the north. As he said (Amos 5:26–7), "I will deport the Sikkut of your King 15 and the Kiyyun of your images away from my tent to Damascus." The books of the law are the Sukkah 16 of the King, as he said, (Amos 9:11), "I will lift up the fallen Sukkah of David." The King 17 is the assembly; and the bases of the images (and the Kiyyun of the images) are the books of the prophets 18 whose words Israel despised. And the star is the Interpreter of the law, 19 who will come to Damascus, as is written (Num 24: 13), "A star moves out of Jacob, and a scepter arises 20 out of Israel." The scepter is the prince of the whole congregation and when he rises he will destroy 21 all the sons of Seth. ...

IX 1 Every man who gives a human person to anathema[125] shall be executed according to the laws of the gentiles. 2 And what it says (Lev. 19:18), "Do not avenge yourself or bear resentment against the sons of your people": everyone of those who entered 3 the covenant who brings an accusation against his fellow, unless it is with reproach before witnesses, 4 or who brings it when he is angry, or he tells it to his elders so

---

125. This text probably imposes the death penalty for turning over a fellow Jew to non-Jewish courts to stand trial for a capital offense.

that they despise him, he is "the one who avenges himself and bears resentment." 5 Is it not written that only (Nah. 1:2), "he (God) avenges himself and bears resentment against his enemies?" 6 If he kept silent about him from one day to the next, or accused him of a capital offense, 7 he has witnessed against himself, for he did not fulfill the commandment of God which tells him (Lev. 19:17), "You shall 8 reproach your fellow so as not to incur sin because of him." Concerning the oath: as for what he 9 said (1 Sam. 25:26), "You shall not do justice with your (own) hand," but whoever forces the making of an oath in the open field, 10 not in the presence of judges or at their command, has done justice for himself with his hand.

Every lost object 11 about which it is not known who stole it from the property of the camp in which it was stolen—its owner should make a maledictory 12 oath; whoever hears it, if he knows and does not say it, is guilty. 13 Every illegal object[126] which should be given back and has no owner—he who gives it back should confess to the priest 14 and it will be for himself, apart from the ram of the sin-offering. And in the same way, every lost object which has been found and has 15 no owner, will be for the priests, for he who found it does not know the regulation in its regard; 16 if its owner is not found, they shall keep it.

Any matter in which a man sins 17 against the law, and his fellow sees him and he is alone; if it is a capital matter, he shall denounce him 18 in his presence, with reproach, to the Inspector, and the Inspector shall write with his hand until he commits it 19 again in the presence of someone alone, and he denounces him to the Inspector; if he returns and is surprised in the presence of 20 someone alone, his judgment is complete;[127] but if they are two who testify about 21 a different matter, the man is only to be excluded from the pure food on condition that 22 they are trustworthy, and that on the same day on which he saw him, he denounces him to the Inspector.[128] And concerning property, they shall accept two 23 trustworthy witnesses, and one to exclude from the holy food.[129] A witness is not to be accepted X 1 by the judges to condemn to death on his word, if he has not completed his days to pass 2 among those

---

126. An object acquired in a dishonest fashion, through deception.

127. The testimony of three witnesses to separate occurrences of the same transgression is sufficient for punishment. Capital cases always required three witnesses according to this approach.

128. Two witnesses testifying in this fashion cannot cause the transgressor to be punished except by being excluded from the pure food of the community.

129. In non-capital crimes, two witnesses are required, but the complaint of one is enough to lead to separation from the pure food of the community.

who are recruited and is fearful of God. No one 3 who has consciously transgressed anything of a precept is to be believed as a witness against his fellow, until he has been purified to return.

4 And this is the rule of the judges of the congregation. Ten men in number, chosen 5 from among the congregation, for a period; four from the tribe of Levi and of Aaron and six from Israel; 6 learned in the book of Hagy[130] and in the principles of the covenant; between 7 twenty-five and sixty years. And no one over 8 sixty years should hold the office of judging the congregation, for on account of man's sin 9 his days were shortened, and because of God's wrath against the inhabitants of the earth, he decided to remove knowledge 10 from them before they completed their days.

Concerning purification with water: 11 no one should bathe in water which is dirty or which is less than the amount which covers a man. 12 No one should purify a vessel in it. And every cavity in the rock in which there is not the amount 13 which covers, if an impure person has touched it, he has defiled the water like the water of a vase.

14 Concerning the Sabbath, to observe it in accordance with its regulation: no one should do 15 work on the sixth day, from the moment when the sun's disc is 16 at a distance of its diameter from the gate, for this is what he says (Deut. 5:12), "Observe the 17 Sabbath day to keep it holy."

And on the day of the Sabbath, no one should say a 18 useless or stupid word. He is not to lend anything to his fellow. He is not to discuss riches or gain. 19 He is not to speak about matters of work or of the task to be carried out on the following day. 20 No one is to walk in the field to do the work which he wishes 21 [on] the Sabbath. He is not to walk more than one thousand cubits outside the city, 22 No one is to eat on the Sabbath day except what has been prepared; and from what is lost 23 in the field, he should not eat. And he should not drink except of what there is in the camp. XI 1 On the road, if he goes down to bathe, he should drink where he stands. But he is not to draw it with 2 any vessel. He is not to send a foreigner to do what he wishes on the Sabbath day. 3 No one is to wear dirty clothes or (clothes) which are in the chest, unless 4 they have been washed with water or rubbed with incense. No one should fast voluntarily 5 on the Sabbath.

No one should go after an animal to pasture it outside his city, except for 6 a thousand cubits. He is not to raise his hand to strike with the fist. If 7 it is stubborn, he should not remove it from his house. No one should remove anything from the house 8 to outside, or from outside to the

---

130. Most probably the Torah or a sectarian book of law.

house. Even if he is in a hut, he should remove nothing from it 9 nor bring anything into it. He is not to open a sealed vessel on the Sabbath. No one should wear 10 perfumes on the Sabbath, to go out or come in. In his dwelling no one should lift 11 a stone or dust. The wet-nurse should not lift the baby to go out or come in on the Sabbath. 12 No one should press his servant or his maidservant or his employee on the Sabbath. 13 No one should help an animal give birth on the Sabbath day, and if he causes it to fall into a well 14 or a pit, he should not take it out on the Sabbath. No one should stay in a place close 15 to gentiles on the Sabbath.

No one should profane the Sabbath by riches or gain on the Sabbath. 16 And any living man who falls into a place of water or into a place. . ., 17 no one should take him out with a ladder or a rope or a utensil. No one should offer anything upon the altar on the Sabbath, 18 except the sacrifice of the Sabbath, for thus is it written (Lev. 23:38), "except your offerings of the Sabbath."

No one should send 19 to the altar a sacrifice, or an offering, or incense, or wood, by the hand of a man impure from any 20 of the impurities, thus allowing him to defile the altar, for it is written (Prov. 15:8), "the sacrifice 21 of the wicked is an abomination, but the prayer of the just is like an agreeable offering." And everyone who enters 22 the house of prostration should not enter with impurity requiring washing; and when the trumpets of the assembly sound, 23 he may advance or retreat, but the whole service should not stop. . . XII 1 it is holy. No man should sleep with his wife in the city of the temple, defiling 2 the city of the temple with their impurity. Every man over whom the spirit of Belial dominates 3 and he preaches apostasy, will be judged according to the regulation of the necromancer or the diviner. But everyone who goes astray, 4 defiling the Sabbath and the festivals, shall not be executed, for guarding him 5 belongs to men; and if he is cured of it, they shall guard him for seven years and afterwards 6 he shall enter the assembly.

He is not to stretch out his hand to shed the blood of one of the gentiles 7 for the sake of riches and gain. Neither should he take any of his riches, so that they do not 8 blaspheme, except on the advice of the company of Israel. No one should sell an animal, 9 or a clean bird, to the gentiles lest they sacrifice them. 10 And he should not sell them anything from his granary or his press, at any price. And his servant and his maidservant: he should not sell them, 11 for they entered the covenant of Abraham with him.

No one should defile his soul 12 with any living being or one which creeps, by eating them, from the larvae of bees to every living 13 being which creeps in water. And fish, they should not eat them unless they have been opened up 14 alive, and the[ir blood poured] away. And all the locusts, according to their kind, shall be put into fire or into water 15 while they are still alive, as this is the regulation for their species. And all the wood and the stones 16 and the dust which are defiled by human impurity, by defilement of oil in them, 17 in accordance with their uncleanness will make whoever touches them impure. And every utensil, nail or peg in the wall 18 which is with a dead person in the house will be unclean with the same uncleanness as tools for work.

7

Apocrypha, Pseudepigrapha, and the Dead Sea Scrolls

One of the most significant characteristics of Second Temple Judaism is the wide variety of texts which circulated among different groups of Jews. We are accustomed to treating these documents in classes, based more on their transmission than their literary and theological characteristics. So we speak of Apocrypha, Pseudepigrapha, and Dead Sea Scrolls, designating in the first and last instance specific groups of texts collected in Antiquity. Pseudepigrapha is a catch-all term which has been used with increasing looseness in recent years. Taken together, we gain from these texts a picture of a Jewish community, both in and outside of the Land of Israel, producing literary works of many kinds and involved in vigorous debate about all kinds of religious questions.

For later Rabbinic Judaism, already in the Mishnah Sanhedrin (text 7.1.1), the reading of the Apocrypha and other nonbiblical works was prohibited, and it was understood to lead to loss of one's portion in the world to come. This blanket prohibition may have referred only to public reading of such nonscriptural books. The interpretation of this Mishnah text in the Jerusalem Talmud (text 7.1.2) explicitly refers to Ben Sira, which is included in the Apocrypha, a body of works canonized in the Greek Bible, which served as the basis for the Septuagint. Also forbidden to Jews were the works of early Christians, as explained in the Babylonian Talmud (text

7.1.3). Only the twenty-four books of the Hebrew Bible were to be considered canonical, as explained in *Ecclesiastes Rabbah* (text 7.1.4).

In order to illustrate the material in the Apocrypha, we present several examples. Tobit is set in the Assyrian period but clearly refers to the Seleucid era. The excerpt we have included (text 7.1.5) shows the nature of the religious teachings of this book and the piety which the author attributed to its heroes. Similar is the case of the beautiful tale of Judith (text 7.1.6), which has been the theme of so much European art.

The additions to Esther preserved only in the Septuagint Greek version (text 7.1.7) illustrate the manner in which the expanded Greek version of this text tried to introduce similar piety into the story of Esther, although in the Hebrew version preserved in the Massoretic Bible no such notions are explicit. In this case, virtually all later Jewish traditions followed the same model, introducing God and religious issues into the book of Esther. Similar additions are found in the Greek Daniel. Nonbiblical Qumran manuscripts also preserve some alternative versions of elements of Daniel but these do not parallel the material added in the Greek versions. Among these additions is the Song of the Three Young Men—Hananiah, Mishael, and Azariah—(text 7.1.8), which provides the prayer lacking in the canonical text of Daniel. Another addition to Daniel, the story of Susanna (text 7.1.9), is of an entirely different character. It is intended in context to explain how Daniel was recognized for his wisdom even as a youth, but it is truly the story of a righteous young woman whose virtue is vindicated by God's justice.

Apocryphal literature focused also on more minor biblical characters, and this is the case with Baruch the scribe of Jeremiah, who was also the focus of some pseudepigraphal texts. The book of Baruch (text 7.1.10) was clearly written after the destruction of the Second Temple. In portraying Baruch's reaction to the first destruction in 586 B.C.E., it tries to deal with the theological ramifications of the second. Another work closely linked to the biblical book of Jeremiah is the so-called Letter of Jeremiah (text 7.1.11), which tried to fill in the missing letter which Jeremiah sent to the exiles in Babylonia.

Among the most important of these works is Ben Sira, from which we can only present a small part (text 7.1.12). This book, composed originally in Hebrew, carries on many older wisdom traditions but is clearly a work of Second Temple times. It gives a sense of how by this time wisdom and Torah had been totally melded. Similar is the Wisdom of Solomon (text 7.1.13), except that it was probably composed in Greek and is therefore somewhat more Hellenized in content. Both works represent the common piety that must have been characteristic of most Jews of the Second Temple period, especially of those not involved in apocalyptic movements or members of particular sectarian circles.

When we enter the world of the Pseudepigrapha, for the most part we encounter books which represent particular approaches to Judaism, often stemming from apocalyptic circles. This is certainly the case with the various parts of the book of 1 Enoch, also known as Ethiopic Enoch. The antiquity of the sections of the book discussed here is certain since parts of these sections were preserved in the Qumran manuscripts. The Book of Watchers (text 7.2.1) recorded a variety of traditions about the angels and their marriages with women. Further, here we encounter an early version of the vision of the divine throne, a motif that would continue to be prominent in the long history of Jewish mystical thought. These selections also show the apocalyptic nature of this material as they involve the revelation of heavenly secrets, including those pertaining to the end of days. We also include some material from the Apocalypse of Weeks, toward the end of 1 Enoch (text 7.2.2). This passage is typical of ancient attempts to schematize history in an apocalyptic fashion, and can be compared also with the book of Daniel. The last selection from this book is an account of the birth of Noah (text 7.2.3) which is part of a wider Noah literature that revolved around this ancient and clearly mysterious biblical hero.

Extensive selections are included from the book of Jubilees (text 7.2.4). This book was preserved at Qumran in a number of manuscripts and was explicitly quoted in the sectarian literature. It may have been considered canonical by the sectarians. Whatever the case, its influence on aspects of Jewish law and biblical interpretation, what the Rabbis called halakhah and aggadah, was tremendous. It emphasizes the importance of Moses as a vehicle for God's revelation, as well as the need to strictly observe the laws of the Torah, which are said to have already been observed by the patriarchs—

Abraham, Isaac, and Jacob. Further, it is structured on a chronological system of Jubilee years. Like Enoch, Jubilees calls for the observance of a calendar of solar months and years, in contrast to the lunar months of the Pharisaic-Rabbinic calendar.

The final text in this section is the Testament of Levi (text 7.2.5), a sort of ethical will given by Levi to his descendants at the end of his life. A very similar text, called the *Aramaic Levi Document*, was found at Qumran, showing the early date of this material. It emphasizes the sanctity of the tribe of Levi and its priestly duties, and the need for the priests and Levites to maintain the sanctity of their tribe.

The literature of the Dead Sea Scrolls is so extensive that it would be impossible to provide even a small part of it. Yet certain texts have been important in the ongoing debates over the nature of the scrolls and their significance, and we have endeavored to include some of them. In the preceding chapter the fundamental texts of the *Rule of the Community* and the *Damascus Document (Zadokite Fragments)* were presented.

The *pesher* literature, consisting of contemporizing biblical commentaries that understand the biblical prophets as referring to events taking place in the author's own day, are an important source for the distinctive ideas of the Qumran sect itself as well as for some details of the history of the group. Most significant of these is the *Habakkuk Pesher* (text 7.3.1). Here we see the persecution of the sect's leader, the Teacher of Righteousness, by his opponents as well as the expectation that the Romans were soon to attack Judea. The extent to which the interpretations depart from the plain sense of Scripture should be apparent. The *Thanksgiving Scroll* (also termed *Hodayot Scroll*) contains inspirational poetry which expresses the theological beliefs of the sectarians, such as predestination, as well as the sense of persecution they felt at the hands of their opponents (text 7.3.2).

The sectarians expected to engage in an eschatological war with their opponents and the nations of the world, and this war is described in the *Scroll of the War of the Sons of Light Against the Sons of Darkness* (text 7.3.3). Here we encounter a sort of ritualized war in which the sectarians destroy the forces of evil and emerge victorious at the end of days.

Extremely important for its relevance to biblical studies, Jewish law, and even the history of architecture is the *Temple Scroll*, which presents a plan for a new Temple and its sacrifices, as well as for the polity of Israel. In this excerpt (text 7.3.4), we present the law of the king which is effectively a polemic against the Hasmonean order of government, still in effect when the scroll was compiled, for the most part, from earlier sources.

The recently published *Miqẓat Ma'ase ha-Torah*, otherwise known as the "Halakhic Letter" (text 7.3.5), provides much evidence about the legal polemics about sacrifice and purity which led to the formation of the Dead Sea sect. This text shows us that many of its own halakhic views are Sadducean in character, and it confirms that many legal rulings and interpretations in the *Temple Scroll* are in origin Sadducean. This, in turn, raises the question of the probability of Sadducean origins for the Dead Sea sect.

Much discussion has centered around the possible connection of the scrolls with early Christianity. We include here a dramatic example of the dependence of Christianity on earlier Jewish traditions that were unknown before the discovery of the scrolls. The so-called "Son of God" text, the *Aramaic Apocalypse* (text 7.3.6), provides evidence that some Jews referred to a redeemer figure as "son of God" in the third century B.C.E. We complete this chapter with a beautiful poem (text 7.3.7) found in the *Psalms Scroll* but originally a separate composition, which shows the love for the holy city of Jerusalem that has always been a constant in Jewish life.

All in all, as a result of the discovery and publication of the Dead Sea Scrolls, we now have an expanded notion of the nature of the literature of Second Temple Jews, most of which was already in circulation in the Hasmonean period. This literature has provided a much deeper understanding of the nature of the various approaches to Judaism in this period. Based on this wider picture, we are better able to reconstruct the influence of this literature on the later development of Judaism.

7.1 THE APOCRYPHA

7.1.1 Mishnah Sanhedrin 10:1:
The Status of Those Who Read the Apocrypha[1]

The Mishnah records the opinion of Rabbi Akiva concerning those who read apocryphal books. It is possible that his prohibition refers only to the public reading of these texts.

ༀ

All of Israel has a portion in the World to Come, as it is written, "And your people, all of them are righteous; they will inherit the land forever, the shoot of my planting, the work of my hands in which I exalt myself" (Is. 60:21).

But these are the ones who have no portion in the World to Come: he who says that resurrection of the dead is not attested in the Torah, and [he who says] that the Torah is not from heaven, and an *apikoros*.[2] Rabbi Akiva says: "also one who reads in the external books,[3] and one who murmurs over a wound[4] and says, 'all the diseases which I have set upon Egypt, I will not set upon you for I am the Lord your healer' (Ex. 15:26)." Abba Saul says: "also he who pronounces the Divine name according to its letters."[5]

7.1.2 Jerusalem Talmud Sanhedrin 10:1 (28a):
On the Status of Apocryphal Books[6]

An attempt is made to distinguish the canonized, sacred books from apocryphal books and from ordinary literature.

ༀ

"Rabbi Akiva says: 'also one who reads external books,'"[7] like the books of Ben Sira[8] and the books of Ben La'ana.[9] But the books of

---

1. Trans. S. Berrin.
2. Hebrew adaptation of the Greek for "Epicurean" used as a term for heretic.
3. Those not part of the biblical canon, i.e., apocryphal texts.
4. A healer who uses incantations including biblical verses.
5. It was prohibited to pronounce the divine name as it was spelled except by the high priest on the most holy day of the calendar, Yom Kippur. Therefore, this written name was always "pronounced" by use of a substitute term.
6. Trans. S. Berrin.
7. Mishnah Sanhedrin 10:1.
8. A book in the Apocrypha.
9. The identity of this book is not known.

Homer and all the books which have been written from (the period of the last prophets) and thereafter, one who reads them is like one who reads a letter. What is the reason? "And of more than these, my son, be warned! The making of many books has no end, and much study is wearying of the flesh" (Eccl. 12:12). For reading they were given, but for laborious study they were not given.

7.1.3 Babylonian Talmud Sanhedrin 100b: The Books of the Early Christians

The question arose as to how to treat religious or moral works not in the biblical canon, especially those of the early Christians.

ℭ

"Rabbi Akiva says: 'also one who reads external books. . . .'" A tanna taught: "[this means] the books of the *minim*."[10] Rabbi Joseph said: "It is also forbidden to read from the book of Ben Sira."

7.1.4 *Ecclesiastes Rabbah* 12:12: On the Study of Apocryphal Books[11]

Ecclesiastes Rabbah designates the twenty-four books of the Hebrew Bible as the basic library for study, a closed canon to which all other books are extraneous.

ℭ

"And of more than these (Hebrew: *mhmh*), my son, be warned! The making of many books has no end, and much study is wearying of the flesh" (Eccl.12:12): [Read the word *mhmh* as] *mhwmh* (confusion), because whoever brings into his house more than the 24 books [of the Bible] brings confusion into his house, such as the book of Ben Sira and the book of Ben Tagla.[12] "And much study (*lahag*) is a weariness of the flesh" (ibid.). [These apocryphal books] are given to talk about (*lahagot*) but are not given for the weariness of the flesh.[13]

---

10. Heretics subjected to legal restrictions in an effort to suppress their rejection of Jewish doctrine. In the Rabbinic period, these restrictions were mainly directed against the early Christians.

11. Trans. S. Berrin.

12. The identity of this book is not known.

13. It is not permitted to study them in detail.

7.1.5 Book of Tobit 11–12: The Reward of the Righteous[14]

An example of an apocryphal book, Tobit illustrates the moral that healing and blessing come as a result of righteousness. Although significant parts of the book are preserved in the original Aramaic amongst the Dead Sea Scrolls, the full text of this book is preserved only in Greek. The following excerpt illustrates the pious religious outlook of this book.

※

11:1 After this[15] Tobias went on his way, praising God because he had made his journey a success. And he blessed Raguel and his wife Edna.

So he continued on his way until they came near to Nineveh. 2 Then Raphael[16] said to Tobias, "Are you not aware, brother, of how you left your father? 3 Let us run ahead of your wife and prepare the house. 4 And take the gall of the fish with you." So they went their way, and the dog went along behind them.

5 Now Anna[17] sat looking intently down the road for her son. 6 And she caught sight of him coming, and said to his father, "Behold, your son is coming, and so is the man who went with him!"

7 Raphael said, "I know, Tobias, that your father will open his eyes. 8 You therefore must anoint his eyes with the gall; and when they smart he will rub them, and will cause the white films to fall away, and he will see you."

9 Then Anna ran to meet them, and embraced her son, and said to him, "I have seen you, my child; now I am ready to die." And they both wept. 10 Tobit started toward the door, and stumbled. But his son ran to him 11 and took hold of his father, and he sprinkled the gall upon his father's eyes, saying. "Be of good cheer, father." 12 And when his eyes began to smart he rubbed them, 13 and the white films scaled off from the corners of his eyes. 14 Then he saw his son and embraced him, and he wept and said, "Blessed art thou, O God, and blessed is thy name for ever, and blessed are all thy holy angels. 15 For thou hast afflicted me, but thou hast had mercy upon me; here I see my son Tobias!" And his son went in

---

14. All texts from the Apocrypha taken from the *Revised Standard Version Apocrypha* (New York: National Council of Churches, 1957).

15. Tobias had journeyed to Ecbatana to the house of Raguel to marry his daughter, Sarah.

16. The angel, Raphael, was employed as Tobias' travel guide and helped him to thwart the demon that killed Sarah's previous husbands by burning the heart and liver of a fish. The gall he reserved for curing the blind father of Tobias, Tobit.

17. The mother of Tobias.

rejoicing, and he reported to his father the great things that had happened to him in Media.

16 Then Tobit went out to meet his daughter-in-law at the gate of Nineveh, rejoicing and praising God. Those who saw him as he went were amazed because he could see. 17 And Tobit gave thanks before them that God had been merciful to him. When Tobit came near to Sarah his daughter-in-law, he blessed her, saying, "Welcome, daughter! Blessed is God who has brought you to us, and blessed are your father and your mother." So there was rejoicing among all his brethren in Nineveh. 18 Ahikar and his nephew Nadab came, 19 and Tobias' marriage was celebrated for seven days with great festivity.

12:1 Tobit then called his son Tobias and said to him, "My son, see to the wages of the man who went with you; and he must also be given more." 2 He replied, "Father, it would do me no harm to give him half of what I have brought back. 3 For he has led me back to you safely, he cured my wife, he obtained the money for me, and he also healed you." 4 The old man said, "He deserves it." 5 So he called the angel and said to him, "Take half of all that you two have brought back."

6 Then the angel called the two of them privately and said to them: "Praise God and give thanks to him; exalt him and give thanks to him in the presence of all the living for what he has done for you. It is good to praise God and to exalt his name, worthily declaring the works of God. Do not be slow to give him thanks. 7 It is good to guard the secret of a king, but gloriously to reveal the works of God. Do good, and evil will not overtake you.

11 "I will not conceal anything from you. I have said, 'It is good to guard the secret of a king, but gloriously to reveal the works of God.' 12 And so, when you and your daughter-in-law Sarah prayed, I brought a reminder of your prayer before the Holy One: and when you buried the dead, I was likewise present with you. 13 When you did not hesitate to rise and leave your dinner in order to go and lay out the dead, your good deed was not hidden from me, but I was with you. 14 So now God sent me to heal you and your daughter-in-law Sarah. 15 I am Raphael, one of the seven holy angels who present the prayers of the saints and enter into the presence of the glory of the Holy One."

16 They were both alarmed; and they fell upon their faces, for they were afraid. 17 But he said to them. "Do not be afraid: you will be safe. But praise God for ever. 18 For I did not come as a favor on my part, but by the will of our God. Therefore praise him forever. 19 All these days I merely appeared to you and did not eat or drink, but you were seeing a vision. 20 And now give thanks to God, for I am ascending to him who

sent me. Write in a book everything that has happened." 21 Then they stood up; but they saw him no more. 22 So they confessed the great and wonderful works of God, and acknowledged that the angel of the Lord had appeared to them.

7.1.6 Book of Judith 4–16: The Pious Heroine

The book of Judith, set in an earlier era but clearly written in Hebrew in the second half of the second century B.C.E., tells the story of a heroine who saved her people from danger. It appears to recall the time of the persecutions under Antiochus IV, although there is no specific reference.

⟡

4:1 By this time the people of Israel living in Judea heard of everything that Holofernes, the general of Nebuchadnezzar the king of the Assyrians, had done to the nations, and how he had plundered and destroyed all their temples; 2 they were therefore very greatly terrified at his approach, and were alarmed both for Jerusalem and for the temple of the Lord their God. . . . 6 And Joakim, the high priest, who was in Jerusalem at the time, wrote to the people of Bethulia and Betomesthaim, which faces Esdraelon opposite the plain near Dothan, 7 ordering them to seize the passes up into the hills, since by them Judea could be invaded, and it was easy to stop any who tried to enter, for the approach was narrow, only wide enough for two men at the most. 8 So the Israelites did as Joakim the high priest and the senate of the whole people of Israel, in session at Jerusalem, had given order. 9 And every man of Israel cried out to God with great fervor, and they humbled themselves with much fasting.

5:1 When Holofernes, the general of the Assyrian army, heard that the people of Israel had prepared for war and had closed the passes in the hills and fortified all the high hilltops and set up barricades in the plains, 2 he was very angry. . . . 7:1 The next day Holofernes ordered his whole army, and all the allies who had joined him, to break camp and move against Bethulia, and to seize the passes up into the hill country and make war on the Israelites. . . .

4 When the Israelites saw their vast numbers they were greatly terrified, and every one said to his neighbor, "These men will now lick up the face of the whole land; neither the high mountains nor the valleys nor the hills will bear their weight." 5 Then each man took up his weapons, and when they had kindled fires on their towers they remained on guard all that night. 6 On the second day Holofernes led out all his cavalry in full view of the Israelites in Bethulia, 7 and examined the approaches to the

city, and visited the springs that supplied their water, and seized them and set guards of soldiers over them, and then returned to his army. . . .

19 The people of Israel cried out to the Lord their God, for their courage failed, because all their enemies had surrounded them and there was no way of escape from them. 20 The whole Assyrian army, their infantry, chariots, and cavalry, surrounded them for thirty-four days, until all the vessels of water belonging to every inhabitant of Bethulia were empty; 21 their cisterns were going dry, and they did not have enough water to drink their fill for a single day, because it was measured out to them to drink. 22 Their children lost heart, and the women and young men fainted from thirst and fell down in the streets of the city and in the passages through the gates; there was no strength left in them any longer.

8:1 At that time Judith heard about these things. . . . 2 Her husband Manasseh, who belonged to her tribe and family, had died during the barley harvest. 3 For as he stood overseeing the men who were binding sheaves in the field, he was overcome by the burning heat, and took to his bed and died in Bethulia his city. So they buried him with his fathers in the field between Dothan and Balamon. 4 Judith had lived at home as a widow for three years and four months. 5 She set up a tent for herself on the roof of her house, and girded sackcloth about her loins and wore the garments of her widowhood. 6 She fasted all the days of her widowhood, except the day before the sabbath and the sabbath itself, the day before the new moon and the day of the new moon, and the feasts and days of rejoicing of the house of Israel. 7 She was beautiful in appearance, and had a very lovely face; and her husband Manasseh had left her gold and silver, and men and women slaves, and cattle, and fields; and she maintained this estate. 8 No one spoke ill of her, for she feared God with great devotion. . . .

32 Judith said to them, "Listen to me. I am about to do a thing which will go down through all generations of our descendants. 33 Stand at the city gate tonight, and I will go out with my maid; and within the days after which you have promised to surrender the city to our enemies, the Lord will deliver Israel by my hand. 34 Only, do not try to find out what I plan; for I will not tell you until I have finished what I am about to do."

35 Uzziah and the rulers said to her, "Go in peace, and may the Lord God go before you, to take revenge upon our enemies." 36 So they returned from the tent and went to their posts.

9:1 Then Judith fell upon her face, and put ashes on her head, and uncovered the sackcloth she was wearing; and at the very time when that evening's incense was being offered in the house of God in Jerusalem, Judith cried out to the Lord with a loud voice and said. . . . 7 "Behold now, the Assyrians are increased in their might; they are exalted, with their horses and riders; they glory in the strength of their foot soldiers; they trust in shield and spear, in bow and sling, and know not that thou art the Lord who crushest wars; the Lord is thy name. 8 Break their strength by thy might, and bring down their power in thy anger; for they intend to defile thy sanctuary, and to pollute the tabernacle where thy glorious name rests, and to cast down the horn of thy altar with the sword. 9 Behold their pride, and send thy wrath upon their heads; give to me, a widow, the strength to do what I plan. 10 By the deceit of my lips strike down the slave with the prince and the prince with his servant; crush their arrogance by the hand of a woman. . . .

10:1 When Judith had ceased crying out to the God of Israel, and had ended all these words, 2 she rose from where she lay prostrate and called her maid and went down into the house where she lived on sabbaths and on her feast days; 3 and she removed the sackcloth which she had been wearing, and took off her widow's garments, and bathed her body with water, and anointed herself with precious ointment, and combed her hair and put on a tiara, and arrayed herself in her gayest apparel, which she used to wear while her husband Manasseh was living. 4 And she put sandals on her feet, and put on her anklets and bracelets and rings, and her earrings and all her ornaments, and made herself very beautiful, to entice the eyes of all men who might see her. 5 And she gave her maid a bottle of wine and a flask of oil, and filled a bag with parched grain and a cake of dried fruit and fine bread; and she wrapped up all her vessels and gave them to her to carry.

6 Then they went out to the city gate of Bethulia, and found Uzziah standing there with the elders of the city, Chabris and Charmis. 7 When they saw her, and noted how her face was altered and her clothing changed, they greatly admired her beauty, and said to her, 8 "May the God of our fathers grant you favor and fulfill your plans, that the people of Israel may glory and Jerusalem may be exalted." And she worshipped God.

9 Then she said to them, "Order the gate of the city to be opened for me, and I will go out and accomplish the things about which you spoke with me." So they ordered the young men to open the gate for her, as she had said. 10 When they had done this, Judith went out, she and her maid with her; and the men of the city watched her until she had gone down the mountain and passed through the valley and they could no longer see her.

11 The women went straight on through the valley; and an Assyrian patrol met her 12 and took her into custody, and asked her, "To what peo-

ple do you belong, and where are you coming from, and where are you going?" She replied, "I am a daughter of the Hebrews, but I am fleeing from them, for they are about to be handed over to you to be devoured. 13 I am on my way to the presence of Holofernes the commander of your army, to give him a true report; and I will show him a way by which he can go and capture all the hill country without losing one of his men, captured or slain."

14 When the men heard her words, and observed her face—she was in their eyes marvelously beautiful—they said to her, 15 "You have saved your life by hurrying down to the presence of our lord. Go at once to his tent; some of us will escort you and hand you over to him. 16 And when you stand before him, do not be afraid in your heart, but tell him just what you have said, and he will treat you well."

17 They chose from their number a hundred men to accompany her and her maid, and they brought them to the tent of Holofernes. 18 There was great excitement in the whole camp, for her arrival was reported from tent to tent, and they came and stood around her as she waited outside the tent of Holofernes while they told him about her. 19 And they marveled at her beauty, and admired the Israelites, judging them by her, and every one said to his neighbor, "Who can despise these people, who have women like this among them? Surely not a man of them had better be left alive, for if we let them go they will be able to ensnare the whole world!"

20 Then Holofernes' companions and all his servants came out and led her into the tent. 21 Holofernes was resting on his bed, under a canopy which was woven with purple and gold and emeralds and precious stones. 22 When they told him of her he came forward to the front of the tent, with silver lamps carried before him. 23 And when Judith came into the presence of Holofernes and his servants, they all marveled at the beauty of her face; and she prostrated herself and made obeisance to him, and his slaves raised her up.

11:1 Then Holofernes said to her, "Take courage, woman, and do not be afraid in your heart, for I have never hurt any one who chose to serve Nebuchadnezzar, the king of all the earth. 2 And even now, if your people who live in the hill country had not slighted me, I would never have lifted my spear against them; but they have brought all this on themselves. 3 And now tell me why you have fled from them and have come over to us—since you have come to safety. 4 Have courage; you will live, tonight and from now on. No one will hurt you, but all will treat you well, as they do the servants of my lord King Nebuchadnezzar."

5 Judith replied to him, "Accept the words of your servant, and let your maidservant speak in your presence, and I will tell nothing false to my lord

this night. . . . 10 . . . our nation cannot be punished, nor can the sword prevail against them, unless they sin against their God. 11 And now, in order that my lord may not be defeated and his purpose frustrated, death will fall upon them, for a sin has overtaken them by which they are about to provoke their God to anger when they do what is wrong. 12 Since their food supply is exhausted and their water has almost given out, they have planned to kill their cattle and have determined to use all that God by his laws has forbidden them to eat. 13 They have decided to consume the first fruits of the grain and the tithes of the wine and oil, which they had consecrated and set aside for the priests who minister in the presence of our God at Jerusalem—although it is not lawful for any of the people so much as to touch these things with their hands. 14 They have sent men to Jerusalem, because even the people living there have been doing this, to bring back to them permission from the senate. 15 When the word reaches them and they proceed to do this, on that very day they will be handed over to you to be destroyed.

16 "Therefore, when I, your servant, learned all this, I fled from them; and God has sent me to accomplish with you things that will astonish the whole world, as many as shall hear about them. 17 For your servant is religious, and serves the God of heaven day and night; therefore, my lord, I will remain with you, and every night your servant will go out into the valley, and I will pray to God and he will tell me when they have committed their sins. 18 And I will come and tell you, and then you shall go out with your whole army, and not one of them will withstand you. 19 Then I will lead you through the middle of Judea, till you come to Jerusalem; and I will set your throne in the midst of it; and you will lead them like sheep that have no shepherd, and not a dog will so much as open its mouth to growl at you. For this has been told me, by my foreknowledge; it was announced to me, and I was sent to tell you."

20 Her words pleased Holofernes and all his servants, and they marveled at her wisdom and said, 21 "There is not such a woman from one end of the earth to the other, either for beauty of face or wisdom of speech!"

22 And Holofernes said to her, "God has done well to send you before the people, to lend strength to our hands and to bring destruction upon those who have slighted my lord. 23 You are not only beautiful in appearance, but wise in speech; and if you do as you have said, your God shall be my God, and you shall live in the house of King Nebuchadnezzar and be renowned throughout the whole world."

12:1 Then he commanded them to bring her in where his silver dishes were kept, and ordered them to set a table for her with some of his own food and to serve her with his own wine. 2 But Judith said, "I cannot eat it, lest it be an offense; but I will be provided from the things I have brought with me."

3 Holofernes said to her, "If your supply runs out, where can we get more like it for you? For none of your people is here with us." 4 Judith replied, "As your soul lives, my lord, your servant will not use up the things I have with me before the Lord carries out by my hand what he has determined to do."

5 Then the servants of Holofernes brought her into the tent, and she slept until midnight. Along toward the morning watch she arose 6 and sent to Holofernes and said, "Let my lord now command that your servant be permitted to go out and pray." 7 So Holofernes commanded his guards not to hinder her. And she remained in the camp for three days, and went out each night to the valley of Bethulia, and bathed at the spring in the camp. 8 When she came up from the spring she prayed to the Lord God of Israel to direct her way for the raising up of her people. 9 So she returned clean and stayed in the tent until she ate her food toward evening.

10 On the fourth day Holofernes held a banquet for his slaves only, and did not invite any of his officers. 11 And he said to Bagoas, the eunuch who had charge of his personal affairs, "Go now and persuade the Hebrew woman who is in your care to join us and eat and drink with us. 12 For it will be a disgrace if we let such a woman go without enjoying her company, for if we do not embrace her she will laugh at us."

13 So Bagoas went out from the presence of Holofernes, and approached her and said, "This beautiful maidservant will please come to my lord and be honored in his presence, and drink wine and be merry with us, and become today like one of the daughters of the Assyrians who serve in the house of Nebuchadnezzar."

14 And Judith said, "Who am I, to refuse my lord? Surely whatever pleases him I will do at once, and it will be a joy to me until the day of my death!"

15 So she got up and arrayed herself in all her woman's finery, and her maid went and spread on the ground for her before Holofernes the soft fleeces which she had received from Bagoas for her daily use, so that she might recline on them when she ate. 16 Then Judith came in and lay down, and Holofernes' heart was ravished with her and he was moved with great desire to possess her; for he had been waiting for an opportunity to deceive her, ever since the day he first saw her.

17 So Holofernes said to her. "Drink now, and be merry with us!"

18 Judith said, "I will drink now, my lord, because my life means more to me today than in all the days since I was born."

19 Then she took and ate and drank before him what her maid had prepared. 20 And Holofernes was greatly pleased with her, and drank a great quantity of wine, much more than he had ever drunk in any one day since he was born.

13:1 When evening came, his slaves quickly withdrew, and Bagoas closed the tent from outside and shut out the attendants from his master's presence; and they went to bed, for they all were weary because the banquet had lasted long. 2 So Judith was left alone in the tent, with Holofernes stretched out on his bed, for he was overcome with wine. . . . 6 She went up to the post at the end of the bed, above Holofernes' head, and took down his sword that hung there. 7 She came close to his bed and took hold of the hair of his head, and said, "Give me strength this day, O Lord God of Israel!" 8 And she struck his neck twice with all her might, and severed it from his body. 9 Then she tumbled his body off the bed and pulled down the canopy from the posts; after a moment she went out, and gave Holofernes' head to her maid, 10 who placed it in her food bag. Then the two of them went out together, as they were accustomed to go for prayer; and they passed through the camp and circled around the valley and went up the mountain to Bethulia and came to its gates. 11 Judith called out from afar to the watchmen at the gates, "Open, open the gate! God, our God, is still with us, to show his power in Israel, and his strength against our enemies, even as he has done this day!"

12 When the men of her city heard her voice, they hurried down to the city gate and called together the elders of the city. 13 They all ran together, both small and great, for it was unbelievable that she had returned; they opened the gate and admitted them, and they kindled a fire for light, and gathered around them. 14 Then she said to them with a loud voice, "Praise God, O praise him! Praise God, who has not withdrawn his mercy from the house of Israel, but has destroyed our enemies by my hand this very night!"

15 Then she took the head out of the bag and showed it to them, and said, "See, here is the head of Holofernes, the commander of the Assyrian army, and here is the canopy beneath which he lay in his drunken stupor. The Lord has struck him down by the hand of a woman. 16 As the Lord lives, who has protected me in the way I went, it was my face that tricked him to his destruction, and yet he committed no act of sin with me, to defile and shame me."

17 All the people were greatly astonished, and bowed down and worshiped God, and said with one accord, "Blessed art thou, our God, who hast brought into contempt this day the enemies of thy people. . . ."

14:11 As soon as it was dawn they hung the head of Holofernes on the wall, and every man took his weapons, and they went out in companies to the passes in the mountains. 12 And when the Assyrians saw them they sent word to their commanders, and they went to the generals and the captains and to all their officers. 13 So they came to Holofernes' tent and said to the steward in charge of all his personal affairs, "Wake up our lord, for the slaves have been so bold as to come down against us to give battle, in order to be destroyed completely."

14 So Bagoas went in and knocked at the door of the tent, for he supposed that he was sleeping with Judith. 15 But when no one answered, he opened it and went into the bedchamber and found him thrown down on the platform dead, with his head cut off and missing. 16 And he cried out with a loud voice and wept and groaned and shouted, and rent his garments. 17 Then he went to the tent where Judith had stayed, and when he did not find her he rushed out to the people and shouted, 18 "The slaves have tricked us! One Hebrew woman has brought disgrace upon the house of King Nebuchadnezzar! For look, here is Holofernes lying on the ground, and his head is not on him!"

19 When the leaders of the Assyrian army heard this, they rent their tunics and were greatly dismayed, and their loud cries and shouts arose in the midst of the camp. 15:1 When the men in the tents heard it, they were amazed at what had happened. 2 Fear and trembling came over them, so that they did not wait for one another, but with one impulse all rushed out and fled by every path across the plain and through the hill country. 3 Those who had camped in the hills around Bethulia also took to flight. Then the men of Israel, every one that was a soldier, rushed out upon them. 4 And Uzziah sent men to Betomasthaim and Bebai and Choba and Kola, and to all the frontiers of Israel, to tell what had taken place and to urge all to rush out upon their enemies to destroy them. 5 And when the Israelites heard it, with one accord they fell upon the enemy, and cut them down as far as Choba. Those in Jerusalem and all the hill country also came, for they were told what had happened in the camp of the enemy; and those in Gilead and in Galilee outflanked them with great slaughter, even beyond Damascus and its borders. 6 The rest of the people of Bethulia fell upon the Assyrian camp and plundered it, and were greatly enriched. 7 And the Israelites, when they returned from the slaughter, took possession of what remained, and the villages and towns in the hill

country and in the plain got a great amount of booty, for there was a vast quantity of it.

8 Then Joakim the high priest, and the senate of the people of Israel who lived at Jerusalem, came to witness the good things which the Lord had done for Israel, and to see Judith and to greet her. 9 And when they met her they all blessed her with one accord and said to her, "You are the exaltation of Jerusalem, you are the great glory of Israel, you are the great pride of our nation! 10 You have done all this singlehanded; you have done great good to Israel, and God is well pleased with it. May the Almighty Lord bless you for ever!" And all the people said, "So be it!"

11 So all the people plundered the camp for thirty days. They gave Judith the tent of Holofernes and all his silver dishes and his beds and his bowls and all his furniture; and she took them and loaded her mule and hitched up her carts and piled the things on them. 12 Then all the women of Israel gathered to see her, and blessed her, and some of them performed a dance for her; and she took branches in her hands and gave them to the women who were with her; 13 and they crowned themselves with olive wreaths, she and those who were with her; and she went before all the people in the dance, leading all the women, while all the men of Israel followed, bearing their arms and wearing garlands and with songs on their lips.

16:1 Then Judith began this thanksgiving before all Israel, and all the people loudly sang this song of praise. 2 And Judith said,

> Begin a song to my God with tambourines,
> sing to my Lord with cymbals.
> Raise to him a new psalm;
> exalt him, and call upon his name.
> 3 For God is the Lord who crushes wars;
> for he has delivered me out of the hands of my pursuers,
> and brought me to his camp, in the midst of the people.
> 4 The Assyrian came down from the mountains of the north;
> he came with myriads of his warriors;
> their multitude blocked up the valleys,
> their cavalry covered the hills.
> 5 He boasted that he would burn up my territory,
> and kill my young men with the sword,
> and dash my infants to the ground
> and seize my children as prey,
> and take my virgins as booty.
> 6 But the Lord Almighty has foiled them

by the hand of a woman.
7 For their mighty one did not fall by the hands of the young men,
nor did the sons of the Titans smite him,
nor did tall giants set upon him;
but Judith the daughter of Merari undid him
with the beauty of her countenance.
8 For she took off her widow's mourning
to exalt the oppressed in Israel.
She anointed her face with ointment
and fastened her hair with a tiara
and put on a linen gown to deceive him.
9 Her sandal ravished his eyes,
her beauty captivated his mind,
and the sword severed his neck.
10 The Persians trembled at her boldness,
the Medes were daunted at her daring. . . .
17 Woe to the nations that rise up against my people!
The Lord Almighty will take vengeance on them on the day of judgment;
fire and worms he will give to their flesh;
they shall weep in pain for ever. . . .

19 Judith also dedicated to God all the vessels of Holofernes, which the people had given her; and the canopy which she took for herself from his bedchamber she gave as a votive offering to the Lord. 20 So the people continued feasting in Jerusalem before the sanctuary for three months, and Judith remained with them.

21 After this every one returned home to his own inheritance, and Judith went to Bethulia, and remained on her estate, and was honored in her time throughout the whole country. 22 Many desired to marry her, but she remained a widow all the days of her life after Manasseh her husband died and was gathered to his people. 23 She became more and more famous, and grew old in her husband's house, until she was one hundred and five years old. She set her maid free. She died in Bethulia, and they buried her in the cave of her husband Manasseh, 24 and the house of Israel mourned for her seven days. Before she died she distributed her property to all those who were next of kin to her husband Manasseh, and to her own nearest kindred. 25 And no one ever again spread terror among the people of Israel in the days of Judith, or for a long time after her death.

7.1.7 Greek Esther 13–14:
The Letter and the Prayer

The translator of the book of Esther into Greek, whose work is found in the Septuagint, expanded on the biblical story by adding his own embellishments. His addition was intended to provide the letter of Ahasueras as well as the prayers of Mordecai and Esther not found in the Hebrew text. Here we read his version of the king's letter to the provinces and the text of Esther's prayer for deliverance.

꽃

13:1 This is a copy of the letter: "The Great King, Artaxerxes, to the rulers of the hundred and twenty-seven provinces from India to Ethiopia and to the governors under them, writes thus:

2 "Having become ruler of many nations and master of the whole world, not elated with presumption of authority but always acting reasonably and with kindness, I have determined to settle the lives of my subjects in lasting tranquillity and, in order to make my kingdom peaceable and open to travel throughout all its extent, to reestablish the peace which all men desire.

3 "When I asked my counselors how this might be accomplished, Haman, who excels among us in sound judgment, and is distinguished for his unchanging good will and steadfast fidelity, and has attained the second place in the kingdom, 4 pointed out to us that among all the nations in the world there is scattered a certain hostile people, who have laws contrary to those of every nation and continually disregard the ordinances of the kings, so that the unifying of the kingdom which we honorably intend cannot be brought about. 5 We understand that this people, and it alone, stands constantly in opposition to all men, perversely following a strange manner of life and laws, and is ill-disposed to our government, doing all the harm they can so that our kingdom may not attain stability.[18]

6 "Therefore we have decreed that those indicated to you in the letters of Haman, who is in charge of affairs and is our second father, shall all, with their wives and children, be utterly destroyed by the sword of their enemies, without pity or mercy, on the fourteenth day of the twelfth month, Adar, of this present year, 7 so that those who have long been and are now hostile may in one day go down in violence to Hades, and leave our government completely secure and untroubled hereafter."

---

18. A Hellenistic anti-Semitic accusation.

14:1 And Esther the queen, seized with deathly anxiety, fled to the Lord; 2 she took off her splendid apparel and put on the garments of distress and mourning, and instead of costly perfumes she covered her head with ashes and dung, and she utterly humbled her body, and every part that she loved to adorn she covered with her tangled hair. 3 And she prayed to the Lord God of Israel, and said:

"O my Lord, thou only art our King; help me, who am alone and have no helper but thee, 4 for my danger is in my hand. 5 Ever since I was born I have heard in the tribe of my family that thou, O Lord, didst take Israel out of all the nations, and our fathers from among all their ancestors, for an everlasting inheritance, and that thou didst do for them all that thou didst promise. 6 And now we have sinned before thee, and thou hast given us into the hands of our enemies, 7 because we glorified their gods. Thou art righteous, O Lord! 8 And now they are not satisfied that we are in bitter slavery, but they have covenanted with their idols 9 to abolish what thy mouth has ordained and to destroy thy inheritance to stop the mouths of those who praise thee and to quench thy altar and the glory of thy house, 10 to open the mouths of the nations for the praise of vain idols, and to magnify for ever a mortal king. 11 O Lord, do not surrender thy scepter to what has no being; and do not let them mock at our downfall; but turn their plan against themselves, and make an example of the man who began this against us.

7.1.8 Song of the Three Young Men 1–68: Supplication and Thanksgiving

This composition is an addition to the book of Daniel found in the Septuagint, the Greek translation of the Bible. It purports to give the text of the prayer which the Three Young Men, Hananiah, Azariah, and Mishael recited in the midst of the fiery furnace. The prayer contains the theme of exile as a punishment for sin and the liturgical theme of petitioning God to have mercy on His people because of the merit of their ancestors, Abraham, Isaac, and Jacob.

ॐ

1 And they walked about in the midst of the flames singing hymns to God and blessing the Lord. 2 Then Azariah stood and offered this prayer; in the midst of the fire he opened his mouth and said:

3 "Blessed art thou, O Lord, God of our fathers, and worthy of praise;
and thy name is glorified for ever.
4 For thou art just in all that thou hast done to us,
and all thy works are true and thy ways right,

and all thy judgments are truth.
5 Thou hast executed true judgments
in all that thou hast brought upon us
and upon Jerusalem, the holy city of our fathers,
for in truth and justice thou hast brought all this upon us because of our sins.
9 Thou hast given us into the hands of lawless enemies, most hateful rebels,
and to an unjust king, the most wicked in all the world.
10 And now we cannot open our mouths;
shame and disgrace have befallen thy servants and worshipers.
11 For thy name's sake do not give us up utterly,
and do not break thy covenant,
12 and do not withdraw thy mercy from us,
for the sake of Abraham thy beloved
and for the sake of Isaac thy servant
and Israel thy holy one
13 to whom thou didst promise
to make their descendants as many as the stars of heaven
and as the sand on the shore of the sea.
14 For we, O Lord, have become fewer than any nation,
and are brought low this day in all the world because of our sins.
15 And at this time there is no prince, or prophet, or leader,
no burnt offering, or sacrifice, or oblation, or incense,
no place to make an offering before thee or to find mercy.
16 Yet with a contrite heart and a humble spirit may we be accepted,
as though it were with burnt offerings of rams and bulls,
and with tens of thousands of fat lambs;
17 such may our sacrifice be in thy sight this day,
and may we wholly follow thee, for there will be no shame for those who trust
in thee.
18 And now with all our heart we follow thee,
we fear thee and seek thy face.
19 Do not put us to shame,
but deal with us in thy forbearance and in thy abundant mercy.
20 Deliver us in accordance with thy marvelous works,
and give glory to thy name, O Lord!
Let all who do harm to thy servants be put to shame;
21 let them be disgraced and
deprived of all power and dominion,
and let their strength be broken.
22 Let them know that thou art the
Lord, the only God,
glorious over the whole world."

23 Now the king's servants who threw them in did not cease feeding the furnace fires with naphtha, pitch, tow, and brush. 24 And the flame streamed out above the furnace forty-nine cubits, 25 and it broke through and burned those of the Chaldeans whom it caught about the furnace. 26 But the angel of the Lord came down into the furnace to be with Azariah and his companions, and drove the fiery flame out of the furnace, 27 and made the midst of the furnace like a moist whistling wind, so that the fire did not touch them at all or hurt or trouble them.

28 Then the three, as with one mouth, praised and glorified and blessed God in the furnace, saying:

29 "Blessed art thou, O Lord, God of our fathers,
and to be praised and highly exalted for ever;
30 And blessed is thy glorious, holy name
and to be highly praised and highly exalted for ever;
31 Blessed art thou in the temple of thy holy glory
and to be extolled and highly glorified for ever.
32 Blessed art thou, who sittest upon cherubim and lookest upon the deeps,
and to be praised and highly exalted for ever.
33 Blessed art thou upon the throne of thy kingdom
and to be extolled and highly exalted for ever.
34 Blessed art thou in the firmament of heaven
and to be sung and glorified for ever. . . .

66 Bless the Lord, Hananiah, Azariah, and Mishael,
sing praise to him and highly exalt him for ever;
for he has rescued us from Hades and saved us from the hand of death,
and delivered us from the midst of the burning fiery furnace;
from the midst of the fire he has delivered us.
67 Give thanks to the Lord, for he is good,
for his mercy endures for ever.
68 Bless him, all who worship the Lord, the God of gods,
sing praise to him and give thanks to him,
for his mercy endures for ever."

7.1.9 Book of Susanna 1–64: Daniel Rescues Susanna

The book of Susanna is an exciting tale, set in Babylon, of the narrow escape of the beautiful, innocent heroine from an evil plot to destroy her by vengeful, rejected lovers. This tale is intended to show the wisdom of Daniel even as a youth, and for this reason it was included in the Greek version of the book of Daniel. This story appears at the end of Daniel in the Septuagint and

Latin Bibles. In some other versions, it is the introduction to Daniel. It prob-
ably dates to the second or first century B.C.E.

ᛟ

1 There was a man living in Babylon whose name was Joakim. 2 And
he took a wife named Susanna, the daughter of Hilkiah, a very beautiful
woman and one who feared the Lord. 3 Her parents were righteous, and
had taught their daughter according to the law of Moses. 4 Joakim was
very rich, and had a spacious garden adjoining his house; and the Jews
used to come to him because he was the most honored of them all.

5 In that year two elders from the people were appointed as judges.
Concerning them the Lord had said: "Iniquity came forth from Babylon,
from elders who were judges, who were supposed to govern the people."
6 These men were frequently at Joakim's house, and all who had suits at
law came to them.

7 When the people departed at noon, Susanna would go into her husband's garden to walk. 8 The two elders used to see her every day, going
in and walking about, and they began to desire her. 9 And they perverted
their minds and turned away their eyes from looking to Heaven or
remembering righteous judgments. 10 Both were overwhelmed with passion for her, but they did not tell each other of their distress, 11 for they
were ashamed to disclose their lustful desire to possess her. 12 And they
watched eagerly, day after day, to see her. . . .

15 Once, while they were watching for an opportune day, she went in
as before with only two maids, and wished to bathe in the garden, for it
was very hot. 16 And no one was there except the two elders, who had
hid themselves and were watching her. . . .

19 When the maids had gone out, the two elders rose and ran to her,
and said: 20 "Look, the garden doors are shut, no one sees us, and we are
in love with you; so give your consent, and lie with us. 21 If you refuse,
we will testify against you that a young man was with you, and this was
why you sent your maids away."

22 Susanna sighed deeply, and said, "I am hemmed in on every side.
For if I do this thing, it is death for me; and if I do not, I shall not escape
your hands. 23 I choose not to do it and to fall into your hands, rather
than to sin in the sight of the Lord."

24 Then Susanna cried out with a loud voice, and the two elders
shouted against her. 25 And one of them ran and opened the garden
doors. 26 When the household servants heard the shouting in the garden,
they rushed in at the side door to see what had happened to her. 27 And

when the elders told their tale, the servants were greatly ashamed, for nothing like this had ever been said about Susanna.

28 The next day, when the people gathered at the house of her husband Joakim, the two elders came, full of their wicked plot to have Susanna put to death. 29 They said before the people, "Send for Susanna, the daughter of Hilkiah, who is the wife of Joakim." 30 So they sent for her. And she came with her parents, her children, and all her kindred. . . .

34 Then the two elders stood up in the midst of the people, and laid their hands upon her head. 35 And she, weeping, looked up toward heaven, for her heart trusted in the Lord. 36 The elders said, "As we were walking in the garden alone, this woman came in with two maids, shut the garden doors, and dismissed the maids. 37 Then a young man, who had been hidden, came to her and lay with her. 38 We were in a corner of the garden, and when we saw this wickedness we ran to them. 39 We saw them embracing, but we could not hold the man, for he was too strong for us, and he opened the doors and dashed out. 40 So we seized this woman and asked her who the young man was, but she would not tell us. These things we testify."

41 The assembly believed them, because they were elders of the people and judges; and they condemned her to death.

42 Then Susanna cried out with a loud voice, and said, "O eternal God, who dost discern what is secret, who art aware of all things before they come to be, 43 thou knowest that these men have borne false witness against me. And now I am to die! Yet I have done none of the things that they have wickedly invented against me!"

44 The Lord heard her cry. 45 And as she was being led away to be put to death, God aroused the holy spirit of a young lad named Daniel; 46 and he cried with a loud voice, "I am innocent of the blood of this woman."

47 All the people turned to him, and said, "What is this that you have said?" 48 Taking his stand in the midst of them, he said, "Are you such fools, you sons of Israel? Have you condemned a daughter of Israel without examination and without learning the facts? 49 Return to the place of judgment. For these men have borne false witness against her."

50 Then all the people returned in haste. And the elders said to him, "Come, sit among us and inform us, for God has given you that right." 51 And Daniel said to them, "Separate them far from each other, and I will examine them."

52 When they were separated from each other, he summoned one of them and said to him, "You old relic of wicked days, your sins have now come home, which you have committed in the past, 53 pronouncing

unjust judgments, condemning the innocent and letting the guilty go free, though the Lord said, 'Do not put to death an innocent and righteous person.'[19] 54 Now then, if you really saw her, tell me this: Under what tree did you see them being intimate with each other?" He answered, "Under a mastic tree." 55 And Daniel said, "Very well! You have lied against your own head for the angel of God has received the sentence from God and will immediately cut you in two."

56 Then he put him aside, and commanded them to bring the other. And he said to him, "You offspring of Canaan and not of Judah, beauty has deceived you and lust has perverted your heart. 57 This is how you both have been dealing with the daughters of Israel, and they were intimate with you through fear; but a daughter of Judah would not endure your wickedness. 58 Now then tell me: Under what tree did you catch them being intimate with each other?" He answered, "Under an evergreen oak." 59 And Daniel said to him, "Very well! You also have lied against your own head, for the angel of God is waiting with his sword to saw you in two, that he may destroy you both."

60 Then all the assembly shouted loudly and blessed God, who saves those who hope in him. 61 And they rose against the two elders, for out of their own mouths Daniel had convicted them of bearing false witness; 62 and they did to them as they had wickedly planned to do to their neighbor; acting in accordance with the law of Moses, they put them to death.[20] Thus innocent blood was saved that day.

63 And Hilkiah and his wife praised God for their daughter Susanna, and so did Joakim her husband and all her kindred, because nothing shameful was found in her. 64 And from that day onward Daniel had a great reputation among the people.

7.1.10 Baruch 1–5:
The Destruction of the Temple and the Exile

In the aftermath of the destruction of Jerusalem at the hands of the Romans in 70 C.E., the author, writing thirty to fifty years after the destruction, sought to understand the reasons why this calamity had befallen the Jewish people. His lament, which acknowledges exile as a punishment for transgression, also promises the restoration of Jerusalem. For punishment is only a short-lived phenomenon which, when accomplished, is overridden by God's love and eternal promises of the Land of Israel for his people.

---

19. Ex. 23:7.
20. Cf. Deut. 19:16–21.

꧁

1:1 These are the words of the book which Baruch[21] the son of Nera-iah, son of Mahseiah, son of Zedekiah, son of Hasadiah, son of Hilkiah, wrote in Babylon, 2 in the fifth year, on the seventh day of the month, at the time when the Chaldeans took Jerusalem and burned it with fire. 3 And Baruch read the words of this book in the hearing of Jeconiah the son of Jehoiakim, king of Judah, and in the hearing of all the people who came to hear the book, 4 and in the hearing of the mighty men and the princes, and in the hearing of the elders, and in the hearing of all the peo-ple, small and great, all who dwelt in Babylon by the river Sud.

5 Then they wept, and fasted, and prayed before the Lord; 6 and they collected money, each giving what he could; 7 and they sent it to Jerusa-lem to Jehoiakim the high priest, the son of Hilkiah, son of Shallum, and to the priests, and to all the people who were present with him in Jerusa-lem. 8 At the same time, on the tenth day of Sivan, Baruch took the ves-sels of the house of the Lord, which had been carried away from the temple, to return them to the land of Judah—the silver vessels which Zedekiah the son of Josiah, king of Judah, had made, 9 after Nebuchad-nezzar king of Babylon had carried away from Jerusalem Jeconiah and the princes and the prisoners and the mighty men and the people of the land, and brought them to Babylon.[22]

10 And they said: "Herewith we send you money; so buy with the money burnt offerings and sin offerings and incense, and prepare a cereal offering, and offer them upon the altar of the Lord our God; 11 and pray for the life of Nebuchadnezzar king of Babylon, and for the life of Bel-shazzar his son, that their days on earth may be like the days of heaven. 12 And the Lord will give us strength, and he will give light to our eyes, and we shall live under the protection of Nebuchadnezzar king of Baby-lon, and under the protection of Belshazzar his son, and we shall serve them many days and find favor in their sight. 13 And pray for us to the Lord our God, for we have sinned against the Lord our God, and to this day the anger of the Lord and his wrath have not turned away from us. 14 And you shall read this book which we are sending you, to make your confession in the house of the Lord on the days of the feasts and at appointed seasons.

---

21. This pseudepigraphic book is placed in the mouth of Baruch, son of Neraiah, the legal scribe of the prophet Jeremiah, who himself witnessed the destruction of the first Temple in 586 B.C.E.

22. In 597 B.C.E.

15 "And you shall say: 'Righteousness belongs to the Lord our God, but confusion of face, as at this day, to us, to the men of Judah, to the inhabitants of Jerusalem, 16 and to our kings and our princes and our priests and our prophets and our fathers, 17 because we have sinned before the Lord, 18 and have disobeyed him, and have not heeded the voice of the Lord our God, to walk in the statutes of the Lord which he set before us. 19 From the day when the Lord brought our fathers out of the land of Egypt until today, we have been disobedient to the Lord our God, and we have been negligent, in not heeding his voice. 20 So to this day there have clung to us the calamities and the curse which the Lord declared through Moses his servant at the time when he brought our fathers out of the land of Egypt[23] to give to us a land flowing with milk and honey. 21 We did not heed the voice of the Lord our God in all the words of the prophets whom he sent to us, but we each followed the intent of his own wicked heart by serving other gods and doing what is evil in the sight of the Lord our God.

2:1 "'So the Lord confirmed his word, which he spoke against us, and against our judges who judged Israel, and against our kings and against our princes and against the men of Israel and Judah. 2 Under the whole heaven there has not been done the like of what he has done in Jerusalem, in accordance with what is written in the law of Moses, 3 that we should eat, one the flesh of his son and another the flesh of his daughter.[24] 4 And he gave them into subjection to all the kingdoms around us, to be a reproach and a desolation among all the surrounding peoples, where the Lord has scattered them. 5 They were brought low and not raised up, because we sinned against the Lord our God, in not heeding his voice.'"

4:27 "Take courage, my children, and cry to God,
for you will be remembered by him who brought this upon you.
28 For just as you purposed to go astray from God,
return with tenfold zeal to seek him.
29 For he who brought these calamities upon you
will bring you everlasting joy with your salvation."

30 Take courage, O Jerusalem,
for he who named you will comfort you.
31 Wretched will be those who afflicted you
and rejoiced at your fall.
32 Wretched will be the cities which your children served as slaves;

23. Cf. Deut. 28.
24. Lev. 26:29; Deut. 28:53.

wretched will be the city which received your sons.[25]
33 For just as she rejoiced at your fall and was glad for your ruin,
so she will be grieved at her own desolation. . . .
36 Look toward the east, O Jerusalem,
and see the joy that is coming to you from God!
37 Behold, your sons are coming, whom you sent away;
they are coming, gathered from east and west,
at the word of the Holy One,
rejoicing in the glory of God.

5:1 Take off the garment of your sorrow and affliction, O Jerusalem,
and put on for ever the beauty of the glory from God,
2 Put on the robe of the righteousness from God;
put on your head the diadem of the glory of the Everlasting.
3 For God will show your splendor everywhere under heaven,
4 For your name will for ever be called by God,
"Peace of righteousness and glory of godliness. . . ."

9 For God will lead Israel with joy,
in the light of his glory,
with the mercy and righteousness that come from him.

7.1.11 The Letter of Jeremiah 6:1–7: Prediction of the Babylonian Exile

This letter is a pseudepigraphic composition dating to the Hellenistic period which purports to be the letter Jeremiah sent from Jerusalem to those exiled to Babylon in 597 B.C.E. before the destruction of the Temple in 586 B.C.E. It expresses the belief that exile is a punishment for sins, and exhorts the people not to fall victim to idolatrous practices even in exile.

§℃

6:1 A copy of a letter which Jeremiah sent to those who were to be taken to Babylon as captives by the king of the Babylonians, to give them the message which God had commanded him. 2 Because of the sins which you have committed before God, you will be taken to Babylon as captives by Nebuchadnezzar, king of the Babylonians. 3 Therefore when you have come to Babylon you will remain there for many years, for a long time, up to seven generations; after that I will bring you away from there in peace. 4 Now in Babylon you will see gods made of silver and gold and wood, which are carried on men's shoulders and inspire fear in

---

25. Babylon.

the heathen. 5 So take care not to become at all like the foreigners or to let fear for these gods possess you, when you see the multitude before and behind them worshipping them. 6 But say in your heart, "It is thou, O Lord, whom we must worship." 7 For my angel is with you, and he is watching your lives.

7.1.12 Book of Ben Sira 1–24: The Wisdom of a Sage

Ben Sira, composed by a wisdom sage who led a school for young men in Jerusalem in about 180 B.C.E., survives in Hebrew manuscripts found at Qumran, Masada, and the medieval Cairo genizah—and in Greek as well. Like the biblical Proverbs, much of the material is couched as a father's ethical advice to his son. God created Wisdom, personified as a woman, as a gift to man just as He created Eve as a gift to Adam.

1:1 All wisdom comes from the Lord
and is with him for ever.
2 The sand of the sea, the drops of rain,
and the days of eternity—who can count them?
3 The height of heaven, the breadth of the earth,
the abyss, and wisdom—who can search them out?
4 Wisdom was created before all things,
and prudent understanding from eternity,
6 The root of wisdom to whom has it been revealed?
Her clever devices—who knows them?
8 There is One who is wise, greatly to be feared,
sitting upon his throne.
9 The Lord himself created wisdom;
he saw her and apportioned her,
he poured her out upon all his works.
10 She dwells with all flesh according to his gift,
and he supplied her to those who love him. . . .

22 Unrighteous anger cannot be justified,
for a man's anger tips the scale to his ruin.
23 A patient man will endure until the right moment,
and then joy will burst forth for him.
24 He will hide his words until the right moment,
and the lips of many will tell of his good sense. . . .

2:1 My son, if you come forward to serve the Lord,
prepare yourself for temptation.

2 Set your heart right and be steadfast,
and do not be hasty in time of calamity.
3 Cleave to him and do not depart,
that you may be honored at the end of your life.
4 Accept whatever is brought upon you,
and in changes that humble you be patient.
5 For gold is tested in the fire,
and acceptable men in the furnace of humiliation.
6 Trust in him, and he will help you;
make your ways straight, and hope in him.
7 You who fear the Lord, wait for his mercy;
and turn not aside, lest you fall.
8 You who fear the Lord, trust in him,
and your reward will not fail;
9 you who fear the Lord, hope for good things,
for everlasting joy and mercy.
10 Consider the ancient generations and see:
who ever trusted in the Lord and was put to shame?
Or who ever persevered in the fear of the Lord and was forsaken?
Or who ever called upon him and was overlooked?
11 For the Lord is compassionate and merciful;
he forgives sins and saves in time of affliction. . . .

3:10 Do not glorify yourself by dishonoring your father,
for your father's dishonor is no glory to you.
11 For a man's glory comes from honoring his father,
and it is a disgrace for children not to respect their mother.
12 O son, help your father in his old age,
and do not grieve him as long as he lives;
13 even if he is lacking in understanding, show forbearance;
in all your strength do not despise him.
14 For kindness to a father will not be forgotten,
and against your sins it will be credited to you;
15 in the day of your affliction it will be remembered in your favor;
as frost in fair weather, your sins will melt away.
16 Whoever forsakes his father is like a blasphemer,
and whoever angers his mother is cursed by the Lord.
17 My son, perform your tasks in meekness:
then you will be loved by those whom God accepts.
18 The greater you are, the more you must humble yourself;
so you will find favor in the sight of the Lord.
20 For great is the might of the Lord: he is glorified by the humble. . . .

4:1 My son, deprive not the poor of his living,
and do not keep needy eyes waiting.

2 Do not grieve the one who is hungry,
nor anger a man in want.
3 Do not add to the troubles of an angry mind,
nor delay your gift to a beggar.
4 Do not reject an afflicted suppliant,
nor turn your face away from the poor.
5 Do not avert your eye from the needy,
nor give a man occasion to curse you;
6 for if in bitterness of soul he calls down a curse upon you,
his Creator will hear his prayer.
7 Make yourself beloved in the congregation;
bow your head low to a great man.
8 Incline your ear to the poor,
and answer him peaceably and gently.
9 Deliver him who is wronged from the hand of the wrongdoer
and do not be fainthearted in judging a case.
10 Be like a father to orphans, and instead of a husband to their mother;
you will then be like a son of the Most High,
and he will love you more than does your mother. . . .

23 Do not refrain from speaking at the crucial time,
and do not hide your wisdom.
24 For wisdom is known through speech,
and education through the words of the tongue.
25 Never speak against the truth, but be mindful of your ignorance.
26 Do not be ashamed to confess your sins,
and do not try to stop the current of a river.
27 Do not subject yourself to a foolish fellow,
nor show partiality to a ruler.
28 Strive even to death for the truth
and the Lord God will fight for you. . . .

9:1 Do not be jealous of the wife of your bosom,
and do not teach her an evil lesson to your own hurt.
2 Do not give yourself to a woman so that she gains mastery over your strength.
3 Do not go to meet a loose woman,
lest you fall into her snares. . . .
8 Turn away your eyes from a shapely woman,
and do not look intently at beauty belonging to another;
many have been misled by a woman's beauty,
and by it passion is kindled like a fire.

24:1 Wisdom will praise herself, and will glory in the midst of her people.
2 In the assembly of the Most High she will open her mouth,
and in the presence of his host she will glory:

3 "I came forth from the mouth of the Most High,
and covered the earth like a mist.
4 I dwelt in high places,
and my throne was in a pillar of cloud.
5 Alone I have made the circuit of the vault of heaven
and have walked in the depths of the abyss.
6 In the waves of the sea, in the whole earth,
and in every people and nation I have gotten a possession.
7 Among all these I sought a resting place;
I sought in whose territory I might lodge.
8 Then the Creator of all things gave me a commandment,
and the one who created me assigned a place for my tent.
And he said, 'Make your dwelling in Jacob,
and in Israel receive your inheritance.'
9 From eternity, in the beginning, he created me,
and for eternity I shall not cease to exist.
10 In the holy tabernacle I ministered before him,
and so I was established in Zion.
11 In the beloved city likewise he gave me a resting place,
and in Jerusalem was my dominion.
12 So I took root in an honored people,
in the portion of the Lord, who is their inheritance. . . ."

7.1.13 Wisdom of Solomon 1–6: Righteousness and Foolishness

The Wisdom of Solomon was probably composed in Greek in the second half of the first century B.C.E. Ascribed to King Solomon, this composition assumes the literary form of balanced epigrams. It believes that the righteous, though they suffer in this world, are rewarded after death. Even kings are subject to divine judgment and must be held accountable to do what is upright. Wisdom is portrayed as a beautiful woman with whom the righteous are in love.

৯৫

1:1 Love righteousness, you rulers of the earth,
think of the Lord with uprightness, and seek him with sincerity of heart;
2 because he is found by those who do not put him to the test,
and manifests himself to those who do not distrust him.
3 For perverse thoughts separate men from God,
and when his power is tested, it convicts the foolish;
4 because wisdom will not enter a deceitful soul,
nor dwell in a body enslaved to sin.

5 For a holy and disciplined spirit will flee from deceit,
and will rise and depart from foolish thoughts,
and will be ashamed at the approach of unrighteousness....

3:1 But the souls of the righteous
are in the hand of God,
and no torment will ever touch them,
2 In the eyes of the foolish they seemed to have died,
and their departure was thought to be an affliction,
3 and their going from us to be their destruction:
but they are at peace.
4 For though in the sight of men they were punished,
their hope is full of immortality.
5 Having been disciplined a little, they will receive great good,
because God tested them and found them worthy of himself;
6 like gold in the furnace he tried them,
and like a sacrificial burnt offering he accepted them.
7 In the time of their visitation they will shine forth,
and will run like sparks through the stubble.
8 They will govern nations and rule over peoples,
and the Lord will reign over them for ever.
9 Those who trust in him will understand truth,
and the faithful will abide with him in love,
because grace and mercy are upon his elect,
and he watches over his holy ones.
10 But the ungodly will be punished
as their reasoning deserves,
who disregarded the righteous man
and rebelled against the Lord;
11 for whoever despises wisdom and
instruction is miserable.
Their hope is vain, their labors are unprofitable,
and their works are useless.
12 Their wives are foolish, and their children evil;
13 their offspring are accursed.
For blessed is the barren woman who is undefiled,
who has not entered into a sinful union;
she will have fruit when God examines souls.
14 Blessed also is the eunuch whose hands have done no lawless deed,
and who has not devised wicked things against the Lord;
for special favor will be shown him for his faithfulness,
and a place of great delight in the temple of the Lord.
15 For the fruit of good labors is renowned,
and the root of understanding does not fail.

16 But children of adulterers will not come to maturity,
and the offspring of an unlawful union will perish. . . .

6:1 Listen therefore, O kings, and understand;
learn, O judges of the ends of the earth.
2 Give ear, you that rule over multitudes,
and boast of many nations.
3 For your dominion was given you from the Lord
and your sovereignty from the Most High,
who will search out your works and inquire into your plans.
4 Because as servants of his kingdom you did not rule rightly,
nor keep the law,
nor walk according to the purpose of God,
5 he will come upon you terribly and swiftly,
because severe judgment falls on those in high places.
6 For the lowliest man may be pardoned in mercy,
but mighty men will be mightily tested.
7 For the Lord of all will not stand in awe of any one,
nor show deference to greatness;
because he himself made both small and great,
and he takes thought for all alike.
8 But a strict inquiry is in store for the mighty.
9 To you then, O monarchs, my words are directed,
that you may learn wisdom and not transgress.
10 For they will be made holy who
observe holy things in holiness,
and those who have been taught them will find a defense.
11 Therefore set your desire on my words;
long for them, and you will be instructed.
12 Wisdom is radiant and unfading,
and she is easily discerned by those who love her,
and is found by those who seek her.
13 She hastens to make herself known to those who desire her.
14 He who rises early to seek her will have no difficulty,
for he will find her sitting at his gates.
15 To fix one's thought on her is perfect understanding,
and he who is vigilant on her account will soon be free from care,
16 because she goes about seeking those worthy of her,
and she graciously appears to them in their paths,
and meets them in every thought.
17 The beginning of wisdom is the most sincere desire for instruction,
and concern for instruction is love of her,
18 and love of her is the keeping of her laws,
and giving heed to her laws is assurance of immortality,

19 and immortality brings one near to God;
20 so the desire for wisdom leads to a
kingdom. . . .

7.2 PSEUDEPIGRAPHA

7.2.1 1 Enoch, Book of Watchers: Enoch's Vision[26]

The Book of 1 Enoch is made up of five previously-existing texts, four of which were found among the Dead Sea Scrolls in fragments of the original Aramaic. Four of the parts date from the third to second centuries B.C.E. while one, the Parables (or Similitudes), is probably a Christian work in its present form. The first of these, The Book of Watchers, is certainly a pre-Maccabean composition, and the earliest source for the story of the fallen angels, which continued to influence Jewish and Christian theology through the centuries. This selection narrates an alternate Flood story which lays the blame for corruption on earth at the feet of evil angels, Watchers, who taught mankind the art of war and then took human women for their wives. The second part of the selection is Enoch's hekhalot vision, a mystical vision of God's Temple, based on Ezekiel and heavily influenced by Daniel, which enriched later Jewish mystical literature.

❧

The Righteous and the Wicked

1:1 The blessing of Enoch: with which he blessed the elect and the righteous who would be present on the day of tribulation at (the time of) the removal of all the ungodly ones. 2 And Enoch, the blessed and righteous man of the Lord, took up (his parable) while his eyes were open and he saw, and said, "(This is) a holy vision from the heavens which the angels showed me: and I heard from them everything and I understood. I look not for this generation but for the distant one that is coming. 3 I speak about the elect ones and concerning them." And I took up with a parable (saying), "The God of the universe, the Holy Great One, will come forth from his dwelling. 4 And from there he will march upon Mount Sinai and appear in his camp emerging from heaven with a mighty power. And everyone shall be afraid, and Watchers[27] shall quiver. 5 And

---

26. Trans. E. Isaac, "1 (Ethiopic Apocalypse of) Enoch," in *The Old Testament Pseudepigrapha*, ed. J. H. Charlesworth (Garden City, NY: Doubleday, 1983), vol. 1, pp. 13–18, 20–21, 35–37, 74, 86–87.

27. The fallen angels.

great fear and trembling shall seize them unto the ends of the earth. 6 Mountains and high places will fall down and be frightened. And high hills shall be made low; and they shall melt like a honeycomb before the flame. 7 And earth shall be rent asunder; and all that is upon the earth shall perish. And there shall be a judgment upon all, (including) the righteous. 8 And to all the righteous he will grant peace. He will preserve the elect, and kindness shall be upon them. They shall all belong to God and they shall prosper and be blessed; and the light of God shall shine unto them. 9 Behold, he will arrive with ten million of the holy ones in order to execute judgment upon all. He will destroy the wicked ones and censure all flesh on account of everything that they have done, that which the sinners and the wicked ones committed against him."

The Fall of Angels

6:1 In those days, when the children of man had multiplied, it happened that there were born unto them handsome and beautiful daughters. 2 And the angels, the children of heaven, saw them and desired them; and they said to one another, "Come, let us choose wives for ourselves from among the daughters of man and beget us children." 3 And Semyaz, being their leader, said unto them, "I fear that perhaps you will not consent that this deed should be done, and I alone will become (responsible) for this great sin." 4 But they all responded to him, "Let us all swear an oath and bind everyone among us by a curse not to abandon this suggestion but to do the deed." 5 Then they all swore together and bound one another by (the curse). . . .

7:1 And they took wives unto themselves, and everyone (respectively) chose one woman for himself, and they began to go unto them. And they taught them magical medicine, incantations, the cutting of roots, and taught them (about) plants. 2 And the women became pregnant and gave birth to great giants whose heights were three hundred cubits. 3 These (giants) consumed the produce of all the people until the people detested feeding them. 4 So the giants turned against (the people) in order to eat them. 5 And they began to sin against birds, wild beasts, reptiles, and fish. And their flesh was devoured the one by the other, and they drank blood. 6 And then the earth brought an accusation against the oppressors.

8:1 And Azaz'el taught the people (the art of) making swords and knives, and shields, and breastplates; and he showed to their chosen ones bracelets, decorations, (shadowing of the eye) with antimony, ornamentation, the beautifying of the eyelids, all kinds of precious stones, and all coloring tinctures and alchemy. 2 And there were many wicked ones and they committed adultery and erred, and all their conduct became corrupt. . . .

10:1 And then spoke the Most High, the Great and Holy One! And he sent Asuryal to the son of Lamech, (saying), 2 "Tell him in my name, 'Hide yourself!' and reveal to him the end of what is coming; for the earth and everything will be destroyed. And the Deluge is about to come upon all the earth; and all that is in it will be destroyed. 3 And now instruct him in order that he may flee, and his seed will be preserved for all generations." 4 And secondly the Lord said to Raphael, "Bind Azaz'el hand and foot (and) throw him into the darkness!" And he made a hole in the desert which was in Duda'el and cast him there; 5 he threw on top of him rugged and sharp rocks. And he covered his face in order that he may not see light; 6 and in order that he may be sent into the fire on the great day of judgment. 7 And give life to the earth which the angels have corrupted. And he will proclaim life for the earth: that he is giving life to her. And all the children of the people will not perish through all the secrets (of the angels), which they taught to their sons. . . .

14:1 This is the book of the words of righteousness and the chastisement of the eternal Watchers, in accordance with how the Holy and Great One had commanded in this vision. . . . 5 From now on you will not be able to ascend into heaven unto all eternity, but you shall remain inside the earth, imprisoned all the days of eternity. 6 Before that you will have seen the destruction of your beloved sons and you will not have their treasures, which will fall before your eyes by the sword. 7 And your petitions on their behalf will not be heard—neither will those on your own behalf (which you offer) weeping (and) praying—and you will not speak even a word contained in the book which I wrote.

Enoch's Vision

8 And behold I saw the clouds: And they were calling me in a vision;[28] and the fogs were calling me; and the course of the stars and the lightnings were rushing me and causing me to desire; and in the vision, the winds were causing me to fly and rushing me high up into heaven. 9 And I kept coming (into heaven) until I approached a wall which was built of white marble and surrounded by tongues of fire; and it began to frighten me. 10 And I came into the tongues of the fire and drew near to a great house which was built of white marble, and the inner wall(s) were like mosaics of white marble, the floor of crystal, 11 the ceiling like the path of the stars and lightnings between which (stood) fiery cherubim and their

---

28. Enoch is now shown a vision of God's Temple.

heaven of water; 12 and flaming fire surrounded the wall(s), and its gates were burning with fire. 13 And I entered into the house, which was hot like fire and cold like ice, and there was nothing inside it; (so) fear covered me and trembling seized me. 14 And as I shook and trembled, I fell upon my face and saw a vision.

15 And behold there was an opening before me (and) a second house which is greater than the former and everything was built with tongues of fire. 16 And in every respect it excelled (the other)—in glory and great honor—to the extent that it is impossible for me to recount to you concerning its glory and greatness. 17 As for its floor, it was of fire and above it was lightning and the path of the stars; and as for the ceiling, it was flaming fire. 18 And I observed and saw inside it a lofty throne—its appearance was like crystal and its wheels like the shining sun; and (I heard) the voice of the cherubim; 19 and from beneath the throne were issuing streams of flaming fire. It was difficult to look at it. 20 And the Great Glory was sitting upon it—as for his gown, which was shining more brightly than the sun, it was whiter than any snow. 21 None of the angels was able to come in and see the face of the Excellent and the Glorious One; and no one of the flesh can see him—22 the flaming fire was round about him, and a great fire stood before him. No one could come near unto him from among those that surrounded the tens of millions (that stood) before him. 23 He needed no council, but the most holy ones who are near to him neither go far away at night nor move away from him. 24 Until then I was prostrate on my face covered and trembling. And the Lord called me with his own mouth and said to me, "Come near to me, Enoch, and to my holy Word." 25 And he lifted me up and brought me near to the gate, but I (continued) to look down with my face.

15:1 But he raised me up and said to me with his voice, "Enoch." I (then) heard, "Do not fear, Enoch, righteous man, scribe of righteousness; come near to me and hear my voice. 2 And tell the Watchers of heaven on whose behalf you have been sent to intercede: 'It is meet (for you) that you intercede on behalf of man, and not man on your behalf. 3 For what reason have you abandoned the high, holy, and eternal heaven; and slept with women and defiled yourselves with the daughters of the people, taking wives, acting like the children of the earth, and begetting giant sons? 4 Surely you, you [used to be] holy, spiritual, the living ones, [possessing] eternal life; but (now) you have defiled yourselves with women, and with the blood of the flesh begotten children; you have lusted with the blood of the people, like them producing blood and flesh, (which) die and perish. 5 On that account, I have given you wives in order that (seeds) might be sown upon them and children born by them, so that the deeds that are done upon the earth will not be withheld from you. 6 Indeed you, formerly you were spiritual, (having) eternal life, and immortal in all the generations of the world. 7 That is why (formerly) I did not make wives for you, for the dwelling of the spiritual beings of heaven is heaven.

7.2.2 1 Enoch 93: Enoch's Vision of the Future

This section constitutes the introductory part of the Epistle of Enoch, a letter from him to his spiritual descendants. It contrasts the sinners and the righteous. The initial section schematizes human history from Enoch to the end of days.

The Apocalypse of Weeks

93:1 Then after that Enoch happened to be recounting from the books. 2 And Enoch said, "Concerning the children of righteousness, concerning the elect ones of the world, and concerning the plant of truth, I will speak these things, my children, verily I, Enoch, myself, and let you know (about it) according to that which was revealed to me from the heavenly vision, that which I have learned from the words of the holy angels, and understood from the heavenly tablets." 3 He then began to recount from the books and said, "I was born the seventh during the first week, during which time judgment and righteousness continued to endure. 4 After me there shall arise in the second week great and evil things; deceit should grow, and there the first consummation will take place. But therein (also) a (certain) man shall be saved. After it is ended, injustice shall become greater, and he shall make a law for the sinners.

5 "Then after that at the completion of the third week a (certain) man shall be elected as the plant of the righteous judgment, and after him one (other) shall emerge as the eternal plant of righteousness. 6 After that at the completion of the fourth week visions of the old and righteous ones shall be seen; and a law shall be made with a fence, for all the generations. 7 After that in the fifth week, at the completion of glory, a house and a kingdom shall be built. 8 After that in the sixth week those who happen to be in it shall all of them be blindfolded, and the hearts of them all shall forget wisdom. Therein, a (certain) man shall ascend. And, at its completion, the house of the kingdom shall be burnt with fire; and therein the whole clan of the chosen root shall be dispersed. 9 After that in the seventh week an apostate generation shall arise; its deeds shall be many, and all of them criminal. At its completion, there shall be elected the elect

ones of righteousness from the eternal plant of righteousness, to whom shall be given sevenfold instruction concerning all his flock.

7.2.3 1 Enoch 106: Fragment of the Book of Noah

This section is an account of the miraculous birth of Noah which probably stems from a full book of Noah, which is no longer preserved. It has parallels to the Genesis Apocryphon from Qumran and other early "aggadic" literature.

ᛸ

106:1 And after some days my son, Methuselah, took a wife for his son Lamech, and she became pregnant by him and bore him a son. 2 And his body was white as snow and red as a rose, the hair of his head as white as wool and his *demdema*[29] beautiful; and as for his eyes, when he opened them the whole house glowed like the sun—(rather) the whole house glowed even more exceedingly. 3 And when he arose from the hands of the midwife, he opened his mouth and spoke to the Lord with righteousness. 4 And his father, Lamech, was afraid of him and fled and went to Methuselah his father; 5 and he said to him, "I have begotten a strange son: He is not like an (ordinary) human being, but he looks like the children of the angels of heaven to me; his form is different, and he is not like us. His eyes are like the rays of the sun, and his face glorious. 6 It does not seem to me that he is of me, but of angels; and I fear that a wondrous phenomenon may take place upon the earth in his days. 7 So I am beseeching you now, begging you in order that you may go to his (grand)father Enoch, our father, and learn from him the truth, for his dwelling place is among the angels."

8 When Methuselah heard the words of his son, he came to us at the ends of the earth; for he had heard that I was there. He cried aloud, and I heard his voice and came to him; and I said to him, "Behold, my son, here I am, why have you come here?" 9 Then he answered me and said, "On account of a great distress have I come to you, on account of a grievous vision have I come near here. 10 Now, my father, hear me: For unto my son Lamech a son has been born, one whose image and form are not like unto the characteristics of human beings. . . . 12 Then his father, Lamech, became afraid and fled, and he did not believe that he (the child) was of him but of the image of the angels of heaven. And behold, I have come to you in order that you may make me know the real truth."

---

29. Ethiopic word for "long locks."

13 Then I, Enoch, answered, saying to him, "The Lord will surely make new things upon the earth; and I have already seen this matter in a vision and made it known to you. For in the generation of Jared, my father, they transgressed the word of the Lord, (that is) the law of heaven. 14 And behold, they commit sin and transgress the commandment; they have united themselves with women and commit sin together with them; and they have married (wives) from among them, and begotten children by them. 15 There shall be a great destruction upon the earth; and there shall be a deluge and a great destruction for one year. 16 And this son[30] who has been born unto you shall be left upon the earth; and his three sons[31] shall be saved when they who are upon the earth are dead. 17 And upon the earth they shall give birth to giants, not of the spirit but of the flesh. There shall be a great plague upon the earth, and the earth shall he washed clean from all the corruption.[32] 18 Now, make known to your son Lamech that the son who has been born is indeed righteous; and call his name Noah, for he shall be the remnant for you; and he and his sons shall be saved from the corruption which shall come upon the earth on account of all the sin and oppression that existed, and it will be fulfilled upon the earth, in his days. 19 After that there shall occur still greater oppression than that which was fulfilled upon the earth the first time; for I do know the mysteries of the holy ones; for he, the Lord, has revealed (them) to me and made me know—and I have read (them) in the heavenly tablets."

7.2.4 Book of Jubilees: The Book of Division[33]

The book of Jubilees purports to project those things revealed to Moses during the forty days he spent on Mount Sinai (Ex. 24:18). It opens with God's revealing to Moses the future of the Jewish people. In the persona of an angel recounting Jewish history until the time of Moses, Jubilees retells the biblical stories with embellishments and modifications. The Hebrew text was composed in Palestine before 150 B.C.E.

---

30. Noah.

31. Shem, Ham, and Japhet.

32. A reference to the famous Flood in the time of Noah.

33. Trans. O. S. Wintermute in *The Old Testament Pseudepigrapha*, ed. J. H. Charlesworth (Garden City, NY: Doubleday, 1985), vol. 2, pp. 52–55, 57–58, 68, 94–96, 139–140, 142.

꿏

Moses is Summoned to the Mountain

1:1 In the first year of the Exodus of the children of Israel from Egypt, in the third month on the sixteenth day of that month, the Lord spoke to Moses, saying, "Come up to me on the mountain, and I shall give you two stone tablets of the Law and the commandment, which I have written, so that you may teach them."

2 And Moses went up to the mountain of the Lord. And the glory of the Lord dwelt upon Mount Sinai, and a cloud overshadowed it for six days. 3 And he called to Moses on the seventh day from the midst of the cloud. And the appearance of the glory of the Lord was like fire burning on top of the mountain. 4 And Moses was on the mountain forty days and forty nights.

Moses is Instructed to Write a Book

And the Lord revealed to him both what (was) in the beginning and what will occur (in the future), the account of the division of all of the days of the Law and the testimony. 5 And he said, "Set your mind on every thing which I shall tell you on this mountain, and write it in a book so that their descendants might see that I have not abandoned them on account of all of the evil which they have done to instigate transgression of the covenant which I am establishing between me and you today on Mount Sinai for their descendants. . . .

Moses is Told How the People Will Forsake the Lord in the Land of Promise

7 "And you, write for yourself all of these words which I shall cause you to know today, for I know their rebelliousness and their stubbornness before I cause them to enter the land which I swore to their fathers, Abraham, Isaac, and Jacob, saying, 'I will give to your seed a land flowing with milk and honey.'[34] 8 And they will eat and be satisfied, and they will turn to strange gods, to those who cannot save them from any of their affliction. And this testimony will be heard as testimony against them, 9 for they will forget all of my commandments, everything which I shall command them, and they will walk after the gentiles and after their defilement and shame. And they will serve their gods, and they will become a scandal for them and an affliction and a torment and a snare. 10 And many

---

34. Deut. 31:20.

will be destroyed and seized and will fall into the hand of the enemy because they have forsaken my ordinances and my commandments and the feasts of my covenant and my sabbaths and my sacred place, which I sanctified for myself among them, and my tabernacle and my sanctuary, which I sanctified for myself in the midst of the land so that I might set my name upon it and might dwell (there). 11 And they will make for themselves high places and groves and carved idols. And each of them will worship his own (idol) so as to go astray. And they will sacrifice their children to the demons and to every work of the error of their heart.

The Murder of Prophets, the Captivity, and the Loss of the Cult

12 "And I shall send to them witnesses[35] so that I might witness to them, but they will not hear. And they will even kill the witnesses. And they will persecute those who search out the Law, and they will neglect everything and begin to do evil in my sight. 13 And I shall hide my face from them, and I shall give them over to the power of the nations to be captive, and for plunder, and to be devoured. And I shall remove them from the midst of the land, and I shall scatter them among the nations. 14 And they will forget all of my laws and all of my commandments and all of my judgments, and they will err concerning new moons, sabbaths, festivals, jubilees, and ordinances.

Repentance and Restoration

15 "And afterward they will turn to me from among the nations with all their heart and with all their soul and with all their might. And I shall gather them from the midst of all the nations. And they will seek me so that I might be found by them. When they seek me with all their heart and with all their soul, I shall reveal to them an abundance of peace in righteousness. 16 And with all my heart and with all my soul I shall transplant them as a righteous plant. And they will be a blessing and not a curse. And they will be the head and not the tail. 17 And I shall build my sanctuary in their midst, and I shall dwell with them. And I shall be their God and they will be my people truly and rightly. 18 And I shall not forsake them, and I shall not be alienated from them because I am the Lord their God."

Moses' Prayer of Intercession

19 And Moses fell upon his face, and he prayed and said, "O Lord, my God, do not abandon your people and your inheritance to walk in the error of their heart. And do not deliver them into the hand of their

---

35. Prophets.

enemy, the gentiles, lest they rule over them and cause them to sin against you. . . ."

The Lord Predicts a Restoration of the People

22 And the Lord said to Moses, "I know their contrariness and their thoughts and their stubbornness. And they will not obey until they acknowledge their sin and the sins of their fathers. 23 But after this they will return to me in all uprightness and with all of (their) heart and soul. And I shall cut off the foreskin of their heart and the foreskin of the heart of their descendants. And I shall create for them a holy spirit, and I shall purify them so that they will not turn away from following me from that day and forever. 24 And their souls will cleave to me and to all my commandments. And they will do my commandments. And I shall be a father to them, and they will be sons to me. 25 And they will all be called 'sons of the living God.'[36] And every angel and spirit will know and acknowledge that they are my sons and I am their father in uprightness and righteousness. And I shall love them.

Moses Told Again to Write

26 "And you write down for yourself all of the matters which I shall make known to you on this mountain: what (was) in the beginning and what (will be) at the end, what will happen in all of the divisions of the days which are in the Law and testimony and throughout their weeks (of years) according to the jubilees forever, until I shall descend and dwell with them in all the ages of eternity."

The Angel of the Presence is Instructed to Write the History for Moses

27 And he said to the angel of the presence, "Write for Moses from the first creation until my sanctuary is built in their midst forever and ever. 28 And the Lord will appear in the sight of all. And everyone will know that I am the God of Israel and the father of all the children of Jacob and king upon Mount Zion forever and ever. And Zion and Jerusalem will be holy."

The Angel of the Presence Receives the Tablets Containing the History

29 And the angel of the presence, who went before the camp of Israel, took the tablets of the division of years from the time of the creation of the law and testimony according to their weeks (of years), according to

---

36. Hos. 2:1 (1:10 in English Bibles).

the jubilees, year by year throughout the full number of jubilees, from [the day of creation until] the day of the new creation when the heaven and earth and all of their creatures shall be renewed according to the powers of heaven and according to the whole nature of earth, until the sanctuary of the Lord is created in Jerusalem upon Mount Zion. And all of the lights will be renewed for healing and peace and blessing for all of the elect of Israel and in order that it might be thus from that day and unto all the days of the earth.

Description of the Six Days of Creation

2:1 And the angel of the presence spoke to Moses by the word of the Lord, saying, "Write the whole account of creation, that in six days the Lord God completed all his work and all that he created. And he observed a sabbath the seventh day, and he sanctified it for all ages. And he set it (as) a sign for all his works."

2 For on the first day he created the heavens, which are above, and the earth, and the waters and all of the spirits which minister before him:

> the angels of the presence,
> and the angels of sanctification,
> and the angels of the spirit of fire,
> and the angels of the spirit of the winds,
> and the angels of the spirit of the clouds and darkness
>   and snow and hail and frost,
> and the angels of resoundings and thunder and lightning,
> and the angels of the spirits of cold and heat and winter and
>   springtime and harvest and summer,
> and all of the spirits of his creatures which are in heaven and on earth.

And (he created) the abysses and darkness—both evening and night—and light—both dawn and daylight—which he prepared in the knowledge of his heart. 3 Then we saw his works and we blessed him and offered praise before him on account of all his works because he made seven great works on the first day. . . .

The Significance of the Sabbath

17 And he gave us a great sign, the sabbath day, so that we might work six days and observe a sabbath from all work on the seventh day. 18 And he told us—all of the angels of the presence and all of the angels of sanctification, these two great kinds—that we might keep the sabbath with him in heaven and on earth. 19 And he said to us, "Behold I shall separate for myself a people from among all the nations. And they will also keep the sabbath. And I will sanctify them for myself, and I will bless them. Just as I

have sanctified and shall sanctify the sabbath day for myself thus shall I bless them. And they will be my people and I will be their God. 20 And I have chosen the seed of Jacob from among all that I have seen. And I have recorded him as my firstborn son, and have sanctified him for myself forever and ever. And I will make known to them the sabbath day so that they might observe therein a sabbath from all work."

21 And thus he created therein a sign by which they might keep the sabbath with us on the seventh day, to eat and drink and bless the one who created all things just as he blessed and sanctified for himself a people who appeared from all the nations so that they might keep the sabbath together with us. 22 And he caused their desires to go up as pleasing fragrance,[37] which is acceptable before him always. . . .

The Laws for Keeping the Sabbath

25 He created heaven and earth and everything which he created in six days. And the Lord made the seventh day holy for all of his works. Therefore he commanded concerning it, "Let everyone who will do any work therein die. And also whoever defiles it let him surely die."[38]

26 And you, command the children of Israel, and let them guard this day so that they might sanctify it and not do any work therein, and not defile it because it is more holy than any day. 27 And everyone who pollutes it let him surely die. And anyone who will do any work therein, let him surely die forever so that the children of Israel might guard this day throughout their generations and not be uprooted from the land because it is a holy day and a blessed day. 28 And every man who guards it and keeps therein a sabbath from all his work will be holy and blessed always like us.

29 Make known and recount to the children of Israel the judgment of the day that they should keep the sabbath thereon and not forsake it in the error of their hearts. And (make known) that it is not permitted to do work thereon which is unlawful, (it being) unseemly to do their pleasure thereon. And (make known) that they should not prepare thereon anything which will be eaten or drunk, which they have not prepared for themselves on the sixth day. And (make known that it is not lawful) to draw water or to bring in or to take out any work within their dwellings which is carried in their gates. 30 And they shall not bring in or take out from house to house on that day because it is more holy and it is more blessed than any day of the jubilee of jubilees. On this day we kept the

---

37. As a sacrifice on the altar.

38. The text enjoins the death penalty not only for all Sabbath violations but even for ritual impurity on that day.

sabbath in heaven before it was made known to any human to keep the Sabbath thereon upon the earth. . .

The Danger in Failing to Observe a 364-Day Calendar

6:32 And you (Moses), command the children of Israel so that they shall guard the years in this number, three hundred and sixty-four days, and it will be a complete year. And no one shall corrupt its (appointed) time from its days or from its feasts because all (of the appointed times) will arrive in them according to their testimony, and they will not pass over a day, and they will not corrupt a feast. 33 But if they are transgressed, and they do not observe them according to his commandment, then they will corrupt all of their (fixed) times, and the years will be moved from within this (order), and they will transgress their ordinances. 34 And all of the sons of Israel will forget, and they will not find the way of the years. And they will forget the new moons and (appointed) times and sabbaths. And they will set awry all of the ordinances of the years. 35 For I know and henceforth I shall make you know—but not from my own heart, because the book is written before me and is ordained in the heavenly tablets of the division of days—lest they forget the feasts of the covenant and walk in the feasts of the gentiles, after their errors and after their ignorance.

36 And there will be those who will examine the moon diligently because it will corrupt the (appointed) times and it will advance from year to year ten days.[39] 37 Therefore, the years will come to them as they corrupt and make a day of testimony reproach and a profane day a festival, and they will mix up everything, a holyday (as) profaned and a profane (one) for a holy day, because they will set awry the months and sabbaths and feasts and jubilees. 38 Therefore, I shall command you and I shall bear witness to you so that you may bear witness to them because after you have died your sons will be corrupted so that they will not make a year only three hundred and sixty-four days. . . .

Abraham's Farewell Testimony for Isaac

21:1 And in the sixth year of the seventh week of this jubilee Abraham called Isaac, his son, and he commanded him, saying, "I am old and I do not know the day of my death and I am filled with my days. 2 Behold I am one hundred and seventy-five years old, and throughout all of the

---

39. The author argues against the use of lunar months since 12 lunar months equal 354 days, 10 days less than the author's incorrect solar year of 364 days. In fact, the Rabbinic Jewish calendar intercalated extra months every three years or so, so as to synchronize with the correctly calculated solar calendar of 365¼ days.

days of my life I have been remembering the Lord and sought with all my heart to do his will and walk uprightly in all his ways. 3 I hated idols, and those who serve them I have rejected. And I have offered my heart and spirit so that I might he careful to do the will of the one who created me 4 because he is the living God. And he is holy, and faithful, and he is more righteous than all (others) and there is no accepting of persons with him or accepting of gifts because he is a righteous God and he is the one who executes judgment with all who transgress his commandments and despise his covenant. 5 And you, my son, keep his commandments and ordinances and judgments, and do not follow pollutions or graven images or molten images. 6 And do not eat any blood of beasts or cattle or any bird which flies in heaven.

7 And if you slaughter a sacrifice as an acceptable burnt offering of peace, slaughter it, but pour out its blood on the altar. And offer up all the fat of the burnt offering on the altar with fine flour kneaded with oil, together with its libation. You will offer it all together on the altar (as) a burnt offering, (as) a sweet aroma before the Lord, 8 and the fat of the thanksgiving offering you will place upon the fire which is on the altar. You shall remove the fat which is on the belly, all of the fat of the internal organs and the two kidneys, all of the fat which is on them and on the thighs and the liver together with the kidneys. 9 And you will offer all of this up as a sweet aroma which is acceptable before the Lord together with its (fruit) offering and its libation for a sweet odor, the bread of a burnt offering to the Lord. 10 And eat its flesh on that day and on the second (day), but do not let the sun of the second (day) set upon it until it is consumed. And do not let it remain until the third day because it will not be acceptable since it was not chosen. Therefore, it will not be eaten. And all of those who eat it will raise up sin against themselves. Because thus I have found written in the books of my forefathers and in the words of Enoch and in the words of Noah. 11 And you shall put salt in all of your offerings, and you shall not omit the salt of the covenant from any of your offerings before the Lord. . . .

16 And at all of the (appointed) times be pure in your body and wash yourself with water before you go to make an offering upon the altar. And wash your hands and your feet before you approach the altar. And when you have completed making the offering, wash your hands and feet again. 17 And let there not be seen any blood upon you or your garments. Be careful, my son, be extremely careful of blood. Cover it in the earth. 18 And, therefore, do not eat blood because it is life, and you shall not eat any blood. . . .

21 I see, my son,
every deed of mankind, that (they are) sins and evils;
and all of their deeds are defilement and corruption and contamination;
and there is no righteousness with them.
22 Be careful not to walk in their ways,
and to tread in their path,
or to commit a mortal sin before God Most High
so that he will hide his face from you,
and deliver you into the power of your sin,
and uproot you from the earth,
and your seed from beneath the sky,
and your name and seed will perish from all the earth.
23 Turn yourself aside from all their deeds and from all their defilement;
and keep the commands of God Most High,
and perform his will, and act uprightly in all things.
24 And he will bless you in all your deeds,
and he will raise up from you a righteous plant in all the earth throughout all
the generations of the earth; and my name and your name shall not cease from
beneath heaven forever.

Moses' Experience in Midian and Encounter with Mastema[40]

48:1 And on the sixth year of the third week of the forty-ninth jubilee
you went and dwelt in the land of Midian five weeks and one year and
you returned to Egypt on the second week in the second year in the fiftieth jubilee. 2 And you know what was related to you on Mount Sinai,
and what Prince Mastema desired to do with you when you returned to
Egypt, on the way when you met him at the shelter. 3 Did he not desire
to kill you with all of his might and save the Egyptians from your hand
because he saw that you were sent to execute judgment and vengeance
upon the Egyptians? 4 And I delivered you from his hand and you did the
signs and wonders which you were sent to perform in Egypt against Pharaoh, and all his house, and his servants, and his people. . . .

The Escape from Egypt and Mastema's Deeds

9 And Prince Mastema stood up before you and desired to make you
fall into the hand of Pharaoh. And he aided the magicians of the Egyptians, and they stood up and acted before you. 10 Thus we let them do
evil, but we did not empower them with healing so that it might be done
by their hands. 11 And the Lord smote them with evil wounds and they
were unable to stand because we destroyed (their ability) to do any single
sign. 12 And despite all the signs and wonders, Prince Mastema was not

---

40. Another name for Beliar (Belial), the chief of the forces of evil.

shamed until he had become strong and called to the Egyptians so that they might pursue after you with all the army of Egyptians, with their chariots, and with their horses, and with all the multitude of the peoples of Egypt.

13 And I stood between the Egyptians and Israel, and we delivered Israel from his hand and from the hand of his people. And the Lord brought them out through the midst of the sea as through dry land. 14 And all of the people whom he brought out to pursue after Israel the Lord our God threw into the middle of the sea, into the depths of the abyss beneath the children of Israel. Just as the men of Egypt cast their sons into the river he avenged one million. And one thousand strong and ardent men perished on account of one infant whom they threw into the midst of the river from the sons of your people.

15 And on the fourteenth day, and on the fifteenth, and on the six-teenth, and on the seventeenth, and on the eighteenth Prince Mastema was bound and shut up from (coming) after the children of Israel so that he might not accuse them. 16 And on the nineteenth day we released them so that they might help the Egyptians and pursue after the children of Israel. 17 And he hardened their hearts and strengthened them. And it was conceived of by the Lord our God that he might smite the Egyptians and throw them into the midst of the sea. 18 And on the fourteenth day we bound him so that he might not accuse the children of Israel on the day when they were requesting vessels and clothing from the men of Egypt—vessels of silver, and vessels of gold, and vessels of bronze—so that they might plunder the Egyptians in exchange for the servitude which they subjected them to by force. 19 And we did not bring the children of Israel from Egypt in their nakedness.

The Sabbath and Jubilee Years

50:1 And after this law I made you know the days of the sabbaths in the wilderness of Sin which is between Elim and Sinai. 2 And I also related to you the sabbaths of the land on Mount Sinai. And the years of jubilee in the sabbaths of years I related to you. 3 But its year I have not related to you until you enter into the land which you will possess. And the land will keep its sabbaths when they dwell upon it. And they will know the year of jubilee.

4 On account of this I ordained for you the weeks of years, and the years, and the jubilees (as) forty-nine jubilees from the days of Adam until this day and one week and two years. And they are still forty further years to learn the commands of the Lord until they cross over the shore of the land of Canaan, crossing over the Jordan to its western side. 5 And jubilees

will pass until Israel is purified from all the sin of fornication, and defilement, and uncleanness, and sin and error. And they will dwell in confidence in all the land. And then it will not have any Satan or any evil (one). And the land will be purified from that time and forever. . . .

7.2.5 Testament of Levi 1–13:
The Sanctity of the Priesthood[41]

The Testaments of the Twelve Patriarchs were preserved in a Greek text containing testaments for each of the twelve sons of Israel. Each recounts his life and gives ex eventu (after the fact) prophecy to his children. Only Testaments of Levi and Naphtali have parallels in the Dead Sea Scrolls, and it seems that these two are the earliest. The Testament of Levi sees the priesthood as the primary leadership role in Israel, reflecting an important sacerdotal trend in Second Temple Judaism.

⁊℣

1:1 A copy of the words of Levi: the things that he decreed to his sons concerning all they were to do, and the things that would happen to them until the day of judgment. 2 He was in good health when he summoned them to him, but it had been revealed to him that he was about to die. When they all were gathered together he said to them:

2:1 "I, Levi, was born in Haran and came with my father to Shechem. 2 I was a youth, about twenty years old. It was then that, together with Simeon, I performed vengeance against Hamor because of our sister, Dinah. 3 As I was tending the flocks in Abel-Maoul a spirit of understanding from the Lord came upon me, and I observed all human beings making their way in life deceitfully. Sin was erecting walls and injustice was ensconced in towers. 4 I kept grieving over the race of the sons of men, and I prayed to the Lord that I might be delivered. 5 Then sleep fell upon me, and I beheld a high mountain, and I was on it. 6 And behold, the heavens were opened, and an angel of the Lord spoke to me: 'Levi, Levi, enter!' 7 And I entered the first heaven, and saw there much water suspended. 8 And again I saw a second heaven much brighter and more lustrous, for there was a measureless height in it. 9 And I said to the angel, 'Why are these things thus?' And the angel said to me, 'Do not be amazed concerning this, for you shall see another heaven more lustrous and beyond compare. 10 And when you have mounted there, you shall stand

41. Trans. H. C. Kee, "Testaments of the Twelve Patriarchs," in *The Old Testament Pseudepigrapha*, ed. J. H. Charlesworth (Garden City, NY: Doubleday, 1985), vol. 1, pp. 788, 791–93.

near the Lord. You shall be his priest and you shall tell forth his mysteries to men. You shall announce the one who is about to redeem Israel. . . .

9:1 "And after two days Judah and I went with our father, Jacob, to Isaac, our grandfather. 2 And my father's father blessed me in accord with the vision that I had seen. And he did not want to go with us to Bethel. 3 When we came to Bethel my father, Jacob, saw a vision concerning me that I should be in the priesthood. 4 He arose early and paid tithes for all to the Lord, through me. 5 And thus we came to Hebron to settle there. 6 And Isaac kept calling me continually to bring to my remembrance the Law of the Lord, just as the angel had shown me. 7 And he taught me the law of the priesthood: sacrifices, holocausts, voluntary offerings of the first produce, offerings for safe return. 8 Day by day he was informing me, occupying himself with me. And he said to me, 9 'Be on guard against the spirit of promiscuity, for it is constantly active and through your descendants it is about to defile the sanctuary. 10 Therefore take for yourself a wife while you are still young, a wife who is free of blame or profanation, who is not from the race of alien nations. 11 Before you enter the sanctuary, bathe; while you are sacrificing, wash; and again when the sacrifice is concluded, wash. 12 Present to the Lord the twelve trees that have leaves,[42] as Abraham taught me. 13 And from every clean living animal and bird, bring a sacrifice to the Lord. 14 And of all your first produce and wine bring the very first as a sacrifice to the Lord God. And salt with salt every sacrificial offering. . . .'"

13:1 "And now, my children, I command you:
Fear the Lord your God with your whole heart,
and walk according to his Law in integrity.
2 Teach your children letters also,
so that they might have understanding throughout all their lives
as they ceaselessly read the Law of God.
3 For everyone who knows the Law of God shall be honored wherever he goes, he shall not be a stranger.
4 He shall acquire many more friends than his parents, and many men will want to serve him and to hear the Law from his mouth.
5 Therefore, my sons, do righteousness on earth
in order that you might find it in heaven.
6 Sow good things in your souls
and you will find them in your lives.
If you sow evil,
you will reap every trouble and tribulation.

---

42. The text refers to the wood used for the burning of sacrifices which was to be selected only from these trees which would be unlikely to contain worms.

7 Acquire wisdom in fear of the Lord
because if a captivity occurs,
if cities and territories are laid waste,
if silver and gold and every possession are lost,
nothing can take away the wisdom of the wise man
except the blindness of impiety and the obtuseness of sin.
8 For if anyone preserves himself from these evil deeds, his wisdom shall be
glorious, even among his opponents;
it will be found to be a homeland in a foreign territory, and a friend in the
midst of his enemies.
9 Whoever teaches good things and practices them
shall be enthroned with kings,
as was Joseph my brother."

7.3 DEAD SEA SCROLLS

7.3.1 *Habakkuk Pesher* I–XI:
The Coming of the Final Age[43]

*This scroll, typical of the pesher texts, interprets the parables of the biblical
book of Habakkuk to refer to events in the writer's own times. The scroll mentions the Teacher of Righteousness, the leader of the sect, and the traitors who
opposed him. The Chaldeans of Habakkuk's time are transposed into the
Romans who are presented as the mighty army that God uses to exact revenge
on His enemies.*

ॐ

I 1 [Hab. 1:1–2, "Oracle received by the prophet Habakkuk in a vision.
For how long, Lord] will I ask for help without 2 [your hearing me;
shout: Violence! to you without your saving me?" The interpretation of
this concerns the beg]inning of the [final] generation . . . ; II 1 Hab. 1:5,
"You reported it." [The interpretation of the word concerns] the traitors
with the Man of 2 Lies, since they do not [believe in the words of the]
Teacher of Righteousness from the mouth of 3 God; (and it concerns) the
traito[rs of the] new [covenant] since they did not 4 believe in the covenant of God [and dishonored] his holy name. 5 Likewise: The interpretation of the word [concerns the trai]tors in the 6 last days. They shall be
violators of [the coven]ant who will not believe 7 when they hear all that
is going [to happen to] the final generation, from the mouth of the

---

43. García Martínez, *The Dead Sea Scrolls Translated: The Qumran Texts in English,*
W.G.E. Watson, translator (Leiden: E. J. Brill, 1994), pp. 197–202, with minor revisions by
L. H. Schiffman.

8 Priest whom God has placed wi[thin the Community,] to foretell the fulfillment of all 9 the words of his servants, the prophets, [by] means of whom God has declared 10 all that is going to happen to his people [Israel]. Hab. 1:6, "For see, I will mobilize 11 the Chaldaeans, a cru[el and determined] people." 12 Its interpretation concerns the Kittim,[44] who are swift and powerful 13 in battle, to slay many [with the edge of the sword] in the kingdom of 14 the Kittim; they will vanquish [many countries] and will not believe 15 in the precepts of [God . . .]

III 1 and they will advance over the plain, to destroy and pillage the cities of the country. 2 For this is what he has said: Hab. 1:6, "To vanquish foreign habitations." Hab. 1:7, "It is terrible 3 and terrible; from his very self his justice and his preeminence arise." 4 The interpretation of this concerns the Kittim. Due to the fear and dread they provoke in all 5 the peoples; their intrigues are planned ahead, and with cunning and treachery 6 they behave towards all the peoples. Hab. 1:8, "Their horsemen are swifter than panthers; they are more savage 7 than wolves at night. Their riders leap and hurl themselves from afar. 8 They will fly like the eagle stooping to gorge itself." Hab. 1:9, "All of them resort to force; the breath of 9 their faces is like the East wind." [Its inter]pretation concerns the Kittim, who 10 trample the land with their horses and their animals 11 and come from far off, from the islands of the sea, to devour all the peoples, like an eagle, 12 insatiable. With fury [they will assemble, and with bu]rning wrath 13 and livid faces they will speak to all [the peoples.] For this is what 14 he has said: [Hab. 1:9, "The breath of their faces is like the East wind. And they amass] captives [like sa]nd. . . ."

V 8 . . . Hab. 1:13, "Why are you staring, traitors, and you maintain your silence when 9 a wicked person consumes someone more upright than himself?" Its interpretation concerns the House of Absalom 10 and the members of his council, who kept silent at the time of the reproach of the Teacher of Righteousness, 11 and did not help him against the Man of Lies, who rejected 12 the Law in the midst of their whole Comm[unity.] . . . VI 2 And what it says: Hab. 1: 16, "For this he sacrifices to his net 3 and burns incense to his seine." Its interpretation: they 4 offer sacrifices to their standards, and their weapons are 5 the object of their worship. . . ."

VIII 3 Hab. 2:5–6, "Surely wealth will corrupt the boaster 4 and one who distends his jaws like the abyss and is as greedy as death will not be

---

44. Kittim, probably designating Cyprus, was a code word in the scrolls used to refer to the Romans who were gradually closing in on the Near East when this text was written. The sectarians expected the great messianic war to be fought against them.

restrained. 5 All the nations ally against him, all the peoples collaborate against him. 6 Are they not all, perhaps, going to chant verses against him, explaining riddles at his expense? 7 They shall say: 'Ah, one who amasses the wealth of others! How long will he load himself 8 with debts?'" Its interpretation concerns the Wicked Priest, who 9 was called by the name of loyalty at the start of his office. However, when he ruled 10 over Israel his heart became conceited, he deserted God and betrayed the laws for the sake of 11 riches. And he stole and hoarded wealth from the brutal men who had rebelled against God. 12 And he seized public money, incurring additional serious sin. 13 And he performed repulsive acts of every type of filthy licentiousness. (Hab. 2:7–8): 14 "Will your creditors not suddenly get up, and those who shake you wake up? You will be their prey. 15 Since you pillaged many countries, the rest of the peoples will pillage you." 16 The interpretation of the word concerns the Priest who rebelled 17 [. . .] the precepts of [God. . . .]

IX 1 being distressed by the punishments of sin; the horrors of 2 terrifying maladies acted upon him, as well as vengeful acts on his fleshly body. And what 3 it says: Hab. 2:8, "Since you pillaged many countries, 4 the rest of the peoples will pillage you." Its interpretation concerns the last priests of Jerusalem, 5 who will accumulate riches and loot from plundering the peoples. 6 However, in the last days their riches and their loot will fall into the hands 7 of the army of the Kittim. . . . XI 1 Afterwards knowledge will be revealed to them, as plentiful as the water 2 in the sea. Hab. 2:15, "Woe to anyone making his companion drunk, spilling out 3 his anger! He even makes him drunk to look at their festivals!" 4 Its interpretation concerns the Wicked Priest who 5 pursued the Teacher of Righteousness to consume him with the ferocity 6 of his anger in the place of his banishment, in festival time, during the rest 7 of the Day of Atonement. He paraded in front of them, to consume them 8 and make them fall on the day of fasting, the Sabbath of their rest.

7.3.2 *Thanksgiving Scroll* V–VII: A Hymn of Praise[45]

The Thanksgiving Scroll (Hodayot Scroll) from Qumran was one of the seven original scrolls found by the Bedouin shepherd at Qumran. It is a series of plaintive hymns expressing the religious ideas of the Dead Sea sect. Some scholars have assigned the authorship of some of the hymns to the Teacher of Righteousness, the leader of the sect in its formative years. These hymns

---

45. García Martínez, *The Dead Sea Scrolls Translated,* pp. 319, 322–4.

emphasize the sectarians' belief in ethical dualism and predestination as well as the group's sense of being a persecuted minority.

৯৫

V 13 ... These are those you fou[nded before] the centuries,
14 to judge through them all your works before creating them,
together with the host of your spirits and the assembly of [the gods,][46]
with the holy vault and all its hosts,[47]
15 with the earth and all its produce,
in the seas and in the deeps,
according to all their designs for all the eternal ages
16 and the final visitation.[48]
For you have established them
before the centuries,
and [in them you have enha]nced the action of [man]
17 so that they can recount your glory throughout all your kingdom;
for you have shown them what they had never seen,
[overcoming] what was there from of old
and creating new things,
18 demolishing ancient things
and erecting what would exist for ever.
For you have established them
and you will exist for ever and ever.

VI 23 I give you thanks, Lord,
according to your great strength
and your abundant wonders
from eternity and for eternity.
You are lofty, great, lavish in favors,
24 you are someone who forgives those who turn away from sin
and someone who punishes the depravity of the wicked.
[You love the truth] with a generous heart
25 and you hate depravity, for ever.
And myself your servant, you have favored me
with the spirit of knowledge
[so that I can love] truth [and justice,]
26 so that I loathe all the paths of wickedness.
I love you liberally, with (my) whole heart,
27 [with (my) whole soul I look for] your wisdom,
because these things happen at your hand

---

46. The angels.
47. The heavens and the angelic hosts.
48. In the end of days when God will punish the evildoers and reward the righteous.

and without [your approval nothing exists.]
VII 16 … But I,
I have known, thanks to your intellect,
that it is not by a hand of flesh that the path of man [is straightened out,]
17 nor can a human being establish his steps.
I know that every spirit is fashioned by your hand,
18 [and all its travail] you have established
even before creating him.
How can anyone change your words?
You, you alone, have created the just man.
19 For him, from the womb, you determined the period of approval,
so that he will keep your covenant and walk on all (your paths),
20 to [empty] upon him your plentiful compassion,
to open all the narrowness of his soul to eternal salvation
and endless peace, without want.
21 Over flesh you have raised his glory.
But the wicked you have created for the time of wrath,
from the womb you have predestined them for the day of annihilation.
22 For they walk on paths that are not good,
they reject your covenant,
their soul loathes your decrees,
they take no pleasure in what you command,
23 instead they choose what you hate.
You have established all those [who hate your law]
to carry out great judgments against them
24 in the eyes of all your creatures,
so they will be a sign and an omen
[for] eternal [generations,]
so that all will know your glory
25 and your great might.
What, then, is flesh, to understand [your wonders?]
And how can dust direct its steps?
26 You have fashioned the spirit
and have organized its task.
From you comes the path of every living being.
But I, I have known
27 that utter wealth cannot compare to your truth,
and I have […] your holiness.
I know that you have chosen them above all
28 and they will serve you forever.
You do not take [gifts for evil deeds,]
or accept a bribe for wicked acts.
29 For you are God of truth
and you [destroy] all sin.

7.3.3 *The Scroll of the War of the Sons of Light Against the Sons of Darkness I–II:* **The Thirty-Five Year's War**[49]

This scroll describes the ultimate battle between the forces of good (the sons of light) and evil (the sons of darkness) in which those on the side of good will prevail, but the nations of the world and the evil enemies of the Dead Sea sectarians will perish. Then the messianic era will be ushered in. Apart from its eschatological content, the scroll informs us of military weaponry, battle plans, and strategy in Roman times.

꽃

I 1 For the Ins[tructor: The Rule] of the War. The first attack by the sons of light will be launched against the lot of the sons of darkness, against the army of Belial,[50] against the company of Edom and of Moab and of the sons of Ammon 2 and the comp[any of . . . and of] Philistia, and against the companies of the Kittim of Ashur[51] and [those who assist them from among the wicked] who violate the covenant. The sons of Levi, the sons of Judah and the sons of Benjamin, the exiled of the desert, will wage war against them. 3 [. . .] against all their companies, when the exiled sons of light return from the desert of the peoples to camp in the desert of Jerusalem. And after the war, they shall go up from there 4 [. . .] of the Kittim in Egypt. And in his time, he will go out with great rage to wage war against the kings of the North, and his anger will exterminate and cut off the horn of 5 [. . . There] will follow a time of salvation for the people of God and a period of rule for all the men of his lot, and of everlasting destruction for all the lot of Belial. There will be 6 g[reat] panic [among] the sons of Japhet, Ashur shall fall and there will be no help for him; the rule of the Kittim will come to an end, wickedness having been defeated, with no remnant remaining, and there will be no escape 7 [for the so]ns of darkness.

8 And [the sons of jus]tice shall shine in all the corners of the earth. They shall go on illuminating, up to the end of all the periods of darkness; and in the time of God, his exalted greatness will shine for all the [eternal] times, 9 for peace and blessing, glory and joy, and long days for all the sons of light. And on the day on which the Kittim fall, there will be a battle, and savage destruction before the God of 10 Israel, for this will be the day determined by him[52] since ancient times for the war of extermina-

---

49. García Martínez, *The Dead Sea Scrolls Translated*, pp. 95–96.
50. Belial was the mythical head of the forces of evil.
51. The Roman province of Syria.
52. That is, predestined.

tion against the sons of darkness. On this (day), the assembly of the angels and the congregation of men shall confront each other for great destruction. 11 The sons of light and the lot of darkness shall battle together for God's might, among the roar of a huge multitude and the shout of angels and of men, on the day of the calamity. It will be a time of 12 suffering fo[r al]l the people redeemed by God. Of all their sufferings, none will be like this, from its onset until eternal redemption is fulfilled.

And on the day of their war against the Kittim, 13 they [shall go out to destr]uction. In the war, the sons of light will be the strongest during three lots,[53] in order to strike down wickedness; and in three (others), the army of Belial will gird themselves in order to force the lot of 14 [...] to retreat. There will be infantry battalions to melt the heart, but God's might will strengthen the hea[rt of the sons of light.] And in the seventh lot, God's great hand will subdue 15 [Belial, and a]ll the angels of his dominion and all the men of [his lot.].

II 1 ... They shall arrange the chiefs of the priests behind the high priest and his second (in rank), twelve chiefs to serve 2 in perpetuity before God. And the twenty-six chiefs of the divisions shall serve in their divisions and after them the chiefs of the Levites to serve always, twelve, one 3 per tribe. And the chiefs of their divisions shall each serve in their place. The chiefs of the tribes, and after them the fathers of the congregation, shall have charge of the sanctuary gates in perpetuity. 4 And the chiefs of the divisions with their enlisted shall have charge of their feasts, their new moons and their sabbaths and all the days of the year—those fifty years of age and upwards. 5 These shall have charge of the burnt offerings and the sacrifices, in order to prepare the pleasant incense for God's approval, to atone for all his congregation and in order to grow fat in perpetuity before him 6 at the table of his glory.

They shall arrange all these during the appointed time of the year of release. During the remaining thirty-three years of the war, the famous men 7 called to the assembly, and all the chiefs of the fathers of the congregation, shall choose for themselves men of war for all the countries of the nations; from all the tribes of Israel they shall equip for them 8 intrepid men, in order to go out on campaign according to the directives of war, year after year. However, during the years of release they shall not equip themselves in order to go out on campaign, for it is a sabbath of 9 rest for Israel. During the thirty-five years of service, the war will be prepared during six years; and all the congregation together will

---

53. Stages in the war.

prepare it. 10 And the war of the divisions (will take place) during the remaining twenty-nine years. . . .

7.3.4 *The Temple Scroll* LVI–LVII: The Law of the King[54]

The Temple Scroll is a rewriting and reediting of the Torah from the command to build the Temple at the end of Exodus through the end of the laws of Deuteronomy. This part of the scroll emphasizes the selection of a king who is a native, married to a Jewish woman, a follower of the Torah, and one who does not aggrandize himself with wealth for its own sake. This passage is a polemic against the Hasmonean kings of the writer's own time, and the scroll as a whole dates to the Hasmonean era.

𝕾

LVI 12 When you enter the land which I give you, and own it and live 13 in it and say to yourself: "I shall set a king over myself like all the peoples which surround me,"[55] 14 then you shall set a king over yourself, a king whom I shall choose. From among your brothers you shall set over yourself a king; 15 you shall not set a foreign man who is not your brother over yourself. But he is not 16 to increase the cavalry or make the people go back to Egypt on account of war in order to 17 increase the cavalry, or the silver and gold. I told you, "You 18 shall not go back again on this path." He is not to have many wives or 19 let his heart go astray after them. He is not to have much silver and gold. 20 When he sits upon the throne of his kingdom they shall write 21 for him this law according to the book which is in front of the priests.

LVII 1 This is the law [...] the priests. 2. On the day when they proclaim him king, the children of Israel [shall assemble], from those 3 more than twenty years old up to those of sixty years, according to their banners. And he shall appoint 4 at their head chiefs of a thousand, chiefs of a hundred, chiefs of fifty 5 and chiefs of ten in all their cities. From them he shall select a thousand, a thousand 6 from each tribe, to be with him: twelve thousand men of war 7 who will not leave him on his own, so that he will not be seized by the hands of the nations. All those 8 selected, which he selects, shall be men of truth, venerating God, 9 enemies of bribery, skilled men in war; and they shall always be with him 10 day and night and they shall guard him from every act of sin 11 and from the foreign nations so that he does not fall into their hands. He will have twelve 12 princes of his people with him and twelve priests 13 and twelve levites

---

54. García Martínez, *The Dead Sea Scrolls Translated*, pp. 173–5.
55. Cf. Deut. 17: 14–20.

who shall sit next to him for judgment 14 and for the law. He shall not divert his heart from them or do anything 15 in all his councils without relying on them.

He shall not take a wife from among all 16 the daughters of the nations, but instead take for himself a wife from his father's house, 17 from his father's family. He shall take no other wife apart from her 18 because only she will be with him all the days of her life. If she dies, he shall take 19 for himself another from his father's house, from his family. He shall not pervert justice, 20 or accept a bribe to pervert correct judgment. He shall not crave 21 the field, the vineyard, the wealth, the house or any valuable thing in Israel or purloin....

And if he sallies out to war against 16 his enemies, a fifth part of the people shall sally out with him, the men of war, the mighty men of 17 valor. And they shall refrain from every impurity and every immodesty and from every sin and fault. 18 They are not to sally forth until he has entered the presence of the high priest and he has consulted for him the decision of the Urim 19 and Tummim. On his orders he shall sally out and on his orders he shall (re-)enter, he and all the children of Israel who 20 are with him; he shall not sally out on the advice of his heart until he has consulted the decision of the Urim 21 and Thummim. He will have success in all his paths as long as he goes out in accord with the decision which....

The king who 14 prostitutes his heart and his eyes, removing them from my commandments, will not find someone who will sit on the throne 15 of his fathers for ever, because over the centuries I shall prevent his line from governing again in Israel. 16 But if he walks according to my precepts and keeps my commandments and does 17 what is upright and good before me, there will not be lacking one of his sons who sits on the throne of the kingdom 18 of Israel for ever. I shall be with him and free him from the hand of those who hate him and from the hand 19 of those who seek his life in order to destroy it; I shall place in front of him all his enemies and he will govern them 20 as he pleases and they shall not govern him. I shall make him improve and not diminish, [I shall place him] at the head 21 and not at the tail, and he will extend his kingdom for many days, he and his sons after him.

7.3.5 *Miqzat Ma'ase ha-Torah*:
Laws of Sacrifice and Purity[56]

This fragmentary text (also known as MMT) outlines the halakhic dis-agreements of the Dead Sea sectarians with the ruling Hasmoneans and the Pharisaic teachers in Jerusalem concerning the Temple service. It appears that the sectarians took the views of the Sadducean priesthood which was ousted from prominence in Temple affairs in 152 B.C.E. Their inability to control Temple ritual to their satisfaction caused them to leave Jerusalem and to estab-lish their sect in the Judean Desert. For this reason, MMT may be viewed as a foundation document for the Dead Sea sect. The text shows that the schism leading to the formation of the Dead Sea sect was over issues of Jewish law which was at the center of religious life in Second Temple times.

🙊

These are some of our regulations [concerning the law of G]od, which are pa[rt of] 5 the precepts we [are examining and] they [a]ll relate to . . . 6 and the purity of [...] ... [Concerning the offering of the] wheat of the Gen[tiles which they . . .] 7 and they touch it [...] and they defi[le it: you shall not eat it.] 8 [None] of the wheat of the Gentiles shall be brought into the temple. . . . And concerning the sacrifice] 9 which they cook in vessels [of bronze . . .] 10 the flesh of their sacrifices and [...] in the courtyard the [...] 11 with the broth of their sacrifices. And concerning the sacrifice of the Gentiles: [we say that they sacrifice] 12 [...] [And con-cerning the thank-offerings] 13 which they postpone from one day to another, w[e think] 14 that the ce[real]-offering [should be eaten] with the fats and the meat on the day of their sa[crifice, and that the] 15 priests should oversee in this matter in such a way that the [sons of Aaron] do not 16 lead the people into error.

And also in what pertains to the purity of the red heifer in the sin-offering: 17 that whoever slaughters it and whoever burns it and whoever collects the ash and whoever sprinkles the [water of] 18 purification, all these ought to be pure at sunset, 19 so that whoever is pure sprinkles the impure. For the sons of 20 [Aaron] ought [to be . . .] 21 [And concerning the] hides of cat[tle and the flocks, we think that. . .] 22 the vessels of

---

56. García Martínez, *The Dead Sea Scrolls Translated*, pp. 77–9.

[hide...] 23 [in order to bring] them into the tem[ple...] 24 [...] And
also concerning the hid[es and the bones of the unclean animals; they shall
not make,] 25]from their bones] and from their hides, handles of ves[sels.
And also, concerning the carcasses] 26 [of the] clean [animals]: the one
who [carries] its carcass [shall not approach the holy purity] 27 [...] And
also concerning [...] which they [...] 28 [... for] 29 the priests ought
to com[ply with all these] things [so that they do not] 30 lead the people
into sin.

And concerning what is written: Lev 17:3, ["When a man slaughters
within the camp"—they] 31 [slaughter] outside the camp—"a bull, or a
[she]ep or a she-goat": the pl[ace of slaughter is to the north of the camp.]
32 And we think that the temple [is the place of the tent of meeting, and
Je]rusalem 33 is the camp; and outside the camp is [outside Jerusalem;] it
is the camp of 34 their cities. Outside the ca[mp ...] [...] You shall
remove the ashes 35 from the altar and bur[n there the sin-offering, for
Jerusalem] is the place which 36 [he chose from among all the tribes of
Israel...] 37 [...] 38 [... they] do not slaughter in the temple [...]
39 [And concerning pregnant animals, we think that] the mother and offspring [should not be sacrificed] on the same day 40 [... And concerning
who eats, w]e think that one can eat the offspring 41 [which was in the
womb of his mother after she has been slaughtered; and you know that]
this is so and that this matter is written down; the pregnant 42 [... And
concerning the Ammonite and the Moabite and the bastard and the one
with crushed testicles and one with sever]ed penis, if these enter 43 [the
assembly ... and] take a bone 44 [...] 45 [...] we think 46 [...] concerning these 47 [... that they should not] join them and make them 48 [...]
and not be brou[ght] 49 [into the temple.... And you know that some]
of the people 50 ... some associating with others. 51 [Because the sons of
Israel ought to keep themselves from all] uncleanness of the male 52 and
be respectful towards the temple.

And also concerning flowing liquids: we say that in these there is no
59 purity. Even flowing liquids cannot separate unclean 60 from clean
because the moisture of flowing liquids and their containers is 61 the same
moisture. And into the holy camp dogs should not be brought which
62 could eat some of the bones from the te[mple...] the flesh on them.
Because 63 Jerusalem is the holy camp, the place 64 which He has chosen from among all the tribes of Is[rael, since Jer]usalem is the head 65 of
the camps of Israel....

92 [And you know that] we have segregated ourselves from the rest of
the peop[le and (that) we avoid] 93 mingling in these affairs and associating with them in these things. And you k[now that there is not] 94 to be

found in our actions deceit or betrayal or evil, for concerning [these things w]e give [. . . and further] 95 to you we have wr[itten] that you must understand the book of Moses [and the words of the pro]phets and of David [and the annals] 96 [of eac]h generation.

And in the book it is written [...] not to 97 [...] And further it is written that [you shall stray] from the path and you will undergo evil. And it is written 98 [...] and we determined [...] 99 [...] And it is written that 100 [all] these [things] shall happen to you at the end of days, the blessing 101 and the curse [. . . and you shall ass]ent in your heart and turn to me with all your heart 102 [and with a]ll your soul [. . . at the e]nd [of time] and you shall be [...] 103 [And it is written in the book of] Moses and in [the words of the prop]hets that [blessings and curses] will come upon you which [...] 104 [the bl]essings which c[ame upon] him in the days of Solomon the son of David and also the curses 105 which came upon him from the [days of Je]roboam son of Nebat right up to the capture of Jerusalem and of Zedekiah, king of Judah 106 [that] he should bring them in [...].

And we are aware that part of the blessings and curses have occurred 107 that are written in the b[ook of Mo]ses. And this is the end of days, when they will repent in Israel 108 for [ever. . .] and not backslide [...] but the wicked will act wickedly and [...] 109 And [...] remember the kings of Israel and reflect on their deeds, how whoever of them 110 who respected [the Torah] was freed from his afflictions; those who sought the Torah 111 [were forgiven] their sins. Remember David, one of the "pious," and he, too, 112 was freed from his many afflictions and was forgiven.

And also we have written to you 113 some of the precepts of the Torah which we think are good for you and for your people, for in you [we saw] 114 intellect and knowledge of the Torah. Reflect on all these matters and seek from him so that he may support 115 your counsel and keep far from you the evil scheming and the counsel of Belial, 116 so that at the end of time, you may rejoice in finding that some of our words are true. 117 And it shall be reckoned to you as just when you do what is upright and good before him, for your good 118 and that of Israel.

7.3.6 *Aramaic Apocalypse* I–II: The "Son of God" Text[57]

The so-called Son of God text, an Aramaic apocalypse, provides a vision of Israel's redemption which terms a messianic figure "son of God," showing that

---

57. García Martínez, *The Dead Sea Scrolls Translated*, p. 138.

such a designation existed among Jews in the third or early second century
B.C.E.

꙰

I 1 [...] settled upon him and he fell before the throne 2 [...] eternal
king. You are angry and your years 3 [...] they will see you, and all shall
come for ever. 4 [...] great, oppression will come upon the earth 5 [...]
and great slaughter in the city 6 [...] king of Assyria and of Egypt 7 [...]
and he will be great over the earth 8 [...] they will do, and all will serve
9 [...] great will he be called and he will be designated by his name.

II 1 He will be called son of God, and they will call him son of the
Most High. Like the sparks 2 of a vision, so will their kingdom be. They
will rule several years over 3 the earth and crush everything. A people
will crush another people, and a city another city, 4 until the people of
God arises and makes everyone rest from the sword. 5 His kingdom will
be an eternal kingdom, and all his paths in truth and uprigh[tness]. 6 The
earth (will be) in truth and all will make peace. The sword will cease in
the earth, 7 and all the cities will pay him homage. He is a great God
among the gods. 8 He will make war with him; he will place the peoples
in his hand and cast away everyone before him. His kingdom will be an
eternal kingdom, and all the abysses. . . .

7.3.7 *Psalms Scroll* 22:1–15: Apostrophe to Zion[58]

*This stirring poem eloquently expresses the dream of the Jewish people for
the city of Jerusalem, from the time of King David to the end of days. The
poem was apparently part of the liturgy of the Qumran sect, as it was included
in their Psalms Scroll.*

꙰

I will remember you for a blessing, O Zion
I have loved you with all my might;
May your memory be blessed for ever!

Great is your hope, O Zion
That peace and your longed-for salvation will come.

Generation after generation will dwell in you,
And generations of the pious will be your glory.

---

58. Trans. L. H. Schiffman, *Reclaiming the Dead Sea Scrolls* (Philadelphia: Jewish Publication Society, 1994), pp. 392–3.

Those who yearn for the day of your redemption,
That they may rejoice in your great glory.

They are nourished from the abundance of your glory,
And in your beautiful squares they walk.

You will remember the kindness of your prophets,
And in the deeds of your pious ones you will glory.

Purge violence from your midst,
Falsehood and dishonesty should be eradicated from you.

Your children will rejoice in your midst,
And your friends will join together with you.

How many have hoped for your redemption,
And your pure ones have mourned for you.

Your hope, O Zion, shall not perish,
Nor will your longing be forgotten.

Who is it who has ever perished in righteousness,
Or who is it that has ever escaped in his iniquity?

A person is tested according to his way(s),
One will be requited according to his deeds.

All around your enemies are cut off, O Zion,
And all those who hate you have scattered.

Praise of you is pleasing, O Zion,
Cherished throughout the world.

Many times will I remember you for a blessing,
With all my heart I will bless you.

May you attain everlasting justice,
And may you receive the blessings of magnates.

May you merit the fulfillment of the vision prophesied about you,
The dream of the prophets which was sought for you.

Be exalted and spread far and wide, O Zion,
Praise the Most High, your Redeemer.
May my soul rejoice at (the revelation of) your glory!

8

The Jewish-Christian Schism

The early period of Roman domination of the Land of Israel would eventually yield far-reaching events for the history of Judaism, in particular the destruction of the Second Temple and the various adjustments and accommodations that would transform Judaism into the nonsacrificial religion it became. But even before this, Roman rule would lead to the development out of Judaism of another religious community—the early Christians.

Roman rule in Judea began with the stamping out of the last revolts of the Hasmoneans, described by Josephus in *Wars* (text 8.1.1). The fall of the Hasmoneans made it possible for the pro-Roman Antipater, father of Herod, to rise to power in the guise of advisor to Hyrcanus II, the Hasmonean prince backed by the Romans, as recorded also by Josephus (text 8.1.2). It was in this way that Herod and his brothers rose to positions of authority. Herod would eventually parlay his role as a governor into rule over an independent Roman client kingdom of Judea.

Josephus devotes a tremendous amount of space to the rule of Herod, and we present only a small part of his detailed account in the shorter and earlier version contained in *War* (text 8.2.1). This ancient ruler and his complex story still fascinate readers. Here were combined consummate political acumen with a self-destructive inability to maintain normal human relations, even with his own children, some of whom he killed. Yet he created architectural wonders and advanced his kingdom to a leading position among the client kingdoms of Rome.

After his death Judea was governed by procurators, under whose rule there were constant disturbances. A brief account of the transition from Herodian to direct Roman rule is provided by the Roman historian Tacitus (text 8.3.1). The difficulties of direct Roman rule were well explained by Josephus, who pointed to the clashes between the Romans and the Jews' desire to observe their ancestral laws (text 8.3.2). Here we see the infamous Pontius Pilate, the Roman procurator who ordered the crucifixion of Jesus, in confrontation with the Jews. All in all, the procurators failed completely to understand how to rule the Jews, who, with the exception of some extreme nationalists motivated by apocalyptic tendencies, desired only to be allowed religious freedom.

It was in this context that the early church developed as a group of Jews who came to see the messiah in the person of Jesus. There is no question but that the early Christians were influenced by the apocalyptic trends which we have seen in Second Temple literature. The basic teachings of Jesus and his community are described in the excerpts from the Gospel of Mark from the New Testament (text 8.4.1). Jesus preached the social message of Pharisaic Judaism in an environment in which Roman oppression had led to poverty and degradation for many. On some ritual matters, he differed with the Pharisees, the most prominent legal authorities of the day, yet he and his early followers remained observant Jews.

But circumstances soon led to great tensions between the followers of Jesus and the other Jews, and Christianity soon began to develop into a separate religious community. The Rabbis initially saw it as a form of Jewish heresy and included a benediction against the early Christians in the Amidah prayer, as noted in the Babylonian Talmud Berakhot (text 8.5.1). We present the text of this benediction as well (text 8.5.2). Various other laws, such as those found in the Tosefta Ḥullin (text 8.5.3), were enacted or strengthened to distance Jews from the early Christians with whom they lived in close proximity.

Relations between Jews and Christians often involved interreligious discussion, as evidenced in the narrative from Tosefta Ḥullin (text 8.5.4), but this text also shows the attitude of the Rabbis that the early Christians were heretics and that it was forbidden to benefit from their teachings. The Jerusalem Talmud Berakhot (text 8.5.5) testifies to the need on the part of the Rabbis to refute the idea of the trinity in amoraic times, indicating that Jews were very much aware of the developing theology of Christianity. Further, this passage testifies again to the direct debates that occurred between Jews and Jewish Christians in Palestine. The Rabbis opposed Jewish Christianity so strongly that they even considered a Torah scroll copied by a member of the Jewish Christian community to have no sanctity, as the Babylonian Talmud Gittin rules (text 8.5.6).

As time went on, Jewish-Christian relations became more strained, for Christianity gradually ceased to be a Jewish phenomenon. The Church increasingly turned its message toward and indeed had greater success with non-Jews, who joined the new religious movement in large numbers. Yet debate and discussion continued, even with these Gentile Christians, as can be seen in the excerpts from the *Dialogue with Trypho* of Justin Martyr (text 8.6.1). Here we find the Christian notion of supercessionism, according to which God's covenant with the Jews is effectively abrogated by their refusal to accept the messiahship of Jesus. It was this notion that underlay much of the antagonism that Christians displayed to Jews throughout the centuries. By this time, Christianity had taken a position of opposition to the observance of Jewish law, following the teachings of Paul.

The same kind of antagonism faced the Jews in the east, including the large community of talmudic Jews in Babylonia. In the works of the Christian Bishop Aphrahat (text 8.6.2), written in the Syriac dialect of Aramaic, we see the basic claim that the Jews had forfeited the status of the true "Israel" and had been replaced by the Christians as God's chosen people.

Despite the turn away from Jewish law and away from the Jewish form of Christianity on the part the Church, some Jewish Christians persisted in following Jewish law, as documented in the work of Epiphanius (text 8.6.3). This document already suggests links between the Essenes and Jesus. The Nazarenes and other "Jewish Christians" he describes were actually Judaizing Christians, not descendants of Jews, who sought to turn back the clock and to return to the Jewish roots of Christianity.

The rise of Christianity ultimately inaugurated a long history of religious persecution for the Jewish people. This was a history that never should have been, in light of the common heritage which Jews and Christians shared in Second Temple Judaism.

8.1 JUDEA UNDER ROMAN RULE

8.1.1 Josephus, *War* I, 160–79:
The Last Revolts of the Hasmoneans[1]

Josephus tells us of the last attempts by the Hasmoneans to wrest control from Rome and from Hyrcanus II, the Hasmonean high priest the Romans had appointed. Aristobulus, brother of Hyrcanus, and his son Alexander, both at the same time, fought valiantly against all odds and to no avail, to regain Jewish independence after the Roman conquest of 63 B.C.E.

৯৫

(160) But as for Alexander, that son of Aristobulus who ran away from Pompey, in the course of time, he got a considerable band of men together, and seriously annoyed Hyrcanus, by overrunning Judea.[2] He was likely to overthrow him quickly, and indeed he had come to Jerusalem and had ventured to rebuild its wall that was thrown down by Pompey, had not Gabinius,[3] who was sent to Syria as successor to Scaurus,[4] shown his bravery, as on many other occasions, by making an expedition against Alexander. . . .

(171) Aristobulus afforded a new foundation for other disturbances.[5] He fled from Rome and got together again many of the Jews who were eager for a revolution and who had been his past supporters. He first took Alexandrium[6] and attempted to build a wall around it, but as soon as Gabinius sent an army against him under Sisenna, Antonius, and Servilius, he became aware of it, and retreated to Macherus.[7] (172) He dis-

---

1. All passages from Josephus trans. W. Whiston, *The Works of Josephus* (Peabody, MA: Hendrickson, 1987), revised by L. H. Schiffman in consultation with H. St. J. Thackeray, Ralph Marcus, Allen Wikgren, and L. H. Feldman, trans., *Josephus: in Nine Volumes* (Loeb Classical Library; Cambridge: Harvard University Press, 1976–79).

2. 57 B.C.E.

3. Aulus Gabinius, Roman governor of Syria, 57–55 B.C.E.

4. M. Aemilius Scaurus had been governor of Syria 65–62 B.C.E. Josephus ignores two intermediary governors.

5. Josephus is describing events which took place in 56 B.C.E.

6. A fortress on the edge of the Jordan Plain, north of Jericho.

7. A fortress east of the Dead Sea.

missed the unprofitable multitude and only marched on with those who were armed, numbering eight thousand, among whom was Pitholaus who had been the lieutenant at Jerusalem but who had deserted to Aristobulus with a thousand of his men. So the Romans followed him, and when it came to a battle, Aristobulus's party for a long time fought courageously. But at length they were overcome by the Romans. Five thousand of them fell, and about two thousand fled to a certain little hill. But the thousand that remained with Aristobulus broke through the Roman army and marched together to Macherus.

(173) When the king lodged for the first night among its ruins, he was in hopes of raising another army if the war would but cease for a while. Accordingly, he fortified that stronghold, though it was done in a weak manner. But when the Romans fell upon him, he resisted, even beyond his abilities, for two days, and then was taken and brought as a prisoner to Gabinius, with Antigonus his son, who had fled together with him from Rome, and from Gabinius he was taken to Rome again. (174) There the senate imprisoned him but sent his children back to Judea, because Gabinius informed them by letters that he had promised Aristobulus's mother to do so in exchange for her delivering the fortresses up to him.

(175) But now, as Gabinius was marching to the war against the Parthians . . . [8] (176) . . . the other part of Syria was in commotion, and Alexander, the son of Aristobulus, brought the Jews to revolt again. Accordingly, he got together a very great army and set about killing all the Romans who were in the country. (177) Then Gabinius was afraid . . . and sent Antipater who prevailed upon some of the rebels to desist. However, thirty thousand still remained with Alexander, who was himself also eager to fight. Accordingly, Gabinius went out to fight, the Jews met him, and a battle was fought near Mount Tabor. Ten thousand of them were killed, and the rest of the multitude dispersed themselves and fled.

(178) Then Gabinius came to Jerusalem and settled the government according to Antipater's wishes. . . . (179) In the meantime, Crassus[9] arrived as successor to Gabinius in Syria. He took away all the gold belonging to the Temple of Jerusalem in order to furnish his expedition against the Parthians. He also took away the two thousand talents which Pompey had not touched.[10]

---

8. In 55 B.C.E.

9. M. Licinius Crassus, governor of Syria, 54–53 B.C.E., as part of the first triumvirate—Caesar, Pompey, and Crassus.

10. Cf. *War* I, 152–3.

8.1.2 Josephus, *War* I, 199–358:
Antipater and Herod's Rise to Power

The scene was set for the rise of Herod by the conquest of Judea by the Romans in 63 B.C.E. Despite the attempts of the Hasmonean prince Aristobulus and his son Antigonus to resist Roman rule, the Romans reorganized Judea under the high priest Hyrcanus who was controlled by Antipater, father of Herod. It was not long before Herod would, therefore, take control of Judea. It is generally agreed by scholars that Josephus' narrative pertaining to the Herodian dynasty was derived almost verbatim from the work of Nicolaus of Damascus, Herod's non-Jewish secretary of state. Nicolaus (born ca. 64 B.C.E.) was the author of a universal history, but his work did not survive.

※

(199) Caesar[11]. . . declared Hyrcanus to be the most worthy for the high priesthood and allowed Antipater to choose his own appointment, but [Antipater] left the determination of such office to him who bestowed the office upon him. So he was appointed procurator of all Judea and obtained permission moreover to rebuild those walls of his country that had been thrown down. (200) Caesar sent orders to have these honorary grants engraved in the Capitol so that they might stand there as indications of his own justice and of the virtue of Antipater.

(201) As soon as Antipater escorted Caesar out of Syria, he returned to Judea, and the first thing he did was to rebuild that wall of his own capital [Jerusalem] which Pompey had overthrown,[12] and then to traverse the country and to quiet the local tumults. He partly threatened and partly advised everyone, and told them that if they would submit to Hyrcanus, they would live happily and peaceably and enjoy what they possessed in universal peace and quiet. (202) But that, if they hearkened to those who had some vain hopes that by raising new troubles they might get themselves some gain, they should then find him to be their lord instead of their procurator, and find Hyrcanus to be a tyrant instead of a king, and both the Romans and Caesar to be their enemies instead of rulers, for [the Romans] would not allow their governor to be removed. (203) At the same time that he said this, he settled the affairs of the country by himself because he saw that Hyrcanus was inactive and unfit to manage the affairs of the kingdom. So he appointed his eldest son, Phasaelus, governor of

---

11. Sextus Julius Caesar, governor of the Roman province of Syria from 47–44 B.C.E., was not the famous Julius Caesar but a relative.

12. Pompey had conquered Jerusalem in 63 B.C.E.

Jerusalem and of the region around it. He also sent his next son, Herod, who was very young, with equal authority into Galilee.[13]

(204) Herod was an active man and soon found proper material for his active spirit to work upon. As he found that Hezekias, the head of the robbers,[14] was overrunning the neighboring parts of Syria with a great band of men, he caught him and killed him, and many more of the robbers with him. (205) This exploit was so very much admired by the Syrians that hymns were sung in Herod's commendation, both in the villages and in the cities, as having procured peace for them and having preserved their possessions. On this occasion he became acquainted with Sextus Caesar, a kinsman of the great Caesar, and governor of Syria.[15]

(206) A just emulation of [Herod's] glorious actions excited Phasaelus also to imitate him. Accordingly he procured the good will of the inhabitants of Jerusalem by his own management of the city affairs and did not abuse his power in any disagreeable manner. (207) As a result, the nation paid Antipater the respects that were due only to a king. . . . (208) However, he found it impossible to escape envy even in his prosperity, for the glory of these young men affected even Hyrcanus himself already privately, though he said nothing of it to anybody. But what principally grieved him were the great actions of Herod, and that so many messengers came one after another and informed him of the great reputation he had won in all his undertakings. There were also many people in the royal palace itself who inflamed his envy; those, I mean, who were obstructed in their designs by the prudence either of the young men or of Antipater. (209) These men said that by committing the public affairs to the management of Antipater and his sons, he [Hyrcanus] remained content with nothing but the bare name of a king without any of its authority. They asked him how long he would be so mistaken as to rear kings against his own interest, for they [Herod and Phasaelus] no longer concealed their government of affairs any longer, but were plainly lords of the nation and had thrust him out of his authority; seeing that this was the case when Herod killed so many men without his giving him any command to do it, either by word of mouth or by his letter, in contradiction to the law of the Jews. Therefore, [they said,] in case he were not a king, but a private man, [Herod] still ought to come to trial and answer for his conduct and

---

13. These appointments took place ca. 47 B.C.E.

14. The Greek word for "robbers" here also denotes revolutionaries. This Hezekias was part of a family that consistently opposed Roman rule over the Jews.

15. Sextus Caesar, as a relative of Caesar's and a political appointee, had great power and influence which he later brought to bear to save Herod from being convicted for murder.

to the laws of his country which do not permit anyone to be killed unless he has been convicted by trial.[16]

(210) Now Hyrcanus was gradually inflamed with these discourses, and at length could bear it no longer, but summoned Herod to trial. Accordingly, by his father's advice, and as soon as the affairs of Galilee would allow him, he came up [to Jerusalem] after he had first placed garrisons in Galilee. However, he came with a sufficient body of soldiers, calculated so that he might not appear to have with him an army able to overthrow Hyrcanus's government, nor yet so few as to expose himself to the insults of those who envied him. (211) However, Sextus Caesar was in fear for the young man, lest he should be taken by his enemies and brought to punishment. So he sent express orders to Hyrcanus that he should acquit Herod of the capital charge against him. He acquitted him accordingly, being otherwise inclined also to do so, for he loved Herod.

(212) But Herod, supposing that he had escaped punishment without the consent of the king [Hyrcanus], retired to Sextus, to Damascus, and got everything ready in order not to obey him if he should summon him again.... (213) And now, since Herod was made general of Celesyria[17] and Samaria by Sextus Caesar, he was formidable not only because of the good will which the nation bore him, but by the power he himself had. As a result, Hyrcanus fell into the utmost degree of terror and expected that he (Herod) would immediately march against him with his army.

(214) Nor was he mistaken in the conjecture he made, for Herod got his army together, out of the anger he bore him for his threatening him with the accusation in a public court, and led it to Jerusalem in order to depose Hyrcanus from his kingdom. He would have soon done this except that his father and brother went out together and broke the force of his fury by exhorting him to carry his revenge no further than to threatening and frightening, but to spare the king, under whom he had been advanced to such a degree of power. Provoked as he might be at his being tried, he should not forget to be thankful that he was acquitted; nor think so long upon the bleak prospect of condemnation as to be ungrateful for his deliverance.... (215) ... So Herod was prevailed upon by these arguments and supposed that what he had already done was sufficient for his future hopes, and that he had shown his power to the nation sufficiently....

(225) In the war between Cassius and Brutus on one side, against the young Caesar [Augustus] and Antony on the other,[18] Cassius and Marcus

---

16. A more detailed account of Herod's trial is found in *Antiquities* (text 10.1.2).
17. Syria and Palestine.
18. 44 B.C.E.

got together an army in Syria. Because Herod was likely to have a great share in providing assistance, they then made him procurator of all Syria and gave him an army of foot soldiers and cavalry. Cassius promised him also that after the war was over, he would make him king of Judea. (226) But it so happened that the power and hopes of this son became the cause of his father's destruction. For, as Malichus[19] was afraid of this, he bribed one of the king's cup-bearers with money to give a poisoned potion to Antipater. So he became a sacrifice to Malichus's wickedness and died at a feast. . . .

(242) But when Caesar and Antony had killed Cassius near Philippi, and Caesar had gone to Italy and Antony to Asia, amongst the rest of the cities which sent ambassadors to Antony to Bithynia,[20] the great men of the Jews also came and accused Phasaelus and Herod of holding power by force and of leaving to Hyrcanus no more than an honorable name. Herod appeared ready to answer this accusation; and, having made Antony his friend by the large sums of money he gave him, he caused him not to hear the others speak against him. So, for the time being, the enemies (of Herod) departed.

(243) However, after this there came a hundred of the principal men among the Jews to Daphne beside Antioch to Antony, who was already in love with Cleopatra to the degree of slavery. These Jews put foremost those men that were the most powerful, both in dignity and eloquence, and accused the brothers [Herod and Phasaelus]. But Messala[21] opposed them, and defended the brothers, and Hyrcanus stood by him on account of his relation to them. (244) When Antony had heard both sides, he asked Hyrcanus which party was the fittest to govern. He replied that Herod and his party were the fittest. Antony was glad of that answer for he had been formerly treated in a hospitable and obliging manner by [Herod's] father Antipater when he marched into Judea with Gabinius. So he appointed the brothers tetrarchs,[22] and committed to them the government of Judea.[23]

(245) But when the ambassadors were indignant at this procedure, Antony took fifteen of them and put them into custody, whom he was also going to kill immediately, and the rest he drove away with disgrace.

---

19. The Nabatean Arab king.

20. A region in northwest Asia Minor.

21. Marcus Valerius Mesalla Corvinus (ca. 70–3 B.C.E.), author, orator, and patron of literature, was a friend of Antony's.

22. This title designated a secondary ruler, immediately under the high priest.

23. The appointment dates to 42–41 B.C.E.

As a result, a still greater tumult arose in Jerusalem, so they sent again a thousand ambassadors to Tyre where Antony now abode, as he was marching to Jerusalem. Against these men who made a clamor he sent out the governor of Tyre, and ordered him to punish all that he could catch of them, and to support the authority of those whom he had made tetrarchs.

(246) But before this, Herod and Hyrcanus went out to the seashore, and earnestly requested of these ambassadors that they should neither bring ruin upon themselves nor war upon their native country by their rash contentions. But when they grew still more outrageous, Antony sent out armed men and killed a great many and wounded more of them. Those who were slain were buried by Hyrcanus, as were the wounded put under the care of physicians by him. (247) Yet those who escaped would not be silenced but put the affairs of the city into such disorder, and so provoked Antony, that he killed those whom he had taken prisoner also.

(248) Now two years afterward,[24] Barzapharnes, a satrap among the Parthians, and Pacorus, the king's son, occupied Syria. Lysanias, who had already succeeded to the government [of Chalcis] upon the death of his father Ptolemy, son of Menneus, convinced the satrap by a promise of a thousand talents and five hundred women, to bring back Antigonus[25] to his kingdom and to depose Hyrcanus. (249) Pacorus was by these means induced to advance through the interior. . . .

(250) . . . Many of the Jews flocked to Antigonus and showed themselves ready to make an incursion into the country, so he sent them forward into that place called Drymus [the woodland] to seize the place. There a battle was fought, and they drove the enemy away and pursued them, ran after them as far as Jerusalem, and as their numbers increased, proceeded as far as the king's palace. (251) But as Hyrcanus and Phasaelus received them with a strong body of men, a battle took place in the marketplace, in which Herod's party beat the enemy, shut them up in the Temple, and set sixty men in the houses adjoining as a guard over them. (252) But the people that were in league against the brothers came in and burned those men. As a result, Herod, in his rage for killing them, attacked and killed many of the people. Every day one party sallied out against the other by turns, and the slaughter was continuous among them.

(253) Now, when that festival which we call Pentecost (Shavuot) was at hand, all the places around the Temple and the entire city were full of country-folk, most of whom were armed also, at which time Phasaelus

---

24. 40 B.C.E.
25. The Hasmonean prince, Son of Aristobulus.

guarded the wall, and Herod with a small force guarded the royal palace. Then he made an assault upon his enemies, as they were out of their ranks in the north quarter of the city, and he killed a very great number of them and put them all to flight. Some of them he shut up within the city and others within the outward rampart. (254) In the meantime, Antigonus desired that Pacorus might be admitted as a reconciler between them, and Phasaelus was prevailed upon to admit the Parthian into the city with five hundred horsemen and to treat him in a hospitable manner. He pretended that he came to quell the tumult, but in reality he came to assist Antigonus. (255) However, Pacorus laid a plot for Phasaelus and persuaded him to go as an ambassador to Barzapharnes in order to put an end to the war. Herod, however, was very earnest with him to the contrary, and exhorted him to kill the plotter but not expose himself to the snares he had laid for him because the barbarians are naturally perfidious. However, Pacorus left and took Hyrcanus with him. So that he might be the less suspected, he also left some of the horsemen, called the Freemen by the Parthians,[26] with Herod, and escorted Phasaelus with the rest.

(256) But now, when they arrived at Galilee, they found that the people of that region had revolted and were up in arms. The satrap [Barzapharnes], with whom they had an audience, sought to conceal his treacherous intentions by obliging behavior toward them. Accordingly, he at first gave them presents, and afterward, as they left, laid ambushes for them. (257) So when they came to one of the maritime cities called Ecdippon,[27] they perceived that a plot was laid for them. . . . (259) . . . Phasaelus went up to the Parthian governor and reproached him to his face for laying this treacherous plot against them, chiefly because he had done it for money, and he promised him that he would give him more money for their preservation than Antigonus had promised to give for the kingdom. (260) But the sly Parthian endeavored to remove all his suspicion by apologies and by oaths, and then went to [the prince] Pacorus. Immediately afterwards those Parthians who had been left behind, and had orders to do so, seized Phasaelus and Hyrcanus who could do no more than curse their perfidiousness and their perjury.

(261) In the meantime the cup-bearer was sent [back] and laid a plot to seize Herod by deluding him and getting him out of the city, as he was commanded to do. But Herod suspected the barbarians from the beginning, and then received intelligence that a messenger, who was to bring him letters that informed him of the intended treachery, had fallen into

---

26. Most of the Parthian soldiers were slaves, but these were apparently free men.
27. Achziv, halfway between Tyre and present-day Haifa.

the hands of the enemy, and so he would not go out of the city. This was despite the fact that Pacorus said very positively that he ought to go out and meet the messengers who brought the letters, for the enemy had not taken them, and that their contents were not accounts of any plots upon them but of what Phasaelus had done. (262) Yet he had heard from others that his brother had been seized, and Alexandra, the shrewdest woman in the world, Hyrcanus's daughter, begged of him that he would not go out nor trust himself to those barbarians who now had come to make an attempt upon him openly.

(263) While Pacorus and his friends were considering how they might bring their plot to fruition privately, because it was not possible to circumvent a man of such great prudence by openly attacking him, Herod prevented them and went off by night to Idumea[28] with the persons who were most closely related to him without their enemies being apprised of it. (264) But as soon as the Parthians perceived it, they pursued them. Then he gave orders for his mother, sister, and the young woman who was betrothed to him, with her mother, and his youngest brother, to continue their journey, while he himself with his servants secured their retreat holding off the barbarians. After every assault he killed a great many of them, and then he came to the stronghold of Masada.[29]

(265) Indeed, he found by experience that the Jews were more troublesome to him than the Parthians and perpetually created trouble for him. Even after he had traveled sixty furlongs[30] from the city, they fought a regular battle which lasted a considerable time. So where Herod beat them and killed a great number of them, he subsequently built a citadel in memory of the great actions he did there, adorned it with the most costly palaces, erected very strong fortifications, and called it by his own name, Herodium.[31] (266) Now, as they were in flight, many joined themselves to him every day; and at a place called Rhesa in Idumea,[32] his brother Joseph met him and advised him to send away a great number of his followers because Masada would not contain so many people—over nine thousand. (267) Herod . . . arrived safely at the fortress with his nearest relations and retained with him only the stoutest of his followers. There he left eight

28. The present-day region of the Negev.
29. A fortress in the Judean Desert, south of Jerusalem on the western shore of the Dead Sea.
30. 7.5 miles.
31. A Judean fortress located about 7 miles south of Jerusalem
32. Some texts have Thressa.

hundred of his men as a guard for the women and provisions sufficient for a siege, but he himself hastened to Petra in Arabia.[33]

(268) The Parthians in Jerusalem then began to plunder and fall upon the houses of those who had fled and upon the king's palace, and they spared nothing but Hyrcanus's money which amounted to no more than three hundred talents. They lighted on other men's money also, but not so much as they hoped for. For Herod, having for a long while had a suspicion of the perfidiousness of the barbarians, had taken care to have the most splendid of his treasures removed to Idumea, and every one of his men had likewise done so. (269) But the Parthians proceeded to so great a degree of injustice as to fill all the country with undeclared war and to demolish the city Marissa.[34] Not only did they set up Antigonus as king, but they delivered Phasaelus and Hyrcanus bound into his hands for torture. (270) Antigonus himself bit off Hyrcanus's ears with his own teeth, as he fell down upon his knees to him, so that he might never be able upon any change of affairs to assume the high priesthood again, for the high priests who officiated were to be perfect and without blemish.[35]

(271) However, he failed in his purpose of abusing Phasaelus, by reason of his courage, for though he had the command of neither his sword nor his hands, he prevented all abuses by dashing his head against a stone. In this way, he showed himself to be Herod's own brother, and Hyrcanus a most degenerate relation, and he died with great bravery, in keeping with his life's career. . . . (273) This was the death of Phasaelus; but the Parthians . . . put the government of Jerusalem into the hands of Antigonus and took away Hyrcanus, bound him, and carried him to Parthia. . . .

(281) Herod went to Rome with all speed. There he first of all went to Antony, on account of the friendship his father had enjoyed with him, and laid before him his misfortunes and those of his family; and that he had left his nearest relations besieged in a fortress and had sailed to him through a storm to make supplication to him for assistance.

(282) Thereupon Antony was moved to compassion at the change that had taken place in Herod's affairs, both upon his calling to mind how hospitably he had been treated by Antipater,[36] but more especially on account

---

33. Hebrew, *Sela*, the rock-cut city of the Nabateans located 140 miles south of Amman and 60 miles north of Eilat.

34. Maresha, ca. 25 miles southwest of Jerusalem. Recent excavations have shown that this was a major city in the Greco-Roman period.

35. Cf. Lev. 21:17–21.

36. Herod's father.

of Herod's own virtue. He then resolved to have him made king of the Jews, whom he had himself formerly made tetrarch. Also the conflict that he had with Antigonus was another inducement and of no less weight than the great regard he had for Herod, for he looked upon Antigonus as a seditious person and an enemy of the Romans. (283) As for Caesar, Herod found him more ready than Antony, remembering the wars he had gone through together with his father, the hospitable treatment he had received from him, and the entirely good will he had shown to him, besides the enterprising character which he saw in Herod himself. (284) So he called the senate together where Messalas, and after him Atratinus, presented Herod before them, and gave a full account of the merits of his father and of his own good will to the Romans. At the same time, they demonstrated that Antigonus was their enemy, not only because he had earlier quarreled with them, but because he now overlooked the Romans and accepted the government of the Parthians. These reasons greatly moved the senate, so that when Antony came in and told them that it was to their advantage in the Parthian war that Herod should be king, they all cast their votes for it. (285) When the senate was adjourned, Antony and Caesar went out with Herod between them, while the consul and the rest of the magistrates went before them in order to offer sacrifices and to deposit the decree in the Capitol. Antony also made a feast for Herod on the first day of his reign. . . .

(288) In the meantime Ventidius, the Roman general, was sent from Syria to restrain the incursions of the Parthians. After he had done that, he came into Judea on the pretense of assisting [Herod's brother] Joseph and his party, but in reality to extort money from Antigonus. (289) He pitched his camp very near Jerusalem, and as soon as he had received enough money, he departed with the greatest part of his forces. Yet he still left Silo[37] with some part of them, for if he had taken them all away, his taking of bribes might have been too openly discovered. Now Antigonus hoped that the Parthians would come again to his assistance and, therefore, cultivated a good understanding with Silo in the meantime, to prevent any trouble from him before his expectations were realized.

(290) Now by this time Herod had sailed from Italy and arrived at Ptolemais.[38] As soon as he had gotten together a considerable army of foreigners and of his own countrymen, he marched through Galilee against Antigonus, wherein he was assisted by Ventidius and Silo . . . (291) The number of his forces increased every day as he went along, and all Galilee,

---

37. Ventidius' second-in-command.
38. Present-day Akko on the Mediterranean, south of Haifa.

with few exceptions, joined themselves to him. . . . (294) He easily recovered his relatives who were in Masada, as well as the fortress Rhesa, and then marched to Jerusalem where the soldiers who were with Silo joined themselves to his own, as did many of the citizens out of dread of his power.

(295) Now, when he had pitched his camp on the west side of the city, the guards who were there shot their arrows and threw their darts at them, while others ran out in companies and attacked those in the forefront. But Herod ordered a proclamation to be made at the wall that he had come for the good of the people and the preservation of the city, without any design to take revenge on his avowed enemies, but to grant amnesty to them, though they had been the most obstinate against him. (296) Antigonus made a contrary exhortation and did not permit anybody to hear that proclamation nor to change sides. So Herod at once gave the order to his forces to beat the enemy back from the walls. Accordingly, they soon threw their darts at them and put them to flight from the towers. . . .

(349) To stop the raiders, the king contrived that ambushes should be laid so that they might restrain their incursions. As for the lack of provisions, he provided that they should be brought to them from great distances. He was also too powerful for the Jews because of the Romans' skill in the art of war. (350) Although they were bold to the utmost degree, they dared not engage in direct battle with the Romans which was certain death. But through their mines under the ground they would appear in the midst of them suddenly, and before they could batter down one wall, they built them another in its stead. To sum up all at once, they did not show any lack either of action or ingenuity, having resolved to hold out to the very last.

(351) Indeed, though they had so great an army besieging them, they bore a siege of five months, until some of Herod's chosen men ventured to climb up the wall and jump down into the city, as did Sossius'[39] centurions after them. They first seized the area around the Temple and when the army poured in, there was slaughter of vast multitudes everywhere because of the rage of the Romans due to the length of the siege and because the Jews who were with Herod were determined that none of their adversaries might remain alive. (352) So great multitudes were cut to pieces as they were crowded together in narrow streets and in houses or running away to the Temple. Nor was there any mercy shown either to infants, or to the aged, or to the weaker sex. Although the king sent a message that he desired them to spare the people, nobody could be per-

---

39. Socius was governor of Syria, 38–37 B.C.E.

suaded to withhold his hand from slaughter, but like madmen they killed people of all ages. (353) Then Antigonus, without any regard to his former or to his present fortune, came down from the citadel and threw himself down at Sossius' feet. Without pitying him at all upon the change in his condition, he laughed at him beyond measure and called him Antigonia.[40] Yet he did not treat him like a woman by letting him go free, but put him into bonds and kept him in custody.

(354) But Herod's concern at present, now that he had his enemies under his power, was to restrain the zeal of his foreign auxiliaries, for the multitude of the foreigners were very eager to see the Temple and what was sacred in the holy house itself. But the king endeavored to restrain them, partly by his exhortations, partly by threats, indeed, partly by force, thinking that the victory would be worse than a defeat for him, if anything that ought not to be seen were seen by them.[41] (355) He also forbade, at the same time, the despoiling of the city, asking Sossius in the most earnest manner whether the Romans, by thus emptying the city of money and men, had a mind to leave him king of a desert. He told him that he judged the dominion of the habitable earth too small a compensation for the slaughter of so many citizens. (356) And when Sossius said that it was just to allow the soldiers this plunder as a reward for what they had suffered during the siege, Herod answered that he would give every one of the soldiers a reward out of his own money. So he purchased the deliverance of his country and kept his promises to them, and made presents in a magnificent manner to each soldier and proportionately to their commanders with a most royal bounty to Sossius himself, so that nobody went away unprovided. (357) Then Sossius dedicated a crown of gold to God and then withdrew from Jerusalem, leading Antigonus away in chains to Antony. Then the ax brought to his end one who still had a fond desire of life and some vain hopes of it to the last, but who, by his cowardly behavior, well deserved to die by it.

(358) Thereupon king Herod made a distinction among the population in the city. For those who were on his side, he made them still more his friends by the honors he conferred on them. But for those of Antigo-

---

40. The feminine equivalent of his name.

41. Because this would be seen as so great an offense against the Jews that revolt might begin anew.

nus' party, he killed them. As his money now ran low, he turned all the ornaments he had into money and sent it to Antony and to his staff.

8.2 HERODIAN RULE

8.2.1 Josephus, *War* I, 386–673: Personal Life and Rule of Herod

Only a small part of the account of Herod's long and complex reign by Josephus can be presented here. Like the previous excerpt, it was authored by the statesman and historian Nicolaus of Damascus and taken over virtually verbatim by Josephus. For this reason, it tends to be very favorable to Herod, even excusing some of the horrible excesses of his reign.

৯৫

(386) But now Herod was immediately concerned about a most important affair on account of his friendship with Antony who had been overcome at Actium by Caesar. . . .[42] (387) However, the king resolved to confront the danger. Accordingly, he sailed to Rhodes where Caesar then lived, and came to him without his diadem and in the clothing and appearance of a private person, but with the proud spirit of a king. So he concealed nothing of the truth, but spoke thus without reserve:[43]

(388) "O Caesar, as I was made king of the Jews by Antony, so do I profess that I have used my royal authority in the best manner and entirely to his advantage. Nor will I conceal that you would certainly have found me in arms and an inseparable companion of his had not the Arabians hindered me. However, I sent him as many auxiliaries as I was able, and many tens of thousands of measures of grain. Indeed, I did not desert my benefactor after his defeat at Actium, but I gave him the best advice I was able (389) when I was no longer able to assist him in the war. I told him that there was but one way of recovering his affairs and that was to

---

42. In 31 B.C.E. Actium is in northwest Greece. Herod had supported Antony who had been defeated, and he now faced retribution from Julius Caesar who had been victorious.

43. This speech and the words attributed below to Caesar reflect the assumptions of Josephus' source, Nicolaus of Damascus, about what Herod would have said. But his close association with Herod makes it possible that it may reflect the basic argument that Herod made.

kill Cleopatra, and I promised him that if she were dead, I would provide him money and walls for his security, with an army and myself to assist him in his war against you. (390) But his affections for Cleopatra stopped up his ears, as did God himself also who has bestowed the government on you. I myself also share his defeat, and with his defeat I have laid aside my diadem. I have come here to you, resting my hopes of safety in your virtue, and I ask that you first consider how faithful a friend, and not whose friend, I have been."

(391) Caesar replied to him thus: "Indeed, you shall not only be in safety but shall be a king, more firmly than you were before; for you are worthy to reign over a great many subjects by reason of the steadfastness of your friendship. So endeavor to be equally constant in your friendship to me upon my good success, which is what I depend upon from the generosity of your disposition. However, Antony has done well in preferring Cleopatra to you. For by this means we have gained you by her madness. (392) Thus you have begun to be my friend before I began to be yours, for Quintus Didius has written to me that you sent him assistance against the gladiators.[44] I therefore assure you that I will confirm the kingdom to you by decree. I shall also endeavor to do you some further kindness afterwards so that you may not feel the loss of Antony."

(393) When Caesar had spoken such gracious things to the king and had put the diadem again on his head, he proclaimed what he had bestowed on him by a decree, in which he enlarged on the commendation of the man in a magnificent manner. . . . (396) When Caesar came to Egypt, and Cleopatra and Antony were dead, not only did he bestow other marks of honor upon [Herod], but he made an addition to his kingdom by giving him not only the territory which had been taken from him by Cleopatra,[45] but, besides that, Gadara, Hippos,[46] and Samaria; and moreover, the maritime cities, Gaza, Anthedon, Joppa, and Strato's Tower.[47] (397) He also made him a present of a bodyguard of four hundred Gauls, who had been Cleopatra's before. Nor did anything so strongly induce Caesar to make these presents as the generosity of him that received them.

---

44. The gladiators were sent for by Cleopatra after the battle of Actium but were intercepted.

45. Including towns in the interior of the country as well as on the Mediterranean Sea. Strato's tower was later called Caesarea.

46. These two cities are in northern Jordan.

47. Cleopatra convinced Antony to present her with some of Herod's territory, including Jericho and some areas to the north. This was now restored to him.

(398) Moreover, after the first games at Actium,[48] he added to his kingdom both the region called Trachonitis and what lay in its neighborhood, Batanea, and the country of Auranitis. . . . [49] (399) He also made him a procurator of all Syria on the tenth year afterward[50] when he again came into that province, and the other procurators could not do anything in the administration without his advice. (400) When Zenodorus[51] died, Caesar bestowed on him all that land which lay between Trachonitis and Galilee. Yet, still of more consequence to Herod, he was beloved by Caesar next after Agrippa,[52] and by Agrippa next after Caesar. As a result, he attained at a very great degree of prosperity, yet the greatness of his ambition exceeded it, and his lofty ambition was extended to works of piety.

(401) Accordingly, in the fifteenth year of his reign,[53] Herod rebuilt the Temple and encompassed the piece of land about it with a wall, enlarging the surrounding area to double its former extent. The expenses he devoted to it were incalculable, and its riches were unspeakable. A sign of this you have in the great colonnades that were erected around the Temple and the citadel which was on its north side. The colonnades he built from the foundation, but the citadel he repaired at tremendous expense in a style in no way inferior to that of a royal palace, and he called it Antonia in honor of Antony. (402) He also built himself a palace in the upper city, containing two very large and most beautiful apartments, to which the Temple itself could not be compared [in size]. One apartment he named Caesareum, and the other Agrippium, for his [two great] friends.

(403) Yet he did not preserve their memory only by giving their names to particular buildings, but his generosity went as far as entire cities. For he built a most beautiful wall around a town in Samaria, twenty furlongs long,[54] brought six thousand inhabitants into it, and allotted to it a most fruitful piece of land. In the midst of the city thus built, he erected a very large temple to Caesar and laid round about it a portion of sacred land of three and a half furlongs.[55] He called the city Sebaste,[56] and the inhabitants were given a privileged constitution. . . .

---

48. 28 B.C.E.

49. To the east of Lake Tiberius.

50. Ca. 20 B.C.E.

51. A chieftain who had become tetrarch of this territory.

52. Caesar's friend, Marcus Vipsanius Agrippa (63–12 B.C.E.).

53. 20 B.C.E.

54. 2½ miles.

55. Outside the Jewish area of his kingdom, Herod built pagan temples and gave financial support to pagan rites.

56. From Sebastus, meaning the same as Augustus.

(408) And when he observed that there was a city by the seaside that was much decayed (its name was Strato's Tower) but that the place, by the advantage of its location, was capable of great improvements through his liberality, he rebuilt it all with white stone and adorned it with several most splendid palaces wherein he especially demonstrated his magnanimity. (409) For the entire seashore between Dora and Joppa,[57] between which this city is situated, had no good harbor, so that everyone who sailed from Phoenicia to Egypt had to lie at anchor in the stormy sea because of the south-west winds that threatened them. . . . (410) But the king, by his expenditures and enterprise, overcame nature and built a harbor larger than Piraeus [at Athens]; and in the inner recesses of the water he built other deep stations [for the ships also]. . . ? (414) . . . So he dedicated the city to the province, and the harbor to the sailors there, but the honor of the new foundation he ascribed to Caesar and named it Caesarea accordingly. (415) He also built the other edifices—the amphitheater, theater, and marketplace—in a manner worthy of the name which the city bore, and instituted games every fifth year, and called them, in like manner, Caesar's Games. He himself first offered the largest prizes upon the hundred ninety-second Olympiad[58] in which not only the victors themselves, but those who came in second, and even those who came in third place, were partakers of his royal bounty. . . .

(422) And when he had built so much, he showed the greatness of his soul to no small number of foreign cities. He built gymnasia at Tripoli, Damascus, and Ptolemais. He built a wall around Byblos, large rooms, porticoes, temples, and marketplaces at Berytus (Beirut) and Tyre, with theaters at Sidon and Damascus. He also built aqueducts for those Laodiceans who lived by the seaside, and for those of Ascalon[59] he built baths and costly fountains, and also colonnades that were admirable both for their workmanship and size. Moreover, he dedicated groves and meadows to some people; (423) indeed, not a few cities received grants of land as if they were parts of his own kingdom. . . .

(431) However, fortune took revenge on Herod for his great successes by visiting on him domestic troubles, and he began to have wild disorders in his family on account of his wife of whom he was so very fond. (432) For upon ascending the throne, he divorced the wife whom he had married before when he was a private person, a native of Jerusalem whose name was Doris, and married Mariamne, the daughter of Alexander, the

---

57. Present-day Dor and Jaffa on the Mediterranean shore.
58. 10–9 B.C.E.
59. Ashkelon, in modern spelling, on the shore of the Mediterranean.

son of Aristobulus.[60] On her account disturbances arose in his family, which, beginning at an early date, were aggravated greatly after his return from Rome. (433) First of all, for the sake of his sons by Mariamne, he expelled Antipater the son of Doris, from the city and permitted him to enter at no times other than at the festivals. After this he killed his wife's grandfather, Hyrcanus, when he returned from Parthia to him, under the pretense that he suspected him of plotting against him. . . .

(435) Of the five children which Herod had by Mariamne, two of them were daughters and three were sons. The youngest of these sons was educated at Rome, and died there, but the two eldest he treated as those of royal blood on account of the nobility of their mother and because they were not born until he was king. (436) But what was stronger than all this was the love that he bore to Mariamne which inflamed him every day to a great degree, and so far conspired with the other motives that he was insensitive to the troubles of which his beloved was the cause, for Mariamne's hatred of him was as great as his love for her. (437) She had indeed just cause for indignation because of what he had done, while her boldness proceeded from his affection for her. So she openly reproached him with what he had done to her grandfather Hyrcanus and to her brother Aristobulus,[61] for he had not spared this Aristobulus though he was but a youth. For although he had given him the high priesthood at the age of seventeen, he killed him quickly after he had conferred that dignity upon him. When Aristobulus had put on the holy vestments and had approached the altar at a festival, the multitude in great crowds fell into tears. Thereupon the youth was sent by night to Jericho, and was plunged there by the Gauls, at Herod's command, in a pool until he drowned.[62]

(438) For these reasons Mariamne reproached Herod, and his sister and mother, in a most abusive manner while he was paralyzed on account of his affection for her. But the women seethed with indignation at her and raised a charge against her that she was adulterous, which they thought most likely to move Herod to anger. . . . (440) This charge fell like a thunderbolt upon Herod and put him into disorder, especially because his love of her occasioned him to be jealous. . . .

(441) When, therefore, he was about to take a journey abroad, he committed his wife to Joseph, his sister Salome's husband, as to one who

---

60. Brother of Hyrcanus II.

61. Aristobulus III, died 35 B.C.E.

62. The public saw Aristobulus as a continuator of his great Hasmonean heritage, and this inspired fear in Herod, so he had him killed.

would be faithful to him and bore him good will on account of their being related. He also gave him a secret injunction that if Antony killed him, he should kill her. But Joseph, without any ill design, and only in order to demonstrate the king's love to his wife and how he could not bear to think of being separated from her even by death itself, revealed this grand secret to her. (442) When Herod came back, and as they talked together and he confirmed his love to her by many oaths and assured her that he had never had such affection for any other woman as he had for her, "Yes," said she, "you did, to be sure, demonstrate your love to me by the injunctions you gave Joseph, when you commanded him to kill me."

(443) When he heard that this grand secret was revealed, he was beside himself, and he said that Joseph would never have disclosed that injunction of his unless he had debauched her. His passion also made him stark mad and, leaping out of his bed, he ran about the palace in a wild manner. His sister Salome took the opportunity also to slander Mariamne and confirmed his suspicion about Joseph. Then, out of his ungovernable jealously and rage, he commanded both of them to be killed immediately. (444) But as soon as his passion was over, he repented of what he had done, and as soon as his anger was worn off, his affections were kindled again. Indeed, the flame of his desires for her was so ardent that he could not think she was dead, but he would appear, under his disorders, to speak to her as if she were still alive, until time taught him the reality of his loss when his grief appeared as great as his affection had been for her while she was living.

(445) Mariamne's sons were heirs to that hatred which had been borne by their mother, and when they considered the greatness of Herod's crime towards her, they were suspicious of him as of an enemy of theirs, at first while they were educated at Rome but still more when they returned to Judea. This antagonism of theirs increased as they grew up to be men. (446) When they came to an age fit for marriage, one of them married the daughter of their aunt Salome (who had had been the accuser of their mother); the other married the daughter of Archelaus, king of Cappadocia.[63] And now they spoke boldly and bore hatred in their minds. (447) Their boldness lent a handle to those who slandered them, and some of them related now more plainly to their king that there were treacherous designs laid against him by both his sons, and that the one who was a son-in-law to Archelaus, relying upon his father-in-law, was preparing to flee in order to accuse Herod before Caesar. (448) When Herod's head had been filled with these calumnies long enough, he brought Antipater,

---

63. A country in eastern Asia Minor.

whom he had by Doris, into favor again, as a defense to him against his other sons, and began in all the ways he possibly could to prefer him over them. . . .

(467) But now the quarrel that was between them still accompanied these brothers when they parted, and the suspicions they had one of the other grew worse. Alexander and Aristobulus were much grieved that the privilege of the firstborn was confirmed to Antipater, as was Antipater very angry at his brothers that they were to succeed him. (468) The latter, being of a disposition that was mutable and politic, knew how to hold his tongue and used a great deal of cunning, and thereby concealed the hatred he bore to them. But the former, depending on the nobility of their births had everything upon their tongues which was in their minds. Many also provoked them further, and many of their [seeming] friends insinuated themselves into their friendship to spy out what they did. (469) Now everything that was said by Alexander was instantly brought to Antipater, and from Antipater it was brought to Herod with additions. . . . (470) Antipater also was perpetually setting his agents on to provoke him to speak so that his lies might seem to have some foundation of truth. . . .

(495) . . . as for the king, he was brought to such a degree of terror by those prodigious slanders and fabrications that he fancied that he saw Alexander coming to him with a drawn sword in his hand. (496) So he caused him to be seized immediately and bound, and proceeded to examine his friends by torture, many of whom died [under the torture] but would reveal nothing nor say anything against their consciences. But some of them, being forced to speak falsely by the pains they endured, said that Alexander and his brother Aristobulus plotted against him and waited for an opportunity to kill him as he was hunting and then flee to Rome. (497) These accusations, though they were of an incredible nature and only invented because of the great distress they were in, were readily believed by the king who thought it some comfort to him, after he had bound his son, that it might appear he had not done so unjustly. . . .

(551) He also sent his sons to Sebaste,[64] a city not far from Caesarea, and ordered them to be strangled there. The order was executed immediately, and he commanded that their dead bodies should be brought to the fortress Alexandrium to be buried with Alexander, their grandfather on their mother's side. Such was the end of Alexander and Aristobulus. . . .

(647) Herod's illness became more and more severe because these disorders fell upon him in his old age and when he was in a melancholy condition. For he was already almost seventy years of age and had been brought

---

64. Biblical Samaria.

low by the calamities that happened to him regarding his children from whom he had no pleasure in life even when he was in good health. Also the fact that Antipater was still alive aggravated his disease, and he resolved to put him to death now, not at random, but as soon as he should be well again; and he resolved to have him executed [in a public manner].

(648) There also now happened to him, among his other calamities, a popular revolt. There were two men of learning in the city [Jerusalem] who were thought the most skillful in the laws of their country and were on that account held in very great esteem all over the nation. They were, the one Judas, the son of Sepphoraeas, and the other Matthias, the son of Margalus. (649) There was a great assembly of young men when these men expounded the laws, and every day there assembled a kind of army of their followers who were in their prime. When these men were informed that the king was wearing away with melancholy and disease, they dropped hints to their friends that it was now a very proper time to defend the cause of God and to pull down what had been erected contrary to the laws of their country, (650) for it was unlawful that there should be anything in the Temple such as images, or faces, or a representation of any animal whatsoever.[65] Now the king had put up a golden eagle over the great gate of the Temple, and these learned men exhorted their followers to cut it down and told them that if any danger should arise, it was a glorious thing to die for the laws of their country because the soul was immortal, and an eternal enjoyment of happiness did await those who died on that account. . . .

(651) At the same time that these men made this speech to their disciples, a rumor was spread abroad that the king was dying which made the young men set about the work with greater boldness. They therefore let themselves down from the top of the Temple with thick cords at midday while a great number of people were in the Temple, and cut down that golden eagle with axes. (652) This was immediately reported to the king's captain of the Temple who came running with a great body of soldiers and caught about forty of the young men, and brought them to the king. (653) When he asked them, first of all, whether they had dared to cut down the golden eagle, they confessed that they had done so. When he asked them by whose command they had done so, they replied, at the command of the law of their country. When he further asked them how could they be so joyful when they were to be put to death, they replied, because they should enjoy greater happiness after they were dead.

---

65. Cf. Ex. 20:4–5, Deut. 5:7–8.

(654) At this the king was in such a fury that he overcame his disease [for the time] and went out and spoke to the people. He made a terrible accusation against those men of being guilty of sacrilege under the pretense of zeal for the law, and he demanded that they be punished for their impiety. (655) The people, afraid of wholesale prosecutions, requested that he first punish those that put them up to this action and then those who were caught in it, so that he would forgo his anger against the rest. With this the king complied, though not without difficulty, and he ordered those that had let themselves down, together with their teachers, to be burnt alive. Then he delivered the rest who were caught to the proper officers to be put to death by them.

(656) After this, the disease seized his entire body and greatly plagued all its parts with various symptoms. For he had a gentle fever and an intolerable itch over all the surface of his body, continual pains in his colon, dropsical tumors on his feet, an inflammation of the abdomen, and a putrefaction of his privy member that produced worms. Besides this he had difficulty breathing and could not breathe except when he sat upright, and had a convulsion of all his limbs. The diviners said those diseases were a punishment upon him for what he had done to the teachers.

(657) Yet he struggled with his numerous disorders and still had a desire to live, and since he hoped for recovery, he considered several methods of cure. Accordingly, he crossed the Jordan and made use of those hot baths at Callirrhoe which run into the lake Asphaltitis[66] but are themselves sweet enough to be drunk. Here the physicians thought it proper to raise the temperature of his whole body by letting it down into a large vessel full of warm oil. Then he fainted and raised his eyes as if he were dying, (658) and as a tumult was then made by his servants, at their voice he revived again. Yet after this he despaired of recovery and gave orders that each soldier should have fifty drachmae each, and that his commanders and friends should have great sums of money given to them.

(659) He then returned to Jericho in such a melancholy state of body as almost threatened him with immediate death, so he proceeded to attempt a horrible scheme. He got together the most illustrious men of the entire Jewish nation, out of every village, into the hippodrome[67] and there shut them in. (660) He then called for his sister Salome and her husband Alexas and made this speech to them:[68] "I know well enough that

---

66. Callirrhoe is located at the northeast end of the Dead Sea, termed here the Lake of Asphalt.

67. The race-course for chariots.

68. This speech must represent the essence of his words since Nicolaus was so close to him.

the Jews will keep a festival upon my death. However, it is in my power to be mourned for on other accounts and to have a splendid funeral, if you will but be subservient to my commands. Take care to send soldiers to surround these men now in custody and kill them immediately upon my death, and then all Judea, every family of them, will weep at it whether they wish to or not. . . ."

(662) He revived for a little while and had a desire to live, but soon after he was overcome by his pains and was disordered by want of food and by a convulsive cough, and so endeavored to prevent a natural death. He took an apple and asked for a knife, for he used to pare apples and eat them. He then looked round about to see if there was anybody to hinder him, and lifted up his right hand as if he would stab himself. But Achiabus, his first cousin, came running to him, held his hand, and hindered him from so doing. (663) Immediately, a very great lamentation was made in the palace as if the king were expiring. As soon as Antipater heard that, he took courage, and with joy in his looks, asked his keepers, for a sum of money, to release him and let him go. But the principal keeper of the prison not only prevented him in that intention, but ran and told the king what his designs were. (664) Thereupon the king cried out louder than his disease would well bear, and immediately sent some of his guards and killed Antipater. He also gave an order to have him buried at Hyrcanium[69] and altered his testament again making Archelaus, his eldest son and the brother of Antipas,[70] his successor and made Antipas tetrarch.

(665) Herod died, having survived the slaughter of his son five days, having reigned thirty-four years since he had caused Antigonus to be killed[71] and obtained his kingdom, but thirty-seven years since he had been made king by the Romans.[72] Now, as for his fortune, it was prosperous in all other respects, if ever any other man could be so, since, from a private man he rose to the throne and kept it so long and left it to his own sons. But still in his domestic affairs, he was a most unfortunate man.[73]

(666) Before the soldiers knew of his death, Salome and her husband came out and released those who were in bonds and whom the king had commanded to be killed, and told them that he had changed his mind and would have every one of them sent to their own homes. When these men were gone, Salome told the soldiers that [the king was dead] and got them and the rest of the multitude together to an assembly in the amphitheater

---

69. Khirbet Mird in the Judean Desert.

70. Herod Antipas, mentioned in the New Testament as the killer of John the Baptist.

71. 37 B.C.E.

72. 40 B.C.E.

73. This moral judgment was probably added by Josephus to the material available to him in the writings of Nicolaus of Damascus.

at Jericho, (667) where Ptolemy, who was entrusted by the king with his signet ring, came before them and spoke of the happiness the king had attained, comforted the multitude, and read the epistle which had been left for the soldiers wherein he earnestly exhorted them to bear good will to his successor. (668) After he had read the epistle, he opened and read his testament wherein Philip was to inherit Trachonitis[74] and the neighboring countries, Antipas was to be tetrarch, as we said before, and Archelaus was made king. (669) He had also been commanded to carry Herod's ring to Caesar, and the settlements he had made, sealed up, because Caesar was to be in control of all the settlements he had made and was to confirm his will; and he ordered that the dispositions he had made were to be kept as they were in his previous will.

(670) So there was an acclamation made to Archelaus to congratulate him upon his advancement, and the soldiers, with the multitude, surrounded him in troops and promised him their good will, and besides prayed to God to bless his government. After this they prepared for the king's funeral. (671) Archelaus omitted nothing of magnificence therein, but brought out all the royal ornaments to augment the pomp of the deceased. There was a bier all of gold, embroidered with precious stones, and a purple covering embroidered with various colors, with the dead body upon it, covered with purple. A diadem was put upon his head and a crown of gold above it, and a scepter in his right hand. (672) Near the bier were Herod's sons and a great number of his relatives. Next came his guards, and the regiments of Thracians, Germans, and Gauls all accoutred as if they were going to war. (673) The rest of the army marched in front, armed and following their captains and officers in a regular manner, after whom five hundred of his domestic servants and freedmen followed with sweet spices in their hands. The body was carried two hundred furlongs[75] to Herodium where he had given an order to be buried. And this shall suffice for the conclusion of the life of Herod.

8.3 JUDEA UNDER THE PROCURATORS

8.3.1 Tacitus, *Historiae* V, 9:1–3:
The Roman Conquest of Judea[76]

Tacitus, the first-century Roman historian, described Roman rule in Palestine briefly. His account highlights the disturbances after Herod's death and

---

74. The area to the east of the Sea of Galilee.

75. 25 miles.

76. Trans. C. H. Moore, *Tacitus III: Histories 4–5 and Annals 1–3* (Loeb Classical Library; Cambridge: Harvard University Press, 1931), pp. 191–3.

the transition to procuratorial administration which paved the way for the eventual outbreak of the Great Revolt of 66–73 C.E.

๙

9:1 The first Roman to subdue the Jews and set foot in their Temple by right of conquest was Gnaeus Pompey:[77] thereafter it was a matter of common knowledge that there were no representations of the gods within, but that the place was empty and the secret shrine contained nothing. The walls of Jerusalem were razed, but the Temple remained standing. Later, in the time of our civil wars, when these eastern provinces had fallen into the hands of Mark Antony, the Parthian prince, Pacorus, seized Judea,[78] but he was slain by Publius Ventidius, and the Parthians were thrown back across the Euphrates: the Jews were subdued by Gaius Sosius.[79] 2 Antony gave the throne to Herod, and Augustus, after his victory, increased his power. After Herod's death, a certain Simon assumed the name of king without waiting for Caesar's decision.[80] He, however, was put to death by Quintilius Varus, governor of Syria; the Jews were repressed; and the kingdom was divided into three parts and given to Herod's sons. Under Tiberius[81] all was quiet. Then, when Caligula[82] ordered the Jews to set up his statue in their Temple,[83] they chose rather to resort to arms, but the emperor's death put an end to their uprising. 3 The princes now being dead or reduced to insignificance, Claudius[84] made Judea a province and entrusted it to Roman knights or to freedmen;[85] one of the latter, Antonius Felix,[86] practiced every kind of cruelty and lust, wielding the power of a king with all the instincts of a slave; he married Drusilla, the granddaughter of Cleopatra and Antony, and so was Antony's grandson-in-law, while Claudius was Antony's grandson.

---

77. In 63 B.C.E. after the conquest of Jerusalem.

78. In 40 B.C.E.

79. 37 B.C.E.

80. Simon was one of three leaders who stirred the nation to revolt in 4 B.C.E. after the death of Herod.

81. 14–37 C.E.

82. 37–41 C.E.

83. 39/40 C.E.

84. 41–54 C.E.

85. After the death of Agrippa I in 44 B.C.E., Judea was returned to provincial administration.

86. Procurator, 52–60 C.E.

8.3.2 Josephus, *War* II, 167–404:
Jewish Law Clashes with Roman Rule

Pontius Pilate, the infamous procurator who crucified Jesus, seemed to have been oblivious to the religious sensibilities of the people he governed and defended his actions with arms. The emperor Gaius expected the Jews to worship him in their Temple, and even ordinary Romans were disrespectful of Judaism. There was a visible deterioration in the relationship between the Jewish population and their Roman rulers which eventually declined into pure corruption and exploitation.

⚜

(167) When the ethnarchy of Archelaus was converted into a Roman province,[87] the other sons of Herod—Philip, and that Herod who was called Antipas—each took upon himself the administration of their respective tetrarchies. . . . 168) But when the Roman empire was passed to Tiberius, the son of Julia, upon the death of Augustus,[88] who had reigned fifty-seven years, six months and two days, both Herod [Antipas] and Philip continued in their tetrarchies. The latter built the city of Caesarea at the fountains of Jordan and in the region of Paneas as well as the city of Julias in Lower Gaulanitis. Herod [Antipas] also built the city Tiberias in Galilee, and in Perea [beyond Jordan] another that was also called Julias.

(169) Pilate,[89] who had been sent as procurator into Judea by Tiberius, sent those images of Caesar called standards into Jerusalem by night. (170) This aroused a very great tumult among the Jews when day broke, for those who were near them were astonished at the sight of the images as indications that their laws were trampled underfoot, for those laws do not permit any sort of image to be brought into the city. Indeed, besides the indignation which the citizens themselves had at the procedure, a vast number of people came running out of the country. (171) These came zealously to Pilate in Caesarea and besought him to take those standards out of Jerusalem and to preserve inviolably for them their ancient laws. But upon Pilate's denial of their request, they fell down prostrate upon the ground and remained immovable in that posture for five days and as many nights.

---

87. 6 C.E.

88. August 19, 14 C.E.

89. Pontius Pilate, prefect of Judea from 26–36 C.E., reacted with violence to serious disturbances which occurred when the Romans violated the religious sensibilities of the Jews.

(172) On the next day Pilate sat upon his tribunal[90] in the open marketplace and called the multitude to him as if desirous to give them an answer, and then gave a signal to the soldiers that they should all by agreement at once surround the Jews with their weapons. (173) So the band of soldiers stood around about the Jews in three ranks. The Jews were under the utmost consternation at that unexpected sight. Pilate also said to them that they would be cut in pieces unless they would admit Caesar's images and he gave intimation to the soldiers to draw their swords. (174) Thereupon the Jews, as it were at one signal, fell down in vast numbers together and exposed their bare necks, and cried out that they were sooner ready to be killed than that their law should be transgressed. Pilate was greatly surprised at their religious zeal, and gave the order that the standards should be taken immediately out of Jerusalem.

(175) After this he caused another disturbance by expending that sacred treasure which is called Korban[91] on aqueducts, whereby he brought water from the distance of four hundred furlongs.[92] At this the people were greatly angered, and when Pilate came to Jerusalem, they surrounded his tribunal with an angry clamor. (176) Apprised beforehand of this disturbance, he mixed his own armed soldiers with the multitude, and ordered them to conceal themselves in the clothing of private men and not to use their swords, but with their staves to beat those who made the clamor. He then gave the signal from his tribunal. (177) The Jews were so sadly beaten that many of them perished by the blows they received, and many of them perished by being trampled to death. Therefore, the multitude was astonished at the calamity of those who were killed and held their peace.

(178) In the meantime, Agrippa, son of Aristobulus[93]. . . cultivated a friendship with Gaius, son of Germanicus, . . . (179) and openly wished that Tiberius might die so that he [Agrippa] might quickly see him [Gaius,] emperor of the world. (180) This was told to Tiberius. . . who. . ordered Agrippa bound and had him very ill treated in prison for six months until Tiberius died. . . . (181) But when Gaius was made Caesar,[94] he released Agrippa from his bonds and made him king of Philip's tetrarchy,[95] for Philip was now dead. . . .

---

90. The platform on which Roman officials sat.
91. Sacrificial funds to be used for Temple offerings.
92. Equivalent to 5 miles.
93. Aristobulus was a son of Herod, and Agrippa was Herod's grandson.
94. 37 C.E.
95. The Golan Heights and the surrounding regions.

(184) Gaius Caesar so grossly abused the fortune he had arrived at as to represent himself to be a god and to desire to be so called. . . . (185) He sent Petronius[96] with an army to Jerusalem to place his statues in the Temple and commanded him that, in case the Jews would not admit them, he should kill those who opposed it and carry all the rest of the nation into captivity. . . . (192) The Jews got together in great numbers with their wives and children. . . and begged Petronius first for their laws, and in the next place, for themselves. (195) And when they insisted on their law and the custom of their country, and how it was not only not permitted for them to make either an image of God or indeed any man and put it in any lesser part of the country, much less in the Temple itself, Petronius replied, "And am I not also," said he, "bound to keep the laws of my own lord? For if I transgress his orders and spare you, I will perish, . . . for I am under command as much as you. . . . Will you then make war against Caesar?" (197) The Jews said, "We offer sacrifices twice a day for Caesar and for the Roman people," but that if he would place the images among them, he must first sacrifice the whole Jewish nation. . . . (198) At this Petronius was astonished and had sympathy for them on account of the inexpressible sense of religion the men were under and their courage which made them ready to die for it. . . . (202) Petronius immediately sent a letter to Caesar and informed him. . . that. . . he must permit them to observe their law and countermand his previous orders. (203) Gaius answered that letter in a violent way and threatened to have Petronius put to death for his being so late in the execution of his orders. But it happened that those who brought Gaius's letter were tossed by a storm and were detained on the sea for three months, while others who brought the news of Gaius's death had a good voyage.[97]

(204) When Gaius had reigned three years and eight months and was killed in a treacherous manner,[98] Claudius was hurried away by the armies at Rome to take charge of the government. . . . (215) He bestowed on Agrippa[99] his whole paternal kingdom[100] immediately and added to it, besides those regions which had been given by Augustus to Herod, Trachonitis, Auranitis, and the kingdom of Lysanius. . . .[101] (217) He bestowed on his brother Herod, who was also his son-in-law by marriage

---

96. Publius Petronius, governor of Syria, 39?–41/2 C.E.

97. According to *Ant.* XVIII, 304, Gaius ordered Petronius to kill himself. The news of Gaius's death, however, reached Petronius before the order to kill himself.

98. January 24, 41 C.E.

99. Agrippa I, ruled as king of Judea 41–44 C.E.

100. The kingdom of his grandfather Herod.

101. Abila, northwest of Damascus and part of Lebanon.

to his daughter Bernice, the kingdom of Chalcis.[102] (218) So now riches flowed in to Agrippa by his enjoyment of so large a dominion. Nor did he abuse the money he had on small matters, but he began to encompass Jerusalem with a wall which, had it been completed, would have made it impossible for the Romans to take it by siege. (219) But his death at Caesarea,[103] before he had raised the walls to their proposed height, ended his plan. He had then reigned three years. . . . (220) He left behind him three daughters. . . and one son, Agrippa. . . . [104]

(221) Now after this, Herod the king of Chalcis died. . . [and] (223) Claudius set Agrippa (II), the son of Agrippa, over his uncle's kingdom. Cumanus took upon himself the office of procurator of the rest of the Roman province,[105] and therein he succeeded [Tiberius] Alexander.[106] Under Cumanus troubles began which resulted in another large loss of Jewish lives. (224) It happened that when the people gathered together in Jerusalem for the Feast of Unleavened Bread,[107] and as the Roman troops stood over the porticoes of the Temple (for they always were armed and kept guard at the festivals to prevent any disorders), one of the soldiers pulled back his garment, stooped down in an indecent manner, and turned his backside to the Jews, and made such a noise as you might expect upon such a posture. (225) At this the entire multitude was indignant and cried out to Cumanus to punish the soldier, while the rasher part of the youth and such as were naturally the most tumultuous fell to fighting, picked up stones, and threw them at the soldiers. (226) Upon this Cumanus was afraid lest all the people should make an assault upon him, and so he sent for more armed men who, when they came in great numbers into the porticoes, caused the Jews very great consternation. Being beaten out of the Temple, they ran into the city, (227) and the urgency with which they crowded to get out was so great that they trod upon each other and squeezed one another until ten thousand of them were killed, so much so that this feast became a cause of mourning for the whole nation, and every family lamented [their own relatives]. . . .

(228) Now there followed after this another calamity. . . in which

---

102. Claudius appointed this Herod, a brother of Agrippa, to rule the kingdom of Chalcis, a region in southern Lebanon.

103. In 44 C.E.

104. He was 17 years old, and the Romans considered him too young to inherit the kingdom.

105. 48–52 C.E.

106. He had served in 46–48 C.E.

107. The holiday of Passover.

(229) a certain soldier found in one village a sacred book of the law,[108] tore it to pieces, and threw it into the fire. (230) Thereupon the Jews were in great disorder, as if their whole county were aflame, and so many of them assembled in their zeal for their religion as by some instrument and ran together with united clamor to Caesarea, to Cumanus, and made supplication to him that he not overlook this man who had offered such an affront to God and to his law, but punish him for what he had done. (231) Accordingly, perceiving that the multitude would not be quiet unless they had a suitable answer from him, he gave an order that the soldier be executed. After this was done, the Jews went their ways. . . .

(248) Claudius, when he had administered the government for thirteen years, eight months, and twenty days, died and left Nero to be his successor in the empire. . . .[109] (252) Nero bestowed the kingdom of Lesser Armenia upon Aristobulus, the son of Herod [of Chalcis], and he added to Agrippa's kingdom four cities with their toparchies . . . , but over the rest of Judea he made Felix procurator.[110] (253) This Felix captured alive Eleazar the arch robber and many of his followers. . . .[111]

(254) When the country was purged of these, there sprang up another sort of robbers in Jerusalem, called Sicarii,[112] who slew men in the daytime in the midst of the city. (255) This they did chiefly at the festivals, when they mingled among the multitude and concealed daggers under their garments with which they stabbed those who were their enemies. When any fell down dead, the murderers joined in the cries of indignation, by which means they appeared persons of such reputation that they could by no means be discovered. (256) The first man killed by them was Jonathan the high priest,[113] after whose death many were killed every day, while the fear men were in of being attacked was more afflicting than the calamity itself. . . .

(258) There was also another body of wicked men who banded together, not so impure in their actions but more wicked in their intentions, who destroyed the tranquillity of the city no less than did these murderers. . . . (259) These were such men as deceived and deluded the people under pretense of divine inspiration, but were for procuring revo-

---

108. A Torah scroll.

109. 54 C.E.

110. He confirmed his earlier appointment. Felix served 52–60 C.E.

111. These so-called "robbers" were really revolutionaries who fought against Roman rule.

112. From Latin *sica*, "dagger."

113. Jonathan, son of Ananus, was high priest from 36 until his murder in 37 C.E. *Ant.* XX, 162–4 implicates the procurator Felix in his death.

lutionary changes in the government. . . . (261) There was an Egyptian false prophet who did the Jews even more mischief for he was a cheat and pretended to be a prophet, and gathered together thirty thousand men who were deluded by him. (262) These he led round about from the wilderness to the mount which was called the Mount of Olives, and he was ready to break into Jerusalem by force from that place. If he could but once conquer the Roman garrison and the people, he intended to set himself up as tyrant over them with the assistance of guards who were to break into the city with him. (263) But Felix prevented his attempt and met him with his Roman soldiers, and all the people assisted him in the defense. . . .

(264) Now, when these were quieted, it happened, as it does in a diseased body, that another part was subject to an inflammation. A company of deceivers and robbers got together and persuaded the Jews to revolt, and exhorted them to assert their liberty, inflicting death on those who continued in obedience to the Roman government and saying that those who willingly chose slavery ought to be prevented forcibly from such inclinations. (265) They divided themselves into different bodies, lay in wait up and down the country, plundered the houses of the great men, killed the men themselves, and set the villages on fire until all Judea was filled with the effects of their madness. Thus the flame was every day fanned more and more until it came to a direct war. . . .

(271) Now Festus[114] succeeded Felix as procurator and made it his business to attack the principal plague of the country. So he caught a huge number of the robbers and destroyed a great many of them. (272) But then Albinus,[115] who succeeded Festus, did not execute his office as the other had done. There was no sort of wickedness that could be named which he did not have a hand in. (273) Accordingly, not only in his political capacity did he steal and plunder private property and burden the whole nation with taxes, but he also permitted the relatives of those put in prison for robbery, either by the local councils or by the former procurators, to ransom them for money, and nobody remained in the prisons as a malefactor except him who gave him nothing. (274) At this time, the enterprises of the revolutionaries at Jerusalem were stimulated. The principal men among them purchased immunity from Albinus to go on with their rebellious practices, while that part of the people who delighted in disturbances joined themselves to the accomplices of Albinus. (275) Every one of these wicked wretches was surrounded by his own band of robbers,

---

114. 60–62 C.E.
115. 62–64 C.E.

while he himself, like an arch robber or a tyrant towering above his company, abused his authority over those about him in order to plunder those who lived quietly. . . . (276) On the whole, nobody dared speak his mind for tyranny was generally tolerated; and at this time were those seeds sown which brought the city to destruction.

(277) Although such was the character of Albinus, Gessius Florus,[116] who succeeded him, showed him to have been a most excellent person upon comparison. For the former committed the greatest number of his crimes in private and with a sort of dissimulation, but Gessius committed his unjust actions to the harm of the nation in a pompous manner. As though he had been sent as an executioner to punish condemned malefactors, he omitted no sort of robbery or violence. (278) Where the case was really pitiable, he was most barbarous, and in things of the greatest turpitude, he was most impudent. No one could outdo him in disguising the truth, nor could anyone contrive more subtle ways of deceit than he did. He indeed thought it but a petty offense to get money out of individuals, so he despoiled whole cities and ruined entire populations at once, and publicly proclaimed almost all over the country that all were at liberty to turn to robbery upon condition that he might share with them in the spoils. (279) Accordingly, his greed caused entire cities to be brought to desolation, and a great many of the people left their own country and fled to foreign provinces. (280) While Cestius Gallus was ruler of the province of Syria, nobody dared do so much as send an embassy to him against Florus. But when he came to Jerusalem upon the occasion of the Feast of Unleavened Bread (Passover),[117] the people assembled around him, no fewer than three million,[118] implored him to ameliorate the calamities of their nation, and cried out against Florus as the ruin of their country.

(281) But as Florus was present and stood next to Cestius, he laughed at their words. However, Cestius, when he had quieted the multitude and had assured them that he would take care that Florus should hereafter treat them in a more gentle manner, returned to Antioch. (282) Florus also escorted him as far as Caesarea and deluded him, though he had at that very time the purpose of showing his anger at the nation and making war upon them, by which means alone he supposed he might conceal his enormous crimes. (283) For he expected that if peace continued, the Jews would accuse him before Caesar, but if he could make them revolt,

---

116. 64–66 C.E.
117. Probably in 65 C.E.
118. Clearly an exaggerated number.

he would divert inquiry into less serious charges by a crime that was so much greater. He therefore exacerbated their sufferings every day in order to induce them to rebellion....

(293) Moreover, as to the citizens of Jerusalem, although they took this matter[119] very badly, they restrained their passion. But Florus acted as if he had been hired to fan the flames of war and sent some men to take seventeen talents out of the Temple treasury pretending that Caesar wanted them. (294) At this the people were immediately outraged and ran together to the Temple with piercing cries, called upon Caesar by name, and besought him to free them from the tyranny of Florus. (295) Some of the rebellious also cried out against Florus and heaped the greatest reproaches upon him, and carried a basket about and begged for some copper coins for him, as for one that was destitute and in miserable condition. Yet he was not ashamed of his love of money, but was more enraged, and provoked to acquire still more. (296) Instead of coming to Caesarea as he ought to have done, and quenching the flames of war which was beginning there, and so eliminating the cause of this disturbance (which was his job for which he had been paid), he marched hastily with his cavalry and infantry against Jerusalem so that he might attain his goal by the arms of the Romans and might, by his terror and by his threats, bring the city into subjection....

(301) At this time Florus lodged at the palace. On the next day he had his tribunal placed before it, sat upon it, and the high priests and the men of power and those of the greatest eminence in the city all came before that tribunal. (302) Florus commanded them to deliver up to him those who had reproached him and told them that they would themselves partake of his vengeance if they did not produce the criminals. But they declared that the people were peaceably disposed, and they begged forgiveness for those who had spoken disrespectfully. (303) For it was no wonder at all, they said, that in so great a multitude there should be some more daring, and because of their young age foolish also, than they ought to be, and that it was impossible to distinguish those who offended from the rest, while every one was sorry for what he had done and denied it out of fear of what would follow. (304) He ought, however, to provide for the peace of the nation and take such counsel as might preserve the city for the Romans and, rather for the sake of a great number of innocent people, forgive a few that were guilty, than for the sake of a few of the wicked, bring trouble upon so large and good a population.

---

119. Referring to disturbances which took place in Caesarea.

(305) Florus was more provoked at this, and called out aloud to the soldiers to plunder that which was called the Upper Marketplace and to kill whomever they met. So the soldiers, taking this exhortation of their commander to be in agreement with their desire of gain, not only plundered the place they were sent to, but forcing themselves into every house, they killed its inhabitants. (306) The citizens fled along the narrow lanes, and the soldiers killed those they caught, and no method of plunder was omitted. They also caught many of the peaceable citizens and brought them before Florus who at first had them chastised with stripes and then crucified. (307) Accordingly, the total number of those who were destroyed that day with their wives and children (for they did not spare even the infants themselves) was about three thousand six hundred. . . .

(333) Florus contrived yet another way to oblige the Jews to begin the war by sending a message to Cestius accusing the Jews falsely of revolting [against the Roman government]. He imputed the beginning of the earlier fight to them and pretended that they had been the authors of that disturbance in which they were only the victims. Yet the magistrates of Jerusalem were not silent upon this occasion, but themselves wrote to Cestius, as did Bernice[120] also, about the illegal practices of which Florus had been guilty against the city. (334) Cestius, upon reading both accounts, consulted with his officers. Some of them thought it best for Cestius to go up with his army, either to punish the revolt, if it was real, or to confirm the Jews in their allegiance to Rome. But he thought it best himself to send one of his intimate friends beforehand to investigate the state of affairs and to give him a faithful account of the intentions of the Jews. (335) Accordingly he sent one of his tribunes, whose name was Neopolitanus, who met with King Agrippa at Jamnia[121] as he was returning from Alexandria, and told him who it was that sent him and on what errand he was sent.

(336) Here the high priests and men of power among the Jews, as well as the Sanhedrin, came to congratulate the king [upon his safe return]. After they had paid him their respects, they lamented their own calamities and related to him what barbarous treatment they had met with from Florus . . . , (339) and they showed him, when they came into the city (Jerusalem), how the marketplace was made desolate and the houses plundered. (340) They then persuaded Neopolitanus, with the help of

---

120. The sister of King Agrippa who had pleaded for clemency for the Jews before Florus.

121. Yavneh, near the Mediterranean coast.

Agrippa, to walk around the city with only one servant as far as Siloam,[122] so that he might assure himself that the Jews submitted to all the rest of the Romans and were displeased only at Florus because of his excessive barbarity to them. So he walked around and had sufficient experience of the good spirit the people were in, and then went up to the Temple (341) where he called the multitude together, highly commended them for their fidelity to the Romans, and earnestly exhorted them to keep the peace. Having performed divine worship in those areas of the Temple as were permitted, he returned to Cestius.

(342) But as for the multitude of the Jews, they addressed themselves to the king and to the high priests and desired to send ambassadors to Nero against Florus and not to remain silent after such great slaughter which would leave a suspicion that the Jews were disposed to revolt. . . . (343) . . . But Agrippa (II), although he thought it too dangerous a thing for them to appoint men to go as the accusers of Florus, yet did not think it fit for him to overlook them, as they were in a disposition for war. (344) He therefore called the multitude together into a large gallery. . . and spoke to them. . . .[123]

(348) "I am well aware that many wax eloquent concerning the injuries that have been offered to you by your procurators and concerning the glorious advantages of liberty. . . . (352) . . . let us take it for granted that the Roman ministers are injurious to you and are incurably severe. Yet it is not all the Romans who thus injure you; nor has Caesar, against whom you are going to make war, injured you. It is not by their command that any wicked governor is sent to you, for they who are in the west cannot see those who are in the east, nor indeed is it easy for them at a distance even to hear what is done in these parts. (353) Now it is absurd to make war with a great many for the sake of one, to do so with such mighty people for a small cause. . . . (354) Indeed, such crimes as we complain of may soon be corrected, for the same procurator will not continue forever, and it is probable that his successors will come with more moderate inclinations. But as for war, once begun, it is not easily ended, nor borne without calamities. . . .

(361) "Moreover, there are ten thousand other nations who had even greater reason than we to claim their liberty [from Rome] and yet do submit. You are the only people who think it a disgrace to be servants to those to whom all the world has submitted. What sort of an army do you rely on? What are the arms you depend on? Where is your fleet to sweep

---

122. The pool of Siloam (Shiloah) at the southeast corner of the city.

123. The speech that follows, composed by Josephus, reflects the historian's opposition to the revolt and so cannot be taken as the words of Agrippa.

the Roman seas, and where is the treasury which will be sufficient for your undertakings? (362) . . . for the power of the Romans is invincible in all parts of the habitable earth. . . . (380) Now, when almost all people under the sun submit to Roman arms, will you be the only people that make war against them?. . .

(390) "What remains, therefore, is only recourse to divine assistance, but this is already on the side of the Romans, for it is impossible that so vast an empire should be built up without God's providence. (391) Reflect upon how impossible it would be for the zealous observance of your religious customs to be preserved, for they are hard to observe even when you fight against those whom you are able to conquer. How can you then most of all hope for God's assistance when, by being forced to transgress his law, you will make him turn his face from you? (392) And if you do observe the custom of the Sabbath days and cannot be prevailed upon to do anything on the Sabbath, then you will easily be defeated as were your forefathers by Pompey who was the busiest in his siege on those days on which the besieged rested.[124] (393) But if in time of war you transgress the law of your country, I cannot tell for what further reason you will go to war since your one concern is to preserve inviolate all the institutions of your forefathers. . . ."

(402) When Agrippa had spoken thus, both he and his sister wept, and by their tears repressed a great deal of the violence of the people, but still they cried out that they would not fight against the Romans but against Florus on account of what they had suffered under him. (403) To this Agrippa replied, "But your actions are already acts of war against the Romans, for you have not paid the tribute which is due to Caesar, and you have cut down the porticoes [of the Temple] leading to the tower Antonia.[125] (404) You can therefore prevent any charge of revolt only if you will rebuild these and if you will pay your tribute. For the citadel does not now belong to Florus, nor is the tribute money due to Florus."

8.4 THE RISE OF THE EARLY CHURCH

8.4.1 Mark 1–13: The Teachings of Jesus[126]

Mark's version of the career and teachings of Jesus, probably completed around 70 C.E., is generally regarded as the earliest of the Gospel accounts. It

---

124. That is, on the Sabbaths and festivals.

125. Cutting off the Roman forces stationed in the fortress from access to the Temple.

126. *Revised Standard Version of the Bible* (New York: National Council of Churches, 1971).

provides a picture of the early Jesus movement emerging within Judaism and chronicles the teachings of early Christianity and the life of Jesus. We present here excerpts providing a sense of the fundamental teachings of the new movement which would soon constitute a distinct religious community.

🙟

1:1 The beginning of the gospel[127] of Jesus Christ, the Son of God. 2 As it is written in Isaiah the prophet,

> "Behold, I send my messenger before thy face,[128]
> who shall prepare thy way;
> 3 the voice of one crying in the wilderness:
> Prepare the way of the Lord,
> make his paths straight."[129]

4 John the baptizer appeared in the wilderness, preaching a baptism of repentance for the forgiveness of sins. 5 And there went out to him all the country of Judea, and all the people of Jerusalem; and they were baptized by him in the river Jordan, confessing their sins. . . .

9 In those days Jesus came from Nazareth of Galilee and was baptized by John in the Jordan. 10 And when he came up out of the water, immediately he saw the heavens opened and the Spirit descending upon him like a dove; 11 and a voice came from heaven, "Thou art my beloved Son; with thee I am well pleased. . . ."

14 Now after John was arrested, Jesus came into Galilee, preaching the gospel of God, 15 and saying, "The time is fulfilled, and the kingdom of God is at hand; repent, and believe in the gospel."

16 And passing along by the Sea of Galilee, he saw Simon and Andrew the brother of Simon casting a net in the sea; for they were fishermen. 17 And Jesus said to them, "Follow me and I will make you become fishers of men." 18 And immediately they left their nets and followed him. 19 And going on a little farther, he saw James the son of Zebedee and John his brother, who were in their boat mending the nets. 20 And immediately he called them; and they left their father Zebedee in the boat with the hired servants, and followed him.

---

127. Literally, "good news," referring in Christian usage to the good news that the kingdom of God is at hand.

128. Mal. 3:1.

129. Is. 40:3.

21 And they went into Capernaum;[130] and immediately on the sabbath he entered the synagogue and taught. 22 And they were astonished at his teaching, for he taught them as one who had authority, and not as the scribes. 23 And immediately there was in their synagogue a man with an unclean spirit; 24 and he cried out, "What have you to do with us, Jesus of Nazareth? Have you come to destroy us? I know who you are, the Holy One of God." 25 But Jesus rebuked him, saying, "Be silent, and come out of him!" 26 And the unclean spirit, convulsing him and crying with a loud voice, came out of him. 27 And they were all amazed, so that they questioned among themselves, saying, "What is this? A new teaching! With authority he commands even the unclean spirits, and they obey him." 28 And at once his fame spread everywhere throughout all the surrounding region of Galilee. . . .

6:1 He went away from there and came to his own country; and his disciples followed him. 2 And on the sabbath he began to teach in the synagogue; and many who heard him were astonished, saying, "Where did this man get all this? What is the wisdom given to him? What mighty works are wrought by his hands! 3 Is not this the carpenter, the son of Mary and brother of James and Joses and Judas and Simon, and are not his sisters here with us?" And they took offense at him. 4 And Jesus said to them, "A prophet is not without honor, except in his own country, and among his own kin, and in his own house." 5 And he could do no mighty work there, except that he laid his hands upon a few sick people and healed them. 6 And he marveled because of their unbelief. And he went about among the villages teaching.

7 And he called to him the twelve, and began to send them out two by two, and gave them authority over the unclean spirits. . . . 12 So they went out and preached that men should repent. 13 And they cast out many demons, and anointed with oil many that were sick and healed them.

14 King Herod[131] heard of it; for Jesus's name had become known. Some said, "John the baptizer has been raised from the dead; that is why these powers are at work in him." 15 But others said, "It is Elijah." And others said, "It is a prophet, like one of the prophets of old." 16 But when Herod heard of it he said, "John, whom I beheaded, has been raised." 17

---

130. Kefar Naḥum, on the northern shore of the Sea of Galilee.

131. Herod Antipas, son of Herod the Great, tetrarch of Galilee and Perea, 4 B.C.E.–39 C.E.

For Herod had sent and seized John, and bound him in prison for the sake of Herodias, his brother Philip's[132] wife; because he had married her.[133] 18 For John said to Herod, "It is not lawful for you to have your brother's wife."[134] 19 And Herodias had a grudge against him, and wanted to kill him. But she could not, 20 for Herod feared John, knowing that he was a righteous and holy man, and kept him safe. When he heard him, he was much perplexed; and yet he heard him gladly. 21 But an opportunity came when Herod on his birthday gave a banquet for his courtiers and officers and the leading men of Galilee. 22 For when Herodias' daughter came in and danced, she pleased Herod and his guests; and the king said to the girl, "Ask me for whatever you wish, and I will grant it." 23 And he vowed to her, "Whatever you ask me, I will give you, even half of my kingdom." 24 And she went out, and said to her mother, "What shall I ask?" And she said, "The head of John the baptizer." 25 And she came in immediately with haste to the king, and asked, saying, "I want you to give me at once the head of John the Baptist on a platter." 26 And the king was exceedingly sorry; but because of his oaths and his guests he did not want to break his word to her. 27 And immediately the king sent a soldier of the guard and gave orders to bring his head. He went and beheaded him in the prison, 28 and brought his head on a platter, and gave it to the girl; and the girl gave it to her mother. 29 When his disciples heard of it, they came and took his body, and laid it in a tomb. . . .

7:14 And he (Jesus) called the people to him again, and said to them, "Hear me, all of you, and understand: 15 there is nothing outside a man which by going into him can defile him; but the things which come out of a man are what defile him." 17 And when he had entered the house, and left the people, his disciples asked him about the parable. 18 And he said to them, "Then are you also without understanding? Do you not see that whatever goes into a man from outside cannot defile him, 19 since it enters, not his heart but his stomach, and so passes on?" (Thus he declared all foods clean.) 20 And he said, "What comes out of a man is what defiles a man. 21 For from within, out of the heart of man, come evil thoughts, fornication, theft, murder, adultery, 22 coveting, wickedness, deceit, licentiousness, envy, slander, pride, foolishness. 23 All these evil things come from within, and they defile a man. . . ."

---

132. Herod Philip, Tetrarch of Batanaea, Trachonitis, Auronitis, and the east shore of the Dead Sea from 4 B.C.E.–34 C.E. But this is an error as actually she was married to a half uncle of her father Aristobulus, also named Herod.

133. After she had left her first husband.

134. Lev. 18:16. This law was set aside only in the case of levirate marriage (Deut. 25:5–6).

8:27 And Jesus went on with his disciples, to the villages of Caesarea Philippi;[135] and on the way he asked his disciples, "Who do men say that I am?" 28 And they told him, "John the Baptist; and others say, Elijah; and others one of the prophets." 29 And he asked them, "But who do you say that I am?" Peter answered him, "You are the Christ."[136] 30 And he charged them to tell no one about him.

31 And he began to teach them that the Son of man must suffer many things, and be rejected by the elders and the chief priests and the scribes, and be killed, and after three days rise again. 32 And he said this plainly. And Peter took him, and began to rebuke him. 33 But turning and seeing his disciples, he rebuked Peter, and said, "Get behind me, Satan! For you are not on the side of God, but of men. . . ."

9:1 And he said to them, "Truly, I say to you, there are some standing here who will not taste death before they see that the kingdom of God has come with power."

2 And after six days Jesus took with him Peter and James and John, and led them up a high mountain apart by themselves; and he was transfigured[137] before them, 3 and his garments became glistening, intensely white, as no fuller[138] on earth could bleach them. 4 And there appeared to them Elijah[139] with Moses; and they were talking to Jesus. . . .

9 And as they were coming down the mountain, he charged them to tell no one what they had seen, until the Son of man should have risen from the dead. 10 So they kept the matter to themselves, questioning what the rising from the dead meant.

10:1 And he left there and went to the region of Judea and beyond the Jordan, and crowds gathered to him again; and again, as his custom was, he taught them.

2 And Pharisees came up and in order to test him asked, "Is it lawful for a man to divorce his wife?" 3 He answered them, "What did Moses command you?" 4 They said, "Moses allowed a man to write a certificate of divorce, and to put her away."[140] 5 But Jesus said to them, "For your hardness of heart he wrote you this commandment. 6 But from the beginning of creation, 'God made them male and female.'[141] 7 'For this reason a man

---

135. A town on the southern slope of Mt. Hermon in the upper Galilee.

136. Literally, "anointed messiah."

137. Attaining a non-earthly appearance.

138. Launderer.

139. The prophet Elijah was expected to appear on earth before the messiah appeared (Mal. 4:5–6).

140. Cf. Deut. 24:1–4.

141. Gen. 1:27; 5:2.

shall leave his father and mother and be joined to his wife, 8 and the two shall become one flesh.'[142] So they are no longer two but one flesh. 9 What therefore God has joined together, let not man put asunder."

10 And in the house the disciples asked him again about this matter. 11 And he said to them, "Whoever divorces his wife and marries another, commits adultery against her; 12 and if she divorces her husband and marries another, she commits adultery."

13 And they were bringing children to him, that he might touch them; and the disciples rebuked them. 14 But when Jesus saw it he was indignant, and said to them, "Let the children come to me, do not hinder them; for to such belongs the kingdom of God. 15 Truly, I say to you, whoever does not receive the kingdom of God like a child shall not enter it." 16 And he took them in his arms and blessed them, laying his hands upon them.

17 And as he was setting out on his journey, a man ran up and knelt before him, and asked him, "Good Teacher, what must I do to inherit eternal life?" 18 And Jesus said to him, "Why do you call me good? No one is good but God alone. 19 You know the commandments: 'Do not kill, Do not commit adultery, Do not steal, Do not bear false witness, Do not defraud, Honor your father and mother.'"[143] 20 And he said to him, "Teacher, all these I have observed from my youth." 21 And Jesus looking upon him loved him, and said to him, "You lack one thing; go, sell what you have, and give to the poor, and you will have treasure in heaven; and come, follow me." 22 At that saying his countenance fell, and he went away sorrowful; for he had great possessions.

23 And Jesus looked around and said to his disciples, "How hard it will be for those who have riches to enter the kingdom of God!" 24 And the disciples were amazed at his words. But Jesus said to them again, "Children, how hard it is to enter the kingdom of God! 25 It is easier for a camel to go through the eye of a needle than for a rich man to enter the kingdom of God."[144] 26 And they were exceedingly astonished, and said to him, "Then who can be saved?" 27 Jesus looked at them and said, "With men it is impossible, but not with God; for all things are possible with God. . . ."

13:1 And as he came out of the Temple, one of his disciples said to him, "Look, Teacher, what wonderful stones and what wonderful buildings!" 2

---

142. Gen. 2:24.

143. Ex. 20:12–16; Deut. 5:16–20.

144. It was supposed that wealth made possible the performance of religious duties. Jesus' point is that wealth prevents man from submitting to God's rule.

And Jesus said to him, "Do you see these great buildings? There will not be left here one stone upon another, that will not be thrown down." 3 And as he sat on the Mount of Olives opposite the Temple, Peter and James and John and Andrew asked him privately, 4 "Tell us, when will this be, and what will be the sign when these things are all to be accomplished?" 5 And Jesus began to say to them, "Take heed that no one leads you astray. 6 Many will come in my name, saying, 'I am he!' and they will lead many astray. 7 And when you hear of wars and rumors of wars, do not be alarmed; this must take place, but the end is not yet. 8 For nation will rise against nation, and kingdom against kingdom; there will be earthquakes in various places, there will be famines; this is but the beginning of the birth-pangs.

9 "But take heed to yourselves; for they will deliver you up to councils; and you will be beaten in synagogues; and you will stand before governors and kings for my sake, to bear testimony before them. 10 And the gospel must first be preached to all nations. 11 And when they bring you to trial and deliver you up, do not be anxious beforehand what you are to say; but say whatever is given you in that hour, for it is not you who speak, but the Holy Spirit. 12 And brother will deliver up brother to death, and the father his child, and children will rise against parents and have them put to death; 13 and you will be hated by all for my name's sake. But he who endures to the end will be saved. . . .

19 "For in those days there will be such tribulation as has not been from the beginning of the creation which God created until now, and never will be. 20 And if the Lord had not shortened the days, no human being would be saved; but for the sake of the elect, whom he chose, he shortened the days. 21 And then if any one says to you, 'Look, here is the Christ!' or 'Look, there he is!' do not believe it. 22 False Christs and false prophets will arise and show signs and wonders, to lead astray, if possible, the elect. 23 But take heed; I have told you all things beforehand.

24 "But in those days, after that tribulation, the sun will be darkened, and the moon will not give its light, 25 and the stars will be falling from heaven, and the powers in the heavens will be shaken. 26 And then they will see the Son of man coming in clouds with great power and glory. 27 And then he will send out the angels, and gather his elect from the four winds, from the ends of the earth to the ends of heaven.

28 "From the fig tree learn its lesson: as soon as its branch becomes tender and puts forth its leaves, you know that summer is near. 29 So also, when you see these things taking place, you know that he is near, at the very gates. 30 Truly, I say to you, this generation will not pass away before

all these things take place. 31 Heaven and earth will pass away, but my
words will not pass away. . . .

8.5 PARTING OF THE WAYS

8.5.1 Babylonian Talmud Berakhot 28b:
The Composition of the Blessing against the Heretics[145]

*After discussing the significance of the number eighteen regarding the prayer
of the "Eighteen Benedictions," the Babylonian Talmud discusses the origin
of what it considered to be the additional nineteenth blessing, denouncing non-
believers, which has been incorporated into the prayer.*

ℵ

These eighteen [benedictions] are [really] nineteen. Rabbi Levi said:
The blessing against the heretics (*minim*) was innovated at Yavneh. . . .

Our Rabbis taught: Simon ha-Pakoli arranged the Eighteen Benedictions in order before Rabban Gamliel at Yavneh.[146] Rabban Gamliel said
to the Sages: "Is there nobody who knows how to innovate a blessing
against the heretics? Samuel ha-Qatan arose and innovated it. The following year he forgot it and he concentrated for two or three hours [to
remember it] but they did not remove him [from leading the prayer].

Why did they not remove him? Did not Rabbi Judah say that Rav
said: "If he erred in any one of the blessings you do not remove him, but if
[he erred] in the blessing against the heretics, you do remove him, [for]
you suspect that he is a heretic?"

[They did not remove him because] Samuel ha-Qatan is different, for
he innovated it. But should we not suspect that he might have changed his
mind? Abaye has said: We learn [in a tradition] "one who is good does
not become bad." Can he not? Is it not written, "And when a righteous
man turns from his righteousness and does wickedness" (Ezek. 18:24)?[147]
This refers to one who is originally evil, but one who is originally righteous will not [become evil]. No? But we learn in a Mishnah, "Do not
trust in yourself until the day of your death,"[148] for Yoḥanan the High
Priest[149] served in the high priesthood for eighty years, and in the end he
became a Sadducee.

---

145. Trans. S. Berrin.
146. Ca. 80 C.E.
147. Implying that a righteous person can become evil.
148. Mishnah Avot 2:4.
149. John Hyrcanus.

Abaye said, "Yannai[150] is the same as Yoḥanan."

Rava said, "Yannai and Yoḥanan are separate individuals. Yannai was originally evil and Yoḥanan was originally righteous."

It makes sense according to Abaye (that they did not suspect the originally good Samuel ha-Qatan of turning evil), but according to Rava it is a problem [that they did not remove Samuel ha-Qatan].

Rava would say to you: an originally righteous man may also change his mind.

If so, then why did they not remove him? Samuel ha-Qatan is different because he began [to recite] the blessing. For Rabbi Judah said that Rav said, and some teach Rabbi Judah ben Levi: "They only taught this rule [of removing one who erred in the blessing against the heretics] in a case in which he did not [even] begin [to recite] it. But if he began [to recite] it, he may finish it.

8.5.2 The Eighteen Benedictions: The Benediction against the Heretics[151]

Palestinian texts of the Amidah preserve an early form of the Benediction against Heretics which includes both minim, Jewish Christians, and noẓerim, Gentile Christians. The Benediction's recitation was intended to bring about the separation of Christians from the synagogue. Such a procedure is mentioned in the Gospel of John and in the writings of the Church Fathers.

ﷺ

For the apostates[152] may there be no hope unless they return to Your Torah. As for the *noẓerim* and the *minim*, may they perish immediately. Speedily may they be erased from the Book of Life and may they not be registered among the righteous. Blessed are You, O Lord, Who subdues the wicked.

8.5.3 Tosefta Ḥullin 2:20–21: Laws Distancing Jews from the Heretics[153]

The Tosefta presents a list of regulations put together from previously existing statements, reflecting tannaitic steps to distance Jews from the early Chris-

---

150. Rabbinic tradition (Babylonian Talmud Kiddushin 66a) relates that Yannai massacred the Sages of Israel. See text 6.2.12 in this volume. If they are the same person, then he was originally evil, so his Sadducean conversion is not surprising.

151. Trans. L. H. Schiffman, *Who Was a Jew?* (Hoboken, NJ: Ktav, 1985), p. 55.

152. Jews who no longer practice Judaism.

153. Schiffman, *Who Was a Jew?* p. 64.

tians who were increasingly regarded as members of a separate religious community.

𝕾

If meat is found in the hand of a non-Jew, it is permitted to derive benefit from it. [If it is found] in the hand of a *min*,[154] it is forbidden to derive benefit from it. That which comes forth from the house of a *min*, indeed it is the meat of sacrifices to the dead (idolatrous worship), for they said: The slaughtering of a *min* is idolatry; their bread is the bread of a Samaritan; their wine is the wine of [idolatrous] libation; their fruits are untithed; their books are the books of diviners, and their children are *mamzerim*.[155] We do not sell to them, nor do we buy from them. We do not take from them, nor do we give to them, and we do not teach their sons a craft. We are not healed by them, neither healing of property nor healing of life.[156]

8.5.4 Tosefta Ḥullin 2:24: Rabbi Eliezer and the Heretic[157]

This narrative indicates that even Rabbis were in contact with Jewish Christians and that they exchanged interpretations and teachings.

𝕾

It happened that Rabbi Eliezer[158] was arrested on charges of *minut* (heresy), and they brought him up to the platform to be tried. The governor said to him, "Does an elder like yourself busy himself with things like these?"

He (Rabbi Eliezer) said to him (the governor), "The judge is reliable concerning me."

The governor thought that he was referring to him, but he intended to refer to his Father Who is in Heaven.

He (the governor) said to him (Rabbi Eliezer), "Since you have accepted me as reliable concerning yourself, thus I have said: It is possible that these gray hairs are in error concerning these charges. *Dimissus*.[159] You are released."

---

154. "Heretic," referring here to a Jewish Christian.

155. Progeny of a forbidden marriage, such as that of adultery or incest.

156. By "healing of property," the text refers to cases in which there is no mortal danger. "Healing of life" refers to cases in which a life is at stake.

157. Schiffman, *Who Was a Jew?* p. 71.

158. Rabbi Eliezer ben Hyrcanus, who lived at the end of the first and beginning of the second century.

159. The accused is acquitted.

After he (Rabbi Eliezer) left the platform, he was troubled that he was arrested on charges of *minut*. His disciples came in to console him, but he would not take [consolation].

Rabbi Akiva entered and said to him, "My teacher, may I say before you something so that perhaps you will not grieve?"

He said to him, "Say [it]."

He (Rabbi Akiva) said to him (Rabbi Eliezer), "Perhaps one of the *minim* said a word of *minut* which gave you pleasure?"

He (Rabbi Eliezer) said, "By Heaven, you have reminded me. Once I was walking in the street of Sepphoris. I chanced upon Jacob of Kefar Sikhnin, and he said a word of *minut* in the name of Yeshua ben Pantira (Jesus), and it gave me pleasure. I was arrested on charges of *minut*, for I have transgressed the words of the Torah, 'Keep your path far from her and do not draw near to the entrance of her house (Prov. 5:8), for she has brought down many victims [and numerous are those whom she has killed] (Prov. 7:26).'"

For Rabbi Eliezer used to say: "Stay away from ugliness and from that which resembles ugliness."

8.5.5 Jerusalem Talmud Berakhot 9:1 (12d–13a): Rabbi Simlai Refutes the Trinity[160]

Christians often confronted Rabbis and engaged them in debate. Here we see a third century Rabbi's refutation of the trinity, by then a fundamental Christian doctrine.

ৡৢ

Said Rabbi Simlai: "In every instance that the *minim* have asked a question (based upon a verse), the answer is right next to it. . . ."

[The *minim*] asked him: "What is this that is written, 'God, the Lord God, He knows. . . '?" (Josh. 22:22) [161]

He said to them: "It is not written, 'They know,' but 'He knows.'"[162]

His students said to him: "Rabbi, you deflected them with a straw, but how will you answer us?"

He said to them: "These are three titles for a single Being, just as a person says *basileus* (Greek for 'king'), Caesar (and) Augustus."

---

160. Trans. S. Berrin.

161. The repetition of phrases mentioning God three times seemed to the Christians to imply a trinity of three divinities.

162. The subject of the verb is singular, not plural, confirming unity.

The *minim* again asked him: "What is this that is written, 'God, the Lord God? spoke and summoned the world. . . '?" (Ps. 50:1)

He said to them: "'Spoke and summoned' was not written here in the plural, but rather 'He spoke and summoned the world' (was written) in the singular."

His students said to him: "Rabbi, you deflected them with a straw, but how will you answer us?"

He said to them: "These are three titles for the same thing, just as a person says artisan, builder (and) architect."

8.5.6 Babylonian Talmud Gittin 45b: A Torah Written by a Heretic[163]

The Rabbis went so far as to require the destruction of a Torah scroll written by a Jewish Christian, seeing it as having no sanctity.

༄

Rabbi Naḥman said, "We have a tradition that a Torah scroll written by a *min* must be burnt, and one written by an idolator must be stored away. One that is found with a *min* must be stored away, and one that is found with an idolator, some say it must be stored away and others say that it may be read.

8.6 JEWISH-CHRISTIAN RELATIONS IN THE EARLY CENTURIES

8.6.1 Justin Martyr, *Dialogue with Trypho*: Proofs of Christianity from the Old Testament[164]

Justin Martyr (100–165 C.E.) composed a Greek record of a supposed dialogue with a Jew. Apparently, this work is a literary device, purporting to be a dialogue with the famous Mishnaic sage Rabbi Tarfon. The debate shows that the theological battle lines between Jews and Christians had already been drawn by the mid-second century C.E., and Christian hostility to Judaism was already normative.

༄

Trypho then said . . . "Prove to us that Jesus Christ is the one about whom these prophecies were spoken."

---

163. Trans. S. Berrin.

164. Trans. T. B. Falls, *Writings of St. Justin Martyr* (New York: Christian Heritage, 1948), pp. 202, 204–8, 212–4.

"At the proper time," I replied, "I will supply the proofs you wish, but for the present permit me to quote the following prophecies to show that the Holy Spirit by parable called Christ God, and Lord of hosts and of Jacob. God Himself calls your interpreters stupid (Jer. 4:22) because they claim that these prophecies were not spoken of Christ, but of Solomon, when he transported the ark of testimony into the temple built by himself...."

"It would be better for us," Trypho concluded, "to have obeyed our teachers who warned us not to listen to you Christians, nor to converse with you on these subjects, for you have blasphemed many times in your attempt to convince us that this crucified man was with Moses and Aaron, and spoke with them in the pillar of the cloud; that He became man, was crucified, and ascended into Heaven, and will return again to this earth; and that He should be worshipped."

"I am aware," I replied, "that, as the Word of God testifies, this great wisdom of Almighty God, the Creator of all, is concealed from you. It is, therefore, with feelings of pity that I exert every possible effort to help you understand our teachings, which to you seem paradoxical. If I fail, then I shall not be held accountable on judgment day. I shall recount to you other doctrines which may seem even more paradoxical to you, but don't be disturbed; instead of leaving me, become more zealous and inquisitive listeners. At the same time, forsake the tradition of your teachers, for they are convicted by the Prophetic Spirit of being incapable of understanding the truths spoken by God, and of preferring to spread their own opinions...."

"It is small wonder," I continued, "that you Jews hate us Christians who have grasped the meaning of these truths, and take you to task for your stubborn prejudice. Indeed, Elijah, when interceding for you before God, spoke thus.: 'Lord, they have slain Your prophets, and have destroyed Your altars; and I am left alone, and they seek my life.' And God answered: 'I still have seven thousand men, whose knees have not been bowed before Baal' (1 Kings 19:18). Therefore, just as God did not show His anger on account of those seven thousand men, so now He has not yet exacted judgment of you, because He knows that every day some of you are forsaking your erroneous ways to become disciples in the name of Christ, and this same name of Christ enlightens you to receive all the graces and gifts according to your merits. One receives the spirit of wisdom, another of counsel, another of fortitude, another of healing, another of foreknowledge, another of teaching, and another of the fear of God."

"Don't you realize," interposed Trypho, "that you are out of your mind to say such things?"

"Listen to me, my friend," I retorted, "and I'll prove that I'm not out of my mind when I mention these special gifts. For it was predicted that, after His Ascension into Heaven, Christ would free us from the captivity of error and endow us with gifts. Here are the words of the prophecy: 'He ascended on high; He led captivity captive; He gave gifts to men' (Ps. 67[68]:19). Thus, having received gifts from Christ, who ascended into Heaven, we can show from the prophecies that you 'who are wise in your own eyes and prudent in your own sight' (Is. 5:21), are in reality stupid, for you honor God and His Christ only with your lips. We, on the other hand, who have been well instructed in His whole truth, honor Them with our actions, our knowledge, and our hearts, even unto death. . . ."

"Prove to us," interrupted Trypho, "that this man who you claim was crucified, and ascended into Heaven, is the Christ of God. It has indeed been proved sufficiently by your Scriptural quotations that it was predicted in the Scriptures that Christ should suffer, and that He should come again in glory to accept the eternal kingdom over all nations, and that every kingdom should be made subject to Him.[165] But what we want you to prove is that this Jesus is the Christ spoken of in the Scriptures."

"My dear friends," I replied, "anyone with ears would know that I have already proved that very point, and it can be shown also from the facts which you yourselves have admitted. But, lest you think that I am not able to furnish further proof that Jesus is the Messiah, I renew my promise to produce additional arguments in their proper place. For the present, however, I would like to continue on the same subject we were discussing. . . ."

"As circumcision originated with Abraham, and the Sabbath, sacrifices, oblations, and festivals with Moses (and it has already been shown that your people were commanded to observe these things because of their hardness of heart), so it was expedient that, in accordance with the will of the Father, these things should have their end in Him who was born of the Virgin, of the race of Abraham, of the tribe of Judah, and of the family of David: namely, in Christ, the Son of God, who was proclaimed as the future Eternal Law and New Testament for the whole world (as the above-quoted prophecies clearly show). We, indeed, who have come to God through Jesus Christ, have received not a carnal, but a spiritual, circumcision, as did Enoch and those like him. Through God's mercy we

---

165. Justin falsely attributes to Trypho belief in certain Christian doctrines.

received this by means of baptism, since we had become sinners, and all men should likewise receive it. . . ."

"Now, it is clear to all that no one of the race of Abraham was ever born, or even said to be born, of a virgin, except of our Christ. But, since you and your teachers venture to assert that the real words of Isaiah are not 'Behold, a virgin shall conceive,' but 'Behold a young woman shall conceive, and bear a son;' (Is. 7:14) and since you refer this prophecy to your king Hezekiah, I will attempt to answer you and show that this prophecy applies to Him whom we profess as our Christ."

"I will be absolutely without blame in my obligations to you, if I endeavor to convince you with every possible proof. But, if you persist in your obstinacy of heart and feebleness of mind, or if you refuse to agree to the truth through fear of the death which awaits every Christian (i.e. the death penalty for being a Christian), you will have only yourselves to blame. And you are sadly mistaken if you think that, just because you are descendants of Abraham according to the flesh, you will share in the legacy of benefits which God promised would be distributed by Christ. No one can by any means participate in any of these gifts, except those who have the same ardent faith as Abraham, and who approve of all the mysteries. For I say that some precepts were given for the worship of God and the practice of virtue, whereas other commandments and customs were arranged either in respect to the mystery of Christ [or] the hardness of your people's hearts. . . . As men who have cut your souls off from this hope, it is necessary that you know how to obtain pardon of your sins and a hope of sharing in the promised blessings. There is no other way than this, that you come to know our Christ, be baptized with the baptism which cleanses you of sin (as Isaiah testified), and thus live a life free of sin."

8.6.2 Aphrahat: The Rejection of Israel[166]

Aphrahat was a fourth-century bishop of the Syrian Church at Mar Mattai near Nineveh in what was Assyria. In this treatise, written in Syriac in 344 C.E., the author tries to prove that the one, chosen people was rejected because of sin and was replaced in God's plan by the Gentile nations of the earth. All the proofs except the last few are from the Hebrew Bible, reinterpreted in a Christian light. Here the Church sees itself as having replaced the Jews as the true Israel.

---

166. Trans. J. Neusner, *Aphrahat and Judaism* (Leiden: E. J. Brill, 1971), pp. 60–61.

꘡

The peoples which were of all languages were called first, before Israel, to the inheritance of the Most High, as God said to Abraham, "I have made you the father of a multitude of peoples" (Gen. 17:5). Moses proclaimed, saying, "The peoples will call to the mountain, and there will they offer sacrifices of righteousness" (Deut. 33:19)....

Isaiah said, "The mountain of the house of the Lord will be established at the head of the mountains and high above the heights. All the peoples will look to it, and many peoples from a distance will come and say, Come, let us go up to the mountain of the Lord, to the house of the God of Jacob. He will teach us his ways, and we shall walk in his paths. For from Zion law will go forth, and the word of the Lord from Jerusalem. He will judge among peoples and will correct all the distant peoples" (Is. 2:2–4). When he judges and corrects them, then will they accept instruction, be changed, and be humbled from their hard-heartedness. "And they shall beat their swords into ploughshares, and their spears into pruning hooks. No longer will a nation take the sword against a nation; no longer will they learn how to make war" (Is. 2:4)....

See, my beloved, that the vocation of the peoples was recorded before the vocation of the people. When they sinned in the wilderness, he said to Moses, "Let me blot out this people, and I shall make you into a people which is greater and more worthy than they" (Ex. 32:10). But because the time of the peoples had not come, and another was [to be] their redeemer, Moses was not persuaded that a redeemer and a teacher would come for the people which was of the peoples, which was greater and more worthy than the people of Israel. On this account it is appropriate that we should name the son of God [with] great and abundant praise, as Isaiah said, "This thing is too small, that you should be for me a servant and restore the scion of Jacob and raise up the staff of Israel. But I have made you a light for the peoples, that you may show my redemption until the ends of the earth" (Is. 49:6)....

Concerning the children of Israel he said, "I shall send a famine in the land, not that they shall hunger for bread, nor that they shall thirst for water, but for hearing the word of the Lord. They shall go from the west to the east and from the south to the north to seek the word of the Lord, but they shall not find it, for he has withdrawn it from them" (Amos 8:11, 12). Moses earlier wrote about them, "When in the end of days many evil things will happen to you, you will say, Because the Lord is not in my midst, these evil things have happened to me" (Deut. 31:17). So it was that they said in the days of Ezekiel, "The Lord has abandoned the land,

and the Lord no longer sees us" (Ez. 8:12). Isaiah said about them, "Your sins have separated between you and your God, and your iniquities have held back good things from you" (Is. 59:2). Again he said, "You will call in my ears with a loud voice, but I shall not hear you" (Ezek. 8:18). Concerning the people which is from the peoples David said, "All you peoples clap hands, and praise God with the sound of praise" (Ps. 47:1). Again he said, "Hear this, all of you peoples, and pay attention, all who dwell on earth" (Ps. 49:1). . . .

Furthermore Isaiah said concerning our redeemer, "I have set you as a covenant for the people and as a light for the peoples" (Is. 42:6). Now how was this covenant for the people? From the time that the light and the redeemer of the peoples came, from that time Israel was restrained from the worship of idols, and they had a true covenant. Concerning this matter Moses said, "I shall provoke you with a people which is no people, and with a foolish people I shall anger you" (Deut. 32:21). By us they are provoked. On our account they do not worship idols, so that they will not be shamed by us, for we have abandoned idols and call lies the thing which our fathers left us. They are angry, their hearts are broken, for we have entered and have become heirs in their place. For theirs was this covenant which they had, not to worship other gods, but they did not accept it. By means of us he provoked them, and ours was the light and the life, as he preached, saying when he taught, "I am the light of the world" (John 8:12). Again he said, "Believe while the light is with you, before the darkness overtakes you" (John 12:35). And again he said, "Walk in the light, so that you may be called the children of light" (John 12:36). And further he said, "The light gave light in the darkness" (John 1:5). This is the covenant which the people had, and the light which gave light for all the peoples, and lamed and hindered them from crooked ways, as it is written, "In his coming the rough place will be smooth, and the high place will be plain, and the glory of the Lord will be revealed, and all flesh will see the life of God" (Is. 40:4, 5; Luke 3:5, 6).

This brief memorial I have written to you concerning the peoples, because the Jews take pride and say, "We are the people of God and the children of Abraham." But we shall listen to John [the Baptist] who, when they took pride [saying], "We are the children of Abraham," then said to them, "You should not boast and say, Abraham is father unto us, for from these very rocks can God raise up children for Abraham" (Matthew 3:9). Our redeemer said to them, "You are the children of Cain, and not the children of Abraham" (John 8:39, 44). The apostle said, "The branches which sinned were broken off. We were grafted on in their place and are partners in the fat of the olive tree. Now let us not take pride and sin so that we too may not be broken off. Lo, we have been grafted onto the olive tree" (Rom. 11:17, 18). This is the apology against the Jews, because they take pride saying, "We are the children of Abraham, and we are the people of God."

The demonstration on the people and the peoples is completed.

8.6.3 Epiphanius, *Panarion* 29: The Nazarenes[167]

Epiphanius (ca. 315–402 or 3) studied in Egypt, led a monastery in his native Palestine, and then relocated to Cyprus. He devoted his life to fighting heresy and in this connection composed the Panarion, generally known as the Refutation of All Heresies. His account testifies to the existence of Judaizing Christian groups which attempted to combine adherence to the commandments of the Hebrew Bible with belief in the messiahship of Jesus. His attacks on these groups, however, betray the theological anti-Judaism that was typical of Byzantine Christianity.

(1,3) All Christians were called Nazarenes once. For a short time they were also given the name Iessaians, before the disciples in Antioch began to be called Christians. (1,4) And they were called Iessaians because of Jesse, it seems to me, since David was from Jesse, and by lineage Mary was of the seed of David, fulfilling the holy scriptures according to the Old Testament when the Lord said to David (Ps. 131:11 [Greek=Hebrew 132:11]), "From the fruit of your loins will I set upon your throne. . . ."

(3,3) With the coming of Christ, the succession of leaders of Judah came to an end. Until him the anointed kings ruled, but the order crumbled and ceased when he was born in Bethlehem of Judaea, in the time of Alexander,[168] who was of priestly and royal stock. After Alexander, this office crumbled, from the time of Salina (also called Alexandra),[169] during the years of Herod the king and Augustus the Roman emperor. This same Alexander, one of the anointed rulers, also placed the diadem on himself. (3,5) For joining together the two tribes, both royal and priestly, in other words Judah and Aaron and the whole tribe of Levi, he became king and priest. For not one of the figurative sayings of holy scripture has gone astray. (3,6) Moreover, the foreign king Herod then assumed the diadem, and there were no longer any descendants of David. (3,7) And after the

---

167. Trans. R. Pritz, *Nazarene Jewish Christianity*, (Jerusalem–Leiden: Magnes Press, E.J. Brill, 1988), pp. 30–35.

168. Alexander Janneus ruled 103–76 B.C.E., so Epiphanius' chronology is not correct.

169. Salome Alexandra ruled 76–67 B.C.E.

royal seat was changed, the royal honor was transferred in Christ from its fleshly dwelling of Judah and Israel to the Church, and the throne has been established forever in the holy church of God. It holds this honor from two aspects, both royal and high-priestly—(3,8) that is, it holds the royal honor from our Lord Jesus Christ according to two ways: both because he is from the seed of King David according to the flesh and because he is the very one who is the greater eternal king by virtue of his divine nature. The priestly honor it holds, because he who is high priest and chief of high priests afterward was installed as the first bishop: James, (3,9) called apostle and brother of the Lord. (He was the physical son of Joseph by lineage and called 'the brother of the Lord' because he lived closely together with him.). . . .

(4,9) There is also much to say about this; however, I have come to the passage because of which those who had believed in Christ were called Iessaians[170] before they were called Christians, and because of this I said that Jesse was the father of David; and either on the basis of this Jesse or from the name of Jesus our Lord they were named Iessaians—because they began from Jesus, being his disciples, or because of the etymology of the name of the Lord, for Jesus in the Hebrew dialect means either healer or physician and savior.[171] (4,10) Be that as it may, they acquired this name before they were called by the name Christians. But in the time of Antioch, as if we were named from above and because our way of life had to do with the truth, the disciples and all the church of God began to be called Christians.

(5,1) But you may also find, O Philologist, the way of life of these we are discussing in the writings of Philo, in his book written about the Iessaioi.[172] When he relates in full their custom in words of praise, depicting their monasticism in the area surrounding the Mareotis Lake, the man is not telling about Christians. (5,2) For he was in the region [the area is called Mareotis], and staying for a while among them, he was helped in the monasteries of the region. (5,3) And as he was there during the days of Pascha (Passover), he even observed their customs, how some extended their fast right through the holy week of Pascha,[173] while others were eating every second day, and still others were eating evening by evening. But,

---

170. Here he relates the early Christians to the Essenes, termed here Iessaians, whose name he falsely relates to that of Jesse, father of King David. Behind this etymology is the claim that the Essenes were forerunners of Christianity.

171. Two roots are confused here, since *ysh'*, the root of *yeshua'*, Jesus, means "save," and *'sy*, the supposed root of Iessaians, means "heal."

172. Essenes. See Philo's description above, text 6.3.4.

173. In truth, Jews do not fast during Passover.

as I said, all of these matters have been worked out by the man in his treatise pertaining to the faith and the practices of the Christians.[174] (5,4) When they were once called Iessaians during a short period, some again withdrew at that time after the ascension of the Lord when Mark preached in the land of Egypt. They were so-called followers of the apostles, but I suppose that they were Nazarenes[175] who are described by me here. By birth they are Jews and they dedicate themselves to the Law and submit to circumcision. . . . (5,6) For after having heard the name of Jesus only and having seen the divine signs performed by the hands of the apostles, they also believed in Jesus. When they came to know that he was conceived in Nazareth and had grown up in the house of Joseph and therefore is called Jesus the Nazarene in the Gospel, as also the apostles say: "Jesus the Nazarene, a man made known by signs and miracles," etc., they gave themselves this name calling themselves Nazarenes—(5,7) not Naziraeans, which translated means sanctified ones. . . .[176]

(6,1) But they also did not call themselves Nasaraeans, for the heresy of the Nasaraeans existed before Christ and they did not know him. (6,2) However, everyone called the Christians Nazarenes, as I said before. . . .

(6,7) Likewise the holy disciples of Christ called themselves disciples of Jesus, which they really were. When they heard the name Nazarenes from others, they did not reject it, because they saw what was meant by those who called them by this name, viz., that they called them by this name because of Christ, since our Lord himself was also called Jesus the Nazarene, as appears from the Gospels and the Acts of the Apostles. (6,8) For he grew up in the city of Nazareth, at the time a village, in the house of Joseph after being born according to the flesh in Bethlehem of Mary, ever virgin, who was betrothed to Joseph. He moved to that same Nazareth when he settled down in Galilee after his departure from Bethlehem.

(7,1) These heresies, just mentioned, of which we here are giving a brief sketch, passing over the name of Jesus, did not call themselves Iessaians and did not keep the name Jews; they did not call themselves Christians, but Nazarenes, taking this name from the place Nazareth, but actually they remained wholly Jewish and nothing else. (7,2) For they use not only the New Testament but also the Old, like the Jews. For the Legislation and the Prophets and the Scriptures, which are called the Bible by the Jews, are not rejected by them as they are by those mentioned above. They are not at all mindful of other things but live according to the

---

174. No such treatise exists.
175. A group of Jewish Christians of his own day.
176. Naziraeans is said to designate Nazirites. Cf. Num. 6:1–21.

preaching of the Law as among Jews: there is no fault to find with them apart from the fact that they have come to believe in Christ. (7,3) For they also accept the resurrection of the dead and that everything has its origin in God. They proclaim one God and his Son Jesus Christ. (7.4) They have a good mastery of the Hebrew language. For the entire Law and the Prophets and what is called the Scriptures, I mention the poetical books, Kings, Chronicles and Esther and all the others, are read by them in Hebrew as is the case with the Jews, of course.

(7,5) Only in this respect they differ from the Jews and Christians: with the Jews they do not agree because of their belief in Christ, with the Christians because they are trained in the Law, in circumcision, the Sabbath and the other things. . . . (7,7) This heresy of the Nazarenes exists in Beroea[177] in the neighborhood of Coele Syria and the Decapolis in the region of Pella[178] and in Basanitis[179] in the so-called Kokabe, Chochabe in Hebrew. (7,8) For from there it took its beginning after the exodus from Jerusalem when all the disciples went to live in Pella because Christ had told them to leave Jerusalem and to go away since it would undergo a siege. Because of this advice they lived in Perea after having moved to that place, as I said. There the Nazarene heresy had its beginning. . . .

(9,1) The brevity of this exposition will also be sufficient for this heresy. For such people make a fine object to be refuted and are easy to catch, for they are rather Jews and nothing else. (9,2) However, they are very much hated by the Jews. For not only the Jewish children cherish hate against them but the people also stand up in the morning, at noon, and in the evening, three times a day and they pronounce curses and maledictions over them when they say their prayers in the synagogues.[180] Three times a day they say: "May God curse the Nazarenes." (9,3) For they are more hostile against them because they proclaim as Jews that Jesus is the Christ, which runs counter to those who still are Jews who did not accept Jesus.

---

177. Territory east of the Jordan River, more generally known as Perea.
178. In Transjordan.
179. The region of the Bashan in upper Transjordan, east of the Sea of Galilee.
180. A reference to the benediction against the Jewish Christians. See above, text 8.5.2.

9

Revolt and Restoration

The Great Revolt of the Jews against Rome in 66–73 C.E. was a turning point for Judaism in many ways. Many scholars have greatly exaggerated the changes which resulted from the Revolt, seeing the very development of Judaism as we know it as postdating the destruction of the Temple in 70 C.E. While such highly exaggerated conclusions should be rejected in light of the increasing evidence for continuity between the pre- and post-destruction eras, the other extreme should also be avoided. One cannot deny the essential differences between the Judaism of the Second Temple period and that which emerged from the embers of the destruction of the Temple. Accordingly, we present in this chapter a variety of sources relating to the revolt itself as a political and military event and then texts pertaining to the impact of these events on the religious history of the Jews.

Our primary source for the beginnings of the Revolt is Josephus, *War* (text 9.1.1) wherein he describes the outbreak of the Revolt amongst a group of lower clergy around whom there soon assembled revolutionary forces that had been continually opposing Roman rule since its onset in 63 B.C.E. When it became clear that the Revolt was a serious matter, Nero, the Roman emperor, appointed Vespasian, one of his leading generals, to quell the Revolt, as described also by Josephus (text 9.1.2.).

A full description of the military details of the Revolt is not possible in this context, but a number of important battles as well as the story of the fall of Jerusalem are included here. In *War* Josephus gives a detailed account of the battle for Gamala (text 9.1.3) in which we get a sense of his own ambivalence to his early career as a commander of rebel forces. Josephus' involvement in the uprising and his eventual decision to support the Romans in their efforts to quell the violence led to his ambiguous position in Jewish tradition. His own writings seem to have been rejected, whereas Hebrew chronicles derived from his work circulated extensively in the Middle Ages. Josephus describes in great detail the battle for Jerusalem (text 9.1.4), which eventually led to the destruction of the Temple. By this time, Vespasian had become emperor, and his son, Titus, was now prosecuting the war.

All the rebel groups and parties had now regrouped in Jerusalem, yet Josephus provides evidence of their inability to cooperate—a claim also alluded to by talmudic sources as a reason for the failure of the Revolt. Further, he provides ample evidence of the complex military tactics and extensive machinery used by the Romans. The siege eventually led to horrible conditions inside Jerusalem as also described by Josephus (text 9.1.5). Josephus dwelled upon the misery of the inhabitants, believing as he did that the Revolt had been a tragic error brought upon the nation by extremist elements. The general course of the Revolt is described as well by the Roman historian Tacitus (text 9.1.6) but with much less detail. Tacitus' account, however, does not support Josephus' tendency to exonerate the Romans from cruelty and brutality.

The Babylonian Talmud Gittin (text 9.1.7) presents an aggadic account of the siege which extracts from it the lesson of the need for Jewish unity while emphasizing the horrible conditions the rebels faced. This account also explains the continuation of Rabbinic tradition at Yavneh by telling the story of the smuggling of Rabbi Yoḥanan ben Zakkai out of Jerusalem on the eve of the destruction. It was he, according to this text, who asked the Roman general Vespasian to allow him to continue the Rabbinic tradition at the Yavneh academy. This narrative clearly places Rabbi Yoḥanan ben Zakkai in the camp of those who preferred accommodation to Rome rather than the destructive pursuit of rebellion.

Josephus in *War* (text 9.1.8) describes the final defeat of the Jews and the destruction of the Jerusalem Temple. His account portrays the Romans as seeking to spare the Temple but being forced by the actions of the Jews to allow it to burn. Here Josephus is following his basic inclination to exonerate the Romans and blame Jewish extremists for the national tragedy. But Dio Cassius (text 9.1.9), writing from a Roman point of view and describing as well the details of the difficult battle which the Romans were forced to fight, says that the Temple was set afire by the Romans in the course of the battle.

After the destruction of the Temple, the Romans were faced with conquering one final Jewish stronghold, the fortress of Masada on the shore of the Dead Sea. Josephus' description of this siege in *War* (text 9.1.10) has become a literary classic despite the fact that scholars have disputed its veracity. Josephus tells the dramatic story of the suicide of the Sicarii who defended the fortress, preferring death to capture by the Romans. Regardless of the heroism of the defenders, Masada fell to the Romans; the Revolt had finally been crushed.

The destruction of the Temple and the nation led to a number of subsequent developments. The Roman author Suetonius (text 9.2.1) tells of how the Temple tax, the half-shekel which Jews donated annually to the Jerusalem Temple, was now turned into a tax on all Jews throughout the Roman Empire, for whom this new tax, the *Fiscus Judaicus*, was a sign of disgrace and conquest. That Jews initially went to extremes in mourning for the destruction of the Temple is shown in Tosefta Sotah (text 9.2.3.). Yet Rabbinic authority was marshaled to place limits on the extent of such mourning and the interruption of normal life. Indeed, the Rabbis seem to have succeeded in balancing grief for the tragic outcome of the Revolt against the need to face the challenges of the coming centuries.

In fact, it is in this period, immediately after the destruction of the Temple, that we first encounter epigraphical Rabbis, that is, those mentioned in inscriptions found in archaeological context. Such a Rabbi appears in the inscription from the Bet Alpha Synagogue (text 9.3.1). The synagogue as an institution was already in existence before the destruction of the Temple, but its growth thereafter as the fundamental Jewish place of worship and holy place in the absence of a sacrificial Temple is documented in this and many other inscriptions. The inscription from the Ein Gedi Synagogue (text 9.3.2), like that of the Galilean synagogues, describes not only biblical motifs but also calendrical matters and the names of the builders or donors. This inscription, however, is unique for the curse upon anybody who reveals the secret of the town to the Gentiles.

Synagogues were also found in the Diaspora among Greek-speaking Jews. The inscription from Corinth (text 9.3.3) shows the presence there of a synagogue in a community which was also central to the development of Gentile Christianity. The term "synagogue," however, as used in Greek, designated the Jewish communal organization, and inscriptions show that women could serve as archisynagogue, the head of the synagogue, as is shown in an inscription from Rome (text 9.3.4). Exceedingly important is the Theodotus inscription from Jerusalem (text 9.3.5), which proves the existence of the synagogue as an institution in Jerusalem before the destruction of the Temple. It also attests to the functions of the synagogue, including the reading of the Torah, the study of the commandments, the housing of guests, and provision for those in need.

It was not long until the Romans restored a modicum of Jewish autonomy, placing control of Jewish affairs in the hands of the Rabbis, who were the successors to the Pharisees of Second Temple times. According to many scholars, the patriarchs, leaders of the Rabbinic academy, already enjoyed formally recognized authority under Roman rule in the late first century. If so, this would explain the very strong hand exercised by Rabban Gamliel II, as described in the Babylonian Talmud Berakhot (text 9.4.1). Even if Rabban Gamliel was attempting to maintain firm control because of the need to preserve Jewish authority under Rome, this account makes clear that his colleagues would not tolerate his overbearing rule and sought to impeach him. The narrative also includes many details of importance for understanding the Rabbinic movement and its leadership.

We should pause to consider briefly Josephus himself, the historian without whose work it would be impossible to understand the Revolt and its aftermath. Indeed, he himself was a product of the Revolt and the years following it. He provides us in *Life* (text 9.5.1) with numerous details of his autobiography in which he unstintingly praises his own wisdom. Perhaps more importantly here, he portrays himself as having known all along that the Revolt was a catastrophic mistake. Josephus tells us (text 9.5.2) that after the Revolt, Titus and

Vespasian brought him to Rome where he enjoyed royal patronage while writing the rest of his works. From his Preface to *War* (text 9.5.3), we learn of Josephus' dedication to establishing historical truth, but we must read such passages with a full understanding that Greco-Roman historiography allowed greater latitude of interpretation than do contemporary academic standards. In one passage in *Antiquities* (text 9.5.4), we learn that even an accurate historical account must be written in a style that makes it pleasant to read. Modern scholarship has, for the most part, agreed with Josephus about the need for accurate historical accounts and has dedicated itself extensively to ferreting out the accurate details from the sometimes tendentious historiographic writing of Josephus and other ancient authors.

Despite the return to normalcy soon after the Great Revolt, it was not long until the very same social, political, and religious forces which had led the Jews of Palestine into revolt against Rome would once again flare up. But the sources for the Bar Kokhba Revolt are nowhere near as extensive as the account which Josephus provides us of the earlier rebellion. A short account is, however, given by Dio Cassius (text 9.6.1). Eusebius (text 9.6.2), a Christian writer, also documents the suffering and death brought on by the Roman victory in 135 C.E. and the renaming of Jerusalem as Aelia Capitolina.

Archaeological excavation has revealed perhaps the most exciting evidence of the Bar Kokhba revolt, namely, letters from the leader of the revolt, Simeon bar Kosiba (text 9.6.3). These dramatic documents throw light on the administration of Judea during the Revolt as well as on the steps taken by the rebel leaders as Roman forces began to gain the upper hand. The Jerusalem Talmud Ta'anit testifies to a debate as to whether to support the Bar Kokhba rebellion or not (text 9.6.4). This text clearly indicates that some tannaim believed Bar Kokhba to be the messiah, and there is good reason to believe that many Jews who participated in the Revolt were motivated by messianic fervor. The horrible destruction brought about by the Roman suppression of the Revolt is highlighted in this account, as it is in the Church Fathers. This text further tries to explain Bar Kokhba's defeat as resulting from the death of an innocent Rabbi who was suspected of being an informer. This indicates the inability of the Rabbis to understand why the Revolt was not

successful. Indeed, the destruction is also documented in the Babylonian Talmud Gittin (text 9.6.5) which discusses the final conquest
of the rebels' last stronghold, Betar.

Just as recovery had been swift after the Great Revolt, so again the
land began to recover after the Bar Kokhba Revolt. The Romans
relied upon Rabbinic sages to maintain the internal administration
of Jewish affairs. Soon after the Bar Kokhba Revolt, the sages reas-
sembled at Usha, which became the seat of the Rabbinic academy,
as indicated in *Song of Songs Rabbah* (text 9.7.1). The edict against
circumcision was reversed, but it was nonetheless forbidden, as
Modestinus testifies (text 9.7.2), for the Jews to circumcise Gentiles
who sought to convert to Judaism.

By the time the dust had settled, recovery had proceeded quickly
enough that by the end of the century the Rabbis of Roman Palestine would be prepared to edit the Mishnah, the fundamental compilation of tannaitic law. With the political independence of the
Jewish state at an end after two unsuccessful revolts, Judaism turned
to the building of the talmudic edifice.

9.1 THE GREAT REVOLT

9.1.1 Josephus, *War* II, 405–48:
The First Stage of the Revolt

Josephus tells the story of how Jewish discontent with Roman rule soon
flared into open revolt. He chronicles the inner Jewish struggle between the
incipient Jewish revolutionaries and the pro-Roman aristocracy.

৯৫

(405) This advice the people hearkened to,[1] and they went up into the
temple with the king[2] and Bernice and began to rebuild the porticoes.
The magistrates and members of the council also divided themselves into
the villages and collected the tribute, and soon got together forty talents
which was the sum that was owed. (406) Thus did Agrippa then put a stop
to that war which was threatened. Later he attempted to persuade that
multitude to obey Florus until Caesar would send someone to succeed
him. But they were thereby more provoked, cast reproaches upon the

---

1. Agrippa advised the people to avoid war with Rome by paying their taxes and
rebuilding the porticoes they had destroyed.
2. Agrippa II (28–92 C.E.), the last Herodian king.

king, and had him excluded from the city. Indeed, some of the rebellious had the impudence to throw stones at him. (407) So when the king saw that the violence of those who were for revolution was not to be restrained, and being very angry at the insults he had received, he sent their magistrates together with their men of power to Florus, to Caesarea, so that he might appoint whom he thought fit to collect tribute in the country. [Agrippa] then retired into his own kingdom.[3]

(408) At this time, some of those that principally excited the people to go to war made an assault upon a certain fortress called Masada. They took it by treachery, killed the Romans who were there, and installed a garrison of their own party in their place. (409) At the same time, Eleazar, the son of Ananias the high priest,[4] a very bold youth who was at that time governor of the temple, persuaded those who officiated in the divine service to receive no gift or sacrifice from any foreigner. This was the true beginning of our war with the Romans for they rejected the sacrifice of Caesar on this account. (410) When many of the high priests and principal men besought them not to omit the sacrifice which it was customary for them to offer for their rulers, they would not be prevailed upon. They relied much upon their numbers, for the stalwarts of the revolutionaries assisted them, but they relied above all on the authority of Eleazar, the governor of the temple.

(411) Then the men of power got together and conferred with the high priests, as did also the most notable of the Pharisees, and thinking that all was at stake and that their calamities were becoming incurable, they took counsel as to what was to be done. Accordingly, they determined to try an appeal to the revolutionaries. . . .

(417) As they spoke, they produced those priests who were expert in the traditions of their country, who reported that all their forefathers had received sacrifices from foreign nations. But still not one of the revolutionaries would hearken to what was said: Indeed, those who ministered in the temple failed to come to their support but were preparing matters for beginning the war. . . .

(422) Upon this the men of power with the high priests, and the part of the multitude who were desirous of peace, took courage and seized the upper city [Mount Zion]; for the revolutionaries held the lower city and the temple in their power. (423) They constantly made use of stones and slings against one another, and threw darts continually on both sides, and sometimes it happened that they made excursions by troops and fought it

---

3. At this time Agrippa II ruled over what is today the Golan Heights and part of the Galilee. He also had the right to appoint high priests in Jerusalem.

4. Ananias had served as high priest from 47–59 C.E.

out hand to hand. The revolutionaries were superior in boldness, but the king's soldiers[5] in skill. (424) The latter strove chiefly to gain the temple and to drive out of it those who profaned it. Eleazar and the rebels labored to gain the upper city in addition to what they held already. Thus there were continual slaughters on both sides for seven days, but neither side would surrender the portion of town they had seized.

(425) The next day was the festival of wood-offering[6] on which the custom was for everyone to bring wood for the altar (so that there might never be a lack of fuel for that fire which was unquenchable and always burning). On that day, the Jews in the temple excluded the opposite party from the ceremony. And when they had joined to themselves many of the Sicarii (that was the name for such robbers as had under their bosoms swords called *sicae*) who crowded in among the weaker people, they grew bolder and carried their undertakings further. (426) Since the king's soldiers were overpowered by their multitude and boldness, they gave way and were driven out of the upper city by force. The others then set fire to the house of Ananias the high priest and to the palaces of Agrippa and Bernice. (427) Then they carried the fire to the place where the archives were deposited, and made haste to burn the contracts belonging to their creditors in order to dissolve their obligations to pay their debts. This was done in order to gain the support of the multitude of those who had been debtors, to persuade the poorer sort to join in their insurrection with safety against the more wealthy; so the keepers of the records fled away and the rest set fire to them. (428) When they had thus burned down the nerve center of the city, they fell upon their enemies. This time some of the men of power and the high priests went into the vaults under ground and concealed themselves, (429) while others fled with the king's soldiers to the upper palace and shut the gates immediately, among whom were Ananias the high priest, his brother Hezekiah, and the ambassadors that had been sent to Agrippa. Now the revolutionaries were content with the victory they had achieved and the buildings they had burned down and proceeded no further.

(430) But on the next day, which was the fifteenth of the month Lous [Ab],[7] they made an assault upon Antonia and besieged the garrison which was in it for two days. They then took the garrison, killed them, and set the citadel on fire. (431) After this they marched to the palace, to

---

5. The soldiers of Agrippa II.

6. Although wood was brought several times during the year, Josephus is referring to the 15th of Av (July/August). The events, however seem to have taken place on the 14th in light of section 430.

7. July/August.

which the king's soldiers had fled, divided themselves into four bodies, and made an attack upon the walls. As for those who were within it, no one had the courage to sally out, because those who assaulted them were so numerous. But they posted themselves in the breast-works and turrets and shot at the besiegers, whereby many of the robbers fell beneath the walls. (432) Nor did they cease to fight one another by night or by day since the revolutionaries supposed that those within would grow weary for lack of food, and those outside supposed that the others would do the same by the fatigue of the siege.

(433) In the meantime, one Menaḥem the son of Judas, called the Galilean (who was a very cunning sophist and had formerly reproached the Jews under Quirenius, that after God they were subject to the Romans) took some of the men of note with him and retired to Masada (434) where he broke open King Herod's armory and gave arms not only to his own people but to other robbers[8] also. These he made use of for a bodyguard and returned in the state of a king to Jerusalem. He became the leader of the revolt and gave orders for continuing the siege. (435) But they lacked proper equipment, and it was not practicable to undermine the wall because the darts came down upon them from above. But still they dug a tunnel from a great distance under one of the towers and made it totter, and, having done that, they set on fire what was combustible and left it. (436) When the foundations were burnt below, the tower fell down suddenly. Yet they then met with another wall that had been built inside, for the besieged were aware beforehand of what they were doing, and probably the tower shook as it was being undermined, so they provided themselves with another fortification. (437) When the besiegers unexpectedly saw it, although they thought they had already conquered the place, they were in considerable consternation. However, those who were within sent to Menaḥem and to the other leaders of the revolt requesting that they might leave upon capitulation. This was granted to the king's soldiers and their own countrymen only, who went out accordingly, (438) but the Romans who were left alone were greatly dejected for they were not able to force their way through such a multitude. To sue for terms they thought would be a reproach to them and, besides, if they should give it to them, they dared not depend upon them. (439) So they deserted their camp, as easily taken, and ran away to the royal towers—that called Hippicus, that called Phasael, and that called Mariamne. (440) But Menaḥem and his party fell upon the place from which the soldiers had fled, and killed as many of them as they could catch before they

---

8. The term "robber" often refers to revolutionaries.

got up to the towers, plundered what they had left behind them, and set
fire to their camp. This took place on the sixth day of the month Gor-
pieus [Elul].[9]

(441) But on the next day the high priest was caught where he had
concealed himself in an aqueduct; he was killed together with Hezekiah
his brother by the robbers. Then the revolutionaries besieged the towers
and kept them guarded, lest any one of the soldiers should escape. (442)
Now the overthrow of the strongholds and the death of the high priest
Ananias so puffed up Menaḥem that he became barbarously cruel and, as
he thought he had no antagonists to dispute the management of affairs
with him, he was no better than an insufferable tyrant. (443) But Eleazar
and his party, when words had passed between them, remarked how it was
not proper when they had revolted against the Romans out of the desire
for liberty to betray that liberty to any of their own people, and to bear a
lord who, though he should be guilty of no violence, was yet inferior to
themselves. If they were obliged to set someone over their public affairs,
it was fitter they should give that privilege to anyone rather than to him.
Accordingly, they assaulted him in the temple (444) for he had gone there
to worship in a pompous manner, adorned with royal garments, and had
his followers with him in their armor. (445) But Eleazar and his party fell
violently upon him, as did the rest of the people, and taking up stones to
attack him, they threw them at the sophist [Menaḥem], and thought that
if he were once ruined, his downfall would crush the entire revolt. (446)
Now Menaḥem and his party offered resistance for a while, but when
they perceived that the whole multitude was falling upon them, they fled
wherever they could. Those who were caught were killed, and those who
hid themselves were searched for. (447) There were a few of them who
privately escaped to Masada, among whom was Eleazar, the son of Yair,
who was a relative of Menaḥem's, and he acted the part of a tyrant at Masada afterward.[10] (448) As for Menaḥem himself, he ran away to the place
called Ophla,[11] and there lay hiding in private. But they took him alive
and dragged him out before them all. They then tortured him with many
sorts of torments and afterwards killed him, as they did to those who
were captains under him also, and particularly to the principle supporter
of his tyranny whose name was Absalom.

---

9. August/September.

10. It was Eleazar ben Yair who convinced the defenders of Masada, in Josephus's
account, to commit mass suicide.

11. The Ophel, a place in the lower city.

9.1.2 Josephus, *War* III, 1–7:
The Appointment of Vespasian as General

The emperor Nero feared that the Jewish revolt and the initial successes of the Jews would serve as a stimulus to the Eastern provinces to rise against their Roman conquerors. Accordingly, for strategic reasons he determined to send his best general, Vespasian, to put down the revolt in Judea. Josephus, attributing to God historical causation, suggests that Vespasian was chosen in order that he could be prepared to become emperor.

જે

(1) When Nero was informed of the Romans' reverses in Judea, . . . (3) as he was deciding to whom he should commit the care of the east which was in so great a commotion, and who might be best able to punish the Jews for their rebellion and might prevent the same revolt from spreading to the neighboring nations also, (4) he found no one but Vespasian equal to the task. . . .

(6) So Nero saw that Vespasian's age gave him sure experience and great skill, and that he had his sons as hostages for his fidelity to himself, and that the flourishing age they were in would make them fit instruments under their father's guidance. Perhaps also there was some interposition of Providence which was paving the way for Vespasian himself becoming emperor afterwards. (7) He sent this man to take upon him the command of the armies in Syria. . . .

9.1.3 Josephus, *War* IV, 1–82: The Battle at Gamala

In the account of the battle for Gamala, we encounter Josephus' description of his own involvement as a rebel commander, a role he claimed he never really pursued wholeheartedly. Gamala was an impregnable fortress located in the lower Golan, and its conquest by the Romans was a harbinger of their conquest of the rest of Judea.

જે

(1) Now all those Galileans who, after the taking of Jotapata,[12] had revolted against the Romans, upon the conquest of Taricheae[13] surrendered to them again. And the Romans received all the fortresses and the

---

12. Hebrew, Yodefat, a Galilean fortress 6 miles north of the talmudic period town of Sepphoris.
13. On the southern end of Lake Tiberias.

cities, excepting Gischala[14] and those who had occupied Mount Tabor.[15]
(2) Gamala[16] also, which is a city across from Taricheae, but on the other
side of the lake,[17] conspired with them. . . .

(4) Agrippa had come to terms with Sogana and Seleucia[18] at the very
beginning of the revolt, but Gamala did not accede to them, but relied
upon the difficulty of its position which was greater than that of Jotapata,
(5) for it was situated upon a rough ridge of a high mountain with a kind
of hump in the middle. . . .

(9) Although this city was naturally impregnable, Josephus made it still
stronger by building a wall about it and by ditches and mines under
ground. (10) The people who were in it were made more bold by the
nature of the place than the people of Jotapata had been, but it had much
fewer fighting men in it. They had such confidence in the location of the
place that they did not permit any more fighters to enter. For the city had
been filled with those who had fled to it for safety on account of its
strength, because of which they had been able to resist those whom
Agrippa sent to besiege it for seven months. . . .

(11) But Vespasian moved his camp from Ammathus[19] where he had last
pitched his camp before the city Tiberias . . . and came to Gamala. . . .
(17) Now when the earthworks were finished, which was done rapidly
by a multitude of hands which were accustomed to such work, they
brought the machines. (18) Chares and Joseph, who were the most prominent men of the city, set their armed men in order, though already they
were afraid because they did not suppose that the city could hold out
long since they did not have a sufficient quantity either of water or of
other supplies. (19) However, their leaders encouraged them and brought
them out upon the wall, and for a while indeed they drove away those
who were bringing the machines. But when those machines threw darts
and stones at them, they retired into the city. (20) Then the Romans
brought battering rams to three different places and made the wall shake
[and fall]. They then poured in over the parts of the wall that were thrown
down with a mighty sound of trumpets and noise of armor and with a
shout of the soldiers, and they broke in by force upon those who were in
the city. (21) But these men fell upon the Romans for some time at their

---

14. Hebrew, Gush Ḥalav, an ancient city in the upper Galilee, 5 miles northwest of
Safed.
15. A mountain in the northeast part of the Jezreel Valley in the Galilee.
16. A fortress in the Golan Heights.
17. Lake Tiberias, also known as the Sea of Galilee.
18. These cities did not participate in the revolt.
19. South of Tiberias, known today as Ḥamat Tiberias.

first entrance and prevented their going any farther, and with great courage beat them back.

(22) The Romans were so overpowered by the greater multitude of the people, who beat them on every side, that they were obliged to run into the upper parts of the city. Then the people turned about and fell upon their enemies who had attacked them and thrust them down to the lower parts, and as they were impeded by the narrowness and difficulty of the place, killed them. (23) As these Romans could neither beat back those who were above them, nor escape the force of their own men who were forcing their way forward, they were compelled to flee into their enemies' houses which were on the ground. (24) These houses, being thus full of soldiers whose weight they could not bear, fell down suddenly; and when one house fell, it pushed down a great many of those that were under it, as those did to those that were under them. (25) By this means a vast number of the Romans perished. For they were so terribly distressed that although they saw the houses collapsing, they were compelled to leap upon their rooftops. A great many were buried by these ruins, and a great many of those who escaped from under them lost some of their limbs, but still a greater number were suffocated by the dust that arose from the ruins. (26) The people of Gamala supposed this to be an assistance afforded them by God, and without regard for the damage they suffered, they pressed forward and thrust the enemy upon the tops of their houses; and when they stumbled in the narrow streets, they threw their stones or darts at them, and killed them. . . .

(62) But of the people of Gamala, those that were of the bolder sort fled and hid themselves, while the more infirm perished by famine; (63) but the men of war sustained the siege till the twenty-second day of the month Hyperberetaeus [Tishri],[20] when three soldiers of the fifteenth legion, about the time of the morning watch, crept up to a high tower that was near and undermined it without making any noise. . . . (70) . . . Titus . . . took two hundred chosen horsemen and some footmen with him and entered without noise into the city. . . .

(74) Now the upper part of the city was rocky all over, difficult of ascent, elevated to a vast height, very full of people on all sides, and encompassed with precipices. (75) Here the Jews cut off those who advanced against them and did much mischief to others by their darts and the large stones which they rolled down upon them, while they were themselves so high that the enemy's darts could hardly reach them. (76) However, there arose a miraculous storm against them which was instru-

---

20. November 9, 67 C.E.

mental in their destruction. It carried the Roman darts upon them and made those which they threw return back. (77) Nor could the Jews indeed stand upon their precipices, because of the violence of the wind, having nothing that was stable to stand on, nor could they see the approaching enemy. (78) The Romans got up and surrounded them. Some they killed before they could defend themselves, and others as they were surrendering, and the remembrance of those who were killed at their initial entrance into the city increased their rage against them now. (79) A great number also of those who were surrounded on every side, despairing of escape, threw their children and their wives, and themselves also, down the precipices, into the valley beneath which, near the citadel, had been dug hollow to a vast depth. (80) So it happened that the anger of the Romans appeared not to be as great as the madness of those who were now conquered. While the Romans killed only four thousand, the number of those who had thrown themselves over the cliff was found to be five thousand. (81) Nor did anyone escape except two women who were nieces on the mother's side of Philip, the son of an eminent man called Jacimus, who had been general of King Agrippa's army. (82) They escaped because they lay concealed from the sight of the Romans when the city was taken, for otherwise they spared not so much as the infants, of whom many were flung down by them from the citadel. . . .

9.1.4 Josephus, *War* V, 1–84, 269–88:
The Battle of Jerusalem

After subduing the entire country, the Romans turned toward Jerusalem, the conquest of which would decide the war. Josephus' detailed narrative is an eyewitness account of that battle, although it was clearly shaped by his own pro-Roman prejudices. Clearly, Jewish disunity in the revolt was one of the causes of its failure, as seen in this selection.

ℵ

(1) When, therefore, Titus[21] had marched over that desert which lies between Egypt and Syria, in the manner described above, he came to Caesarea, having resolved to set his forces in order at that place, before he began the war. (2) But while he was assisting his father (Vespasian) at Alexandria in settling that government which had been newly conferred upon them by God, it so happened that the revolt at Jerusalem was

---

21. The son of Vespasian who took over for him as general after his father was named emperor in 69 C.E.

revived, and parted into three factions, one faction fighting against the other. . . .

(5) Eleazar, the son of Simon,[22] who caused the first separation of the Zealots from the people and made them retire into the temple, appeared very angry at John's[23] insolent attempts which he made every day upon the people, for this man never left off murdering. But the truth was that he could not bear to submit to a tyrant who had arisen after him. (6) So being desirous of gaining the entire power and dominion for himself, he revolted against John, and took with him Judas the son of Chelcias and Simon the son of Ezron who were among the men of greatest power. There was also with him Hezekiah the son of Chobar, a person of eminence. (7) Each of these was followed by a great many of the Zealots, and they seized the inner court of the temple and laid their arms upon the holy gates and over the holy fronts of that court. (8) Because they had plenty of provisions, they were of good courage, for there was a great abundance of what was consecrated for sacred use, and they had no compunctions about making use of it. Yet they were afraid on account of their small number, and when they had laid up their arms there, they did not stir from the place they were in. . . .

(71) Whereas beforehand the several parties in Jerusalem had been dashing one against another perpetually, the war from outside, which had now suddenly come upon them in a violent manner, put the first stop to their contentions one against another. (72) The rebels now saw with astonishment the Romans pitching three different camps, so they began to think of an awkward sort of alliance and said one to another, (73) "What are we doing here, and what do we mean when we allow three fortified walls to be built to coop us in so that we will not be able to breathe freely? The enemy is securely building a kind of city in opposition to us while we sit still within our own walls and become mere spectators of what they are doing, with our hands idle and our armor laid by as if they were about something that was for our good and advantage. (74) We are, it seems," so did they cry out, "only courageous against ourselves, while the Romans are likely to gain the city without bloodshed because of our strife." (75) Thus did they encourage one another when they had gotten together. Then they immediately took their armor and ran out against the Tenth Legion, and fell upon the Romans with great eagerness and with a prodigious shout while they were fortifying their camp. (76) These Romans were caught in different groups, organized in order to perform

---

22. A priest who was a Zealot leader.
23. John of Gischala, leader of one of the rebel groups.

their different tasks, and for this reason, they had to a great extent laid aside their arms, for they thought the Jews would never venture to make a sally upon them. And had they been disposed to do so, they supposed that their dissension would distract them. So they were put into disorder unexpectedly. (77) Some of them left their work and immediately marched off, while many ran to their arms but were smitten and killed before they could turn back upon the enemy. . . .

(81) Indeed, things looked as though the entire legion would have been in danger had not Titus been informed of the position they were in and come to their aid immediately. So he reproached them for their cowardice and brought those back who were running away, (82) and fell himself upon the Jews on their flank, with those select troops who were with him, killed a considerable number, wounded more of them, put them all to flight, and made them run away hastily down the valley. (83) Now as these Jews suffered greatly in the declivity of the valley, so, when they had gotten over it, they turned about, and stood against the Romans, having the valley between them, and there fought with them. (84) Thus they continued the fight till noon. When it was already a little after noon, Titus deployed his reinforcements along with those who belonged to the auxiliary cohorts, to prevent the Jews from making any more sallies, and then he sent the rest of the legion to the upper part of the mountain to fortify their camp. . . .

(269) The engines that all the legions had ready prepared for themselves were admirably designed, but still more extraordinary ones belonged to the Tenth Legion. Those that threw darts and those that threw stones were more powerful and larger than the rest. With these they not only repelled the excursions of the Jews, but also drove those away who were upon the walls. (270) The stones that were cast were of the weight of a talent[24] and were carried two furlongs[25] and farther. The blow they gave could in no way be sustained, neither by those who stood first in the way nor by those who were beyond them at a great distance. (271) As for the Jews, they at first watched the coming of the stone, for it was of a white color and could therefore not only be perceived by the great noise it made, but it could be seen also before it came by its brightness. (272) Accordingly, the watchmen upon the towers gave them notice when the engine was fired and the stone came from it, and cried out aloud in their own country's language, "The son is coming!"[26] so that those who were in its way stood

---

24. Approximately 20 kilograms.
25. One-fourth mile.
26. A corruption of Hebrew ha-'even, "the stone," into ha-ben, "the son."

aside and threw themselves down upon the ground so that by their thus guarding themselves, the stone fell down and did them no harm. (273) But the Romans contrived to prevent that by blackening the stone which they then could aim at them with success, for the stone was not discerned beforehand as it had been until then. So they destroyed many of them at one blow. (274) Yet the Jews, under all this distress, did not permit the Romans to raise their embankments easily, but they shrewdly and boldly exerted themselves and repelled them both by night and by day.

(275) And now, when the Roman earthworks were finished, the workmen measured the distance from the wall by lead and line which they threw to it from their embankments. For they could not measure it otherwise because the Jews would shoot at them if they came to measure it themselves. When they found that the battering-rams could reach the wall, they brought them there. (276) Then Titus set his engines at proper distances nearer to the wall so that the Jews might not be able to repel them, and gave orders that they should strike. (277) Thereupon a terrific noise echoed round about from three places, and suddenly there was a great cry made by the citizens within the city, and terror fell upon the rebels as well. Then both groups, seeing the common danger they were in, contrived to make a joint defense. (278) So those of different factions cried out one to another that they were acting entirely in concert with their enemies, whereas, even if God did not grant them lasting agreement, in their present circumstances they ought to lay aside their enmities against one another and unite together against the Romans. Accordingly, Simon proclaimed that those who came from the temple had permission to go upon the wall. John also, though he could not believe Simon was in earnest, gave them the same permission. (279) So both sides laid aside their hatred and their private quarrels and formed themselves into one body. They then ran around the walls, and having a vast number of torches with them, threw them at the machines and shot darts continually upon those who controlled those engines battering the wall. (280) The bolder sort leaped out in bands upon the hurdles that covered the machines and pulled them to pieces, and attacked those operating them and beat them, not so much by any skill they had as by the boldness of their attacks. (281) However, Titus himself sent assistance to those who were the hardest hit, placed both horsemen and archers on the several sides of the engines, and thereby beat off those who shot stones or darts from the towers, and then set the battering-rams to work in earnest. (282) Yet the wall did not yield to these blows, except that the battering-ram of the Fifteenth Legion dislodged the corner of a tower. . . .

(284) The Jews suspended their sallies for a while. However, when they observed the Romans dispersed about the works and in their several camps (for they thought the Jews had retired out of weariness and fear) they suddenly dashed out at the tower Hippicus through a concealed gate, and at the same time brought fire to burn the seige-works, and went boldly up to the Romans—to their very fortifications. (285) At their shouts, the legionaries nearby came immediately to their assistance, and those farther off came running up after them. Here the boldness of the Jews was too much for the good discipline of the Romans. They beat those whom they first fell upon and pressed on against the assembling troops. (286) A fierce conflict took place around the machines, for one side tried hard to set them on fire and the other side to prevent it. On both sides there were confused cries, and many of those in the forefront of the battle were killed. (287) However, the Jews were now too difficult for the Romans to resist due to the furious assaults they made like madmen. The fire caught hold of the siege-works, and both all those works and the engines themselves were in danger of being burnt. But many of the select soldiers from Alexandria stood in opposition and prevented it, and they behaved with greater courage than they themselves supposed they could have done. For in this fight they outdid those who had an even greater reputation than they. This was the state of things until Caesar (Titus) took the stoutest of his horsemen and attacked the enemy. (288) He himself killed twelve of those in the forefront of the Jewish line. The death of these men, when viewed by the rest, caused the remainder to give way so that Caesar pursued them and drove them all into the city, and saved the siege-works from the fire. . . .

9.1.5 Josephus, *War* X, 420–565: The Siege of Jerusalem

In what follows, Josephus describes the horrible conditions the Jews faced in the city as the siege progressed. His own pro-Roman feelings and his deep disgust with the rebel factions comes out clearly in this passage.

❦

(420) As Josephus was speaking thus with a loud voice, the revolutionaries would neither yield to what he said, nor did they deem it safe for them to change their conduct, but as for the people, they had a great inclination to desert to the Romans. . . . (422) For Titus let a great number of them go away into the country to wherever they pleased. They were so ready to desert in order to be freed from those miseries which they had endured in the city and yet not be enslaved by the Romans.

(423) However, John and Simon and their factions watched for these men's escape more carefully than they did the coming in of the Romans, and, if any one afforded the least shadow of suspicion of such an intention, his throat was cut immediately.

(424) But as for the well-to-do, it proved equally fatal to remain in the city or to attempt to get out of it, for every such person was put to death under the pretense that he was going to desert, but in reality the robbers murdered them for their property. . . . (427) There were many who sold what they had for one measure of wheat if they were of the richer sort, or of barley if they were poorer. Then they shut themselves up in the innermost rooms of their houses and ate the grain they had gotten. Some did it without grinding it, because of their extreme hunger, and others baked bread of it as necessity and fear dictated. (428) A table was nowhere laid for a meal, but they snatched the bread out of the fire, half-baked, and ate it very hastily.

(429) It was now a miserable case and a sight that would justly bring tears into our eyes, how the more powerful had more than enough food while the weaker were lamenting (for lack of it). But the famine was too strong for all other passions, and it was destructive to nothing so much as to respect. For what was otherwise worthy of reverence was in this case despised. (430) Children pulled the very morsels that their fathers were eating out of their mouths and, what was still more to be pitied, so did the mothers do to their infants. When those who were most dear were perishing in their arms, they were not ashamed to take from them the very last drops that might preserve their lives. (431) While they ate in this manner, they were not able to conceal their actions, so the rebels everywhere came upon them immediately and snatched away from them what they had gotten from others. (432) For when they saw any house shut up, this was to them a signal that the people within had gotten some food, whereupon they broke open the doors, ran in and took pieces of what they were eating, almost up out of their very throats by force. (433) The old men, holding their food tightly, were beaten, and if the women hid what they had within their hands, they were dragged by their hair to yield it up. Nor was there any commiseration shown either to the aged or to infants, but they lifted up children from the ground as they hung upon the morsels they had gotten and threw them down upon the floor. (434) But they were still more barbarously cruel to those who had anticipated their coming and had actually swallowed down their expected spoil, as if they had been unjustly defrauded of their due. . . .

(439) These were the afflictions which the lower classes suffered from these tyrants' guards, but the men who were dignified and rich were

brought before the tyrants themselves. Some of them were falsely accused of laying treacherous plots and so were executed; others were charged with designs of betraying the city to the Romans; but the easiest way of all was to suborn somebody to testify that someone had decided to desert to the enemy. (440) He who was utterly despoiled of what he had by Simon was sent back again to John, just as from those who had been already plundered by John, Simon got what remained. . . .

(446) So now Titus' earthworks were progressing greatly, notwithstanding that his soldiers had been very much harassed from the wall. He then sent a party of horsemen and ordered that they should lay ambushes for those who went out into the valleys to gather food. (447) Some of these were indeed fighting men who were not content with what they got by plunder, but the majority of them were poor people who were deterred from deserting by the concern for their own relatives. (448) For they could not hope to escape together with their wives and children without the knowledge of the rebels. Nor could they think of leaving their relatives to be slain by the robbers. . . .

(491) And now Titus consulted with his commanders what was to be done. . . . (499) . . . his opinion was that if they aimed at speed joined with security, they must build a wall around the whole city. This was, he thought, the only way to block every exit so that then the Jews would either entirely despair of saving the city, and so would surrender it to him, or be still more easily conquered when the famine had further weakened them. . . .

(508) . . . Now outside this wall were erected thirteen places in which to keep garrisons, the circumference of which, taken together, amounted to ten furlongs.[27] (509) The whole was completed in three days so that what would naturally have required some months was done in so short an interval as to be incredible. . . .

(512) So all hope of escaping was now cut off from the Jews, together with their freedom to go out of the city. Then the famine widened its progress and devoured the people by whole houses and families. (513) The upper stories were full of women and children dying by famine, and the lanes of the city were full of the dead bodies of the aged. The children also and the young men wandered about the marketplaces like shadows, all swollen with the famine, and fell down dead wherever their misery seized them. (514) As for burying them, those who were sick themselves were not able to do it, and those who were hearty and well were deterred from doing it by the great multitude of those dead bodies and by the uncer-

---

27. 1¼ miles.

tainty there was as to how soon they would die themselves. . . . (518) The rebels at first gave orders that the dead should be buried out of the public treasury, for they were not able to endure the stench of the dead bodies. But afterwards, when they could not do that, they had them cast down from the walls into the valleys below.

(519) However, when Titus, in making his rounds along those valleys, saw them full of dead bodies and the thick putrefaction running from them, he groaned. Spreading out his hands to heaven, he called God to witness that this was not his doing. (520) Such was the sad case of the city itself. But the Romans were very joyful since none of the rebels could now make sallies out of the city because they were themselves disconsolate. The Romans, meanwhile, had a great supply of grain and other supplies from Syria and the neighboring provinces. (521) Many of them would stand near the wall of the city and show the people what great quantities of provisions they had, and so make the enemy more aware of their famine by the great superabundance which they had themselves. (522) However, when the rebels still showed no inclination of yielding, Titus, out of his commiseration for the people who remained and his earnest desire to rescue those who still survived, began to raise his earthworks again, although materials for them were hard to come by (523) since all the trees that were around the city had already been cut down to make the earlier earthworks. Yet the soldiers brought with them other materials from the distance of ninety furlongs[28] and thereby raised earthworks in four sections, much larger than the previous works, though this was done only at the tower of Antonia.[29] (524) So Caesar (Titus) made his rounds through the legions and expedited the siege-works, and showed the robbers that they were now in his hands. . . .

(548) Then some of the deserters, having no other way, leaped down from the wall immediately, while others went out of the city with stones, as if they would fight them, but they then fled to the Romans. There a worse fate accompanied them than what they had found within the city, and they met with a quicker dispatch from the great abundance they had among the Romans than they could have from the famine among the Jews. (549) For when they first came to the Romans, they were puffed up by the famine and swollen like men afflicted with dropsy. Then they all of a sudden over-filled those bodies that were before empty, and so burst asunder, except only those who were skillful enough to restrain their appetites and by degrees took in their food into bodies unaccustomed to

---

28. 11¼ miles.
29. A fortress north of the Temple Mount.

it. (550) Yet another plague seized those who were thus preserved. For there was found among the Syrian deserters a certain person who was caught gathering pieces of gold out of his excrement. For the deserters used to swallow such pieces of gold, as we told you before, when they came out. . . . (551) When this contrivance was discovered in one instance, the report that the deserters came to them full of gold filled their several camps. So the multitude of the Arabs with the Syrians cut up those that came as supplicants and searched their bellies. (552) Nor does it seem to me that any misery befell the Jews that was more terrible than this, since in one night's time about two thousand of these deserters were thus dissected. . . .

(562) But as for John, when he could no longer plunder the people, he had recourse to sacrilege. He melted down many of the sacred utensils which had been given to the temple as well as many of those vessels which were necessary for public worship—the cauldrons, the dishes, and the tables. Nor did he abstain from the pouring-vessels that were sent by Augustus and his wife. (563) For the Roman emperors always had both honored and adorned this temple, whereas this man, who was a Jew, seized upon what were the donations of foreigners (564) and said to those who were with him that it was proper for them to use divine things while they were fighting for the Divinity without fear, and that those whose warfare is for the temple should live at the expense of the temple. (565) Accordingly, he emptied the vessels of that sacred wine and oil which the priests kept to be poured on the burnt offerings and which lay in the inner court of the temple, and distributed it among the multitude, who, without hesitation, anointed themselves and drank of them. . . .

9.1.6 Tacitus, *Historiae* V, 10–14:
The Roman Earthworks at Jerusalem[30]

Tacitus, the Roman historian (ca. 56–ca. 118 C.E.), describes the siege of Jerusalem from the Roman point of view. While Josephus described Titus as hastening the battle out of compassion for the starving Jews, Tacitus ascribes it to base instincts. He accents as well the difficulties of the siege.

꿏

10 Still the Jews' patience lasted until Gessius Florus became procurator:[31] in his time war began. When Cestius Gallus, governor of Syria,

---

30. Trans. C. H. Moore, *Tacitus III, Histories 4–5 and Annals 1–3* (Loeb Classical Library; Cambridge: Harvard University Press, 1931), pp. 193–9.
31. 64–66 C.E.

tried to stop it, he suffered varied fortunes and met defeat more often than he gained victory. On his death, whether in the course of nature or from vexation, Nero sent out Vespasian, who, aided by his good fortune and reputation as well as by his excellent subordinates, within two summers occupied with his victorious army the whole of the level country and all the cities except Jerusalem. 2 The next year was taken up with civil war, and thus was passed in inactivity so far as the Jews were concerned. When peace had been secured throughout Italy, foreign troubles began again; and the fact that the Jews alone had failed to surrender increased our resentment; at the same time, having regard to all the possibilities and hazards of a new reign, it seemed expedient for Titus to remain with the army.

11 Therefore, as I have said above, Titus pitched his camp before the walls of Jerusalem and displayed his legions in battle array: the Jews formed their line close beneath their walls, being thus ready to advance if successful, and having a refuge at hand in case they were driven back. Some horse and light-armed foot [soldiers] were sent against them, but fought indecisively; later the enemy retired, and during the following days they engaged in many skirmishes before their gates until at last their continual defeats drove them within their walls. 2 The Romans now turned to preparations for an assault; for the soldiers thought it beneath their dignity to wait for the enemy to be starved out, and so they began to clamor for danger, part being prompted by bravery, but many were moved by their savage natures and their desire for booty. Titus himself had before his eyes a vision of Rome, its wealth and its pleasures, and he felt that if Jerusalem did not fall at once, his enjoyment of them was delayed. 3 But the city stands on an eminence, and the Jews had defended it with works and fortifications sufficient to protect even level ground; for the two hills that rise to a great height had been included within walls that had been skillfully built, projecting out or bending in so as to put the flanks of an assailing body under fire. The rocks terminated in sheer cliffs, and towers rose to a height of sixty feet where the hill assisted the fortifications, and in the valleys they reached one hundred and twenty; they presented a wonderful sight, and appeared of equal height when viewed from a distance. An inner line of walls had been built around the palace, and on a conspicuous height stands Antony's Tower, so named by Herod in honor of Mark Antony.

12 The temple was built like a citadel, with walls of its own, which were constructed with more care and effort than any of the rest; the very colonnades about the temple made a splendid defense. Within the enclosure is an ever-flowing spring; in the hills are subterraneous excavations,

with pools and cisterns for holding rain-water. 2 The founders of the city had foreseen that there would be many wars because the ways of their people differed so from those of the neighbors: therefore they had built at every point as if they expected a long siege; and after the city had been stormed by Pompey,[32] their fears and experience taught them much. Moreover, profiting by the greed displayed during the reign of Claudius, they had bought the privilege of fortifying their city, and in time of peace had built walls as if for war.

The population at this time had been increased by streams of rabble that flowed in from the other captured cities, for the most desperate rebels had taken refuge here, and consequently sedition was the more rife. 3 There were three generals, three armies: the outermost and largest circuit of the walls was held by Simon, the middle of the city by John, and the temple was guarded by Eleazar. John and Simon were strong in numbers and equipment, Eleazar had the advantage of position: between these three there was constant fighting, treachery, and arson, and a great store of grain was consumed. 4 Then John got possession of the temple by sending a party, under pretense of offering sacrifice, to slay Eleazar and his troops. So the citizens were divided into two factions until, at the approach of the Romans, foreign war produced concord.

13 Prodigies[33] had indeed occurred, but to avert them either by victims[34] or by vows is held unlawful by a people which, though prone to superstition, is opposed to all propitiatory rites. Contending hosts were seen meeting in the skies, arms flashed, and suddenly the temple was illumined with fire from the clouds. Of a sudden the doors of the shrine opened and a superhuman voice cried: "The gods are departing": at the same moment the mighty stir of their going was heard. 2 Few interpreted these omens as fearful; the majority firmly believed that their ancient priestly writings contained the prophecy that this was the very time when the East should grow strong and that men starting from Judea should possess the world. This mysterious prophecy had in reality pointed to Vespasian and Titus, but the common people, as is the way of human ambition, interpreted these great destinies in their own favor, and could not be turned to the truth even by adversity. 3 We have heard that the total number of the besieged of every age and both sexes was six hundred thousand: there were arms for all who could use them, and the number ready to fight was larger than could have been anticipated from the total popula-

---

32. In 63 B.C.E. when the Romans first conquered Judea.
33. Prophetic signs or omens.
34. Animal sacrifices.

tion. Both men and women showed the same determination; and if they were to be forced to change their home, they feared life more than death.

14 Such was the city and people against which Titus Caesar now proceeded; since the nature of the ground did not allow him to assault or employ any sudden operations, he decided to use earthworks and mantlets:[35] the legions were assigned to their several tasks, and there was a respite of fighting until they made ready every device for storming a town that the ancients had ever employed or modern ingenuity invented.

9.1.7 Babylonian Talmud Gittin 56a–b: The Rabbinic Account of the Siege[36]

The Babylonian Talmud includes a long account of the siege which emphasizes the difficult conditions of the majority of the people and which claims Rabbinic opposition to the revolt. This passage also tells the story of the escape of Yohanan ben Zakkai and the transfer of the seat of Rabbinic leadership to Yavneh after the debacle.

࿐

[Bar Kamza] went and said to Caesar, "The Jews have rebelled against you."

[Caesar] said to him, "How can I tell?"

[Bar Kamza] said to him, "Send a sacrifice to them and see whether they offer it."

[Caesar] sent a young calf with [Bar Kamza]. While on the way, [Bar Kamza] made a blemish on its upper lip, or as some say, on the white of its eye, in a place which is considered a blemish to [the Jews], but not to [the Romans].

The Rabbis considered sacrificing it for political peace, (but) Rabbi Zechariah ben Abkulas said, "They will say that blemished animals may be slaughtered on the altar."

They considered killing [Bar Kamza] so that he not go and inform, (but) Rabbi Zechariah said to them, "They will say that one who blemishes a consecrated animal shall be killed."

Rabbi Yohanan said, "The discretion of Rabbi Zechariah ben Abkulas destroyed our House, burned our Temple, and exiled us from our Land."

He sent Vespasian Caesar against them. He came and besieged [Jerusaglem] for three years. There were three rich men there. . . . These men had enough to feed [Jerusalem] for twenty-one years.

---

35. A movable shelter used to protect besiegers.
36. Trans. S. Berrin.

There were among them those rebels. The Rabbis said to them, "Let us go out and make peace with them [the Romans]." [The rebels] would not allow them.

[The rebels] said to [the Rabbis], "Let us go out and make war against them."

The Rabbis said to them, "It will not succeed [for lack of divine support]."

They [the rebels] arose and burned the provisions of wheat and barley, and there was famine.

Martha the daughter of Boethus was one of the rich women of Jerusalem. She sent her servant, saying to him, "Go and bring me some fine flour."

While he was on his way [to the market], it [the fine flour] was bought up.

He [the servant] said to her [Martha], "They have no fine flour; they have white flour."

She said to him, "Go bring me [white flour]."

While he was on his way [to the market], it [the white flour] was bought up.

He said to her, "They have no white flour; they have dark flour."

She said to him, "Go bring me [dark flour]."

While he was on his way [to the market], it [the dark flour] was bought up.

He said, "They have no dark flour, they have barley flour."

She said to him, "Go bring me [barley flour]."

While he was on his way [to the market], it [the barley flour] was bought up.

Although she had taken off her shoes, she said, "I will go out and see if I can find something to eat." Some excrement stuck to her foot and she died.

Rabban Yoḥanan ben Zakkai applied the verse to her: "The gentlest woman among you and the most delicate who has not ventured to set a foot upon the ground" (Deut. 28:56). There are those who say that she ate a fig left by Rabbi Zadok and she became sick and died. For Rabbi Zadok sat forty years in fasting, so that Jerusalem would not be destroyed. When he used to eat something, the food could be seen [passing through his throat]. When he wanted to restore himself, they would bring him a fig; he would suck out the juice and throw the rest away.

When Martha was about to die, she took out all her gold and silver and threw it down in the marketplace. She said, "Why do I need these?"

And this is as is written, "Their silver they will throw in the streets" (Ezek. 7:19).

Abba Sikara, the head of the rebels of Jerusalem, was the nephew of Rabban Yoḥanan ben Zakkai. [Rabban Yoḥanan ben Zakkai] sent for him [saying,] "Come secretly to me."

He [Abba Sikara] came [to Rabban Yoḥanan ben Zakkai] who said to him, "Until when will you do this, killing everybody with famine?"

He [Abba Sikara] said to him: "What should I do? For if I say anything to them, they will kill me."[37]

He [Rabban Yoḥanan ben Zakkai] said to him, "Devise a plan for me that I may go out; maybe there could at least be a small [chance for] salvation."

[Abba Sikara] said to him: "Let it be known that you are deathly ill and everybody will come to ask about you. Take a stinking object and keep it by you, so that they will say that you have died.[38] Let your students bear you, and let no other man bear you so that none may sense how light you are, for they [the rebels] know that a live man is lighter than a dead one."

[Rabban Yoḥanan ben Zakkai] did so. Rabbi Eleazar carried him on one side and Rabbi Joshua on the other side. When they came to the city entrance, [the rebel guards] wanted to pierce the [body to ensure that he was dead].

[Abba Sikara] said to them, "[The Romans] will say that [the rebels even] pierced their [own] Rabbi!"

They wanted to push him [to see if he would cry out].

[Abba Sikara] said to them, "[The Romans] will say that they pushed their [own] Rabbi!"

[The guards] opened the gate and they went out.

When [Rabban Yoḥanan ben Zakkai] arrived [at the Roman camp], he said, "Peace unto you, King; Peace unto you, King!"

[Vespasian] said to him, "You are twice guilty of a capital crime. Once, because I am not a king and you called me king. And further, because if I am a king, why did you not come to me until now?"

[Rabban Yoḥanan ben Zakkai] said to [Vespasian], "That which you have said, 'I am not a king,' certainly you are a king! If you were not a king, Jerusalem would not have been given into your hands. For it is written, 'And Lebanon by a mighty one will fall' (Is. 10:34). 'A mighty one' is none other than a king, for it is written, 'their mighty one shall be of

---

37. His rebel followers would kill even their leader if they suspected him of moving toward conciliation.

38. Believing the stench to come from your corpse.

themselves [and its ruler shall go out from its midst]' (Jer. 30:21). And Lebanon is none other than the Temple, for it is said, 'This good mountain and the Lebanon' (Deut 3:25). And as to what you have said, 'If I am a king why did you not come to me until now?' Until now, the rebels among us would not permit it."

[Vespasian] said to [Rabban Yoḥanan ben Zakkai], "If there is a jug of honey and a serpent is coiled upon it, do they not break the jug in order to kill the snake?"[39]

[Rabban Yoḥanan ben Zakkai] was silent.

Rabbi Joseph, and some say Rabbi Akiva, applied this verse to him: "He sends sages backward and confuses their minds" (Is. 44:25). [Rabban Yoḥanan ben Zakkai] should have said, "We take tongs and grip the snake and kill it, and the jug we may retain for ourselves."

Meanwhile, a messenger came to him [Vespasian] from Rome. He said to him, "Rise, because Caesar has died and the prominent men of Rome have decided to seat you at their head [as the new Caesar]. . . ."[40]

[Vespasian] said to him, "And now that you are so smart, why did you not come to see me until now?"

[Rabban Yoḥanan ben Zakkai] said to him, "Did I not tell you?"

[Vespasian] said to him, "I also answered you."[41]

[Vespasian] said, "I will go and send someone to take my place. But ask something of me that I may grant it to you."

[Rabban Yoḥanan ben Zakkai] said to him, "Give me Yavneh[42] and its sages, the chain of Rabban Gamliel,[43] and doctors to cure Rabbi Zadok."[44]

Rabbi Joseph, and some say Rabbi Akiva, applied this verse to him: "He sends sages backward and confuses their minds" (Is. 44:25). He should have asked that [Jerusalem] be left alone this once. But [Rabban

---

39. Indicating that he must destroy Jerusalem to conquer the rebels inside it.

40. Actually, upon the death of the emperor Nero in 68 C.E., Vespasian halted his campaign in Judea. Then a succession of short-term emperors attempted unsuccessfully to take control. At the advice of the Roman governors of Syria and Egypt, Vespasian was made emperor in July of 69 by the legions of Syria, Egypt, and Judea. The Senate then recognized him as emperor.

41. "I already told you what I have to say, namely that we have no choice but to destroy Jerusalem."

42. Yavneh, on the Mediterranean coast, was already the seat of a group of sages, and Rabbi Yoḥanan asked that it be preserved.

43. The dynasty of the patriarchate, the line of the descendants of Hillel who, according to tradition, headed the Rabbinic Sanhedrin.

44. From the fasting he had done for the sake of Jerusalem.

Yoḥanan ben Zakkai must have] thought, "Lest all this not be granted and then there may not be even a small [chance for] salvation. . . ."

[Vespasian the king] sent for Titus. "He will say, 'Where is their God, the rock upon whom they relied?'" (Deut. 32:37).[45] This is the wicked Titus who blasphemed and profaned Heaven. What did he do? He grabbed a harlot by the hand and he went into the Holy of Holies [of the Temple] and spread out a Torah scroll and performed a sinful act upon it. Then he drew a sword and pierced the curtain [of the ark]. A miracle occurred, and blood spurted out, and he thought he had killed [the Deity] himself. . . . [Then] what did he do? He took the curtain and made it into a sort of basket and he brought all the vessels in the Temple and put them into it, and he put them on a ship to go and celebrate a triumph in his city [Rome].

9.1.8 Josephus, *War* VI, 149–266: The Final Roman Victory

The Romans finally overcame the Jews amid great slaughter. The final battle was for the Temple. Josephus portrays Titus as wanting to spare it, but in the end it was destroyed nonetheless.

༄

(149) In the meantime, the rest of the Roman army in seven days' time had overthrown the foundations of the tower of Antonia, and had made ready a broad ascent to the temple. (150) Then the legions approached the first court and began to raise their embankments. . . . (157) Now, a day after the Romans ascended the breach, many of the rebels were so pressed by the famine because of the lack of plunder that they got together and made an attack on those Roman guards on the Mount of Olives at about the eleventh hour of the day, supposing first that they would not expect such an advance, and, second, that they were then taking refreshments and therefore that they could very easily beat them. (158) But the Romans were apprised of their coming to attack beforehand, and running together suddenly from the neighboring camps, they prevented them from scaling their fortification or cutting through the wall that was built around them. (159) This led to a sharp fight, and here many gallant feats were performed on both sides. . . .

(164) In the meantime, the Jews were so distressed by the fights they had been in, as the war advanced further and further, creeping up to the

---

45. The Rabbis understood "he will say . . ." to refer to Titus who was so irreverent of God.

holy house [the temple] itself, that they, as it were, cut off those limbs of their body which were infected in order to prevent the further spread of the disease. (165) So they set on fire the northwest portico, which was joined to the tower of Antonia, and after that broke off about twenty cubits of that portico, thereby beginning the burning of the sanctuary.[46] (166) Two days after that, on the twenty-fourth day of the aforementioned month [Panemus or Tamuz], the Romans set fire to the adjoining portico. When the fire went fifteen cubits further,[47] the Jews, in like manner, cut off its roof, and with no reverence at all for the works of art, severed the tower of Antonia from the temple. (167) Even though it was in their power to have stopped the fire, rather, they lay still while the temple was first set on fire since they deemed this spreading of the fire to be to their own advantage. (168) Then the armies fought against each other around the temple incessantly, and the war was conducted by continual sallies of each party against the other. . . .

(177) The rebels in the temple every day openly endeavored to beat off the soldiers on the embankments, and on the twenty-seventh day of the aforementioned month [Panemus, or Tamuz], they contrived such a stratagem as this: (178) They filled that part of the western portico which was between the beams and the roof under them with dry materials and also with bitumen and pitch, and then retired from that place as though they were totally exhausted. (179) Thereupon, many of the most inconsiderate among the Romans, who were carried away with violent passions, followed immediately after them as they were retiring, applied ladders to the portico, and sprang upon it suddenly. But the prudent ones, suspicious of this unaccountable retreat of the Jews, stood still where they were before.

(180) However, the portico was full of those who had gone up the ladders. Then the Jews set it all on fire, and as the flames burst out everywhere all of a sudden, the Romans who were out of danger were seized with very great consternation, as were those who were in the midst of the danger in the utmost distress. (181) So when they perceived themselves surrounded with the flames, some of them threw themselves down backwards into the city, and some into the midst of their enemies [in the temple]; many leaped down to their own men and broke their limbs. But a great number were caught in the fire in their rush to escape, though some anticipated the fire with their own swords. . . .

---

46. Here Josephus, true to his political and religious views, blames the Jews for the destruction of the Temple.

47. About 22 feet.

(191) Now this portico was burned down as far as John [of Giscala's] tower which he had built in the war he waged against Simon [ben Giora] over the gates that led to the Xystus.[48] The Jews also cut off the rest of that portico from the temple after they had destroyed those who got up to it. . . . (192) But the next day the Romans burned down the northern portico entirely as far as the east portico, the common angle of which was built over the valley that was called Kedron where the depth was frightful. And this was the state of the temple at that time. (193) The number of those who perished by famine in the city was countless and the miseries they underwent were unspeakable. . . .

(220) And now two of the legions had completed their embankments on the eighth day of the month Lous [Ab],[49] so Titus gave orders that the battering-rams should be brought and set over against the western edifice of the inner temple. (221) For before these were brought, the firmest of all the other engines had battered the wall for six days together without ceasing yet without making any impression upon it. But the vast size and strong connection of the stones were superior to that engine and to the other battering-rams also. (222) Other Romans did indeed undermine the foundations of the northern gate, and, after great exertions, removed the outermost stones. Yet the gate was still upheld by the inner stones and still stood undamaged, until the workmen, despairing of all such attempts by engines and crowbars, brought their ladders to the porticoes. (223) Now the Jews did not interrupt them in so doing, but when they had climbed up, they fell upon them and fought with them. Some of them they thrust down and threw backwards headlong; others of them they met and killed. . . .

(225) . . . those who bore the [Roman] standards fought hard for them, deeming it a terrible thing which would redound to their great shame if they permitted them to be stolen away. (226) Yet the Jews did at length get possession of these standards, and destroyed those who had gone up the ladders, while the rest were so intimidated by what those suffered who were killed that they retreated, (227) although none of the Romans died without having done good service before his death. Of the rebels, those who had fought bravely in the former battles did the same now as did Eleazar, the nephew of Simon the tyrant. (228) But when Titus perceived that his endeavors to spare a foreign temple led only to the damage of his soldiers and caused them to be killed, he gave orders to set the gates on fire. . . .

---

48. Cf. *War* IV, 580–1.
49. July/August.

(232) Now the soldiers had already set fire to the gates, and the silver that was over them quickly carried the flames to the wood that was within it, whence it spread itself all of a sudden and caught hold of the porticoes. (233) Upon the Jews' seeing this fire all around them, they were deprived of all energy of body and mind, and they were so astounded that not one of them hurried either to defend himself or to quench the fire, but they stood only as mute spectators. (234) However, they did not so grieve at the loss of what was now burning as to grow wiser thereby for the time to come, but as though the holy house itself had been on fire already, they whetted their passions against the Romans. (235) This fire prevailed during that day and the next also, for the soldiers were not able to burn all the porticoes that were round about all at one time, but only by sections.

(236) But then, on the next day, Titus commanded part of his army to quench the fire and to make a road to facilitate the marching up of the legions while he himself gathered the commanders together. . . . (238) . . . Titus proposed to these that they should give him their advice what should be done about the holy house. (239) Now, some of them thought it would be best to act according to the rules of war [and demolish it] because the Jews would never cease rebelling while that house was standing, for it was there that they used to gather together. (240) Others were of the opinion that if the Jews would leave it and none of them would lay their arms up in it, he should save it. But if they mounted it to fight any more, he ought to burn it because it must then be looked upon not as a holy house, but as a citadel. The impiety of burning it would then belong to those who forced this to be done and not to them. (241) But Titus said, "Although the Jews should mount that holy house and fight us from it, yet we ought not to revenge ourselves on things that are inanimate instead of on the men themselves," and that he was not in any case for burning down so vast a work as that was because this would be a loss to the Romans themselves, as it would be an ornament to their government if it stood. . . . (243) Then this assembly was dissolved as Titus gave orders to the commanders that the rest of their forces should lie still, but that they should make use of those who were most courageous in this attack. So he commanded that the chosen men from the cohorts should make their way through the ruins and quench the fire.

(244) Throughout that day, the Jews were so weary and under such consternation that they refrained from any attacks, but on the next day they gathered their whole force together and sallied forth very boldly against those who guarded the outward court of the temple, through the east gate at about the second hour of the day. (245) These guards withstood their attack with great bravery, and by covering themselves with

their shields in front as if with a wall, they drew their squadrons close together. Yet it was evident that they could not hold together there very long but would be overcome by the great number of their attackers and by the heat of their passion. (246) However, Caesar, seeing from the tower of Antonia that this squadron was likely to give way, sent some chosen horsemen to support them. (247) Thereupon the Jews found themselves not able to sustain their attack, and, upon the slaughter of those in the forefront, many of the rest were put to flight. (248) But as the Romans were moving back, the Jews turned back upon them and fought them. And when those Romans came back upon them, they retreated again, until about the fifth hour of the day when they were overcome and shut themselves up in the inner [court of the] temple.

(249) So Titus retired into the tower of Antonia and resolved to storm the temple the next day, early in the morning, with his whole army, and to encamp around the holy house. (250) But, as for that house, God had for certain long ago doomed it to the fire, and now that fatal day had come according to the revolution of years. It was the tenth day of the month Lous [Ab] upon which it was formerly burnt by the king of Babylon.[50] (251) These flames, however, were ignited by the Jews themselves and were occasioned by them. For upon Titus' retiring, the rebels lay still for a little while and then attacked the Romans again when those who guarded the holy house fought with those who quenched the fire that was burning in the inner [court of the] temple. But these Romans put the Jews to flight and proceeded as far as the holy house itself. (252) At that time, one of the soldiers, without waiting for any orders and without any concern or dread upon him at so great an undertaking, being hurried on by a certain divine fury, snatched a brand out of the materials that were on fire. Lifted up by another soldier, he set fire to a golden window through which there was a passage to the rooms that were around the holy house on the north side of it. (253) As the flames went upward the Jews made a clamor such as so great a tragedy required and ran together to prevent it. They did not spare their lives any longer nor allow anything to restrain their force since that holy house which they had guarded so carefully was about to be destroyed.

(254) And now someone came running to Titus and told him of this fire as he was resting in his tent after the last battle. Thereupon he arose in great haste and, just as he was, ran to the holy house in order to put the fire out. . . .

---

50. In 587 B.C.E.

(260) And now, since Caesar was in no way able to restrain the enthusiastic fury of the soldiers, and the fire proceeded on more and more, he went into the holy place of the temple with his commanders, and saw it with what it contained, which he found to be far superior to what the reports of foreigners contained, and not inferior to what we ourselves boasted of and believed about it. (261) But as the flame had not as yet reached its interior but was still consuming the rooms that were around the holy house, and Titus supposed that the house itself might still be saved, (262) he came in haste and endeavored to persuade the soldiers to quench the fire and gave orders to Liberalius, the centurion of his bodyguard of spearmen, to beat the soldiers who disobeyed orders with staves and to restrain them. (263) Yet their passions were too strong for the regard they had for Caesar and the dread they had of him who forbade them, as was their hatred of the Jews and a certain vehement inclination to fight them which was too strong for them also. (264) Moreover, the hope of plunder induced many to go on who thought that all the places within were full of money, seeing that all around it was made of gold. (265) Besides, when Caesar ran out so hastily to restrain the soldiers, one of those who went into the place threw the fire upon the hinges of the gate in the dark. (266) Then the flame burst out immediately from within the holy house itself, and when the commanders withdrew, Caesar with them, nobody any longer forbade those who were outside to set fire to it. Thus the holy house burned down without Caesar's approval....

9.1.9 Dio Cassius, *Historia Romana* LXVI, 4–7: A Roman Account of the Revolt[51]

The Roman historian Dio Cassius (ca. 164–after 229 C.E.) gives an account which in the main agrees with that of Josephus, except that he sees Titus as encouraging the destruction of the Temple, as did Tacitus.

༅

(4:1) Titus, who had been assigned to the war against the Jews, undertook to win them over by certain representations and promises; but, as they would not yield, he now proceeded to wage war upon them. The first battles fought were indecisive; then he got the upper hand and proceeded to besiege Jerusalem. This city had three walls, including the one that surrounded the temple. (2) The Romans, accordingly, heaped up mounds against the outer wall, brought up their engines, joined battle

---

51. Trans. E. Cary, *Dio's Roman History* (Loeb Classical Library; Cambridge: Harvard University Press, 1925), vol. 8, pp. 264–70.

with all who sallied forth to fight and repulsed them, and with their slings and arrows kept back all the defenders of the wall; for they had many slingers and bowmen who had been sent by some of the barbarian kings. (3) The Jews also were assisted by many of their countrymen from the region round about and by many who professed the same religion, not only from the Roman Empire but also from beyond the Euphrates; and these, also, kept hurling missiles and stones with (4) no little force on account of their higher position, some being flung by the hand and some hurled by means of engines. They also made sallies both night and day, whenever occasion offered, set fire to the siege engines, slew many of their assailants, and undermined the Romans' mounds by removing the earth through tunnels driven under the wall. As for the battering rams, sometimes they threw ropes around them and broke them off, sometimes they pulled them up with hooks, and again they used thick planks fastened together and strengthened with iron, which they let down in front of the wall and thus fended off the blows of still others. (5) But the Romans suffered most hardship from the lack of water; for their supply was of poor quality and had to be brought from a distance. The Jews found in their underground passages a source of strength; for they had these tunnels dug from inside the city and extending out under the walls to distant points in the country, and going out though them, they would attack the Romans' water carriers and harass any scattered detachments. But Titus stopped up all these passages.

(5:1) In the course of these operations many on both sides were wounded and killed. Titus himself was struck on the left shoulder by a stone, and as a result of this accident that arm was always weaker. (2) In time, however, the Romans scaled the outside wall, and then, pitching their camp between this and the second circuit,[52] proceeded to assault the latter. But here they found the conditions of fighting different; for now that all the besieged had retired behind the second wall, its defense proved an easier matter because its circuit was shorter. (3) Titus therefore once more made a proclamation offering them immunity. But even then they held out, and those of them who were taken captive or deserted kept secretly destroying the Romans' water supply and slaying any troops whom they could isolate and cut off from the rest; hence Titus would no longer receive any Jewish deserters. (4) Meanwhile some of the Romans, too, becoming disheartened, as often happens in a protracted siege, and suspecting, furthermore, that the city really was impregnable, as was commonly reported, went over to the other side. The Jews, even though they

---

52. The second set of walls.

were short of food, treated these recruits kindly, in order to be able to show that there were deserters to their side also.

(6:1) Though a breach was made in the wall by means of engines, nevertheless, the capture of the place did not immediately follow even then. On the contrary, the defenders killed great numbers who tried to crowd through the opening, and they also set fire to some of the buildings near by, hoping thus to check the further progress of the Romans. (2) Nevertheless, the soldiers, because of their superstition, did not immediately rush in; but at last, under compulsion from Titus, they made their way inside. Then the Jews defended themselves much more vigorously than before, as if they had discovered a piece of rare good fortune in being able to fight near the temple and fall in its defense. The populace was stationed below in the court, the senators on the steps, and the priests in the sanctuary itself. (3) And though they were but a handful fighting against a far superior force, they were not conquered until a part of the temple was set on fire. Then they met death willingly, some throwing themselves on the swords of the Romans, some slaying one another, others taking their own lives, and still others leaping into the flames. And it seemed to everybody, and especially to them, that so far from being destruction, it was victory and salvation and happiness to them that they perished along with the temple. (7:1) Yet even under these conditions many captives were taken, among them Bargiora,[53] their leader; and he was the only one to be executed in connection with the triumphal celebration.

(2) Thus was Jerusalem destroyed on the very day of Saturn,[54] the day which even now the Jews reverence most. From that time forth it was ordered that the Jews who continued to observe their ancestral customs should pay an annual tribute of two *denarii* to Jupiter Capitolinus. In consequence of this success both generals[55] received the title of *imperator*, but neither got that of *Judaicus*, although all the other honors that were fitting on the occasion of so magnificent a victory, including triumphal arches, were voted to them.

9.1.10 Josephus, *War* VII, 252–404: The Siege of Masada

The final chapter in the Great Revolt was the battle for Masada. Here, according to Josephus, the rebels faced certain defeat and so elected to deny their captors the opportunity to deprive them of their freedom by killing themselves. In recent years, scholars have debated the historicity of this account.

---

53. Simon bar Giora, leader of one of the revolutionary factions.
54. Saturday, the Sabbath.
55. Vespasian and Titus.

꣠

(252) When Bassus[56] had died, Flavius Silva[57] succeeded him as procurator in Judea. When he saw that all the rest of the country was subdued in this war, and that there was only one stronghold that was still in rebellion, he got together all his army from various places and made an expedition against it. This fortress was called Masada.[58] (253) It was Eleazar, a man of influence and the commander of the Sicarii,[59] who had seized it. He was a descendant of that Judas who had persuaded multitudes of Jews, as we have previously related, not to submit to the taxation when Quirinius was sent into Judea to collect it. . . . .[60]

(275) For now it was that the Roman general came and led his army against Eleazar and those Sicarii who held the fortress of Masada together with him. He immediately conquered the whole country adjoining it and put garrisons into the most suitable places in it. (276) He also built a wall all around the entire fortress so that none of the besieged might easily escape, and he also set his men to guard it. (277) He himself pitched his camp in an agreeable place which he had chosen for the siege, where the rock belonging to the fortress abutted the neighboring mountain, which yet was a place of difficulty for obtaining sufficient provisions. (278) For it was not only food that had to be brought from a great distance [to the army], and this with a great deal of hard labor for those Jews who were appointed for that purpose, but water also had to be brought to the camp because the place afforded no nearby water source. (279) Therefore when Silva had completed the arrangements beforehand, he turned to the siege which was likely to demand a great deal of skill and exertion because of the strength of the fortress. . . .

(295) As for the stores that were within this fortress, they was still more wonderful on account of its splendor and the length of time that it stood. (296) For here was stored grain in large quantities and supplies which would allow men to subsist for a long time. Here also were wine and oil in abundance with all kinds of pulse[61] and piles of dates, (297) all of which

---

56. Lucilius Bassus had been sent as governor to Judea. Cf. *War* VII, 162.

57. L. Flavius Silva was governor 73/4–81 C.E.

58. Located on top of an isolated rock on the western shore of the Dead Sea, 15½ miles south of the oasis of Ein Gedi.

59. Literally, "dagger carriers," one of the groups of rebels against Rome.

60. P. Sculpicius Quirinius was a Roman commander and administrator. In 6 C.E. he was appointed governor of Syria. He soon conducted a property census of Judea which generated much opposition among anti-Roman elements. Luke 2:1–2 links this census with the birth of Jesus.

61. The seeds of legumes such as peas and beans.

Eleazar found there when he and his Sicarii got possession of the fortress by treachery. . . . (299) There was also found here a large quantity of all sorts of weapons of war which had been hoarded by king [Herod] and which were sufficient for ten thousand men. . . .

(304) After the Roman commander Silva had built a wall on the outside, around this whole place, as we have said already, and had thereby taken the greatest precautions to prevent any of the besieged from running away, he undertook the siege itself. He found only one single place capable of supporting the earthworks he was to raise. . . .

(315) When Silva saw this, he thought it best to try taking the wall[62] by setting fire to it So he gave the order that the soldiers should throw a great number of burning torches upon it. (316) Accordingly, as it was chiefly made of wood, it soon caught fire, and once it was set on fire, its hollowness made that fire spread into a mighty flame. (317) Now, at the very beginning of this fire, a north wind that then blew proved terrible to the Romans, for by bringing the flame downward, it drove it upon them, and they were almost in despair of success, fearing that their machines would be burned. (318) But after this, suddenly the wind changed to the south as if it were done by divine Providence, blew strongly the other way, and carried the flame and drove it against the wall which was now on fire through its entire thickness. (319) So the Romans, having now assistance from God, returned to their camp with joy and resolved to attack their enemies the very next day. Because of this, they set their watch more carefully that night lest any of the Jews should run away from them without being discovered.

(320) However, Eleazar never once thought of fleeing, nor would he permit anyone else to do so. (321) But when he saw their wall burned down by the fire, and could devise no other way of escaping or opportunity for their further courage, and imagining what the Romans would do to them, their children, and their wives if victorious, he consulted about having them all slain. (322) Now, as he judged this to be the best thing they could do in their present circumstances, he gathered the most courageous of his companions together and encouraged them to take that course by a speech which he made to them. . . .

(326) ". . . Nor can we propose to ourselves any more to fight them and beat them. (327) It would have been proper indeed for us to have conjectured the purpose of God much sooner, at the very first, when we were so desirous of defending our liberty and when we received such

---

62. The wall around Masada protecting the defenders.

hard treatment from one another, and worse treatment from our enemies, and to have been aware that the same God, who had of old taken the Jewish nation into his favor, had now condemned them to destruction. (328) For had he either continued to be favorable or had he been in a lesser degree displeased with us, he would not have overlooked the destruction of so many people or delivered his most holy city to be burned and demolished by our enemies. (329) To be sure, we weakly hoped to have preserved ourselves—and ourselves alone—still in a state of freedom, as if we had been guilty of no sins ourselves against God nor taken part in those of others; we also taught other men to preserve their liberty. (330) Wherefore, consider how God has convinced us that our hopes were in vain by bringing such distress upon us in the desperate state we are now in which is beyond all our expectations. (331) For the nature of this fortress, which was in itself unconquerable, has not proved a means of our deliverance. And even while we still have a great abundance of food and a great quantity of arms and other necessities more than we need, we are openly deprived by God Himself of all hopes of deliverance. (332) For that fire which was driven upon our enemies did not, of its own accord, turn back upon the wall which we had built. This was the effect of God's anger against us for our manifold sins of which we have been guilty in a most insolent and extravagant manner with regard to our own countrymen.

(333) "Let us not receive the punishments for them from the Romans, but from God Himself, as executed by our own hands, for these will be more moderate than the other. (334) Let our wives die before they are abused and our children before they have tasted of slavery. After we have slain them, let us bestow that glorious benefit upon one another mutually and preserve ourselves in freedom, as an excellent funeral monument for us. (335) But first let us destroy our property and the fortress by fire, for I am well assured that it will be a great source of grief to the Romans that they will not be able to seize our bodies and our wealth as well. (336) Let us spare nothing but our provisions, for they will be a testimonial when we are dead that we were not subdued for lack of provisions but that, according to our initial resolution, we have preferred death over slavery. . . ."

(389) Even as Eleazar was exhorting them, they all cut him off short and made haste to do the deed, full of an unconquerable impulse, and moved with a demoniacal fury. So they went their ways each endeavoring to outdo the other, and thinking that this eagerness would be a demonstration of their courage and good conduct if they could avoid appearing among the last. So great was the zeal they were in to slay their wives and

children and themselves also! (390) Nor, indeed, when they came to the deed itself did their courage fail them, as one might imagine it would have, but they then held fast to the same resolution, without wavering, which they had upon hearing Eleazar's speech. Even though every one of them still retained the natural passion of love for themselves and their families, the reasoning they followed still appeared to them to be very just, even with regard to those who were dearest to them.

(391) For the husbands tenderly embraced their wives, took their children into their arms, and gave the longest parting kisses to them with tears in their eyes. (392) Yet at the same time they completed what they had resolved upon as if they had been executed by the hands of strangers, and they had nothing else to console them but the necessity they were in of doing this execution to avoid that prospect they had of the miseries they would suffer from their enemies. (393) Nor was there in the end any one of these men who hesitated to act their part in this terrible execution, but every one of them dispatched his dearest relatives. Wretched victims indeed were they, whose distress forced them to kill their own wives and children with their own hands, as the least of those evils that were before them. (394) Being no longer able to bear the grief they were under for what they had done, and considering it an injury to those they had killed to live even the shortest space of time after them, they quickly laid all they had in a heap and set fire to it. (395) They then chose ten men by lot to kill all the rest, every one of whom laid himself down next to his wife and children on the ground, and threw his arms about them, and they offered their necks to the stroke of those who by lot executed that melancholy office. (396) And when these ten had, without fear, killed them all, they made the same rule for casting lots for themselves, that he whose lot it was should first kill the other nine, and last of all should kill himself. Accordingly, all these had courage sufficient to be in no way behind one another in doing or suffering. (397) Finally, the nine offered their necks to the executioner, and he who was the last of all surveyed all the other bodies, lest perchance some one among so many who were slain should want his assistance to be dispatched. When he perceived that they were all dead, he set fire to the palace, and with the great force of his hands ran his sword entirely through himself and fell down dead near his own relatives.

(398) These people died with this intention, that they would not leave alive even one soul among them all to be subject to the Romans. (399) Yet there was an old woman and another who was related to Eleazar, superior to most women in prudence and learning, with five children, who had

concealed themselves in the subterranean aqueducts, and who were hidden there when the rest were intent upon the slaughter of one another. (400) Those others were nine hundred and sixty in number, including the women and children. (401) This calamitous slaughter occurred on the fifteenth day of the month Xanthicus [Nisan].[63]

(402) The Romans expected that they would be fought in the morning. Accordingly, they put on their armor and laid bridges of planks upon their ladders from their embankments to make an assault upon the fortress. (403) But they saw nobody as an enemy, only a terrible solitude on every side with a fire within the place as well as a perfect silence. So they were at a loss to guess at what had happened. At length they made a shout, as if it had been at a blow given by the battering-ram, to try to see whether they could bring anyone out who was inside. (404) The women heard this noise, came out of their underground cavern, and informed the Romans of what had been done. One of the two clearly described all that was said and what was done and the manner of it. . . .

9.2 DESTRUCTION AND ITS AFTERMATH

9.2.1 Suetonius, *Life of Domitian* 12:2:
The Jewish Tax and Hidden Jews[64]

Suetonius (ca. 70–ca. 130), known for his biographies of the caesars, testifies to the Fiscus Judaicus, the Jewish tax that replaced the voluntary tax paid by Jews throughout the Roman Empire for the Temple. After the destruction, this tax was paid to the Roman imperial treasury.

❧

Besides other taxes, that on the Jews was levied with the utmost rigor, and those were prosecuted who without publicly acknowledging that faith yet lived as Jews, as well as those who concealed their origin and did not pay the tribute levied upon their people. I recall being present in my youth when the person of a man ninety years old was examined before the procurator and a very crowded court, to see whether he was circumcised.

---

63. May 2, 73 C.E.

64. Trans. J. C. Rolfe, *Suetonius II* (Loeb Classical Library; Cambridge: Harvard University Press, 1979).

9.2.2 Mishnah Gittin 5:6:
Restoring the Land to the Jewish People[65]

The Mishnah records a number of rulings designed to aid in the reestablish-
ment of the Jewish community of Palestine after the Great Revolt of 66–73
C.E. and the attendant destruction of the land.

The law of the *sikarikon*[66] did not apply in the days of the war [against
Titus] in Judah,[67] but after the war and following it applied. What was this
law? [If a Jew] bought land from a *sikarikon* and subsequently bought the
land from its original [Jewish] owner, the sale is void.[68] If he bought the
land from the original owner and then paid the *sikarikon*, the sale is valid.
[Similarly, if a Jew] bought land belonging to a woman from her husband,
and subsequently bought it from her, the sale is void.[69] [If he bought it]
from the woman and then from the husband, the sale is valid.

This is the teaching of the earlier Rabbis. A later Rabbinic court said:
Whoever buys land from a *sikarikon* must pay the original owner a fourth
[of the value of the land].[70] When is this? When they [the original owners]
do not have [the sum of the value of the land] in their possession, but if
they do have [the sum of the value of the land] in their possession they
precede any man [in the right to buy back the land]. Rabbi [Judah the
Prince][71] convened his court [to discuss this law] and they decided that if
the land was in the possession of the *sikarikon* for twelve months, whoever bought the land first has the rights to it, but he must pay the original
owners a fourth.

---

65. Trans. Hadassah Schiffman Levy.

66. *Sikarikon* is a Greek word meaning "thief." The *sikarikon* referred to here is a
Roman soldier who acquired land from Jews in exchange for sparing their lives. He then
sold the land in order to make a profit.

67. 66–73 C.E.

68. Since the original owner sold it out of fear of the *sikarikon* and did not intend the
sale to be final.

69. Since she can say that she only sold it in order not to upset her husband, and not
because she wanted to sell it.

70. Since the *sikarikon* generally sold the land for three quarters of its value, the buyer
was required to pay the original owner the rest of the actual value.

71. The editor of the Mishnah, d. ca. 225.

9.2.3 Tosefta Sotah 15:10–15:
Mourning for the Destroyed Temple[72]

Those Rabbis who lived through the destruction of the Temple had to come to terms with it and to decide how it would be commemorated henceforth. Resisting the impulse of depression which decreed the halting of ordinary activities, they affirmed that life must go on and daily affairs must be restored to normal.

10 Rabban Simeon ben Gamliel said, "From the day that the Temple was destroyed, it would have been logical that we not eat meat and not drink wine. However, the court may not decree upon the congregation things to which they are unable to adhere."

He used to say, "Since they are uprooting the Torah from our midst, let us decree upon the world that it should be desolate: that one may not marry a wife, nor have children, nor celebrate the circumcision feast, until the seed of Abraham disappears on its own."

They said to him, "Rather, it is better for the community that they act in error rather than intentionally."

11 From the time when the latter (Second) Temple was destroyed, ascetics became numerous in Israel, and they would not eat meat and they would not drink wine. Rabbi Joshua went to address them. He said to them, "My children, why do you not eat meat?"

They said to him, "How can we eat meat? Every day the daily sacrifice used to be offered upon the altar, and now it is no longer [offered]."

He said to them, "Why do you not drink wine?"

They said to him, "How can we drink wine? Every day it was poured out for libation on the altar, and now it is no longer [poured]."

12 He said to them, "Let us not eat even figs and grapes, for they used to bring first-fruits from them on Shavuot. Let us not eat bread, for they used to bring the two loaves[73] and the showbread from them. Let us not drink water, for they used to offer libations from it on Sukkot."

They were silent.

---

72. Trans. S. Berrin from S. Lieberman, ed., *Tosefta, Nashim* 2 (New York: Jewish Theological Seminary of America, 1973) 242–244. The text presented here is a reconstruction from Manuscripts Erfurt and Vienna.

73. Offered also on Shavuot.

He said to them, "Not to mourn at all is not feasible, for the decree has already been decreed. But further, to mourn excessively (also) is not feasible. Rather, thus the sages have said, 'A man shall plaster his home with plaster and leave over a small bit as a remembrance of Jerusalem.

13 'A man may prepare all the needs of a meal, and leave off a little bit as a remembrance of Jerusalem.

14 'A woman may prepare all her ornaments and leave off a little bit as a remembrance of Jerusalem,' as it is said, 'If I forget you, O Jerusalem, let my right hand forget its cunning; let my tongue cleave to my palate if I do not remember you, if I do not set Jerusalem above my highest joy.' (Ps. 137:5)."

15 All who mourn over Jerusalem will merit to see her joy, as it is said, "Rejoice with Jerusalem and be glad for her, all who love her, join in her jubilation all who mourn over her" (Is. 66:10).

9.3 FROM TEMPLE TO SYNAGOGUE

9.3.1 Beth Alpha Synagogue: A "Rabbi"[74]

This inscription, dating probably to the reign of Justin I, 517–28 C.E., mentions a "Rabbi," indicating the links between the synagogues of Palestine and the Rabbinic class.

৯৫

1. [This mosa]ic was composed in the year
2. [ ] of the reign of Emperor Justin
3. [with the proceeds] of the sale of wheat, one hundred
4. [se'ahs . . .] which all the [to]wnspeople volunteered
5. [ ] Rabbi
6. [ ] may there be remembered for good all
7. the t[ownspeople . . . may there be remembered for go]od

9.3.2 The Inscription in the Ein Gedi Synagogue: The "Secret of the Town"[75]

The fifth- to seventh-century C.E. inscription preserved in the mosaic floor of the narthex to the west of the Ein Gedi synagogue sanctuary contains 18 lines and 118 words. Until the discovery of the Reḥov inscription (text

---

74. Trans S. Berrin and L. H. Schiffman from J. Naveh, *'Al Pesipas va-'Even* (Jerusalem: Israel Exploration Society, 1977/8), p. 72.

75. Trans. L. I. Levine, "The Inscription in the 'En Gedi Synagogue," in *Ancient Synagogues Revealed*, ed. L. I. Levine (Jerusalem: Israel Exploration Society, 1981), p. 140.

12.2.1), this was the longest synagogue inscription known from Roman Palestine.

𝕾

1. Adam,[76] Seth, Enosh, Kenan, Mahalalel, Jared,
2. Enoch, Methuselah, Lamech, Noah, Shem, Ham and Japheth.
3. Aries,[77] Taurus, Gemini, Cancer, Leo, Virgo,
4. Libra, Scorpio, Sagittarius, Capricorn, and Aquarius, Pisces.
5. Nisan,[78] Iyar, Sivan, Tammuz, Av, Elul,
6. Tishri, Marheshvan, Kislev, Tevet, Shevat
7. and Adar, Abraham, Isaac, Jacob.[79] Peace.[80]
8. Hananiah, Mishael, and ʿAzariah.[81] Peace unto Israel.
9. May they be remembered for good: Yose and ʿEzron and Hizziqiyu the sons of Hilfi.
10. Anyone causing a controversy between a man and his friend, or whoever
11. slanders his friend before the Gentiles, or whoever steals
12. the property of his friend, or whoever reveals the secret of the town[82]
13. to the Gentiles—He Whose eyes range through the whole earth
14. and Who sees hidden things, He will set His face on that
15. man and on his seed and will uproot him from under the heavens.
16. And all the people said: Amen and Amen Selah.[83]
17. Rabbi Yose the son of Hilfi, Hiziqiyu the son of Hilfi, may they be remembered for good,[84]
18. for they did a great deal in the name of the Merciful, Peace.

---

76. Lines 1–2 name the thirteen ancestors of the human race.

77. Lines 3–4 list the twelve signs of the zodiac.

78. Lines 5–6 contain the names of the twelve months of the Jewish lunar calendar.

79. The three patriarchs.

80. The use of the expression "Peace" or "Peace unto Israel" marks the closure of a thought in Jewish inscriptions, much like the end of a paragraph.

81. The three heroic young men who survived the fiery furnace of King Nebuchadnezzar. The king had them thrown in it in an attempt to punish them for not publicly worshipping the golden image he had set up (Dan. 3:1–30).

82. A most intriguing phrase, the "secret of the town" is still unrevealed. Various theories having to do with commercial matters or the security of the community have been suggested.

83. "Amen" or "Amen Selah" signifies agreement to the previous statement, so that when the people answer "Amen" to the curse in lines 10–15, they accept its validity. This expression is from 1 Chron. 16:36 where it refers to the song of praise to God at the dedication ceremony of the ark by King David.

84. Dedication in honor of the donors.

9.3.3 Corinth: A Synagogue[85]

*This inscription from the fourth to sixth centuries C.E. confirms the termi-
nology we are accustomed to using to refer to Jewish houses of worship.*

꙳

"[syna]gogue of the Hebr[ews]"

9.3.4 Rome: An Archisynagogue[86]

*The following, from a catacomb inscription, refers to an archisynagogue, lit-
erally, "head of the synagogue." It was not unusual for women to serve in this
role which involved heading the Jewish community, not the conduct of religious
services.*

꙳

Here lies Salo the daughter of Gad, archisynagogue of the Jews. She
[lived] 41 years. May she rest in peace.

9.3.5 The Theodotus Inscription in Jerusalem:
The Functions of the Synagogue[87]

*This inscription, of the mid-first century C.E., not only introduces us to a
family of archisynagogues but explains some of the purposes of the synagogue
itself. The early date of this inscription testifies to the presence of a synagogue
in Jerusalem even before the destruction of the Second Temple.*

꙳

Theodotus, son of Vettenus, priest and archisynagogue, son of an archisynagogue, grandson of an archisynagogue, built the synagogue for the
reading of the Law and the teaching of the commandments, and the
guest-house and the rooms and the water supplies for the lodging of
strangers in need, which his fathers founded and the Elders and Simonides.

---

85. Trans. S. Berrin from J.-B. Frey, *Corpus Inscriptionum Iudaicarum* II (Rome: Pontificio Istituto di Archeologia Cristiana, 1952), no. 718.

86. Trans. S. Berrin from J.-B. Frey, *Corpus Inscriptionum Iudaicarum*, no. 510.

87. Trans. S. Berrin from J.-B. Frey, *Corpus Inscriptionum Iudaicarum*, no. 1404.

9.4 RESTORATION OF AUTONOMY: THE AUTHORITY OF THE RABBIS

9.4.1 Babylonian Talmud Berakhot 27b–28a: The Impeachment of Rabban Gamliel[88]

After the destruction of the Temple and the failure of the Great Revolt of 66–73 C.E., the Romans placed the Rabbis in charge of the internal affairs of the Jews of Palestine. Rabban Gamliel, who from about 80 C.E. headed the academy at Yavneh, seems to have had formal recognition as patriarch. He felt constrained to rule with a heavy hand in order to maintain the vestiges of Jewish freedom. This account, however, shows that his colleagues rose up against his heavy hand and impeached him, only to restore him afterwards, probably for fear of the political consequences of their actions.

ﷺ

Our Rabbis taught: Once, a student[89] came before Rabbi Joshua, and said to him, "Are the evening prayers optional or mandatory?"

[Rabbi Joshua] said to him, "[They are] optional."

[The same student] came before Rabban Gamliel and said to him, "Are the evening prayers optional or mandatory?"

[Rabban Gamliel] said to him, "[They are] mandatory."

[The student] said to [Rabban Gamliel], "But Rabbi Joshua told me they are optional!"

[Rabban Gamliel] said to [the student], "Wait until the shield-bearers[90] enter the House of Study."

When the shield-bearers entered, the questioner stood and asked, "Are the evening prayers optional or mandatory?"

Rabban Gamliel told him, "[They are] mandatory."

Rabban Gamliel said to the sages, "Is there anybody at all who disagrees in this matter?"

Rabbi Joshua said to him, "No."

[Rabban Gamliel] said to [Rabbi Joshua], "But in your name they have told me, 'they are optional.'"

[Rabban Gamliel] said to [Rabbi Joshua], "Joshua, stand on your feet and they will testify against you."

---

88. Trans. S. Berrin.
89. Rabbi Simeon bar Yoḥai.
90. A term for the sages.

Rabbi Joshua stood on his feet, and said, "If I were alive and [the student] were dead, then the live person could contradict the dead one, but since he is alive and I am alive, how can one live man contradict another live man?"[91]

Rabban Gamliel was sitting and expounding, while Rabbi Joshua stood on his feet,[92] until all the people shouted and told Ḥuzpit the translator, "Stop [repeating aloud the words of Rabban Gamliel]!"[93] and he stopped.

They said, "How long will [Rabban Gamliel] go on harassing [Rabbi Joshua]? He harassed him last year in Tractate Rosh Hashanah;[94] he harassed him in Tractate Bekhorot about the matter of Rabbi Zadok;[95] and here too he is harassing him. Come let us depose him.

"Whom will we appoint [to serve as patriarch]?"

"Let us appoint Rabbi Joshua. [No,] he is involved in the matter [and therefore inappropriate]. Let us appoint Rabbi Akiva. [No,] he may be susceptible to [Rabban Gamliel's] punishment as he does not have the merit of [righteous] ancestors.[96]

"Rather, let us appoint Rabbi Eleazar ben Azariah, for he is wise, and rich, and a tenth (generation descendant) from Ezra." "He is wise," so that if someone questions him, he will respond. "He is rich," so that if he must serve the House of Caesar,[97] he may go and serve. "And he is tenth from Ezra," so that he has the merit of [righteous] ancestors, and [Rabban Gamliel] will not harm him.

They came and said to [Rabbi Eleazar ben Azariah], "[Would] it please you, sir, to be head of the academy?"

He said, "I will go and consult my household."

He went and consulted his wife. She said, "Maybe they will remove you."

---

91. He admits to having said that the evening prayer is optional.

92. Out of respect for the patriarch, Rabbi Joshua remained standing. Rabban Gamliel did not give him permission to sit as a punishment.

93. Who continued to teach while Rabbi Joshua remained standing, humiliating him in public.

94. When Rabban Gamliel forced Rabbi Joshua to appear before him with his walking stick on the day that Rabbi Joshua had calculated was Yom Kippur.

95. He forced him to remain standing because he differed with him regarding the status of a first-born animal belonging to Rabbi Zadok.

96. Rabbi Akiva was a descendant of converts and therefore did not have worthy deceased ancestors whose merit could protect him from Rabban Gamliel, who was of the patriarchal family.

97. By paying tribute to the Roman authorities as the representative of the Jewish people.

He said to her, "(Better for) a person to use an expensive cup for one day, even if it breaks the next day."

She said to him, "You have no white hair."[98]

That day he was eighteen years old, and a miracle happened to him, and eighteen rows of his hair turned white. This is as Rabbi Eleazar ben Azariah said, "Behold I am *as* one who is seventy years old," and not "I *am* seventy years old."[99]

(A tanna) taught: That day, they removed the entrance guard and gave permission to [the students] to enter, for Rabban Gamliel used to announce, "Any student whose inside is not like his outside may not enter the House of Study."

That day they added a number of benches. Rabbi Yoḥanan said, "Abba Joseph ben Dostai and the Rabbis dispute over this, one saying 'they added four hundred benches,' and one saying, 'they added seven hundred benches.'"

Rabban Gamliel was upset. He said: "Perhaps, God forbid, I have withheld Torah from Israel?" He was shown in his dream white casks filled with ashes.[100] But it was not so; this was only shown to him to reassure him.

(A tanna) taught: "The tractate Eduyot was taught on that day," and wherever [something] is taught [preceded by] *on that day*, it refers to this day. And there was no legal decision which had been undecided in the House of Study that they did not resolve. And even Rabban Gamliel did not hold himself back from the House of Study even for one hour, as we learn:[101] *On that day*, Judah the Ammonite proselyte came before them to the House of Study. He said to them: "What is the ruling about my entry to the congregation?"[102]

Rabban Gamliel said to him, "You are forbidden to enter into the congregation."

Rabbi Joshua said, "You are permitted to enter the congregation."

Rabban Gamliel said to [Rabbi Joshua], "But does it not say, 'An Ammonite and a Moabite shall not enter the congregation of the Lord?'" (Deut. 23:4).

---

98. Since it would not seem respectful that a young person should stand at the head of the academy.

99. Mishnah Berakhot 12:2.

100. As though the students being allowed entry were pure only externally, but not internally.

101. Mishnah Yadayim 4:4.

102. Am I permitted to marry a Jewish woman?

Rabbi Joshua said to him, "And are Ammon and Moab settled in their (original) places? Sennacherib the king of Assyria already arose and confused all the nations as it is said, 'I have removed the borders of the nations, and I have plundered their treasures, and have exiled the mighty numbers of inhabitants' (Is. 10:13), and anybody who separates himself, [is understood to] separate from the majority."[103]

Rabban Gamliel said to him, "But does it not say, 'And afterward I will return the captivity of Ammon, the word of God' (Jer. 49:6), and they have already returned."[104]

Rabbi Joshua said to him, "But does it not say, 'And I will return the captivity of my nation Israel' (Amos 9:14), and they have not yet returned!"[105] Immediately, they permitted [Judah the Ammonite proselyte] to enter the congregation.[106]

Rabban Gamliel said, "Since it is thus, I will go and appease Rabbi Joshua."

When [Rabban Gamliel] came to [Rabbi Joshua's] house, he saw that the walls of his house were black. He said to him, "From the walls of your house, it is evident that you are a blacksmith."

[Rabbi Joshua] said to him, "Woe unto the generation whose leader you are, for you do not know the troubles of scholars, by what means they provide for themselves, and by what means they feed themselves."[107]

He said to him: "I beg you, forgive me."

He paid no attention to him.

"Do it for my father's honor."[108]

He was appeased.

They said, "Whom shall we send to inform the sages?"[109]

---

103. And is therefore not assumed to be descended from the original inhabitants of Ammon or Moab.

104. Therefore, the current Ammonites are the original inhabitants, and they are forbidden to marry Jews.

105. Since Israel has not yet been returned to its land, we may assume that the original Ammonites have also not yet returned, and therefore, Judah the Ammonite proselyte is not considered to be of the original Ammonite stock.

106. That is, to marry a Jewish woman after his conversion.

107. The black walls resulted from his abject poverty, not his profession.

108. His father was Rabban Simeon ben Gamliel, who died during the Great Revolt (66–73 C.E.).

109. Having resolved the issue, it was obvious that they should return Rabban Gamliel to his place at the head of the academy. Apparently none of the sages wanted to accept this responsibility because it would mean that Rabbi Eleazar ben Azariah would be removed as the head.

A certain launderer said to them, "I will go."

Rabbi Joshua sent [him] to the House of Study [saying], "Let him who wore the garments wear the garments, and he who does not wear the garments, may he say to the one who wears the garments, remove your garments and I will wear them?"[110]

Rabbi Akiva said to the sages, "Lock the doors, so that Rabban Gamliel's servants will not come and disturb the sages."

Rabbi Joshua said, "I (myself) had better get up and go to them." He went and knocked on the door and said to them, "Let the Sprinkler,[111] the son of the Sprinkler sprinkle,[112] but shall one who is not a Sprinkler or [even] the son of a Sprinkler say to the Sprinkler the son of a Sprinkler, 'Your water is cave water, and your ashes are stove ashes?'"[113]

Rabbi Akiva said to him, "Rabbi Joshua are you appeased? We have done nothing except for your honor. Tomorrow you and I will rise early at [Rabbi Eleazar ben Azariah's] door."

They said, "What shall we do? Shall we completely remove [Rabbi Eleazar ben Azariah]? 'We may only raise levels of holiness, not diminish them.' Shall one teach for one week and one teach on another? That will cause envy! Rather, Rabban Gamliel will teach for three weeks and Rabbi Eleazar ben Azariah for one week."

9.5 JOSEPHUS: HISTORIAN OF THE GREAT REVOLT

9.5.1 Josephus, *Life* 1–24, 80–83: The Autobiography of a Historian

In the Life, Josephus gives some details of his biography and the perspective from which he wrote. His picture is self-glorifying and at times even tendentious, yet when critically evaluated it provides an important perspective on his historical works. The Life probably was written in Rome toward the very end of the first century C.E.

---

110. Using the analogy of the high priestly garments to show that authority should be retained by the one who inherited it, i.e., Rabban Gamliel.

111. The priest, who sprinkles the ashes of the red heifer to make the waters of purification from impurity of the dead (Numbers 19).

112. Rabban Gamliel who is of the patriarchal family should be head of the academy.

113. Should one who is not of the patriarchal line dispute the rulings of one who is? The analogy here is to somebody who accuses the high priest of substituting ordinary still water and oven ashes for the biblically required running water and ashes of the red heifer required for purification.

ₛ᳇

(1) The family from which I am derived is not an ignoble one. . . . (2) I am not only descended from a priestly family, but from the first of the twenty-four courses . . . ,[114] and I am of the chief family of that first course also. Further, by my mother I am of royal blood, for the children of Hasmoneus[115] from whom that family was derived, had both the office of the high priesthood and the dignity of a king for a long time. . . .

(9) When I was a child of about fourteen years of age, I was commended by all for the love I had of learning. For this reason the high priests and leading men of the city came frequently to me in order to know my opinion about the accurate understanding of points of the law. (10) When I was about sixteen years old, I had a mind to gain personal experience of the several sects that were among us. These sects are three: the first is that of the Pharisees, the second that of the Sadducees, and the third that of the Essenes, as we have frequently told you. For I thought that by this means I might choose the best, once I was acquainted with them all. (11) So I submitted myself to hard training and underwent great difficulties, and went through them all. Nor did I submit myself to these trials only. But when I was informed that one whose name was Banus lived in the desert, and that he used no other clothing other than what grew on trees, and had no other food other than what grew of its own accord, and bathed himself in cold water frequently, both by night and by day, in order to preserve his chastity, I imitated him in those things (12) and stayed with him for three years. So when I had accomplished my purposes, I returned to the city, being now nineteen years old, and began to conduct myself according to the rules of the sect of the Pharisees, which resembles the sect of the Stoics, as the Greeks call them.

(13) Soon after I was twenty-six years old, I took a voyage to Rome on the occasion which I shall now describe: When Felix was procurator of Judea,[116] there were certain priests of my acquaintance, very excellent persons, whom on a small and trifling occasion he had put into bonds, and whom he had sent to Rome to plead their cause before Caesar.[117] (14) I was desirous to procure deliverance for them, especially because I was informed that they were not unmindful of piety towards God, even under

---

114. The priests were divided into twenty-four "courses" which served in the temple alternately for one-week periods.

115. The father of the Hasmoneans. Josephus' mother was of the Hasmonean family.

116. Antoninus Felix was procurator from 52 to 60 C.E. These events occurred at the end of his term.

117. Nero, 37–68 C.E., became the Roman emperor in 54.

their afflictions, but supported themselves with figs and nuts.[118] Accordingly I came to Rome by sea after a great number of hazards. (15) For our ship sank in the Adriatic Sea, and we who were in it, about six hundred in number, swam for our lives all night. Then upon the first appearance of the day, we sighted a ship of Cyrene, and I and some others, eighty in all, by God's providence, were taken up into the other ship. (16) And when I had thus escaped and had come to Dicearchia, which the Italians call Puteoli, I became acquainted with Aliturius, an actor of plays and much beloved by Nero, but a Jew by birth. Through his interest I became known to Poppea, Caesar's wife, and took care, as soon as possible, to entreat her to arrange that the priests might be set free. When, besides this favor, I had obtained many presents from Poppea, I returned home again.

(17) And now I perceived that revolutionary movements had already begun and that there were a great many people very much elated in hopes of a revolt against the Romans. I therefore endeavored to put a stop to these tumultuous persons and to persuade them to change their minds. I laid before their eyes against whom it was that they were going to fight, and told them that they were inferior to the Romans not only in martial skill but also in good fortune. (18) I warned them against rashly and in the most foolish manner bringing on the dangers of the most terrible perils upon their country, their families, and themselves. (19) This I said with vehement exhortation because I foresaw that the end of such a war would be most unfortunate for us. But I could not persuade them for the madness of desperate men was far too strong for me.[119]

(20) I was then afraid, lest by repeating these things so often, I should incur their hatred and their suspicions, as if I were of our enemies' party, and should run into the danger of being seized by them and killed since they already possessed the Antonia which was the citadel. So I retired into the inner court of the temple. (21) Yet I did go out of the temple again after Menaḥem and the chief of the band of robbers were put to death,[120] when I stayed among the high priests and the chiefs of the Pharisees. (22) But no small fear took hold of us when we saw the people in arms, while we ourselves knew not what we should do and were not able to restrain the rebels. However, as the danger was directly upon us, we pretended that we were of the same opinion as they but only advised them to be

---

118. Observing the Jewish prohibitions on forbidden foods even in captivity.

119. Despite Josephus' unsuccessful service as one of the rebel commanders in Galilee, he writes here and throughout his works as if he had always opposed the revolt.

120. Cf. *War* II, 433–48. Menaḥem, head of the anti-Roman party, was murdered by a rival faction.

quiet for the present and to let the enemy go away, (23) still hoping that Cestius[121] would not be long in coming with great forces and so put an end to these rebellious proceedings. (24) But upon his coming and fighting, he was beaten, and a great many of those that were with him fell; and this disgrace which Cestius received became the calamity of our whole nation. . . .

(80) I was now about thirty years old when it is a hard thing for anyone to escape the calumnies of the envious even if he restrains himself from fulfilling any unlawful desires, especially if a person is in great authority. Yet I did preserve every woman's honor, and as to the presents offered me, I rejected them as I did not need them; nor, indeed, would I take those tithes which were due to me as a priest, from those who brought them. (81) Yet I do confess that I took part of the spoils of those Syrians who inhabited the cities that adjoined us when I had conquered them, and that I sent them to my relatives in Jerusalem. (82) However, when I twice took Sepphoris by force, Tiberias four times, and Gadara once, and when I had subdued and taken John [of Gischala][122] who often laid treacherous snares for me, I did not punish [with death] either him or any of the aforementioned communities, as the continuation of this discourse will show. (83) And on this account, I suppose, it was that God, Who is never unacquainted with those who do as they ought, delivered me still out of the hands of my enemies and afterwards preserved me when I fell into those many dangers which I shall relate.

9.5.2 Josephus, *Life* 414–30: Josephus after the Revolt

Josephus served as a rebel commander in the Galilee. After the fall of Jotapata, Josephus found shelter with some comrades in a cave and wished to surrender to the Romans, but his companions insisted that lots be drawn, and the besieged killed one another until he and one other were the last alive. They decided to surrender to the Romans. Whether this account is accurate or not, Josephus then took up the cause of the Romans, arguing that submission to Roman rule was the wisest course for Judea.

꿎

(414) When the siege of Jotapata was over and I was among the Romans, I was kept with much care because of the great respect that Vespasian showed me. Moreover, at his command I married a virgin, one of

---

121. Gaius Cestius Gallus, legate of Syria from 63–67 C.E. In 66 he marched into Palestine to restore calm, but he was defeated at Bet Horon and died in 67 C.E.
122. One of the revolutionary leaders with whom Josephus was in conflict.

the women taken captive at Caesarea.[123] (415) But she did not live with me long, but was divorced upon my being freed from my bonds and my going to Alexandria. However, I married another wife at Alexandria, (416) and was thence sent, together with Titus[124] to the siege of Jerusalem and was frequently in danger of being killed. The Jews were very desirous to get me under their power, in order to have me punished.[125] The Romans also, whenever they were beaten, supposed that it was occasioned by my treachery, and made continual complaints to the emperors to bring me to punishment as a traitor to them. (417) But Titus Caesar was well acquainted with the uncertain fortune of war and did not respond to the soldiers' vehement solicitations against me. Moreover, when the city of Jerusalem was taken by force, Titus Caesar persuaded me frequently to take whatever I would of the ruins of my country, and say that he gave me permission to do so. (418) But when my country was destroyed, I thought nothing else to be of any value which I could take and keep as a comfort for my calamities. So I made this request of Titus, that my family might have their liberty. I also received a gift of holy books by Titus's concession. (419) Nor was it long after that I asked him for the life of my brother and fifty friends of his and was not denied. When I also went once to the temple, by the permission of Titus, where there were a great multitude of captive women and children, I got all those whom I remembered among my own friends and acquaintances to be set free, being in number about one hundred and ninety. So I delivered them, without their paying any price of redemption, and restored them to their former fortune. . . .

(422) But when Titus had quelled the troubles in Judea and conjectured that the lands which I had in Judea would bring me no profit because a garrison to guard the country was going to be quartered there, he gave me another parcel of land in the plain. And when he was going away to Rome, he asked me to sail along with him and paid me great respect. (423) When we came to Rome, I had great care taken of me by Vespasian, for he gave me an apartment in his own house in which he had lived before he became emperor. He also honored me with the privilege of Roman citizenship, gave me an annual pension, and continued to respect me until the end of his life, without any abatement of his kindness to me. . . .

---

123. A Jewish woman.
124. Vespasian's son who succeeded him as the Roman commander in Judea after Vespasian was made emperor in 69 C.E. In 70 he captured Jerusalem.
125. The Jews regarded him as a traitor for having surrendered to the Romans.

(425) When those who envied my good fortune frequently brought accusations against me, by God's providence I escaped them all. I also received from Vespasian no small quantity of land in Judea as a free gift. (426) About that time I divorced my wife as I was not pleased with her behavior, though not until she had given birth to three children, two of whom are dead and one, whom I named Hyrcanus, is alive.

(427) After this I married a wife who had lived at Crete, but a Jewess by birth. She was a woman of eminent parents, and such as were the most illustrious in all the country, and whose character was beyond that of most other women as her future life did demonstrate. By her I had two sons. The name of the elder was Justus, and the next Simonides who was also named Agrippa; (428) these were the circumstances of my domestic affairs. However, the kindness of the emperor to me continued still the same. When Vespasian died,[126] Titus, who succeeded him in the government,[127] kept up the same respect for me which I had from his father; and when I had frequent accusations laid against me, he would not believe them. (429) Domitian,[128] who succeeded him, still showed great respect for me for he punished those Jews who were my accusers and commanded that a servant of mine, who was a eunuch and my son's tutor, should be punished. He also made that parcel I had in Judea tax free which is a mark of the greatest honor to him who has it. Indeed, Domitia, the wife of Caesar, continued to do me kindnesses. (430) And this is the account of the actions of my whole life. Let others judge my character by them as they please.

9.5.3 Josephus, *War*, Preface 6–16: Writing the History of the Jewish War

In the preface to the Jewish War, written in Rome between 75 and 79 C.E., Josephus sets forth the principles on which he proposed to write on accurate history of the Jewish war with Rome. From it we learn much about his concept and attitude as a historian. Apparently, the work was written to correct other accounts which Josephus regarded as false.

---

126. In 79 C.E.

127. Titus was emperor from 79 to 81 C.E.

128. Domitian, brother of Titus, was born in 51 C.E., succeeded as emperor upon his brother's death in 81 C.E., and was murdered in 96 C.E., perhaps in a plot aided by his wife, Domitia.

꽝

(6) I thought it an absurd thing to see the truth falsified regarding affairs of such great consequence and to take no notice of it, but to allow those Greeks and Romans who were not in the wars to be ignorant of these things, and to read either flatteries or fictions, while the Parthians, the Babylonians, the remotest Arabians and those of our nation beyond the Euphrates with the Adiabenians by my means knew accurately both whence the war began, what miseries it brought upon us, and how it ended.[129]

(7) It is true that these writers have the confidence to call their accounts histories, but they seem to me to fail at their own purpose as well as to relate nothing that is sound. For they have a mind to demonstrate the greatness of the Romans, while they still diminish and lessen the actions of the Jews, (8) as not discerning how it cannot be that those must appear to be great who have only conquered those who were small. Nor are they ashamed to overlook the length of the war, the multitude of the Roman forces who so greatly suffered in it, or the might of the commanders—whose great labors around Jerusalem will be deemed inglorious if what they achieved be reckoned to be only a small matter.

(9) However, I will not go to the other extreme out of opposition to those men who extol the Romans, nor will I determine to raise the actions of my countrymen too high. But I will faithfully relate the actions of both parties with accuracy. Yet I shall suit my language to the passions I am under, as to the affairs I describe, and must be allowed to indulge some lamentations upon the miseries undergone by my own country. (10) For it was a seditious spirit of our own that destroyed it, and it was the tyrants among the Jews who brought the Roman power upon us, who unwillingly attacked us, and occasioned the burning of our holy temple. Titus Caesar who destroyed it, himself a witness during the entire war, pitied the people who were at the mercy of the revolutionaries and often voluntarily delayed the taking of the city and allowed time to the siege in order to let the culprits have the opportunity for repentance. . . .

(15) But then, an undertaking to preserve the memory of what has not been before recorded, and to represent the affairs of one's own time to those who come afterwards, is really worthy of praise and commendation.

---

129. Josephus is explaining his decision to issue *War* in Greek after an earlier edition, most probably in Aramaic, had circulated.

Now, he is to be esteemed to have taken good pains in earnest not who does no more than change the disposition and order of other men's works, but he who not only relates what had not been related before, but composes an entire body of history of his own. (16) Accordingly, I have been at great charges and have taken very great pains [about this history] though I be a foreigner,[130] and dedicate this work, as a memorial of great actions, both to the Greeks and to the barbarians. But for some of our own principal men, their mouths are wide open and their tongues loosed presently for gain and lawsuits, but quite muzzled up when they are to write history where they must speak the truth and gather the facts together with a great deal of effort. So they leave the writing of such histories to inferior people and to such as are not acquainted with the actions of princes. Yet the real truth of historical facts shall be preferred by us, no matter how much it may be neglected among the Greek historians.

9.5.4 Josephus, *Antiquities* XIV, 1–3: Josephus' Philosophy of History

Josephus tells us that he sought to present a historically accurate work even while using literary techniques to create an enjoyable book.

※

(1) We have related the affairs of Queen Alexandra and her death in the foregoing book, and will now speak of what followed immediately thereafter, declaring, before we proceed, that we have nothing so much at heart as this, that we may omit no facts either through ignorance or laziness. (2) For we are dealing with the history and explication of such things as most people are unacquainted with because of their distance from our times. We aim to do it with a proper beauty of style, so far as that is derived from proper words harmonically arranged, and also from such ornaments of speech as may contribute to the pleasure of our readers, (3) so that they may receive the knowledge of what we write with some agreeable satisfaction and pleasure. But the principal goal that authors ought to aim at, above all the rest, is to speak accurately and to speak truly for the satisfaction of those who are otherwise unacquainted with such matters and who are obliged to believe what these writers inform them of.

---

130. That is, one for whom Greek is not his native language.

9.6 THE BAR KOKHBA REVOLT

9.6.1 Dio Cassius, *Historia Romana* LXIX, 12–14: A Roman Account of the Bar Kokhba Revolt[131]

In his account, Dio Cassius says that the building of the Temple of Jupiter was the cause, rather than the result, of the Bar Kokhba Revolt. Bar Kokhba himself does not appear in this account. The author knows of the hideouts built by the Jews, some of which have been excavated in Israel recently. In addition, Dio Cassius records the advance preparation of weapons, indicating that this was a planned uprising.

※

(12:1) At Jerusalem [Hadrian] founded a city in place of the one which had been razed to the ground, naming it Aelia Capitolina, and on the site of the temple of the god he raised a new temple to Jupiter. This brought on a war of no slight importance nor of brief duration, (2) for the Jews deemed it intolerable that foreign races should be settled in their city and foreign religious rites planted there. So long, indeed, as Hadrian was close by in Egypt and again in Syria, they remained quiet, save in so far as they purposely made of poor quality such weapons as they were called upon to furnish, in order that the Romans might reject them and they themselves might thus have the use of them; but when he went farther away, they openly revolted. (3) To be sure, they did not dare try conclusions with the Romans in the open field, but they occupied the advantageous positions in the country and strengthened them with mines and walls, in order that they might have places of refuge whenever they should be hard pressed, and might meet together unobserved under ground; and they pierced these subterranean passages from above at intervals to let in air and light.

(13:1) At first the Romans took no account of them. Soon, however, all Judea had been stirred up, and the Jews everywhere were showing signs of disturbance, were gathering together, and giving evidence of great hostility to the Romans, partly by secret and partly by overt acts; (2) many outside nations, too, were joining them through eagerness for gain, and the whole earth, one might almost say, was being stirred up over the matter. Then indeed, Hadrian sent against them his best generals. First of these was Julius Severus, who was dispatched from Britain, where he was governor, against the Jews. (3) Severus did not venture to attack his oppo-

---

131. Trans. Cray, pp. 447–51.

nents in the open at any one point, in view of their numbers and their desperation, but by intercepting small groups, thanks to the number of his soldiers and his under-officers, and by depriving them of food and shutting them up, he was able, rather slowly, to be sure, but with comparatively little danger, to crush, exhaust and exterminate them. (14:1) Very few of them in fact survived. Fifty of their most important outposts and nine hundred and eighty-five of their most famous villages were razed to the ground. Five hundred and eighty thousand men were slain in the various raids and battles, and the number of those who perished by famine, disease and fire was past finding out. (2) Thus nearly the whole of Judea was made desolate, a result of which the people had had forewarning before the war. For the tomb of Solomon, which the Jews regard as an object of veneration, fell to pieces of itself and collapsed, and many wolves and hyenas rushed howling into the cities. (3) Many Romans, moreover, perished in this war. Therefore Hadrian in writing to the senate did not employ the opening phrase commonly affected by the emperors, "If you and your children are in health, it is well; I and the legions are in health."

9.6.2 Eusebius, *The Ecclesiastical History* IV, 6: A Christian Account of the Bar Kokhba Revolt[132]

Eusebius (260–339 C.E.), bishop of Caesarea, writing in the first quarter of the fourth century, relates the story of the revolt. According to him, Bar Kokhba was executed by the Romans and the building of the Roman temple in Jerusalem was a result of the war, rather than a cause. He notes that another consequence of the war was that henceforth the bishop of Jerusalem would be a Gentile Christian as the Romans prohibited Jews from living in the holy city.

꿇

6 The rebellion of the Jews once more progressed in character and extent, and Rufus,[133] the governor of Judaea, when military aid had been sent him by the Emperor, moved out against them, treating their madness without mercy. He destroyed in heaps thousands of men, women, and children, and, under the law of war, enslaved their land. The Jews were at that time led by a certain Bar Chochebas, which means "star," a man who

---

132. Trans. K. Lake, *Eusebius: The Ecclesiastical History* (Loeb Classical Library; Cambridge: Harvard University Press, 1980), vol. 1, pp. 311–13.

133. Tinneus Rufus, Roman governor of Judea at the outbreak of the Bar Kokhba Revolt in 132 C.E.

was murderous and a bandit, but relied on his name, as if dealing with slaves, and claimed to be a luminary who had come down to them from heaven and was magically enlightening those who were in misery. The war reached its height in the eighteenth year of the reign of Hadrian in Beththera,[134] which was a strong citadel not very far from Jerusalem; the seige lasted a long time before the rebels were driven to final destruction by famine and thirst and the instigator of their madness paid the penalty he deserved. Hadrian commanded that by a legal decree and ordinances the whole nation should be absolutely prevented from entering from henceforth even the district round Jerusalem, so that not even from a distance could it see its ancestral home. Ariston of Pella[135] tells the story. Thus when the city came to be bereft of the nation of the Jews, and its ancient inhabitants had completely perished, it was colonized by foreigners, and the Roman city which afterwards arose changed its name, and in the honor of the reigning Emperor Aelius Hadrian was called Aelia. The church, too, in it was composed of Gentiles, and after the Jewish bishops the first who was appointed to minister those there was Marcus.

9.6.3 The Bar Kokhba Letters: Day-to-Day Conduct of the Revolt

One of the most dramatic archaeological discoveries is the letters written by Bar Kokhba himself (whose real name was Simeon bar Kosiba) during the revolt. They are, for the most part, military dispatches and they confirm the historicity of the revolt while casting light on the nature of the administration of Judea by the rebels.

🐚

Simeon Bar Kosiba to Yehonathan and to Masabala, a letter:
That every man from Tekoa and from Tel Adirin who is with you, you shall send them to me without delay. And if you shall not send them, let it be known to you, that I will exact punishment from you.
Salisa [son of] Yose, wrote it.[136]

Simeon, son of Kosiba, the ruler over Israel, to Jonathan and Masabala, peace!

---

134. Hebrew, Betar.
135. A mid-second century Christian author whose work is not preserved.
136. Trans. J. Fitzmyer, D. J. Harrington, *A Manual of Palestinian Aramaic Texts* (Rome: Biblical Institute Press, 1978), p. 161, no. 59 with restorations from K. Beyer, *Die aramäischen Texte vom Toten Meer* (Göttingen: Vandenhoeck & Ruprecht, 1994), p. 216.

That you should inspect and take the wheat which Hanan bar Yishma'el has brought, and send me, after inspection, one hundred. And you should give them with assurance for they have been found to be stolen. And if you do not do this, then retribution will be exacted from you. And send me the man immediately with assurance.

And every Tekoan man who is with you, the houses in which they dwell will be burned down, and from you I will exact retribution.

(As for) Joshua, son of the Palmyrene, you shall seize him and send him to me with assurance. Do not hesitate to seize the sword which is upon him. You shall send him.

Samuel, son of Ammi.[137]

Letter of Simeon bar Kosiba, peace!

To Yehonathan son of Ba'aya [my order is] that whatever Elisha tells you do for him and help him [in every] action. Be well.[138]

From the Administrators of Beth Mashko, from Yeshua and from Eleazar to Yeshua ben Galgoula chief of the camp, peace.

Let it be known to you that the cow which Yehoseph ben Ariston took from Ya'akov ben Yehudah, who dwells in Beth Mashko, belongs to him [i.e. to Ya'akov] by purchase. Were it not for the Gentiles [i.e. the Romans] who are near us, I would have gone up and satisfied you concerning this, lest you will say that it is out of contempt that I did not go up to you. Be you well and the whole House of Israel.

Yeshua ben Elazar has written it [i.e. dictated it]
Eleazar ben Yehoseph has written it
Ya'akov ben Yehudah, for himself
Sha'ul ben Eliezer, witness
Yehoseph ben Yehoseph, witness
Ya'akov ben Yehoseph, testifies [scribe or notary?].[139]

Simeon, son of Kosiba, to Jonathan, son of Ba'yan, and Masabala, son of Simeon:

You are to send to me Eleazar, son of Ḥitta, immediately before the Sabbath . . .

---

137. Fitzmyer and Harrington, p. 159, no. 53 with restorations from Beyer, pp. 213–14.
138. Y. Yadin, *Bar-Kokhba* (New York: Random House, 1971), p. 126.
139. Yadin, p. 136 with modifications by L. H. Schiffman.

Simeon, son of Judah, wrote it.[140]

Simeon, son of Kosiba, to Jonathan, son of Ba'yan, and Masabala who is in Ḥotah and to Masabala on the frontier, my brothers, peace. . . .

. . . the Romans. You are to take Tirsos, son of Tinianos, and let him come with you, because we are in need of him. . . . Be in peace.[141]

Simeon to Yehudah bar Menashe to Qiryath 'Arabaya:

I have sent to you two donkeys so that you shall send with them two men to Yehonathan bar Ba'ayan and to Masabala in order that they shall pack and send to the camp, to you, palm branches [*lulavin*] and citrons [*ethrogin*]. And you, from your place, send others who will bring you myrtles [*hadasin*] and willows [*'aravin*]. See that they are tithed and send them to the camp. (The request is made) since the army is large. Be well.[142]

From Simeon ben Kosiba to Yeshua ben Galgoula and to the men of the fort, peace!

I take heaven to witness against me that unless you mobilise [destroy?] the Galileans who are with you every man, I will put fetters upon your feet as I did to ben Aphlul.

[Si]meon be[n Kosiba wrote it].[143]

From Simeon bar Kosiba to the people of Ein Gedi, to Masabala and Yonathan bar Ba'ayan, peace.

In comfort you sit, eat and drink from the property of the House of Israel, and care nothing for your brothers . . . [144]

. . . my house . . . till the end . . . , [send] me grain, for there is no bread [in their] district . . . they have [fl]ed [to] your father . . . to the Fortress of the Hasidim. And my brothers in the sou[th] . . . [Many] of these were lost by the sword . . . these my brothers . . .[145]

9.6.4 Jerusalem Talmud Ta'anit 4:6 (68d–69a): Rabbi Akiva and Bar Kokhba[146]

The Jerusalem Talmud gives evidence of the inner Rabbinic debate over the messianic status of Bar Kokhba. Unable to understand his defeat after the ini-

---

140. Fitzmyer and Harrington, p. 161, no. 56 with slight revisions by L.H. Schiffman.
141. Fitzmyer and Harrington, p. 161, no. 58 with modifications by L.H. Schiffman.
142. Yadin, p. 129.
143. Yadin, p. 137 with additions by L. H. Schiffman.
144. Yadin, p. 133.
145. Yadin, p. 139.
146. 4:5 in other editions. Trans. S. Berrin. Note that below the Hebrew "Ben"= "son of" and the Aramaic equivalent "Bar" are interchanged in the text.

tial success of the rebellion, the Rabbis attributed it to the killing of Rabbi Eleazar of Modiin. The passage also indicates the terrible death and destruction that the revolt brought in its wake.

꙼

Rabbi Simeon bar Yoḥai taught, "Akiva, my master, expounded, 'A star will go forth from Jacob' (Num. 28:17), (as) 'Koziba has come forth from Jacob.'" When Rabbi Akiva would see Bar Koziba, he would say, "This is the King Messiah!" Rabbi Yoḥanan ben Torta said to him, "Akiva, grass will grow on your cheeks and still the Son of David will not have come."

Rabbi Yoḥanan said, "At Hadrian's command, they killed 800,000 in Betar. . . ."

Hadrian besieged Betar for three and a half years.[147] Rabbi Eleazar of Modiin used to sit on sackcloth and ashes and pray every day, saying, "Master of the Universe! Do not sit in judgment today, do not sit in judgment today."[148]

Hadrian wanted to go to him.[149] One Samaritan said to him, "Do not go, for I will go and see what can be done to deliver the city to you."

[The Samaritan] went through the city's drain pipe. He went and found Rabbi Eleazer of Modiin standing and praying. He pretended to whisper in his ear. The people of the city saw him and brought him to Ben Koziba. They said to [Ben Koziba], "We saw this old man conversing with your uncle."[150]

[Ben Koziba] said to [the Samaritan], "What did you say to him, and what did he [Rabbi Eleazer of Modiin] say to you?"

He said to him, "If I tell you, the king will kill me, and if I do not tell you, you will kill me. I prefer that the king should kill me, and not you." [The Samaritan continued and] said to him, "He [Rabbi Eleazer of Modiin] said to me, 'I will surrender the city.'"

[Ben Koziba] went to Rabbi Eleazer of Modiin, [and] said to him, "What did that Samaritan tell you?"

[Rabbi Eleazer] said to him, "Nothing."

[Ben Koziba] said, "What did you say to [the Samaritan]?"

[Rabbi Eleazer] said to him, "Nothing."

[Bar Koziba] gave [Rabbi Eleazer] one kick and he killed him. Immediately, a heavenly voice went forth saying: "'Woe to the worthless shep-

---

147. Betar was the last rebel stronghold to resist Roman conquest.

148. For if God sat in judgment, the Romans would be victorious and Betar would be destroyed.

149. To Rabbi Eleazar to stop him from praying to prevent the destruction of Betar.

150. Rabbi Eleazar of Modiin was Bar Kokhba's uncle.

herd who abandons his flock! Let a sword descend upon his arm and his right eye. His arm will wither and his right eye will be blinded' (Zech. 11:17). You have killed Rabbi Eleazar of Modiin, the arm of Israel and their right eye. Thus, your arm will wither, and your right eye will be blinded." Immediately, Betar was captured and Ben Koziba was killed.

They brought his head to Hadrian. [Hadrian] said, "Who killed him?"

One Samaritan said to him, "I killed him."

[Hadrian] said, "Show me his corpse."

He looked at the corpse and found a serpent coiled around it. [Hadrian] said, "If God had not killed him, who would have been able to kill him?" He applied to him the verse, "Unless their Rock had sold them, and God had given them over" (Deut. 32:30).

The [Romans] went on killing [Jews] until a horse was sunk in blood up to its nose. And the blood was turning over forty-*se'ah* boulders, until the blood flowed forty Roman miles into the sea. . . .

They said that the brains of 300 children were found on one rock. They found 300 baskets of tefillin each of nine *se'ahs*. And some say nine baskets, each weighing three *se'ahs*.

It was taught: Rabbi Simeon ben Gamliel says, "[There were] 500 schools in Betar and the smallest of them had no fewer than 500 children. [The children] used to say, 'If the enemy comes upon us, we will go out against them with our quills and poke out their eyes.' And as a result of the sins [of Israel, the Romans] wrapped each one in his book, and they burned them. From all of them none remained but me." He applied to himself the verse, "My eyes have caused me grief from all the daughters of my city" (Lam. 3:51).

The evil Hadrian had a large vineyard, eighteen Roman miles by eighteen Roman miles, the dimension of the distance from Tiberias to Sepphoris. They surrounded it with a wall made of the victims of Betar as high as a man and his extended arms. And he did not decree that they may be buried until a different king arose and decreed that they might be buried.

9.6.5 Babylonian Talmud Gittin 57a: The Destruction of Betar[151]

The Babylonian Talmud also narrated the horrible destruction of the Bar Kokhba war. Apparently, however, the Babylonian sages thought that the war had begun at Betar and sought to explain its cause.

---

151. Trans. S. Berrin.

𝕊

Because of the shaft of a litter Betar was destroyed. For they had a custom that when a baby boy was born they planted a cedar tree, and for a baby girl they planted a pine tree, and when they would marry, they would cut them down and make a marriage canopy [of the branches]. One day, the daughter of Caesar was passing and the shaft of her litter broke. They cut down a cedar and brought it to her. [The Jews of Betar] fell upon them and beat them. They reported to Caesar that the Jews were rebelling and he marched against them.

"He cut off in fierce anger all the horn of Israel" (Lam. 2:3). Said Rabbi Zeira, said Rabbi Abahu, said Rabbi Yoḥanan, "These are the eighty[152] battle horns which they brought into the city of Betar at the time it was captured. And they killed there men, women and children until their blood flowed into the Mediterranean Sea. Lest you think it was near, it was a Roman mile away."

It has been taught: Rabbi Eliezer the Elder said, "There are two streams in the Valley of Yadayim,[153] one running in one direction, and one running in the other direction, and the sages estimated that they ran two parts water to one part blood."

It was taught in a baraita: For seven years the Gentiles cultivated their vineyards with the blood of Israel without requiring manure (for fertilizer).

9.7 REBUILDING FOR THE FUTURE

9.7.1 *Song of Songs Rabbah* to 2:5 (no. 3): The Sages of Usha[154]

This midrashic text testifies to the immediate effect made after the defeat of Bar Kokhba to reinstate Torah study at Usha, the new seat of the Rabbinic academy.

𝕊

At the end of the Persecution,[155] our teachers gathered at Usha, and these are they: Rabbi Judah, Rabbi Neḥemiah, Rabbi Meir, Rabbi Yose, Rabbi Simeon bar Yoḥai, Rabbi Eliezer ben Rabbi Yose the Galilean, and

---

152. The exaggerated number of 80,000 found in some texts is incorrect.
153. A valley close to Betar.
154. Trans. S. Berrin.
155. The Hadrianic persecutions connected with the aftermath of the Bar Kokhba Revolt. After Hadrian's death in 138 C.E., the persecutions ended.

Rabbi Eliezer ben Jacob. They sent to the Elders of the Galilee saying, "Whoever has learned, let him come and teach; whoever has not learned, let him come and learn." They gathered, and learned, and they took care of all their needs.[156]

9.7.2 Modestinus, *Corpus Jurus Civilis*: Digesta 48:8:11: Circumcision Limited to Jews[157]

The following rescript, recorded by the lawyer Herennius Modestinus (first half of the third century C.E.) and included in the Justinian Code, effectively made it impossible for non-Jews to convert to Judaism since it forbade them to undergo circumcision.

ﷺ

By a rescript[158] of the deified Pius[159] it is allowed only to Jews to circumcise their own sons; a person not of that religion who does so suffers the penalty of one carrying out a castration.

---

156. Taking the steps necessary to restore the orderly function of the halakhic system.

157. Trans. S. Berrin.

158. A rescript is a reply to the request of an individual or administrator for the opinion of the emperor on a legal matter.

159. Antoninus Pius, emperor from 138–161 C.E., was deified upon his death.

10

Mishnah: The New Scripture

The creation and redaction of the Mishnah and the other texts of what has come to be called tannaitic literature represented a major turning point in the development of postbiblical Judaism. To be sure, the collecting and editing of these texts resulted in large part from historical processes set off by the destruction of the Temple. In the aftermath of the destruction, Judaism somehow intrinsically moved toward a process of unification around the teachings of the Pharisaic-Rabbinic tradition. The many and variegated forms which Judaism took in the Second Temple period and the warring factions of the years leading up to the destruction now gave way to the mishnaic tradition, which would serve as a unifying factor for the Jewish people. This is not to say that all Jews, whether in the Land of Israel or outside, immediately adopted the Rabbinic tradition, but rather that the creation of the Mishnah and related texts through a long oral process of collection and redaction was the beginning of this unifying process. This process would culminate first in the editing of the Mishnah ca. 200 C.E., and then with the editing of the other tannaitic corpora certainly by ca. 450 C.E., and finally with the sustained examination of these traditions in the Jerusalem and Babylonian Talmuds.

The tannaim traced the history of the Pharisaic tradition by listing in the Mishnah a series of sages who served as patriarchs and heads of the court. Ostensibly, this list (Tosefta Ḥagigah [text 10.1.1]) presented a history of the views of these sages regarding the permissibility of the laying on of hands on festival sacrifices. This list traces Pharisaic tradition from soon after the Maccabean Revolt (168–164 B.C.E.) until the time of the great sages Hillel and Shammai, whose students laid the basis for the halakhic debates of the Mishnah and Tosefta.

It was only natural that these sages would come into conflict with those Jews who were aligned with the Roman occupiers of the country. In 47 B.C.E., Pharisaic leaders were among the members of the Sanhedrin who summoned Herod, then a governor of the Galilee, to trial for his summary execution of "robbers" who may, in fact, have been anti-Roman revolutionaries. As Josephus tells us in *Antiquities* (text 10.1.2), the hero of this narrative was Sameas, probably the Pharisaic sage Shemaiah, who was willing to stand up to Herod and his Hasmonean backer, Hyrcanus II. Later on, Josephus (text 10.1.3) relates that when Herod became king, he honored the Pharisees Pollio and Sameas, probably Abtalion and Shemaiah, known from Rabbinic sources.

The apogee of the development of Pharisaism was perhaps its final stage as it gave way to tannaitic Judaism. Indeed, we may consider Hillel and Shammai to be the last of the Pharisees, and at the same time, they or their students, the Houses of Hillel and Shammai, are the first of the tannaim. The rise to power of Hillel, a sage of Babylonian origin, is related in several versions in Rabbinic literature of which we have provided Tosefta Pesaḥim (text 10.1.4) and Jerusalem Talmud Pesaḥim (text 10.1.5). In both of these narratives, involving questions concerning how to offer the Passover sacrifice so as to avoid conflict with the laws of the Sabbath, the message was the same. Hillel's ability to marshal all the logical techniques of the hermeneutical rules of tannaitic tradition was of no use. Only when he declared that he had learned the ruling from his teachers, Shemaiah and Abtalion, was his view accepted. This appeal to authority in the face of convincing logic may be seen as an assertion by our sources that ultimately oral tradition is the validator of Rabbinic teaching.

Yet Hillel, whose students would soon attain the dominant position, at least in the eyes of later amoraic sages, was an innovator as well. Faced with the challenge posed by an absence of lenders resulting from the specific laws of the Sabbatical year, he ordained the *prozbul*, a legal device to avoid the remission of debts every seventh year. The scriptural basis for this innovation is discussed by the *Sifre Deuteronomy* (text 10.1.6). Later Babylonian amoraic tradition preserved in the Babylonian Talmud Shabbat (text 10.1.7) told a number of stories about Hillel, emphasizing his kindness and patience.

According to Rabbinic sources, the later patriarchal family traced itself through Hillel to King David. In the case of Rabban Gamliel I, the New Testament in the book of Acts (text 10.1.8) testifies to the significance of this Pharisaic teacher and the honored position that he held. Josephus, *Life* (text 10.1.9), in discussing his own involvement in the Great Revolt (66–73 C.E.), describes Simeon ben Gamliel I, a leading Pharisee. Josephus depicts the earlier return of the Pharisees to power during the reign of Salome Alexandra in *War* (text 10.1.10) in which he paints them as effectively taking over political power from the queen. Their political success, however, can also be explained as due to their popularity with the masses.

Central to Pharisaic-Rabbinic Judaism was the dual-Torah concept. According to this notion, found in tannaitic literature but developed fully only in amoraic texts, God gave two Torahs to Israel at Sinai—the oral and the written. One of the components of what the Rabbis called the oral Torah was tradition. Already in the Hasmonean period, according to Josephus' *Antiquities* (text 10.2.1), this was an object of debate between the Pharisees, who accepted traditions handed down by their ancestors, and the Sadducees, who denied the authority of laws which could not be traced to the biblical text. In the Hellenistic Jewish works, such traditions merged with the concept of unwritten law as seen in Philo, *The Special Laws* (text 10.2.2). Especially significant in the Pharisaic nonbiblical tradition were the purity laws, as we can gather from the New Testament Gospel of Mark (text 10.2.3), which confirms the picture derived from mishnaic literature. While contemporary sources give us little information about the particular Pharisee-Sadducee debates on matters of Jewish law, the seventh- or eighth-century scholion of *Megillat Ta'anit* (text 10.2.4) attempts to provide an understanding of how these groups differed regarding the interpretation of the Torah. This account, however, dates to so long after the events it describes that it cannot be accepted at face value.

By amoraic times, the concept of the oral law had attained significant development so that we can even observe a variety of points of view about how extensive the revelation of this second Torah was. In addition, we can see how influential the concept of oral law was on the development of Rabbinic tradition. The Targum, the Aramaic translation of the Bible, was likewise considered to be part of the oral law, and according to Jerusalem Talmud Megillah (text 10.2.5) it was forbidden to read an Aramaic translation from a book during formal instruction or as part of the synagogue Torah-reading service. Further, the Babylonian Talmud (text 10.2.6) strongly makes the point that because the written law was given in writing, it must be transmitted in writing, and because the oral law was given orally, it must be transmitted orally. The sages all agreed with the view of *Sifre Deuteronomy* (text 10.2.7) that the Torah itself confirmed the validity of the dual-Torah concept.

The tannaim followed a complex procedure for teaching the oral law, according to which tradition was passed on orally from teacher to student. In reconstructing the manner in which Moses would have taught the oral law that he had received at Sinai, the tannaitic tradition in Babylonian Talmud Eruvin (text 10.3.1) is reflecting the procedures for teaching and memorizing which were followed in tannaitic academies. This is not to say that written notes and, in some cases, texts did not exist in tannaitic times, but rather that the formal process of instruction was conducted orally and mnemonically. Mishnah Avot (text 10.3.2) specifically refers to the passing of the oral and written law from Sinai, tracing it through Rabbi Judah the Prince, the editor of the Mishnah. Besides teaching the Rabbis and their students how to conduct themselves as sages, teachers, and judges, Avot sought to assert to validity of the Mishnah as the authoritative summary of the oral law.

According to tannaitic belief, the development and interpretation of the oral law had been given to the Jewish people. This meant that authority to interpret the written law now rested in the Rabbis. The point is dramatically illustrated by the narrative preserved in Babylonian Talmud Bava Meẓia (text 10.3.3). Based on talmudic evidence, Rav Sherira Gaon, writing in the tenth century, traces the early history of the tannaitic movement (text 10.3.4). Despite the late date of this account and the presence of some ahistorical details, this pioneering historiographic work has served as the basis for all later reconstructions of tannaitic history.

Characteristic of tannaitic and amoraic teaching is the dichotomy between Midrash, the exegesis of Scripture, and Mishnah, the statement of abstract law. But these two forms of Rabbinic teaching were understood by the tannaim to constitute a unified whole, bound together by hermeneutical (interpretive) rules such as those compiled by Rabbi Ishmael, presented at the beginning of the *Sifra* (text 10.4.1), a halakhic Midrash on Leviticus. In some cases, tannaitic Midrashim make reference to or even quote the very same laws found in the Mishnah or Tosefta. While in some cases this is because the Midrashim already had before them tannaitic legal statements which they sought to justify by scriptural allusion, the reverse is also the case: that often the halakhic Midrashim preserve the scriptural basis upon which laws found in the Mishnah or Tosefta were derived. To exemplify this complex relationship, we present an excerpt from Mishnah Bava Qamma (text 10.4.2) dealing with damage by fire to the field of another and the corresponding midrashic passage from the *Mekhilta of Rabbi Ishmael* (text 10.4.3).

A second dichotomy is between halakhah—law, and aggadah— stories, ethical teachings, and theology. Aggadah is characterized by the Babylonian Talmud Ḥagigah (text 10.5.1) as the most attractive or inspiring part of the tradition. To the Rabbis, the totality of both of these aspects (as was the case with oral and written law, and Mishnah and Midrash) constituted the entirety of Torah, as emphasized in Jerusalem Talmud Ḥagigah (text 10.5.2). Some sages even saw aggadah as sometimes providing a deeper understanding of Judaism than the study of the legal traditions, as evidenced by Jerusalem Talmud Horayot (text 10.5.3). It appears from a variety of sources, including Jerusalem Talmud Sheqalim (text 10.5.4), that it was customary in tannaitic circles to separate the study of halakhah and aggadah in the curriculum, as it was also the practice to organize study on the basis of either Scriptural interpretation or Mishnah-like tradition.

The complex process of redacting (collecting and editing) the contents of the Mishnah and at the same time deciding what to exclude, effected by Rabbi Judah the Prince ca. 200 C.E., is the subject of a detailed discussion by Rav Sherira Gaon (text 10.6.1). He raises practically all the historical questions to which medieval and modern scholars would return in discussing the history and development of the Mishnah.

Although numerous mishnaic passages are given in this book in various contexts, we present here a few samples to illustrate some central features of the Mishnah. The first example from Mishnah Shabbat (text 10.6.2) illustrates how the Mishnah legislates for an ideal Jewish society at a time in which the Temple would be standing. An excerpt from Mishnah Bava Meẓia (text 10.6.3) exemplifies the concern of Jewish law for all matters and the inclusion in the halakhic system of all aspects of civil law. Here we see an anonymous mishnah commented on by a specific tanna, a feature typical of tannaitic texts. The excerpt from Mishnah Rosh ha-Shanah (text 10.6.4) illustrates the Mishnah's reckoning with the destruction of the Temple in adapting the law to the new circumstances. Further, it preserves a dispute between the Houses of Hillel and Shammai which typifies earlier strata of the Mishnah. This passage also gives a sense of the role of the tannaim in controlling the calendar and so regulating the festivals of the Jewish people. It is important to remember, as noted in Jerusalem Talmud Horayot (text 10.6.5), that the Mishnah redacted by Rabbi Judah the Prince did not constitute the only collection of tannaitic traditions deemed authoritative by its redactors, Other such collections circulated, and their influence is evident in the traditions of the amoraim.

Besides the Mishnah, during the amoraic period a number of collections were made of earlier material, for the most part emerging out of tannaitic academies and study circles. These texts were an important supplement to the Mishnah, and yet their specific relationship to the later talmudic and midrashic collections is very much a matter of scholarly debate.

The nature of the Tosefta and its relationship to the Mishnah is discussed at length by Rav Sherira Gaon (text 10.7.1). As an example of a Tosefta text, we present Tosefta Rosh ha-Shanah (text 10.7.2), which can be compared with its mishnaic parallel included above. The Tosefta, the earliest commentary to the Mishnah, expands upon and explicates the Mishnah, often presenting parallel traditions and differing attributions. Other tannaitic traditions include *baraitot* (individual traditions preserved in various corpora), and the halakhic Midrashim. Rav Sherira Gaon discusses matters pertaining to these as well (text 10.7.3). Although the *Mekhilta* texts, *Sifra*, and *Sifre* are often termed halakhic Midrashim, they contain much aggadah. The *Mekhilta*, for example, is actually three-fifths aggadah. An example of such tannaitic aggadah, from *Mekhilta of Rabbi Ishmael* to *Beshallaḥ*, is presented here (text 10.7.4). The major contents of the *Sifra*, on the other hand, a complex and difficult work, are constituted of careful halakhic interpretation and argumentation as illustrated in the discussion in *Sifra Emor* (text 10.7.5). The complex textual tradition that emerged from the work of the tannaim in the form of the Mishnah, redacted at the end of the tannaitic period, and the other texts redacted somewhat later, constituted a firm intellectual basis for what would be the greatest achievement of Rabbinic Judaism, the creation of the Babylonian and Jerusalem Talmuds.

10.1 FROM PHARISEES TO RABBIS

10.1.1 Mishnah Ḥagigah 2:2–3, Tosefta Ḥagigah 2:8, 10: Rabbinic Traditions about the Pharisees[1]

Later Rabbinic tradition traced the official nasi (patriarch) and head of the court all the way back to the Hasmonean and Herodian periods. In these passages, in which there appear lists of those who prohibited and permitted the laying on of hands on sacrifices offered on festivals, we observe the claim of continuity of the chain of tradition between the Pharisaic sages and the early tannaim, the teachers of the Mishnah.

꧁

Mishnah Ḥagigah 2:2–3

2 Yose ben Yoezer says [on a festival day] not to lay [hands on the offering before it is slaughtered]. Yose ben Yoḥanan says to lay [hands].

Joshua ben Peraḥiah says not to lay [hands]. Nittai the Arbelite says to lay [hands].

---

1. Trans. J. Neusner, *From Politics to Piety: The Emergence of Pharisaic Judaism* (Englewood Cliffs, NJ: Prentice Hall, 1973), pp. 104, 106–7.

Judah ben Tabbai says not to lay [hands]. Simeon ben Shetaḥ says to lay [hands].

Shemaiah says to lay [hands]. Abtalion says not to lay [hands].

Hillel and Menaḥem did not differ, but Menaḥem went forth, and Shammai entered in.[2]

Shammai says not to lay [hands]. Hillel says to lay [hands].

The former were *nasis* [patriarchs], and the latter, fathers of the court [chief magistrates].

3 The House of Shammai say, "They may bring peace-offerings [on a festival day] and do not lay the hands thereon; but [they do] not [bring] burnt-offerings."

And the House of Hillel say, "They may bring [both] peace-offerings and burnt-offerings and lay their hands thereon."

Tosefta Ḥagigah 2:8, 10

8 They differed only on the laying of hands.

"They are five pairs. The three of the first pairs who said not to lay on hands, and the two of the last pairs who said to lay on hands were *nasis*. The second ones [mentioned] were heads of the court," so Rabbi Meir.

Rabbi Judah [bar Ilai] said, "Simeon ben Shetaḥ [was] *nasi*. Judah ben Tabbai [was] head of the court. . . ."

10 What is the laying on of hands concerning which they differed? The House of Shammai say, "They do not lay on hands on the festival, and as to peace-offerings, the one who celebrates through them lays hands on them on the day *before* the festival."

The House of Hillel say, "They bring peace-offerings and burnt-offerings and lay hands on them [as in the Mishnah]."

10.1.2 Josephus, *Antiquities* XIV, 168–84: Herod's Trial before the Sanhedrin[3]

In an attempt to maintain order and control of the Galilee where he was governor from 47 B.C.E., Herod summarily killed those rebels whom he regarded as robbers without trial. He was tried for this offense before the Sanhedrin, but due to a powerful ally, Herod was able to escape a death sentence. The Sanhedrin before which Herod appeared was no doubt made up of repre-

---

2. Menaḥem left office and was replaced by Shammai.

3. All passages from Josephus trans. W. Whiston, *The Works of Josephus* (Peabody, MA: Hendrickson, 1987), revised by L. H. Schiffman in consultation with H. St. J. Thackeray, Ralph Marcus, Allen Wikgren, and L. H. Feldman, trans., *Josephus: In Nine Volumes* (Loeb Classical Library; Cambridge: Harvard University Press, 1976–79).

sentatives of a variety of parties. Sameas, the central figure in that body, was
certainly an early Pharisaic sage.

☙

(168) When Hyrcanus heard this[4] he was persuaded by them. In addition, the mothers of those who had been killed by Herod raised his indignation, for every day in the temple those women kept begging the king and the people that Herod should undergo a trial before the Sanhedrin for what he had done. (169) Hyrcanus was so moved by these complaints that he summoned Herod to come to his trial for the crimes of which he was accused. Accordingly, he came, but his father (Antipater) had persuaded him to come not like a private individual, but with a guard for the security of his person [and that] when he had settled the affairs of the Galilee in the best manner he could to his own advantage, he should come to his trial, but still with a body of men sufficient for his security on his journey, yet with not so great a force as might look terrifying to Hyrcanus, but still a sufficient one as might not leave him unarmed and unprotected [to his enemies]. (170) However, Sextus, governor of Syria, wrote to Hyrcanus and asked him to clear Herod and acquit him at his trial, and threatened him beforehand if he did not do so. This letter of his gave Hyrcanus a pretext for delivering Herod from suffering any harm from the Sanhedrin, for he loved him as his own son. (171) In addition, when Herod stood before the Sanhedrin with his body of men around him, he frightened them all. None of his former accusers dared after that to bring any charge against him. There was instead a deep silence, and nobody knew what was to be done.

(172) While they were in this state, one whose name was Sameas,[5] a righteous man above all fear, rose up and said, "O, you who are councilors with me, and you, our king, I have myself never known such a case nor do I suppose that any one of you can name its parallel. One who was called to stand trial never stood in such a manner before us. But everyone, whoever he may be, who comes to be tried by this Sanhedrin, presents himself in a submissive manner, like one who is in fear of his life and who endeavors to move us to compassion, with his hair disheveled and in a black mourning garment. (173) But this fine fellow Herod, who is accused of murder and called to answer so serious an accusation, stands here clothed in purple with the hair of his head finely trimmed and with

---

4. In *Ant.* XIV, 165–7 the "chief Jews" lodged their accusation with Hyrcanus II that Herod had executed alleged criminals without trial, in violation of the law.

5. Probably the Pharisaic sage Shemaiah, known from Mishnaic sources.

his armed men about him. If we condemn him according to our law, he may kill us and by overpowering justice may himself escape death. (174) Yet I do not make this complaint against Herod himself. He is, to be sure, more concerned for himself than for the laws. But my complaint is against yourselves and your king who give him a license to do so. However, take notice that God is great, and that this very man, whom you are going to absolve and dismiss for the sake of Hyrcanus, will one day punish both you and your king also."

(175) Sameas did not make a mistake in any part of this prediction. For when Herod had received the kingdom, he killed all the members of this Sanhedrin and Hyrcanus, except for Sameas. (176) For he had great respect for him on account of his righteousness and because when the city was afterwards besieged by Herod and Sossius,[6] he persuaded the people to admit Herod into it and told them that for their sins they would not be able to escape his hands—matters which will be related by us in their proper places.[7]

(177) But when Hyrcanus saw that the members of the Sanhedrin were ready to pronounce the sentence of death upon Herod, he put off the trial to another day and sent privately to Herod, advising him to flee from the city in order to escape. (178) So he retired to Damascus, as though he fled from the king. When he had been with Sextus and had made his own affairs secure, he resolved to do this—that in case he were again summoned before the Sanhedrin to stand trial, he would not obey the summons. (179) Thereupon, the members of the Sanhedrin became very indignant at this state of affairs, and endeavored to persuade Hyrcanus that all these things were directed against him. Of this state of affairs he was not ignorant, but his temperament was so unmanly and so foolish that he was incompetent to do anything.

(180) But when Sextus made Herod general of the army of Celesyria, for he sold him that post for money, Hyrcanus was in fear lest Herod should make war upon him. The effect of what he feared was not long in coming, for Herod came and brought an army along with him to fight against Hyrcanus, being angry because of the trial he had been summoned to undergo before the Sanhedrin. (181) But his father Antipater and his brother [Phasaelus] met him and prevented him from assaulting Jerusalem. They also pacified his vehement temper and persuaded him to undertake no violent action but only to frighten them with threats and to

---

6. 39 B.C.E.
7. *Ant.* XV, 3–4.

proceed no further against one who had given him the dignity he had.[8] (182) They also asked him not to be angry that he was summoned and obligated to come to his trial but to remember that he was dismissed without condemnation, and that he ought to give Hyrcanus thanks for that and that he should not consider only what was disagreeable to him and be ungrateful for his deliverance.... (184) Herod was persuaded by these arguments and believed that it was sufficient for his future hopes merely to have made a show of his strength before the nation. This, then, was the state of affairs in Judea.

10.1.3 Josephus, *Antiquities* XV, 2–3, 368–70: Sameas and Pollio

Josephus provides a brief report about Sameas and Pollio, two Pharisaic leaders. Most scholars see them as identical to Shemaiah and Abtalion mentioned in the Mishnah as teachers of Hillel and Shammai.

෴

(2) ... Since Herod now had the government of all Judea in his hands, he promoted those men of the city as had been on his side when he was a commoner, but never stopped avenging and punishing every day those who had chosen to be on the side of his enemies. (3) But Pollio the Pharisee and Sameas, a disciple of his, were honored by him above all the rest, for when Jerusalem was besieged, they advised the citizens to receive Herod, for which advice they were well rewarded. ...

(368) As for those who obstinately refused to acquiesce to his scheme of government, he persecuted them in every way. But for the rest of the populace, he required that they take an oath of fidelity to him, and at the same time compelled them to swear that they would bear him good will in his management of the government. (369) Indeed, most of them, either to please him or out of fear of him, yielded to what he required of them. But as for those who were of a more open and generous disposition, and were indignant at the force he used against them, he by one means or another got rid of them. (370) He endeavored also to persuade Pollio the Pharisee, Sameas, and most of their disciples to take the oath, but these would neither submit to do so nor were they punished together with the rest, out of the reverence he bore to Pollio.

---

8. Hyrcanus had previously appointed Herod governor of the Galilee.

10.1.4 Tosefta Pesaḥim 4:13: Hillel's Rise to Power[9]

Rabbinic literature preserves several versions of the narrative of Hillel's rise to power as leader of the Pharisaic-Rabbinic sages ca. 30 B.C.E. According to this account, Hillel's attempt to prove his views regarding the Passover sacrifice was of no avail until he cited a tradition from his teachers. Only the force of tradition was able to sway the argument. He explained the proper way to present a Passover-offering on the Sabbath, in view of the prohibition of carrying the sacrificial knife on that day from outside the sanctuary.

⌘

One time the fourteenth [of Nisan, the eve of Passover] fell on the Sabbath. They asked Hillel the Elder, "Does the *Pesaḥ* [Passover-offering] override the Sabbath? [That is, is the Passover-sacrifice offered on the Sabbath?]"

He said to them "And do we have only one *Pesaḥ* in the year which overrides the Sabbath? We have many more than three hundred *Pesaḥs* in the year, and they override the Sabbath."[10]

The whole courtyard collected against him.

He said to them, "The continual offering[11] is a community sacrifice, and the *Pesaḥ* is a community sacrifice. Just as the continual offering, a community sacrifice, overrides the Sabbath, so the *Pesaḥ* is a community sacrifice and overrides the Sabbath.

"Another matter: It is said concerning the continual offering: 'In its season' (Num. 28:2), and it is said with reference to the *Pesaḥ*: 'In its season' (Num. 9:2). Just as the continual offering, concerning which 'In its season' is said, overrides the Sabbath, so the *Pesaḥ* concerning which 'In its season' is said, overrides the Sabbath.

"And furthermore [it is a] *qal va-ḥomer* [argument *a fortiori*]: Although the continual offering, which does not produce the [severe] liability of *cutting off*,[12] overrides the Sabbath, the *Pesaḥ*, which *does* produce the liability of *cutting off*—is it not logical that it should override the Sabbath?

"And further, I have received from my masters [the tradition] that the *Pesaḥ* overrides the Sabbath, and not [merely] the first *Pesaḥ*[13] but the sec-

---

9. Trans. Neusner, *From Politics to Piety*, pp. 23–4.

10. Numerous sacrifices are offered on the Sabbath each week, so why should we consider the *Pesaḥ* offering to be any different?

11. The burnt offering sacrificed twice daily.

12. Excision, understood by the Rabbis as either dying young or childless.

13. On the fourteenth of Nisan.

ond,[14] and not [merely] the community *Pesah* but the individual *Pesah* [as well]."

They said to him, "What will be the rule for the people who on the Sabbath did not bring knives and *Pesah*-offerings to the sanctuary?"

He said to them, "Leave them alone. The holy spirit is upon them. If they are not prophets, they are disciples of the prophets." What did Israel [the Jews] do in that hour? He whose *Pesah* was a lamb hid it in its wool; if it was a kid, he tied it between its horns; so they brought knives and *Pesahs* to the sanctuary and slew their *Pesah*-sacrifices.

On that very day they appointed Hillel as *nasi*, and he would teach to them concerning the laws of the *Pesah*.

10.1.5 Jerusalem Talmud Pesahim 6:1 (33a): Another Version of Hillel's Rise to Power[15]

The Jerusalem Talmud presents an alternative version of this same story, the rise of Hillel to Pharisaic-Rabbinic leadership. Here also, no amount of logic was acceptable. Hillel won the argument only by appealing to the authority of his teachers. The message is clear: tradition, not original logical deduction, is the true authority of the oral law.

༄

This law was lost from the Elders of Bathyra.[16] One time the fourteenth [of Nisan] turned out to coincide with the Sabbath, and they did not know whether the *Pesah* [Passover offering] overrides the Sabbath or not. They said, "There is here a certain Babylonian, and Hillel is his name, who studied with Shemaiah and Abtalion. [He] knows whether the *Pesah* overrides the Sabbath or not. Perhaps there will be profit from him."[17] They sent and called him.

They said to him, "Have you ever heard, when the fourteenth [of Nisan] coincides with the Sabbath, whether it overrides the Sabbath or not?"

---

14. The observance of a second Passover a month later on the fourteenth of Iyyar to allow those impure or not able to reach the Temple to offer their Passover offering (Num. 9:9–14).

15. Trans. Neusner, *From Politics to Piety*, pp. 27–8.

16. "Bathyrans were Babylonian Jewish immigrants who came at the time of Herod and were settled in frontier regions, northeast of the Sea of Galilee, to protect the border. They founded the town of Bathyra, whence the name. Herod put some of them into the Temple hierarchy" (Neusner, p. 27).

17. Perhaps he can provide a solution to the problem.

He said to them, "And do we have only one *Pesah* alone that overrides the Sabbath in the whole year? And do not many *Pesahs* override the Sabbath in the whole year?"[18] (Some Tannaim teach a hundred, and some Tannaim teach two hundred, and some Tannaim teach three hundred. He who said "one hundred" [refers to] continual offerings. He who said "two hundred" [refers to] continual offerings and Sabbath additional-offerings. He who said "three hundred" [refers to] continual offerings, Sabbath additional-offerings, [and those] of festivals, and of New Moons, and of seasons.[19])

They said to him, "We have already said that there is profit with you."

He began expounding for them by means of arguments based on *heqqesh, qal va-homer* and *gezerah shavah*:

Heqqesh:[20] Since the continual offering is a community sacrifice and the *Pesah* is a community sacrifice, just as the continual offering, a community sacrifice, overrides [the] Sabbath, so the *Pesah*, a community sacrifice, overrides the Sabbath.

Qal va-homer:[21] If doing the continual offering [improperly], which does not produce the penalty of cutting off, overrides the Sabbath, doing the *Pesah* sacrifice [improperly], which *does* produce the liability of cutting off, all the more so should override the Sabbath.

Gezerah shavah:[22] Concerning the continual offering, "In its season" is said (Num. 28:2), and concerning the *Pesah*, "In its season" is said (Num. 9:3). Just as the continual offering, concerning which is said "In its season" overrides the Sabbath, so the *Pesah*, concerning which "In its season" is said, overrides the Sabbath.

They said to him, "We have already said, 'There is no profit [benefit] from the Babylonian.'[23] As to the *heqqesh* which you said, there is a rebuttal: for if you (use the status of) the continual offering (in your argument), (then you must acknowledge that) there is a limit to the continual offering,[24] but (then you cannot compare the status of) the *Pesah* which has no limit.[25] [Since the two are different, the same rule therefore cannot apply.]

---

18. Therefore it is permissible to sacrifice the Passover offering on the Sabbath.

19. The intermediate days of Passover and Sukkot.

20. This method of exegesis makes an analogy from one set of circumstances to another.

21. An *a fortiori* argument from a stricter to a more lenient case.

22. The use of a common expression in the Bible referring to two matters links the two so that it follows that the same law must apply to both.

23. After listening to his argument from logic, they deny the value of his teachings.

24. Only two are offered.

25. Since innumerable offerings must be made by the entire Jewish people.

"The *qal va-ḥomer* which you stated has a rebuttal: What you say concerning the continual offering, which is the most sacred, can you apply it to the *Pesaḥ,* which is of lesser sanctity? [So the argument collapses.]

"As to the *gezerah shavah* that you stated: A man may not reason a *gezerah shavah* on his own [but must cite it from tradition]. . . ."

Even though he sat and expounded for them all day, they did not accept [it] from him, until he said to them, "May [evil] come upon me![26] Thus have I heard from Shemaiah and Abtalion!" When they heard this from him, they arose and appointed him *nasi* (patriarch) over them.

When they had appointed him *nasi* over them, he began to criticize them, saying, "Who caused you to need this Babylonian? Is it not because you did not serve the two great men of the world, Shemaiah and Abtalion, who were sitting with you?" Since he criticized them, the law was forgotten by him.[27]

They said to him, "What shall we do for the people who did not bring their knives?"

He said to them, "This law have I heard, but I have forgotten [it]. But leave Israel [alone]. If they are not prophets, they are disciples of prophets."

Forthwith, whoever had a lamb as his *Pesaḥ* sacrifice would hide it [the knife] in its wool; [if] it was a kid, he would tie the knife between its horns. So their *Pesaḥ* sacrificial animals turned out to be bringing their own knives with them. When he saw the deed, he remembered the law. He said, "Thus have I heard from Shemaiah and Abtalion."

10.1.6 Sifre Deuteronomy 113: Hillel as Legislator[28]

Hillel, the first century B.C.E. sage, enacted the prozbul, a legislative decree, in order to encourage people to make loans to one another even though there was an upcoming sabbatical year. In the sabbatical year, debts which had been contracted were annulled according to the laws of the Torah (Deut. 15:1–2). By transferring the debt to the court, it remained collectible.

৯৫

"Whatever of yours that is with your brothers your hand should release" (Deut. 15:3), but not one who gives his mortgages to the court. On this basis, they said: Hillel ordained the *prozbul,* on account of the order of the world. He saw that (people) held back from lending to one

---

26. An oath formula indicating the truth of what follows.
27. As a punishment for his arrogant behavior.
28. Trans. L. H. Schiffman.

another and transgressed what is written in the Torah, so he arose and ordained the *prozbul*.

And this is the formula of the *prozbul*: "I give to you, so-and-so and so-and-so, the judges in such-and-such place, every debt which I have, so that I may collect it whenever I wish," and the judges sign below, or the witnesses.

10.1.7 Babylonian Talmud Shabbat 30b–31a: The Patience of Hillel[29]

The Babylonian Talmud preserves a group of stories that circulated in the amoraic period (after 200 C.E.) in Babylonia. These stories contrast Hillel with his colleague Shammai. The stories picture Hillel as patient and Shammai as abrupt. These stories clearly reflect the fact that it was by and large the House of Hillel whose views dominated in halakhah. One of the stories is particularly important in that it emphasizes the need for an oral law to accompany the written.

ਙ

Our Rabbis taught: A man should always be gentle like Hillel, and not impatient like Shammai.

It once happened that two men made a wager with each other, saying, "He who goes and makes Hillel angry shall receive four hundred *zuz*."

Said one, "I will anger him."

That day was the Sabbath eve, and Hillel was washing his head. He went, passed by the door of his house, and called out, "Is Hillel here? Is Hillel here?"

Thereupon he robed and went out to him, saying, "My son, what do you seek?"

"I have a question to ask," said he.

"Ask, my son," he said to him.

He asked, "Why are heads of the Babylonians round?"

"My son, you have asked a great question," he said. "Because they have no skillful midwives."

He departed, tarried a while, returned, and said, "Is Hillel here? Is Hillel here?"

He robed and went out to him, saying, "My son, what do you seek?"

"I have a question to ask," said he.

"Ask, my son," he said.

---

29. Trans. Neusner, *From Politics to Piety,* pp. 37–9.

He asked, "Why are the eyes of the Palmyreans bleared?"

"My son, you have asked a great question," said he. "Because they live in sandy places."

He departed, tarried a while, returned, and said, "Is Hillel here? Is Hillel here?"

He robed and went out to him, saying, "My son, what do you seek?"

"I have a question to ask," said he.

"Ask, my son," he said.

He asked, "Why are the feet of the Africans wide?"

"My son, you have asked a great question," said he. "Because they live in watery marshes."

"I have many questions to ask," said he, "but fear that you may become angry."

Thereupon he robed, sat before him and said, "Ask all the questions you have to ask."

"Are you the Hillel whom they call the *nasi* of Israel?"

"Yes," he said.

"If that is you," he said, "may there not be many like you in Israel."

"Why, my son?" said he.

"Because I have lost four hundred *zuz* through you," complained he.

"Be careful of your moods," he answered.

"Hillel is worthy that you should lose four hundred *zuz* and yet another four hundred *zuz* through him, yet Hillel shall not lose his temper."

Our Rabbis taught: A certain heathen once came before Shammai and asked him, "How many Torahs have you?"

"Two," he replied, "The Written Torah and the Oral Torah."

"I believe you with respect to the Written Torah, but not with respect to the Oral Torah. Make me a proselyte on condition that you teach me the Written Torah [only]." He scolded and repulsed him in anger.

[When] he went before Hillel, he accepted him as a proselyte. On the first day he taught him, *Alef, bet, gimmel, delet* [= A, B, C, D]; the following day he reversed [them] to him.

"But yesterday you did not teach them to me thus," he said.

"Must you not rely upon me? Then rely upon me with respect to the Oral [Torah] too."[30]

On another occasion it happened that a certain heathen came before Shammai and said to him, "Make me a proselyte, on condition that you

---

30. The ability to read the written Torah depends on the oral tradition.

teach me the whole Torah while I stand on one foot." Thereupon he repulsed him with the builder's cubit[31] which was in his hand.

[When] he went before Hillel, he converted him. He said to him, "What is hateful to you, do not do to your neighbor. That is the whole Torah, while the rest is the commentary thereof; go and learn [it]."

On another occasion it happened that a certain heathen was passing behind a school and heard the voice of a scribe reciting, "And these are the garments which they shall make: a breastplate, and an ephod."[32]

Said he, "For whom are these?"

"For the high priest," they said.

Then said that heathen to himself, "I will go and become a proselyte, that I may be appointed a high priest."

So he went before Shammai and said to him, "Make me a proselyte on condition that you appoint me a high priest." But he repulsed him with the builder's cubit which was in his hand.

He then went before Hillel. He made him a proselyte.

Said he to him, "Can any man be made a king but he who knows the arts of government? Go and study the arts of government!"

He went and read. When he came to "And the stranger that comes nigh shall be put to death" (Num. 1:51), he asked him, "To whom does this verse apply?"

"Even to David, King of Israel," was the answer.

Thereupon that proselyte reasoned within himself *a fortiori* [*qal va-homer*]: "If Israel, who are called sons of the Omnipresent, and whom in His love for them he designated 'Israel is my son, my first born'(Ex. 4:22), yet it is written of them, 'And the stranger that comes nigh shall be put to death'—how much more so a mere proselyte, who comes with his staff and wallet!"[33]

Then he went before Shammai and said to him, "Am I then eligible to be a high priest? Is it not written in the Torah, 'And the stranger that comes nigh shall be put to death?'"

He went before Hillel and said to him, "O gentle Hillel: blessings rest on your head for bringing me under the wings of the *Shekhinah* [divine Presence]!"

Some time later the three met in one place. Said they, "Shammai's impatience sought to drive us from the world, but Hillel's gentleness brought us under the wings of the *Shekhinah*."

---

31. Measuring rod.
32. Ex. 28:4.
33. Lacking any previous merit, having only material posessions.

10.1.8 Acts 5: Words of Rabban Gamaliel I[34]

The book of Acts pictures Rabban Gamliel I as reacting to the arrest of the Christian apostles. This passage has him reviewing the history of messianic pretenders in the Second Temple period.

ﷺ

33 When they heard this they were enraged and wanted to kill them. 34 But a Pharisee in the council named Gamaliel,[35] a teacher of the law, held in honor by all the people, stood up and ordered the men to be put outside for a while. 35 And he said to them, "Men of Israel, take care what you do with these men. 36 For before these days Theudas arose,[36] giving himself out to be somebody, and a number of men, about four hundred, joined him; but he was slain and all who followed him were dispersed and came to nothing. 37 After him Judas the Galilean arose in the days of the census[37] and drew away some of the people after him; he also perished, and all who followed him were scattered. 38 So in the present case I tell you, keep away from these men and let them alone; for if this plan or this undertaking is of men, it will fail; 39 but if it is of God, you will not be able to overthrow them. You might even be found opposing God!"

10.1.9 Josephus, *Life* 191–8: Simeon ben Gamliel I

In the course of relating his role in the Great Revolt against Rome (66–73 C.E.), Josephus refers to Simeon ben Gamliel (I) who was the son of the Gamliel mentioned in the New Testament. Simeon (Simon) was a leading Pharisee and apparently fell during the war. This account shows the extent of Pharisaic involvement in political affairs during the revolt.

ﷺ

(191) This Simon was of the city of Jerusalem and of a very noble family, of the sect of the Pharisees, who are supposed to excel others in the accurate knowledge of the laws of their country. (192) He was a man of great wisdom and reason, and capable of restoring public affairs by his

---

34. All New Testament passages in this chapter are from the *Revised Standard Version of the Bible* (New York: National Council of Churches, 1971).

35. Gamaliel and Gamliel are alternative spellings. "Gamliel" appears in Hebrew texts and "Gamaliel" in Greek texts.

36. Theudas, according to Josephus, *Ant.* XX, 97–104, rebelled in 45–46 C.E., some ten years after the dating of this scene in Acts.

37. Judas revolted in 6 C.E.

prudence, when they were in an unfortunate position. He was also an old friend and companion of John,[38] and at that time he had a difference with me. (193) When, therefore, he received such an exhortation, he persuaded the high priests, Ananus, and Jesus the son of Gamala, and some others of the same seditious faction, to cut me down, as I was growing so great, and not to allow me to attain the height of glory. He said that it would be to the advantage of the Galileans if I were deprived of my government there. He urged them to make no delay about the matter, for fear I would get wind of their plans and make an assault upon the city (Jerusalem) with a great army. (194) Such was Simon's advice, but Ananus the high priest demonstrated to them that this was not an easy thing to be done, because many of the high priests and the rulers of the people bore witness that I had acted like an excellent general, and that it was the work of ill men to accuse one against whom they had nothing to say.

(195) When Simon heard Ananus say this, he desired that the messengers should conceal the thing, and not let it come among many; for that he would take care to have Josephus removed out of Galilee very quickly. So he called for John's brother [Simon], and charged him that they should send presents to Ananus and his friends; for, as he said, they might probably, by that means, persuade them to change their minds. (196) And indeed Simon did at length thus accomplish his goal: for Ananus, and those with him, being corrupted by bribes, agreed to expel me from Galilee without making the rest of the citizens acquainted with what they were doing. Accordingly they resolved to send men of distinction as to their learning also.

(197) Two of these, Jonathan and Ananias, were of the populace, by sect Pharisees, while the third, Jozar, was of the stock of the priests and a Pharisee also. Simon, the last of them, was descended from the high priests. (198) Their instructions were that they were to come to the multitude of the Galileans and ask them what was the reason for their devotion to me? If they said that it was because I was born in Jerusalem, they should reply that they four were all born in the same place. If they should say that it was because I was well versed in their law, they should reply that neither were they unacquainted with the practices of their country. But if, besides these, they should say that they loved me because I was a priest, they should reply that two of them were also priests.

---

38. John of Gischala, one of the rebel leaders, who sought to deprive Josephus of his command of the Galilee and take the post for himself.

10.1.10 Josephus, *War* I, 110–12: The Pharisees in Power

Josephus here gives his opinion about how the Pharisees came to be the dominant party in the time of the Hasmonean queen, Salome Alexandra (76–67 B.C.E.). Again we see the Pharisaic role in political affairs.

༄

(110) And now the Pharisees joined themselves to her,[39] to assist her in the government. These are a certain sect of the Jews that appear more religious than others and seem to interpret the laws more accurately. (111) Alexandra hearkened to them to an extraordinary degree, being herself a woman of great piety towards God. But these Pharisees artfully insinuated themselves into her favor little by little, and became themselves the real administrators of public affairs. They banished and reduced whomever they pleased and bound and loosed [men] at their pleasure. In short, they enjoyed royal authority, while the expenses and the difficulties of it belonged to Alexandra. (112) She was a sagacious woman in the management of great affairs, and intent always upon gathering soldiers, she doubled her army, and collected a great body of foreign troops, so that her nation became not only very powerful at home, but a formidable foe even to foreign potentates. But while she governed other people, the Pharisees governed her.

10.2 WRITTEN AND ORAL TORAH

10.2.1 Josephus, *Antiquities* XIII, 297: The Pharisees and Sadducees on the Traditions of the Fathers

The traditions of the fathers, or elders, mentioned by Josephus, are an important component of what the Rabbis later called oral law. The traditions were a hallmark of the Pharisaic approach to Torah and continued into Rabbinic tradition as it was later enshrined in the Mishnah.

༄

(297) . . . What I would now explain is this, that the Pharisees have passed on to the people a great many observances handed down by their fathers, which are not written down in the law of Moses. For this reason the Sadducees reject them and say that we are to consider to be obliga-

---

39. The Pharisees became allies of Queen Salome Alexandra, after the death of her husband, Alexander Janneus, who ruled between 103 and 76 B.C.E.

tory only those observances which are in the written word, but need not observe those which are derived from the tradition of our forefathers.

10.2.2 Philo, *The Special Laws* IV, 143–150: Written and Unwritten Law[40]

Philo discusses both the immortality of the written law, and the obligation of observing the customs, the unwritten law. Although the Greek world had a concept of unwritten law, Philo's view is clearly informed by Jewish tradition and by the Pharisaic concept of tradition.

෨

Another most admirable injunction is that nothing should be added or taken away,[41] but all the laws originally ordained should be kept unaltered just as they were. For what actually happens, as we clearly see, is that it is the unjust which is added and the just which is taken away, for the wise legislator has omitted nothing which can give possession of justice whole and complete. Further he suggests also that the summit of perfection had been reached in each of the other virtues. For each of them is defective in nothing, complete in its self-wrought consummateness, so that if there be any adding or taking away, its whole being is changed and transformed into the opposite condition. . . .

In the same way too if one adds anything small or great to the queen of virtues' piety or on the other hand takes something from it, in either case he will change and transform its nature. Addition will beget superstition and subtraction will beget impiety, and so piety too is lost to sight, that sun whose rising and shining is a blessing we may well pray for, because it is the source of the greatest of blessings, since it gives the knowledge of the service of God, which we must hold as lordlier than any lordship, more royal than any sovereignty. Much the same may be said of the other virtues, but as it is habit to avoid lengthy discussions by abridgment I will content myself with the aforesaid examples which will sufficiently indicate what is left unsaid.

Another commandment of general value is "Thou shalt not remove thy Neighbor's landmarks which thy forerunners have set up."[42] Now this law, we may consider, applies not merely to allotments and boundaries of land in order to eliminate covetousness but also to the safeguarding of

---

40. Trans. F. H. Colson, *Philo* (Loeb Classical Library; Cambridge: Harvard University Press, 1968), vol. 8, 97–103.

41. Deut. 4:2.

42. Deut. 19:14.

ancient customs. For customs are unwritten laws, the decisions approved by men of old, not inscribed on monuments nor on leaves of paper which the moth destroys, but on the souls of those who are partners in the same citizenship. For children ought to inherit from their parents, besides their property, ancestral customs which they were reared in and have lived with even from the cradle, and not despise them because they have been handed down without written record. Praise cannot be duly given to one who obeys the written laws, since he acts under the admonition of restraint and the fear of punishment. But he who faithfully observes the unwritten deserves commendation, since the virtue which he displays is freely willed.

10.2.3 Mark 7: The Pharisees and Purity

This passage from the New Testament testifies to the Pharisaic customs of washing the hands before eating and of requiring the purification of vessels. This passage suggests that the Pharisees followed the requirement of eating non-sacred meals in a state of purity similar to that of the priests. Such oral laws were as much a part of Pharisaic-Rabbinic practice as was the written law.

༄

7:1 Now when the Pharisees gathered together to him, with some of the scribes, who had come from Jerusalem, 2 they saw that some of his disciples ate with hands defiled, that is, unwashed. 3 (For the Pharisees, and all the Jews, do not eat unless they wash their hands, observing the tradition of the elders; 4 and when they come from the market place, they do not eat unless they purify themselves; and there are many other traditions which they observe, the washing of cups and pots and vessels of bronze.[43]) 5 And the Pharisees and the scribes asked him, "Why do your disciples not live according to the tradition of the elders, but eat with hands defiled?" 6 And he said to them, "Well did Isaiah prophesy of you hypocrites, as it is written,

'This people honors me with their lips,
but their heart is far from me;
7 in vain do they worship me,
teaching as doctrines the precepts of men.'[44]

---

43. A reference to the Pharisaic-Rabbinic laws pertaining to the purification of vessels.
44. Is. 29:13, according to the Septuagint.

8 You leave the commandment of God, and hold fast the tradition of men. . . ."

10.2.4 Megillat Ta'anit:
The Law of the Sadducees and the Boethusians[45]

Megillat Ta'anit is a list of days on which fasting and mourning were not permitted. To this list was appended a "scholion," a commentary explaining each of the entries. The scholion, a compilation of Rabbinic traditions, was probably completed in the seventh or eighth century. Here, we see how the scholion understood the dispute of the Pharisees and Sadducees (and the related sect of the Boethusians) about the oral law.

"On the fourteenth of Tammuz the *Sefer Gezerata*[46] was removed"— because there was written and deposited by the Sadducees a Book of Decrees (*Sefer Gezerata*) of who is stoned and who is burned, who is to be killed and who is to be strangled.[47] And when they would sit (in judgment) and a man would ask, then they would show him in the book. If he would say to them, "From whence is it that this one deserves stoning, and this one deserves burning, and this one deserves strangulation?" they did not know how to bring a proof from the Torah. The sages said to them, "Is it not written, 'According to (literally, on the mouth of) the law that they shall teach you' (Deut. 17:11)? This teaches that we do not write laws (halakhot) in a book."

Another interpretation: The Book of Decrees (*Sefer Gezerata*) in which the Boethusians had "An eye for an eye, a tooth for a tooth" (Ex. 21:24, Lev. 24:20). If a man had knocked out the tooth of his fellow, let him knock out his tooth. If he had blinded the eye of his fellow, let him blind his eye. Let them be equal to each other.[48] "And they shall spread the sheet out before the elders of the city" (Deut. 22:17), the words as they are

---

45. Trans. L. H. Schiffman.

46. The *Sefer Gezerata,* "Book of Decrees," was understood here to be a compilation of laws of Sadducean character. No book of this title is known, but such legal compilations are found in the Dead Sea Scrolls.

47. Many scholars have accepted the interpretation of the scholion that this book was a Sadducean book of penalties relating to capital crimes.

48. The Boethusians are portrayed as adopting a literal interpretation of the Bible according to which "an eye for an eye" refers not to financial penalties but to the physical infliction of equivalent damage.

written.[49] "And she should spit before him" (Deut. 25:9), that she should spit in his face.[50]

The sages said to them: "Is it not written, 'The law and the commandment which I have written to teach them' (Ex. 24:12)? And it is written, 'And now write for yourself this song and teach it to the children of Israel; put it in their mouths' (Deut. 31:19). 'Teach it to the children of Israel,' this is Scripture, 'Put it in their mouths,' these are the laws (halakhot)."[51] They made the day on which they abolished it a holiday.

10.2.5 Jerusalem Talmud Megillah 4:1 (74a): Oral and Written Transmission of the Law[52]

Even the Targumim, the Aramaic translations of the Bible, were regarded as part of the oral law. Hence, it was forbidden to teach them from a written text. This passage does show, however, that written Targum texts were available in the Land of Israel in the Byzantine period.

೬೨

Rabbi Haggai said to Rabbi Ishmael, "When Rabbi Isaac entered the synagogue, he saw one Bible teacher reading the Targum from a book. He said to him, 'It is forbidden to you. Words that were said (given) orally, [should be transmitted] orally, and words that were said (given) in writing [should be transmitted] in writing.'"

10.2.6 Babylonian Talmud Temurah 14b: Prohibition on the Writing of the Oral Law[53]

This passage represents the classic formulation by the amoraim of the Scriptural basis for the prohibition of the writing of the oral law. This passage here refers to halakhot (legal traditions), but in the view of the Rabbis, it also holds true for other aspects of oral tradition as well.

---

49. In regard to a claim of non-virginity made after a marriage, the Torah used this expression which Rabbinic tradition understood figuratively, indicating investigation. The Boethusians are portrayed as taking this literally.

50. The ceremony of *ḥaliẓah* for avoiding levirate marriage requires spitting which the Rabbinic tradition understood to be done "in front of" the man. The Boethusians took the expression "in his face" literally.

51. The oral law without which no literal interpretation can be considered authoritative.

52. Trans. L. H. Schiffman.

53. Trans. L. H. Schiffman.

꿏

Rabbi Abba son of Rabbi Ḥiyya son of Abba said (in the name of) Rabbi Yoḥanan: "Those who write the laws are as if they burn the Torah, and he who learns from them (the books) does not receive reward."

Rabbi Judah the son of Naḥmani, the translator of Rabbi Simeon son of Lakish expounded, "It is written (Ex. 34:27), 'Write yourselves these words. . .' and it is written (ibid.), 'For according to (literally, by the mouth of) these words. . . .' How can this be? Words which are in writing you are not permitted to transmit orally, and words which are [transmitted] oral[ly], you may not transmit in writing."

[A teacher] of the school of Rabbi Ishmael taught, "'These' (ibid.), these [words] you may write, but you may not write halakhot."

10.2.7 *Sifre Deuteronomy* 351:
The Antiquity of the Concept of Oral Law

Tannaitic tradition understood the dual-Torah concept to be confirmed by the Bible. This concept shows that the tannaim maintained that both Torahs had been given by God to Israel.

꿏

"And thy law to Israel" (Deut. 33:10): This teaches that two laws were given to Israel, one orally and the other in writing.

Agnitos[54] the general asked Rabban Gamliel,[55] "How many laws were given to Israel?"

[Rabban Gamliel] said to him, "Two; one in writing and one orally."

10.3 TANNAITIC ACADEMIES

10.3.1 Babylonian Talmud Eruvin 54b:
The Teaching of the Oral Law[56]

The Talmud relates several descriptive stories and events to show how the study of the oral law was conducted. These stories reveal that it was a detailed and tedious process which could only be accomplished when a dedicated teacher expended much time and effort on each student. The material was transmitted orally, and the student had to memorize the teachings.

---

54. This official cannot be identified.
55. Most probably Gamliel II, who served as patriarch between 96 and 115 C.E.
56. Trans. S. Berrin.

Our Rabbis taught, "What was the system for teaching the Oral Law?[57]

"Moses learned from the mouth of the Almighty. Then Aaron came in and Moses taught him his lesson. Aaron then rose and sat down on Moses' left. Aaron's sons entered and Moses taught them their lesson. His sons then rose, and Eleazar sat at Moses' right and Ithamar at Aaron's left."

Rabbi Judah said, "Certainly, Aaron went around to Moses' right. The Elders entered and Moses taught them their lesson. The Elders arose, and all the people entered and Moses taught them their lesson. Thus, it was presented to Aaron four times, to his sons three times, to the Elders twice, and to all the people once. Then, Moses left and Aaron taught them his lesson; Aaron left and his sons taught them their lesson; his sons left and the Elders taught them their lesson. Thus, it was presented to everybody four times."

Based on this, Rabbi Eleazar said, "A man must teach his student four times. A *qal va-ḥomer*[58] can be applied: If Aaron who learned from Moses who learned from the Almighty had to learn it four times, then all the more so must an ordinary student from an ordinary teacher."

Rabbi Akiva said, "From where do we know that a man must repeat his teaching to his student until he has learned it? For it is written, 'And teach it to the children of Israel' (Deut. 31:19). And from where do we know [that he must repeat it] until it is established in the mouths of the students? For it is written, 'Put it in their mouths' (ibid.). And from where do we know that he must show reasons (literally faces) for his teachings? For it is written, 'Now these are the rules which you shall set before them (literally before their faces)' (Ex. 21:1)."

10.3.2 Mishnah Avot 1–5: The Ethics and Wisdom of the Rabbis[59]

The Mishnah includes one tractate, Avot, known also as Pirqe Avot, "Chapters of the Fathers," which provides a chain of tradition for Rabbinic Judaism, tracing the authority of both the written and the oral laws from Moses at Mount Sinai to Rabbi Judah the Prince. In many respects, this tractate may be regarded as a wis-

---

57. This section is based on the belief that the oral law was revealed to Moses at Sinai and then passed on by him immediately to Aaron and his sons. This passage surely reflects the procedure for transmission of oral tradition current in Rabbinic circles.

58. In Rabbi Ishmael's thirteen rules (text 10.4.1) by means of which the Torah is interpreted, the first rule is *qal va-ḥomer*, an inference drawn from a more important premise to a less important premise.

59. Trans. H. Danby, *The Mishnah* (London: Oxford, 1933), pp. 446–48. 455. 457–8.

dom text, advice for judges, scholars, and to a great extent the common man, show-
ing the persistence of this trend in later Jewish tradition.

꣹

1:1 Moses received the Law[60] from Sinai and committed it to Joshua, and Joshua to the elders, and the elders to the Prophets; and the Prophets committed it to the men of the Great Synagogue.[61] They said three things: "Be deliberate in judgment, raise up many disciples, and make a fence around the Law."[62]

2 Simeon the Just[63] was of the remnants of the Great Synagogue. He used to say: "By three things is the world sustained: by the Law, by the Temple service, and by deeds of loving-kindness."

3 Antigonus of Soko received [the Law] from Simeon the Just. He used to say: "Be not like slaves who minister to the master for the sake of receiving a bounty, but be like slaves who minister to the master not for the sake of receiving a bounty; rather let the fear of Heaven be upon you."

4 Yose ben Yoezer of Zeredah and Yose ben Yoḥanan of Jerusalem received [the Law] from them. Yose ben Yoezer of Zeredah said: "Let your house be a meeting-house for the sages, and sit amid the dust of their feet and drink in their words with thirst."

5 Yose ben Yoḥanan of Jerusalem said: "Let your house be opened wide and let the needy be members of your household; and talk not much with womankind."[64] They said this of a man's own wife, how much more of his fellow's wife! Hence the sages have said: "He that talks much with womankind brings evil upon himself and neglects the study of the Law and at the last will inherit Gehenna."[65]

6 Joshua ben Peraḥyah and Nittai the Arbelite received [the Law] from them. Joshua ben Peraḥyah said: "Provide yourself with a teacher and get yourself a fellow[-disciple];[66] and when you judge any man, incline the balance in his favor."

---

60. Both the oral and written Torahs.

61. Or "Men of the Great Assembly," a group of 120 sages which, according to Rabbinic tradition, existed in Judea in the Persian period.

62. Add restrictions to the law in order to ensure that its essentials will be properly observed.

63. High priest, ca. 250 B.C.E.

64. This sage's view, while shared by some of his colleagues, should be contrasted with statements taking a much more positive view of women. Although the status of women was evolving in the Rabbinic period, there certainly were some who continued to hold older views.

65. Punishment after death.

66. With whom to study.

7 Nittai the Arbelite said: "Keep yourself far from an evil neighbor and do not consort with the wicked, and lose not belief in (divine?) retribution."

8 Judah ben Tabbai and Simeon ben Shetaḥ received [the Law] from them. Judah ben Tabbai said: "Do not make yourself like those who would influence the judges; and when the litigants stand before you, let them be in your eyes as wicked men, and when they have departed from before you, let them be in your eyes as innocent, as soon as they have accepted the judgment.[67]

9 Simeon ben Shetaḥ said: "Examine the witnesses diligently and be cautious in your words lest from them they learn to swear falsely."

10 Shemaiah and Abtalion received [the Law] from them. Shemaiah said: "Love labor and hate mastery and do not seek acquaintance with the ruling power."

11 Abtalion said: "You sages, give heed to your words lest you incur the penalty of exile and you be exiled to a place of evil waters,[68] and the disciples that come after you drink [of them] and die, and the name of Heaven be profaned."

12 Hillel and Shammai received [the Law] from them. Hillel said: "Be of the disciples of Aaron, loving peace and pursuing peace, loving mankind and bringing them near to the Law."

13 He used to say: "A name made great is a name destroyed; he who does not increase, decreases; he who does not learn is worthy of death; and he who makes worldly use of the crown[69] shall perish.

14 He used to say: "If I am not for myself who is for me? And being for my own self what am I? And if not now, when?"

15 Shammai said: "Make your [study of the] Law a fixed habit; say little and do much, and receive all men with a cheerful countenance."

16 Rabban Gamaliel said: "Provide yourself with a teacher and remove yourself from doubt, and tithe not overmuch by guesswork."[70]

17 Simeon his son said: "All my days have I grown up among the sages and I have found naught better for a man than silence; and not the expounding [of the Law] is the chief thing but the doing [of it]; and he that multiplies words occasions sin."

---

67. Examine both sides strictly and be suspicious of both. But once they have accepted your judgment, treat them as righteous people.

68. False teachings and interpretations of the Torah.

69. The crown of the knowledge of the Torah.

70. Give exact tithes rather than estimated amounts.

18 Rabban Simeon ben Gamaliel said: "By three things is the world sustained: by truth, by judgment, and by peace, as it is written, 'Execute the judgment of truth and peace' (Zech. 8:16)."

2:1 Rabbi[71] said: "Which is the straight way that a man should choose? That which is an honor to him and gets him honor from men. And be as heedful of a light precept as of a weighty one, for you do not know the reward of each precept; and reckon the loss through [the fulfilling of] a precept against its reward, and the reward [that comes] from transgression against its loss. Consider three things and you will not fall into the hands of transgression: know what is above you—a seeing eye, a hearing ear, and all your deeds written in a book. . . ."

4 He[72] used to say: "Do His will as if it were your will so that He may do your will as if it were His will. Make your will of no effect before His will so that He may make the will of others of no effect before your will.

5:1 By ten Sayings[73] was the world created. And what does the Scripture teach thereby? Could it not have been created by one Saying? But this was to requite the ungodly who destroy the world that was created by ten Sayings, and to give a goodly reward to the righteous which sustain the world that was created by ten Sayings. . . .

10 There are four types among men: he who says, 'What is mine is mine and what is yours is yours'—this is the common type, and some say that this is the type of Sodom;[74] [he who says,] 'What is mine is yours and what is yours is mine'—he is an ignorant man; [he who says,] 'What is mine is yours and what is yours is your own'—he is a saintly man; [and he who says,] "What is yours is mine, and what is mine is my own'—he is a wicked man. . . .

17 Any controversy that is for God's sake shall in the end be of lasting worth,[75] but any that is not for God's sake shall not in the end be of lasting worth. Which controversy was for God's sake? Such was the controversy of Hillel and Shammai.[76] And which was not for God's sake? Such was the controversy of Korah and all his company.[77]

---

71. Rabbi Judah the Prince, editor of the Mishnah.
72. Rabban Gamliel, the son of Rabbi Judah the Prince.
73. Divine commands.
74. The residents of Sodom were said to be totally selfish.
75. The differing views will be transmitted to later generations.
76. Where many disputes are preserved in Rabbinic literature.
77. Korah's rebellion against the leadership of Moses (Numbers 16) had no purpose except to wrest power from Moses.

10.3.3 Babylonian Talmud Bava Meẓia 59a–b: The Bet Midrash and Divine Law[78]

The following passage in the Babylonian Talmud highlights the human element in the interpretation and application of the divinely written Torah. Even God, as it were, accepts the authority of the Rabbis to interpret the law.

ﳸ

We learned elsewhere:[79] "If he cut it into separate tiles, placing sand between each tile: Rabbi Eliezer declared it clean, and the sages declared it unclean; and this was the oven of 'Aknai."[80] Why [the oven of] 'Aknai?—Said Rav Judah in Samuel's name: "[It means] that they encompassed it with arguments as a snake,[81] and proved it unclean."

It has been taught: On that day Rabbi Eliezer brought forward every imaginable argument, but they did not accept them. Said he to them: "If the halakhah agrees with me, let this carob-tree prove it!"

Thereupon the carob-tree was torn a hundred cubits out of its place. Others affirm, four hundred cubits.

"No proof can be brought from a carob-tree," they retorted.

Again he said to them: "If the halakhah agrees with me, let the stream of water prove it!"—whereupon the stream of water flowed backwards.

"No proof can be brought from a stream of water," they rejoined.

Again he urged: "If the halakhah agrees with me, let the walls of the schoolhouse prove it," whereupon the walls inclined to fall.

But Rabbi Joshua rebuked them, saying: "When scholars are engaged in a halakhic dispute, what have you to interfere?"

Hence they did not fall, in honor of Rabbi Joshua, nor did they resume their upright position, in honor of Rabbi Eliezer; and they are still standing thus inclined.

Again he said to them: "If the halakhah agrees with me, let it be proved from Heaven!"

Whereupon a Heavenly Voice cried out: "Why do you dispute with Rabbi Eliezer, seeing that in all matters the halakhah agrees with him!"

---

78. Trans. I. Epstein, *The Babylonian Talmud* (London: Soncino Press, 1935–52), 35 vols.

79. Mishnah Kelim 5:10.

80. The issue concerns whether after cutting an impure oven into pieces and reassembling it in this manner, it remains susceptible to ritual impurity (as would a complete oven) or if it is not susceptible to impurity like a broken oven. Cf. Lev. 11:35.

81. Aramaic *'akhna'* means "snake."

But Rabbi Joshua arose and exclaimed: "It is not in heaven."[82]

What did he mean by this? Said Rabbi Jeremiah: That the Torah had already been given at Mount Sinai; we pay no attention to a Heavenly Voice, because You have long since written in the Torah at Mount Sinai, "After the majority must one incline."[83]

Rabbi Nathan met Elijah (the prophet) and asked him: "What did the Holy One, Blessed be He, do in that hour?—He laughed [with joy]," he replied, "saying, 'My sons have defeated Me, My sons have defeated Me.'"

It was said: On that day all objects which Rabbi Eliezer had declared clean were brought and burnt in fire. Then they took a vote and excommunicated him.[84] Said they, "Who shall go and inform him?"

"I will go," answered Rabbi Akiva, "lest an unsuitable person go and inform him, and thus destroy the whole world."[85]

What did Rabbi Akiva do? He donned black garments and wrapped himself in black, and sat at a distance of four cubits from him.

"Akiva," said Rabbi Eliezer to him, "what has particularly happened today?"

"Master," he replied, "it appears to me that your companions hold aloof from you."[86]

Thereupon he too rent his garments, put off his shoes, removed [his seat] and sat on the earth,[87] while tears streamed from his eyes. The world was then smitten: a third of the olive crop, a third of the wheat, and a third of the barley crop. Some say, the dough in women's hands swelled up.[88]

A tanna taught: Great was the calamity that befell that day, for everything at which Rabbi Eliezer cast his eyes was burned up. Rabban Gamaliel too was traveling in a ship, when a huge wave arose to drown him.

"It appears to me," he reflected, "that this is on account of none other but Rabbi Eliezer ben Hyrcanus."

Thereupon he arose and exclaimed, "Sovereign of the Universe! You know full well that I have not acted for my honor, nor for the honor of my paternal house, but for Yours, so that strife may not multiply in Israel!"

At that the raging sea subsided.[89]

---

82. Deut. 30:12.

83. Ex. 23:2.

84. For refusing to accept the ruling of the majority of sages.

85. If Rabbi Eliezer should choose to, he could call down divine wrath just as he had received divine support for his halakhic view.

86. For they have excommunicated you.

87. As a sign of mourning as is required of one who is excommunicated.

88. Became spoiled.

89. The continuation of the story in the Babylonian Talmud is an amoraic addition to the tannaitic material presented here.

10.3.4 *Iggeret Rav Sherira Gaon* 1–2:
The First Generations of the Tannaim[90]

Rav Sherira Gaon, who wrote in ca. 987, provides an idealized account of the history of the tannaitic movement from the time of Hillel and Shammai up to the generation before Rabbi Judah the Prince, editor of the Mishnah. Sherira pictures the Rabbis as solving all problems and resolving all doubts, a view difficult to accept in light of the state of tannaitic literature and talmudic descriptions of amoraic debate.

🕮

The early sages were not known by their names, except for the *nesi'im* and the presidents of the *bet din*,[91] because there were no disputes among them. Instead, they knew clearly all the explanations of the Torah. They also knew the Talmud[92] clearly, with all its detailed discussions and inferences. . . .

As long as the Temple was standing, each one of the sages taught his students the explanations of Scripture, Mishnah, and Talmud, using words which he composed for the occasion; and the sages would render halakhic decisions for their students as they saw fit. Wisdom was abundant, and they were not troubled by other distractions. Only the *semikhah* controversy[93] existed among the early sages. And when Shammai and Hillel came, they, too, only argued on three points, as we say: "Rav Huna said: 'Shammai and Hillel were in disagreement on three issues.'"[94]

When the Temple was destroyed, the sages moved to Betar,[95] and when Betar was also destroyed, they dispersed in every direction. On account of all these upheavals, persecutions, and disturbances, the students did not serve the sages sufficiently,[96] and disputes increased.

---

90. Trans. N. D. Rabinowich, *The Iggeres of Rav Sherira Gaon* (Jerusalem: Moznaim, 1988), pp. 4–14.

91. The Rabbinic court.

92. The explanation of the oral traditions in their possession.

93. About a detail of the procedure for sacrificing the festival offering. See text 10.1.1.

94. Babylonian Talmud Shabbat 14b. The three controversies concerned the minimum quantity of dough requiring the separation of the priests' portion (*ḥallah*), the amount of drawn water poured into a ritual bath that might render it unfit, and the determination of the onset of menstruation for observance of the purity laws.

95. The stronghold of Bar Kokhba.

96. The intricate details of the law were not studied thoroughly enough and some were even forgotten.

After the death of Rabban Yoḥanan ben Zakkai,[97] Rabban Gamliel[98] as well as Rabbi Dosa ben Hyrcanus were still alive as were others from the earlier period. Nevertheless, the disputes between the Houses of Shammai and Hillel took place. And although the House of Shammai was overruled, and it was established that the halakhah follows the House of Hillel, there still were other disputes in the time of Rabban Gamliel [such as] those between Rabbi Eliezer . . . and Rabbi Joshua. Both these sages were former students of Rabban Yoḥanan ben Zakkai. . . .

Second to them, [in] that they were [first] students but [later] became related to them both as students and as colleagues, were Rabbi Akiva, Rabbi Eliezer ha-Modaʿi, Rabbi Judah ben Bava, and Rabbi Ishmael. Moreover, at that time Rabbi Judah was in Nisibis.[99] Although he was there during the Temple period, he was also there after the Destruction. The reprieve after the destruction of the Temple was an important time, for the sages then convened in order to retrieve the laws that were nearly lost in the turmoil and persecutions and as a result of the strife between the Houses of Shammai and Hillel.

There were many sages at that time. Some of them had seats in the House of Study and others sat before them. On the day when Rabbi Eleazar ben Azariah was inaugurated as *nasi,* we say in Tractate Bera-khot:[100] "That day, many seats were added to the House of Study. Rabbi Yoḥanan said: 'Abba Yose ben Dustai and the sages disagree. One says that four hundred seats were added, and one says seven hundred.'" If so many were added, certainly many more were there originally.

Rabbi Akiva sacrificed his life after the death of Rabbi Yose ben Kisma; and then Rabbi Ḥannina ben Teradion was executed.[101] The wisdom of the sages decreased after the passing [of these great men]. Rabbi Akiva had trained many students, but there was a persecution against the students of Rabbi Akiva [and they died].[102] Thus, the authority over Israel was entrusted to his latter students. . . .[103]

---

97. Who led the sages after the destruction of the Temple in 70 C.E.

98. Rabban Gamliel II of Yavneh became *nasi* and the leading sage after Rabban Yoḥanan ben Zakkai ca. 80 C.E.

99. A city in the northeast corner of Mesopotamia.

100. Babylonian Talmud Berakhot 28a.

101. During the Bar Kokhba Revolt of 132–5 C.E.

102. This passage has given rise to the view that Rabbi Akiva's students died at the hands of the Romans as a result of their participation in the Bar Kokhba Revolt.

103. Babylonian Talmud Yevamot 62b.

During that generation,[104] Rabban Simeon ben Gamliel was *nasi*. Rabbi Nathan came up from Babylonia and served as *av bet din*. . . . Rabbi Meir was the wisest sage of the generation: "When Rabbi Meir and Rabbi Nathan entered the house of study, the entire academy stood before them."[105] That generation also had many great sages constantly promulgating Torah. . . .[106]

During all these years [the sages] clarified all the laws which had been left unresolved in the academies due to the great loss that took place because of the Temple's destruction and the unresolved halakhic questions that had arisen during those troubled and confused times. All the halakhic disputes that had come into existence during those three generations were decided. The individual and majority opinions were made known after our sages had diligently and completely analyzed and investigated them. They thoroughly examined all the traditions and *mishnayot*[107] in order to establish the correct version. They did not add to the earlier teachings of the Men of the Great Assembly. But they toiled mightily and examined the material until they understood what the earlier masters had said and had practiced. Thus they finally resolved all their doubts.

10.4 MIDRASH AND MISHNAH

10.4.1 *Sifra*:
The Thirteen Hermeneutical Rules of Rabbi Ishmael[108]

Rabbi Ishmael, who lived in the first half of the second century, compiled a list of hermeneutical rules which govern the legal interpretation of the Torah. Modern scholars have noted the resemblance of some of these rules to the interpretive principles in use in the Greek world. These principles and their application are responsible for much of the halakhic Midrash in Rabbinic texts.

ॐ

Rabbi Ishmael says: There are thirteen rules by means of which the Torah is interpreted:

---

104. The second generation of tannaim after the destruction of the Temple.

105. Babylonian Talmud Horayot 13b.

106. Here Rav Sherira Gaon lists twenty-six prominent sages.

107. Paragraphs of the Mishnah.

108. Interpretive translation by Hadassah Schiffman Levy, based on P. Birnbaum, *Daily Prayer Book* (New York: Hebrew Publishing, 1949), pp. 42–6.

1. Inference is drawn from a less important premise to a more important premise, or vice versa.

2. From the similarity of words or phrases in separate texts it is inferred that the law expressed in the one must also be applied to the other.

3. A comprehensive principle, as contained in one or two biblical laws, is applicable to all related laws.

4. When a generalization is followed by specification, the specification applies instead of the generalization.

5. When a specification is followed by a generalization, the generalization then applies.

6. If a generalization is followed by a specification and then treated again by a general term, one must interpret according to what the specification implies.

7. When, however, the specification or generalization is necessary for the sake of clarity, rules 4 and 5 do not apply.

8. Whatever is first implied in a generalization and afterwards specified to provide new information concerning it, is stated not only for its own sake, but to teach something additional concerning the general proposition.

9. Whatever is first implied in a general law and afterwards specified to prove another similar provision, is specified in order to alleviate, and not to increase the severity of that provision.

10. Whatever is first implied in a general law and is afterwards specified to prove another provision which is not similar to the general law, is specified in order to alleviate the severity in some respects, but to increase it in other respects.

11. Whatever is first implied in a general law and is afterwards specified to determine a new matter, cannot be applied to the general proposition, unless the text expressly states that it can.

12. An ambiguous word or passage may be interpreted from its context or from a subsequent expression in the text.

13. Similarly, when two biblical texts contradict each other, they can be reconciled only by a third text.

10.4.2 Mishnah Bava Qamma 6:4–5: Restitution for Damage by Fire[109]

Often Mishnah passages are closely paralleled by the halakhic Midrashim. In this example, Mishnah Bava Qamma and Mekhilta of Rabbi Ishmael, the following passage, present parallel laws, each in its own characteristic format.

---

109. Trans. H. Danby, *The Mishnah* (London: Oxford University Press, 1958), pp. 339–40.

꠸

6:4 If a man caused fire to break out at the hand of a deaf-mute, an imbecile, or a minor, he is not culpable by the laws of man, but he is culpable by the laws of Heaven. If he caused it to break out at the hand of one of sound senses, this one[110] is culpable. If one brought the fire and then another brought wood, he that brought the wood is culpable.

If one brought wood and then another brought the fire, he that brought the fire is culpable. If the wind set it ablaze none of them is culpable.

If a man caused a fire to break out and it consumed wood or stones or dust, he is culpable, for it is written, "If a fire breaks out and catches in thorns so that the shocks of corn (grain) or the standing corn or the field be consumed, he that kindles the fire shall surely make restitution"(Ex. 22:5). If it passed over a fence four cubits high, or over a public way or a river, he that caused it is not culpable.[111]

If a man kindled fire within his own domain, how far may it spread?[112] Rabbi Eleazar ben Azariah says: It is looked upon as though it was in the midst of a *kor's* space[113] of land. Rabbi Eliezer says: Sixteen cubits[114] [in every direction], like a public highway.[115] Rabbi Akiva says: Fifty cubits.[116] Rabbi Simeon says: [It is written,] "He that kindled the fire shall surely make restitution" (Ex. 22:5).—all is in accordance with the nature of the fire.[117]

5 If a man set fire to a stack and in it there were utensils and these caught fire, Rabbi Judah says: He must make restitution for what was therein. But the sages say: He need only make restitution for a stack of wheat or barley.[118] If a kid was fastened to it and a bondman stood near by, and they were burnt together, he that kindled the fire is liable [for the kid but not for the bondman].[119] If the bondman was bound and a kid stood near by and they were burnt together, he that kindled the fire is not

---

110. The agent.

111. Because he could not expect that it would travel so far.

112. At what distance is he no longer culpable, since he had no reason to suspect that the fire might spread so far?

113. 75,000 square cubits. (A cubit is about 18 inches.) This is equivalent to a distance of about 137 cubits, approximately 245 feet.

114. 24 feet.

115. Like the width of a public thoroughfare.

116. 75 feet.

117. His view is that it depends on the size of the fire he kindled and the material he was burning. To whatever extent such a fire might normally spread, he is responsible.

118. Since he could not know what was inside.

119. The slave would have fled from the danger.

liable [financially for either].[120] And the sages agree with Rabbi Judah that if a man set fire to a large building he must make restitution for everything therein; for such is the custom among men to leave [their goods] in their houses.[121]

10.4.3 *Mekhilta of Rabbi Ishmael*, Nezeqin 14: Restitution for Damage by Fire[122]

As opposed to the Mishnah which only rarely quotes Scriptural proof texts, the halakhic Midrashim provide what is constructed as a sustained biblical commentary, showing how tannaitic law was derived from the Torah. In so doing, halakhic Midrashim, like the Mekhilta, emphasize the unity of the written and oral Torahs, which, to the Rabbis, were considered to be one whole.

܍

"If fire breaks out," etc. (Ex. 22:5). Why is this said? Even if it had not been said I could have reasoned: Since he is liable for damage done by what is owned by him, shall he not be liable for damage done by himself? If, then, I succeed in proving it by logical reasoning, what need is there of saying: "If fire break out"? Simply this: Scripture comes to declare that in all cases of liability for damage mentioned in the Torah, one acting under duress is regarded as one acting of his own free will, one acting unintentionally is regarded as one acting intentionally, and the woman is regarded like the man.

"And catches in thorns." Behold, thorns are mentioned only with regard to fixing the distance within which one is liable. If there are thorns around, there is a certain distance within which one is liable. If there are no thorns around, there is no such distance. Hence the sages said: If the fire gets across a river, or a road, or a stone fence higher than ten hand-breadths and causes damage, he is not liable. How do we determine the matter? We regard him as standing in the center of a field, requiring a *kor* of seed, and lighting the fire. These are the words of Rabbi Eleazar ben Azariah. Rabbi Eliezer says: The distance within which he is liable is 16 cubits, the usual width of a public road. Rabbi Akiva says: The distance

---

120. Since he is criminally liable for the death of the slave, he bears no financial penalty, according to an established principle of halakhah. He is exempt from liability for the kid since it could have fled the fire.

121. The arsonist would have known in advance about the presence of these possessions.

122. Trans. J. Z. Lauterbach, *Mekilta de-Rabbi Ishmael* (JPS Library of Jewish Classics; Philadelphia: Jewish Publication Society, 1976), vol. 3, pp. 110–12.

is fifty cubits. Rabbi Simon says: "He that kindled the fire shall surely make restitution:" it all depends on the size of the fire. It happened once that a fire spread across the Jordan and did damage there, since it was a big fire. When does this obtain? When the fire jumps. But if it keeps close to the ground and spreads that way, even though it go a distance of a mile, he is liable.

"So that the stack . . . be consumed." This means any kind of a pile. It also includes a row of reeds or of beams, and likewise a heap of stones or of pebbles prepared to be used for plastering.

"Or the standing corn (grain)." Trees are also included.

"Or the field." That is, even if it just dried up the ground. May it not mean, even if there were implements hidden in the stacks and they were burnt? It says: "Or the standing corn or the field." Just as the field is open, so also what stands in it must be open.

"The one that kindled the fire shall surely make restitution." Why is this said? Because it says: "A man" (v. 4), from which I know only about a man. But how about a woman, a *tumtum*[123] or a hermaphrodite? It says: "The one that kindled the fire shall surely make restitution"—whoever it may be.

I thus far know only about damage caused by grazing or by burning. How about all other kinds of damage mentioned in the Torah? Behold, you reason and establish a general rule on the basis of what is common to these two: The peculiar aspect of damage by grazing is not like the peculiar aspect of damage by burning, nor is the peculiar aspect of damage by burning like the peculiar aspect of damage by grazing. What is common to both of them is: that it is their characteristic to do damage, they are your property, and it is incumbent upon you to guard them. And when damage is done, the one causing the damage is liable to pay for the damage from the best of his land.[124]

10.5 HALAKHAH AND AGGADAH

10.5.1 Babylonian Talmud Ḥagigah 14a: Defining the Aggadah[125]

The following excerpt shows that the sages understood the word aggadah ("telling") as if derived from a root meaning "draw," in that it drew the heart to the study of Torah and its observance.

---

123. One whose sexual characteristics cannot be determined.

124. Therefore, anyone who causes damage in any way at all is liable to pay for the damage.

125. Trans. S. Berrin.

⚜

"Every support of water" (Is. 3:1): This refers to the Masters of aggadah, for they draw the hearts of men like water by means of aggadah.

10.5.2 Jerusalem Talmud Ḥagigah 1:8 (76a): Revelation of the Oral Law[126]

This passage shows how the Rabbis understood both halakhah and aggadah to be part of the oral Torah, given by God at Sinai.

⚜

Rabbi Joshua ben Levi said, "'Upon them'—'*And* upon them'; 'all'—'*according* to all'; 'words'—'*the* words.' Scripture, Mishnah, Talmud, halakhah, and aggadah. Even that which an experienced student will teach, has already been taught to Moses at Sinai."[127]

10.5.3 Jerusalem Talmud Horayot 3:5 (48c): The Power of Aggadah[128]

These amoraic passages emphasize the power of aggadah to provide an understanding even deeper than that of Talmud, logical deduction from legal teachings. Further, the text notes the non-halakhic character of aggadah which cannot lead to legal rulings.

⚜

Rabbi Samuel son of Rabbi Yose son of Rabbi Abun expounded: "A rich man is wise in his own eyes, but an understanding poor man will probe him" (Prov. 28:11). "A rich man" refers to a Master of the Talmud. "But an understanding poor man will probe him" refers to a Master of Aggadah.

[It is comparable] to two who entered a city. One had bars of gold and one had small change. The man with the bars of gold could not spend and

---

126. Trans. S. Berrin.

127. Deut. 9:10, describing the writing on the tablets of the Ten Commandments, says, "And on them was written according to all the words which the Lord spoke with you on the mountain." Rabbi Joshua noted that it does not simply say "Upon them" but "*And* upon them"; not simply "all" but "*according* to all"; not simply "words" but "*the* words." He says that these apparently superfluous words were added to teach that the revelation at Sinai included much more than the Ten Commandments themselves, namely, Scripture, Mishnah, etc.

128. Trans. S. Berrin.

sustain himself; the man with the small change could spend and sustain himself. . . .

Rabbi Abba bar Kahana went to a place and he found Rabbi Levi sitting and expounding: "A man to whom God gives riches, property and wealth so that his soul does not lack anything he may desire, but God does not permit him to eat of it, for a foreigner will eat of it" (Eccl. 6:2). "Does not permit him to eat of it" refers to a Master of Aggadah who does not forbid and does not permit, does not declare pure and does not declare impure. . . .

10.5.4 Jerusalem Talmud Sheqalim 5:1 (48c): Separation of Halakhah and Aggadah[129]

The role of Rabbi Akiva in organizing the separate disciplines of aggadah and halakhah is asserted here, although some held that these approaches were already distinguished by the Persian period. Modern scholars assume that these distinctions were made only in the tannaitic period.

৯৫

Rabbi Jonah said: "It is written, 'Therefore I will give him a portion with the great, and with the mighty shall he divide the spoils' (Is. 53:12). This refers to Rabbi Akiva who organized the learning of Midrash, Halakhah, and Aggadah."

But some say: "The Men of the Great Assembly organized these. So what did he organize? [Rabbi Akiva] organized generalizations and particularizations."[130]

10.6 THE REDACTION OF THE MISHNAH

10.6.1 *Iggeret Rav Sherira Gaon* 3: The Mishnah[131]

Rav Sherira Gaon was the first post-talmudic authority to deal systematically with the question of how the Mishnah, Tosefta, baraitot and Talmud were compiled. This section of his work deals with the Mishnah.

৯৫

---

129. Trans. S. Berrin.

130. This latter opinion would date the organization of the corpus of tradition to the Persian period rather than the Roman period.

131. Trans. Rabinowich, *The Iggeres of Rav Sherira Gaon,* pp. 20–32.

The days of Rabbi,[132] the son of Rabban Simeon ben Gamliel, were an opportune time.[133] Rabbi arranged . . .[134] the Mishnah. The words of the Mishnah can be compared to the words of the Almighty to Moses: they were like a sign and a wonder.[135] Rabbi did not produce these words with his own mind; rather, they were the teachings of the early sages who preceded him. How do we know this?

The Mishnah says, "It once happened that Ben Zakkai examined [witnesses] regarding the stems of the fig."[136] The Talmud suggests,[137] "This reference is probably to a different Ben Zakkai; for if Rabban Yoḥanan ben Zakkai were meant, would Rabbi have called him merely 'Ben Zakkai?' [The Talmud now refutes the above statement by quoting a *baraita* which parallels the mishnah and which includes the title, "Rabban":] Yet has it not been taught: "It once happened that Rabban Yoḥanan ben Zakkai examined witnesses regarding the stems of the fig"?

The Talmud now finds a different way to reconcile the mishnah and *baraita*: "He [Rabban Yoḥanan ben Zakkai] must therefore have been a disciple sitting before his master[138] when he made this suggestion. His reasoning was so acceptable to his master that he [the master] perpetuated [the incident] in his [the disciple's] name."[139] Thus, from the time of Hillel and Shammai, our sages had already taught this mishnah with the plain name "Ben Zakkai," and Rabbi also taught it this way, without modifying it. . . .

The Mishnah was even divided into tractates before the time of Rabbi; for Rabbi Meir told Rabbi Nathan: "Let us ask Rabban Simeon ben Gamliel to open [his lectures] with [Tractate] Uqzin, with which he is unfamiliar. . . ." The story continues: "Rabbi Jacob ben Karshai went and sat by the upper room where Rabban Simeon ben Gamliel was studying,

---

132. Rabbi Judah the Prince.

133. The end of a period of persecution.

134. This text is available in two versions. The Spanish recension does indeed claim here that the Mishnah was written down, but virtually all scholars acknowledge the primacy of the French recension which sees the editorial and transmissional activity of Rabbi as oral.

135. Rav Sherira Gaon is drawing a parallel between the divine inspiration of Moses and that of Rabbi.

136. Mishnah Sanhedrin 5:2: Witnesses testified that someone had committed murder under a certain fig tree. To test the validity of their testimony, Ben Zakkai questioned them about the appearance of small details such as the stems of the figs.

137. Babylonian Talmud Sanhedrin 41a.

138. Probably Hillel.

139. The mishnah used the plain "Ben Zakkai," since he had not yet been given the title "Rabban," "our teacher." But in the *baraita,* which was composed later, the title "Rabban" is used.

and he recited [Tractate] Uqẓin again and again. Rabban Simeon ben Gamliel thought: 'Is someone asking questions about Uqẓin?' He turned his attention to it and studied it."[140]

There are places where Rabbi added commentary. For example, the mishnah says: "Boys may go out with garlands and royal children may go out with bells."[141] This is the way the mishnah was taught by the early sages.[142] Then Rabbi added the following explanation: "Everyone else [likewise may go out with bells]; but the sages spoke in terms of the usual situation."[143]

An exception is those things which were taught in his day[144] and in the days after him, as we say: "This is [what is taught in] the early mishnah; but the later mishnah [on the same subject] says. . . ."

Likewise, Eduyot was established[145] on the day that Rabbi Eleazar ben Azariah was inaugurated (as *nasi*), as we say: "Eduyot was also learned that day." And we learn, "The term, 'that day' always means the day Rabbi Eleazar ben Azariah was seated[146] in the yeshivah."[147]

Rabbi afterwards included material which was taught in his father's time.[148] For example: "Rabbi Yose says, 'In six instances the House of Shammai holds the lenient opinion while the House of Hillel holds the stringent opinion.'"[149] Another example: "Rabbi Judah said, 'God forbid that Akavyah ben Mehallalel was ever excommunicated; for no man of Israel is a better example of a bastion of wisdom and fear of sin than Akavyah ben Mehallalel."[150]

However, with other tractates, even though their basic principles had already been taught by the early sages, Rabbi arranged their halakhot—some of them he taught in the original wording, and others he worded as

---

140. Babylonian Talmud Horayot 13b.

141. This mishnah concerns the prohibition of carrying from the private to the public domain on the Sabbath. Since garlands and bells were usual items of clothing for boys, wearing them is not considered carrying.

142. Those who first formulated the halakhot of the Mishnah.

143. Mishnah Shabbat 6:9: Since it is usually royal children who go out with bells, the sages put the mishnah in these terms.

144. Teachings which were formulated as *mishnayot* only in Rabbi's day. In fact, there are *mishnayot* which incorporate decisions by his sons and even by his grandsons.

145. This could mean that the *mishnayot* were given their final form at this time, or that individual *mishnayot* were first organized into a tractate.

146. As Rosh Yeshivah, Head of the Academy.

147. Babylonian Talmud Berakhot 28a.

148. The following statements by Rabbi Yose and Rabbi Judah were made by Rabbis who were contemporaries of Rabban Simeon ben Gamliel, Rabbi's father.

149. Mishnah Eduyot 5:2.

150. Mishnah Eduyot 5:6.

he saw fit. Every anonymous mishnah is [the teaching of] Rabbi Meir. But he did not create them from his own heart. Rather, Rabbi Meir had a certain way of teaching the *mishnayot* to his disciples; and Rabbi chose and established this way to teach [the *mishnayot*] to everyone. Rabbi Meir had received his way of learning [the Mishnah] from his teacher, Rabbi Akiva; and Rabbi Akiva had received it from his teachers, the earlier sages. Thus, we say: "Rabbi Yoḥanan said, 'An anonymous Mishnah is Rabbi Meir. An anonymous Tosefta is Rabbi Nehemiah. An anonymous *Sifra* is Rabbi Judah. An anonymous *Sifre* is Rabbi Simeon. And all of them taught in the way of Rabbi Akiva.'"[151]

These *baraitot* of Tosefta, *Sifra*, and *Sifre* were all taught by the earlier sages. Then Rabbi Judah, Rabbi Nehemiah, and Rabbi Simeon came, and each made his own compilation of [the *baraitot*]. Sifra [was compiled by] Rabbi Judah; Tosefta, by Rabbi Nehemiah; and *Sifre*, by Rabbi Simeon; and the Mishnah, by Rabbi Meir. And all of them follow the method of Rabbi Akiva, for all were disciples of Rabbi Akiva.

But other *baraitot* do not interest us, because these [just mentioned] were selected and compiled by leading sages who were the foremost disciples of Rabbi Akiva. Thus, Rabbi Simeon told his students: "My sons, learn my principles for my principles are the cream of the cream of Rabbi Akiva's principles."[152] We say:[153] "The hearts of the early ones are like the entrance to the great hall [of the Holy Temple] and the hearts of the later ones [are] like the entrance to the antechamber." And [the Talmud] goes on to explain: "'The early ones' means Rabbi Akiva."[154]

Our sages explain that even Adam, the first man, rejoiced in the wisdom of Rabbi Akiva when the Holy One, Blessed is He, showed [Adam] the sages of each generation.[155] And in [Tractate] Yevamot Rabbi Dosa ben Harkinas said to Rabbi Akiva, "Are you Akiva ben Joseph, whose name goes from one end of the world to the other?"[156]

The greatest of all Rabbi Akiva's students was Rabbi Meir, as we learn in [Tractate] Eruvin: "Rav Aḥa ben Ḥanina said, 'It is revealed and known before Him Who spoke and the world came into existence, that in the generation of Rabbi Meir there was none equal to him. Then why was

---

151. Babylonian Talmud Sanhedrin 86a.
152. Babylonian Talmud Gittin 67a.
153. Using the following passages, Rav Sherira Gaon describes the greatness of Rabbi Akiva and his disciple, Rabbi Meir, in order to explain why Rabbi chose their way of teaching the Mishnah over that of other tannaim.
154. Babylonian Talmud Eruvin 53a.
155. Babylonian Talmud Sanhedrin 38b.
156. Babylonian Talmud Yevamot 16b.

not the halakhah fixed in agreement with his views? Because his colleagues could not fathom the depths of his mind, for he would declare the
ritually unclean to be clean and the ritually clean to be unclean and he
would supply plausible proof.'"[157] Therefore Rabbi Akiva was fond of him
and ordained him in his youth.

In his halakhot Rabbi chose the way [of teaching] of Rabbi Meir,
which was the way of Rabbi Akiva, because Rabbi saw that Rabbi Meir's
way was succinct and easy to teach. His statements were well composed,
each topic [placed] with that which was similar to it. His teachings were
more exact than any of the other tannaim, without superfluous language.
Each word makes a vital point without unnecessary exaggeration. Nothing was missing or extra, except in a few instances. The way [of presenta-
tion] was concise. Great and wondrous things were included in every
single word. Not everyone who is learned knows how to create such a
composition, as it is said: "A man may arrange his thoughts, but what he
says depends on God"(Prov. 16:1). All the Rabbis shared the same under-
lying principles; nevertheless, since Rabbi Akiva possessed a broad heart[158]
and his disciple Rabbi Meir also possessed a broad heart, they arranged
[the material] in an excellent manner, and they were preferable to all the
other tannaim.

Therefore, Rabbi gathered [their arrangement]. To it he added [hala-
khot] that were [formulated] in his time. He arranged it as he saw fit. He
also explained the essence and the main principles behind disputes of the
Rabbis. Since there were Rabbis who had heard from great sages a different opinion [from that in the Mishnah] or who taught minority opinions
anonymously, if someone heard about this he could become confused
[when studying the Mishnah]. [But] when Rabbi explained the matter, no
doubt [regarding the halakhah] could set in. Thus we learn in the Mishnah:[159] Rabbi Judah said: "Why is the opinion of the minority recorded
along with the majority? In order to nullify it, so that if a man says this,
[one can] say to him: 'Where did you hear this?' If he replies: 'I received it
[as a tradition from my teachers],' one can say to him: 'Perhaps what you
heard was the opinion of so-and-so.'"[160]

When everybody saw the form of the Mishnah, the truthfulness of its
teachings and the exactness of its words, they abandoned their previous
formulations and compilations. These halakhot were disseminated

---

157. Babylonian Talmud Eruvin 13b.
158. The capacity to understand and remember.
159. Mishnah Eduyot 1:6.
160. I.e., the minority.

throughout the Jewish people while the other halakhot were shunted aside and became like a *baraita*. They are utilized as a commentary or for their more elaborate style. However, the Jewish people gave [only] these halakhot [binding] authority. They accepted it faithfully when they saw it, and no one has disputed its authority.

Using this approach [of Rabbi Akiva and Rabbi Meir], Rabbi arranged the six orders of the Mishnah. This does not mean that the more numerous earlier sages were abandoned for the later ones. Rather, the earlier sages had no need for compiled material and the things that we learn by memory. Every single one of the [earlier] Rabbis knew these things through a chain of transmission. They had no need to compile them and write them down among themselves until the Temple's destruction. Then came [these earlier sages'] students, who were not as knowledgeable, and found it necessary to make compilations. . . .

Therefore Rabbi had to compile and arrange the six orders of the Mishnah after a respite of two generations from the persecutions that took place during the Temple's destruction. . . .

When Rabbi arranged the Mishnah, he did not place the tractates in a specific order, one after another. [Rather] he arranged [and taught] each tractate separately in whatever order was convenient for him. We do not know which he taught first. However, the halakhot [in each chapter] and the chapters of each tractate were arranged in a specific order. Thus Rav Huna said: "In one tractate we do not say, 'There is no order to Mishnah,' but regarding two tractates we do say, 'There is no order to Mishnah.'"[161] One could say about either of [the two tractates] that Rabbi might have taught it first.

Sometimes we find a mishnah [on a certain halakhic topic] which gives only one opinion (*stam*) without attributing it to a specific tanna or mentioning any tanna who disagrees. Later in the same tractate we may find another mishnah [on the same topic] which presents the opinion of the earlier mishnah as subject to dispute. In such a case, referred to as "*stam* and later disputed," the halakhah does not follow the earlier (*stam*) mishnah. On the other hand, if the reverse situation is found within one tractate—"disputed and later *stam*"—we say that the halakhah follows the *stam* mishnah. However, if the two *mishnayot* in question are found in two different tractates, the above rules do not apply; for [the tractates] have no order.[162] Rav Joseph also agrees [with these rules], except he says that the three "Bavas" of Order Neziqin are to be considered one tractate.

---

161. Babylonian Talmud Bava Qamma 102a.

162. There is no way of verifying which was arranged first, the disputed or the *stam* opinion, and therefore we cannot establish preference.

As for your question why [Tractate] Kippurim (Yoma) was placed before Shekalim: We in our *bet midrash*[163] study Sheqalim before Kippurim, but certainly we study Sukkah before Yom-Tov (Beẓah). This is followed by Rosh ha-Shanah. However, perhaps [in Rabbi's day] they studied them in the opposite order. However, it can be reasoned that Shabbat should be first, since it is so important,[164] followed by Tractate Eruvin which is similar to [Shabbat] and on the same subject.[165] Then follows Tractate Pesaḥim, since Passover is the first of all the festivals; [this is] followed by Sheqalim, [the subject matter of which] comes [directly] before [that of Pesaḥim] and is one of its aspects. After Sheqalim we study Seder Yoma, which is similar to Shabbat. After Seder Yoma we study Tractate Sukkah because it follows *Yom ha-Kippurim*[166] and is a major festival. After Tractate Sukkah we study Tractate Yom-Tov (Beẓah) because it is on the same subject. After Yom-Tov we study Tractate Rosh ha-Shanah so that we can study Tractate Taʿanit right after it, since after Rosh ha-Shanah is the time of the first rainfall and the time of sowing, and it is like the same subject.

This is how the Rabbis usually study; but if someone finds it convenient to follow a different order, he may do so, even though we see in certain tractates that we say: "Now that the tanna finished Tractate. . . ." For example, in Tractate Sotah: "Now that the tanna has finished [Tractate] Nazir. . . ." And in Tractate Shevuʿot: "Now that the tanna has finished [Tractate] Makkot. . . ." [These passages] prove that there is a specific order.

10.6.2 Mishnah Shabbat 23:1–2: Permitted Activities on the Sabbath[167]

This section illustrates the many Mishnah passages stated anonymously in which ritual laws are prescribed. The Mishnah includes rulings for the Temple even though it had been destroyed before the redaction of the Mishnah (ca. 200 C.E.).

𐤔

---

163. House of study.

164. Shabbat introduces the topic of forbidden types of labor, most of which are also forbidden on the holidays.

165. Eruvin discusses laws pertaining to carrying on the Sabbath. From here on, Rav Sherira Gaon tries to link the different tractates in some logical order, relating each to the one previous and the one after.

166. The Day of Atonement.

167. Trans. S. Berrin.

1 One may borrow jars of wine and jars of oil from his neighbor on the Sabbath, as long as he does not say, "Lend me." So too, a woman [may borrow] loaves of bread from her neighbor. If [the lender] does not trust [the borrower], [the borrower] may leave his garment with him, and settle the account after the Sabbath. So too, in Jerusalem, when Passover eve is on the Sabbath, one may leave his garment with [the seller of sacrificial animals] and take his Passover lamb, and settle the account after the Festival.

2 One may count how many guests and how many delicacies, [only] by mouth, but not from a written document. One may cast lots among his children and the rest of his household for the [food on the] table, but only as long as he has not intended to make larger and smaller portions, for that would be like gambling with dice [on the Sabbath]. In the Temple, lots may be cast for sacrificial meat, but not for other portions.

10.6.3 Mishnah Bava Meẓia 1:2–4: Property Disputes[168]

The following selections illustrate civil law as included in the Mishnah. Oaths were an important tool for guaranteeing ownership in Jewish law.

ﱢﱠ

1:2 Two men were riding on an animal or one was riding the animal and one was leading it; if one says: "It is all mine" and the other says "it is all mine,"[169] then one must swear that he does not own less than half, and the other must swear that he does not own less than half, and they divide it[s value]. If they both agree or if they have witnesses, they divide it without an oath.

3 One said to two men: [I know] I have stolen a *maneh*[170] from one of you, but I do not know which one; or [one says]: The father of one of you deposited a *maneh* with me, but I do not know which one. He must give a *maneh* to each one, since he himself confessed.

4 Two men deposited some money with a third man; one [gave] a *maneh* (=100 *zuz*), and one [gave] 200 *zuz*. One says: the 200 *zuz* are mine, and the other says: the 200 *zuz* are mine. He must give each of them a *maneh*, and the rest should be set aside until Elijah comes.[171] Rabbi

---

168. Trans. S. Berrin.
169. Each claims ownership of the entire animal.
170. A *maneh* is equal to 100 *zuz* (*denarii*).
171. The harbinger of the Messiah who will settle all halakhic disputes.

Yose said: If so, then what is the liar losing?! [He gets back his full 100 *zuz* deposit.] Rather, all the money should be set aside until Elijah comes.

10.6.4 Mishnah Rosh ha-Shanah 1:1–9: The Fixing of the Calendar[172]

The Mishnah deals with the fixing of the calendar, specifying four New Year periods and prescribing the manner of observing the moon to determine the lunar months. This passage illustrates disputes between the Houses of Hillel and Shammai and between later tannaim.

ಜಿ

1:1 There are four "New Year" days: on the first of Nisan is the New Year for kings and feasts; on the first of Elul is the New Year for the Tithe of Cattle (Rabbi Eleazar and Rabbi Simeon say: The first of Tishre); on the first of Tishre is the New Year for [the reckoning of] the year [of foreign kings], of the Years of Release[173] and Jubilee years, for the planting [of trees] and for vegetables;[174] and the first of Shevat is the New Year for [fruit-]trees (so the School of Shammai, and the School of Hillel say: On the fifteenth thereof).

2 At four times in the year is the world judged: at Passover, regarding grain; at Pentecost, regarding the fruits of the tree; on New Year's Day all that come into the world pass before Him like legions of soldiers, for it is written, "He that fashions the hearts of them all, that considers all their works" (Ps. 33:15); and at the Feast [of Tabernacles] they are judged regarding water.

3 Because of six New Moons do messengers go forth [to proclaim the time of their appearing]: because of Nisan, to determine the time of Passover, because of Av, to determine the time of the Fast; because of Elul, to determine the New Year; because of Tishre, to determine aright the set feasts; because of Kislev, to determine the time of [the feast of] the Dedication (Hanukkah); and because of Adar, to determine the time of Purim. And while the Temple still stood they went forth also because of Iyyar, to determine the time of the Second Passover.[175]

---

172. Danby, *The Mishnah*, pp. 188–9.
173. The Sabbatical year.
174. For reckoning the years for the purpose of tithing fruits and vegetables.
175. Num. 9:9–14.

4 Because of two New Moons may the Sabbath be profaned:[176] [the New Moon] of Nisan and [the New Moon] of Tishre, for on them messengers used to go forth to Syria, and by them the set feasts were determined. And while the Temple still stood the Sabbath might also be profaned because of any of the New Moons, to determine aright the time of the offerings.

5 Whether [the New Moon] was manifestly visible or not, they may profane the Sabbath because of it. Rabbi Yose says: If it was manifestly visible they may not profane the Sabbath because of it.

6 Once more than forty pairs [of witnesses] came forward, but Rabbi Akiva in Lydda restrained them. Rabban Gamliel sent to him [saying]: "If you restrain the multitude, you will put a stumbling-block in their way for the future."[177]

7 If a father and his son saw the New Moon they may [both] go [to bear witness]; not that they can be included together [as a valid pair of witnesses], but that if one of them is found ineligible, the other may be included to make a pair with some other [witness]. Rabbi Simeon says: A father and his son, and any that are near of kin, are eligible to bear witness about the New Moon. Rabbi Yose said: Once Toviah the Physician saw the New Moon in Jerusalem together with his son and his freed slave; and the priests accepted him and his son but pronounced his freed slave ineligible. And when they came before the court, they accepted him and his slave but declared his son ineligible.

8 These are they who are ineligible (as witnesses): a dice-player, a usurer, pigeon-flyers, traffickers in Seventh Year produce, and slaves. This is the general rule; any evidence that a woman is not eligible to bring, these are not eligible to bring.

9 If a man saw the New Moon but could not walk, he may be taken on an ass [on the Sabbath] or even on a bed; and if any lie in wait for them, they may take staves in their hands. If it was a far journey, they may take food in their hands, since for a journey enduring a night and a day they may profane the Sabbath and go forth to bear witness about the New Moon, for it is written, "These are the set feasts of the Lord, even holy convocations which you shall proclaim in their appointed season" (Lev. 23:4).

---

176. In order to testify about the appearance of the New Moon.

177. They will hesitate to travel on the Sabbath in order to testify to seeing the New Moon, assuming that others have already done so.

10.6.5 Jerusalem Talmud Horayot 3:5 (48c): Alternative Mishnah Collections[178]

This passage is important as it indicates that among the tannaitic texts there were Mishnah collections other than the authoritative Mishnah redacted by Rabbi Judah the Prince.

※

"A man to whom God gives riches, properties and honor so that he does not lack anything which his appetite may crave, but God does not permit him to enjoy it . . ." (Eccl. 6:2). "Wealth": this is Scripture; "properties": these are halakhot; and "honor": this is Tosefta; "he does not lack anything which his appetite may crave": these are the "Great Mishnahs"[179] such as the Mishnah of Rav Huna, the Mishnah of Rabbi Hoshaia, and the Mishnah of Bar Kappara.

10.7 OTHER TANNAITIC TEXTS

10.7.1 *Iggeret Rav Sherira Gaon* 4: The Tosefta[180]

Rav Sherira Gaon explains the relation of the Tosefta to the Mishnah and summarizes the later talmudic view of the superior authority of the Mishnah to the Tosefta.

※

Concerning the Tosefta: Certainly Rabbi Ḥiyya arranged it,[181] but there is no definite indication whether he arranged it during Rabbi's lifetime or afterwards. However, it undoubtedly was arranged after the halakhot of our Mishnah. It is clear that the teachings of the Tosefta are based upon our Mishnah and teach about [its halakhot].

We do not know whether Rabbi Ḥiyya died during Rabbi's lifetime or after him. In Chapter *ha-Nose*[182] Rabbi instructs that: "Ḥannina bar Ḥama shall preside."

The Talmud asks: "Was there not Rabbi Ḥiyya, who was greater than he?"

---

178. Trans. S. Berrin.
179. Mishnah collections.
180. Trans. Rabinowich, *The Iggeres of Rav Sherira Gaon*, pp. 34–48.
181. This view has been disputed by modern scholars who see it as a later collection. Some agree that Rabbi Ḥiyya created a proto-Tosefta.
182. Babylonian Talmud Ketubot 103b.

The reply is: "Rabbi Ḥiyya had already died."

Regarding this reply, the Talmud now offers a series of three proofs that Rabbi Ḥiyya in fact outlived Rabbi: But Rabbi Ḥiyya said: "I saw Rabbi's tomb and shed tears on it." Moreover, did not Rabbi Ḥiyya say: "On the day when Rabbi died, priesthood ceased"? And elsewhere: "When Rabbi took ill Rabbi Ḥiyya entered to visit him. . . ." Thus, we see from the Talmud that it was doubtful who died first.

Our sages maintain, however, that the Tosefta was arranged during Rabbi's lifetime, and from that time it was taught in Rabbi's *bet midrash.* This is seen from the episode cited in Tractate Ḥagigah[183] concerning two deaf-mutes who lived in Rabbi's neighborhood. They were the sons of Rabbi Yoḥanan ben Gudgeda's sister; some say, the sons of Rabbi Yoḥanan ben Gudgeda's daughter: "Whenever Rabbi would enter the *bet midrash,* they would come and sit before him, move their lips and shake their heads. Rabbi prayed for them and they were healed. It was found that they were well versed in halakhah, *Sifra, Sifre,* Tosefta, and all of the Talmud."

As for your question, "What was Rabbi Ḥiyya's reason for writing the Tosefta, and why did Rabbi not write it?" Had Rabbi sought to write down and order all the material extant during his lifetime, it would have been too lengthy and would have been forgotten. Instead, Rabbi prepared and wrote the essential topics and the general rules in an abbreviated language, in which even one word can be the source for a number of fundamental principles and an abundance of profound and wonderful halakhot and aggadot; for the Mishnah was composed with divine aid.

Then Rabbi Ḥiyya came and, in the *baraitot,* set forth the particulars and the various aspects of these essential topics and general rules. Most of the principles which are proliferated and elaborated in the *baraitot* have their root in the Mishnah, and rely upon it as their basis. Thus we say in Ta'anit:[184] "Ilfa balanced himself at the top of the ship's mast and declared: 'If anyone asks me a question regarding a statement of Rabbi Ḥiyya and Rabbi Oshaya and I am unable to answer it from our Mishnah, I will throw myself from the mast and drown.'" Thus we see that any teaching of Rabbi Ḥiyya and Rabbi Oshaya can be derived from the Mishnah.[185]

---

183. Babylonian Talmud Ḥagigah 3a.
184. Babylonian Talmud Ta'anit 21a.
185. The Talmudic passage about Ilfa is intended as evidence for Rav Sherira Gaon's point. He now goes on to discuss the passage in more detail.

Ilfa wished to exhibit his wisdom, because of the incident with Rabbi Yoḥanan. [In response to Ilfa's challenge,] a certain old man came and recited a halakhah from the Tosefta: "If a man says, 'Give my sons one shekel a week,' but they need to be given a *sela,* we give them a *sela.*"[186]

Ilfa replied, "Whose opinion is this?"

And he proceeded to show that it is the opinion of Rabbi Meir, who said, "It is a mitzvah to fulfill the wishes of the deceased."[187]

We do not follow the opinion of Rabbi Ḥiyya, as expressed in a *baraita,* if he disputes with Rabbi. For example, let us suppose that a certain halakhah had originally been a matter of dispute between Rabbi Meir and Rabbi Yose; but Rabbi decided to record in the Mishnah only Rabbi Meir's opinion. Rabbi Ḥiyya then came, in the Tosefta, and stated that the halakhah had originally been a matter of dispute.

Now, the Talmud[188] gives us a rule about disputes among the sages: "When Rabbi Meir and Rabbi Yose disagree, the halakhah follows Rabbi Yose." Nevertheless, since in the Mishnah, Rabbi mentioned only Rabbi Meir's opinion, we follow Rabbi Meir.

Or, let us suppose that Rabbi in the Mishnah records a dispute between Rabbi Meir and Rabbi Yose. However, Rabbi Ḥiyya prefers Rabbi Meir's argument, and therefore records it in a *baraita* without mentioning Rabbi Yose's opposing view. In such a case, we do not accept [Rabbi Ḥiyya's] decision.

Thus, in Yevamot,[189] Rabbi Abbahu's servant asked him: "If only one side of a dispute is given in the Mishnah, and a *baraita* gives both sides, which do we follow?"

He answered: "We follow the Mishnah which presents only the one view." [He asked:] "When the Mishnah records both sides of a dispute and the *baraita* records only one side, which do we follow?"

He answered: "If Rabbi did not teach it, how would Rabbi Ḥiyya know about it?" For Rabbi Ḥiyya was Rabbi's student. He said what Rabbi taught him. Thus, Rabbi Ḥiyya had no information that Rabbi did not also have.[190]

Even an implication in a mishnah overrules an explicit statement of a *baraita.*

---

186. Tosefta Ketubot 6:10.

187. Rav Sherira Gaon now explains further how the Tosefta is subordinate to the Mishnah.

188. Babylonian Talmud Eruvin 46b.

189. Babylonian Talmud Yevamot 42b.

190. Hence, his inclusion of only one view cannot indicate an authoritative ruling.

10.7.2 Tosefta Rosh ha-Shanah 1:1–14:
More on the Fixing of the Calendar[191]

This Tosefta passage, when compared with the Mishnaic parallel presented above (text 10.6.4), shows how the Tosefta constitutes the earliest commentary to the Mishnah, assembling earlier versions of some traditions and later expansions as well in approximately the same order as that of the Mishnah.

🙚

1:1 Nisan is the New Year for kings and festivals, for the sequences of the months and for the heave-offering of the shekels. And some say, also for rent of houses. How so for kings? [If the king] died in Adar, and another took power in his place in Adar, they count the year as part of the reign of both this one [who died] and that one [who now reigns]. [If the king] died in Nisan, and another took power in his place in Nisan, they count the year as part of the reign of both this one [who died] and that one [who now reigns]. [If the king] died in Adar, and another took power in his place in Nisan, the former is counted in the reign of the first, and the latter is counted in the reign of the second.

2 How so for festivals? All the same are one who vows, one who pledges a valuation, and one who consecrates an object [but have not yet carried out what they have said in each case]: One violates the law against postponing the keeping of one's obligations only once the festivals of an entire year have gone by. Rabbi Simeon says, "[This is so in the case of] three festivals in their proper order, with the festival of unleavened bread coming first." And so did Rabbi Simeon say, "Sometimes they are three, sometimes they are four, and sometimes they are five. "How so? [If] one vowed before Passover, [he violates the law] only after Passover, Pentecost (Shavuot), and the Festival (Sukkot) will have passed. [If] he vowed before Pentecost, [he will have violated his vow] only after Pentecost, the Festival, Passover, Pentecost, and the Festival will have passed. [If] he vowed before the Festival, [he will have violated his vow] only after the Festival, Passover, Pentecost, and the Festival will have passed."

3 How so for months? Even though it is said concerning the first month,[192] "In the second month,[193] on the twenty-seventh day of the month, the earth was dry"[194] (Gen. 8:14), they begin to count only from

---

191. Trans. J. Neusner, *Tosefta* (New York: Ktav, 1977–80), pp. 249–52.

192. Counting from Tishre in the fall.

193. Marḥeshvan, after Tishre.

194. At the end of the flood, from which you might deduce that Tishre is the first month.

Nisan,[195] as it is said, "This month shall be for you the beginning of the months; it shall be the first month of the year for you" (Ex. 12:2).

4 How so for the heave-offering of shekels? All public offerings are offered on the first of Nisan. If the new shekels come on time,[196] [the public offerings] are offered [from beasts purchased from] the new [heave-offering of the shekels]. And if not, they are offered [from beasts purchased] from the old [heave-offering of the shekels].

5 How so for the rent for houses? He who rents out a house to his fellow for a year collects rent from him for twelve months, reckoned from day to day. If he said, "[It is rented] for this year," even though he rented it from him only on the first of Adar, he has a right to the house only to the first of Nisan.[197]

6 "The first day of Elul is the new year for tithing cattle. Rabbi Eleazar and Rabbi Simeon say, 'It is on the first day of Tishre.'"[198] Said Rabbi Simeon ben Azzai, "Since these rule that it is on the first day of Elul, and those rule that it is on the first day of Tishre, let the ones born in Elul be tithed by themselves. "How so? [If] they were born on the fifth day of Av and the fifth day of Elul, on the fifth day of Elul and on the fifth day of Tishre, on the fifth day of Av and on the fifth day of Tishre, they will not join together [for the purposes of tithing]. [But if they were born] on the fifth day of Tishre and on the fifth day of Av, lo, these will then join together for the purposes of tithing."

7 "[The first day of] Tishre is the new year for the reckoning of years, for Sabbatical years, for Jubilees, for planting [trees], and for vegetables,"[199] for tithes and for vows. How so for "for the reckoning of years, for Sabbatical years, and for Jubilees"? They begin counting for years, Sabbatical years, and Jubilees, only from Tishre.

8 How so for "planting trees"? All the same are the ones who plant a tree, plant a shoot, and graft a branch onto a tree thirty days before the New Year: It [the planting] gets credit for a whole year, and it is permitted to allow them to continue to grow in the seventh year. [If it is] less than this, it does not get credit for a whole year, and it is not permitted to let them continue to grow in the seventh year. [In any year in which a tree is planted within thirty days of the *new* year], the produce of such a sapling are forbidden until the fifteenth of Shevat [of the year in which the tree's produce becomes permitted for common use]. [If the tree is] *orlah* [that is,

---

195. In the spring.
196. Before Nisan 1.
197. When the year draws to a close.
198. Mishnah Rosh ha-Shanah 1:1.
199. Mishnah Rosh ha-Shanah 1:1.

within the first three years of its growth], [it is still continued to be considered as] *'orlah* [until the fifteenth of Shevat]. [If the tree is] in the fourth year [of its growth], [it is still considered to be subject to the prohibition of a tree] in the fourth year of its growth [until the fifteenth of Shevat].

9 How so for "vegetables?" [If] one gathered vegetables on the eve of the new year before sunset, and then he went and gathered more after sunset, they do not take heave-offering or give tithes from this [gathered before sunset] for that [gathered afterward], because the latter is new and the former is old. [If] it was the second year of the Sabbatical cycle and the third year then was coming on, then that which is gathered first is tithed as second-year-tithe, and that which is gathered second is tithed as poor man's tithe. [If] one picked a citron (*etrog*) on the eve of the fifteenth of Shevat before sunset, and then went and picked another one after sunset, they do not take heave-offering or give tithes from this one [gathered before sunset] for that one [gathered afterward], because the latter is new and the former is old. [If] it was the third year [of the cycle] and the fourth year was coming on, then that which is picked first is tithed as poor man's tithe, and that which is picked second is tithed as second tithe.

10 How so for "vows"? He who is prohibited by vow from deriving benefit from his fellow for a year—[If] he vowed not to derive benefit from him for twelve months, these are reckoned from day to day. But if he said, "For this year," even if he vowed not to derive benefit from him only on the first day of Elul, he is subject to the vow only up to the first day of Tishre.

11 "At the New Year all who enter the world pass before him like troops, since it is said, 'He who fashions the hearts of them all, who considers all their works'" (Ps. 33:15). And it says, "Blow the trumpet at the New Moon, at the full moon, on our feast day. For it is a statute for Israel, and ordinance of the God of Jacob" (Ps. 81:3–4). [If] the court has sanctified the day, [the heavenly] court enters before Him (God). And if not, [the heavenly] court does not enter before him.

12 And so you find with reference to the *omer* of *manna*: If [the New Moon] comes at its proper time, it is forthwith used up. And if not, it is held back for thirty days. Said Rabbi Akiva, "Bring an *omer* of barley at Passover, which is the season of the ripening of barley, so that the harvest will be blessed for you. Bring fruit as first fruits on Pentecost, which is the season of the ripening of orchards, so that the produce of the orchards will be blessed for you. Bring a water-offering at the Festival, so that the rains will be blessed for you."[200] Say before him sovereignty-verses, remem-

---

200. Tosefta Sukkah 3:18.

brance-verses, and shofar-verses:[201] sovereignty-verses, so that you will make him ruler over them; remembrance-verses, so that your remembrance will come before him for good; shofar-verses, so that your prayer will go up with the quavering sound of the shofar before him.

13 "All are judged on the New Year, and the decree is sealed on the Day of Atonement," the words of Rabbi Meir. Rabbi Judah says, "All are judged on the New Year, and the decree of each and every one of them is sealed in its own time: at Passover for grain, at Pentecost for fruits of the orchard, at the Festival for water. And the decree of man is sealed on the Day of Atonement." Rabbi Yose says, "Man is judged every single day, since it says, 'What is man, that You make so much of him, and that You set Your mind upon him, visit him every morning, and test him every moment?'" (Job 7:17–18).

14 "On the occasion of six New Moons messengers go forth."[202] Rabbi made the rule that they should go forth also on the occasion of the New Moon of the Second Adar.[203]

10.7.3 *Iggeret Rav Sherira Gaon* 5: The *Baraitot, Sifra,* and *Sifre*[204]

Rav Sherira attests to the slow diffusion of those traditions found in the halakhic Midrashim. This would explain the absence of some of the baraitot found in these collections from relevant passages in the Jerusalem and Babylonian Talmuds.

ৡৄ

Unlike the *baraita* [collection] of Rabbi Ḥiyya and Rabbi Oshaya,[205] these [other] *baraitot* were not established so as to be studied by everyone. Nor do we refer to them with the [introductory] expression, *tanu rabbanan*.[206] Rather, [they are introduced] by: *tanya*[207] and *tanna tuna*.[208]

The *Sifra* and *Sifre* also did not originally become as widely known among the sages as the Mishnah, which from the time of its completion spread throughout Israel. Rather, [the *Sifra* and *Sifre* spread] little by little.

---

201. In the Rosh ha-Shanah liturgy. See text 12.6.3.
202. Mishnah Rosh ha-Shanah 1:3.
203. During the leap-year when an extra Adar is intercalated.
204. Trans. Rabinowich, *The Iggeres of Rav Sherira Gaon,* pp. 43–4.
205. The Tosefta.
206. Used to introduce material from Tosefta, Sifra and Sifre.
207. "It was taught."
208. "The tanna taught."

Thus we say in Yevamot: "Rabbi Yoḥanan said to Resh Lakish: 'I observed that the son of Pedat was sitting and making expositions like Moses from the mouth of the Almighty.'[209]

"And [Resh Lakish] replied, 'It [his exposition] is not his, it is a *baraita*; and where was it taught? In *Torat Kohanim* [*Sifra*].' Rabbi Yoḥanan went and learned it [the *Sifra*] in three days, and analyzed it for three months."

Afterwards,[210] *Sifra*, *Sifre*, and Tosefta became established so as to be studied by the sages, and this remains the ordinance until the present day, as Rav Naḥman said there, "Here are Rav Sheshet and I who have studied halakhot [Mishnah], *Sifra*, *Sifre*, Tosefta, and the whole Talmud."[211]

10.7.4 *Mekhilta of Rabbi Ishmael, Beshallaḥ*: Moses and the Bones of Joseph[212]

This Midrash expands the verse in Exodus (Ex. 13:19) which states tersely of Moses that upon the Exodus from Egypt, Moses took the remains of Joseph with the Israelites. It is an excellent example of the many extended aggadic passages present in what claims to be a halakhic Midrash.

꙳

"And Moses took the bones of Joseph with him" (Ex.13:19).

This demonstrates the wisdom and piety of Moses. For all Israel was busy with the spoils while Moses was busy fulfilling the commandment concerning the bones of Joseph. The verse says of him, "The wise of heart accepts commands, but he whose speech is foolish comes to grief" (Prov. 10:8).[213] And how did Moses know where Joseph was buried? They said that Seraḥ, the daughter of Asher, remained from that generation and she showed Moses the grave of Joseph. She said to him, "They put him in this place. The Egyptians made him a metal coffin and they sank it in the Nile."

So Moses went and stood by the Nile. He took a pebble, threw it in, and cried out, saying, "Joseph, Joseph, the time has come for the [fulfillment] of the oath which the Holy One Blessed be He swore to our father Abraham, for He is redeeming His children. Honor the Lord, God

---

209. Babylonian Talmud Yevamot 72b.

210. After these collections became more widespread.

211. Babylonian Talmud Shevu'ot 41b.

212. Trans. S. Berrin based on the text of H. S. Horovitz and I. A. Rabin, *Mekhilta' de-Rabbi Ishmael* (Jerusalem: Bamberger & Wahrman, 1960), pp. 78–80.

213. Moses, the wise of heart, immediately undertook to fulfill the command of Joseph to bring his bones back to the Land of Israel.

of Israel, and do not delay the redemption, for because of you we are delayed. Otherwise, we will be exempted from your oath." Immediately, Joseph's coffin floated to the surface and Moses took it.

Do not be surprised at this. Behold it is written, "As one of them was felling a tree-trunk, the iron ax-head fell into the water, and he cried out, 'Alas, master, it was borrowed!'

" 'Where did it fall?' asked the man of God.

"He showed him the spot and he cut off a stick and threw it in and he made the ax-head float" (2 Kings 6:5–6). These things are a case of *a fortiori* reasoning:[214] If Elisha, the disciple of Elijah, could make the iron rise to the surface, then all the more so could Moses, the master of Elijah, do so.[215]

Rabbi Nathan said: "Joseph was buried in the necropolis of Egypt in order to teach you that according to the measure which man metes out, so do they mete out unto him. Miriam waited for her brother a while as it is said, 'And his sister stood far off' (Ex. 2:4). So, in the wilderness God made the ark, the Divine Presence, the priests, the Levites, all Israel and the seven clouds of glory all wait for her, as it is written, 'And the people did not travel on until Miriam was readmitted' (Num. 12:15).[216] Joseph was privileged to bury his father, for there was none greater than he among his brothers, as it is said, 'and Joseph went up to bury his father. . . and chariots and horsemen went up with him' (Gen. 50:7–9). Who do we have as great as Joseph, with whom none other than Moses busied himself? Moses busied himself with the bones of Joseph, and there is none greater than he in Israel, as it is said, 'And Moses took the bones of Joseph with him' (Ex. 13:19). Whom do we have greater than Moses, with whom none other than the Divine Presence busied itself?, as it is said, 'And He [God] buried him [Moses] in the valley' (Deut 34:6).

"Furthermore, with Jacob Pharaoh's servants and the elders of his house went up, as it is said, 'And with him all the servants of Pharaoh and all the elders of his house went up' (Gen. 50:7). And with Joseph the ark, the Divine Presence, the priests, the Levites, all of Israel and the seven clouds of glory went up. Furthermore, Joseph's coffin (Hebrew *'aron*) was traveling with the Ark (Hebrew *'aron*) of the Eternal Living One. Passersby said, 'What is the nature of these two *'aronot*?'

---

214. *Qal va-ḥomer*: see 10.4.1.

215. To recover the metal coffin of Joseph.

216. Miriam had contracted the skin disease *ẓara'at*, usually mistranslated "leprosy," and the people waited during her period of quarantine and purification.

"They said to them, 'This is the *'aron* of a dead man, and this is the *'aron* of the Eternal Living One.'

"They said, 'How is it that a dead man is going with the *'aron* of the Eternal Living One?'

"They said to him, 'He who is lying in this *'aron* (Joseph) fulfilled that which is written on what is lying in this *'aron* (the Ten Commandments).'"[217]

On that which is lying in this *'aron* it is written, "I am the Lord your God" (Ex. 21:2). About Joseph it is written, "Am I a substitute for God?" (Gen. 50:19). On that which is lying in this *'aron* it is written, "You shall have no other gods besides Me" (Ex. 20:3). About Joseph it is written, "I fear God" (Gen. 42:18). It is written, "You shall not swear [by the name of the Lord your God]" (Ex. 20:7). Concerning Joseph it is written, "By Pharaoh's life" (Gen. 42:16). It is written, "Remember the Sabbath day to keep it holy" (Ex. 20:8). Of Joseph it is written, "slaughter and prepare an animal" (Gen. 43:16), and "prepare" indicates nothing other than the Sabbath, as it is said, "but on the sixth day, they should prepare" (Ex. 16:5). It is written, "Honor your father" (Ex. 20:12). Of Joseph it is written, "Israel said to Joseph, 'Your brothers are pasturing at Shechem. Come, I am sending you to them.' And he said, 'I am ready'" (Gen. 37:13). It is written, "You shall not murder" (Ex. 20:13); he did not murder Potiphar.[218] It is written, "You shall not commit adultery" (Ex. 20:13); he did not commit adultery with the wife of Potiphar. It is written, "You shall not steal" (Ex. 20:13). He did not steal, as it is said, "Joseph gathered in all the money. . . [and Joseph brought the money into Pharaoh's house]" (Gen. 47:14). It is written, "You shall not bear false witness against your neighbor" (Ex. 20:13). And behold these things are a case of *a fortiori* reasoning: since he did not say even a true thing, all the more so [did he not say] a false one! It is written, "You shall not covet" (Ex. 20:14); he did not covet the wife of Potiphar. It is written, "You shall not hate [your brother in your heart]" (Lev. 19:17). Of Joseph it is said, "And he reassured them and he spoke to their hearts" (Gen. 50:21).[219] It is written, "You shall not take vengeance and shall not bear a grudge" (Lev. 19:18). And it is written, "Although you intended evil for me, God

---

217. The Mekhilta compares each of the Ten Commandments to events in the life of Joseph to show how Joseph fulfilled them.

218. According to midrashic tradition, the wife of his master Potiphar tried to convince Joseph to murder her husband.

219. Even after his father's death, Joseph reassured his brothers that he held no grudge or hatred for their having sold him into slavery in Egypt.

intended it for good" (Gen. 50:20). It is written, "Let your brother live with you" (Lev. 25:35); and "Joseph sustained his father and his brothers, and all his father's household" (Gen. 47:12).

When [Joseph] made them swear [to bring up his bones for burial in the Land of Israel], he made them swear that they would have their children swear. Rabbi Nathan said, "Why did he make his brothers swear but did not make his (own) children swear? He said, 'If I make my children swear, the Egyptians will not permit them. And if they say, "Our father (Joseph) brought up his father (Jacob)" they will immediately tell them, "Your father was a king."'"

Thus, he made his brothers swear and not his sons. Joseph said to them, "My father came down here voluntarily and I brought him up; I came down here against my will and I will have you swear that you will return me to the place from which you stole me." And so they did for him, as it is said, "And the bones of Joseph which the Israelites had brought up from Egypt were buried at Shechem, in the plot of ground which Jacob had bought for a hundred *qesitah* from the children of Hamor, Shechem's father, and it was an inheritance to the sons of Joseph" (Josh. 24:32).

"God will surely remember you" (Ex. 13:19). He remembered you in Egypt, He will remember you at the Red Sea; He remembered you at the Sea, He will remember you in the desert; He remembered you in the desert, He will remember you at Naḥal Arnon; He remembered you in this world, He will also remember you in the World to Come.[220]

10.7.5 *Sifra Emor* 5: Logic and Scripture[221]

This passage from the Sifra, the halakhic Midrash on Leviticus, is typical of the complex logical argumentation of this work. The Sifra makes a sustained argument that Scriptural sources are necessary for the derivation of halakhah because logical deduction alone is always open to refutation. In this passage, the Sifra explains the application of the principle that wives of priests may eat of the priestly rations while wives of Israelites may not.

ૐ

7 If a priest's daughter is married to a man who is an outsider [she may not eat of the sacred (priestly) rations]" (Lev. 22:12); I know that this applies if she has married a person of irreparably tainted genealogy

---

220. This is an example of the messianic peroration (conclusion) with which many homiletical sections of Midrash end.

221. Trans. L. H. Schiffman.

[*mamzer*].[222] How do I know that it applies even [if she married] a Levite or an Israelite? Scripture says, "to an outsider."[223] How do I know that if a widow is married to a high priest, or a divorcee or a woman who has performed the rite of removing the shoe[224] [is married to] to an ordinary priest, [they may not eat of the priestly rations]?[225] Scripture says, "to a man," to a man [husband] who bestows upon her the right to eat [priestly rations].[226]

8 But is that not a matter of logic?[227] If in the case of [the marriage of the daughter of a priest to] an Israelite with whom sexual relations does not invalidate her [later on from returning] to the priestly caste [should her husband die and she have no children], yet [having had] sexual relations with him does invalidate her from eating priestly rations, then a high priest [or a divorcee or a woman who has performed the rite of removing the shoe who is married to an ordinary priest], with whom [having had] sexual relations invalidates her from [ever entering] the priestly caste [again],[228] is it not logical that it should invalidate her from eating priestly rations? No![229] If you have said this regarding an Israelite who does not bestow on any woman the right to eat priestly rations, will you say the same of the high priest [or the ordinary priest] who certainly does bestow on other women the right to eat priestly rations?[230]

Since[231] he bestows the right on other women to eat priestly rations, sexual relations with him should not invalidate this woman from eating priestly rations. [Accordingly,] Scripture states, "to a man," a man who bestows upon her the right of eating [priestly rations].[232]

9 "She may not eat of the sacred (priestly) rations": She may not eat priestly rations, but she may bestow that right on her mother.

---

222. A *mamzer* is the descendant of an adulterous or incestuous marriage and is forbidden to marry a priest, Levite, or free Israelite.

223. Meaning anyone who is not a priest.

224. Cf. Deut. 25:5–10. This rite was performed in a case of refusal to perform levirate marriage.

225. Because such a marriage violates the law of the Torah.

226. A priest who marries her in violation of the law does not have that right.

227. If so, then why do we need a verse to explain the law?

228. She may never marry a priest.

229. This law cannot be derived from logic.

230. You may not derive anything regarding the law of priests by deduction from that of ordinary Israelites. Hence, we need a Scriptural verse to tell us that a woman married to a priest whom she is forbidden to marry may not eat of the priestly rations.

231. The text now sets out what you might think if not for the biblical command of Lev. 22:12.

232. Excluding the marriage to a priest who may not legally marry her.

10 How so? An Israelite woman who married a priest[233] and gave birth to a daughter with him, and then the daughter went and married an Israelite,[234]—I might have said that just as she does not have the right to eat [priestly rations], so her mother may not eat [priestly rations]. Scripture says, "*she* may not eat of the sacred (priestly) rations": [while] she may not eat [priestly rations], her mother may eat [priestly rations].[235]

---

233. And so is permitted to eat priestly rations.

234. And so she may no longer eat priestly rations since she has left her father's house.

235. Even though her daughter has married, she may still eat priestly rations by right of her marriage to a priest.

11

Formative Judaism Comes of Age

The years following the redaction of the Mishnah saw the gradual expansion of the hegemony of the emerging talmudic system of Judaism to large parts of the communities in the Palestinian center and the Babylonian Diaspora. In the areas of the Greco-Roman Diaspora, Hellenistic Judaism began to wane and was gradually replaced by an approach to Judaism derived ultimately from the Land of Israel. Jews faced new political and, as a result, religious challenges with the rise of the Byzantine Christian Empire in Palestine and the Sassanian rulers in Babylonia. The events and trends chronicled here provide the background for the immense growth of Rabbinic tradition and literature.

Throughout the Greco-Roman Diaspora, Hellenistic Judaism was on the decline. To some extent, this development was encouraged by the spread of Christianity, which competed for the allegiance of Jews and of those Gentiles attracted to monotheism. The decision of the Church, as chronicled in Acts 15 (text 11.1.1), to accept Gentile converts without conversion to Judaism must have hastened this process. Another significant factor must have been the debacle that ensued after the failed Jewish uprising which took place throughout the Diaspora between 115 and 117 C.E., and which is reflected in the work of Dio Cassius (text 11.1.2). The enormous ramifications which he sketches may be exaggerated, but the account by Eusebius in his *Ecclesiastical History* (text 11.1.3) indicates the consequences for the Jewish communities, the scale of the revolt, and the likelihood that anti-Jewish feeling among Greco-Roman pagans must have risen considerably as a result. Echoes of these events are also heard in Mishnah Sotah (text 11.1.4) and *Seder Olam Rabbah* (text 11.1.5), both of which term this disturbance a "war."

The Christianization of the Eastern Roman Empire, completed in 324 C.E., placed the Jews of Palestine in a new position. They were now a minority group in the emerging Christian world. Yet they continued to be led, on the one hand, by the patriarch, and on the other hand, by the Rabbinic sages, who sometimes exhibited rivalry with one another as described in Jerusalem Talmud Sanhedrin (text 11.2.1). During this period Jews recalled the high status in local affairs that Rabbi Judah the Prince had enjoyed as patriarch, protected as he was by his close relationship with Roman officials. The memory of this period inspired such—to some extent fanciful—accounts as that of the relationship of Rabbi to a Roman official, Antoninus, as related in the Babylonian Talmud Avodah Zarah (text 11.2.2). Later patriarchs also enjoyed good relations with important non-Jews, as evidenced in the letters which the rhetor Libanius wrote to the patriarch in the fourth century C.E. (text 11.2.3).

The legal status of the Jews during this period was complex, as is clear from the selections presented from *Codex Theodosianus* (text 11.2.4), which are representative of Byzantine legislation on Jewish affairs. We find that Judaism and its leaders were at times outlawed and at times protected. We hear of Jews who converted to Christianity and of Christians who converted to Judaism. Synagogues were to be burned in one excerpt and were to be protected in another. It is here that we see the legal status of the patriarch formally reduced in the early fifth century so that this institution would soon be dismantled. It is interesting that this code prohibited intermarriage between Jews and Christians. Further examples of a similar nature are found in the *Novels of Theodosius* (text 11.2.5). Here we find the total delegitimization of Judaism and even the dehumanization of its followers, termed "heretical monsters" along with Samaritans and pagans.

In view of the anti-Semitic legislation imposed by the Byzantine Empire, it is no surprise that Jews took up arms in revolt in 352 C.E. The Gallus Revolt, as it is called, was described by Jerome in his *Chronicon* (text 11.2.6), in which he testifies to the widespread character of the violence. Similar is the account of Socrates Scholasticus in his *Ecclesiastical History* (text 11.2.7).

When the emperor Julian ascended the throne in 361, he attempted to reimpose paganism on the empire. As part of his anti-Christian policy, he encouraged the Jews to rebuild their Temple, as described by Sozomenus in his *Ecclesiastical History* (text 11.2.8). The failure of this program was understood by Christian sources to have been a miracle. Julian may even have extended various privileges to the Jews in an attempt to attract them to his plan to rebuild the Temple, as is mentioned in a supposed letter of his to the Jewish community (text 11.2.9).

Yet anti-Jewish legislation continued, as evidenced in *Codex Justinianus* (text 11.2.10). Jews were prohibited from observing their marriage laws and were denied equal rights in court in this sixth-century C.E. legal collection. Such legal disabilities, no doubt, related to Samaritans as well, so that in 484 C.E. the Samaritans were in open revolt, as documented in the *Chronicon Paschale* (text 11.2.11). This revolt is also described by Procopius of Caesarea (text 11.2.12), indicating that the rebels lashed out against the bishop of Nablus, and the Christian rulers gave the Samaritan cult-place on Mount Gerizim to Christians for the building of a church. Procopius criticizes (text 11.2.13) the persecution of non-Christians in the Byzantine Empire, among them the Samaritans, claiming that it was undertaken primarily for financial gain and not for religious reasons. By 529, the Samaritans were again in revolt, as shown in *Chronicon Paschale* (text 11.2.14), which claims that Samaritans were living as converts to Christianity externally while privately continuing to observe their brand of Israelite religion.

Jews and Samaritans both experienced a hopeful sign when in 614 the Persians conquered Jerusalem as described by Antiochus Strategos (text 11.2.15), but it was not long until the Byzantine Christians regained control of Palestine only to lose it to the Moslems in the Arab Conquest of 638.

The conventional wisdom that Babylonian Jewry enjoyed a freer environment in which to develop its intellectual and religious tradition during this period has much to recommend it, although the great strides made in Palestine even under difficult conditions should not be minimized. The development of Judaism in this period may effectively be seen as a partnership of these two great centers.

Already in the pre-Christian period, as reported by Josephus in *Antiquities* (text 11.3.1), an independent Jewish principality led by two Jewish swashbucklers was in existence in Babylonia. The inability of Asineus and Anileus to move from a life of predation to one of political leadership soon spelled the end of this principality. By the time this episode ended, however, considerable antipathy to the Jews had developed.

By the middle of the first century C.E., tannaitic Judaism had already been transplanted to Babylonia, as related in Jerusalem Talmud Yevamot (text 11.3.2). Babylonian Talmud Sanhedrin (text 11.3.3), looking back at the history of Rabbinic centers of learning, listed Nisibis in Mesopotamia, and Babylonia in general, as major centers of Rabbinic teaching. Babylonian Jewry even boasted a tanna who, according to Mishnah Yevamot (text 11.3.4), preserved traditions from Rabban Gamliel I that were not known in the Land of Israel. We should in no way be surprised by this in light of the presence in the Babylonian Talmud of numerous Palestinian traditions, and vice-versa.

In treating the early history of Babylonian Jewry above (chapter 5), we presented Josephus' account of the conversion of the royal House of Adiabene. A Palestinian midrashic tradition from the Byzantine period in *Genesis Rabbah* (text 11.3.5) expounded upon these events, about which it had limited historical information. Later on, in geonic Babylonia, Rav Sherira Gaon (text 11.3.6) surveyed the detailed chronology of the Babylonian amoraim whose work created the Babylonian Talmud. Along the way he recounted numerous historical traditions, some of which derived from archives available in early medieval Babylonia. In contrast, the list of the exilarchs and the sages who guided them, presented in the medieval chronicle *Seder Olam Zuta* (text 11.3.7), does not allow a reconstruction of a correct historical sequence, since the author lacked sufficient data.

Both the Palestinian and Babylonian Jewish communities had their institutions of self-government, the patriarchate and the exilarchate, respectively. Throughout this period a rivalry existed between these two institutions which itself reflected the local patriotism of the two communities. This debate is taken up in Babylonian Talmud Horayot (text 11.3.8) in the context of the discussion of the sacrifice of the "ruler" for an accidental transgression. Some clearly took the two institutions to be of equal status, as is noted in Babylonian Talmud Ḥullin (text 11.3.9). The exilarchs, just like the patriarchs, were increasingly distant from Rabbinic learning, as we see in Babylonian Talmud Bava Qamma (text 11.3.10), in which the exilarch is said to judge according to Persian law and not Jewish law. Babylonian amoraim also noted laxity in the observance of Sabbath laws at the home of the exilarch, as told in Babylonian Talmud Shabbat (text 11.3.11).

Essential to the ability of Jews to live under talmudic law throughout the ever-widening Diaspora was a principle enunciated by the Babylonian amora Samuel in Babylonian Talmud Bava Batra (text 11.3.12). Samuel ruled that the law of the land applied in matters of business and civil law, a ruling which was a fundamental pillar of the adjustment to life under non-Jewish governments.

Rav Sherira Gaon (text 11.3.13), again with help from talmudic sources, archival materials, and local traditions, provided a detailed account of the chronology of the last of the amoraim and of the savoraim, those who completed the process of editing the Babylonian Talmud. He also testified to the tensions between the Rabbis and the exilarch.

Babylonian Jewry understood fully the immense contribution that the Babylonian amoraim had made to the final crystalization of Rabbinic Judaism. Their prayer for the scholars of Babylonia (text 11.3.14) also provides some sense of the complexity of Babylonian Rabbinic organization at the end of the talmudic period. By the time this period came to an end, important classics of Rabbinic literature had been edited, the impact of which would transform the nature of the Jewish world.

11.1 DECLINE OF HELLENISTIC JUDAISM

11.1.1 Acts 15:
The Acceptance of Gentile Converts into Christianity[1]

Paul, the apostle (mid-first century C.E.), saw the bulk of Jewish law, including circumcision, as not applicable and welcomed Gentiles who did not

---

1. *Revised Standard Version of the Bible* (New York: National Council of Churches, 1957).

want to observe Mosaic law into the nascent Church. He required them to abstain from idolatry, unchastity, and the eating of blood as the chief rules of Christianity. This turn to Gentile Christianity was formally debated and approved by the Jerusalem Church and led to the spread of Christianity in the Greco-Roman world. Hellenistic Judaism subsequently became a less significant force and was soon to become extinct.

✿

15:1 But some men came down from Judea and were teaching the brethren, "Unless you are circumcised according to the custom of Moses, you cannot be saved." 2 And when Paul and Barnabas had no small dissension and debate with them, Paul and Barnabas and some of the others were appointed to go up to Jerusalem to the apostles and the elders about this question. 3 So, being sent on their way by the church, they passed through both Phoenicia and Samaria, reporting the conversion of the Gentiles, and they gave great joy to all the brethren. 4 When they came to Jerusalem, they were welcomed by the church and the apostles and the elders, and they declared all that God had done with them. 5 But some believers who belonged to the party of the Pharisees rose up,[2] and said, "It is necessary to circumcise them, and to charge them to keep the law of Moses."

6 The apostles and the elders were gathered together to consider this matter. 7 And after there had been much debate, Peter rose and said to them, "Brethren, you know that in the early days God made choice among you, that by my mouth the Gentiles should hear the word of the gospel and believe. 8 And God who knows the heart bore witness to them, giving them the Holy Spirit just as he did to us; 9 and he made no distinction between us and them, but cleansed their hearts by faith. 10 Now therefore why do you make trial of God by putting a yoke upon the neck of the disciples which neither our fathers nor we have been able to bear? 11 But we believe that we shall be saved through the grace of the Lord Jesus, just as they will."[3]

12 And all the assembly kept silence; and they listened to Barnabas and Paul as they related what signs and wonders God had done through them among the Gentiles. 13 After they finished speaking, James replied, "Brethren, listen to me. 14 Symeon[4] has related how God first visited the

---

2. Jewish Christians who continued to observe the law.

3. Arguing that observance of the law is not necessary for Gentiles.

4. Also called Peter.

Gentiles, to take out of them a people for his name. 15 And with this the words of the prophets agree, as it is written,

16 'After this I will return,
and I will rebuild the dwelling of David, which has fallen;
I will rebuild its ruins,
and I will set it up,
17 that the rest of men may seek the Lord,
and all the Gentiles who are called by my name,

18 says the Lord, who has made these things known from of old.'[5]

19 Therefore my judgment is that we should not trouble those of the Gentiles who turn to God, 20 but should write to them to abstain from the pollutions of idols and from unchastity and from what is strangled[6] and from blood. 21 For from early generations Moses has had in every city those who preach him, for he is read every sabbath in the synagogues."[7]

22 Then it seemed good to the apostles and the elders, with the whole church, to choose men from among them and send them to Antioch with Paul and Barnabas. They sent Judas called Barsabbas, and Silas, leading men among the brethren, 23 with the following letter: "The brethren, both the apostles and the elders, to the brethren who are of the Gentiles in Antioch and Syria[8] and Cilicia,[9] greeting. 24 Since we have heard that some persons from us have troubled you with words, unsettling your minds, although we gave them no instructions, 25 it has seemed good to us, having come to one accord, to choose men and send them to you with our beloved Barnabas and Paul, 26 men who have risked their lives for the sake of our Lord Jesus Christ. 27 We have therefore sent Judas and Silas, who themselves will tell you the same things by word of mouth. 28 For it has seemed good to the Holy Spirit and to us to lay upon you no greater burden than these necessary things: 29 that you abstain from what has been sacrificed to idols and from blood and from what is strangled and from unchastity. If you keep yourselves from these, you will do well. Farewell."

30 So when they were sent off, they went down to Antioch; and having gathered the congregation together, they delivered the letter. 31 And

---

5. Cf. Amos 9:11–12.

6. Meat not ritually slaughtered.

7. The reading of the Torah, the Five Books of Moses, occurs every week in the synagogue.

8. That is, Antioch and the rest of Syria.

9. A district of southern Asia Minor, now located in Turkey.

when they read it, they rejoiced at the exhortation. 32 And Judas and Silas, who were themselves prophets, exhorted the brethren with many words and strengthened them. 33 And after they had spent some time, they were sent off in peace by the brethren to those who had sent them. 35 But Paul and Barnabas remained in Antioch, teaching and preaching the word of the Lord, with many others also.

11.1.2 Dio Cassius, *Historia Romana* LXVIII, 32:1–3: The Jewish Uprising[10]

This selection from a Roman historian who lived ca. 160–230 C.E. describes the Diaspora Revolt of 115–117 C.E. In Dio Cassius' view, strong measures against the Jews were justified by their ruthlessness in the conduct of the rebellion. While this account is certainly greatly dramatized and exaggerated, it does indicate the extent of the revolt and the seriousness with which it was considered in the Greco-Roman world.

꿨

(1) Trajan[11] therefore departed thence,[12] and a little later began to fail in health. Meanwhile the Jews in the region of Cyrene[13] had put a certain Andreas at their head, and were destroying both the Romans and the Greeks. They would eat the flesh of their victims, make belts for themselves of their entrails, anoint themselves with their blood and wear their skins for clothing; many they sawed in two, from the head downwards; (2) others they gave to wild beasts, and still others they forced to fight as gladiators.[14] In all two hundred and twenty thousand persons perished. In Egypt, too, they perpetrated many similar outrages and in Cyprus under the leadership of a certain Artemion. There, also, two hundred and forty thousand perished, (3) and for this reason no Jew may set foot on this island, but if one of them is driven upon its shores, he is put to

---

10. Trans. E. Cary, *Dio's Roman History* (Loeb Classical Library; Cambridge: Harvard University Press, 1925), vol. 8, pp. 421–3.

11. Born ca. 53 C.E., he was an experienced military officer who later became a popular Roman emperor in 98. In 116 and 117, having conquered Armenia, he was conducting a military campaign against the Parthians in Mesopotamia, but his successes were marred by the revolt of the Jews which spread to Mesopotamia. He took ill and died in 117.

12. From Hatra in the steppe west of the Tigris, which Trajan unsuccessfully besieged as part of the Parthian campaign he conducted toward the end of his reign.

13. A Greek colony in North Africa the prosperity of which was interrupted by the Jewish revolt which began there in 115 C.E.

14. These mythic exaggerations are thought by some scholars to have been derived by Dio Cassius from anti-Semitic Greek sources.

death. Among others who subdued the Jews was Lusius,[15] who was sent
by Trajan.

11.1.3 Eusebius, *Ecclesiastical History* IV, 1–5: The Jewish Uprising[16]

*Eusebius, born in Caesarea in Palestine, lived between ca. 260 and 339.
He was a prolific writer, biblical scholar, bishop of Caesarea, and the first
Church historian. In his Ecclesiastical History his main point is to demonstrate that God's plan for salvation subsumed the whole of history. Basing
himself on Greek sources, Eusebius describes the Diaspora Revolt in a realistic
manner, emphasizing its wide scope.*

✺

(1) While the teaching of our Savior and the church were flourishing
daily and moving on to further progress the tragedy of the Jews was reaching the climax of successive woes. In the course of the eighteenth year of
the reign of the Emperor[17] a rebellion of the Jews again broke out and
destroyed a great multitude of them. (2) For both in Alexandria and in the
rest of Egypt and especially in Cyrene, as though they had been seized by
some terrible spirit of rebellion, they rushed into sedition against their
Greek fellow citizens, and increasing the scope of the rebellion in the following year started a great war while Lupus was governor of all Egypt. (3)
In the first engagement they happened to overcome the Greeks, who fled
to Alexandria and captured and killed the Jews in the city, but through
thus losing the help of the townsmen, the Jews of Cyrene continued to
plunder the country of Egypt and to ravage the districts in it under their
leader Lucuas. The Emperor sent against them Marcius Turbo with the
land and sea forces including cavalry. (4) He waged war vigorously against
them in many battles for a considerable time and killed many thousands of
Jews, not only those of Cyrene but also those of Egypt who had rallied to
Lucuas, their king. (5) The Emperor suspected that the Jews in Mesopota-

---

15. Lusius Quietus, a Moorish cavalry commander who accompanied Trajan in the
conquest of Parthia. In 116 C.E. he was brought in to Mesopotamia to suppress the Jewish
revolt there which he did with ruthless brutality. He subsequently rose to various positions
in Roman politics, including governor of Judea. He was removed from the governorship
by the Emperor Hadrian and executed in 118, supposedly for conspiracy against the
emperor.

16. Trans. K. Lake, *Eusebius: The Ecclesiastical History* (Loeb Classical Library; Cambridge: Harvard University Press, 1926) vol. 1, pp. 305–7.

17. Trajan, 115 C.E.

mia would also attack the inhabitants and ordered Lusius Quietus to clean them out of the province. He organized a force and murdered a great multitude of the Jews there, and for this reform was appointed governor of Judea by the Emperor. The Greek authors who chronicle the same period have related this narrative in these very words.

11.1.4 Mishnah Sotah 9:14: Persecutions under Quietus[18]

Lusius Quietus governed Judea in 117 C.E. during the reign of Trajan. He was appointed as a result of his success in subduing the Jews in Mesopotamia who opposed Roman rule. He apparently also subdued a Jewish revolt against Rome in Judea at about the same time, and references to this revolt have been preserved in Rabbinic literature.

ॐ

In the War of Quietus[19] they decreed against the garlands of brides[20] and that a person may not teach his son Greek.

11.1.5 *Seder Olam Rabbah* 30: Chronology of Revolts[21]

The Seder Olam Rabbah, a Jewish chronological work, ascribed by the Talmud to a second-century C.E. tanna, related the sequence of revolts of the Jews against Rome.

ॐ

From the war of Vespasian[22] to the war of Quietus[23] is twenty-four (years),[24] from the war of Quietus to the war of Ben Koziba[25] is sixteen years.[26]

---

18. Trans. L. H. Schiffman.
19. Reading with Manuscripts Cambridge and Kaufmann. Other manuscripts read "Titus."
20. As a sign of mourning.
21. Trans. L. H. Schiffman from ed. B. Ratner, *Seder Olam Rabbah* (New York: Talmudical Research Institute, 1966), pp. 143–6.
22. The Great Revolt, 66–73 C.E.
23. Emending from "Titus," following Ratner, p. 146.
24. This interval was actually longer, at least 42 years.
25. The Bar Kokhba Revolt of 132–135 C.E.
26. This number is reasonably correct.

11.2 UNDER BYZANTINE CHRISTIANITY

11.2.1 Jerusalem Talmud Sanhedrin 2:1 (19d–20a): The Patriarchate and the Sages[27]

Under the Byzantine Christians, the Jews were organized around two primary institutions, the house of the patriarch and the academy of the sages. That tensions arose between these two elites is clear from this passage in the Jerusalem Talmud.

🐾

Resh Laqish said: "A *nasi* (patriarch) who has sinned is to be flogged in a court of three (Judges)" . . . Rabbi Judah Nesiah[28] learned of this and became angry. He sent his servants to apprehend Resh Laqish who was troubled and fled to Migdal (Just north of Tiberias); some say to Kefar Ḥittim (east of Tiberias). The next day, Rabbi Yoḥanan came to the academy and Rabbi Judah Nesiah also came to the academy. He (Rabbi Judah) asked: "Why does our master not teach us Torah?" He (Rabbi Yoḥanan) began clapping with one hand. He asked him: "Does one clap with one hand?" He (Rabbi Yoḥanan) replied: "No, but without Resh Laqish, I do not" (i.e. I cannot clap with two, he is like my second hand). He (Rabbi Judah) said: "Tomorrow you and I will go meet him." (In the meantime) Rabbi Yohanan sent to Resh Laqish: "Prepare a word of Torah for the *nasi* is coming out to meet you." (Resh Laqish) came out to greet them and said: "The example you set is comparable to that of your Creator. When God wished to save Israel he sent neither a messenger nor an angel, but He Himself (went), as it is written: 'And I will pass through all the land of Egypt' (Ex. 12:12)—He and all His entourage." He (either Rabbi Yoḥanan or Rabbi Judah) said: "And why did you see it fitting to say this?" He replied to them: "What do you think? Would I desist from teaching the word of God because I am afraid of you?"

---

27. Trans. L. I. Levine in *The Rabbinic Class of Roman Palestine in Late Antiquity* (Jerusalem: Yad Izhak ben-Zvi; New York: Jewish Theological Seminary of America, 1989), pp. 187–8.
28. Grandson of Rabbi Judah the Prince, 230–270 C.E.

11.2.2 Babylonian Talmud Avodah Zarah 10a–11a: Antoninus and Rabbi[29]

The Babylonian Talmud includes a collection of stories about the relationship between Rabbi Judah the Prince and a supposed Roman emperor named Antoninus. Scholars have debated whether to identify this Antoninus with one of the emperors of the Severan dynasty, perhaps Antoninus Pius (ruled 138–161 C.E.), or to understand these texts as relating to some Roman official, but not the emperor. Behind these clearly mythic descriptions lies the notion of a close relationship between the patriarchal house and the Roman government. This passage also deals with other instances of Romans who were said to have befriended the Jews.

🕱

Antoninus once said to Rabbi: "It is my desire that my son Asverus[30] should reign instead of me and that Tiberias should be declared a Colony.[31] Were I to ask one of these things it would be granted while both would not be granted."

Rabbi thereupon brought a man, and having made him ride on the shoulders of another, handed him a dove bidding the one who carried him to order the one on his shoulders to liberate it. The Emperor perceived this to mean that he was advised to ask [of the Senate] to appoint his son Asverus to reign in his stead, and that subsequently he might get Asverus to make Tiberias a free Colony.

[On another occasion] Antoninus mentioned to him that some prominent Romans were annoying him. Rabbi thereupon took him into the garden and, in his presence, picked some radishes, one at a time. Said [the Emperor to himself] his advice to me is: Do away with them one at a time, but do not attack all of them at once. But why did he not speak explicitly? — He thought his words might reach the ears of those prominent Romans who would persecute him. Why then did he not say it in a whisper? — Because it is written: "For a bird of the air shall carry the voice" (Ezek. 10:20).

The Emperor had a daughter named Gilla who committed a sin,[32] so

---

29. Trans. I. Epstein, ed., *The Babylonian Talmud* (London: Soncino Press, 1935–52), 35 vols.

30. I.e., Severus, the dynastic name of the Roman emperors who ruled 193–235.

31. Given special status that extended Roman citizenship to its inhabitants and set up a government under two magistrates.

32. She had illicit sexual relations.

he sent to Rabbi a rocket-herb,[33] and Rabbi in return sent him corian-der.[34] The Emperor then sent some leeks[35] and he sent lettuce in return.[36] Many a time Antoninus sent Rabbi gold-dust in a leather bag filled with wheat at the top, saying [to his servants]: "Carry the wheat to Rabbi!" Rabbi sent word to say. "I need it not, I have quite enough of my own," and Antoninus answered: "Leave it then to those who will come after you that they might give it to those who will come after me, for your descendants and those who will follow them will hand it over to them."

Antoninus had a cave which led from his house to the house of Rabbi. Every time [he visited Rabbi] he brought two slaves, one of whom he slew at the door of Rabbi's house and the other [who had been left behind] was killed at the door of his own house.[37]

Said Antoninus to Rabbi: "When I call, let none be found with you."

One day he found Rabbi Ḥaninah bar Ḥama sitting there, so he said: "Did I not tell you no man should be found with you at the time when I call?"

And Rabbi replied, "This is not an [ordinary] human being."

"Then," said Antoninus, "let him tell that servant who is sleeping out-side the door to rise and come in."

Rabbi Ḥaninah bar Ḥama thereupon went out but found that the man had been slain. Thought he, "How shall I act now? Shall I call and say that the man is dead?—but one should not bring a sad report; shall I leave him and walk away?—that would be slighting the king."

So he prayed for mercy for the man, and he was restored to life. He then sent him in. Said Antoninus: "I am well aware that the least one among you can bring the dead to life, still when I call let no one be found with you."

Every time [he called] he used to attend on Rabbi and wait on him with food or drink. When Rabbi wanted to get on his bed, Antoninus crouched in front of it saying. "Get on to your bed by stepping on me."[38]

Rabbi, however, said, "It is not the proper thing to treat a king so slightingly."

---

33. Indicating that she had committed this offense. Antoninus and Rabbi both made use of devices to conceal the content of their messages from Antoninus' messengers.
34. Hinting that she should be executed.
35. Indicating that his progeny would be cut off.
36. Saying that if so, Antoninus ought to be merciful to his daughter.
37. To maintain the secrecy of their meetings.
38. Showing his subservience to the patriarch.

Whereupon Antoninus said: "Would that I served as a mattress unto thee in the world to come!"

Once he asked him: "Shall I enter the world to come?"

"Yes!" said Rabbi.

"But," said Antoninus, "is it not written, 'There will be no remnant to the house of Esau?'" (Obad. 18).

"That," he replied, "applies only to those whose evil deeds are like those of Esau."

We have learned likewise: "There will be no remnant to the House of Esau," might have been taken to apply to all, therefore Scripture says distinctly—"To the house of Esau," so as to make it apply only to those who act as Esau did.

"But" said Antonius, "is it not also written: 'There [in the nether world] is Edom, her kings, and all her princes'" (Ezek. 32:29).[39]

"There, too," Rabbi explained, "[it says:] 'her kings,' it does not say 'all her kings;' 'all her princes,' but not all her officers!"

This . . . excludes Antoninus the son of Asverus.

Antoninus attended on Rabbi: Artaban[40] attended on Rav.[41] When Antoninus died, Rabbi exclaimed: "The bond is snapped!"[42]

[So also] when Artaban died, Rav exclaimed: "The bond is snapped!"

"And the Lord said to her: Two nations [Goyim] are in thy womb"(Gen. 25:23). Said Rav Judah in the name of Rav: "Read not *goyim* [nations] but *ge'im* [lords]. This refers to Antoninus and Rabbi." [43]

11.2.3 Libanius, *Letter to the Patriarch*: The Politics of Byzantine Rule[44]

Libanius of Antioch, the most famous rhetorician of the fourth century C.E., had many opportunities to meet Jews on economic, social and cultural levels. Here Libanius addresses the patriarch with words indicating deep respect and a sympathetic understanding of the common plight of Jews and "Hellenes" under the yoke of Christian emperors. His letters to the patriarch

39. Hence, I will not go to the world to come but to the netherworld.

40. Artabanus V, the last significant Parthian king, ruled ca. 213–227 C.E.

41. The early third-century Babylonian amora.

42. Referring both to the personal bonds and to the protection that the Jewish people received as a result.

43. Archetypal representatives of the best of Rome and Israel relating like children of the same mother.

44. Trans. M. Stern, *Greek and Latin Authors on Jews and Judaism* (Jerusalem: The Israel Academy of Sciences and Humanities, 1980), vol. 2, p. 590.

are an important source of information on the status of the patriarch in eastern Roman society in the Byzantine period.

§৻

To the Patriarch:[45]

That which was told to me in your letter, I knew in part before, and in part I have learned now. And my pain has been aggravated by the addition of the letter.[46] Who will not be grieved that such a nation has suffered for so long a time? Nobody spoke to me through letters on behalf of those who wronged you.[47] Even if many had done this, they would not have succeeded, for I would not wrong myself in wronging you. Concerning the man who you think was to obtain the rule over your country and who is somehow near to us, a false rumor deceived you, as it did me.[48] I have, however, become undeceived, as you should also, if it has not yet happened.

To the Patriarch:[49]

You would be worried about the affairs of Theophilius,[50] a very wise and just man whose place is among books both when he is awake and sleeping, even if I did not write to you at all. For such people you are who belong to that nation.[51] Since it is your habit to help everybody, but above all to help the best, taking care of all as human beings, but of the best as living a life of virtue.[52] Yet fearing that you may think that I am not a friend of his or that I am lazy about my friends, I have sent you this letter, not in order to convince one that has already been convinced, but to gain myself a reputation in your eyes by helping such a man. I wish him success in business, while my gain will consist in your letter.[53] I would rather have

---

45. The name of the patriarch is nowhere mentioned in the correspondence, but he appears to be a close friend of Libanius whom Libanius thinks of as a man of accomplished Greek education.

46. The patriarch wrote a previous letter to Libanius regarding an injustice done to the Jews.

47. He denies having received letters from the opponents of the Jews seeking his help against them.

48. Regarding an appointment of a new governor for Syria.

49. Trans. S. Stern, *Greek and Latin Authors*, vol. 2, p. 593.

50. A pagan, born in Palestine, who was on friendly terms with Libanius. Theophilius had a court case pending for which he wanted help from the patriarch.

51. He assumes that Jews would have sympathy for a lover of books and learning.

52. Libanius praises the character of the Jews, describing them as giving aid to all people, and especially the good ones, so that he feels that his request to the patriarch for help is superfluous, as the patriarch would have given it in any event.

53. He hopes to get a letter of reply from the patriarch.

a double gain, the letter that I shall receive and the defeat of those who insult him who imitates the son of Lysimachus.[54]

11.2.4 *Codex Theodosianus*: Laws Concerning the Jews[55]

While Judaism was not technically outlawed in the Byzantine Christian Empire, there were nevertheless discriminatory laws against Jews, limiting their rights and imposing special taxes on them. Many of these were brought together in the Codex Theodosianus by the emperor Theodosius II (408–450 C.E.). The law was particularly strict in prohibiting Jews from holding Christian slaves or circumcising Christians. Some Byzantine rulings, however, protected the Jews and asserted their right to practice their religion. A sampling of such regulations from the fourth and fifth century Theodosian Code is given here. Especially significant is Book 16, Title 8, Section 22 which reflects the Byzantine cancellation of the privileges and status of the patriarch, a process soon to lead to eliminating self-government for the Jews of the Byzantine Empire.

⚜

Book 16. Title 8
1 Emperor Constantine Augustus to Evagrius.[56]
It is Our will that Jews and their elders and patriarchs shall be informed that if, after the issuance of this law, any of them should dare to attempt to assail with stones or with any other kind of madness—a thing which We have learned is now being done—any person who has fled their feral sect and has resorted to the worship of God,[57] such assailant shall be immediately delivered to the flames and burned, with all his accomplices.

Moreover, if any person from the people should betake himself to their nefarious sect and should join their assemblies, he shall sustain with them the deserved punishments.

Given on the fifteenth day before the kalends of November at Murgillum in the year of the fourth consulship of Constantine Augustus and Licinius.—October 18 (19), 315; August 13, 339.

---

54. Aristedes, the son of Lysimachus, was famous for his honesty. The use by Libanius of this allusion without any explanation indicates that he considered the Greek education of the patriarch to be quite considerable.

55. Trans. C. Pharr, *The Theodosian Code and Novels and the Sirmondian Constitutions* (New York: Greenwood Press, 1969), pp. 467–72.

56. A praetorian prefect.

57. That is, who has converted to Christianity.

4 The same Augustus to the Priests, Rulers of the Synagogues, Fathers of the Synagogues, and all others who serve in the said place.

We command that priests, rulers of the synagogues, fathers of the synagogues, and all others who serve the synagogues shall be free from every compulsory public service of a corporal nature.

Given on the kalends of December at Constantinople in the year of the consulship of Bassus and Ablavius.—December 1, 331; 330.

5 The same Augustus to Felix, Praetorian Prefect.

(After other matters.) Jews shall not be permitted to disturb any man who has been converted from Judaism to Christianity or to assail him with any outrage. Such contumely shall be punished according to the nature of the act which has been committed. (Etc.)

Given on the eleventh day before the kalends of November at Constantinople. —October 22 (21), (335). Posted on the eighth day before the ides of May at Carthage[58] in the year of the consulship of Nepotianus and Facundus.—May 8, 336.

7 The same Augustus and Julian Caesar to Thalassius, Praetorian Prefect.

In accordance with the venerable law which has been established, We command that if any person should be converted from Christianity to Judaism and should join their sacrilegious gatherings, when the accusation has been proved, his property shall be vindicated to the ownership of the fisc.[59]

Given on the fifth day before the nones of July at Milan in the year of the ninth consulship of Constantius Augustus and the second consulship of Julian Caesar.—July 3, 357; 352; 353.

9 The same Augustuses to Addeus, Count and Master of both branches of the Military Service in the Orient.

It is sufficiently established that the sect of the Jews is forbidden by no law. Hence We are gravely disturbed that their assemblies have been forbidden in certain places. Your Sublime Magnitude will, therefore, after receiving this order, restrain with proper severity the excesses of those persons who, in the name of the Christian religion, presume to commit certain unlawful acts and attempt to despoil the synagogues.

---

58. Note how these decrees were spread throughout the Byzantine Empire.
59. The imperial treasury.

Given on the third day before the kalends of October at Constantinople in the year of the third consulship of Theodosius Augustus and the consulship of Abundatus. —September 29, 393

11 The same Augustuses to Claudianus, Count of the Orient.

If any person should dare in public to make an insulting mention of the Illustrious patriarchs, he shall be subject to a sentence of punishment.

Given on the eighth day before the kalends of May at Constantinople in the year of the fourth consulship of Arcadius Augustus and the third consulship of Honorius Augustus.—April 24, 396.

12 The same Augustuses to Anatolius, Praetorian Prefect of Illyricum.

Your Exalted Authority shall direct that the governors shall be notified, so that they shall know on receipt of this notice that all insults of persons attacking the Jews shall be averted and that their synagogues shall remain in their accustomed quietude.

Given on the fifteenth day before the kalends of July at Constantinople in the year of the consulship of Caesarius and Atticus. —June 17, 397.

14 The same Augustuses to Messala, Praetorian Prefect.

It is characteristic of an unworthy superstition that the rulers of the synagogues or the priests of the Jews or those whom they themselves call apostles, who are dispatched by the patriarch at a certain time to collect gold and silver, should bring back to the patriarch the sum which has been exacted and collected from each of the synagogues. Wherefore, everything that We are confident has been collected, taking into consideration the period of time, shall be faithfully dispatched to Our treasury. For the future, moreover, We decree that nothing shall be sent to the aforesaid patriarch.[60] The people of the Jews shall know, therefore, that We have abolished the practice of such depredation. But if any persons should be sent on such a mission of collection by that despoiler of the Jews, they shall be brought before the judges, in order that a sentence may be pronounced against them as violators of Our laws.

Given on the third day before the ides of April at Milan in the year of the consulship of the Most Noble Theodorus.—April 11, 399.

17 The same Augustuses to Hadrianus, Praetorian Prefect.

We had formerly ordered[61] that what was customarily contributed by

---

60. With this order, the patriarch's right to collect funds in the Diaspora, a holdover from the half-shekel tax collected for the Jerusalem Temple, was canceled.

61. In 14, according to which the money that the patriarch collected from each of the synagogues was to be dispatched to the imperial treasury.

the Jews of these regions[62] to the patriarchs should not be contributed. Now We revoke the first order in accordance with the statutory privileges granted by the early Emperors, and it is Our will that all men shall know that the privilege of sending this contribution is hereby conceded to the Jews by Our Clemency.

Given on the eighth day before the kalends of May at Rome in the year of the sixth consulship of Honorius Augustus and the consulship of Aristaenetus.—July 25, 404.

18 Emperors Honorius and Theodosius Augustuses to Anthemius, Praetorian Prefect.

The governors of the provinces shall prohibit the Jews, in a certain ceremony on their festival of Haman in commemoration of some former punishment, from setting fire to and burning a simulated appearance of the holy cross,[63] in contempt of the Christian faith and with sacrilegious mind, lest they associate the sign of Our faith with their places. They shall maintain their own rites without contempt of the Christian law, and they shall unquestionably lose all privileges that have been permitted them heretofore unless they refrain from unlawful acts.

Given on the fourth day before the kalends of June at Constantinople in the year of the consulship of Bassus and Phillipus. —May 29, 408.

20 The same Augustuses to Johannes, Praetorian Prefect.

If it should appear that any places are frequented by conventicles of the Jews and are called by the name of synagogues, no one shall dare to violate or to occupy and retain such places, since all persons must retain their own property in undisturbed right, without any claim of religion or worship.

Moreover, since indeed ancient custom and practice have preserved for the aforesaid Jewish people the consecrated day of the Sabbath, We also decree that it shall be forbidden that any man of the aforesaid faith should be constrained by any summons on that day, under the pretext of public or private business, since all the remaining time appears sufficient to satisfy the public laws, and since it is most worthy of the moderation of Our time that the privileges granted should not be violated, although sufficient provision appears to have been made with reference to the aforesaid matter by general constitutions of earlier Emperors.

---

62. The western part of the Roman Empire.

63. This refers to the Jewish custom of hanging Haman in effigy as part of the celebration of the festival of Purim, which the Christians misunderstood as an attack on Christianity.

Given on the seventh day before the kalends of August at Ravenna in the year of the ninth consulship of Honorius Augustus and the fifth consulship of Theodosius Augustus.—July 26, 412.

21 The same Augustuses to Philippus, Praetorian Prefect of Illyricum.

No person shall be trampled upon when he is innocent, on the ground that he is a Jew, nor shall any religion cause any person to be exposed to contumely. Their synagogues and habitations shall not be burned indiscriminately, nor shall they be injured wrongfully without any reason, since, moreover, even if any person should be implicated in crimes, nevertheless, the vigor of Our courts and the protection of public law appear to have been established in Our midst for the purpose that no person should have the power to seek his own revenge.

But just as it is Our will that the foregoing provision shall be made for the persons of the Jews, so We decree that the Jews shall also be admonished that they perchance shall not become insolent and, elated by their own security, commit any rash act in disrespect of the Christian religion.

Given on the eighth day before the ides of August at Constantinople in the year of the ninth consulship of Honorius Augustus and the fifth consulship of Theodosius Augustus.—August 6, 412; 418; 420.

22 The same Augustuses to Aurelianus, Praetorian Prefect for the second time.

Since Gamaliel[64] has supposed that he could do wrong with impunity, all the more because he has been elevated to the pinnacle of honors, Your Illustrious Authority shall know that Our Serenity has dispatched instructions to the Illustrious master of offices that Gamaliel shall be deprived of the imperial letters patent conferring on him the rank of honorary prefect, so that he shall remain with that honor which he had before he was appointed to the prefecture. Hereafter[65] he shall cause no synagogues to be founded, and if there are any synagogues in desert places which can be destroyed without sedition, he shall have it done. He shall have no power to judge between Christians; and if a dispute should arise between them and the Jews, it shall be decided by the governor of the province. If he himself or any other of the Jews should attempt to pollute a Christian or a man of any sect, freeborn or slave, with the Jewish stigma,[66] he shall be subjected to the severity of the laws. Moreover, if he retains in his power

---

64. Gamaliel VI, Jewish patriarch from 400 to 425, who had become an honorary praetorian prefect. This decree was the beginning of the end of the officially recognized patriarchate, a process completed by 425 C.E.

65. What follows is probably a list of the offenses of Gamaliel VI.

66. Circumcision.

any slaves of the Christian faith, according to the law of Constantine, they shall be delivered to the Church.

Given on the thirteenth day before the kalends of November at Constantinople in the year of the tenth consulship of Honorius Augustus and the sixth consulship of Theodosius Augustus.—October 20, 415.

25 The same Augustuses to Asclepiodotus, Praetorian Prefect.

It is Our pleasure that in the future no synagogue at all of the Jews shall be indiscriminately taken away from them or consumed by fire, and that if, after the issuance of this law, there are any synagogues which by recent attempt have been thus seized, vindicated to the churches, or at any rate consecrated to the venerable mysteries, the Jews shall be granted as compensation therefor, place in which they can construct synagogues commensurate, of course, with those that were taken away. 1. If any offertories have been removed, they shall be restored to the aforesaid Jews if they have not yet been dedicated to the sacred mysteries, but if venerable consecration does not permit their return, a price equal to the value thereof shall be paid as compensation for them. 2. In the future no synagogues shall be constructed, and the old ones shall remain in their present condition.

Given on the fifteenth day before the kalends of March at Constantinople in the year of the consulship of Asclepiodotus and Marinianus.—February 15, 423.

28 Emperors Theodosius and Valentinian Augustuses to Bassus, Praetorian Prefect.

If a son, daughter, or grandchild, one or more, of a Jew or of a Samaritan, with better counsel should turn to the light of the Christian religion from the darkness of his own superstition, their parents, that is, father, mother, grandfather, or grandmother, shall not be permitted to disinherit them or to pass over them less than they should obtain if they were called to the inheritance on intestacy.[67] But if such a contingency should occur, We order that the will shall be rescinded and that the aforesaid persons shall succeed as though on intestacy. The grants of freedom made in the said testament, however, if within the statutory number, shall retain their validity. If it can be clearly proved that such children or grandchildren have committed a very grave crime against their mother, father, grandfather, or grandmother, the statutory punishment against the offenders shall remain valid even if accusation has been legally made in the meantime. Nevertheless, under such a statement, which shall be supported by prov-

---

67. If they had died without a will.

able and manifest documents, parents shall leave them only the Falcidian fourth of the due inheritance,[68] so that they may appear to have gained this at least in honor of the chosen religion. As We have said, the punishment for any crimes shall remain if they should be proved. (Etc.)

Given on the sixth day before the ides of April at Ravenna in the year of the twelfth consulship of Theodosius Augustus and the second consulship of Valentinian Augustus. —April 8 (7), 426.

Book 16. Title 9

1 Emperor Constantine Augustus to Felix, Praetorian Prefect.[69]

If any Jew should purchase and circumcise a Christian slave or a slave of any other sect whatever, he shall not retain in slavery such a circumcised person. But the person who endured such treatment shall obtain the privilege of freedom. (Etc.)

Given on the twelfth day before the kalends of November at Constantinople. —October 21, (335). Posted on the eighth day before the ides of May at Carthage in the year of the consulship of Nepotianus and Facundus. —May 8, 336.

2 Emperor Constantius Augustus to Evagrius.

If any Jew should suppose that he should purchase the slave of another sect or people, such slave should be immediately vindicated to the fisc.[70] If the Jew should purchase a slave and circumcise him, he shall be penalized not only with the loss of the slave, but he shall also be visited with capital punishment. But if a Jew should not hesitate to purchase slaves who are adherents of the venerable faith (Christianity), he shall immediately be deprived of all such slaves found in his possession, nor shall any delay be interposed in depriving him of the possession of those men who are Christians. (Etc.)

Given on the ides of August in the year of the second consulship of Constantius Augustus and the consulship of Constans Augustus. — August 13, 339.

3 Emperors Honorius and Theodosius and Augustuses to Annas, Didascalus, and the Elders of the Jews.

We direct that the Jewish masters without any fear of chicanery may have Christian slaves, on the sole condition that they permit such slaves to retain their own religion. Therefore, judges of the provinces shall care-

---

68. The fourth of the estate to which the children were entitled by the Falcidian Law, even in opposition to a will.

69. Trans. Pharr, *The Theodosian Code*, p. 471.

70. The imperial treasury.

fully inspect the trustworthiness of the information that is lodged before them and shall know that they must repress the insolence of those persons who suppose that by means of timely supplications they may accuse the Jews. We decree that all rescripts that have been surreptitiously and fraudulently elicited hereafter shall be annulled. If any person should violate these regulations, he shall be punished as though guilty of sacrilege.

Given on the eighth day before the ides of November at Ravenna in the year of the tenth consulship of Honorius Augustus and the sixth consulship of Theodosius Augustus. —November 6, 415.

5 The same Augustuses to Asclepidotus, Praetorian Prefect.

(After many other matters.) No Jew shall dare to purchase Christian slaves.[71] For We consider it abominable that very religious slaves should be defiled by ownership of very impious purchasers. If any person should commit this offense, he shall be subject to the statutory punishment without any delay. (Etc.)

Given on the fifth day before the ides of April at Constantinople in the year of the consulship of Asclepiodotus and Marinianus. —April 9, 423.

Book 3. Title 7

2 Emperors Valentian, Theodosius, and Arcadius Augustuses to Cynegius, Praetorian Prefect.[72]

No Jew shall receive a Christian woman in marriage, nor shall a Christian man contract a marriage with a Jewish woman. For if any person should commit an act of this kind, the crime of this misdeed shall be considered as the equivalent of adultery, and freedom to bring accusation shall be granted to the voices of the public.

Given on the day before the ides of March at Thessalonica in the year of the second consulship of Theodosius Augustus and the consulship of the Most Noble Cynegius.—March 14, 388.

11.2.5 *The Novels of the Sainted Theodosius Augustus*: Treatment of Jews, Samaritans, Heretics and Pagans[73]

Novels (Novellae) were new constitutions, that is, laws issued after the compilation of the Theodosian Code and not included in it. These Novels extend from 438 to 468 C.E. The legislation against non-Christians is justified here by the desire to foster the "true religion" and to defend it against sav-

---

71. It is interesting to note that in the preceding section, Jews were permitted by law to own Christian slaves. This is indicative of the fluctuation in legal attitudes toward Jews.

72. Trans. Pharr, *The Theodosian Code*, p. 70.

73. Trans. Pharr, *The Theodosian Code*, pp. 488–9.

age and corrupting unbelievers. *Note the dehumanizing language with which Jews, Samaritans, and pagans are condemned. Judaism was totally delegitimated in the Novels.*

৻৶

Book 1. Title 3
Emperors Theodosius and Valentinian Augustuses to Florentius, Praetorian Prefect.

Among the other anxieties which Our love for the State has imposed upon Us for Our ever watchful consideration, We perceive that an especial responsibility of Our Imperial Majesty is the pursuit of the true religion. If We shall be able to hold fast to the worship of this true religion, We shall open the way to prosperity in human undertakings. This We have learned by the experience of Our long life, and by the decisions of Our pious mind. We decree that the ceremonies of sanctity shall be established by a law of perpetual duration, even to posterity.

1 For who is so demented, so damned by the enormity of strange savagery, that, when he sees the heavens with incredible swiftness define the measures of time within their spaces under the sway of the divine guidance, when he sees the movements of the stars which control the benefits of life, the earth richly endowed with the harvests, the waters of the sea, and the vastness of this immense achievement confined within the boundaries of the natural world, he does not seek the author of so great a mystery, of so mighty a handiwork? We learn that the Jews, with blinded senses, the Samaritans, the pagans, and the other breeds of heretical monsters dare to do this. If We should attempt by a remedial law to recall them to the sanity of an excellent mind, they themselves will be blameworthy for Our severity, since they leave no place for pardon by the obstinate wickedness of their unyielding arrogance.

2 Wherefore, since according to the ancient maxim, no cure must be employed for hopeless diseases, in order that these deadly sects, oblivious of Our age, may not spread too wantonly into the life of Our people like an indistinguishable confusion, We finally sanction by this law destined to live in all ages, that no Jew, no Samaritan, who does not rely on either law[74] shall enter upon any honors or dignities; to none of them shall the administration of a civil[75] duty be available, nor shall they perform even

---

74. There are two possible explanations for this passage. Either it refers to the law of the eastern or of the western part of the Empire, or it refers to either Jewish or Roman law, for the Samaritans did not follow Jewish law as defined by the Rabbis.

75. Municipal.

the duties of a defender. Indeed We believe that it is wrong that persons hostile to the Supernal Majesty and to the Roman laws should be considered avengers of Our laws under the protection of a surreptitious jurisdiction; that they should be protected by the authority of a dignity thus acquired; that they should have the power to judge or to pronounce whatever sentence they may wish against the Christians and very often against the bishops themselves of the holy religion, as if they were insulting Our faith.

5 If any person of these sects, therefore, has assumed the insignia of office, he shall not possess the dignities which he has acquired, and if he has erected a synagogue, he shall know that he has labored for the profit of the Catholic Church. Furthermore, if any of these persons has stolen into a position of honor, he shall be considered, as previously, of the lowest condition, even though he should have obtained an honorary dignity. If any one of them should begin the building of a synagogue, not with the desire merely to repair it, in addition to the loss of fifty pounds of gold, he shall be deprived of his audacious undertaking. Besides, he shall perceive that his goods are proscribed and that he himself shall immediately be destined to the death penalty, if he should overthrow the faith of another by his perverted doctrine.[76]

11.2.6 Jerome, *Chronicon* for 352: The Gallus Revolt[77]

The Church Father Jerome (342–420 C.E.) described the Gallus Revolt, dating it to 352 C.E. From his description one gains a sense of the wide scope of the uprising and the Roman response to it. The revolt was no doubt provoked by the persecution of the Jews by the Christians.

✥

Gallus[78] crushed the Jews, who had murdered the soldiers in the night, seizing arms for the purpose of rebellion, even many thousands of men, even innocent children and their cities of Diocaesarea,[79] Tiberias, and Diospolis[80] and many villages he consigned to flames.

---

76. Any Jew who converts a Christian to his own religion is subject to capital punishment.

77. Trans. B. H. Geller, *The Fourth-Century Jewish "Revolt" During the Reign of Gallus: Archaeological and Literary Evidence and Background Issues* (unpublished), p. 57.

78. Vice-Emperor of the East under Emperor Constantius II.

79. Sepphoris.

80. Lydda; Lod in Hebrew.

11.2.7 Socrates Scholasticus, *Ecclesiastical History* II, 33: The Gallus Revolt[81]

Socrates Scholasticus, writing in the 440s, was a careful historian who gathered his material from a wide variety of sources. He also testifies to the widespread nature of the revolt.

꿎

While at the same time there came to pass in the East another internal war. For the Jews in Diocaesarea of Palestine raised up arms against the Romans and overran them near those places. But then Gallus, who was also Constantius, whom the Emperor appointed Caesar and sent to the East, dispatched a force [which] prevailed against them. And their city Diocaesarea he ordered to be razed to the ground.

11.2.8 Sozomenus, *Ecclesiastical History* V, 22: Julian the Apostate Tries to Rebuild the Temple[82]

Sozomenus, a native of Palestine writing in the latter half of the fifth century, questions the motives of the Emperor Julian, known as Julian the Apostate (ruled 361–3), in attempting to rebuild the Jewish Temple and rejoices over his failure, which he tendentiously attributes to supernatural events leading many to convert to Christianity.

꿎

Though the emperor hated and oppressed the Christians, he manifested benevolence and humanity towards the Jews. He wrote to the Jewish patriarchs and leaders, requesting them to pray for him, and for the prosperity of the empire. In taking this step he was not actuated, I am convinced, by any respect for their religion; for he was aware that it is, so to speak, the mother of the Christian religion, and he knew that both religions rest upon the authority of the patriarchs and prophets; but he thought to grieve the Christians by favoring the Jews who are their most inveterate enemies. But perhaps he also calculated upon persuading the Jews to embrace paganism and sacrifices; for they were only acquainted with the mere letter of scripture, and could not, like the Christians and a few of the wisest among the Hebrews, discern the hidden meaning.

---

81. Trans. Geller, p. 70.
82. Trans. E. Walford, *The Ecclesiastical History of Sozomen* (London: H. G. Bohn, 1855), pp. 240–2.

Events proved that this was his real motive; for he sent for some of the chiefs of the race and exhorted them to return to the observance of the laws of Moses and the customs of their fathers. On their replying that because the Temple in Jerusalem was overturned, it was neither lawful nor ancestral to do this in another place than the metropolis out of which they had been cast, he gave them public money, commanded them to rebuild the Temple, and to practice the cult similar to that of their ancestors, by sacrificing after the ancient way. The Jews entered upon the undertaking,[83] without reflecting that according to the prediction of the holy prophets, it could not be accomplished. They sought for the most skillful artisans, collected materials, cleared the ground, and entered so earnestly upon the task, that even the women carried heaps of earth, and brought their necklaces and other female ornaments towards defraying the expense.

The emperor, the other pagans, and all the Jews regarded every other undertaking as secondary in importance to this. Although the pagans were not well-disposed towards the Jews, yet they assisted them in this enterprise, because they reckoned upon its ultimate success and hoped by this means to falsify the prophecies of Christ. Besides this motive, the Jews themselves were impelled by the consideration that the time had arrived for rebuilding their Temple.

When they had removed the ruins of the former building, they dug up the ground and cleared away its foundation, it is said that on the following day . . . a great earthquake occurred, and by the violent agitation of the earth, stones were thrown up from the depths, by which those of the Jews who were engaged in the work were wounded. . . .

When God caused the earthquake to cease, the workmen who survived again returned to their task, partly because thus was the edict of the emperor, and partly because they were themselves interested in the undertaking. Men often, in endeavoring to gratify their own passions, seek what is injurious to them, reject what would be truly advantageous, and are deluded by the idea that nothing is really useful except what is agreeable to them. . . . The Jews, I believe, were just in this state; for instead of regarding this unexpected earthquake as a manifest indication that God was opposed to the re-erection of their Temple, they proceeded to recommence the work. But all parties relate that they had scarcely returned to the undertaking when fire burst suddenly from the foundations of the Temple, and consumed several of the workers.

---

83. Apparently in the year 363 C.E.

This fact is fearlessly stated, and believed by all; the only discrepancy in the narrative is that some maintain that the flame burst from the interior of the Temple, as the workmen were striving to force an entrance, while others say that the fire proceeded directly from the earth. In whichever way the phenomenon might have occurred, it was equally wonderful.

If one does not feel disposed to believe my narrative, let him go and be convinced by those who heard the facts I have related from the eye-witnesses of them, for they are still alive. Let him inquire also of the Jews and pagans who left that work in an incomplete state, or who, to speak more accurately, were unable to commence it.

11.2.9 Emperor Julian, *To the Community of the Jews*: The Redress of Oppressive Measures[84]

In the following letter, the authenticity of which is uncertain, Julian the Apostate purports to offer to the Jews numerous privileges and tax abatements. If authentic, this letter would represent Julian's attempt to garner support from the Jewish masses after his plan to rebuild the Temple was coldly received by the Jewish leadership.

In times past, by far the most burdensome thing in the yoke of your slavery has been the fact that you were subjected to unauthorized ordinances and had to contribute an untold amount of money to the accounts of the treasury. Of this I used to see many instances with my own eyes, and I have learned more, by finding the records which are preserved against you. Moreover, when a tax was about to be levied against you again I prevented it, and compelled the impiety of such obloquy to cease here; and I threw into the fire the records against you that were stored in my desks; so that it is no longer possible for anyone to aim at you such a reproach of impiety. My brother Constantius[85] of honored memory was not so much responsible for these wrongs of yours as were the men who used to frequent his table,[86] barbarians in mind, godless in soul. These I seized with my own hands and put them to death by thrusting them into the pit, that not even memory of their destruction might still linger amongst us.

And since I wish that you should prosper yet more, I have admonished

---

84. Trans. W. C. Wright, *The Works of the Emperor Julian*, The Letters of Julian #51 (Loeb Classical Library; Cambridge: Harvard University Press, 1990), vol. 3, pp. 177–81.

85. Constantius II, emperor of the Eastern Roman Empire, ruled from 337–61.

86. His advisors.

my brother Iulus, your most venerable patriarch,[87] that the levy which is said to exist among you should be prohibited,[88] and that no one is any longer to have the power to oppress the masses of your people by such exactions; so that everywhere, during my reign, you may have security of mind, and in the enjoyment of peace may offer more fervid prayers for my reign to the Most High God, the Creator, who has deigned to crown me with his own immaculate right hand. For it is natural that men who are distracted by any anxiety should be hampered in spirit, and should not have so much confidence in raising their hands to pray; but that those who are in all respects free from care should rejoice with their whole hearts and offer their suppliant prayers on behalf of my imperial office to Mighty God, even to him who is able to direct my reign to the noblest ends, according to my purpose. This you ought to do, in order that, when I have successfully concluded the war with Persia, I may rebuild by my own efforts the sacred city of Jerusalem, which for so many years you have longed to see inhabited, and may bring settlers there, and, together with you, may glorify the Most High God therein.

11.2.10 *Codex Justinianus* 1: Anti-Jewish Legislation[89]

Justinian I, emperor of the Eastern Roman Empire, 527–65 C.E., was a zealous persecutor of all non-Christians in the Byzantine Empire. He confirmed and extended the anti-Jewish laws of Theodosius II, determining the legal status of Jews in the Byzantine Empire for the next seven hundred years. These laws intended to prohibit the Jewish marriage ceremony itself and all laws pertaining to marriage, and abrogate the Jewish legislation regarding the legal age of marriage and degrees of permitted kinship. Codex Justinianus restricted not only Jewish religious life, but also the civil rights of Jews as citizens in a Christian society.

🦂

The same three Augusti to Infantius, Comes of the East:

9:7 None of the Jews shall keep his custom in marriage unions, neither shall he contract nuptials according to his law, or enter into several matrimonies at the same time.[90]

---

87. Apparently referring to the Patriarch Hillel II (320–65 C.E.).

88. Referring to the collection of the half-shekel for the support of the patriarchate.

89. Trans. A. Linder, *The Jews in Roman Imperial Legislation* (Detroit: Wayne State University; Jerusalem: Israel Academy of Sciences and Humanities, 1987), pp. 193, 373–4.

90. Prohibiting polygamy, which was still permissible according to Jewish law.

Given on the Third Day Before the calends of January at Constantinople, in the Consulate of Theodosius Augustus for the third time and Abundantius [30 December 393].

5:21 The same Augustus to Johannes, Pretorian Prefect:
Since many judges in course of determining litigation addressed us, needing our oracle in order that it will be revealed to them what must be decided about heretic witnesses, whether their testimonies should be accepted or rejected, we determine that there should be no participation of a heretic, or even of those who practice the Jewish superstition, in testimonies against Orthodox litigants, whether one party to the trial is Orthodox or the other. We grant, however, to the heretics and to the Jews, that whenever they shall deem fit to have litigation among themselves they shall have mixed agreement and even witnesses worthy of the litigants.... On the other hand, we allow their testamentary testimonies and those found in last wills or in contracts without any discrimination, because of the benefit of this necessary usage, lest the means of demonstration be reduced.

Given on the fifth day before the calends of August at Constantinople, after the consulate of the illustrious Lampadius and Orestes [28 July 531].

11.2.11 *Chronicon Paschale*:
The Samaritan Rebellion of 484[91]

The Chronicon Paschale is an anonymous Byzantine Greek chronology from the early 7th century which presents an account of world history up to that time from a Christian viewpoint. It provides a rather one-sided account of the Samaritan revolt against Christian Byzantine rule which took place and was suppressed in 484 C.E.

૬૭

In these times the people of the Samaritan race in Palestine seized a pretext and rebelled, and crowned a Samaritan brigand chief named Justasas. And he came to Caesarea and watched chariot races and murdered many people while he was ruler in Palestine. And the same Justasas also burnt the church of St. Probus, in the time of Timothy bishop of Cae-

---

91. Trans. M. and M. Whitby, *Chronicon Paschale, 284–628 AD* (Liverpool: Liverpool University, 1989), pp. 95–6.

sarea. And immediately Asclepiades, the *dux*[92] of Palestine and dignitary of Caesarea, came with his forces to hunt the brigand, together with the *Arcadianae*;[93] and he set out against the same Justasas and engaged with him, and the same Justasas was beheaded and his head was sent along with his diadem to the emperor Zeno.[94] The emperor Zeno immediately made their synagogue, which was in the place called Gargarides,[95] into a great house of prayer for Our Lady the Mother of God and ever-Virgin Mary, and he also restored the church of St. Procopius;[96] he issued an edict that a Samaritan should not hold an administrative post, and he confiscated the property of their wealthy men. And there was fear and peace.

11.2.12 Procopius of Caesarea, *Buildings* V, vii: The First Samaritan Rebellion[97]

This description of the first Samaritan rebellion by Procopius of Caesarea, a Byzantine historian, was written between 559 and 560 C.E. This account highlights the religious nature of the struggle, supporting the notion that Christian persecution of the Samaritans led to the unleashing of the revolt.

In Palestine there is a city named Neapolis,[98] above which rises a high mountain, called Garizin. This mountain the Samaritans originally held; and they had been wont to go up to the summit of the mountain to pray on all occasions, not because they had ever built any temple there, but because they worshipped the summit itself with the greatest reverence. . . .

During the reign of Zeno, the Samaritans suddenly banded together and fell upon the Christians in Neapolis in the church while they were celebrating the festival called Pentecost,[99] and they destroyed many of them. They struck with their swords the man who at that time was their

---

92. Latin title for the military commander of a frontier province of the Byzantine Empire.

93. A body of troops.

94. Ruled 474–91 C.E.

95. Mt. Gerizim in Samaria, near Shechem, known today as Nablus. This was the location of the Samaritan temple.

96. Apparently destroyed during the revolt.

97. Trans. H. B. Dewing, *Procopius, with an English Translation, The Anecdota or Secret History* (Loeb Classical Library; Cambridge: Harvard University Press, 1971), vol. 7, pp. 349–55.

98. Modern Nablus.

99. A Christian festival celebrated fifty days after Easter Sunday.

Bishop, Terebinthius by name, finding him standing at the holy table as he performed the mysteries. They slashed at him and cut off the fingers of his hand, and they railed at the mysteries, as is natural for Samaritans to do, while we honor them with silence. And this priest straightaway came to Byzantium and appeared before the ruling emperor and displayed what he had suffered, setting forth what had happened and reminding the emperor of the prophecy of Christ,[100] and he begged him to avenge all that had been done.

The Emperor Zeno was greatly disturbed by what had happened, and with no delay inflicted punishment in due measure upon those who had done the terrible thing. He drove out the Samaritans from Mt. Garizin and straightaway handed it over to the Christians, and building a church on the summit, he dedicated it to the Mother of God, putting a barrier, as it was made to appear, around this church, though in reality he erected only a light wall of stone. And he established a garrison of soldiers, placing a large number in the city below, but not more than ten men at the fortifications and the church. The Samaritans resented this, and chafed bitterly in their vexation and deplored their condition, but through fear of the emperor they bore their distress in silence.

But at a later time, when Anastasius was holding the imperial office,[101] the following happened. Some of the Samaritans, incited by a woman's suggestion, unexpectedly climbed the steep face of the mountain, since the path which leads up from the city was carefully guarded, and it was impossible for them to attempt the ascent by that route. Entering the church suddenly, they slew the guards there and with a mighty cry summoned the Samaritans in the city. They, however, through fear of the soldiers, were by no means willing to join the attempt of the conspirators. And not long afterwards the governor of the district (he was Procopius of Edessa, a man of learning) arrested the authors of the outrage and put them to death. Yet even after that no thought was taken for the fortifications, and no provision for proper defense was made at that time by the emperor. But during the present reign, although the emperor Justinian has converted the Samaritans for the most part to a more pious way of life and has made them Christians, he left the old fortification around the church on Garizin in the form in which it was, that is merely a barrier, as I have said. But by surrounding this with another wall on the outside he made the place absolutely impregnable. There too he restored five shrines of the Christians which had been burned down by the Samaritans.

---

100. That the Samaritans would no longer worship on Mt. Gerizim but that the Christians would worship there (John 4:21–4).

101. 491–518 C.E.

11.2.13 Procopius of Caesarea, *Anecdota* XI, 13–31: Religious Compulsion in the Christian Roman Empire[102]

Procopius here accuses the emperor Justinian of forcing religious conversion to Christianity for ulterior motives—the plunder of the property of his non-Christian subjects. In his view, this policy was ultimately injurious to the Christians who lost their churches and their income from agricultural lands as the result of the exile of their tenant farmers. This text also testifies to the persecution of Samaritans by the Byzantine Christians.

﷽

And while he[103] was stirring up the evils of faction and of war for the Romans and fanning the flames, with the one thought in mind that the earth should by many a device be filled with human blood and that he should plunder more money, he contrived another massacre of his subjects on a large scale, in the following manner.

There are in the whole Roman Empire many rejected doctrines of the Christians, which they are accustomed to call "heresies". . . . All these heretics he commanded to change their earlier beliefs, threatening many things in case of their disobedience, and in particular that it would be impossible for them in the future to hand down their property to their children or other relatives. Now the shrines of these heretics, as they are called, . . . contained wealth unheard of. . . . So the Emperor Justinian began by confiscating the properties of these sanctuaries, thus stripping them suddenly of all their wealth. From this it came about that thereafter most of them were cut off from their livelihood.

And many straightaway went everywhere from place to place and tried to compel such persons as they met to change from their ancestral faith. And since such action seemed unholy to the farmer class, they all resolved to make a stand against those who brought this message. So then, while many were being destroyed by the soldiers and many even made away with themselves,[104] thinking in their folly that they were doing a most righteous thing, and while the majority of them, leaving their homelands, went into exile, the Montani,[105] whose home was in Phrygia,[106] shutting themselves up in their own sanctuaries, immediately set

---

102. Trans. Dewing, *Procopius*, vol. 6, pp. 135–9.

103. Emperor Justinian (527–65 C.E.).

104. Committing suicide.

105. Members of a Christian prophetic sect which believed that the New Jerusalem was soon to descend.

106. A region in Asia Minor, now Turkey.

their churches on fire, so that they were destroyed together with the buildings in senseless fashion, and consequently the whole Roman Empire was filled with murder and with exiled men.

And when a similar law was immediately passed touching the Samaritans also, an indiscriminate confusion swept through Palestine.[107] Now all the residents of my own Caesarea and of all the other cities, regarding it as a foolish thing to undergo any suffering in defense of a senseless dogma, adopted the name of Christians in place of that which they then bore and by this pretence succeeded in shaking off the danger arising from the law. And all those of their number who were persons of any prudence and reasonableness showed no reluctance about adhering loyally to this faith, but the majority, feeling resentment that, not by their own free choice, but under compulsion of the law, they had changed from the beliefs of their fathers, instantly inclined to the Manichaeans[108] and to the Polytheists, as they are called.

And all the farmers, having gathered in great numbers, decided to rise in arms against the Emperor, putting forward as their Emperor a certain brigand, Julian by name, son of Savarus. And when they engaged with the soldiers, they held out for a time, but finally they were defeated in the battle and perished along with their leader. And it is said that one hundred thousand men perished in this struggle, and the land, which is the finest in the world, became in consequence destitute of farmers. And for the owners of the land who were Christians this led to very serious consequences. For it was incumbent upon them, as a matter of compulsion, to pay to the Emperor everlastingly, even though they were deriving no income from the land, the huge annual tax, since no money was shown in the administration of this business.

11.2.14 *Chronicon Paschale*: The Samaritan Revolt of 529[109]

Again the ancient sources reflect the dubious effect of the forced conversions of the Samaritans who became Christians after their failed rebellion.

꿎

In this year,[110] when the Samaritans revolted and created for themselves an emperor and Caesar, Irenaeus the son of Pentadia was sent as

---

107. The rest of this account seems to concern the Samaritans.

108. Adherents of a gnostic religion. Manichaeanism was founded by the Babylonian Mani (216–76 C.E.).

109. Whitby and Whitby, *Chronicon Paschale*, p. 111.

110. 530 C.E.

magister militum[111] and put many to death. And certain of them in fear came to Christianity under compulsion, and were received and baptized, and up till the present day they waver between the two: under stringent officials they deceive by appearance and they falsely and wickedly manifest themselves as Christians, but under lax and greedy officials, they conduct themselves as Samaritans and haters of Christians and as if ignorant of Christianity, persuading the officials by means of money to favor Samaritans.

11.2.15 Antiochus Strategos: The Persian Conquest of Jerusalem in 614[112]

This description of the Persian conquest of Jerusalem in 614 C.E. shows that by this time, most of the inhabitants of the city were Christians. The terrible destruction wreaked by the Persians did not secure the city for them, and it soon fell again to Byzantine rule. Palestinian Jewry looked upon the Persian conquest as an opportunity for deliverance from anti-Semitic Byzantine rule. Some even saw it as the sign that messianic redemption was soon to come.

ॶ

The beginning of the struggle of the Persians with the Christians of Jerusalem was on the fifteenth of April, in the second Indiction, in the fourth year of Emperor Heraclius.[113] They spent twenty days in the struggle. And they shot from their ballistas with such violence that on the twenty-first day they broke down the city wall. Thereupon the evil foemen entered the city in great fury, like infuriated wild beasts and irritated serpents. The men however who defended the city wall fled and hid themselves in caverns, fosses, and cisterns in order to save themselves; and the people in crowds fled into churches and altars; and there they destroyed them. For the enemy entered in mighty wrath, gnashing their teeth in violent fury; like evil beasts they roared, bellowed like lions, hissed like ferocious serpents, and slew all whom they found. Like mad dogs they tore with their teeth the flesh of the faithful, and respected none at all, neither male nor female, neither young nor old, neither child nor baby, neither priest nor monk, neither virgin nor widow. . . .

---

111. Chief of the army.

112. Trans. F. Conybeare, "Antiochus Strategos' Account of the Sack of Jerusalem in A.D. 614," *English Historical Review* 25 (1910), pp. 506–13.

113. Ruled 610–41 C.E.

When the Persians had entered the city and slain countless souls and blood ran deep in all places, the enemy in consequence no longer had the strength to slay, and much Christian population remained that was unslain. So when the ferocity of the wrath of the Persians was appeased, then their leader, whom they called Rasmi Ozdan, ordered the public criers to go forth and to make proclamation saying, "Come out, all of you that are in hiding. Fear not. For the sword is put away from you and by me is granted peace." Then, as soon as they heard that, a very numerous crowd came forth that had been hidden in cisterns and fosses. But many of them were already dead within them, some owing to the darkness, others from hunger and thirst. Who can count the number of those who died? For many tens of thousands were destroyed by the number of privations and diversity of hardships, before those in hiding came out owing to the number of their privations; and they abandoned themselves to death when they heard the chief's command, as if he was encouraging them for their own good and they would get alleviation by coming out. But when those in hiding came out, the prince summoned them and began to question the whole people as to what they knew of the art of building. When they had one by one specified their crafts, he bade those be picked out on one side who were skilled in architecture, that they might be carried captive to Persia; but he seized the remainder of the people and shut them up in the reservoir of Mamel,[114] which lies outside the city at a distance of about two stades[115] from the tower of David. And he ordered sentinels to guard those thus confined in the moat. . . .

11.3 BY THE RIVERS OF BABYLON

11.3.1 Josephus, *Antiquities* XVIII, 310–79: A Jewish Babylonian Principality[116]

Josephus, apparently basing himself on a preexistent source, relates the story of two brothers who in the first century C.E. created an independent Jewish principality in Babylonia. This short-lived attempt at Jewish independence, while obviously not typical, provides some sense of the scope and influential character of the Jewish community in Babylonia in the early centuries of our era.

---

114. Present-day Mamilla, opposite Jaffa gate.

115. About one quarter of a mile.

116. Trans. W. Whiston, *The Works of Josephus* (Peabody, MA: Hendrickson, 1987), revised by L. H. Schiffman in consultation with H. St. J. Thackeray, Ralph Marcus, Allen Wikgren, and L. H. Feldman, trans., *Josephus: In Nine Volumes* (Loeb Classical Library; Cambridge, MA: Harvard University, 1976–79).

🙐

(310) A very sad calamity now befell the Jews who were in Mesopotamia, and especially those who dwelled in Babylonia. Inferior it was to none of the calamities which had gone before. It was accompanied by a great slaughter of them, greater than any previously recorded. Concerning all this I shall speak accurately and shall explain the reasons for which these miseries came upon them.

(311) There was a city in Babylonia called Neerda,[117] not only a very populous one, but one that had a good and large territory around it. (314) There were two brothers, Asineus and Anileus, of the city Neerda by birth. They had lost their father, and their mother sent them to learn the art of weaving curtains, for it was not considered a disgrace among them for men to be weavers of cloth. He that taught them that art and was set over them complained that they came too late to their work and punished them with lashes. (315) But they took this just punishment as an affront, and carried off all the weapons which were kept in that house, which were not a few, and went to a certain place where there was a partition of the rivers,[118] a place naturally very fit for feeding cattle and for preserving such fruits as were usually stored for winter. The worst sort of young men also gathered around them, and they armed them with the weapons they had gotten and became their captains. Nothing hindered them from leading them into mischief. (316) For after they became invincible and had built themselves a citadel, they sent for the herdsmen and ordered them to pay them so much tribute from their flocks as might be sufficient for supporting them, proposing also that they would be their friends if they would submit to them and that they would defend them from all their other enemies on every side, but that they would kill the cattle of those who refused to obey them. (317) So they hearkened to their proposals (for they could do nothing else), and sent them as many sheep as were required of them. As a result, their forces grew greater, and they became lords over all they pleased because they marched suddenly and made sudden raids so that everybody who had to do with them chose to pay them respect. They became formidable to anyone who came to assault them until the report about them came to the ears of the king of Parthia himself.

(318) But the governor of Babylonia understood this and had a mind to put a stop to them before they grew greater and before greater mischiefs should arise from them. He assembled as great an army as he could, both

---

117. Nehardea.
118. Or, to a place called "Parting of the Rivers."

of Parthians and Babylonians, and marched against them, thinking to attack them and destroy them before anyone could report to them that he had raised an army. (319) He then encamped at a marsh and lay still. But on the next day (It was the Sabbath which is among the Jews a day of rest from all sorts of work.) he supposed that the enemy would not dare to fight him thereon, but that he would seize them and carry them away as prisoners without fighting. He therefore proceeded gradually, and planned to fall upon them suddenly.

(320) Now Asineus was sitting with the rest, and their weapons lay near them when he said, "Men, I hear a neighing of horses, not of ones who are feeding, but those who have men on their backs, and I also hear a noise of their bridles. So I am afraid that some enemies are coming upon us to surround us. However, let somebody go to look around and make a report of the present state of things, and may what I have said prove a false alarm!" (321) And when he had said this, some of them went out to spy out what was the matter. They came back again immediately and said to him, "Neither have you been mistaken in telling us what our enemies were doing, nor will those enemies permit us to be injurious to people any longer. (322) We are caught by their trap like wild animals, and there is a large body of cavalry marching upon us, while our hands are tied from defending ourselves because we are restrained from doing so by the prohibition of our law which obligates us to rest [on this day]." (323) But Asineus did not by any means agree with the opinion of his spy as to what was to be done, but thought it more agreeable to the law to take courage in this circumstance they had fallen into and break their law by avenging themselves, although they should die in the action, than by doing nothing so as to please their enemies by allowing themselves to be killed by them. Accordingly, he took up his weapons and infused courage into those who were with him to act as courageously as himself. (324) So they fell upon their enemies who came as if to certain victory and killed a great many of them because they despised them, and they put the rest to flight.

(325) But when the news of this fight came to the king of Parthia, he was surprised at the boldness of the brothers and was desirous to see them and speak with them. He therefore sent the most trustworthy of all his guards to say to them: (326) "King Artabanus,[119] although he had been unjustly treated by you who have made an attempt against his government, still has more regard for your courageous behavior than for the anger he bears to you, and has sent me to give you his right hand and security."

---

119. Artabanus III, ruled 12–ca. 38 C.E.

(327) Asineus himself put off his journey there, but sent his brother Anileus with such presents as he could procure. So he went and was admitted to the king's presence. When Artabanus saw Anileus coming alone, he inquired into the reason why Asineus declined to come along with him. (328) When he understood that he was afraid and that he stayed by the marsh,[120] he took an oath by the gods of his country that he would do them no harm if they came to him upon the assurances he gave them, and he gave him his right hand. (329) When Artabanus had done this, he sent away Anileus to persuade his brother to come to him. (330) The king did this because he wanted to curb his own provincial governors by the courage of these Jewish brothers, lest they should make an alliance with them. For some were already in revolt, and some were disposed to rebel, and he was ready to march against them.

(332) Since the king had these intentions, he sent away Anileus; and Anileus prevailed upon his brother [to come to the king], by relating to him the king's good will and the oath that he had taken. Accordingly they made haste to go to Artabanus (333) who received them when they had arrived with pleasure, and admired Asineus's courage in the actions he had taken.

(336) Then at dawn the king called for Asineus and said to him, "It is time for you, O young man, to return home and not provoke the indignation of my generals in this place any further lest they attempt to murder you without my approval. (337) I commit to you the country of Babylonia in trust that it may, by your care, be kept free of robbers and from other mischief. I have kept my faith inviolable to you, not in trifling affairs but in those that concerned your safety, and I therefore deserve that you should be kind to me." (338) When he had said this and given Asineus some presents, he sent him away immediately. When he arrived home, he built fortresses and became great in a short time, and managed things with such courage and success, as no other person, who had no higher a beginning, ever did before him.

(340) But although their affairs were in so flourishing a state, there sprang up among them a problem for the following reason: When once they had deviated from that course of virtue whereby they had gained so much power, they affronted and transgressed the laws of their forefathers and fell under the dominion of their lusts and pleasures. A certain Parthian, who came as general of an army into those regions, (341) had a wife accompanying him, who had a vast reputation for other accomplishments and particularly was admired above all other women for her

---

120. Where he and his men lived.

beauty. (342) Anileus, the brother of Asineus, either heard of her beauty from others or perhaps also saw her himself, and so became at once her lover and her enemy, partly because he could not hope to enjoy this woman except by obtaining power over her as a captive, and partly because he thought he could not conquer his inclinations for her. (343) As soon, therefore, as her husband had been declared an enemy to them and had fallen in battle, the widow of the deceased was married to her lover.

However, this woman did not come into their house without producing great misfortunes, both to Anileus himself and also to Asineus. Rather, she brought great misfortune upon them for the following reason: (344) When she was led away captive on the death of her husband, she concealed the images of her ancestral gods, belonging to her husband and herself. It is the custom of that country for all to have the idols they worship in their own houses and to carry them along with them when they go to a foreign land. In accord with this custom of theirs, she carried her idols with her. At first she performed her worship of them privately, but when she had become Anileus's wife, she worshipped them in her accustomed manner and with the same appointed ceremonies which she had practiced in her former husband's days. (345) Their most esteemed friends blamed him at first that he did not act in the manner of the Hebrews nor perform what was consonant with their laws in marrying a foreign wife, one that transgressed the strict rules of their sacrifices and religious ceremonies. He ought to consider lest, by indulging himself in many pleasures of the body, he might lose his principality on account of the beauty of a wife and that high authority which, by God's blessing, he had attained. (346) The appeal was fruitless, and he even put to death one of them for whom he had had the greatest respect because of the liberty he took with him.

(348) But when they also heard of the worship of those gods whom the Parthians adore, they thought that the injury that Anileus offered to their laws was to be borne no longer. A great number of them came to Asineus and loudly complained about Anileus, (349) and told him that it would have been well had he himself seen what was advantageous to them. However, it was now high time to correct what had been done before the crime that had been committed proved the ruin of himself and all the rest of them. They added that the marriage to this woman was done without their consent and without regard to their ancient laws, and that the worship which this woman performed [to her gods] was a reproach to the God whom they worshipped. (350) Asineus was aware of his brother's offense, and that it had already been the cause of great misfortune and would be so for the future. Yet he tolerated it because of the good will he

had to so near a relative and excused it on account of his brother's being quite overcome by his wicked inclinations. (351) But as more and more men came to him every day, and the clamors about it became greater, he at length spoke to Anileus about these complaints, reproving him for his former actions and urging him for the future to put an end to them and send the woman back to her relations. (352) But nothing was gained by these reproofs. As the woman perceived what a tumult occurred among the people on her account, and she was afraid for Anileus lest he should come to any harm because of his love for her, she infused poison into Asineus's food and thereby did away with him and was now sure of prevailing, since her lover was to be the judge of what should be done about her.

(353) So Anileus took the government upon himself alone and led his army against the villages of Mithridates, who was a man of principal authority in Parthia and had married King Artabanus's daughter. He also plundered them, and among that prey was found a great deal of money, many slaves, a great number of sheep, and many other things which add to the prosperity of those who possess them. (354) When Mithridates, who was there at this time, heard that his villages were taken, he was very much displeased to find that Anileus had first begun to do him wrong, and to disregard his high rank when he had not at all done him wrong beforehand. So he amassed the greatest body of horsemen he could, selected those out of that number who were of an age fit for war, and came to fight Anileus. When he had arrived at a certain village of his own, he rested there, intending to fight him on the following day because it was the Sabbath, the day on which the Jews rest. (355) And when Anileus was informed of this by a Syrian stranger from another village, who not only gave him an exact account of the circumstances of the other army but also told him where Mithridates would have a feast, he took his supper at a proper time and marched by night, with the intent of falling upon the Parthians while they were unaware of what he was doing. (356) So he fell upon them about the fourth watch of the night.[121] Some of them he killed while they were asleep, and others he put to flight. He took Mithridates alive and set him naked upon an ass which among the Parthians is considered the greatest reproach possible.

(357) And when he had brought him into a forest in this insulting way, his friends asked him to kill Mithridates. He soon told them his own opinion to the contrary and said that it was not right to kill a man who was of one of the principal families among the Parthians and greatly hon-

---

121. 3:00 A.M.

ored by marrying into the royal family. (360) So Mithridates was let go. But, after he had gotten away, his wife reproached him that although he was a son-in-law to the king, he neglected to avenge himself on those who had injured him, not caring about it, (361) but was content to have been made a captive by the Jews and to have escaped them. She bade him either to go back like a man of courage, or else she swore by the gods of their royal family that she would certainly dissolve her marriage with him. (362) Partly because he could not bear her daily taunting, and partly because he was afraid of her insolence lest she should in earnest dissolve their marriage, he unwillingly, and against his inclinations, again assembled as great an army as he could and marched along with them.

(363) But as soon as Anileus understood that Mithridates was marching with a great army against him, he thought it inglorious to tarry about the marshes and not to take the first opportunity of meeting his enemies, and he hoped to have the same success and to beat their enemies as they did before. Accordingly he led out his army. (364) A great many more joined that army in order to plunder other people's property and in order to terrify the enemy again by their numbers. (365) But when they had marched ninety furlongs,[122] since there was no water along the road and it was now mid-day, they became very thirsty. Then Mithridates appeared and fell upon them since they were in distress for lack of water because of which, and on account of the time of the day, they were not able to wear their armor. (366) So Anileus and his men were put to a disgraceful rout since men who were exhausted were fighting those who were fresh and in good condition. Then a great slaughter took place, and many tens of thousands of men fell.

Anileus and all who stood firm about him ran away as fast as they were able into a forest and afforded Mithridates the pleasure of having gained a great victory over them. (367) But there now came to Anileus a horde of evil men who valued their own lives very little if they might but gain some present benefit, and they, by thus coming to him, made up for the multitude of those who had perished in the fight. Yet these men were not like those who fell, because they were rash and untrained in war. (368) However, with these he came upon the villages of the Babylonians, and great devastation of all things took place there by the violence that Anileus perpetrated. (370) The Babylonians, upon taking a view of his situation, and having learned where Anileus and his men lay, fell secretly upon them as they were drunk and asleep, and fearlessly killed all whom they caught, including Anileus himself.

---

122. 11¼ miles.

(371) The Babylonians were now freed from Anileus's heavy incursions which had been a great restraint upon the hatred they bore to the Jews. For they were almost always in conflict with them because of the conflict of their laws, and whichever party grew bolder than the other assaulted the other. At this time in particular, upon the ruin of Anileus's party, the Babylonians attacked the Jews. (372) The Jews vehemently resented the injuries they received from the Babylonians, but, being neither able to fight them nor considering it tolerable to live with them, went to Seleucia,[123] the principal city of the region, which was founded by Seleucus Nicator.[124] It was inhabited by many Macedonians but by more Greeks, and not a few Syrians also held civic rights[125] there. (373) The Jews fled and lived there for five years without any problems. . . .[126]

(376) When [the Greeks and the Syrians] had agreed [to a reconciliation], they both knew that the uniting factor of their union would be their common hatred of the Jews. Accordingly they fell upon them and killed about fifty thousand of them. Indeed, the Jews were all destroyed except for a few who escaped by the compassion which their friends or neighbors afforded them in order to let them flee.

(377) Those who escaped retired to Ctesiphon, a Greek city situated near Seleucia. (379) Most of the Jews gathered together and went to Neerda and Nisibis and gained safety there because of the strength of those cities. Besides which, their inhabitants, who were a great many, were all warlike men.

11.3.2 Jerusalem Talmud Yevamot 12:1 (12c): The Tannaitic Movement in Babylonia[127]

Already in the tannaitic period, Rabbinic sages were to be found in Babylonia. Most prominent among them was Rabbi Judah ben Bathyra I (mid-first century C.E.) settled in Nisibis before the destruction of the Temple.

ﭪ

Rabbi Yose said, "Once I visited Nisibis,[128] and I saw an old man there, and I said to him, 'Have you ever been expert in the teachings of Rabbi

---

123. On the Tigris River.

124. The founder of the Seleucid dynasty who ruled 312–280 B.C.E.

125. Rights of citizenship.

126. 35/36–40/41 C.E.

127. Trans. J. Neusner, *A History of the Jews in Babylonia*, vol. 1 (Leiden: E. J. Brill, 1969), p. 48.

128. A trade center in northern Mesopotamia.

Judah Ben Bathyra?' and he said to me, 'Rabbi, I was a money-changer in my city, and he used to change money at my table.'"

11.3.3 Babylonian Talmud Sanhedrin 32b: The Great Tannaitic Sages[129]

Later traditions recognized the importance of Rabbi Judah ben Bathyra I's teachings in Babylonia as can be seen from his presence in this list with the great figures of tannaitic tradition and their centers of learning.

𝕾

"Righteousness, righteousness, pursue!" (Deut. 16:20). Go after the sages to the academy, after Rabbi Eliezer to Lud, after Rabbi Yoḥanan ben Zakkai to Beror Ḥail, after Rabbi Joshua to Peki'in, after Rabban Gamliel to Yavneh, after Rabbi Akiva to Bene Brak, after Rabbi Mattiah to Rome, after Rabbi Ḥananiel ben Teradion to Sikhnin, after Rabbi Yose to Sepphoris, after Rabbi Judah ben Bathyra to Nisibis, after Rabbi Ḥananiah nephew of Rabbi Joshua to the golah,[130] after Rabbi [Judah the Prince] to Bet She'arim, after the sages to the Hewn-Stone chamber.[131]

11.3.4 Mishnah Yevamot 16:7: The Tannaitic Tradition in Babylonia[132]

Rabbi Akiva met a tanna in Babylonia, Nehemiah of Bet Deli, who had been a student of Rabban Gamliel I in the Land of Israel. He still was able to transmit traditions from his teacher that were not known in the Land of Israel.

𝕾

Rabbi Akiva said, "When I went down to Nehardea[133] to intercalate the year, Nehemiah of Bet Deli met me, and he said to me, 'I have heard that in the Land of Israel, the sages, excepting Rabbi Judah ben Bava, do not allow a woman to marry again on the evidence of one witness [that her first husband is dead].' I answered, 'It is so.' 'Tell them in my name,' he said, 'I received a tradition from Rabban Gamliel the Elder[134] that they may allow a woman to remarry on the evidence of one witness.' And when I came and recounted the matter before Rabban Gamliel II, he

---

129. Trans. Neusner, *A History of the Jews in Babylonia* I, p. 49.
130. The "Exile," that is, Babylonia.
131. The meeting place of the Sanhedrin in the last years of the Second Temple period.
132. Trans. Neusner, *A History of the Jews in Babylonia* I, p. 52.
133. A major center of Jewish population in Babylonia.
134. Rabban Gamliel I.

rejoiced at my words, and said, 'We have now found a fellow for Rabbi Judah ben Bava.'"

11.3.5 *Genesis Rabbah* 46:11: The Circumcision of the Sons of Ptolemy[135]

The events described in Josephus regarding the conversion of the royal house of Adiabene (text 5.1.1) are reflected as well in a short account in Genesis Rabbah which reflects how the events were seen by the Jews of Byzantine Palestine. Here the willingness of the two princes to undergo circumcision is emphasized.

᛫ᛇ᛫

"You shall circumcise the flesh of your foreskin" (Gen. 17:11); like a sore it [the foreskin] is attached to the body. And it happened that Monobazus and Izates, the sons of Ptolemy the King,[136] were sitting and reading the book of Genesis when they came to this verse, "You shall circumcise." One turned his face to the wall and began to cry. One went and circumcised himself. After a few days, they were sitting and reading the Book of Genesis, and when they reached the verse, "You shall circumcize," one said to his companion, "Woe to you, my brother." He said, "Woe to you, my brother, and not to me." They revealed the matter one to another. When their mother became aware, she went and said to their father, "A sore has developed on their flesh, and the physician has prescribed that they be circumcised." He [their father] said that they should be circumcised. How did the Holy One, blessed be He, repay him? Said Rabbi Pinḥas: When he went forth to war, an ambush was set for him, but an angel descended and saved him.

11.3.6 *Iggeret Rav Sherira Gaon* 9–10: The Amoraim[137]

Rav Sherira Gaon's systematic chronological list of the Babylonian sages classifies each authority in relation to his teachers, disciples, or colleagues and so traces the chain of transmission of Rabbinic tradition. For this part of his work, he drew on talmudic sources as well as archival material available in the Babylonian academies.

---

135. Trans. L. H. Schiffman, "The Conversion of the Royal House of Adiabene in Josephus and Rabbinic Sources," in *Josephus, Judaism, and Christianity*, ed. L. H. Feldman and G. Hata (Detroit: Wayne State University Press, 1987), p. 301.

136. The aggadah made use here of the dynastic name of the rulers of Hellenistic Egypt.

137. Trans. N. D. Rabinowich, *The Iggeres of Rav Sherira Gaon* (Jerusalem: Moznaim, 1988), pp. 93–4, 101–5.

ς͡ζ

When Rav Shila passed away, Rav and Samuel were [already] here [in Babylonia]. Rav gave precedence to Samuel and did not want to be his superior and have him sit before him. Nor did Samuel want to be Rav's superior and have Rav sit before him, for Rav was much older than Samuel, as we say in the Gemara *Merubah*:[138]

"Rav, Samuel and Rav Assi once met at the celebration of a circumcision, or as some say, of the redemption of a firstborn son. Rav would not enter before Samuel nor Samuel before Rav Assi, nor Rav Assi before Rav. They said: 'Who should encourage [the other to go first]'? [It was decided that] Samuel should encourage [Rav to go first]. But why should not Rav have encouraged [Samuel]? [Because] it was Rav who had granted Samuel precedence."

Therefore, Rav left Samuel in Nehardea which was his [Samuel's] place and a place of Torah, and distanced himself to a place which had no Torah. That was Sura, which is Mata Meḥasya.[139] There were many Jews there and yet there were some who did not even know the prohibition against [combining] milk and meat. He said: "I will settle here so that there will be Torah in this place." This is in accordance with the episode explained in [Chapter] *Kol ha-Basar*:[140]

"Rav found an open space and put a fence around it,[141] and when he came to Tatlafush[142] he taught them and declared the udder forbidden to them."[143]

And [Rav] was called the "*Resh Sidra*," as Rabbi Yoḥanan said to Isi bar Hini:

"Who is the *Resh Sidra* in Babylonia?"

He replied, "Abba Arikha."[144]. . . .

Rav Judah lived after [Rav Huna] for two years, and all the Rabbis came before him at Pumbeditha. After Rav Judah, who died in the year 610 [of the Seleucid Era; 299 C.E.], Rav Ḥisda ruled in Sura for ten years and died in the year 620 [of the Seleucid Era; 309 C.E.].

---

138. Babylonian Talmud Bava Qamma 80a.

139. On the outskirts of Sura.

140. Babylonian Talmud Ḥullin 110a.

141. He came to a place where the people were negligent in their religious observance and he therefore placed upon them additional restrictions.

142. A place near Sura.

143. Rav taught them the basic laws of milk and meat and then instituted a new halakhic ordinance.

144. Full name of Rav.

Rabbah and Rav Joseph, who had been in Pumbeditha with Rav Judah, each said to the other: "You rule," and they would not take authority for themselves by becoming the head [of the academy]. This is explained at the end of [Tractate] *Horayot*[145] and at the end of [Tractate] *Berakhot*:[146]

"The time came[147] when Rabbah or Rav Joseph was required [to be head of the academy]. They sent [an answer] from [the Land of Israel]:[148] 'Rav Joseph has preference because he is Sinai,[149] and all require the owner of wheat.'[150] Nevertheless, Rav Joseph would not accept [the post] because the astrologers had told his mother that Rav Joseph would rule for [only] two and one-half years. Rabbah [thereupon] ruled for twenty-two years and Rav Joseph after him for two years and a half."

But since each one deferred to the other, their matter remained [in abeyance]. For several years, Rabbah would go to Rav Ḥisda, to Sura. At the end of the days of Rav Ḥisda, when Rabbah saw that the time had come when he was very much needed, he accepted the head position. He ruled for twenty-two years, and died in the year 631 [of the Seleucid Era; 320 C.E.].

And we have heard from the Rabbis of our academy [Pumbeditha] that in those years after Rav Judah, when Rabbah did not accept the head position, Rav Huna bar Ḥiyya ruled in Pumbeditha and had there a great *bet midrash*.[151]

When he [Rav Huna bar Ḥiyya] died, and the times required Rabbah to become the head, he accepted the leadership so that Torah would not cease in Pumbeditha, for most of the Rabbis of Israel were there.

And Rabbah, who is Rabbah bar Naḥmani, ruled in Pumbeditha and disseminated much Torah. He died in a religious persecution,[152] for he was denounced [to the king] for causing twelve thousand men to be idle during a month in summer and a month in winter, the two months of the

---

145. Babylonian Talmud Horayot 14a.

146. Babylonian Talmud Berakhot 64a.

147. After Rav Judah passed away and there was a leadership void.

148. The Babylonian community had sent a question to Palestine: who should become the leader, Rabbah, whose greatest strength was astute reasoning, or Rav Joseph whose greatest strength was his unfailing memory?

149. Rav Joseph was called "Sinai" because of his encyclopedic knowledge of the talmudic material.

150. That is, one who knows the authentic traditions.

151. House of study.

152. This was the period of the Sassanian monarchs who, though shielding the Jews against the Roman/Christian threat, considered them a fertile field for taxation to supply the ever increasing expenses of war.

Kallah, Adar and Elul.[153] He fled from the police to a marsh were he died. And a message from heaven came down in Pumbeditha: "Rabbah bar Naḥmani has been summoned to the heavenly academy. . . ."

In these years that Rabbah bar Naḥmani was in Pumbeditha, Rabbah bar Ḥiyya was disseminating Torah in Sura.

After Rabbah bar Naḥmani, Rav Joseph ruled in Pumbeditha for two and one-half years and died in the year 634 [of the Seleucid Era; 323 C.E.].

After him, Abbaye ruled for fourteen years and died in the year 648 [of the Seleucid Era; 337 C.E.]. Thus [the Talmud] explains in Chapter *ha-Nizaqin*:[154]

"That shofar[155] was first in the house of Rav Judah, then in the house of Rabbah, then in the house of Rav Joseph and then in the house of Abbaye."

This means that these [sages] were the heads of the academy. The shofar was the moneybox for the Rabbis of the academy. Whatever [money] came for them from the Jewish people was put into it.

After Abbaye, Rava, who was a member of [the academy of] Pumbeditha, ruled in Meḥoza, as is explained in [Chapter] *ha-Ro'eh*:[156]

"Bar Hadaya was a dream interpreter . . . [and said to Rava]: 'Abbaye will die and his academy will come before you.'"

And the Rabbis of the whole world gathered before him.[157]

Although after Ḥisda died there was no gaon[158] in Sura, nevertheless the rule of Rava was much greater and he had great authority and influence. Rav Joseph's blessing of him was fulfilled . . . [when] "Rav Joseph said to him, 'May it be the will [of God] that your head shall rise above the whole city. . . .'"[159] And the years of the rule of Rava were fourteen, and he died in the year 663 [of the Seleucid Era; 352 C.E.].

In all these years there was only one academy, [the one] in Pumbeditha. After Rava they split again into two academies: Rav Naḥman bar Isaac

---

153. This was a time for former students and others to gather at the academy for study during the months in which agricultural activities were slowest.

154. Babylonian Talmud Gittin 60b.

155. A box which was called "shofar" because it resembled the ram's horn, being narrow at the top and wide at the bottom.

156. Babylonian Talmud Berakhot 56a.

157. Rava became the senior sage of all Israel. For the previous thirty years (since 308 C.E.) there had been no head of the academy in Palestine due to the political turbulence brought on by the abdication of the emperor Diocletian in 305 C.E. and then the acceptance of Christianity as the state religion in 325 C.E.

158. Eminent scholar who served as the head of the academy.

159. Babylonian Talmud Yoma 53a.

[ruled] in Pumbeditha for four years, and died in the year 667 [of the Seleucid Era; 356 C.E.]. Rav Papa was in Naresh, near Sura. He ruled nineteen years and died in the year 682 [of the Seleucid Era; 371 C.E.].

After Rav Naḥman bar Isaac a number of geonim ruled in Pumbeditha. Rav Hama [was in] Pumbeditha and died in 688 [of the Seleucid Era 377 C.E.].

11.3.7 *Seder Olam Zuta*, 9–10: History of the Exilarchs[160]

Seder Olam Zuta is an anonymous Hebrew chronicle written in the early Middle Ages, certainly before 804 C.E. It seeks to demonstrate the continuity, legitimacy, and the Davidic descent of the exilarchate. This section traces the exilarchs who served during the talmudic period. This listing cannot be success-fully harmonized with other sources on the chronology of the exilarchate and represents a later memory from a period when the sequence of exilarchs was only partially known.

ॐ

In the year one hundred sixty six after the destruction of the Temple, the Persians attacked the Romans. Shekhaniah died and Hezekiah his son arose after him, and the sages guided him.[161] Hezekiah died. [Aqov] his son arose after him, and the sages guided him. When he died, Nathan was still in his mother's womb. He is Nathan of Zuẓita.[162] Nathan died, and Rav Huna his son arose after him, and the sages guided him. [Rav Huna] died, and Nahum his son arose. The sages guided him. Rav Huna, Rav Ḥanina, and Rav Matana, and Rav Ḥananel were his sages. Nahum died and Yoḥanan arose. The sages directed him. Rav Ḥananel was his sage. Yoḥanan died and Shefet his son arose. The sages guided him, and Rav Ḥananel was his sage.

Shefet died and Anan his son arose after him. The sages guided him, and Rav and Samuel were his sage[s]. And Pa[p]a[163] bar Neẓar came up and destroyed Nehardea. Rav Huna died and was buried in the Land of Israel near Rabbi Ḥiyya the Great. Nathan his son arose, and the sages guided him. Rav Judah bar Ezekiel and Rav Sheshet were his sages.

The Persians inherited the kingdom in the year 245 after the destruc-tion of the Temple [313 C.E.], and the Persians decreed a persecution

---

160. Trans. L. H. Schiffman.

161. These "sages" were probably those who provided guidance in halakhah to the exilarchs.

162. Literally, "Nathan of the ray of light," meaning that he was a repentant sinner.

163. Emending from Pasa, following *Iggeret Rav Sherira Gaon*.

against the Jews. Nathan died, and his son Nehemiah arose, and the sages guided him. Rav Shizbi was his sage. Nehemiah died, and Aqaviah his son arose, and the sages guided him. Rava and Rav Ada were his sages. In his time, Shapur went up against Armenia and conquered it. Mar Uqban of Zuzita died and was buried in the land of Israel. Huna, his nephew, arose after him, and the sages guided him. Abaye, Rabbah and Rav Joseph bar Hama were his sages. In his time, Shapur went up against Nisibis and took it. Huna Mar died, and after him arose Uqba his brother, and the sages guided him. Rav Hananel was his sage. Uqba died and after him arose Abba, his nephew, the son of Mar Uqban. Rava and Ravina were his sages. In the year 416 after the destruction of the Temple [484 C.E.] the world stood without a king. Abba died and Rav Kahana his brother arose. Rav Safra was his sage. Mar Kahana died and Mar Zutra his son arose after him. Rav Aha of Difti was his sage. Mar Zutra died; Kahana his son arose after him. Ravina was his sage. Rav Kahana died and after him arose Rav Huna Mar his brother. Rav Aha of Difti son of Hanilai was his sage. He died and Rav Huna his uncle, the son of Rav Kahana arose after him. Rav Mari and Mar Hanina Rabba were his sages. [164]

11.3.8 Babylonian Talmud Horayot 11b:
The Status of the Exilarch vs. the Patriarch[165]

This passage reflects the rivalry between the Babylonian exilarch and the patriarch in the Land of Israel, each of whom was considered like an independent Jewish ruler.

ૐ

Rabbi inquired of Rav Hiyya, "Is one like myself to bring a hegoat [as a sin-offering of a ruler, according to Lev. 4:23]?"[166]

"You have your rival in Babylonia," he replied.[167]

"The kings of Israel and the kings of the house of David," he objected, "bring sacrifices independently of one another."[168]

---

164. After reaching this point, approximately the end of the fifth century, the chronicle describes the persecution of the exilarchs and the interruption of the institution.

165. Trans. Neusner, *A History of the Jews in Babylonia* I, p. 110.

166. This offering was to be brought by the "ruler" in case of accidental transgression of a biblical ordinance. Since the Temple no longer stood at the time of this debate, this theoretical discussion was intended to clarify the relative status of the two officials.

167. Implying that he does not bring this offering.

168. Even though each ruled part of the Jewish people they were considered under the status of "ruler."

"There,"[169] Ḥiyya replied, "they were not subordinate to one another. Here[170] we are subordinate to them [in Babylonia]."

Rav Safra taught thus, "Rabbi inquired of Rav Ḥiyya, 'Is one like me to bring a hegoat?' There is the scepter, here is only the law giver, as it was taught, 'The scepter shall not depart from Judah' refers to the exilarch in Babylonia who rules Israel with the scepter, 'nor the ruler's staff between his feet' (Gen. 49:10) refers to the grandchildren of Hillel[171] who teach the Torah to Israel in public."[172]

11.3.9 Babylonian Talmud Ḥullin 92a: The Two Princes[173]

This text takes the view that the patriarch and exilarch are of equal status.

෫ෂ

"For you have striven with God and with men and have prevailed" (Gen. 32:39). Rabbah said, "He hinted to him[174] that two princes were destined to go forth from him, the exilarch in Babylonia and the patriarch in Palestine."

11.3.10 Babylonian Talmud, Bava Qamma 58b: Judgment of the Exilarch[175]

The following text shows that the exilarchs were not necessarily experts in Rabbinic law. Rav Naḥman, who served the exilarchate as a judicial officer, effectively reversed the decision.

෫ෂ

A certain person cut down a date tree belonging to a neighbor. When he appeared before the exilarch, the latter said to him, "I myself saw the place. Three date-trees stood close together, and they were worth one hundred zuz. Go therefore and pay the other thirty-three and a third."

The defendant said, "What have I to do with an exilarch who judges

---

169. In the case of the kings of Northern Israel and Judah.

170. In the case of the patriarchate and the exilarchate.

171. The patriarchal house which traced its lineage through Hillel to King David.

172. So both the exilarch and the patriarch are considered to be "rulers" of equal status and both bring the hegoat offering.

173. Trans. J. Neusner, *A History of the Jews in Babylonia* (Leiden: E.J. Brill, 1989), vol. 4, p. 103.

174. The angel hinted to Jacob.

175. Trans. I. Epstein, ed. *The Babylonian Talmud* (London: Soncino Press, 1935–52), 35 vols.

in accordance with Persian law?"[176] He therefore came to Rav Naḥman who said that the valuation should be made in conjunction with sixty [times as much].[177]

11.3.11 Babylonian Talmud Shabbat 48a: Lax Observance in the Home of the Exilarch[178]

The Rabbis criticized the house of the exilarch for lax observance of the law.

꙰

Rabbah and Rav Zera visited the exilarch [on the Sabbath], and saw a slave place a pitcher of water on the mouth of a kettle. [The pitcher contained cold water, and the kettle was hot.][179] Rabbah thereupon rebuked him [the slave].

Said Rav Zera to him, "Wherein does it differ from a boiler upon a boiler [which is permitted]?"

"He preserves the heat there," he replied, "while here he creates it."

Then he saw him spread a turban over the mouth of a cask and place a cup upon it. Thereupon Rabbah rebuked him. Said Rav Zera to him, "Why?"

"You will soon see," he replied. Subsequently he saw him [the slave] wringing it out [which is prohibited on the Sabbath].

11.3.12 Babylonian Talmud Bava Batra 55a: The Law of the Land[180]

Exceedingly important for the orderly functioning of the exilarchate was the recognition of the validity of the law of the Sassanian Persian rulers of Babylonia. Samuel's principle of recognition of the legal system of the dominant ruler was the basis of Jewish life under foreign domination from medieval until modern times.

---

176. The law of the Sassanian Persian rulers of Babylonia.

177. As if the damage had taken place in a field 60 times as large. Therefore, the total damage was actually much less than if the judgment were made on a piece of land that had only three trees.

178. Trans. Neusner, *A History of the Jews in Babylonia* IV, pp. 106–7.

179. Heating water is forbidden on the Sabbath.

180. Trans. Neusner, *A History of the Jews in Babylonia* IV, p. 113.

᛫ᛡ᛫

Rabbah[181] said, "These three things were told to me by Uqban ben Nehemiah the exilarch in the name of Samuel:[182] "The law of the state is law. The Persians acquire ownership by an occupation of forty years. The sale by rich landlords [grandees] of lands bought up in payment of taxes is a valid sale.'"

11.3.13 *Iggeret Rav Sherira Gaon* 11:
The Last of the Amoraim and the Savoraim[183]

For about two hundred years (500–700 C.E.) the final editing of the Talmud continued under a group of scholars known as the savoraim ("interpreters"). They are responsible for much of the anonymous material in the Talmud and for certain complete discussions. The first generation of savoraim were the last sages to insert their discussions into the Gemara. It was during this period also that the Talmud was originally committed to writing as a complete work.

᛫ᛡ᛫

In all those years after Rav Papa,[184] Rav Ashi was gaon in Sura. He came to Mata Meḥasya, tore down the synagogue of Be Rav, and rebuilt it (as we say in [Chapter] *ha-Shutafin*),[185] making a number of fine improvements. He convened [in Mata Meḥasya] festivals and fast days[186] that [until then] had been the prerogative only of the exilarch and in Nehardea. He made it[187] the site of the Festival of the Exilarch,[188] for he [Rav Ashi] was an extraordinary person and was great in Torah and wealth.

Huna bar Nathan, who was the exilarch in those days, and Meremar and Mar Zutra, who were [exilarchs] after him, were subordinate to Rav Ashi, and they convened their festivals at Mata Meḥasya. Thus we say in Gittin:[189]

---

181. Some texts: Rava.
182. The third century amora.
183. Trans. Rabinowich, *Iggeres of Rav Sherira Gaon*, pp. 110–20.
184. He died in 371 C.E.
185. Babylonian Talmud Bava Batra 3b.
186. Perhaps grandiose public observances of the festivals.
187. Mata Meḥasya.
188. This was a display of honor and gratitude towards the exilarch by the Jewish people of Babylonia, including the sages and heads of the academies. It would seem that on these occasions the exilarch lectured, as well as the heads of the academies.
189. Babylonian Talmud Gittin 59a.

"Rav Aḥa bar Rava said: 'We, too, may say that from the days of Rabbi [Judah the Prince] until Rav Ashi we have not found Torah and wealth in one place.' But was there not Huna bar Nathan? Huna bar Nathan is different, [since] he was subordinate to Rav Ashi."

Since the Festival of the Exilarch was established at Mata Meḥasya, the heads of Pumbeditha had to go there for the Shabbat of [the Torah portion] *Lekh Lekha*;[190] for that is the Shabbat on which the Festival of the Exilarch took place. And most of the exilarchs established residence there.

What Rav Ashi accomplished[191] was not undone afterwards,[192] as things were undone in the years of Rav Judah, Rabbah, Rav Joseph, Abbaye, and Rava, when there was only one academy in Pumbeditha. But after Rav Ashi there were [still] two academies. This is the meaning of what Rav Ashi said in Tractate Shabbat:[193] "I brought it about that Mata Meḥasya should not be destroyed."

Every year when there was an exilarch in Mata Meḥasya who convened the Festival at Be Rav,[194] the heads [of the academy] and the Rabbis of Pumbeditha came before [Rav Ashi].

This arrangement had been the custom until about two hundred years ago,[195] because the exilarchs exercised heavy-handed authority and wielded great power in the days of the Persians[196] and in the days of the Ishmaelites.[197] For they [the exilarchs] would buy the exilarchate for large sums of money, and there were those among them who did much to aggrieve and oppress the Rabbis.

Rav Ashi functioned as head of his academy for almost sixty years. This explains why we say in Chapter *Mi She-Met*:[198] "In the first cycle[199] of Rav Ashi he told us [this,] and in the latter cycle of Rav Ashi he told us [something else.]"

For this is what the Rabbis instituted: to study two tractates every year, whether long or short.[200] So he [Rav Ashi] reviewed his entire Talmudic

---

190. Gen. 12–17, read in the fall according to the one-year Torah reading cycle followed in Babylonia.

191. The reestablishment of the Sura academy.

192. The academy continued to function for at least fifty years after Rav Ashi's death.

193. Babylonian Talmud Shabbat 11a.

194. The academy of Sura, now situated at Mata Meḥasya.

195. Ca. 800 C.E.

196. The Sassanian dynasty.

197. The Arab caliphs.

198. Babylonian Talmud Bava Batra 157b.

199. Thirty-year review of the entire Talmud.

200. Whether a leap year, containing an extra month, or a regular year of twelve lunar months.

knowledge in thirty years. Since Rav Ashi ruled close to sixty years,[201] there were two cycles. And he died in the year 738 [of the Seleucid Era; 427 C.E.].

Rav Yemar ruled after him in Mata Meḥasya, and he died in the year 743 [of the Seleucid Era; 432 C.E.].

After him [ruled] Rav Idi bar Abin, and he died in the year 763 [of the Seleucid Era; 452 C.E.].

After him [ruled] Rav Naḥman bar Rav Huna, and he died in the year 766 [of the Seleucid Era; 455 C.E.,] in a time of persecution, when Yezdegird decreed the abolition of the Sabbath.[202]

Then Rav Tavyomi, who is Mar bar Rav Ashi, ruled in Mata Meḥasya, and he died in the year 779 [of the Seleucid Era; 468 C.E.,] on the night following Yom Kippur. After him, Rabbah Tosfa'ah [ruled,] and he died in the year 785 [of the Seleucid Era; 474 C.E.].

On Wednesday, the thirteenth [day] of Kislev, in the year 786 [of the Seleucid Era; 475 C.E.], Ravina bar Rav Huna died. He represents the end of Talmudic halakhic determination.[203]

During those years, [the following] ruled in Pumbeditha: Rav Geviha of Be Kesil; and he died in 744 [of the Seleucid Era; 433 C.E.].

After him, Rafram of Pumbeditha; and he died in the year 754 [of the Seleucid Era; 443 C.E.].

After him, Rav Reḥumi—or, as some have it—Rav Reḥumai, and he died in the year 767 [of the Seleucid Era; 456 C.E.] in the time of persecution decreed by Yezdegird.

After him, Rav Sama the son of Rava ruled. In that same period—that of [Rav Sama] and Mar bar Rav Ashi—we have heard[204] from the earlier sages and have seen it written in their chronicles, that they prayed for mercy regarding [the persecutions of] Yezdegird, and a serpent swallowed him in his bedroom,[205] and the persecution was annulled.

In the days of this Rav Sama, on a Sabbath in Tevet of the year 781 [of the Seleucid Era; 470 C.E., the following sages] were arrested: Rabbana Amemar bar Mar Yenuka; Huna Mari, son of the exilarch; and Mesharshya bar Pakod. On the eighteenth of Tevet, Huna bar Mar Zutra

---

201. Actually 56 years, 371–427 C.E.

202. Yezdegird II (438–457) was a religiously zealous Sassanian king who tried forcing Zoroastrianism upon his subjects.

203. The last of the amoraim whose named statements are quoted in the Babylonian Talmud.

204. By an oral tradition.

205. The "serpent" might be a veiled allusion to a successful conspiracy resulting in the assassination of the king.

the exilarch and Mesharshya were executed. And in Adar of that year, Rabbana Amemar bar Mar Yenuqa was killed. In the year 785 [of the Seleucid era; 474 C.E.] all the Babylonian synagogues were closed,[206] and Jewish infants were handed over to the Magians.[207]

In the year 787 [of the Seleucid Era; 476 C.E.], Rav Sama the son of Rava died.

After him, Rav Yose ruled. In his days was the end of Talmudic halakhic determination and the Talmud was sealed.[208]

Most of the savoraim died within a few years of each other,[209] as the geonim explained in their historical books.[210]

In the year 815 [of the Seleucid Era; 504 C.E.], Rabbana Sama the son of Rabbana Yehudai died in [the month of] Sivan; and they say that he was the Judge of the Gate.[211]

On Sunday, the fourth of Adar, in the year 817 [of the Seleucid Era; 506 C.E.], Rav Aḥai bar Rav Huna died.

In Nissan of that year, Rabbi Reḥumi—or, as some have it, Rabbi Reḥumai—died.

In the year 817 [of the Seleucid Era; 506 C.E.,] in [the month of] Kislev, Rav Samuel bar Abbahu, of Pumbeditha, died.

In Adar, Ravina bar Amatziah died.

In the year 819 [of the Seleucid Era; 508 C.E.], Rav Huna the exilarch died.

In 822 [of the Seleucid Era; 511 C.E.,] on Yom Kippur, there was anger, and Rav Aḥai the son of Rabbah bar Abbuha died.

In 826 [of the Seleucid Era; 515 C.E.], Rav Taḥna and Mar Zutra, the sons of Rav Ḥinnena, died.

Rav Yose remained the gaon in our academy for about forty years.[212]

Afterwards, Rav Eina [was gaon] in Sura, and Rav Simonia [was gaon] in Pumbeditha.

Afterwards [was] Rav Revai of Rov.[213] He was from our academy, and they say[214] that he was a gaon.[215]

---

206. This persecution affected Sura in Babylon, but not Pumbeditha.

207. The priests of the Persian religion.

208. A second step in the redaction of the Talmud was completed.

209. Because of executions.

210. An allusion to the sources available to Rav Sherira in the Babylonian academies of his own day.

211. Chief judge of the Torah court attached to the academy; Hebrew, *av bet din*.

212. 476–514 C.E.

213. He began the second generation of savoraim.

214. It is known from an oral tradition.

215. "Gaon" here possibly means a very prominent person who commanded more authority and prestige than the other heads of academies even though he never formally received any higher appointment (Rabinowich, p. 123 n. 71).

11.3.14 Morning Service for Sabbaths and Festivals: Prayer for the Scholars[216]

The Jewish community in Babylonia was accustomed to praying for their scholars and Rabbinic leaders. This prayer, composed late in the talmudic period, gives some indication of the complex organization of the community which followed the Rabbis.

༅

May salvation arise from heaven. May grace, kindness and mercy—long life, ample sustenance and divine aid; physical health, perfect vision, and healthy children who will never neglect the study of the Torah—be granted to our scholars and teachers, to the holy societies that are in the land of Israel and in the land of Babylon, to the heads of the academies and the chiefs of the captivity, to the presidents of the colleges and the judges of the towns, to their disciples and the disciples of their disciples, and to all who study the Torah. May the King of the universe bless them, prolong their lives, increase their days and add to their years; may they be saved and delivered from all distress and disease. May our Lord who is in heaven be their help at all times; and let us say, Amen.

---

216. Trans. P. Birnbaum, *Daily Prayer Book* (New York: Hebrew Publishing Company, 1949), p. 378.

12

The Sea of the Talmud

Rabbinic literature was produced through a complex process of composition, collection, and redaction, much of which was carried on orally beginning already in the study circles of the amoraim. While recent scholarship has found little evidence for complex institutional structures which might deserve the term "academies" in Babylonia in the talmudic period, there is no question but that scholars and students assembled around masters. These groups we may term study circles or schools. In the Land of Israel more structured academies existed, continuing the practice of the tannaim. After being forced by political events to relocate several times in the tannaitic period, the Palestinian academy came to rest eventually in Tiberias at the southern end of the Sea of Galilee (text 12.1.1). Babylonian sages congregated primarily at the academies of Sura (Mata Meḥasya) and Pumbeditha.

The amoraim taught by oral repetition and detailed analysis. For this purpose, mnemonic devices were used (text 12.1.2), remnants of which are still found in the text of the Talmud. It is clear from the Reḥov inscription (text 12.2.1) that material which eventually was included in the talmudic compilations was already formulated, and even circulated, beforehand. This inscription further testifies to the observance of the agricultural laws of the Mishnah and Jerusalem Talmud by Jews in Byzantine Palestine.

We present an excerpt from the Jerusalem Talmud Berakhot (text 12.3.1) which, like so many other passages from this Talmud, is essentially a series of tannaitic traditions followed by a named amo-

619

raic statement drawing a conclusion. The Jerusalem Talmud, as in this example from Bava Meẓia (text 12.3.2), often preserves narratives which reflect the political, economic, and social life of Palestine during the Byzantine period. The beautiful series of aggadot included in this text testifies to Roman recognition of the honesty of the Jews.

In order to illustrate a sustained talmudic discussion in the Jerusalem Talmud, we have included a selection from Pesaḥim (text 12.3.3). Here we see the interplay of Mishnah, *baraita*, and Palestinian amoraic statement which typifies this Talmud. Somewhat different in character is the Babylonian Talmud, as can be seen in the selection we have presented from Bava Meẓia (text 12.4.1). This passage reflects the much greater dependence of the Babylonian Talmud on logical analysis and deduction, often presented in the voice of the anonymous redactor. Further, this passage features both Babylonian amoraim and their Palestinian counterparts. The passage also demonstrates that, whereas some issues of halakhah were decided by the Talmuds, others were left unresolved. To supplement this picture, we have also included passages from the Babylonian Talmud Qiddushin (text 12.4.2) dealing with a child's responsibilities to his or her parents and Babylonian Talmud Pesaḥim (text 12.4.3), showing Judaism's unbending concern for the sanctity of human life.

The Rabbis of the Land of Israel excelled in the creation of expositional Midrashim in which biblical passages were explained in order to derive religious and ethical lessons. Since many of these exegeses had their origin in public sermons in the Palestinian synagogues of the Byzantine period, they are often arranged in the form of a "proem." This literary form is essentially a midrashic text in which a complex chain of interpretations leads from a seemingly unrelated verse to the beginning of the Torah portion of a Sabbath or festival on which the sermon was given. An example is presented here from *Lamentations Rabbah* (text 12.5.1). An extended midrashic passage dealing with Moses' early years from *Exodus Rabbah* is also included (text 12.5.2). This text is arranged according to the sequence of biblical passages, providing a running commentary. Some Rabbinic Midrashim, however, are collections of homilies for festivals or special Sabbaths, such as *Pesiqta de-Rav Kahana* (text 12.5.3), from which a selection for the High Holy Day season has

been included. These homilies are essentially organized around subjects rather than biblical passages. Subjects of Jewish law could also
be framed as homilies, as in Babylonian Talmud Shabbat (text
12.5.4), in which the Rabbinic principle that the Sabbath must be
violated for the sake of life is discussed.

The Torah reading in both the Land of Israel and Babylonia was
accompanied by translation of the Bible into Aramaic, which was
the spoken language of most Jews in these regions at this time. Aramaic translations of the Bible, such as the *Job Targum*, found among
the Dead Sea Scrolls, had been in use from Second Temple times.
The oral use of such translations in the public Torah-reading ceremony led to their gradual expansion to include midrashic elements.
Examples of such Targumim (Aramaic translations) with aggadic
additions are the Palestinian Targum (also known as *Targum Jonathan*
or *Pseudo-Jonathan*) of the Ten Commandments (text 12.5.5) and
Targum Jonathan to Judges 5 (text 12.5.6).

Another area of literary creativity closely linked to the Rabbinic
corpus was the ongoing process of the canonization of the Jewish
liturgy. In order to expose readers to a sampling of such texts, some
are presented here, although others have been included in the next
chapter because they exemplify aspects of Jewish ritual and practice.
The daily Amidah (text 12.6.1) is at the core of the Jewish prayer
service, praising God and at the same time asking for the needs of
the Jewish people and the individual. The reader's repetition of the
Amidah in morning and afternoon services includes the Qedushah
(text 12.6.2) in which the worshipper, in the presence of a quorum
of ten adult males, joins in the angelic praise of God. Important
aspects of Jewish theology are revealed in the prayers for Rosh ha-
Shanah (text 12.6.3) and Yom Kippur (text 12.6.4). These texts are
written in a poetic style which came to fruition in the third through
sixth centuries in the Land of Israel, although they are based on
liturgical formulations which go back to the tannaitic period and
even earlier.

During the same period, alongside the statutory prayers that we
have been discussing, there grew up numerous poetic additions to
the liturgy known as *piyyutim*. An example is the Qedushta of Yannai (text 12.6.5), which describes the central ritual of the reading of
the Shema. Another example of such poetry is the poem recounting

the miracles of Passover night also composed by Yannai (text 12.6.6). These poems are rich in a complex web of biblical allusions and veiled references to numerous aggadic traditions which we may also find in midrashic texts.

The creation of Rabbinic literature during such turbulent times constitutes one of the great accomplishments of the Jewish people. It was the study of this literature which was the foundation of the giant intellectual enterprise of Torah study throughout Jewish history. Furthermore, this literature served as the basis for the practice of Judaism in the centuries following.

12.1 AMORAIC SCHOOLS

12.1.1 *Genesis Rabbah* 97:13:
The Migrations of the Sanhedrin[1]

The various locations of the Sanhedrin are linked with the verse in Genesis which locates the tribe of Zebulun by the seashore. Genesis Rabbah, a midrash on Genesis edited in the fifth century C.E., *locates the resting place of the Sanhedrin in Zebulun's territory in Sepphoris but was also aware that it later moved to Tiberias.*

ﬡ

"Zebulun shall dwell by the seashore" (Gen. 49:13) in his commerce, and Issachar in his Torah. Together they are in partnership in this world and the next.[2] Another interpretation: "Zebulun by the seashore," why did Jacob first bless Zebulun and only afterwards Issachar? Was not Issachar older and thus worthy of being blessed first? Rather [God] foresaw that the Temple would be destroyed and the Sanhedrin would be uprooted from the tribe of Judah and would be relocated in that of Zebulun. At first when the Sanhedrin was exiled, it resided in Yavneh, and from Yavneh to Usha, and from Usha to Shefar'am, and from Shefar'am to Beth She'arim, and from Beth She'arim to Sepphoris, and Sepphoris was located in the portion of Zebulun.[3] Only afterward did it move to Tiberias.

---

1. Trans. L. I. Levine, *The Rabbinic Class of Roman Palestine in Late Antiquity* (Jerusalem: Yad Izhak Ben-Zvi; New York: The Jewish Theological Seminary of America, 1989), p. 80.

2. The tribe of Zebulun will provide financial support so that the tribe of Issachar can devote itself fully to the study of the Torah.

3. All these towns are located in the Galilee.

12.1.2 Babylonian Talmud Eruvin 54b–55a: Amoraic Pedagogy[4]

The amoraim made use of various techniques to impart the oral Torah to their students. Most prominent was simple repetition. To aid in memorizing, since the oral Torah was transmitted and taught through an oral process, mnemonic devices and other formulations were used.

⟊

Rabbi Peraida had a certain student, [who needed to be] taught four hundred times until he learned. One day [while Rabbi Peraida was teaching this student, he] was requested for a religious matter.[5] He taught [the student four hundred times] but [the student] was unable to learn. [Rabbi Peraida] said to him, "What is different today?"[6]

[The student] said to him, "From the time that my Master was told that there is a religious matter, I did not pay attention. Every moment I said to myself, 'My Master will get up now, my Master will get up now.'"

[Rabbi Peraida] said to him, "Give me your attention and I will teach you."

He went back and taught him four hundred times [more]. A heavenly voice went forth and said to [Rabbi Peraida], "Do you prefer that four hundred years be added to your life, or that you and your generation merit a share in the world to come?"[7]

He said, "[I prefer] that I and my generation merit a share in the world to come."

Said the Holy One Blessed be He, "Give him both."

Rav Ḥisda said, "Torah is only acquired by means of mnemonic symbols.[8] For it is written, 'Put it (*simah*) in their mouths' (Deut. 31:19). Do not read [it as] *simah*, but rather [read it] *simana* (its sign)."

Rabbi Taḥlifa of the west [the Land of Israel] heard this, and said before Rabbi Abahu, "You learn it [the necessity for mnemonics] from that text, and we learn it from the following text: 'Establish for yourselves signs (*ziyyunim*), set up for yourself . . .' (Jer. 31:21). Make markers for the Torah. And how do we know that *ziyyun* denotes a sign? As it is written, 'Anyone who sees a man's bone will put up a sign (*ziyyun*)' (Ezek. 39:15)."

---

4. Trans. S. Berrin.
5. This phrase usually refers to the collecting of charity.
6. That you were unable to learn.
7. As a reward for your dedication in teaching Torah.
8. The word used for symbols is *simanin*, the singular of which is *simana*.

Rabbi Eliezer said, "From here [we learn the necessity for mnemonics]: 'Say to Wisdom, "you are my sister," and call Understanding, "kindred" (*moda'a*)' (Prov. 7:4). Make signs (*moda'im*) for the Torah."

Rava said, "Make appointed times (*mo'adim*) for Torah [study]."

This[9] is [in accordance with] Abdimi bar Ḥama bar Dosa [who] said, "What is the interpretation of the following verse, 'It is not in the heavens ... nor is it across the sea'? (Deut. 30:12–13). 'It is not in the heavens'; for if [the Torah] were in the heavens, you would have to ascend after it, and if it were 'across the sea,' you would have to cross after it."

Rava said, "'It is not in the heavens' [means that] it will not be found with somebody who lifts his head as high as the sky [because of his knowledge of Torah],[10] nor will it be found with somebody whose head swells like the sea [because of his knowledge of Torah]."

Rabbi Yoḥanan said, "'It is not in the heavens' [means that] it will not be found with the arrogant ...; 'nor is it across the sea' [means that] it will not be found with merchants and vendors."[11]

12.2 FROM AMORAIC INTERPRETATION
TO TALMUDIC TEXTS

12.2.1 The Reḥov Inscription:
Agricultural Precepts of the Land of Israel[12]

The Reḥov Inscription, the longest mosaic inscription uncovered in Israel, was found on the floor of the synagogue at Reḥov[13] and dates somewhere between the fifth and seventh centuries C.E. It contains detailed agricultural laws concerning tithes and Sabbatical Year produce. These laws were observed throughout the Holy Land in all Jewish settlements, at least until the early Arab period, despite an increasingly difficult economic situation. The text itself has many parallels with the Tosefta, Sifre Deuteronomy, and Jerusalem Talmud and seems in some respects to represent an alternative recension of the same halakhic traditions.

---

9. This concept of expending effort to provide mnemonics and other aids for the study of the Torah.

10. Who is arrogant because of his knowledge.

11. Implying that merchants and vendors travel across the sea and do not have time to study the Torah sufficiently.

12. Trans. R. Grafman, "The Reḥob Inscription: A Translation," in *Ancient Synagogues Revealed*, ed. L. I. Levine (Jerusalem: Israel Exploration Society, 1981), pp. 152–3.

13. West of the Jordan River south of Beth Shean.

🙌

(1) Shalom! These fruits are forbidden at Beth-Shean in the Seventh Year,[14] and in the other sabbatical cycle years they are tithed (as) *demai*:[15] the marrows,[16] (2) and the melons, and the cucumbers, and the parsnips, and the mint which is bound by itself, and Egyptian beans which are bound (3) in shavings, and leeks from the holiday (of Sukkot) until Hanukkah, and seeds, and dried figs, and sesame, and mustard, and rice, and cummin, and dry lupine, (4) and large peas which are sold by measure, and garlic, and village onions sold by measure, and onions, (5) and pressed dates, and wine, and oil. In the Seventh Year (they are considered) Seventh Year (produce),[17] the other years of the sabbatical cycle (they are tithed as) *demai,* and the bread for *ḥallah* (dough-offering) is eternally (due).[18]

These are the places (6) which are permitted[19] around Beth-Shean: on the south which is the "campus" gate till the "white field"; on the west (7) which is the gate of the (oil-) press till the end of the pavement (?); on the north which is the gate of the watchtower (or "of Sekuta") till Kefar Qarnos, and Kefar Qarnos (8) is as Beth-Shean; and on the east which is the "dung" gate till the tomb of *pnwtyyh,* and the gate of Kefar Zimrin and the gate of the uncleared field (or *'gmh*). (9) Before the gate it is allowed and beyond it is forbidden.

The forbidden towns in the territory of Sussita:[20] Ayyanosh, and *'ynhtrh,* and *dmbr,* (10) Iyyon, and Yaarut, and Kefar Yahtrib, and Nob, and Hasfiya (=Caspein), and Kefar Zemaḥ, and Rabbi permitted Kefar Zemaḥ. The towns which are doubtful within the territory of Naveh: (11)

---

14. Every seven years the land is to lie fallow, and sowing and cultivation are forbidden (Ex. 23:10–11; Lev. 25:2–7). Therefore, the inscription specifies those fruits which are forbidden to be eaten if they are cultivated during the Sabbatical Year as well as the boundaries of the Holy Land within which these laws apply.

15. Since Beth-Shean is close to the boundary, it is not possible to be certain if the produce comes from inside or outside the Land of Israel. Hence, it is treated as *demai,* produce the status of which is uncertain, and it is tithed without reciting a benediction.

16. A type of squash.

17. Hence they are forbidden.

18. *Ḥallah,* the dough offering, was due in any case, as it was not dependent on the locality from which it came, being obligatory even outside the Land of Israel.

19. Areas in which Jews did not live which were considered exempt from the restrictions of Sabbatical produce.

20. These towns were located on the periphery of the Jewish community of Palestine in pagan regions, but they were considered Jewish, that is, subject to the forbidden fruits of the Seventh Year.

Ẓir, and Ẓayyer, and Gasimea, and Zeizun, and Raneb, and Ḥarbata, and *'ygr, ḥwtm,* and Charax of bar *ḥrg.*

The forbidden towns in the territory of Tyre: *ẓẓt,* (12) Bezeth, and Pi Masoba, and Upper Hanotha and lower Hanotha, and *bybrh,* and *r'ẓ myyh,* and *'mwn,* and *mẓh,* which is Castella, and all (the lands) which Jews have purchased, (13) is forbidden.

The territory of Eretz-Israel:[21] the place which they who returned from Babylon [held], the Ascalon junction, and the wall of Strato's Tower, Dor, and the wall of Acco (14) and the head of the waters of Gaaton, and Gaaton proper, and Kabr[atha and B]eth-Zenitha, and the *castrum*[22] of Galila, and *qwb'yyh* ("peaks"?) of Aita, and *mmẓyyh* of Jorcatha, (15) and the fort of Kuryaim, and the neighborhood (or "enclosure") of Jatti[r and the brook] of *bs'l,* and Beth-Aita, and Barshata, and greater Houle, and the channel (?) (16) of Iyyon, and *msb spnḥh,* and Karka of Bar Sangora, and Upper Tarnegola of Caesarea (Paneas), and Beth-Sabal, and Canatha, (17) and Rekem (of) Trachonitis, Zimra of the limits of Bostra, Jabbok, and Heshbon, and the brook Zered, Igar Sahaduta, Nimrin, (18) the fort of Raziza, Rekem of Gaia, and the garden of Ascalon and the great road leading to the desert.

These fruits (19) are forbidden in Paneas in the Seventh Year and in the other years of the sabbatical cycle they are tithed as full (?) *demai:* (20) the rice, and the nuts, and the sesame, and Egyptian beans. Some say even choice plums, (21) for these in the Seventh Year are (considered) Seventh Year (produce) and in the other years of the sabbatical cycle they are tithed as *demai,* and even (22) from Upper Tarnegola and beyond.

These fruits are tithed (as) *demai* at Caesarea (Maritima): the wheat and the bread (23) for *ḥallah* (which is) eternally (due),[23] and the wine, and the oil, and the dates, and the rice, and the cummin for these are permitted in the Seventh Year at Caesarea (24) and in the other years of the sabbatical cycle they are due (as) *demai,* and there are some who forbid white onions from (25) the King's Mountain. And until where is the region of Caesarea? Till Ẓoran, and the inn of Tibetah, and the column, (26) and Dor, and Kefar Saba, and if there is a place which was purchased by Jews our Rabbis are suspicious of it.

---

21. These boundaries of the Land of Israel delineate the boundaries of the territory possessed by the returnees from the Babylonian exile, that is, those regions which were obligated to observe the agricultural precepts applicable in the Holy Land.

22. Latin, "military camp."

23. The dough offering for the priests.

Shalom![24] The towns (27) permitted within the territory of Sebaste: *'yqbyn*, and Kefar Kasdayah and Ẓir, and *'zylyn*, and Safirin, and *'nnyn*, and Upper Jibleam, and Mezḥaru, (28) and Dothan, and Kefar *myyh*, and Silta, and Pentakomias Livias and Pardisalya, and Yazit, and *'rbnwryn*, and Kefar (29) Yehudit, and *mwnryt*, and half of Shalaf.

12.3 THE PALESTINIAN TALMUD

12.3.1 Jerusalem Talmud Berakhot 2:5 (5a): Distraction in Prayer[25]

The Jerusalem Talmud relies heavily on tannaitic traditions (baraitot) and often appears to be a compilation of such traditions with brief amoraic conclusions or explanations. In the excerpt which follows, this is the case as the Gemara emphasizes the need to avoid distraction during prayers and Grace after Meals.

❧

A tanna taught, "One may not wink his eyes while reciting [the Shema]."

A tanna taught, "Workers who were doing work for their employer recite the first blessing [of the Grace after Meals], and then include Jerusalem and the Land[26] in a single blessing ending with a reference to the Land. But if they were working for him in return for their meals, or if their employer ate with them, they recite all four [benedictions].[27]

Rabbi Mana[28] said, "This teaches that it is forbidden to work while reciting the Grace after Meals, for otherwise we would say that they should do their work and recite the [complete] blessings [while working]."

12.3.2 Jerusalem Talmud Bava Meẓia 2:5 (8b): The Return of Lost Articles[29]

In this aggadic passage, the Jerusalem Talmud stresses the importance of the return of lost objects to their owner. Not only is it the honest thing to do, but it brings honor upon God· and His people.

---

24. This "Shalom" indicates a change of subject from the far borders of the land to those quite close to Reḥov itself.

25. Trans. S. Berrin.

26. Usually two separate benedictions.

27. The complete Grace after Meals.

28. A Palestinian amora.

29. Trans. S. Berrin and L. H. Schiffman. The translation follows E. S. Rosenthal, S. Lieberman, *Yerushalmi Neziqin* (Jerusalem: Israel Academy of Sciences and Humanities, 1983), pp. 48, 135–6.

જ૬

Rabbi Ḥanina related this story: "Some old Rabbis bought a pile of wheat from some soldiers[30] and found in it a purse full of dinars, and they returned it to them."

The soldiers said, "Blessed be the God of the Jews."

Abba Oshaya of Tiraya was a laundry-man. Once the queen came to wash in a pool of water and lost her bath clothes. [Abba Oshaya] found them. When she came out, he gave them to her. She said to him, "They are yours. What use have I for them? Of what importance are they to me? I have better ones and I have many more."

He responded to her, "The Torah decrees that we must return [lost property]."

She said, "Blessed be the God of the Jews."

Rabbi Samuel bar Sursetai went to Rome. The queen lost her necklace and he found it. A proclamation was issued throughout the province that whoever returns it within thirty days will receive such-and-such [as a reward], but [whoever returns it] after thirty days will be beheaded. [Rabbi Samuel] did not return it within the thirty days. After the thirty days he returned it.

She said to him, "Were you not in the province?"

He responded to her, "Yes, [I was here]."

She said to him, "Did you not hear the proclamation?"

He said to her, "Yes, [I heard it]."

She said, to him "What was it?"

He responded to her, "Whoever returns it within thirty days will receive such-and-such, but if after thirty days he will be beheaded."

She said to him, "Then why did you not return it within the thirty days?"

He said to her, "So that no one may say that I did it because of fear of you; for, [actually, I did it] because of fear of the All-Merciful."

She said, "Blessed be the God of the Jews."

12.3.3 Jerusalem Talmud Pesaḥim 10:1 (37a–c): Preparing for the Seder[31]

This passage sets forth a particular order for the Passover eve celebration. It discusses the rule that one may not eat on the days preceding Sabbaths and fes-

---

30. The translation of this word is uncertain.

31. Trans. B. Bokser, completed and edited by L. H. Schiffman, *Yerushalmi Pesaḥim* (*The Talmud of the Land of Israel: A Preliminary Translation and Explanation*, vol. 13; Chicago Studies in the History of Judaism; Chicago: University of Chicago Press, 1994), pp. 473–8.

tivals from the time of the afternoon sacrifice until the evening, and mandates that reclining at the Seder not be limited to the rich or intellectuals, who in antiquity predominated at wine parties and symposia and who elsewhere in Rabbinic sources are associated with reclining.

~€

"On the eve of Passover [from] close to [the time of the] *minhah* [afternoon offering = about the ninth hour of the day], until it gets dark a person should not eat. Even a poor person in Israel should not eat until he reclines [at the Seder]. [At the Seder those who serve] should not give him fewer than four cups of wine even if [the funds come] from the charity plate."[32]

The teaching [the Mishnah] represents the position of Rabbi Judah [who holds that one refrains from eating on the eve of all Sabbaths and festivals]. As it is taught:[33] " 'Sabbath eve from *minhah* time onward a person should not taste anything until it gets dark so that he may enter the Sabbath with an appetite'—the words of Rabbi Judah. Rabbi Yose says, '[A person] continues to eat until he finishes [the meal].' 'They interrupt [eating] because of the Sabbath [to welcome it by reciting the Sanctification blessing]'—the words of Rabbi Judah. Rabbi Yose says, 'They do not interrupt.'

"A case concerning Rabban Simeon ben Gamaliel and Rabbi Yose bar Halafta who [prior to *minhah* time] were dining in Akko on the Sabbath eve and the time of Sabbath came. "Said Rabban Simeon ben Gamaliel to Rabbi Yose bar Halafta, 'Do you want us to interrupt [our meal] because of the Sabbath [and thus take Rabbi Judah's position into consideration]?'

"[Rabbi Yose bar Halafta] said to him, 'Every day you would prefer my opinion in the presence of Rabbi Judah and now you prefer Rabbi Judah's in my presence? "Does he mean to ravish the queen in my own palace?" (Est. 7:8)'[34]

"[Rabban Simeon ben Gamaliel] said to him, 'If so, let us not interrupt lest [following our action] the law be fixed in Israel according to Rabbi Judah.' They did not move from there until they fixed the law according to Rabbi Yose."[35]

---

32. Mishnah Pesahim 10:1, which is then discussed in the following Talmudic discussion.

33. Here begins a *baraita* parallel to Tosefta Berakhot 5:1.

34. In my presence, do you wish to follow the view of Rabbi Judah?

35. The *baraita* ends here and amoraic discussion begins.

Rabbi Judah [said] in the name of Samuel, "These [the foregoing] are the opinions of Rabbi Judah and Rabbi Yose. [But] the opinion of the Sages [the law] is: [A person] spreads a napkin [over the bread] and sanctifies [the day by reciting the sanctification blessing]."[36]

What is the law, is it permissible to eat dried fruit [which whets one's thirst]? Rabbi Judah Nesiah [II = Judah the Patriarch III] bathed and became thirsty [in the late afternoon]. He asked Rabbi Mana, "Since I am thirsty, may I drink?"[37]

He said to him, "[No, for] Rabbi Hiyya teaches: 'A person is prohibited from tasting anything until it gets dark.'"[38]

Said Rabbi Levi, "One who eats unleavened bread on Passover eve is like one who has intercourse with his betrothed in his in-laws' [literally: father-in-law's] house, and one who has intercourse with his betrothed in his in-laws' house is liable to lashes." [For both, one must wait for the proper time.]

It is taught:[39] "Rabbi Judah ben Beterah says, 'One is prohibited [from eating] both leavened and unleavened bread.'" Rabbi Simon [said] in the name of Rabbi Joshua ben Levi, "Rabbi [Judah the Patriarch] was accustomed to eat neither leavened nor unleavened bread"—neither unleavened bread because of this [tradition] of Rabbi Levi, nor leavened bread because of this [tradition] of Rabbi Judah ben Beterah."

And was Rabbi a student of Rabbi Judah ben Beterah [that he should follow the latter's opinion in this matter]? Was he not [instead] a student of Rabbi Jacob ben Qorshai? Rather [he refrained from eating leavened bread] because he was a firstborn son [and the firstborn fasted on the day preceding Passover].[40]

Said Rabbi Mana, "Rabbi Jonah, my father, was a firstborn and he ate!"[41]

Said Rabbi Tanhum, "[Rabbi acted thus] not because of this [reason], but because of the following: Rabbi was sickly. When he ate during the day, he would not [be able to] eat in the evening. And why here [in this

---

36. One may eat right up to the time of the beginning of the Sabbath and no waiting period beforehand is required.

37. On Friday afternoon after *minhah*.

38. Until the onset of the Sabbath.

39. In a *baraita*.

40. To commemorate their redemption from the plague of the firstborn, the last of the Ten Plagues against the Egyptians prior to the Exodus.

41. Therefore we must assume that the fast of the firstborn was not yet an accepted custom, and the fact that Rabbi may have been a firstborn is not crucial.

case] would he not eat during the day? In order to enter [upon the eating of] the unleavened bread with an appetite."[42]

Said Rabbi Levi, "Because it is the custom of slaves to eat standing, here [on Passover night, the Mishnah requires people] to eat reclining to proclaim that they have gone out from slavery to freedom." Rabbi Simon [said] in the name of Rabbi Joshua ben Levi, "That olive's amount [of unleavened bread] with which a person fulfills his obligation on Passover—one must eat it reclining."

Rabbi Yose asked before Rabbi Simon, "Does this apply even to a slave in the presence of his master, even to a woman in the presence of her husband?"

He said to him, "Son of the great, until here I have heard [i.e., only what I reported]."

Said Rabbi Ḥiyya bar Adda, "Because it is not pleasant for a person to eat from the communal fund, here [he is required] 'even if [the funds come] from the charity plate.'"[43]

It is taught: "On a festival, a man is required to make his wife and children happy. With what does he make them happy? With wine. Rabbi Judah says, 'Women with what is appropriate for them; and children, with what is appropriate for them'."[44] "Women, with what is appropriate for them"—for example, fine linen garments and belts; "and children, with what is appropriate for them"—for example, walnuts and almonds. They say, "Rabbi Tarfon used to do this."

Whence [did they derive the requirement] for four cups? Rabbi Yoḥanan [said] in the name of Rabbi Benaiah, "[They] correspond to the four redemptions [or acts of redemption, mentioned in reference to Egypt]: 'Say, therefore, to the Israelite people: I am the Lord. I will *take you out* [from under the burdens of the Egyptians and *deliver you* from their bondage. I will *redeem you* with an outstretched arm and through extraordinary chastisements]. And I will *take you* to be my people,' etc. (Ex. 6:6–7). [These verses contain the four terms:] 'I will take out,' 'I will deliver,' 'I will redeem,' 'I will take.'"

---

42. Had he eaten bread in the morning or matzah in the afternoon, he would not have been able to eat matzah at the seder.

43. Because of the importance of drinking four cups, the Mishnah requires a person to take, not just from the communal fund, which provides a weekly allotment, but even from the charity plate, which provides a daily allotment. Since this requires a person to appear daily, it poses an even greater source of embarrassment.

44. A *baraita* parallel to Tosefta Pesaḥim 10:4.

Rabbi Joshua ben Levi said, "[They] correspond to the four cups of [wine mentioned in reference to] Pharaoh: '*Pharaoh's cup* was in my hand, [and I took the grapes,] and I pressed them into *Pharaoh's cup*, and placed the *cup in Pharaoh's hand*' (Gen. 40:11) . . . 'and you will place *Pharaoh's cup* in his hand,' etc. (Gen. 40:13). ['But think of me when all is well with you again so as to free me from this place' (Gen. 40:14).]" [The four cups in the dream and its interpretation brought or preceded a redemption, in this instance that of Joseph.]

Rabbi Levi said, "[They] correspond to the four [world] kingdoms [that have oppressed Israel and that precede the kingdom of God—Babylonia, Media, Greece, and Rome, with each cup perhaps marking the release of Israel from a different oppressor]."

And Rabbis say, "[They] correspond to the four cups of retribution that the Holy One Praised be He will give the nations of the world to drink: 'For thus said the Lord, the God of Israel, to me: "Take from my hand this *cup of wine of wrath* [and make all the nations to whom I send you drink of it]"' (Jer. 25:15); '[Flee from the midst of Babylon for this is a time of vengeance for the Lord, He will deal retribution to her]. *Babylon was a golden cup* in the Lord's hand, [it made the whole earth drunk]' (Jer. 51: 6–7); 'For in the Lord's hand there is a *cup* [*with foaming wine fully mixed*; from this He pours; all the wicked of the earth drink, draining it to the very dregs]' (Ps. 75:9); 'He will rain down upon the wicked blazing coals and sulfur, a scorching wind shall be *the portion of their cup*' (Ps. 11:6)."

[In the last verse,] What is "the portion of their cup"? Rabbi Abin said, "A bowl of poterion[45] like the bowl of poterion after bathing."[46]

[Continuing the words of the Rabbis:] "And corresponding to them [to the four cups of retribution], the Holy One, Praised be He, will give Israel four cups of consolation to drink: 'The Lord is my allotted share and *cup*' (Ps. 16:5); '[You spread a table for me in full view of my enemies;] You anoint my head with oil; my *drink* [*cup*] is abundant' (Ps. 23:5); and this [verse:] 'I raise the *cup of deliverances*' (Ps. 116:13) [provides an additional] two [cups (as "deliverances" is plural), each of which represents a separate act of deliverance]."

---

45. Poterion refers to a potion made from the root of a shrub which was believed to be a healing agent for wounds and used to strengthen weak muscles.

46. Usually given after a bath to relax the muscles but in this case used to bring about a punishment.

12.4 THE BABYLONIAN TALMUD

12.4.1 Babylonian Talmud Bava Meẓia 21b–24a: Lost and Found[47]

Much of the Babylonian Talmud is devoted to the detailed exploration of the legal ramifications of mishnaic rulings in matters pertaining to civil law. The talmudic Rabbis, in cooperation with, and at times in opposition to the exilarchs, were heavily involved in the administration of this aspect of law among Jews. The passage presented here is typical of the careful, logical analysis which became the basis for the study of the Talmud throughout the ages.

§

MISHNAH: "Some finds belong to the finder; others must be announced.[48] The following articles belong to the finder: if one finds scattered fruit, scattered money, small sheaves in a public thoroughfare, round cakes of pressed figs, a baker's loaves, strings of fishes, pieces of meat, fleeces of wool which have been brought from the country, bundles of flax and stripes of purple, colored wool; all these belong to the finder. This is the view of Rabbi Meir. Rabbi Judah says: whatsoever has in it something unusual must be announced, as, for instance, if one finds a round [of figs] containing a potsherd, or a loaf containing money. Rabbi Simeon ben Eleazar says: new merchandise need not be announced."[49]

GEMARA: "If one finds scattered fruit, etc."[50] What quantity [of fruit in a given space] is meant? Rabbi Isaac said: "A *kav*[51] within four cubits."[52] But what kind of a case is meant? If [the fruit appears to have been] dropped accidentally, then even if there is more than a *kav* [it should] also [belong to the finder]. And if it appears to have been [deliberately] put down, then even if there is a smaller quantity it should not [belong to the finder]? Rav Uqba bar Ḥama answered: "We deal here with [the remains of] what has been gathered on the threshing floor: [To collect] a *kav* [scattered over a space] of four cubits is troublesome, and, as people do not

---

47. Trans. I. Epstein, ed., *The Babylonian Talmud* (London: Soncino Press, 1935–52), 35 vols.

48. Publicly, in order that the person who lost something then may come and claim the lost item.

49. Mishnah Bava Metẓia 2:1.

50. Quoting the Mishnah.

51. Approximately a quart and a half.

52. Six square feet. A cubit is about 18 inches.

trouble to come back and collect it, [the owner also] abandons it, but if it is [spread over] a smaller space [the owner] does come back and collect it, and he does not abandon it."

Rabbi Jeremiah inquired: "How is it [if one finds] half a *kav* [scattered over the space] of two cubits? Is the reason why a *kav* within four cubits [belongs to the finder] that it is troublesome [to collect], and therefore half a *kav* within two cubits, which is not troublesome to collect, is not abandoned [and should not belong to the finder], or is the reason [in the case of a *kav* within four cubits] that it is not worth the trouble of collecting [when spread over such a space], and therefore half a *kav* within two cubits, which is still less worth the trouble of collecting, is abandoned [and should belong to the finder]? [Again,] how is it [if one finds] two *kavs* [scattered over the space] of eight cubits? Is the reason why a *kav* within four cubits [belongs to the finder] that it is troublesome to collect, and therefore two *kavs* within eight cubits, which are still more troublesome to collect, are even more readily abandoned [and should certainly belong to the finder], or is the reason [in the case of a *kav* within four cubits] that it is not worth the trouble [of collecting], and therefore two *kavs* within eight cubits, which are worth the trouble [of collecting] are not abandoned [and should not belong to the finder]?" . . . The questions remain unanswered.[53]

It has been stated:[54] "Anticipated abandonment [of the hope of recovering a lost article][55] is, Abaye maintains, no abandonment, but Rava maintains that it is an abandonment." [If the lost article is] a thing which has an identification mark, all agree that [the anticipation of its abandonment by the owner] is no abandonment, and even if in the end we hear him [express regret at his loss in a way that makes it clear] that he has abandoned it, it is not [deemed to be an] abandonment, for when [the finder] took possession of it he had no right to it because [it is assumed that] when [the loser] becomes aware that he lost it, he will not give up the hope [of recovering it] but says [to himself], "I can recognize it by an identification mark; I shall indicate the identification mark and shall take it back." [If the lost article is found] in the intertidal space of the seashore or on ground that is flooded by a river, then, even if it has an identification

---

53. Often talmudic arguments do not reach a conclusion. Medieval codifiers later ruled on many of these issues.

54. This formulation introduces an amoraic statement.

55. "Anticipated abandonment" refers to a presumption that the original owner has given up ownership of a lost object. The issue concerns whether in situations in which a normal owner would have given up ownership if he knew of the loss, we can anticipate that even without knowing of the loss of the object, he would give up ownership.

mark, the Divine Law permits [the finder to acquire it], as we shall explain further on. They[56] differ only where the article has no identification mark. Abaye says: "It is no abandonment," because [the loser] did not know that he lost it; Rava says: "It is an abandonment," because when he becomes aware that he lost it, he gives up the hope [of recovering it] as he says [to himself], "I cannot recognize it by an identification mark," it is therefore as if he had given up hope from the moment [he lost it].[57]

Come and hear:[58] "Scattered money, [etc.] belong to the finder."[59] Why? [Is it not a case in which the loser] did not know that he lost it?[60] There also it is even as Rabbi Isaac said: "A man usually feels for his purse at frequent intervals." So here, too, [we say,] "A man usually feels for his purse at frequent intervals" [and soon discovers his loss].[61]

Come and hear: "Round cakes of pressed figs, a baker's loaves, [etc.] belong to the finder."[62] Why? [Is it not a case in which the loser] did not know that he lost it? There also he becomes aware of his loss, because [the lost articles] are heavy. . . .

Come and hear: "From what time are people allowed to appropriate the gleanings [of a reaped field]? After the 'gropers' have gone through it."[63] Whereupon we asked: "What is meant by the 'gropers?'" and Rabbi Yoḥanan answered: "Old people who walk leaning on a stick," while Resh Laqish answered: "The last in the succession of gleaners." Now why should this be so? Granted that the local poor give up hope [of finding any gleanings], there are poor people in other places who do not give up hope?[64] I will say: Seeing that there are local poor, those [in other places] give up hope right away, as they say. "The poor of that place have already gleaned it"[65]. . . .

Come and hear: Rabbi Yoḥanan said in the name of Rabbi Ishmael ben Jehozadak:[66] "Whence [do we learn] that an article lost through the flood-

---

56. Abaye and Rava.

57. Hence, the finder may keep it.

58. The Talmud now tries to determine the law by quoting and analyzing tannaitic traditions.

59. Quoting the Mishnah.

60. And nevertheless it is assumed that the finder may keep it, proving that anticipated abandonment is valid.

61. Hence, it is not a case of anticipated abandonment.

62. Quoting again from the Mishnah.

63. Mishnah Pe'eh 8:1. The "gropers" are entitled to glean the field due to their poverty.

64. Hence, it should be forbidden for others to take the leftover gleanings, even after the local poor have gleaned.

65. Hence, it is indeed permitted for others to appropriate the remaining gleanings.

66. Manuscripts read: Simeon ben Jehozadak, a tanna who taught Rabbi Yoḥanan.

ing of a river may be retained [by the finder]? It is written, 'And so shall you do with his ass; and so shall you do with his garment; and so shall you do with every lost thing of your brother's, which he has lost and you have found' (Deut. 22:3) [which means to say that only] if the object has been lost by him and may be found by any person [has it to be returned to him, and it follows that] a case like this[67] is exempt [from the biblical law], since it is lost to him and cannot be found by any person."[68] Moreover, the object which is forbidden [to be kept by the finder] is like the object which is permitted [to be kept by the finder]: Just as the permitted object may be kept irrespective of whether it has an identification mark or not, so the forbidden object may not be kept irrespective of whether it has an identification mark or not. [This is] a complete refutation of Rava.[69] And the law is in accordance with Abaye in [the cases indicated by the initials] Y'AL KGM. . . .[70]

"Small sheaves in a public thoroughfare belong to the finder." Rabbah said: Even when they have an identification mark. Consequently [it must be assumed that] Rabbah is of the opinion that an identification mark which is liable to be trodden on[71] is not [deemed to be] an identification mark. Rava said [on the other hand]: [The Mishnah] refers only to things which have no identification mark, but things which have an identification mark have to be announced.[72] Consequently [it must be assumed that] Rava is of the opinion that an identification mark that is liable to be trodden on is [deemed to be] an identification mark. Some teach this as an independent controversy. In regard to an identification mark which is liable to be trodden on, Rabbah says that it is not [deemed to be] an identification mark, but Rava says that it is [deemed to be] an identification mark.

We have learnt: Small sheaves [which are found] in a public thoroughfare belong to the finder, [but if found] on private grounds they have to be taken up and announced. How is this to be understood? If [the

---

67. The loss caused by the flooding of a river.

68. Here the words of Rabbi Ishmael (or Simeon) ben Jehozadak end, and the anonymous gemara continues.

69. Since it indicates that anticipated abandonment of the hope of recovery of the lost object is not considered valid, and the finder may not keep the property.

70. These are initials used as a mnemonic, indicating the six cases in all the Babylonian Talmud in which the law is according to Abaye.

71. And, therefore, which is easily destroyed.

72. One who loses an item with identification will not give up hope of its recovery, assuming that he can provide the identifying mark and claim his property.

sheaves] have no identification mark, what is there to be announced [if they are found] on private grounds? It must therefore be that they have an identification mark, and still it is stated that [if found] in a public thoroughfare they belong to the finder. Consequently [it must be assumed that] an identification mark which is liable to be trodden on is not [deemed to be] an identification mark, which is a refutation of Rava! Rava may answer you: "In reality they have no identification mark; and as to your question, 'What is there to be announced [if they were found] on private grounds?', [the answer is:] The place [where they were found] is announced." But Rabbah says that the place is no identification. . . .

Rav Bibi asked of Rav Naḥman: Is the place [where an article is found] an identification mark or not? [Rav Naḥman] answered him: "You have learned it:[73] 'If one finds barrels of wine, or of oil, or of corn, or of dried figs, or olives, they belong to him.' Now if you were to assume that the place [where an article is found] is an identification mark [the finder] ought to announce the place!"[74] Rav Zebid answered: "Here we deal with [barrels found] on the river-bank."[75] Rav Mari said: "For what reason did the Rabbis maintain that the river-bank does not constitute an identification mark? Because we say to him: As it happened to you, so it may have happened to your neighbor." Some have another version: Rav Mari said: "For what reason did the Rabbis maintain that the place constitutes no identification mark? Because we say to him: As it happened to you in this place, so it may have happened to your neighbor in this [same] place."[76]

12.4.2 Babylonian Talmud Qiddushin 31b: The Proper Treatment of Parents[77]

The Babylonian Talmud includes a long section dealing with relations of parents and children of which we quote a small part. The Talmud is here interpreting the biblical verses referring to revering and honoring one's parents. It spells out the minimum required filial responsibilities.

---

73. In a *baraita*.

74. Hence, location is not considered to be an identification mark.

75. But normally location is an identification mark.

76. Large amounts of merchandise are unloaded at the bank of the river and so there is no way of being sure who the owner is even if the location is known.

77. Trans. S. Berrin.

꽃

Our Rabbis taught:[78] "What is 'reverence'[79] [for parents] and what is 'honor'?[80]

"'Reverence' [refers to one who] does not sit in his [parent's] place and does not stand in his [parent's] place, he does not contradict his [parent's] opinions, and does not judge [his parent's disputes].

"'Honor' [refers to one who] feeds [his father or mother] and gives him (or her) drink; he clothes him (or her) and covers him (or her), and he helps him (or her) to enter and exit."

12.4.3 Babylonian Talmud Pesaḥim 25b: Murder by Command[81]

The Talmud here expresses a very important legal principle: one is forbidden to commit murder even upon pain of death. There can be no excuse of "just following orders." One is required to sacrifice his own life rather than kill an innocent person.

꽃

A man came before Rava and said to him, "The ruler of my town said to me, 'Go kill so-and-so, and if you do not kill him, then I will kill you.'"

Rava replied, "You must let him kill you, but do not kill. How do you know that your blood is redder? Maybe the blood of that man is redder?"

12.5 THE EXEGETICAL AND HOMILETICAL MIDRASHIM

12.5.1 *Lamentations Rabbah,* Proem 21: The Leper and the Temple[82]

This proem to the reading of Lamentations on the Ninth of Av, anniversary of the destruction of the Temple, opens with a passage describing the leper and his impurity which are allegorically interpreted to refer to the Temple. Zion is doomed because, like the leper, she is polluted and disgraced. The

---

78. A standard formula for introducing a tannaitic statement in the Talmud.

79. In the verse, "You shall revere each person his (or her) father and mother" (Lev. 19:3).

80. In the verse, "Honor your father and your mother" (Ex. 20:12).

81. Trans. S. Berrin.

82. J. Heinemann with J. J. Petuchowski, *Literature of the Synagogue* (New York: Behrman House, 1975), pp. 131–3.

unexpected comparison of the leper and the Temple builds up a tension that is resolved only at the end. At the same time, a message of consolation is derived from the notion that the period of exile will last only as long as the period of transgression.

𝕊

Rabbi Alexandri[83] opened his discourse. "And the leper in whom the plague is" (Lev. 13:45): "the leper" refers to the Temple; in whom the plague is—this is idol-worship which defiles like the plague (as it is said, "And they profaned My sanctuary and defiled it").[84] "His clothes shall be rent:" these are the priestly garments; "the hair of his head shall go loose:" as it is said, "And the covering of Judah was laid bare" (Is. 22:8): that which should have been covered,[85] He disclosed. "And he shall cover his upper lip:" When Israel was exiled among the nations of the world, not one of them was able to bring a word of Torah out of his mouth. "And shall cry, 'Unclean, unclean:'" this is the destruction of the First and Second Temples.[86]

Rabbi Yose ben Ḥalafta said: Whoever knows how many years Israel worshipped idols also knows when the son of David will come;[87] and we have three verses to support this statement. The first is, "And I will visit upon her the days of the Baalim,[88] wherein she offered unto them . . . " (Hos. 2:15). The second is, "And it came to pass that, as He called, and they would not hear; so shall they call,[89] and I will not hear" (Zech. 7:13). The third is, "And it shall come to pass that you shall say, 'Wherefore has the Lord our God done all these things to us?' . . . Just as you have forsaken Me, . . . so shall you serve strangers in a land that is not yours" (Jer. 5:19).

Rabbi Yoḥanan and Rabbi Simeon ben Lakish both commented on this matter. Rabbi Yoḥanan said: This point may be derived from "because, even because" (Lev. 26:43), indicating measure for measure.

---

83. He cannot be considered the author of the proem in its entirety, since his exposition is quoted at the end in his name.

84. No such biblical verse exists, so some manuscripts omit it. Cf. Ezek. 5:11, "For you have defiled my sanctuary with all your abominations."

85. Possibly the Holy of Holies, which was uncovered and laid bare at the time of the destruction of the Temple.

86. The aggadists often understood Scripture as hinting at events much later than the text in question.

87. For the total number of years of punishment and exile, after which the messiah will come, will be equal to the number of years Israel worshipped idols.

88. That is, the exact number of days.

89. For the same period of time.

Rabbi Simeon ben Lakish said: It may be derived from "Your land, strangers devour it against you" (Is. 1:7): i.e., corresponding to what you have done, strangers shall devour it. Rabbi Alexandri derived it from this verse, "All the days wherein the plague is in him he shall be unclean . . . he shall dwell alone"[90] (Lev. 13:46). "How does the city dwell alone . . ." (Lam. 1:1).

12.5.2 *Exodus Rabbah*, 1:18–26: The Early Life of Moses[91]

Exodus Rabbah contains two sections, the first finally edited in the tenth century C.E. and the second in the ninth. But the material in these texts stems from the later amoraic period, for the most part. In this extended selection, we see how such texts provide running commentary on the Torah.

�֎

18 "And Pharaoh charged all his people" (Ex. 1: 22)—Rabbi Yose ben Rabbi Ḥanina said: He decreed against his own people too. And why was this? Because his astrologers told him, "The mother of Israel's savior is already pregnant with him, but we do not know whether he is an Israelite or an Egyptian." Then Pharaoh assembled all the Egyptians before him and said: "Lend me your children for nine months that I may cast them in the river," as it is written: "Every son that is born, you shall cast into the river" (Ex. 1:22). It does not say "every son who is an Israelite," but "every son," whether he be Jew or Egyptian. But they would not agree, saying: "An Egyptian son would not redeem them; he must be a Hebrew."

"You shall cast into the river"—Why did they decree that they should cast them into the river? Because the astrologers foresaw that Israel's savior would be undone by means of water, and they thought that he would be drowned in the water; but, as we know, it was only on account of the well of water that the decree of death was pronounced upon him,[92] as it is said: "Because you believed not in Me" (Num. 20:12). The Rabbis say: "They took deep counsel so that God should not exact retribution from them through water. They knew that God repays measure for measure, and they were confident that He would no longer bring a flood upon the world, so they decided to drown them." "And every daughter you shall save alive"— what need did Pharaoh have to save the girls? What they said

---

90. Israel will "dwell alone" in exile for an amount of time corresponding to all the days in which it was polluted by idol-worship.

91. Trans. S. M. Lehrman, *Midrash Rabbah* (London: Soncino Press, 1977) vol. 2, pp. 25–39, 52.

92. Because Moses hit the rock and did not speak to it, as God had instructed.

in fact was: "Let us kill the males so that we may take unto ourselves the females for wives," for the Egyptians were steeped in immorality.

19 "And there went a man of the house of Levi" (2:1)—Where did he go? Rabbi Judah, the son of Rabbi Zebina, said: "He followed his daughter's advice.[93] It was taught: Amram was the leading man of his generation; 'and took to wife a daughter of Levi.' It does not say 'he took her back,' but 'he took,' proving," said Rabbi Judah, the son of Zebina, "that he went through a marriage ceremony with her. He placed her on the bridal litter, Miriam and Aaron dancing before them and the angels saying: 'As a joyful mother of children' (Ps. 113:9)."

"A daughter of Levi"—Is it possible that she was 130 years old and could still be called "a daughter?" for did not Rabbi Ḥama bar Ḥanina say it was Jochebed; and she was conceived on the way, and was born between the walls, as it is said: "And the name of Amram's wife was Jochebed, the daughter of Levi, who was born to Levi in Egypt" (Num. 26:59), which we explain to mean that her birth took place in Egypt, but not her conception, and yet she is called "daughter?"—"This shows," said Rabbi Judah, son of Rabbi Zebina, "that the symptoms of youth came back to her."

20 "And the woman conceived and bore a son" (2:2)—Rabbi Judah said: "Her giving birth is compared to her pregnancy. Just as her pregnancy was painless, so was her giving birth—a proof that righteous women were not included in the decree pronounced on Eve."[94]

"And when she saw him that he was a goodly child—Tob." It was taught: Rabbi Meir says: "His name was Tob." Rabbi Josiah says: "His name was Tobiah." Rabbi Judah says: "He was fit for prophecy." Others say: "He was born circumcised." The sages say: "When Moses was born, the whole house became flooded with light for here it says: 'and she saw him that he was a goodly child,' and elsewhere it says: 'And God saw the light, that it was good' (Gen. 1:40)."

21 "She took for him an ark of bulrushes" (2:3)—Why of bulrushes? Rabbi Eleazar said: "Because the money of the righteous is dearer to them than their persons.[95] Why? Because they do not commit robbery." Rabbi Samuel bar Naḥman explained: "Because a soft thing can withstand the pressure of both soft and hard elements."[96]

---

93. Miriam advised him to return to his wife, from whom he had separated for fear of Pharoah's decree against male children, and to continue to have children.

94. That birth would be painful (Gen. 3:16).

95. Hence, the ark was made of the cheapest material possible.

96. According to his view, they used the best material possible.

"And she daubed it with slime and with pitch"—It was taught: Slime within and pitch without, so that this righteous child should not inhale an evil smell.

"And she put the child therein, and laid it in the rushes (*suf*) by the river's brink" (2:3). Rabbi Eleazar says: "It was the Red Sea, because the Red Sea (*yam suf*)[97] reaches as far as the Nile." Rabbi Samuel bar Naḥman says: "It was a kind of reed, as in the reeds and rushes [*suf*] shall wither" (Is. 19:6). Why did they cast him into the river? So that the astrologers might think that he had already been cast into the water, and would not search for him.

22 "And his sister stood afar off" (2:4)—Why did Miriam stand afar off? Rabbi Amram in the name of Rav said: "Because Miriam prophesied, 'My mother is destined to give birth to a son who will save Israel' and when the house was flooded with light at the birth of Moses, her father arose and kissed her head and said: 'My daughter, your prophecy has been fulfilled.'" This is the meaning of: "And Miriam the prophetess, the sister of Aaron, took a timbrel" (Ex. 15:20)—"The sister of Aaron," but not of Moses?—She is so called because, in fact, she said this prophecy when she was yet only the sister of Aaron, Moses not having been born yet. Now that she was casting him into the river, her mother struck her on the head, saying: "My daughter, what about your prophecy?" This is why it says: "And his sister stood afar off, to know what would be the outcome of her prophecy. . . ."

23 "To bathe in the river" (2:5)—To cleanse herself from the idols of her father's palace. "And her maidens walked along"—Rabbi Yoḥanan said, the expression "walked" here means, walking to meet death, as it is said: "Behold, I am at the point to die" (Gen. 25:32). They said to her: "Your Highness, it is the general rule that when a king makes a decree, his own family will obey that decree even if everyone else transgresses it; but you are flagrantly disobeying your father's command?" Whereupon Gabriel came and smote them to the ground.

"And she sent her handmaid to fetch it. . . . " The Rabbis say that Pharaoh's daughter was leprous and went down to bathe, but as soon as she touched the ark she became healed. For this reason did she take pity upon Moses and loved him with an exceeding love . . . .

26 "And the child grew" (2:10). She[98] suckled him only for twenty-four months, and you say: "And the child grew?" This is to teach you that he grew abnormally.[99] Pharaoh's daughter used to kiss and hug him,

97. Literally, "Sea of Reeds," or rushes.
98. Jochebed, Moses's mother, served as his nurse (Ex. 2:8–9).

loved him as if he were her own son and would not allow him out of the royal palace. Because he was so handsome, everyone was eager to see him, and whoever saw him could not tear himself away from him. Pharaoh also used to kiss and hug him, and Moses used to take the crown of Pharaoh and place it upon his own head, as he was destined to do when he became great. It was this which God said to Miriam: "Therefore have I brought forth a fire from the midst of you" (Ezek. 28:18), and even so did the daughter of Pharaoh bring up him who was destined to exact retribution from her father.

The magicians of Egypt sat there and said: "We are afraid of him who is taking off your crown and placing it upon his own head, lest he be the one of whom we prophesy that he will take away the kingdom from you." Some of them counseled to slay him and others to burn him, but Jethro[100] was present among them and he said to them: "This boy has no sense. However, test him by placing before him a gold vessel and a live coal; if he stretches forth his hand for the gold, then he has sense and you can slay him, but if he makes for the live coal, then he has no sense and there can be no sentence of death upon him."

So they brought these things before him, and he was about to reach forth for the gold when Gabriel came and thrust his hand aside so that it seized the coal, and he thrust his hand with the live coal into his mouth, so that his tongue was burnt, with the result that he became slow of speech and of tongue.[101] "And she called his name Moses"—From here you can infer how great is the reward of those who perform kind acts, for although Moses had many names, the name by which he is known throughout the Torah is the one which Bithia,[102] the daughter of Pharaoh, called him, and even God called him by no other name.

12.5.3 *Pesiqta de-Rav Kahana* 25:1–4: A Penitential Homily[103]

Pesiqta de-Rav Kahana is a collection of homilies grouped around the Torah readings for festivals and special occasions. It is one of the oldest Midrashim, dating to some time in the sixth or early seventh century, predat-

---

99. He grew at a much faster rate than normal.

100. Later to become Moses' father-in-law.

101. Cf. Ex. 4:10.

102. This midrashic name for the daughter of Pharaoh, "Daughter of God," is not in the Bible. It is intended to portray her righteousness in saving Moses and raising him.

103. Trans. W. G. Braude, I. J. Kapstein, *Pesikta de-Rab Kahana, Rav Kahana's Compilation of Discourses for Sabbaths and Festal Days* (Philadelphia: Jewish Publication Society, 1975), pp. 386–9. This section is 26 in the Hebrew printed editions.

ing the Islamic conquest. This homily was intended for the Ten Days of Penitence between Rosh ha-Shanah and Yom Kippur.

৯৫

1 "Yet the righteous holds on his way, and he that has clean hands enhances strength" (Job 17:9). "The righteous" is the Holy One, of whom it is said "The Lord is righteous, He loves righteousness" (Ps. 11:7); "and he that has clean hands" is also the Holy One, to whom it is said "You who are of eyes too clean to behold evil" (Hab. 1:13); "he . . . enhances strength" is again the Holy One who enhances the strength of the righteous to enable them to do His will.

Another comment: "The righteous holds on his way" applies to Moses, of whom it is said "He persisted in executing the righteousness of the Lord, and His ordinances with Israel" (Deut. 33:21); "and he that has clean hands" also applies to Moses who was able to say to the people, "I have not taken one ass from them" (Num. 16: 15); "he . . . enhances strength" also applies to Moses who enhanced the strength of the Almighty, as when he said, "And now, I pray, let the strength of the Lord be enhanced" (Num. 14:17). Thereby—as Rabbi Jacob bar Aba citing Rabbi Yose bar Rabbi Ḥanina, and the Rabbis citing Rabbi Yoḥanan taught—Moses meant: May the strength of Your mercy be enhanced, so that the measure of mercy prevail over the measure of justice: "And now, I pray, let the strength of the Lord be enhanced [to this end]" (ibid.).

Rabbi Yudan told a parable of a strong man who was exercising with a block of stone that came from a stonecutter. A passer-by saw him and said: Your strength is marvelous. May your strength be enhanced by your exercise, as the strength of the Mighty One's mercy is enhanced by His exercise of it: "And now, I pray, let the strength of the Lord be enhanced" (ibid.).

Rabbi Azariah, citing Rabbi Judah bar Rabbi Simon, said: Whenever righteous men do the Holy One's will, they enhance the strength of the Almighty. [This is to say that Moses' doing of God's will gave God the strength to hold back from destroying Israel]. Hence Moses' plea, "And now, I pray, let the strength of the Lord be enhanced" (ibid.), [was answered]. On the other hand, when men do not do His will, then, if one dare say such a thing, "The Rock that begot you, you weaken" (Deut. 32:18).

Rabbi Judah bar Rabbi Simon, citing Rabbi Levi ben Perata, said: Whenever Israel do the Holy One's will, they enhance the power of the Almighty, as shown by the verse "When we are with God, we increase

[His] valor" (Ps. 60:14); but when Israel do not do His will, they "are gone without strength before the persecutor" (Lam. 1:6). Rabbi Aḥa said: Just as when Israel went into exile, they had to yield to the pressure of a powerful persecutor, so, when they are redeemed, they will be redeemed by the pull of a powerful redeemer. Note that the Hebrew word for "persecutor" is given here in the text not in its briefer form *rdf* but in its full form *rwdf* in order to signify the fullness of the persecutor's power; so, too, in order to signify the fullness of the redeemer's power, the Hebrew word for "redeemer" is given here in the text not in its briefer form *g'l*, but in its full form *gw'l*, as in the verse "A redeemer (*gw'l*) will come to Zion" (Is. 59:20).

Rabbi Isaac said: Except for one thing, Moses acknowledged the truth of all God told him. Moses, speaking boldly to the Holy One, complained: Master of universes, when a man sins, You are too patient in punishing him—collect from him at once what is due You. The Holy One replied: As you live, [for Israel's sake] you will have need of such patience from Me. And where in Scripture is Moses shown to have need of God's patience? The place where Scripture tells the incident of the spies who returned with an evil report about the Land—The "Lord be long in acts of patience" (Num. 14:18). We have no verses in Scripture to prove that, except for one thing, Moses admitted the truth of all God had told him. However, as we know from two verses, Moses admitted that God had to have patience. [One of the verses is cited just above: "The Lord be long in acts of patience"]. The other is [the verse "O God, Lord of vengeances" (Ps. 94:1) which is] mentioned by Rabbi Tanḥum bar Ḥanilai in reporting the following incident:

"While passing by a synagogue whose congregation consisted of people who had come from Babylon [to Palestine], I heard the voice of a youngster recite "Your testimonies are very sure . . . O Lord, for prolonging of days" (Ps. 93:5) and go on to recite the verse which directly follows it, "O Lord, God of vengeances" (Ps. 94:1). [It came to me, then, what Moses meant by this verse: not vengeance impatiently taken all at once, but vengeances taken as painlessly as possible—that is, as the plural indicates, vengeance taken only a little at a time]."

That this is the significance of the verse is shown, according to Rabbi Aḥa and Rabbi Tanḥum bar Rabbi Ḥiyya, who cited Rabbi Yoḥanan, [by the fact that the plural "vengeances" is paralleled] by the plural "patiences" in Num. 14:18 where the verse does not say "long in patience," but "long in patiences."

2 [In going on to describe God's attributes, Moses says], "The Lord . . . is plenteous in mercy, lifting up iniquity" (Num. 14:18). Rabbi Eleazar

and Rabbi Yose bar Rabbi Ḥanina differ in their comments on this verse. Rabbi Eleazar said: When both pans of the scale of justice balance exactly, a man's iniquitous deeds on one side and his good deeds on the other, the Holy One lifts out from the pan of iniquities one of the writs attesting the man's guilt, so that the good deeds [in the other pan] tip the balance. Hence we understand that what is meant by the words "lifting up *'awon*" ("iniquity") (Num. 14:18) is "lifting out iniquity, and thus tipping the balance (*'ayin*)."

Rav Huna said in the name of Rabbi Abbahu: If one dare even mention such a thing, forgetfulness is not one of God's attributes. But for Israel's sake He makes Himself be one who forgets. And the proof? The verse "Who is a God like You, who forgets iniquity and passes by transgression" (Mic. 7:18). David said likewise: "You forget the iniquity of Your people, and thus You ever pardon all their sin" (Ps. 85:3).

3 [Continuing, Moses speaks of God as] "Clearing, but not clearing" (Num. 14:18). That is, God clears those who repent of the transgressions they are charged with, but does not clear those who do not repent. God clears [transgressors who repent] in this world, but does not clear [transgressors who wait to repent] in the world-to-come. [Moses goes on furthermore to describe God as] "Visiting the iniquity of the fathers upon the children—upon the third, and upon the fourth generation (ibid.)." Consider the implications of this verse by analogy with a four-level storehouse, one level above the other: on one there is wine; on another, oil; on still another, honey; and on still another, water. If a fire begins on any one of the levels, what is above it will extinguish the fire. But if all four levels should have oil on them, all four will burn down. Likewise, if children persist, generation after generation, in the wicked ways of their forefathers, punishment therefor will be visited upon them. But if there should be an alternating of the generations, with one generation righteous and the next wicked, and so on, then "The fathers shall not be put to death for the children, neither shall the children be put to death for the fathers," etc. (Deut. 24:16). Hearing this, Moses rejoiced, saying, "In Israel there is no destroyer of grape vines who is also the son of a destroyer of grape vines."[104]

4 [Moses prayed to God]: "Pardon, I pray, the iniquity of this people, according unto the greatness of Your lovingkindness" (Num. 14:19). Rabbi Yose bar Rabbi Ḥanina and Rabbi Samuel bar Naḥman differ in their comments on this verse. According to one, the Holy One replied to

---

104. There will be no sinner who will continue in the evil ways of his parent.

Moses, "'From Egypt even till now' (ibid.)—have they not sinned against Me?" But according to the other, it was Moses who, acknowledging Israel's guilt in the words "from Egypt until now," went on to plead with the Holy One: "Master of universes, have You not pardoned and forgiven them in the past? Even so, pardon and forgive them in the future."

Rabbi Alexandri told a parable of two men who presented written petitions to the king. One presented it in his own name; it was granted [not in his name], however, but in the name of his ancestor. The other presented his petition in his ancestor's name, but it was granted to him in his own name.

Thus Hezekiah presented a petition in his own name: "Remember now, O Lord, I beseech You, how I have walked before You in truth," etc. (2 Kings 20:3); but it was granted in the name of his ancestor: "I will defend this city for My own sake, and for My servant David's sake" (2 Kings 20:6). Moses presented a petition in the name of his ancestry, but it was granted in his own name. He presented it in the name of his ancestry: "Remember Abraham, Isaac, and Israel, Your servants," etc. (Ex. 32:13), but it was granted in his own name: "I have pardoned according to your word" (Num. 14:20).

12.5.4 Babylonian Talmud Shabbat 30a–b: The Soul of Man is the Lamp of the Lord[105]

This fascinating example of fourth-century C.E. homiletics from the Land of Israel is preserved in the Babylonian Talmud. It seems to constitute the entire sermon, changed only slightly to fit its new context in the Talmud. The topic of the homily is the permissibility of putting out a lamp on the Sabbath for the benefit of a sick person.

᱖

The question was asked before Rabbi Tanḥum of Nawe: What about extinguishing a burning lamp for the sake of a sick person on the Sabbath? Thereupon he commenced and said:

You, Solomon, where is your wisdom and where is your understanding? It is not enough for you that your words contradict the words of your father David, but they are self-contradictory! Your father David said:[106] "The dead praise not the Lord" (Ps. 115 :17); while you said:[107] "Then I

---

105. Trans. Heinemann and Petuchowski, *Literature of the Synagogue*, pp. 145–8.
106. In the book of Psalms of which David is traditionally said to be the author.
107. In the book of Ecclesiastes, attributed to Solomon.

praise the dead who have died long since more than those who are still living" (Eccl. 4:2), but yet again you said, "For a living dog is better than a dead lion" (Eccl. 9:4).

Yet there is no difficulty.[108] As to what David said, "The dead praise not the Lord," this is what he meant: Let a man always engage in Torah and good deeds before he dies, for as soon as he dies he is restrained from the Torah and good deeds, and the Holy One, blessed be He, finds nothing to praise in him. And this is what Rabbi Yoḥanan said, "What is meant by the verse, 'Among the dead [I am] free' (Ps. 88:6)? Once a man dies he becomes free of the Torah and good deeds." And as to what Solomon said, "Then I praise the dead who have died long since"—When Israel sinned in the wilderness, Moses stood before the Holy One, blessed be He, and spoke many prayers and supplications before Him, but he was not answered. Yet when he exclaimed, "Remember Abraham, Isaac, and Israel, your servants!" (Ex. 32:13), he was immediately answered. Did not then Solomon well say, "Then I praise the dead who have died long since?"

Another interpretation: in worldly affairs, when a king of flesh and blood issues a decree, it is doubtful whether it will be obeyed or not. And even if you say that it is obeyed, it is obeyed during his lifetime but not after his death, whereas Moses our Teacher decreed many decrees and enacted numerous enactments, and they endure for ever and unto all eternity. Did then not Solomon well say, "Then I praise the dead who have died long since?"

Another interpretation: "Then I praise the dead, etc." is in accordance with Rav Judah's dictum in Rav's name: What is meant by, "Show me a token for good that those who hate me may see it, and be ashamed" (Ps. 86:17)? David prayed before the Holy One, blessed be He, "Sovereign of the Universe! Forgive me for that sin!"[109] "It is forgiven," replied He. "Show me a token in my lifetime," he entreated. "In your lifetime I will not make it known, but I will make it known in the lifetime of your son Solomon." For when Solomon built the Temple, he wanted to take the Ark into the Holy of Holies, whereupon the gates stuck to each other. Solomon uttered twenty-four prayers, yet he was not answered. Then he opened [his mouth] and exclaimed, "Lift up your heads, O you gates, and be you lifted up, you everlasting doors, that the King of glory may come in" (Ps. 24:7). They rushed upon him to swallow him up,[110] crying,

---

108. In interpreting this seeming contradiction.
109. The sin he committed with Bathsheba (2 Sam. 1:11–27).
110. They believed that by "King of glory" he was referring to himself.

"Who is the King of glory?" He answered: "The Lord, strong and mighty" (Ps. 24:8). Then he repeated, "Lift up your heads, O you gates; lift them up, you everlasting doors that the King of glory may come in. Who then is the King of glory? The Lord of hosts, He is the King of glory, Selah" (Ps. 24:9–10); yet he was not answered. But as soon as he prayed, "O Lord God, turn not away the face of Your anointed; remember the good deeds of David Your servant" (2 Chron. 6:42), he was immediately answered. In that hour the faces of all David's enemies turned black like the bottom of a pot, and all Israel knew that the Holy One, blessed be He, had forgiven him that sin. Did then not Solomon well say, "Then I praise the dead who have died long since?"

And thus it is written, "On the eighth day he (Solomon) sent the people away, and they blessed the king, and went unto their tents joyful and glad of heart for all the goodness that the Lord had shown unto David his servant, and to Israel his people" (1 Kings 8:66). "And they went unto their tents" means that they found their wives clean;[111] "joyful," because they had enjoyed the luster of the Divine Presence; "and glad of heart," because their wives conceived and each one bore a male child; "for all the goodness that the Lord had shown unto David his servant," that He had forgiven him that sin; "and to Israel his people," for He had forgiven them the sin of the Day of Atonement.[112]

And as to what Solomon said, "for a living dog is better than a dead lion"—that is as Rav Judah said in Rav's name: what is meant by the verse, "Lord, make me know my end, and the measure of my days, what it is; let me know how short-lived I am" (Ps. 39:5)?

David said before the Holy One, blessed be He, "Sovereign of the Universe! 'Lord, let me know my end.'"

"It is a decree before Me," He replied, "that the end of a mortal is not made known." "And the measure of my days what it is"—It is a decree before Me that a person's span [of life] is not made known."

"Let me know how short-lived I am"—He said to him: "You will die on the Sabbath."

"Let me die on the first day of the week!"[113]

"The reign of your son Solomon shall already have become due, and one reign may not overlap another even by a hairbreadth."

---

111. Ritually pure so that sexual relations were permitted.

112. On the occasion of the dedication of the Temple, a feast was held for fourteen days in the seventh month (1 Kings 8:2, 65), which, if it is assumed to have started on the first of the month, must have included the Day of Atonement, which then would not have been observed that year as a fast.

113. On the Sabbath the dead can neither be attended to nor be buried.

"Then let me die on the eve of the Sabbath!"

He said, "For a day in your courts is better than a thousand" (Ps. 84:11): better the one day that you sit and engage in study[114] than the thousand burnt-offerings which your son Solomon is destined to sacrifice before Me on the altar."

Every Sabbath day he (David) would sit and study all day. On the day that his soul was to be at rest, the angel of death stood before him but could not prevail against him, because Torah did not cease from his mouth. "What shall I do to him?" asked he. Now there was a garden before his house; so the angel of death went, ascended, and rustled in the trees. David went out to see; as he was ascending the stairs, they broke under him. Thereupon he became silent and his soul had repose.[115] Then Solomon sent to the house of study: "My father is dead and lying in the sun; and the dogs of my father's house are hungry;[116] what shall I do?" They sent back: "Cut up a carcass[117] and place it before the dogs, and as for your father, put a loaf of bread or a child upon him[118] and carry him away." Did then not Solomon well say, "for a living dog is better than a dead lion?"

And as for the question which I asked before you[119]—a lamp is called a lamp, and the soul of man is called a lamp:[120] better that the lamp of flesh and blood[121] be extinguished than the lamp[122] of the Holy One, blessed be He.[123]

12.5.5 *Targum* to Exodus 20:1–14: The Ten Commandments[124]

The reading of the Torah was accompanied by the oral translation of the text into Aramaic, the vernacular of most Jews in Byzantine Palestine and

---

114. Of the Torah.

115. He stopped studying Torah, and, as a result, the angel of death prevailed and David passed away.

116. They may therefore devour the corpse.

117. Ordinarily not permitted on the Sabbath.

118. Only in this fashion—for the sake of the loaf of bread, as it were—may a corpse be moved on the Sabbath.

119. Actually, "which you asked before me." According to Rashi, this circumlocution is an expression of humility on the part of Rabbi Tanḥum.

120. As it is said, "The soul of man is the lamp of the Lord" (Prov. 20:27). This proof text has, apparently, been omitted through a scribal error.

121. The lamp lit by human beings.

122. The soul of a human being.

123. He concludes that it is permitted to extinguish the physical lamp to protect the spiritual lamp—the live human being.

124. Trans. Leah D. Schiffman.

Sassanian Babylonia. With time, fixed targumic texts grew up which included numerous aggadic expansions of the biblical text. The Ten Commandments are presented here as an example of Palestinian targumic tradition which took final written form only after the end of the Byzantine period.

🔯

1 *And God spoke all these statements, saying:*[125]

2 The first statement, when it came out of the mouth of the Holy One[126]—may His name be blessed—like sparks and like lightening and like blazes of fire, a fiery torch to its right and a fiery torch to its left, sprouted and flew in the air of the heavens, returned and appeared over the camp of Israel, and returned and engraved itself on the Tablets of the Covenant that were placed in the hands of Moses, and went around them from one side to the other.[127] And then it cried out and said: My nation the children of Israel, *I am your God who* redeemed and *took you out* redeemed *from the land of Egypt, from the house of slaves'* slavery.

3 The second statement, when it came out of the mouth of the Holy One—may His name be blessed—like sparks and like lightening and like blazes of fire, a fiery torch to its right and a fiery torch to its left, sprouted and flew in the air of the heavens, returned and appeared over the camp of Israel, returned and engraved itself on the Tablets of the Covenant, and went around them from one side to the other. And then it cried out and said: My nation the children of Israel, *you may have no other gods, except for Me.* 4 *You may not make for yourselves a sculptured image, a form or any image that is in the heavens above, or that is in the earth below, or that is in the water below the earth.* 5 *You may not bow down to them and you may not worship* before *them for I, the Lord your God, am an impassioned* and revenging *God* and I take revenge with passion, *visiting the guilt of* evil *fathers upon* rebellious *children, upon the third* generation *and upon the fourth* generation, *of those who reject Me.* 6 [But I] maintain *kindness* and goodness *for a thousand generations of those who love* righteous ones *and those who observe My commandments* and My Torah.

---

125. Italicized phrases indicate the words of Exodus which the Targum weaves into its commentary.

126. The Targum follows the midrashic view that only the first two commandments were spoken by God himself.

127. The Targum follows the Rabbinic view that the Tablets of the Covenant were engraved from the surface through to the other side and could be read miraculously from both sides.

7 My nation the house of Israel: *not* one of *you shall* swear by any word *of the Lord your God* in vain *for* on the great day of judgment *the Lord will not* acquit any *one who* swears by *His name* in vain.

8 My nation the children of Israel: be mindful of *the Sabbath day to sanctify it.* 9 *Six days you shall labor and do all your work.* 10 *And the seventh day is* sabbath and rest before *the Lord your God. You shall not do any work—you, your sons, your daughters, your slaves, your handmaidens or your proselytes*—in your cities. 11 *For in six days the Lord* created *the heavens and the earth, the sea and all that is in them, and He rested on the seventh day; therefore the Lord blessed the sabbath day and sanctified it.*

12 My nation the house of Israel: be cautious, each one of you, regarding the *honor* of his *father* and the honor of his *mother—so that your days will be extended on the land that the Lord your God is giving you.*

13 My nation the children of Israel: *you shall not* be *murde*rers, nor friends nor partners with murderers. And you shall not appear in the assemblies of Israel with murderers in order that your children do not arise after you and learn themselves to associate with murderers as well. Because of the sin of murderers, the sword [of destruction] is released against the world.

My nation the children of Israel: *you shall not* be *adulte*rers, nor the friends nor partners of adulterers. And you shall not appear in the assemblies of Israel with adulterers in order that your children do not arise after you and learn themselves to associate with adulterers as well. Because of the sin of adulterers, death is released against the world.

My nation the children of Israel: *you shall not* be thieves, not friends or partners with thieves, and you shall not appear in the assemblies of Israel with thieves in order that your children do not arise after you and learn themselves to associate with thieves as well. Because of the sin of thievery, famine is released to the world.

My nation the children of Israel: *you shall not testify against your friends a false testimony.* And [you shall] not [be] friends nor partners with those who testify false testimonies. And you shall not appear in the assemblies of Israel with those who testify false testimonies in order that your children do not arise after you and learn themselves to associate with those who testify false testimonies. Because of the sin of false witnesses, clouds rise and dew does not fall and drought comes upon the world.

14 My nation the children of Israel: *do not* be those who *covet*, nor friends nor partners with those who covet. And you shall not appear in the assemblies of Israel with those who covet in order that your children

do not arise after you and learn themselves to associate with those who covet. And no one of you shall covet your friend's wife, nor his slave, nor his handmaiden, nor his ox, nor his ass, nor anything that he has. Because of the sin of those who covet, the government is jealous of people's property and takes it, and those wealthy in property become poor, and [thus] exile comes upon the world.

12.5.6 *Targum Jonathan* to Judges 5: An Aggadic Translation[128]

The Targum to Prophets was composed, according to talmudic tradition, by the tanna Jonathan ben Uziel (first century B.C.E.–first century C.E.). He was most likely the author of an early translation which appears in our editions with later aggadic additions. The difficult poetry of Judges 5 prompted the translation to provide numerous embellishments and non-literal translations.

🕎

1 *Deborah and Barak the son of Abinoam gave praise* at that time *saying:*[129]

2 *When* the house of Israel rebelled against the Torah, the nations came upon them and banished them from their cities. And when they returned to do the Torah, they prevailed over their enemies and drove them out from the area of the Land of Israel. Therefore, on account of the *punishment* of Sisera[130] and his entire camp, and on account of the miraculous event and redemption that was done to them, *to Israel,* the sages again sat publicly in the houses of assembly and taught *the nation* the words of Torah, and so *bless* and offer thanks before *the Lord.*

3 "*Hear, kings, listen rulers*" says Deborah in prophecy before the Lord, "*I am* praising, thanking and blessing before *the Lord, God of Israel.*"

4 Lord—your Torah which you gave to Israel—when they transgressed it, nations overpowered them. And when they turned to it, they prevailed over their enemies. *Lord,* on the day in which you revealed yourself to teach *from Seir* with appearance of your Presence *in the territory of Edom* the earth trembled and the heavens lowered and the clouds spread raindrops.

---

128. Trans. Leah D. Schiffman.

129. Italicized phrases indicate the words of Exodus which the Targum weaves into its commentary.

130. A Canaanite general.

5 *The mountains trembled from before the Lord. This Sinai* was shaken up; its smoke rose like the smoke of a furnace *because the Lord, God of Israel* was revealed upon it.

6 When they sinned *in the days of Shamgar the son of Anat,*[131] *in the days of Jael, they stopped* traveling *on the roads and those who were walking* on the paths, returned *to go on* roads that were concealed.

7 The ruin of the unwalled cities where they were dwelling *in the Land of Israel* was captured and their *inhabitants* were exiled *until I* was sent—*I, Deborah*—was sent to prophesy with*in* the Children of *Israel.*

8 When the house of Israel *chose* to worship *new gods/idols*[132]—that were made recently—that their fathers had not engaged themselves in,[133] the nations came upon them and banished them from their cities. But when they returned to the Torah, they could not overcome them; such that when the enemies *came upon them* with him [were men] holding *shields and spears with forty thousand* heads of the (military) camps, they were not able to wage war *in Israel.*

9 Says Deborah in prophecy: "I was sent to give praise *to the* scholars *of Israel who,* when that trouble occurred, did not stop studying Torah, and who—as it was appropriate for them—were sitting publicly in the houses of assembly and teaching *the nation* the words of Torah and *bless*ing and giving thanks before *the Lord.*"

10 Those who suspended their affairs and were *riding on donkeys* that were saddled with kinds of embroideries and going through all areas of the Land of Israel and are chosen to sit for judgment, they will be *going on their way* and *tell*ing about the mighty deed that was done for them.

11 From the place where they were attacking them and taking what was in their hands—the place of the publicans' seats[134] and the residence of robbers in back of the water-troughs—there they will offer thanks for the righteousness of the Lord, for the righteousness of him who was dwelling in the unwalled cities in the Land of Israel. Then they went down from the strong fortified cities to dwelling in the unwalled cities, the people of the Lord.

12 Sing praise, sing praise *Deborah,* sing praise and offer thanks, speak praise. *Arise Barak and capture your captives, son of Abinoam.*

13 *Then* one from the camp of Israel *went down* and shattered the strength of the mighty ones of the nations. Behold! It was not from their

---

131. One of the judges who was famed for his exploits against the Philistines.
132. Literally, "errors."
133. Their fathers had not worshipped them.
134. Where the tax collectors operated.

might, but rather the Lord shattered before *His nation* the strength *of the mighty ones* of their enemies.

14 *From* the house of *Ephraim* arose Joshua, son of Nun, the first to wage war against the house of *Amalek. After* him King Saul arose from those of the house of Benjamin. He killed those of the house of Amalek and waged war against the rest of the *nations. From* those of the house of *Machir,* those who were marked *went down* in battle *and from* the tribe of *Zebulun,* they were writing with a (reed) pen of a scribe.

15 *And* the officers of *Issachar* were listening to the words of *Deborah,* and the rest of the tribe of *Issachar* were serving before *Barak*; being *sent* from the cities of the *valley* to every place where it was necessary for him to send them. In the families of *Reuben,* there were many of deceitful *heart.*

16 *Why did you sit* (apart) from the camps of war? To sit *between* the borders *to hear* the good news, to know which camp was victorious, to be with it! Was it right for you to do—those of the house of *Reuben*—did you not know that before Him are revealed thoughts of the *heart*?

17 Those of the house of *Gilead* camped *across the Jordan and* those of the house of *Dan* passed over, crossed over the Jordan, put their possessions in *ships.* Those of the house of *Asher* camped on the *shore of the sea*; cities of the nations that they destroyed—they restored, built them and *dwelled* in them.

18 Those of the house of *Zebulun*—opposite the *nations* that blasphemed—gave their *life* over *to* killing. They *and* those of the house of *Naphtali*—all inhabitants of the land praised them.

19 The *kings came,* waged war. *Then they fought the kings of Canaan in Taanach.* They were camping and pitching their tents *by the waters of Megiddo. Silver* money *they did not take.*

20 *From the heavens,* war was waged with them—from the place where *the stars* come out *of their path* of motion—there the war was waged *with Sisera.*

21 *The Wadi Kishon* broke *them,* the *wadi* in which miracles and mighty acts were done for Israel in ancient times—that *Wadi Kishon*—there *my soul trampled* their mighty ones killed with *strength.*

22 *Then the hooves of their horses slipped,* the driving that drives before the chariots *of his mighty ones.*

23 *"Curse Meroz," said the* prophet *of the Lord, "Curse* and shatter the *inhabitants because they did not come to the assistance of* the nation of *the Lord* when it waged war *with mighty ones.*

24 *May Jael—the wife of Hever* the Shalmaite—*be blessed* with the blessing of good *women.* As one of the *women* who serve in the houses of study,
may she be blessed.

25 *He asked* her *for water, she gave him milk* to drink—to know if his
desire was for *the drinking bowls of the mighty ones,* she *brought* before him
cream cheese.

26 *She stretched her hand out to the tent peg and her right hand to the hammer* to destroy wicked ones and oppressors. *She* struck it down into *Sisera,
she* broke *his head, she crushed* his brain, *she* caused it to pass through *his
temple.*

27 *Between her legs he bent down, he fell, he lay down. Between her legs, he
bent down, he fell.* In the place *where he bent down, there he fell*—Sisera—disgraced.

28 From *the window, the mother of Sisera looked out* and was waiting atten-
tively from between the laths. She was saying, "*Why* are the *chariot*s of my
son *slow to come? Why* are the runners who are bringing me the victory
letter *delayed?*"

29 The wisest of *her chambermaids was answering her. Even she was answering* her by her wisdom, saying *to her:*

30 "*Are they not dividing (up)* what *they are finding,* giving as *loot a man*
and his household to each and every one? (There is) a lot of loot before
Sisera—*loot of colored embroideries* on his *neck,* rich possessions and precious
gifts before his might ones who *looted.*"

31 Like Sisera, *so shall perish all enemies* of *your* nation, O *Lord.* And
may His mercies be ready to give light with the light of His glory 343
times over,[135] *as the sun coming out in its might. And the Land* of Israel *was
quiet for forty years.*

12.6 JEWISH LITURGY

12.6.1 The Weekday Amidah: Themes of Jewish Prayer[136]

*The Amidah, the core of each prayer service, is said by the individual while
standing silently. Also called the "Eighteen Benedictions," it actually features
nineteen essential themes (one was added later), each represented by a blessing*

---

135. According to Is. 30:26, the light of the sun in the end of days will be increased by
seven times seven, that is, forty-nine. This factor multiplied by the seven days of creation
yields the number 343.

136. Trans. Heinemann and Petuchowski, *Literature of the Synagogue,* pp. 33–6 based on
text published by S. Schechter, "Genizah Specimens," *JQR* O.S. 10 (1898), pp. 656–8.

beginning with the formula "Blessed art thou, O Lord." The weekday Amidah includes petitions or requests that are omitted from the Sabbath and holiday Amidah which instead concentrate on the theme of the special occasion. The text reproduced here represents an early version of this prayer representing the liturgy in the Land of Israel.

1 Blessed art thou, O Lord,
Our God and God of our fathers,
God of Abraham, God of Isaac, and God of Jacob,
Great, mighty, and awesome God,
God Most High, creator of heaven and earth,
Our shield and shield of our fathers,
Our refuge in every generation.
Blessed art thou, O Lord, shield of Abraham.

2 Thou art mighty—humbling the haughty,
Powerful—calling the arrogant to judgment,
Eternal—reviving the dead,
Causing the wind to blow and the dew to fall,
Sustaining the living, resurrecting the dead—
O cause our salvation to sprout in the twinkling of an eye!
Blessed art thou, O Lord, who revivest the dead.

3 Thou art holy and thy name is awesome
And there is no god beside thee.
Blessed art thou, O Lord, the Holy God.

4 Graciously favor us, our Father, with understanding from thee,
And discernment and insight out of thy Torah.
Blessed art thou, O Lord, gracious bestower of understanding.

5 "Turn us to thee, O Lord, and we shall return,
Restore our days as of old" (Lam. 5:21).
Blessed art thou, O Lord, who desirest repentance.

6 Forgive us, our Father, for we have sinned against thee,
Erase and blot out our transgressions from before thine eyes,
For thou art abundantly compassionate.
Blessed art thou, O Lord, who forgivest readily.

7 Behold our afflictions and defend our cause,
And redeem us for thy name's sake.
Blessed art thou, O Lord, Redeemer of Israel.

8 Heal us, O Lord our God, of the pain in our hearts,
Remove grief and sighing from us
And cause our wounds to be healed.
Blessed art thou, O Lord, who healest the sick of Israel thy people.

9 Bless this year for us, O Lord our God,
And may its harvest be abundant.
Hasten the time of our deliverance,
Provide dew and rain for the earth,
And satiate thy world from thy storehouses of goodness,
And bestow a blessing upon the work of our hands.
Blessed art thou, O Lord, who blessest the years.

10 Blow a blast upon the great shofar for our freedom
And raise a banner for the ingathering of our exiles.
Blessed art thou, O Lord, who gatherest the dispersed of thy people Israel.

11 Restore our judges as of old,
And our leaders as in days of yore,
And reign over us—thou alone.
Blessed art thou, O Lord, Lover of justice.

12 May there be no hope for the apostates,
And speedily uproot the kingdom of arrogance in our own day.
May the Nazarenes and the sectarians[137] perish in an instant.
May "they be blotted out of the book of living,
And may they not be written with the righteous" (Ps. 69:29).
Blessed art thou, O Lord, who subduest the arrogant.[138]

13 Show abundant compassion to the righteous converts,
And give us a good reward together with those who do thy will.
Blessed art thou, O Lord, Stay[139] of the righteous.

14 Have compassion, O Lord, our God, in thine abundant mercy,
On Israel thy people,
And on Jerusalem thy city,
And Zion, the abode of thy glory,

---

137. Jewish Christians and Gentile Christians.

138. This blessing was modified in the time of the rise of early Christianity to insure that those who were *minim* (Jewish Christians) would not serve as leaders of the prayers in the synagogue. When the separation of the Jewish Christians from the synagogue was accomplished, the prayer was retained as a general malediction against all the enemies of Israel.

139. Supporter, sustainer.

And upon the royal seed of David, thy justly anointed.
Blessed art thou, O Lord, God of David, Rebuilder of Jerusalem.[140]

15 Hear, O Lord, our God, the voice of our prayers,
And have compassion upon us,
For thou art a gracious and compassionate God.
Blessed art thou, O Lord, who hearest prayer.

16 May it be thy will, O Lord, our God, to dwell in Zion,
And may thy servants worship thee in Jerusalem.
Blessed art thou, O Lord, whom we worship with reverence.

17 We thank thee,
Our God and God of our fathers,
For all of the goodness, the lovingkindness, and the mercies
With which thou hast requited us, and our fathers before us.
For when we say, "our foot slips"
Thy mercy, O Lord, holds us up.
Blessed art thou, O Lord, to whom it is good to give thanks.

18 Bestow thy peace
Upon Israel thy people,
And upon thy city,
And upon thine inheritance,
And bless us all, together.
Blessed art thou, O Lord, Maker of peace.

12.6.2 The Qedushah: The Mystical Praise of God[141]

During the morning service the reader or cantor repeats the Amidah before the congregation with the addition of the Qedushah ("Sanctification Prayer") which is recited together with the congregation. The Qedushah is a mystical description of the angels, Seraphim, praising God in the highest heavens just as humans praise Him on earth. This vision of heavenly praise comes from the books of the prophets Isaiah and Ezekiel. The version given here is for the Sabbath and festival additional service.

---

140. This benediction is a prayer for the restoration of the Davidic House and rebuilding of Jerusalem in the messianic era.
141. Trans. Heinemann and Petuchowski, *Literature of the Synagogue*, pp. 78–9.

ॐ

READER: We will reverence and sanctify thee in words of the holy Seraphim, who hallow thy name in the sanctuary, as it is written by thy prophet, "and they called one unto the other and said:

CONGREGATION: Holy, holy, holy is the Lord of hosts: the whole earth is full of his glory" (Is. 6:3).

READER: His glory fills the universe; his ministering angels ask one another, "Where is the place of his glory?" Those over against them say, "Blessed—

CONGREGATION: Blessed be the glory of the Lord from his place" (Ezek. 3:12).

READER: From his place may he turn in mercy and be gracious to the people who, evening and morning, twice every day, proclaim the unity of his name, saying in love, "Hear—"

CONGREGATION: "Hear, O Israel: the Lord our God, the Lord is One" (Deut. 6:4).

READER: One is our God; he is our Father; he is our King; he is our Deliverer; and he in his mercy will let us hear a second time, in the presence of all living [his promise], "To be your God."

CONGREGATION: "I am the Lord your God" (Num. 15:41).

READER: And in thy holy Scriptures it is written, saying,

CONGREGATION: "The Lord will reign for ever, your God, O Zion, unto all generations. Praise the Lord" (Ps. 146: 10).

READER: Through all generations we will declare thy greatness, and to all eternity we will proclaim thy holiness, and thy praise, our God, shall not depart from our mouth for ever, for thou art a great and holy God and King. Blessed art thou, O Lord, the holy God.

12.6.3 The Additional Amidah for Rosh ha-Shanah: Themes of the Day of Remembrance[142]

Each festival features special Amidah themes. In the Musaf (additional) Amidah for Rosh ha-Shanah following the morning service, the themes of the day are connected with God's judgment of the world and the final elimination of evil. Stress is laid on the power and kingship of God, His "remembrance" of every deed so that there can be no secrets from Him, and the shofar, the ram's horn, which symbolizes both God's revelation and the call to repentance. This text reached almost its present form by the end of the Rabbinic period.

---

142. Trans. Heinemann and Petuchowski, *Literature of the Synagogue*, pp. 62–9.

Now, Lord our God, impose thine awe upon all thy works, and thy dread upon all thou hast created, that all works may fear thee and all creatures prostrate themselves before thee, that they may all form a single band to do thy will with a perfect heart, even as we know, Lord our God, that dominion is thine, strength is in thy hand, and might in thy right hand, and that thy name is to be feared above all that thou hast created.

Give then glory, O Lord, to thy people, praise to them that fear thee, hope to them that seek thee, and speech to them that wait for thee, joy to thy land, gladness to thy city, a flourishing horn[143] unto David thy servant, and a clear shining light unto the son of Jesse, thine anointed, speedily in our days.[144]

Then shall the just see this and be glad, and the upright shall exult, and the pious triumphantly rejoice, while iniquity shall close her mouth, and wickedness shall be wholly consumed like smoke, when thou makest the dominion of arrogance to pass away from the earth.[145]

And thou, O Lord, shalt reign, thou alone, over all thy works on Mount Zion, the dwelling place of thy glory, and in Jerusalem, thy holy city, as it is written in thy holy words, "The Lord shall reign for ever, thy God, O Zion, unto all generations, Praise the Lord" (Ps. 146:10).

Thou art holy and thy name is awesome, and there is no god beside thee, as it is written, "And the Lord of hosts is exalted in judgment, and the holy God is sanctified in righteousness" (Is. 5:16). Blessed art thou, O Lord, the holy king.

Thou hast chosen us from all peoples; thou hast loved us and taken pleasure in us, and hast exalted us above all tongues; thou hast sanctified us by thy commandments, and brought us near unto thy service, O our King, and called us by thy great and holy name.

And thou hast given us in love, O Lord our God, this Day of Remembrance, a day of blowing the shofar; a holy festival, as a memorial of the exodus from Egypt.[146]

But on account of our sins we were exiled from our land, and removed far from our country, and we are unable to fulfill our obligations in thy

---

143. A sign of victory and salvation.

144. A reference to the rebuilding of the Temple and the restoration of the Davidic monarchy in the hoped-for messianic age.

145. This paragraph expresses the theme of the utter destruction of evil in the end of days.

146. Rosh ha-Shanah is also a memorial of the Exodus from Egypt because it was after the Exodus that the Jewish people were commanded to observe all the holidays.

chosen house, that great and holy temple which was called by thy name, because of the hand that has been stretched out against thy sanctuary. May it be thy will, O Lord our God and God of our fathers, merciful King, that thou mayest again in thine abundant compassion have mercy upon us and upon thy sanctuary, and speedily rebuild it and magnify its glory. Our father, our king, do thou speedily make the glory of thy kingdom manifest upon us; shine forth and exalt thyself upon us in the sight of all living; bring our scattered ones among the nations near unto thee, and gather our dispersed from the ends of the earth. Lead us with exultation unto Zion thy city, and unto Jerusalem the place of thy sanctuary with everlasting joy;[147] and there we will prepare before thee the offerings that are obligatory for us, the continual offerings according to their order, and the additional offerings according to their enactment; and the additional offerings of this Day of Remembrance, we will prepare and offer unto thee in love according to the precept of thy will, as thou hast prescribed for us in thy Torah through the hand of Moses thy servant, by the mouth of thy glory, as it is said:

"And in the seventh month, on the first day of the month,[148] you shall have a holy convocation; you shall do no servile work: it shall be a day of blowing the shofar unto you. And you shall offer a burnt offering for a sweet savor unto the Lord; one young bullock, one ram, seven he-lambs of the first year without blemish" (Num. 29.1–2). And their meal-offering and their drink-offerings as has been ordained; three tenth parts of an ephah for each bullock; and two tenth parts for the ram, and one tenth part for each lamb, with wine according to the drink-offering thereof, and two he-goats wherewith to make atonement, and the two continual offerings according to their enactment; beside the burnt-offering of the New Moon[149] and the meal-offering thereof, and the continual burnt-offering and the meal-offering thereof, and their drink-offerings, according to their ordinance, for a sweet savor, an offering made by fire unto the Lord.

It is our duty[150] to praise the Master of all things, to ascribe greatness to him who formed the world in the beginning, since he has not made us

---

147. The return to Jerusalem and rebuilding of the Temple will allow the preparation of the sacrificial offerings once part of its ritual. The prayer then continues to enumerate the specific offerings which were part of the divine service for Rosh ha-Shanah.

148. The date designated in the biblical list of holy days as Rosh ha-Shanah.

149. As the first of the month, Rosh ha-Shanah is also the New Moon of the seventh month, so the New Moon offering is also required. See Num. 28:11–15.

150. This and the following paragraph ("We therefore hope . . .") are termed the Alenu prayer. From the Middle Ages, it became customary to end every Jewish service with this proclamation of divine kingship in the present and in the end of days.

like the nations of other lands, and has not placed us like other families of the earth, since he has not assigned unto us a portion as unto them, nor a lot as unto all their multitude. For they bow before those that are vain and of no purpose, and pray unto a god that cannot save. But we bend the knee and bow and acknowledge before the supreme King of kings, the Holy One, blessed be he, who stretched forth the heavens and laid the foundations of the earth, the seat of whose glory is in the heavens above, and the abode of whose might is in the loftiest heights. He is our God; there is none else: in truth he is our King; there is none beside him: as it is written in his Torah, "And you shall know this day, and lay it to your heart, that the Lord he is God in heaven above and upon the earth beneath: there is none else" (Deut. 4:39).

We therefore hope in thee, O Lord our God, that we may speedily behold the glory of thy might, when thou wilt remove the abominations from the earth, and the idols will be utterly cut off, when the world will be perfected under the kingdom of the Almighty, and all the children of flesh will call upon thy name, when thou wilt turn unto thyself all the wicked of the earth. Let all the inhabitants of the world perceive and know that unto thee every knee must bend, every tongue must swear. Before thee, O Lord our God, let them bow and fall; and unto thy glorious name let them give honor; let them all accept the yoke of thy kingdom_and do thou reign over them speedily, and for ever and ever. For the kingdom is thine, and to all eternity thou wilt reign in glory; as it is written in thy Torah, "The Lord shall reign forever and ever" (Ex. 15:18)....[151]

Our God and God of our fathers, reign thou in thy glory over the whole universe, and be exalted above all the earth in thy honor, and shine forth in the splendor and excellence of thy might upon all the inhabitants of thy world, that whatsoever has been made may know that thou hast made it, and whatsoever has been created may understand that thou hast created it, and whatsoever has breath in its nostrils may say, the Lord God of Israel is King, and his dominion rules over all. Sanctify us by thy commandments, and grant our portion in thy Torah; satisfy us with thy goodness, and gladden us with thy salvation: O purify our hearts to serve thee in truth, for thou art God in truth, and thy word is truth, and endures for ever. Blessed art thou, O Lord, King over all the earth, who sanctifiest Israel and the Day of Remembrance.

---

151. After this general introduction to the theme of the Kingship of God, ten verses are quoted from Scripture referring to God as the one king and ruler over all the earth.

Thou rememberest what was wrought from eternity and art mindful of all that has been formed from of old:[152] before thee all secrets are revealed and the multitude of hidden things from the beginning; for there is no forgetfulness before the throne of thy glory, nor is there anything hidden from thy eyes. Thou rememberest every deed that has been done; not a creature is concealed from thee; all things are manifest and known unto thee, O Lord our God, who lookest and seest to the end of all generations. For thou wilt bring the appointed time of remembrance when every spirit and soul shall be visited, and the multitudinous works be remembered with the innumerable throng of thy creatures. From the beginning thou didst make this thy purpose known, and from aforetime thou didst disclose it. This day, on which was the beginning of thy work, is a memorial of the first day, for it is a statute for Israel, a decree of the God of Jacob. On it also sentence is pronounced upon the lands—which of them is destined to the sword and which to peace, which to famine and which to plenty; and each separate creature is visited, and recorded for life or for death. Who is not visited on this day? For the remembrance of every creature comes before thee, each man's deeds and destiny, his works and ways, his thoughts and schemes, his imaginings and achievements. Happy is the man who forgets thee not, and the son of man who strengthens himself in thee; for they that seek thee shall never stumble, neither shall any be put to shame who trust in thee. The remembrance of all works comes before thee, and thou enquirest into the doings of them all. Of Noah also thou wast mindful in thy love, and didst visit him with a promise of salvation and mercy, when thou broughtest the waters of the flood to destroy all flesh on account of their evil deeds. . . .[153]

Our God and God of our fathers, let us be remembered by thee for good: grant us a visitation of salvation and mercy from thy heaven, the heavens of old; and remember unto us, O Lord our God, the covenant and the kindness and the oath which thou didst swear unto Abraham our father on Mount Moriah:[154] and may the binding with which Abraham

---

152. The theme of remembrance is here introduced. This theme includes the declaration that God is the God of history, continually involved in human affairs, knows all deeds, probes all secrets, forgets nothing, and judges the world. Therefore, He is the only one to whom humankind can turn in repentance.

153. Now follow ten quotations from Scripture regarding remembrance, covenant, and God's compassion for His creatures.

154. The theme of remembrance is connected with the theme of the shofar, the ram's horn, by the mention of Abraham and Isaac on Mount Moriah. When God sent an angel to prevent Abraham from sacrificing Isaac, He also provided a ram for the sacrifice. The willingness of Abraham and Isaac to carry out God's order is an example of the merit of the forefathers which reflects positively on his descendents.

our father bound his son Isaac on the altar appear before thee, how he overbore his compassion in order to perform thy will with a perfect heart. So may thy compassion overbear thy anger against us; in thy great goodness may the fierceness of thy wrath turn aside from thy people, thy city (Jerusalem) and thy inheritance. Fulfill unto us, O Lord our God, the word in which thou hast promised us in thy Torah through the hand of Moses thy servant, from the mouth of thy glory, as it is said, "But I will remember unto them the covenant of their ancestors, whom I brought forth out of the land of Egypt in the sight of the nations, that I might be their God: I am the Lord" (Lev. 26:45). For thou art he who remembers from eternity all forgotten things, and before the throne of whose glory there is no forgetfulness. O remember the binding of Isaac this day in mercy unto his seed. Blessed art thou, O Lord, who rememberest the covenant.

Thou didst reveal thyself in a cloud of glory unto thy holy people in order to speak with them.[155] Out of heaven thou didst make them hear thy voice and wast revealed unto them in clouds of purity. The whole world trembled at thy presence, and the works of creation were in awe of thee, when thou didst thus reveal thyself, O our King, upon Mount Sinai to teach thy people the Torah and commandments, and didst make them hear thy majestic voice and thy holy utterances out of flames of fire. Amid thunders and lightnings thou didst manifest thyself to them, and while the shofar sounded thou didst shine forth upon them. . . .[156]

Our God and God of our fathers, sound the great shofar for our freedom, lift up the ensign to gather our exiles; bring our scattered ones among the nations near unto thee, and gather our dispersed from the ends of the earth. Lead us with exultation unto Zion thy city, and unto Jerusalem the place of thy sanctuary with everlasting joy; and there we will prepare before thee the offerings that are obligatory for us, as is commanded us in thy Torah through the hand of Moses thy servant, from the mouth of thy glory, as it is said, "And in the day of your gladness, and in your set feasts, and in the beginnings of your months, you shall blow with the trumpets over your burnt-offerings, and over the sacrifices of your peace-offerings; and they shall be to you for a remembrance before your God: I am the Lord your God" (Num. 10:10). For thou hearest the sound of the shofar and givest heed to the trumpet blast, and there is none like

---

155. The symbolic shofar appears once again at the revelation at Sinai when the Torah was revealed amidst the sound of the shofar.

156. Here follow ten verses regarding the significance of the shofar.

unto thee. Blessed art thou, O Lord, who in mercy hearest the sound of the trumpet of thy people Israel.[157]

12.6.4 Concluding Service for the Day of Atonement: A Last-Minute Prayer for Forgiveness[158]

The Concluding Service of the Day of Atonement, Yom Kippur, is the last moment during the judgment period of the Jewish calendar between Rosh ha-Shanah and Yom Kippur, ten days in all, to pray for complete repentance and the granting of a merciful judgment. God is praised as slow to anger, desiring not the death of the wicked but their penitence.

ॐ

Thou givest a hand to transgressors, and thy right hand is stretched out to receive the penitent; thou hast taught us, O Lord our God, to make confession unto thee of all our sins, in order that we may cease from the violence of our hands, that thou mayest receive us into thy presence in perfect repentance, even as fire-offerings and sweet savors,[159] for thy words' sake which thou hast spoken. Endless would be the fire-offerings required for our guilt, and numberless the sweet savors for our trespasses; but thou knowest that our latter end is the worm,[160] and hast therefore multiplied the means of our forgiveness. What are we? What is our life? What is our piety? What our righteousness? What our helpfulness? What our strength? What our might? What shall we say before thee, O Lord our God and God of our fathers? Are not all the mighty men as nought before thee, the men of renown as though they had not been, the wise as if without knowledge, and the men of understanding as if without discernment? For most of their works are void, and the days of their lives are vanity before thee, and the preeminence of man over the beast is nought, for all is vanity.

Thou hast distinguished man from the beginning, and hast recognized his privilege that he might stand before thee; for who shall say unto thee, What dost thou? and if he be righteous what can he give thee? But thou of thy love hast given us, O Lord our God, this Day of Atonement to be the season of pardon and forgiveness for all our iniquities, that we may cease from the violence of our hands, and may return unto thee to do the

---

157. A reference to the shofar-blowing on Rosh ha-Shanah during the Additional (Musaf) Service.

158. Trans. Heinemann and Petuchowski, *Literature of the Synagogue*, pp. 72–3.

159. Incense offerings.

160. A reference to the decay of the body after death.

statutes of thy will with a perfect heart. In thine abounding compassion, have mercy upon us, for thou delightest not in the destruction of the world, as it is said, "Seek the Lord, while he may be found, call upon him while he is near" (Is. 55:6). And it is said, "Let the wicked forsake his way, and the man of iniquity his thoughts; and let him return unto the Lord, and he will have mercy upon him; and to our God for he will abundantly pardon" (ibid., 7). But thou art a God ready to forgive, gracious and merciful, slow to anger, plentiful in kindness, and abounding in goodness; thou delightest in the repentance of the wicked, and hast no pleasure in their death; as it is said, "Say unto them: As I live, says the Lord God, I have no pleasure in the death of the wicked; but that the wicked turn from his way and live: turn, turn from your evil ways; for why will you die, O house of Israel?" (Ezek. 33:11).

12.6.5 A Qedushta by Yannai: On the Recitation of the Shema[161]

The following is the fourth section of a Qedushta (a liturgical poem for the Sabbath morning service) by Yannai, a poet who lived in Byzantine Palestine. It is meant for recitation on the Sabbath when, according to the 3-year Torah reading cycle followed in the Land of Israel in Late Antiquity, the Torah reading begins with Deut. 6:4 (the Shema). The first two lines end with the word, "Israel." The remaining lines end in "-im," which achieves the rhyme in this poem. Obviously, this structure cannot be reproduced in English, but this rendition tries to preserve something of the flavor of the original.

🦂

How blessed is the fountain of Israel![162]
They say the blessings[163] and recite the "Hear, O Israel."
They sit in Your presence,[164] thinking of Your Name,
Audible to one another, as together they proclaim.

---

161. Trans. Petuchowski, in Heinemann and Petuchowski, *Literature of the Synagogue*, pp. 219–21.

162. The Jewish people.

163. In both the evening service and the morning service, the recitation of the Shema is preceded by two blessings—the first praising God as creator of the heavenly lights, and the second praising God as giver of the Torah. See texts 13.2.2, 13.2.5 in this volume.

164. The Houses of Hillel and Shammai argued whether the Shema should be recited in a sitting or in a standing position. The decision was in accordance with the House of Hillel who contended that if one were standing prior to the Shema one should remain standing; but, if seated, remain seated (Mishnah Berakhot 1:3).

How beautiful they who proclaim it morn and night,
Pleasant their looks, their voices a delight!
Pledged one to another in Unity's affirmation,
They meddle not with those who seek its alteration.

Loving with their heart and soul and might,
They bow their heads in holy fright.
Worshipping, they bend the knee.
Twice every day, perpetually,
They bless and sanctify Your Name, O Holy One.

12.6.6 A Liturgical Poem for the Sabbath Preceding Passover: Miracles that Occurred at Night[165]

The following is a section of a poem composed by Yannai for the Sabbath preceding Passover. It is based on the Rabbinic view that "all the miracles which were wrought for Israel, and the punishment of the wicked on their behalf, took place in the night" (Numbers Rabbah 20:12). This particular section of Yannai's composition has become so popular that it was incorporated into the Ashkenazic version of the Passover Haggadah for recitation on the first Seder night. The first letters of each line form a complete alphabetical acrostic; each line ends with the word "night." The accompanying notes show how heavily these poems rely on biblical allusions.

࿋

And so it came to pass[166] in the middle of the night.
It was then You worked many miracles at night.
At the beginning of the watches[167] on this night,
You gave victory to the convert[168] when
    divided was the night.
And so it came to pass in the middle of the night.

You sentenced the king of Gerar[169] in a dream of the night
You terrorized the Aramean[170] in the yester night.

---

165. Trans. J. Sloan in, Heinemann and Petuchowski, *Literature of the Synagogue*, pp. 223–5. The footnotes, based on the commentary of E. D. Goldschmidt, are by N. N. Glatzer, and appear in his edition of *The Passover Haggadah* (New York: Schocken Books, 1953).

166. Cf. Ex. 12:29.

167. The night is divided into three watches.

168. Abraham, during the battle against the four kings (Gen. 14:15).

169. Abimelech, who "sent and took" Sarah after "Abraham said of Sarah, his wife: 'She is my sister'" (Gen. 20:2–3).

170. Laban, whom God told "yesternight" not to harm Jacob (Gen. 31:29).

And Israel[171] with an angel fought and overcame him at night.
And so it came to pass in the middle of the night.

You crushed the firstborn seed of Pathros[172] in
    the middle of the night.
They found their strength gone when they rose at night.
The lord of Harosheth's[173] host were levelled by
    the stars[174] of night.
And so it came to pass in the middle of the night.

The blasphemer[175] thought to ravage Your chosen;[176]
You rotted his corpses[177] at night.
Bel[178] and his pedestal fell in the middle of the night.
To the greatly beloved man[179] was bared the
    secret vision of night.
And so it came to pass in the middle of the night.

He who grew drunk from the sacred vessels[180]
    was slain[181] on that very night.
He who was saved from the lion's den[182]
    interpreted dread dreams of night.
The Agagite nurtured hate, and wrote scrolls[183] at night.
And so it came to pass in the middle of the night.

You began to overpower him when sleep fled[184] at night.
You will trample down the winepress[185] for him[186]

---

171. Jacob whose name was changed to Israel (Gen. 32:29; Hos. 12:5).

172. Egypt. The firstborn sons were killed in the Tenth Plague (Gen. 10:14; Jer. 44:1).

173. Sisera, the Canaanite general who "dwelt in Harosheth-goiim," and was defeated by Deborah and Barak (Jud. 4:13).

174. "The stars in their courses fought against Sisera" (Jud. 5:20).

175. Sennacherib, king of Assyria, who sent a messenger "to taunt the living God" (Kings 19:4, 22).

176. Zion, the chosen city (Ps. 132:13).

177. "The angel of the Lord went forth, and smote in the camp of the Assyrians..." (2 Kings 19:35).

178. The idol in the book of Daniel.

179. Daniel to whom the interpretation of Nebuchadnezzar's dream was revealed (Dan. 2:19).

180. Belshazzar, the Babylonian king, who "made a great feast for a thousand of his lords" (Dan. 5:1) at which he drank from the vessels of the Temple in Jerusalem (Dan. 5:2–4).

181. Dan. 5:30.

182. Daniel (Dan. 6:20).

183. Haman, who sent letters to the king's provinces to have all the Jews destroyed (Est. 3:13).

184. From Ahasuerus (Est. 6:1).

185. I. e., destroy (cf. Is. 63:3).

186. For the sake of Israel who asks... (Is. 63:3).

who asks, "Watchman, what of the night?"
He will sing out like a watchman, saying,
    "The morning cometh and also the night.[187]

And so it came to pass in the middle of the night.
O bring near the day that is neither day nor night.[188]
O, Most High, announce, yours the day is, yours the night.[189]
Set watchmen[190] to watch your city[191] all the day and all the night.
Brighten, like the light of day, the dark of night.
And so it came to pass in the middle of the night.

---

187. Is. 21:12. The question is taken to mean: "When will the deliverance from the oppressor come?" The answer given is "The morning cometh" for you, "and also the night—" for your oppressors.

188. The day of messianic deliverance (Zech. 14:7).

189. Ps. 74:16.

190. Is. 62:6.

191. Jerusalem.

13

The Life of Torah

By the time the talmudic period drew to a close, the outlines of Rabbinic Judaism had fully taken shape. A developed set of theological beliefs and practices had emerged. Common practices and attitudes were widely held among Palestinian and Babylonian Jews even though differences of opinion and practice certainly remained. But these divergences related to the particular application of an overarching system which was the object of Rabbinic consensus and was, by this time, enshrined in a complex set of textual traditions.

The basic belief of Judaism is God's oneness, as reflected in a text from the Babylonian Talmud Pesaḥim (text 13.1.1), an aggadic explanation of a liturgical addition to the otherwise biblical Shema texts. The Shema occupies a central position in Jewish theology, and was, therefore, the subject of numerous aggadic discussions. We should not be surprised that *Deuteronomy Rabbah* (text 13.1.2) contains an expanded version of this same aggadah. The oneness of God is also the theme of a section of *Midrash Tanḥuma Vayera* 6 (text 13.1.3), which emphasizes God's justice. *Tanḥuma Vayera* 5, an excerpt from a different version of this Midrash (text 13.1.4), describes a dramatic confrontation between Moses and Aaron and Pharaoh in which Pharaoh is taught that the God of Israel rules the universe. God's presence fills the entire world, as asserted by *Exodus Rabbah, Shemot* (text 13.1.5).

Stressing the acceptance of the basic theological beliefs of Judaism, the Rabbis set forth specific requirements regarding the daily recitation of the Shema in Mishnah Berakhot (text 13.2.1). The

Shema was accompanied by benedictions recited before and after. The benedictions before the morning Shema (text 13.2.2) emphasize the acceptance of God and His commandments, and the Sabbath version, presented here, expands on God's role as creator of the heavenly luminaries. This passage also includes a description of the angelic praise of God in the heavens. The Shema itself (text 13.2.3), recited morning and evening, contains three biblical paragraphs which are interpreted in the benedictions that precede and follow them. The Shema is the central proclamation of Jewish faith and commitment. Like the third paragraph of the Shema, the benediction recited afterwards (text 13.2.4) commemorates God's redemption of Israel from slavery in Egypt and assures the Jewish people that He will again redeem them. A similar set of benedictions is recited along with the evening Shema (text 13.2.5). The evening benedictions stress trust in God and include a fourth blessing asking God's protection over Israel.

Rabbinic law required that the Jew pray thrice daily, and the central prayer of each service is the Amidah (Standing Prayer), also known as the Eighteen Benedictions. Exemptions from reciting these prayers are outlined in Mishnah Berakhot (text 13.2.6). The times for these prayers were specifically fixed by Mishnah Berakhot (text 13.2.7) so as to coincide with the times of various sacrifices offered in the Temple. Prayer had to be recited with the proper intention and seriousness according to the same source (text 13.2.8). For Rabbinic Judaism the gift of food from God must always be acknowledged, and the specific benedictions which the Rabbis required before partaking of food are outlined by Mishnah Berakhot (text 13.2.9). To give thanks to God after eating, the Grace after Meals (text 13.2.10) is recited. Made up of four benedictions, the Grace thanks God for sustaining the world, for the Land of Israel, for rebuilding Jerusalem, and for His goodness to all of His creatures.

Mishnah Berakhot also specifies various benedictions to be recited upon experiencing God's greatness in history and nature (text 13.2.11). The obligation to observe the time-bound commandments is generally restricted to males in Rabbinic halakhah (text 13.2.12). Accordingly, women were exempt from a variety of obligations.

The Rabbis expanded on earlier notions which sought to sanctify time. In this respect, they detailed the forms of labor prohibited on the Sabbath (text 13.3.1) so as to recognize God as the creator. The notion that an act of work must be completed in order for a violation to occur is emphasized also by Mishnah Shabbat (text 13.3.2).

The holiday of Passover was of great importance not only because of its biblical character but because its theme of freedom from bondage spoke to the aspirations of generations of Jews. The law required a detailed search for leaven which is described in Mishnah Pesaḥim (text 13.3.3). Leaven was seen as a symbol of the evils of slavery and idolatry. The Passover Seder, the festive meal originally held in the Temple and later in the Jewish home, is described in Mishnah Pesaḥim (text 13.3.4). The commandment to retell the story of the Exodus eventually led to a fixed midrash (text 13.3.5) which later took on the name Haggadah ("telling"). This text provided an opportunity for even the most ignorant Jew to partake of midrashic interpretation of the Torah's account of the Exodus from Egypt.

In the days of the Temple, beautiful ceremonies took place such as the bringing of the First Fruits described in Mishnah Bikkurim (text 13.3.6). The holiday of Sukkot was celebrated by dwelling in a sukkah (booth) commemorating the period of wandering in the desert. The laws for the building of the sukkah are set out in Mishnah Sukkah (text 13.3.7). Only a temporary roof was permitted for the sukkah. During Temple times, impressive processions took place with the *lulav* and *etrog*, and Mishnah Sukkah (text 13.3.8) prescribes the laws pertaining to these four species which continued to be used in the synagogue after the destruction of the Temple. A highlight of the holiday in the Temple period was the Water Drawing Ceremony (text 13.3.9) in which great joy, accompanied by singing and dancing, took place in the Temple on the second night of the eight-day festival.

The holiday of Hanukkah, although not prescribed in the Bible because it commemorates events of later times, was celebrated by the lighting of lamps to symbolize the Jewish victory over the Seleucid forces. The Babylonian Talmud Shabbat (text 13.3.10) sets out the requirements for these lamps as well as summarizing the history of the events that led to the celebration. This account is exceedingly sketchy, and it, along with the formulation of the prayer

'*Al ha-Nissim* (text 13.3.11), indicates that the books of 1 and 2 Maccabees were not available to the Rabbis.

The holiday of Purim, also celebrating deliverance from enemies, is based on the biblical Scroll (Megillah) of Esther. Mishnah Megillah (text 13.3.12) explains the way in which this holiday could be fixed on different days in order to enable all Jews to celebrate it. All Jews were obligated to hear the reading of the entire book from a handwritten scroll copied in accordance with the halakhah as set forth in Mishnah Megillah (text 13.3.13).

Various days were fixed by Jewish tradition as days of national mourning, and these are specified in Mishnah Ta'anit (text 13.3.14). Although additional tragedies may have happened on these days and are also commemorated on them, their fundamental purpose is to commemorate events that led to the destruction of the Jewish Temple and nation by the Babylonians and again by the Romans. Altogether this combination of biblical and postbiblical festive and commemorative days created a ritual calendar which provided the yearly rhythm of life for the Jewish people.

Just as Judaism sought to sanctify time, it also extended holiness to a whole variety of normal human functions. Already in biblical times, the book of Leviticus had prohibited the eating of certain animals (text 13.4.1) which were regarded as impure or, in later terms, unkosher. Specific procedures existed, as explained in Mishnah Ḥullin (text 13.4.2), for the ritual slaughter of animals for either sacrifices (when the Temple still stood) or consumption. The biblical requirement of not seething a kid in its mother's milk was explained by the Mishnah as requiring complete separation of milk and meat foods and utensils. These regulations constitute the laws of *kashrut* (kosher food).

Marriage and family life were the subject of extensive legislation as well. In Second Temple times, spouses were apparently chosenby some in a special ceremony described in Mishnah Ta'anit (text 13.5.1). The remembrance of that occasion taught the Rabbis of the need to accent spiritual values and personality traits in the choice of a wife rather than purely physical attraction. By Rabbinic times marriage was a free act of choice by both parties, although Rabbinic legislation, such as Mishnah Qiddushin (text 13.5.2), continues to use the terminology of acquisition and bride-price. The marriage ceremony included the recital of a series of benedictions which are specified by the Babylonian Talmud Ketubot (text 13.5.3). These benedictions make clear the romantic aspect of the Jewish marriage and also offer a prayer for the redemption of Jerusalem. In order to ameliorate the position of women and to guarantee them sustenance should the marriage end by the death of the husband or divorce, Rabbinic law required a marriage contract (*ketubah*). We present here the marriage contract of Babatha (text 13.5.4), a woman whose business and personal documents were found in the Bar Kokhba caves. Yet in her own family a Greek form of a marriage contract (text 13.5.5) was also used, indicating that some Jews sought the protection of the Roman legal system for their marriages.

Although there was extensive debate in Second Temple and Rabbinic times about how liberally to allow divorce, it was eventually decided that divorce could be initiated by the husband for any reason. Women could demand divorces for certain specific issues, including wife-beating which was strongly condemned by the Rabbis. The laws of divorce required certainty as to the validity of the document, as described in Mishnah Gittin (text 13.5.6), in order to make certain that the divorce document had in fact been written for the specific husband and wife, as required by biblical law. Further, the divorce had to totally sever the relationship between husband and wife so that each was free to remarry. Numerous divorce writs were unearthed among the Bar Kokhba documents (text 13.5.6), and these were generally prepared in accord with Rabbinic law.

In biblical times extensive ritual purity laws had governed the priests and those who sought to visit the Temple. In the Second Temple period, a variety of Jewish groups extended the purity laws to their daily life. With the destruction of the Temple, most of these laws fell into disuse with the exception of menstrual impurity and the washing of hands. Mishnah Niddah (text 13.6.1) deals with the laws of menstrual impurity and informs us that Jewish sectarians did not adhere to the same laws as required by the Rabbis (text 13.6.2). Purification was achieved by bathing in a ritual bath, the laws of which are specified in Mishnah Miqva'ot (text 13.6.3). The laws of ritual hand washing are set out in Mishnah Yadayim (text 13.6.4), although some of the regulations contained here were no longer applicable after the destruction of the Temple.

Rabbinic laws also dealt with all aspects of the life-cycle. Mishnah Shabbat (text 13.7.1) touches on issues pertaining to the raising of children, birth, and circumcision. Just as in Second Temple times, circumcision continued to be a sign of Jewish identity. Mishnah Avot (text 13.7.2) traced a series of ages which were understood to be the normal cycle of life for the Jewish male.

One of the unique aspects of Rabbinic Judaism is its emphasis on study of the Torah in the widest sense, as an act of divine worship. Study is seen as tying the Jew to the giving of the Torah at Sinai, as explained in the chapter *Qinyan Torah* (text 13.8.1), a collection of Rabbinic sayings, which was appended to Mishnah Avot in the early Middle Ages. The Rabbinic system of Judaism required extensive education for its practice, so that study was also seen as facilitating proper observance of the law, and Rabbis, as experts in Torah knowledge, were respected members of the community.

Besides the pursuit of the observance of the law and the study of the Torah, a smaller number of Jews were attracted to mystical approaches to Jewish theology and ritual. Mishnah Ḥagigah (text 13.9.1) already required that esoteric teachings not be expounded even to two students at once lest they be misunderstood. Some Rabbis participated in mystical speculation, as is clear from Jerusalem Talmud Ḥagigah (text 13.9.2) and a number of parallel texts. Yet another passage in Jerusalem Talmud Ḥagigah (text 13.9.3) warns of the dangers of such speculation in the course of explaining the tradition of the four who entered the Pardes, the garden of mystical speculation. This passage emphasized the terrible spiritual fate that befell Elisha ben Abuyah, although the passage readily admits that other factors in his life contributed to his religious downfall. Later mystical traditions in Judaism focused on Rabbi Simeon bar Yoḥai, a tanna whose stay in a cave is described in the Babylonian Talmud Shabbat (text 13.9.4). According to these later traditions, this Rabbi acquired his mystical knowledge while in the cave. Because of the importance of this tradition in later texts, it is included here. Also included here is a mystical prayer from the composition *Ma'aseh Merkavah* (text 13.9.5), which allows us a glimpse of the prayers collected in early Jewish mystical texts that may very well have been recited by mystics already in amoraic times.

Some Jews, as known from numerous talmudic and archaeological sources both in Palestine and Babylonia, were attracted to the practice of apotropaic (protective) magic. Among the texts from the Land of Israel we present an amulet from Ḥorvat Kanaf (text 13.9.6) which seeks protection for a "rabbi" from a variety of demonic forces. This is clearly a monotheistic Jewish text. In Babylonia the use of magic bowls was common. In one bowl (text 13.9.7) Lilith, the female demon, is expelled with a symbolic writ of divorce. In a second bowl (text 13.9.8), protection is sought for a family from all varieties of demonic forces. Such bowls were found buried, for the most part, under the threshold. Clearly, widespread popular magical practices, some of which were even accepted by Rabbinic sages, were part of the popular religion of Jews in Late Antiquity.

The life of Torah was complex and demanding but served to extend sanctity and holiness to every part of human life and to structure the life of the Jewish communities of Palestine and Babylonia. The working out of the details of this complex religious and legal system provided added stimulus for the development of Rabbinic texts and traditions. The Rabbis successfully educated large numbers of Jews to participate in this way of life, thus insuring that Rabbinic halakhah and theology would be the basis for Judaism in the future.

13.1 THE WORLD OF THE AGGADAH

13.1.1 Babylonian Talmud Pesaḥim 56a: The Oneness of God and the Children of Israel[1]

This talmudic aggadah serves to explain Jewish liturgy which requires that after the reading of the first line of the Shema (Deut. 6:5), in which God's oneness is proclaimed, the worshipper recites, "Blessed be the Name of His Royal Glory. . . ." This line is understood here to represent a response of the worshipper to the realization that all the Jewish people have accepted monotheism, and hence, God as ruler of the universe.

৯৫

Rabbi Simeon ben Lakish said: "And Jacob called his sons and said, 'Come together that I may tell you [what is to befall you in days to

---

1. Trans. S. Berrin.

come]'" (Gen. 49:1). Jacob wanted to reveal to his sons the end of days, but the divine presence departed from him.

[Jacob] said, "Perhaps, God forbid, there is a blemish in my progeny, like Abraham, from whom Ishmael came forth, or my father Isaac from whom Esau came forth."

His sons said to him, "'Hear, O Israel, the Lord our God, the Lord is One' (Deut. 6:5). Just as in your heart there is only One, so too in our heart there is only One."

At that moment, Jacob our father opened (his mouth and) said, "Blessed be the name of His royal Glory for ever and ever."

13.1.2 *Deuteronomy Rabbah, Va-Ethanan* 2:35: The Reading of the Shema[2]

Often, midrashic texts preserve expanded versions of traditions found in the Talmud. In this text, we see that the narrative has been expanded, and the connection to the recitation of the Shema had been made explicit. Also, the text mentions the custom of reciting "Blessed be . . ." in a low voice, in order to distinguish it from the words of the Torah which are recited aloud.

Whence has Israel been privileged to recite the Shema? Eleazar the son of Aḥvai said, "From our father Jacob. At the time when he was about to die, he was thinking in his heart and saying: 'Abraham, my grandfather, had two sons, Isaac and Ishmael. Isaac, my father, served the Holy One Blessed be He, and Ishmael served the astral idolatrous deities. In the same way Isaac my father had two sons, myself and Esau. I serve God, and Esau serves idols. I had twelve sons. Perhaps they do not serve the Holy One Blessed be He. Perhaps there is among them an idolater.' What did he do? He called all his sons and assembled them before his bed. As it says: 'Then Jacob called his sons' (Gen. 49:1), and when they had come to him, he said to them: 'Assemble and listen, sons of Jacob, [listen to Israel your father]' (Gen. 49:2).

"What is [meant by] 'assemble and listen'?

"He said to them, 'Listen to what I say to you.'

"They said to him, 'So what do you desire?'

"He said to them, 'Listen to [Hebrew: *el*] Israel your father. Listen to the Holy One Blessed be He [God, Hebrew: *El*] whom your father worships and whom you should worship.'

---

2. Trans. S. Berrin according to S. Lieberman, *Midrash Devarim Rabbah* (Jerusalem: Wahrmann, 1964/5), p. 67.

"They said to him, '[Hear, O Israel], the Lord our God, the Lord is One.' [He said softly, 'Blessed be the name of his royal Glory for ever and ever.']

"And up to now they are accustomed every single day to say 'Hear, O Israel [the Lord our God, the Lord is One' (Deut. 6:5)]. . . .

"Therefore, they merited the reading of the Shema from our forefather Jacob."

13.1.3 *Midrash Tanḥuma, Vayera* 6: The Oneness of God[3]

The following text explains that God's rule over the world is just and that He is not a capricious deity. Even God, we are told, is subject to the law.

శ్రీ

It is written (Job 23:13): "But He has oneness; so who can turn Him? And whatever His soul desires, He does." Rabbi Papias interpreted: "Because he stands alone in his world, there is no one to interfere with him. Whatever he wants, he does." Rabbi Akiva said to him, "Enough from you, Papias! One does not [so] interpret here. Rather, he does everything according to the Law." What is the meaning of "has oneness?" [That just as the petitioner petitions [here] below, so [it is] above. Just as the Sanhedrin conducts proceedings below, so [it is] above, as stated (in 1 Kings 22:19): "I saw the Lord sitting upon His throne, and all the heavenly host was standing by Him to His right and to His left." Is there a left [and right] above? And has it not already been stated (in Exod.15:6): "Your right hand, O Lord, glorious in power, [Your right hand shatters the enemy"]? It is simply that the ones [on the right] tip the balance toward the side of merit, and the ones [on the left] tip the balance toward the side of guilt. Ergo, everything [proceeds] with justice. And, just as one who is a petitioner petitions [here] below, so [it is] above. Where is it shown? Where Daniel has said so (Dan. 4:14): "The ruling is by the decree of the watchers, and the petition [by] the word of the holy ones." Now you say: Because he stands alone in his world, he does whatever he wants! What is the meaning of "has oneness" (in Job 23:13)? Rabbi Pinḥas bar Ḥama the Priest said: "Because he alone in his world knows justice for his creatures." Rabbi Judah ben Rabbi Shallum the Levite [said]: "Because he alone in the world knows the temperament of his creatures. The one to whom he says: Go on my mission, goes." Hence it says (in Job 23:13): "And whatever His soul desires, He does." So Jeremiah stated (Jer. 1:6):

"I am [but] a lad." The Holy One said to him: "Do not say: I am [but] a lad." So also with Sodom, he conducted the proceedings in their court and saw that their guilt merited destruction. Then after that he sent them (the angels) to destroy them. It is therefore stated (Gen. 19:1): "Then the two angels came to Sodom."

13.1.4 *Midrash Tanḥuma, Vayera* 5:
God as the Master of the Universe[4]

This long aggadic narrative emphasizes the notion that one God rules the world by retelling and recasting the confrontation that Moses and Aaron had with Pharaoh (Exod. 5:1–5). It explains the terrible destruction of Egyptians at the sea, resulting from Pharaoh's refusal to accept the authority of the God of Israel.

ۻ

Said Rabbi Ḥiyya bar Abba: Moses and Aaron came to Pharaoh on a day when he was meeting ambassadors. Kings were coming and crowning him supreme ruler over all the kings. While they were crowning him, Moses and Aaron were standing in the doorway of Pharaoh's palace. Pharaoh's servants went in and said to him, "Two old men are standing by the doorway."

He said to them, "Do they have crowns in their hands?"

They said to him, "No."

[Pharaoh] said to them, "Then let them enter last."

When [Moses and Aaron] were standing before Pharaoh, he said to them, "What do you want?"

They said to him, "The God of the Hebrews has sent us to you saying, 'Let my people go that they may worship me.'"[5]

He said to them, "'Who is the Lord that I should listen?' He did not even know to send me a crown, for [you come only] with words. 'I do not know the Lord, [nor will I let Israel go]'" (Ex. 5:2).

Rabbi Levi said: At that time, he brought forth a parchment list of the gods and began to read, "god of Edom, god of Moab, god of Sidon and so all of them. . . ."

He said to them, "I have read my entire list and the name of your God is not in it."

---

4. Trans. S. Berrin, according to *Midrash Tanḥuma*, with commentaries by H. Zundel (Tel Aviv: Pardes, n.d.), Vayera 5, pp. 71a–71b.

5. Instead of Ex. 5:1, the present biblical context, the text quotes Ex. 7:16. Cf. Also Ex. 4:23.

Said Rabbi Levi: To what is this analogous? To a priest who had a foolish servant. The priest left the city, and the servant went to seek him in the cemetery. He started to cry out to the people standing there, "Have you not seen my master here?"

They said to him, "Is not your master a priest?"

He said, "Yes."

They said to him, "Fool! Who has ever seen a priest in a cemetery?"[6]

So did Moses and Aaron say to Pharaoh, "Fool! Those gods which you have mentioned, they are dead, but our God is true. He is the Living God and Eternal King."

Pharaoh said to them, "Is he a young man? Is he an old man? How old is he? How many cities has he vanquished? How many provinces has he conquered? How many years is it since he ascended to the throne?"

They said to him, "Our God—His power and his might fill the universe. He existed before the universe came into being, and will still exist at the end of all eternity. He formed you and gave you your life's-breath."

[Pharaoh] said to them, "What are his works?"

They said to him, "He stretched out the heavens and the earth and his voice flashes forth shafts of fire, shatters mountains, and smashes boulders. His bow is fire, His arrows flames; His javelin is the torch, His shield the clouds, His sword the lightning. He creates the mountains and hills, covers the skies with clouds, brings down rain and dew, makes the grass grow, and ripens fruits. He answers women giving birth, forms the embryo in its mother's womb, and brings it forth to the air of the world. He causes kings to pass away, and establishes kings."

He said to them, "From the start you lie! For I am the Master of the universe, and I created myself and the Nile, as it is said, '[Pharaoh king of Egypt . . . who said, I created myself and the Nile'" (Ezek. 29:3).[7]

At that time, he assembled all the wise men of Egypt. He said to them, "Have you heard tell of the god of these (people)?"

They said to him, "We have heard that he is the son of wise men, son of Eastern kings."

The Holy One Blessed be He said to them, "You call yourselves wise men, and Me you call the son of wise men! I will destroy your wisdom, as it is written, 'The wisest of Pharaoh's advisors have given absurd counsel. How can you tell Pharaoh that I am the son of wise men, the son of East-

---

6. The servant was an obvious fool because he sought his master in a place where he could not possibly be, in a cemetery. Jewish priests were not permitted to come in contact with the dead in any way.

7. Jewish Publication Society translates: "My Nile is my own, I made it for myself." We translate here according to the midrashic understanding of the verse.

ern kings' (Is. 19:11). See what it says of them: 'The wisdom of its wise shall fail and the intelligence of its intelligent will vanish'" (Is. 29:14).

[Pharaoh] responded to [Moses and Aaron], "I do not know what you are saying. Who is God that I should listen to him?" (Ex. 5:2).

The Holy One Blessed be He said to them, "Wicked man! 'Who is God' you said! Who are you?! You will be afflicted with 'Who'" (Hebrew: *mi*). The numerical value of the letters in the word "Who" (*mi*) is fifty. These are the fifty plagues which the Holy Blessed One brought upon the Egyptians in Egypt. Regarding Egypt what does it say? "And the magicians said to Pharaoh: It is the finger of God" (Ex. 8:15). And upon the sea[8] what does it say? "And Israel saw the great hand" (Ex. 14:31). With how many were they afflicted by a finger? Ten plagues. Calculate the five fingers of the great hand; at ten plagues for each finger, behold these are fifty.

13.1.5 *Exodus Rabbah, Shemot* 2:5:
The Revelation at the Thorn Bush[9]

This short narrative of the discussion between a Rabbi and a non-Jew emphasizes the notion that the Shekhinah, the divine presence, fills the entire universe. God is accessible, even in a bush.

༄

A Gentile asked Rabbi Joshua ben Qarḥa, "Why did God speak to Moses from a thorn bush?"

[Rabbi Joshua] said to him, "If [He had spoken] from a carob tree or a sycamore, you would have asked me the same [question]. However, to dismiss you without an answer is impossible. 'Why did God speak from the thorn bush?' To teach that there is no place which is empty of the Shekhinah, not even a thorn bush."

13.2 THE DAILY LIFE OF THE JEW

13.2.1 Mishnah Berakhot 1:1–4:
Laws Regarding Recitation of the Shema[10]

Mishnah Berakhot sets forth the required times for recitation of the evening and morning Shema, in accord with the commandment of Deut. 6:7. It indicates that in tannaitic times the benedictions before and after the Shema were well established parts of Jewish liturgy.

---

8. At the Red Sea.
9. Trans. S. Berrin
10. Trans. S. Berrin.

ॐ

1:1 From what time may the Shema be recited in the evening? "From the time when the priests enter the Temple to eat of their *terumah*[11] until the end of the first watch,"[12] according to Rabbi Eliezer.

But the Sages say: "until midnight."

Rabban Gamliel says: "until the rise of dawn." His sons once returned from a wedding feast and they said to him, "We have not recited the Shema."

He said to them, "If the dawn has not risen, you are obligated to recite it."

Furthermore, any time the Sages say "until midnight," the commandment applies until the rise of dawn. The commandment of burning of the fat and limbs [of the evening sacrifice] applies until the rise of dawn. The commandment of all [sacrifices] which must be consumed within one day applies until the rise of dawn. If this is so, then why did the Sages say, "until midnight?" In order to distance a person from transgression.

2 From what time may the Shema be recited in the morning? From the time that one can discern between blue and white.[13]

Rabbi Eliezer said: "between blue and green."

And it should be completed before sunrise.

Rabbi Joshua said: "[it must be completed] before the third hour,[14] because the way of royalty is to rise at the third hour."

Whoever recites it from that point onward does not lose out, but is like one who reads in the Torah.[15]

4 In the morning, two blessings are said before [the Shema] and one after it; in the evening, two blessings are said before it and two after it, one long and one short. Where they [the Sages] have said to say a long benediction,[16] [one] is not permitted to say a short one;[17] where they have

---

11. The priests' portion which may only be eaten in a state of ritual purity. Priests entered the Temple after completing their purification rites and waiting until nightfall, later understood as the appearance of three stars.

12. One-third of the nighttime hours; night was divided into three watches.

13. The blue and white referred to here are the fringes, *ẓiẓit*, worn on the corner of the garment which had one blue string among the white ones (see the third paragraph of the Shema, below).

14. By the completion of one-fourth of the daylight hours.

15. The reader is credited with the fulfillment of the commandment of Torah study and fulfills the requirement of concentrating on his belief in God and his obligation to observe the commandments.

16. One beginning "Blessed art thou, O Lord . . ." and ending with the same formula.

said to say a short [benediction], [one] is not permitted to say a long one. [A blessing which they have said] to seal (with a concluding formula),[18] one is not permitted not to seal, and [a blessing which they have said] not to seal, one is not permitted to seal.

13.2.2 The Benedictions Before the Morning Shema: Accepting God and His Commandments[19]

The backbone of the daily service, already in the beginning of talmudic times, is the reading of the Shema, three Biblical passages which set forth the basic beliefs and commitments of Judaism. These paragraphs are preceded by two benedictions before and followed by one after. Each benediction emphasized the theme of one of the Biblical passages. The first benediction corresponds to the recital of Deut. 6:5. This passage emphasizes God's sovereignty and this is the meaning of the first benediction regarding the heavenly bodies of which God is the sole creator. The second benediction recalls the Jew's obligation to study the Torah and practice its commandments. This is paralleled in the reading of Deut. 11:13–21 which recalls these same themes. The benediction ends with the ingathering of exiles, just as the biblical passage mentions longevity in the Land of Israel.

🙚

1 Blessed art thou, O Lord our God, King of the universe, who formest light and createst darkness, who makest peace and createst all things.

All shall thank thee, and all shall praise thee, and all shall say, there is none holy like the Lord. All shall extol thee for ever, Creator of all things, O God who openest every day the doors of the gates of the East, and cleavest the windows of the firmament, bringing forth the sun from its place, and the moon from its dwelling, giving light to the whole world and to its inhabitants whom thou hast created in thy mercy. In mercy thou givest light to the earth and to those who dwell on it, and in thy goodness renewest the creation every day continually; O King, who alone was exalted from aforetime, praised, glorified, and extolled from days of old.

Eternal God, in thine abundant mercies, have mercy upon us, Lord of our strength, Rock of our stronghold, Shield of our salvation, thou Stronghold of ours!

---

17. One only concluding "Blessed art thou . . ."

18. Blessed art thou, O Lord. . . .

19. J. Heinemann with J. J. Petuchowski, *Literature of the Synagogue* (New York: Behrman House, 1975), pp. 21–4.

There is none to be compared unto thee, and there is none besides thee; there is none but thee: who is like thee? There is none to be compared unto thee, Lord our God, in this world, and there is none besides thee, our King, in the life of the world to come; there is none but thee, our Redeemer, in the days of the messiah; neither is there any like thee, our Deliverer, in the resurrection of the dead.

God, the Lord over all works,[20]
blessed is he, and ever to be blessed by the mouth of everything that has breath.
His greatness and goodness fill the universe;
knowledge and understanding surround him.

He is exalted above the holy Hayot
and is adorned in glory above the celestial chariot.
Purity and rectitude are before his throne,
kindness and mercy before his glory.

The luminaries are good which our God has created
he formed them with knowledge, understanding and discernment;
He gave them might and power
   to rule in the midst of the world.

They are full of luster, and they radiate brightness:
beautiful is their luster throughout all the world.
They rejoice in their going forth, and are glad in their returning;
They perform with awe the will of their Master.

Glory and honor they render his name,
exultation and rejoicing at the remembrance of his sovereignty.
He called unto the sun, and it shone forth in light
He looked, and ordained the figure of the moon.

All the hosts on high render praise unto him,
the Seraphim, the Ophanim, and the holy Hayot[21] ascribing
   glory and greatness.

To the God who rested from all his works, and on the seventh day exalted himself and sat upon the throne of his glory; who robed himself in glory on the day of rest, and called the Sabbath day a delight. This is the praise of the Sabbath day, that God rested thereon from all his work, when the Sabbath day itself offers praise and says, "A Psalm, a song of the Sab-

---

20. This hymn, *El Adon*, is closely linked to the hymns of praise found in both the Dead Sea Scrolls and *Hekhalot* mystical texts.

21. *Seraphim, Ophanim* and *Hayot* are classes of angels.

bath day, it is good to give thanks unto the Lord" (Ps. 92:1–2). Therefore let all his creatures glorify and bless God; let them render praise, honor, and greatness to the God and King who is Creator of all things, and who, in his holiness, gives an inheritance of rest to his people Israel on the holy Sabbath day. Thy name, Lord our God, shall be hallowed, and thy remembrance, our King, shall be glorified in heaven above and on the earth below. Be thou blessed, our Savior, for the excellency of thy handiwork, and for the bright luminaries which thou hast made: they shall glorify thee for ever.

Be thou blessed, our Rock, our King and Redeemer, Creator of holy beings, praised be thy name for ever, our King; Creator of ministering spirits, all of whom stand in the heights of the universe, and proclaim with awe in unison aloud the words of the living God and everlasting King; all of them are beloved, pure and mighty, and all of them in dread and awe do the will of the Master; and all of them open their mouths in holiness and purity, with song and psalm, while they bless and praise, glorify and reverence, sanctify and ascribe sovereignty to the name of the Divine King, the Great, Mighty, and Dreaded One, Holy is He; and they all take upon themselves the yoke of the kingdom of Heaven one from the other, and give permission to one another to hallow their Creator in tranquil joy of spirit, with pure speech and holy melody they all respond in unison, and exclaim with awe:[22]

"Holy, holy, holy is the Lord of hosts: the whole earth is full of his glory" (Is. 6:3).

And the Ophanim and the holy Ḥayot with a noise of great rushing, upraising themselves toward the Seraphim, over against them offer praise and say:

"Blessed be the glory of the Lord from his place" (Ezek. 3:12).

To the blessed God they offer melodies; to the King, the living and eternal God, they utter hymns and make their praises heard; for he alone performs mighty deeds, and makes new things; he is the Lord of battles; he sows righteousness, causes salvation to spring forth, creates remedies, and is revered in praises. He is the Lord of wonders, who in his goodness renews the creation every day continually, as it is said, "To Him that made great lights, for His mercy endures for ever" (Ps. 136:7). O cause a new

---

22. In what follows, the text recalls the angelic recitation of the Qedushah, the sanctification of God. Just as humanity praise God on earth, so do the angels on high. This notion is closely connected with the early *Hekhalot* mystical literature.

light to shine upon Zion, and may we all be worthy soon to enjoy its brightness. Blessed art thou, O Lord, Creator of the lights.

2 With abounding love hast thou loved us, Lord our God, great and exceeding mercy hast thou bestowed upon us. Our Father, our King, for our fathers' sake, who trusted in thee, and whom thou didst teach laws of life, be gracious unto us and teach us. Our Father, merciful Father, ever compassionate, have mercy upon us and put it into our hearts to understand and to discern, to mark, learn, and teach, to heed, to do, and to fulfill in love all the words of instruction in thy Torah. Enlighten our eyes in thy Torah and let our hearts cleave to thy commandments, and unite our hearts to love and fear thy name, so that we be never put to shame. Because we have trusted in thy holy, great, and revered name, we shall rejoice and be glad in thy salvation. O bring us in peace from the four corners of the earth, and make us go upright to our land; for thou art a God who works salvation. Thou hast chosen us from all peoples and tongues, and hast brought us near unto thy great name for ever in faithfulness, that we might in love give thanks unto thee and proclaim thy unity. Blessed art thou, O Lord, who hast chosen thy people Israel in love.

13.2.3 The Shema:
Affirming Faith in God and His Commandments[23]

Sources as early as the Dead Sea Scrolls testify to the twice-daily recitation of the Shema, the proclamation of Jewish faith. The first paragraph, Deut. 6:4–9, emphasizes the unity and sovereignty of God. The second paragraph, 11:13–21, emphasizes the obligation to observe his commandments, and the third, Num 15:37–41 to remember the experience of slavery in Egypt.

ॐ

HEAR, O ISRAEL, THE LORD OUR GOD, THE LORD IS ONE.[24]
BLESSED BE THE NAME OF HIS GLORIOUS KINGDOM
FOR EVER AND EVER.[25]

You shall love the Lord your God with all your heart, and with all your soul, and with all your might. And these words, which I command you

---

23. Trans. Heinemann and Petuchowski, *Literature of the Synagogue*, pp. 24–5.

24. Here starts the first paragraph of the Shema (Deut. 6:4–9) dealing with God's unity and kingship over the universe.

25. This line derives from the Temple rituals and is recited silently. It serves to highlight the main motif of the Shema—God's kingship over the universe.

this day, shall be in your hearts: and you shall teach them diligently to your children, and shall speak of them when you sit in your house, and when you walk by the way, and when you lie down, and when you rise up. And you shall bind them for a sign upon your hand, and they shall be as front-lets between your eyes. And you shall write them upon the doorposts of your house, and upon your gates.

And it shall come to pass,[26] if you will diligently obey my command-ments which I command you this day, to love the Lord your God, and to serve him with all your heart and with all your soul, that I will give the rain of your land in its season, the former rain and the latter rain, that you may gather in your grain, and your wine, and your oil. And I will give grass in your field for your cattle, and you shall eat and be satisfied. Beware, lest your heart be deceived, and you turn aside, and serve other gods, and worship them; and the anger of the Lord be kindled against you, and he shut up the heaven, that there be no rain, and the land yield not her fruit; and you perish quickly from off the good land which the Lord gives you. Therefore you shall lay up these my words in your heart and in your soul; and you shall bind them for a sign upon your hand, and they shall be as frontlets between your eyes. And you shall teach them to your children, speaking of them when you sit in your house, and when you walk by the way, and when you lie down, and when you rise up. And you shall write them upon the doorposts of your house, and upon your gates: that your days may be multiplied, and the days of your chil-dren, upon the land which the Lord swore to your fathers to give them, as the days of the heavens above the earth.

And the Lord spoke unto Moses, saying,[27] Speak unto the children of Israel, and bid them make for themselves fringes upon the corners of their garments throughout their generations, and put upon the fringe of each corner a cord of blue, and it shall be a fringe unto you, that you may look upon it, and remember all the commandments of the Lord, and do them; that you go not astray after your own heart and your own eyes, after which you used to go astray: that you may remember and do all my com-mandments, and be holy unto your God. I am the Lord your God, who

---

26. Here begins the second paragraph of the Shema (Deut. 11:13–21) in which God's commandments and the concept of reward and punishment are discussed.

27. Here starts the third paragraph of the Shema (Num. 15:37–41) in which the obli-gation to remember the commandments and the Exodus from Egypt is emphasized.

brought you out of the land of Egypt, to be your God: I am the Lord your God.

13.2.4 The Benediction After the Morning Shema: Remembering the Redemption from Egypt[28]

The third benediction recalls the Exodus from Egypt as a conformation of the truth of God's sovereignty. Inherent in remembering the redemption of old is the hope for future redemption in the messianic age. Just as the Exodus is remembered in the third paragraph of the Shema, so it is the main theme of the final benediction which follows here.

꧁

True and firm, established and enduring, right and faithful, beloved and precious, desirable and pleasant, revered and mighty, well-ordered and acceptable, good and beautiful is this word unto us forever and ever. It is true, the God of the universe is our King, the Rock of Jacob, the Shield of our salvation: throughout all generations he endures and his name endures; his throne is established, and his kingdom and his faithfulness endure for ever. His words also live and endure; they are faithful and desirable for ever and to all eternity as for our fathers so also for us, our children, our generations, and for all the generations of the seed of Israel his servants.

For the first and for the last ages thy word is good and endures for ever and ever; it is true and trustworthy, a statute which shall not pass away. True it is that thou art indeed the Lord our God and the God of our fathers, our King, our fathers' King, our Redeemer, the Redeemer of our fathers, our Maker, the Rock of our salvation; our Deliverer and Rescuer from everlasting, such is thy name; there is no God besides thee.

Thou hast been the help of our fathers from of old, a Shield and Protector to their children after them in every generation: in the heights of the universe is thy habitation, and thy judgments and thy righteousness reach to the farthest ends of the earth. Happy is the man who obeys thy commandments, and takes thy Torah and thy word to his heart. True it is that thou art indeed the Lord of thy people, and a mighty King to plead their cause. True it is that thou art indeed the first and thou art the last, and besides thee we have no King, Redeemer, and Deliverer. From Egypt thou didst redeem us, O Lord our God, and from the house of bondmen thou didst deliver us: all their first-born thou didst slay, but thy firstborn

---

28. Trans. Heinemann and Petuchowski, *Literature of the Synagogue*, pp. 25–6.

thou didst redeem; thou didst divide the Red Sea and drown the proud; but thou madest the beloved to pass through, while the waters covered their adversaries, not one of whom was left. Wherefore the beloved praised and extolled God, and offered hymns, songs, praises, blessings and thanksgivings to the King and God, who lives and endures; who is high and exalted, great and revered; who brings low the haughty, and raises up the lowly, leads forth the prisoners, delivers the meek, helps the poor, and answers his people when they cry unto him. Praises to the Most High God, blessed is he, and ever to be blessed. Moses and the children of Israel sang a song unto thee with great joy, saying, all of them:

"Who is like unto thee, O Lord, among the mighty ones? Who is like unto thee, glorious in holiness, revered in praises, doing wonders?" (Ex. 15:11).

With a new song the redeemed people offered praise unto thy name at the seashore; they all gave thanks in unison, and proclaimed thy sovereignty, and said:

"The Lord shall reign for ever and ever" (Ex. 15:18).

Rock of Israel, arise to the help of Israel, and deliver, according to thy promise, Judah and Israel. Our Redeemer, the Lord of hosts is his name, the Holy One of Israel. Blessed art thou, O Lord, who hast redeemed Israel.

13.2.5 Benedictions for the Evening Shema: Liturgy as Interpretation[29]

Each of the themes in this section deals with the waning of day and the oncoming darkness as night envelops the world. The first paragraph acknowledges God's control of the natural processes of the earth. The second expresses the importance of meditation on God's Torah both during the day and at night. The third recalls the Exodus from Egypt, and the fourth petitions God to allow the worshipper "to lie down in peace" and awaken again in peace. As with the benedictions for the daytime, each blessing takes up themes found in one of the paragraphs of the Shema.

꽃

1 Blessed art thou, Lord our God,[30] King of the universe, who at thy word bringest on the evening twilight, with wisdom openest the gates of the heavens, and with understanding changest times and variest the sea-

---

29. Trans. Heinemann and Petuchowski, *Literature of the Synagogue*, pp. 26–8.

30. This benediction on the heavenly lights corresponds to the declaration of God's kingship in the first paragraph of the Shema.

sons, and arrangest the stars in their watches in the sky, according to thy will. Thou createst day and night; thou rollest away the light from before the darkness, and the darkness from before the light; thou makest the day to pass and the night to approach; thou dividest the day from the night, the Lord of hosts is thy name; a God living and enduring continually, mayest thou reign over us forever and ever. Blessed art thou, O Lord, who bringest on the evening twilight.

2 With everlasting love thou hast loved the house of Israel, thy people;[31] Torah and commandments, statutes and judgments hast thou taught us. Therefore, O Lord our God, when we lie down and when we rise up we will meditate on thy law, and rejoice in the words of thy Torah and thy commandments for ever; for they are our life and the length of our days, and we will meditate on them day and night. Mayest thou never take away thy love from us. Blessed art thou, O Lord, who lovest thy people Israel.

"Hear, O Israel. . . ."[32]

3. True and trustworthy[33] is all this, and it is established with us that he is the Lord our God, and there is none besides him, and that we, Israel, are his people. It is he, our King, who redeemed us from the hand of kings, who delivered us from the grasp of all the tyrants. God, who on our behalf dealt out punishment to our adversaries, and requited all the enemies of our soul; who does great things past finding out and wonders without number; who holds our soul in life, and has not suffered our feet to be moved; who made us tread upon the high places of our enemies, and exalted our horn over all that hate us; who wrought miracles for us and vengeance upon Pharaoh, signs and wonders in the land of the children of Ham;[34] who in his wrath smote all the firstborn of Egypt, and brought forth his people Israel among them to everlasting freedom; who made his children pass between the divisions of the sea, but sank their pursuers and their enemies in the depths. Then his children beheld his might; they praised and gave thanks unto his name, and willingly accepted his sovereignty. Moses and the children of Israel sang a song unto thee with great joy, saying all of them:

---

31. This second benediction, like the second paragraph of the Shema, stresses the obligation to observe the commandments.

32. Here the three paragraphs of the Shema (text 13.2.3) are recited.

33. Here starts the third benediction which emphasizes the Exodus from Egypt mentioned in the third paragraph of the Shema.

34. Egypt.

"Who is like unto thee, O Lord, among the mighty ones? Who is like unto thee, glorious in holiness, revered in praises, doing wonders?" (Ex. 15:11).

Thy children beheld thy sovereign power, as thou didst part the sea before Moses. They exclaimed, "This is my God!" and said:

"The Lord shall reign for ever and ever" (Ex. 15:18).

And it is said, "For the Lord has delivered Jacob, and redeemed him from the hand of him that was stronger than he" (Jer. 31:11).

Blessed art thou, O Lord, who hast redeemed Israel.

4 Grant, Lord our God,[35] that we lie down in peace, and raise us again, our King, to life. Spread over us the tabernacle of thy peace, direct us aright through thine own good counsel; save us for thy name's sake, be thou a shield about us; remove from us every enemy, pestilence, sword, famine, and sorrow; remove also the Adversary from before us and from behind us. Shelter us beneath the shadow of thy wings; for thou, O God, art our Guardian and our Deliverer; thou, O God, art a gracious and merciful King. Guard our going out and our coming in unto life and unto peace from this time forth and forevermore. Spread over us the tabernacle of thy peace. Blessed art thou, O Lord, who spreadest the tabernacle of peace over us and over all thy people Israel, and over Jerusalem.

13.2.6 Mishnah Berakhot 3:1–4: Rules of Prayer[36]

The Mishnah discusses who is exempt from various prayers and commandments. Among those exempted are people who are involved with the performance of another commandment, as seen in the first Mishnah.

ᘓ

1. One whose dead [relative] lies unburied before him is exempt from reciting the Shema, from the Tefillah,[37] and from tefillin.[38] As for those carrying the bier and those that relieve them, and those that relieve the relievers; those that precede and those that follow the bier; those who are necessary for the bier are exempt (from reciting the Shema), but those who are not necessary are obligated. Both are exempt from the Tefillah.

---

35. Here begins the fourth benediction which is only added at night. It is a prayer for protection by God from all danger and adversaries.

36. Trans. S. Berrin.

37. The Eighteen Benedictions.

38. Two black leather boxes containing scriptural passages which are bound by black leather straps on the left hand and on the head and worn during morning services, except on Sabbaths and holidays.

2. When they have returned from burying the dead, if they can begin (the Shema) and conclude it before reaching the line of consolers,[39] they begin it, but if they cannot, then they do not begin it. As for those standing in the row: those in the inner line are exempt, but those in the outer line are obligated [to read the Shema].

3. Women, slaves, and minors are exempt from reciting the Shema and from tefillin, but are obligated regarding the Tefillah, *mezuzah*,[40] and Grace after Meals.

4. One who has had a seminal emission should contemplate the words of the Shema in his heart but may not recite the benedictions before or after it. Over a meal, he should say the blessing after it (Grace after Meals) but not the blessing before.

Rabbi Judah says: "He should say both the blessing before and the blessing after (Grace after Meals)."[41]

13.2.7 Mishnah Berakhot 4:1–7: The Times of Prayer[42]

The Mishnah in Berakhot also specifies other times for recital of the Tefillah (Amidah)—the Eighteen Benedictions. These prayers generally correspond to the times of the required sacrifices in the Temple.

꙳

4:1 The morning Tefillah [may be prayed] until midday. Rabbi Judah says: "until the fourth hour."[43] The afternoon Tefillah [may be prayed] until sunset. Rabbi Judah says: "until midway through the [late] afternoon."[44] The evening Tefillah has no set time. The additional Tefillah[45] [may be prayed] the entire day. Rabbi Judah says: "until the seventh hour."[46]

4:3 Rabban Gamliel says, "Every day one should pray the Eighteen [Benedictions]." Rabbi Joshua says, "an abstract of the Eighteen." Rabbi

---

39. The obligation of consoling the mourners supersedes the obligation to say the Shema. However, if it is possible to recite the Shema before reaching the mourners, it is desirable to do so.

40. A parchment scroll affixed to the doorposts of rooms in a Jewish home.

41. In Rabbinic times, the impurity resulting from seminal emissions was still observed. Subsequently, this practice fell into disuse in most segments of the Jewish community.

42. Trans. S. Berrin.

43. Assuming day and night of equal length, until the fourth hour would mean until 10 A.M.

44. 3:30 P.M.

45. The Musaf service of Sabbaths and festivals.

46. 1:00 P.M.

Akiva says, "If the prayer is fluent in his mouth, he should pray the Eighteen, but if not, then the abstract of the Eighteen."

4:7 Rabbi Eleazar ben Azariah says, "The additional Tefillah is said only when there is a local congregation." But the Sages say, "Either with a local congregation or without it." Rabbi Judah says in [Rabbi Eleazar ben Azariah's] name, "Wherever there is a local congregation, the individual is exempt from the additional Tefillah."

13.2.8 Mishnah Berakhot 5:1–3:
The Proper Intentions in Prayer[47]

Intention and seriousness are an important part of Rabbinic prayer. Further, the public prayer had to be recited precisely and in full.

5:1 None may stand up to say the Tefillah except in a sober mood. The Hasidim (pietists) of former days used to wait an hour before they said the Tefillah, so as to direct their hearts to God. Even if a king greets a person, he may not return the greeting. Even if a snake is coiled around his heel, he may not interrupt [his prayer].

5:3 If one prayed: "Your mercies extend to a bird's nest," or "May Your name be remembered for Your good," or "We give thanks, we give thanks,"[48] they silence him. If one went before the Ark (to lead the congregation) and erred, another must replace him, and none may refuse at that time. Where does he begin? At the beginning of the benediction in which the other erred.

13.2.9 Mishnah Berakhot 6:1–4:
The Blessings Over Food[49]

Benedictions before food were required by the Rabbis who considered it to be sacrilege to partake of God's creation without first offering thanks.

6:1 How do we bless over fruits? Over the fruit of trees one says: "[Blessed are You, O Lord, our God] Who creates the fruit of the tree," except over wine, for over wine one says, ". . . Who creates the fruit of the vine." Over the fruit of the earth one says, ". . . Who creates the fruit

---

47. Trans. S. Berrin.
48. These formulae are considered to be heretical or dualistic and are therefore forbidden.
49. Trans. S. Berrin.

of the ground," except over bread, for over bread one says, ". . . Who brings forth bread from the earth." Over vegetables one says, ". . . Who creates the fruit of the ground." Rabbi Judah says: ". . . Who creates various kinds of herbs."

2 If one blessed, ". . . Who creates the fruit of the ground," over fruits of trees, he has fulfilled his obligation; [but if he blessed], ". . . Who creates the fruit of the tree," over fruits of the ground, he has not fulfilled his obligation. Over all of them, if one said, ". . . for all exists by His word," he fulfilled his obligation.

3 Over anything that does not grow from the ground, one says, ". . . for all [exists by His word]." Over vinegar, unripe fallen fruits, or locusts,[50] one says, ". . . for all [exists by His word]." Over milk, cheese, and eggs one says, ". . . for all [exists by His word]. . . ."

Rabbi Judah said: "Over anything that is a sort of curse (like the abovementioned vinegar, unripe fruits, locusts), no blessing should be said."

4 If one has many kinds of food before him: Rabbi Judah says, "If there is among them one of the seven kinds,[51] he recites the benediction over that one." But the Sages say, "He may recite the benediction over whichever one he wants."

13.2.10 Grace After Meals: Thanking God the Provider[52]

The blessing after eating a full meal including bread involves more than simply acknowledging God's responsibility for the creation and provision of food. It also thanks Him for the Land of Israel, asks Him to rebuild the Temple, sustain His people so that they need not be dependent on others, bless the host and hostess of the meal, and send peace to all Israel.

ﭏ

LEADER: Let us say Grace![53]
COMPANY: Blessed be the name of the Lord henceforth and forever.
LEADER: Let us bless our God whose food we have eaten.
COMPANY: Blessed be our God whose food we have eaten and through whose goodness we live.
LEADER: Blessed be he and blessed be his name.

---

50. Certain kinds of locusts were permitted by the Torah (Lev. 11:22) as kosher. With the loss of the tradition of how to identify them, they later became forbidden.

51. Wheat, barley, grapes, figs, pomegranates, olives, and dates, enumerated in Deut. 8:8.

52. Trans. Heinemann and Petuchowski, *Literature of the Synagogue*, pp. 91–3.

53. The formal call to grace is only said when three recite grace after meals together.

1 Blessed art thou, Lord our God, King of the universe, who sustainest the whole world with goodness, kindness, and mercy. He gives food to all creatures, for his mercy endures forever. Through his abundant goodness we have never yet been in want; may we never be in want of sustenance for his great name's sake. For he is God who sustains all, doest good to all, and provides food for all the creatures he has created. Blessed art thou, O Lord, who dost sustain all.

2 We thank thee, Lord our God, for having given a lovely, good, and spacious land to our fathers as a heritage; for having brought us forth from the land of Egypt and freed us from the house of slavery; for thy covenant which thou hast sealed in our flesh;[54] for thy Torah which thou hast taught us; for thy laws which thou hast made known to us, for the life, grace and kindness thou hast bestowed on us; and for the sustenance thou grantest us daily, at every season, at every hour.

For everything, Lord our God, we thank thee and bless thee; be thy name forever blessed by all as it is written: "And you shall eat and be satisfied, and bless the Lord your God for the good land he has given you" (Deut. 8:10). Blessed art thou, O Lord, for the land and the sustenance.

3 Have compassion, Lord our God, on Israel thy people, on Jerusalem thy city, on Zion the abode of thy glory, on the royal house of David thine anointed one, and on the great and holy Temple that bears thy name. O God, our Father, tend and nourish us; sustain and maintain us; grant us deliverance. Speedily, Lord our God, grant us relief from all our troubles. Lord our God, O make us not dependent on the gifts and loans of men but rather on thy full, open and generous hand, that we may never be put to shame and disgrace.

Rebuild Jerusalem thine holy city speedily in our days. Blessed art thou, O Lord, who in his mercy rebuildest Jerusalem. Amen.

4 Blessed art thou, Lord our God, King of the universe, O God, thou art our Father, our King, our Creator, our Redeemer, the Holy One of Jacob, the Shepherd of Israel, the King who art good and doest good to all. Thou bestowest favors on us continuously; thou dost ever confer on us kindness and mercy, relief and deliverance, prosperity and blessing, life and peace and all goodness. Mayest thou never deprive us of any good thing.

May the Merciful One reign over us forever and ever.

May the Merciful One be worshiped in heaven and on earth.

May the Merciful One he praised for countless generations; may he be glorified among us forever and ever; may he be honored in us to all eternity.

---

54. Referring to circumcision.

May the Merciful One grant us a respectable livelihood.

May the Merciful One break the yoke from our neck; may he lead us securely into our land.

May the Merciful One send abundant blessings upon this house and upon this table at which we have eaten.

May the Merciful One send us Elijah the Prophet, of blessed memory, to bring us the good tidings of deliverance and comfort.

May the Merciful One bless the master of this house and the mistress of this house, their entire family and all that is theirs.

May he bless us and all that is ours; may he bless us all alike with a perfect blessing even as our forefathers Abraham, Isaac, and Jacob were blessed in every way; and let us say, Amen.

May they in heaven plead for all of us that we may have enduring peace. May we receive a blessing from the Lord, righteousness from the God of our salvation, may we find grace and good favor in the sight of God and man.

May the Merciful One make us worthy of the days of the messiah and of the life in the world to come.

"He gives great salvation to his king, and shows mercy to his anointed, to David and to his seed forever" (Ps. 18:51).

He who creates peace in his high places, may he create peace for us and for all Israel; and say, Amen.

13.2.11 Mishnah Berakhot 9:1–3: Other Daily Blessings[55]

The Rabbis also required that benedictions be recited to acknowledge God's creation of various natural phenomena, as well as to thank Him for miracles and other signs of personal or communal good fortune.

९४

9:1 One who sees a place where miracles were done for Israel, should say, "Blessed are You, [O Lord, our God,] Who did miracles for our fathers in this place." [If he sees] a place from which idolatry had been uprooted, he should say, "Blessed are You, [O Lord, our God,] Who uprooted idolatry from our Land."

9:2 Over shooting stars, earthquakes, lightning, thunder and storm winds he should say, "Blessed are You, [O Lord, our God,] Whose power and might fill the world." Over mountains, hills, seas, rivers and deserts he should say, "Blessed are You, [O Lord, our God,] Who performs acts of creation." Rabbi Judah says: If a man saw the Mediterranean Sea, he

---

55. Trans. S. Berrin.

should say, "Blessed are You, [O Lord, our God,] Who made the Great Sea" but only if he sees it at intervals.

For rain and for good news he should say, "Blessed are You, [O Lord, our God,] Who is good and does good." For bad tidings he should say, "Blessed are You, [O Lord, our God,] the True Judge."

9:3 One who built a house or bought new vessels should say, "Blessed are You, [O Lord, our God,] Who has kept us alive and sustained us and brought us to this time. . . ."

If a man cries out over the past, this prayer is in vain. In what manner? If his wife was pregnant and he said, "May it be Your will that my wife will bear a male," this prayer is in vain. If he was returning from travel and he heard the sound of shouting coming from the city and he said, "May it be Your will that these should not be members of my household," this prayer is in vain.[56]

13.2.12 Mishnah Qiddushin 1:7: The Obligation of the Commandments[57]

Mishnah Qiddushin specifies the difference in obligations imposed by talmudic law upon women and men.

⁊ℰ

[Concerning] all the commandments regarding a son which are obligatory on the father, men are obligated and women are exempt. [Concerning] all the Torah commandments of a son toward his father, both men and women are obligated. [Concerning] all positive commandments dependent upon time, men are obligated but women are exempt. And [concerning] all positive commandments which are not dependent upon time, both men and women are obligated. But [concerning] all the negative commandments, whether dependent on time or not dependent on time, both men and women are obligated, except [for the commandments], "You shall not destroy [the corners of your beard]" (Lev. 19:27) and "You shall not round [the corners of your head]"[58] and, [for priests:] "you shall not defile yourself for the dead" (Lev. 21:1).[59]

---

56. Because these events have already happened.
57. Trans. S. Berrin.
58. Because women do not have beards or sideburns.
59. Only male descendants of Aaron are considered priests.

13.3 SANCTUARIES IN TIME

13.3.1 Mishnah Shabbat 7:1–2: The Thirty-Nine Acts of Forbidden Labor on the Sabbath[60]

The Torah forbids creative labor on the Sabbath. The Rabbis attempted to carefully define the major categories of work since accidental violation of the Sabbath would require the bringing of a sin offering (when the Temple stood) for each category violated.

7:1 They have laid down a general rule for the Sabbath: Whoever utterly forgets the essence of the Sabbath and commits many acts of (forbidden) labor on many Sabbaths, is liable for only one sin-offering. Whoever is aware of the essence of the Sabbath and commits many acts of (forbidden) labor on many Sabbaths is liable for each and every Sabbath. Whoever knows that it is the Sabbath and commits many acts of (forbidden) labor on many Sabbaths, is liable for each and every category of labor. Whoever commits many acts of (forbidden) labor within one category of work is only liable for one sin-offering.

2 The categories of work are forty less one (i.e., thirty-nine): one who sows, plows, reaps, or gathers; who threshes or winnows; one who selects, grinds, sifts, kneads, or bakes; one who shears wool, washes it, cards it, colors it, spins, or weaves it; one who makes two loops, or weaves two threads, or removes two threads from the loom; one who ties, or unties, or sews two stitches; one who tears in order to sew two stitches; one who traps a deer, slaughters it, skins it, salts it, cures the hide, scrapes it, or cuts it up; one who writes two letters and one who erases in order to write two letters; one who builds or destroys; one who extinguishes or ignites; one who strikes with a hammer; one who carries from one domain to another. Behold, these are the categories of work, forty less one.

13.3.2 Mishnah Shabbat 12:1–3: Sabbath Labor[61]

In order to violate the Sabbath, one must commit a complete act of labor. The Mishnah gives some examples of what constitutes a full measure of forbidden work.

---

60. Trans. S. Berrin.
61. Trans. S. Berrin

᛭

12:1 One who builds [on the Sabbath], how much must he build in order to be liable? Whoever builds anything at all, or hews stone at all, or strikes with a hammer or an adze, or bores a hole at all, is liable. This is the general rule: Whoever commits an act of (forbidden) labor on the Sabbath, and his work will last, is liable.

Rabban Simeon ben Gamliel said: "Even if one just struck a hammer on the anvil during the work, he is liable since he is like one who prepares for (forbidden) labor."

2 Whoever ploughs at all, or weeds at all, or cuts off dead leaves or prunes at all, is liable. Whoever gathers wood, if it is to set it in order, [is liable] for any amount at all. If it is to burn, [he is liable] for an amount sufficient to cook the smallest egg. Whoever gathers herbs, if it is to set the field in order, [is liable] for any amount at all. If it is to feed cattle, [he is liable] for an amount sufficient to fill a kid's mouth.

3 Whoever writes two letters, whether with his right or left hand, whether the same or different letters, whether in different inks, or in any language, is liable. . . .

13.3.3 Mishnah Pesaḥim 1:1–4: The Search for Leaven[62]

The Torah required that all leaven be removed from the home for the entire festival of Passover. In order to accomplish this, the sages prescribed detailed procedures for searching for and disposing of leaven.

᛭

1:1 On the night preceding the fourteenth [of Nisan], they search for leaven by the light of an [oil] lamp. Any place into which they do not [normally] bring leaven does not require searching. And why did they say, "[They search] two rows in the wine vault?" [They refer to] a place into which they bring leaven. The House of Shammai say, "Two rows over the entire surface of [the rack of jars in] the wine-vault." And the House of Hillel say, "The outermost rows which are the uppermost". . . .

3 Rabbi Judah says, "They search out [leaven] on the night of the fourteenth, and on the fourteenth both in the morning and at the time of the destruction [of the leaven]." But the Sages say, "If one did not search on the night of the fourteenth, one should search on the fourteenth. If one

---

62. Trans. B. Bokser, completed and edited by L. H. Schiffman, *Yerushalmi Pesaḥim*, The Talmud of the Land of Israel, vol. 13 (Chicago Studies in the History of Judaism; Chicago: University of Chicago, 1994), pp. 1, 15, 20.

did not search on the fourteenth, one should search during the holiday. If one did not search during the holiday, one should search after the holiday."

And what he leaves [over after searching at night for the next morning prior to the time leaven becomes prohibited], he should set in a hidden place so that it will not require searching after it.

4 Rabbi Meir says, "[They] eat [leaven] throughout the fifth [hour[63] on the fourteenth] and burn [it] at the beginning of the sixth [hour]."[64] Rabbi Judah says, "[They] eat [leaven] throughout the fourth [hour][65] and suspend [it] throughout the fifth [hour][66] and burn [it] at the beginning of the sixth."[67]

13.3.4 Mishnah Pesaḥim 10:2–9: The Passover Seder[68]

The Passover Seder was originally a Temple ritual. After the destruction of the Second Temple in 70 C.E. it became a home ritual and one of Judaism's central educational tools. The mishnah presents a basic outline of its rituals.

𝄞

10:2 They mixed for him the first cup [of wine]: The House of Shammai say, "He says the blessing over the day[69] and afterwards [he] says the blessing over the wine." And the House of Hillel say, "He says the blessing over the wine and afterwards [he] says the blessing over the day."

3 They served him: He dips the lettuce [the vegetable used for the bitter herbs] before he reached the bread condiment. They served him unleavened bread and lettuce and *ḥaroset* [a mixture, e.g. of nuts, fruit, and wine pounded together] even though the *ḥaroset* is not a [biblical] commandment. Rabbi Eleazar ben Zadok says, "It is a [biblical] commandment. And in the Temple they serve him the carcass of the Passover offering.

4 They poured for him the second cup, and here the child asks—and if the child lacks intelligence, his father instructs him—"How is this night different from all the [other] nights? For on all the [other] nights we eat

---

63. Up to 11:00 A.M.

64. 12:00 P.M.

65. Up to 10:00 A.M.

66. 10:00–11:00 A.M.

67. 11:00 A.M.

68. Trans. B. Bokser, *Yerushalmi Pesaḥim*, pp. 473, 485, 488–9, 494, 497–8, 502–4.

69. "Blessed art thou . . . who sanctifies Israel and the festivals," the main benediction of the Kiddush prayer.

leavened and unleavened bread,[70] this night we eat only unleavened. For on all the [other] nights we eat other vegetables, on this night, *maror* (bitter herbs). For on all the [other] nights we eat meat roasted, steamed, or cooked [in a liquid, boiled], this night only [or 'all of it'] roasted. For on all the [other] nights we dip once, this night twice." According to the child's intelligence, his father instructs him. He starts [reading] with the disgrace [section of the Bible] and ends with the glory; and he expounds [the biblical section] from "A wandering Aramean was my father" (Deut. 26:5) until he finishes the entire portion.

5 Rabban Gamaliel said, "Whoever did not say these three things on Passover did not fulfill his obligation: *pesah*, *matzah*, and *merorim* [the Passover offering, unleavened bread, and bitter herbs]. *Pesah*—because the Omnipresent skipped over the houses of our ancestors in Egypt. *Merorim*—because the Egyptians embittered the lives of our ancestors in Egypt. *Matzah*—because they were redeemed. Therefore we are obligated to give thanks, to praise, to glorify, to crown, to exalt, to elevate the One who did for us all these miracles and took us out of slavery to freedom, and let us say before Him, Hallelujah" (Ps. 113:1ff.).

6 Up to what point does he recite [the Hallel]? The House of Shammai say, "Until '[He sets the childless woman among her household] as a happy mother of children' [the end of Ps. 113]." And the House of Hillel say, "Until '[Tremble . . . at the presence of the Lord . . . who turned] the flinty rock into a fountain' [the end of Ps. 124]." And [he] concludes with [the prayer for] "redemption."[71] Rabbi Tarfon says, ". . . Who has redeemed us and redeemed our ancestors from Egypt and brought us to this night [to eat thereon unleavened bread and bitter herbs"[72]—and [he] does not conclude [with a concluding formula].[73]

Rabbi Akiva says, "[One adds to the blessing:] Thus O Lord, our God and God of our ancestors, bring us in peace to the approaching festivals which are coming to meet us, rejoicing in the building of Your city and joyous in Your service, and to eat from the Passover and festive offerings the blood of which will reach the wall of Your altar with favor, and let us thank You for our redemption. Praised art Thou, Lord, Who redeemed Israel."

---

70. The order of the questions here follows the version set forth in the Mishnah for the Temple in which the Paschal lamb was being offered and roasted.

71. He ends with a blessing that has the motif of "redemption."

72. This phrase is added in certain manuscripts of the Mishnah.

73. The benediction does not conclude with "Praised art Thou . . ."

7 [They] poured for him the third cup [of wine]—he says the blessing over his food.[74] [At] the fourth [cup], he finishes the Hallel [through Ps. 118], and says over it the blessing over the song. Between the former cups, if he wants to drink [further] he may drink. Between the third and fourth, he should not drink. After [eating from] the Passover offering, they do not end [with] *afiqomon* [revelry].

8 [If they] fell asleep:[75] [if it was] some of them, they may eat [again because the remaining individuals of the group, who stayed awake, maintained the group]; and [if] all of them [fell asleep], [they] may not eat [again]. Rabbi Yose says, "If they dozed, they may eat [again]. And if they slumbered, [they] may not eat [again]."

9 After midnight the Passover offering imparts uncleanness to the hands; *piggul*[76] [the "offensive" sacrifice] and *notar*[77] [the "remnant"] impart uncleanness to the hands. [If one] said the blessing over the Passover offering, one is exempt from that over the festive offering; [if one said] the [blessing] over the festive offering, one is not exempt from that over the Passover offering"—the words of Rabbi Ishmael. Rabbi Akiva says, "[Saying] the former does not exempt [one from saying] the latter, and [saying] the latter does not exempt [one from saying] the former."

13.3.5 The Passover Haggadah: Retelling the Exodus[78]

Among the earliest of Rabbinic texts is the midrashic exposition of Deut. 26:5–8 and some additional passages. It originated in Second Temple times and was adapted for the Passover Seder in the home after the destruction of the Temple. The basic structure is the quotation of phrases from the Deuteronomic passage followed by other verses, mostly from Exodus, which provide explication.

ॐ

Come and learn what Laban the Syrian tried to do to our father Jacob. While Pharaoh decreed only against the males, Laban desired to uproot all. For so it is written: "A Syrian sought to destroy my father; and he went down to Egypt and dwelled there, a handful, few in number. There he became a nation, great, mighty and numerous" (Deut. 26:5).

---

74. Grace After Meals.

75. If some of those who have joined together to offer a Passover sacrifice (cf. Exod. 12:3–4) fall asleep.

76. Sacrifice offered with the intention to eat it past the proscribed time.

77. Meat from a sacrifice which has been left over after the proscribed time for eating.

78. Trans. N. Goldberg, *Passover Haggadah* (New York: Ktav, 1973), pp. 12–17.

"He went down to Egypt"—Why did he go down to Egypt? He was compelled by God's decree.

"He dwelled there." This means that Jacob our father did not go down to Egypt to settle there but only to stay for a short while; for so it is said, "And they said to Pharaoh, we have come to dwell in the land because there is no pasture for the flocks of your servants, since the famine is very bad in the land of Canaan; and now let your servants dwell in the land of Goshen" (Gen. 47:4).

"Few in number" as it is said: "Your forefathers went down into Egypt with seventy persons. Now the Eternal your God has made you as numerous as the stars in heaven" (Deut. 10:22).

"And there he became a nation"—from this we learn that Israel became a distinct nation in Egypt.

"Great and mighty"—as it is said: "And the children of Israel were fruitful and increased and multiplied and became very strong and numerous, so that the land was full of them" (Ex. 1:7).

"And numerous"—as it is said: "I have increased you as the growth of the field and you have become numerous and grown big and reached to excellence in beauty. You are fully grown, yet you remained naked and bare" (Ezek. 16:7).

"And the Egyptians did evil unto us"—as it is said in the Bible: "Come, let us deal craftily with them, lest they increase yet more, and it may be that when war occurs they will be added to our enemies and fight against us and go up out of the land" (Ex. 1:10).

"And they made us suffer"—as the Bible relates: "So the Egyptians set taskmasters over them in order to oppress them with their burdens; and they built Pithom and Raamses as store cities for Pharaoh" (Ex. 1:11).

"And they set upon us hard work"—as the Bible states: "And Egypt made the children of Israel labor rigorously" (Ex. 1:13).

"So we cried unto the Eternal, the God of our fathers, and the Eternal heard our voice, and He saw our affliction, and our burden, and our oppression" (Deut. 26:7).

"So we cried unto the Eternal, the God of our fathers"—as the Bible recounts: "And it came to pass in the course of those many days that the king of Egypt died, and the children of Israel moaned because of servitude and cried out, and their outcry from servitude came up unto God" (Ex. 2:23).

"And the Eternal heard our voice"—as the Bible tells: "And God heard their groaning, and God remembered His covenant with Abraham, with Isaac and with Jacob" (Ex. 2:24).

"And He saw our affliction"—this phrase suggests the enforced separation of husband and wife under Pharaoh's persecution, as it is written: "And God saw the children of Israel and God understood their plight" (Ex. 2:25).

"And our burden:—this recalls the drowning of the male children, as it is said: "Every son that is born you shall cast into the Nile, but every daughter you may keep alive" (Ex. 1:22). . . .

"And I will pass through the land of Egypt on that night, and I will smite all the first-born in the land of Egypt from man to best, and against all the gods of Egypt I will execute judgments. It is I, the Eternal" (Ex. 12:12)"—I and not a ministering angel; "and I will smite the first-born in the land of Egypt"—I and not a fiery angel; "And against all the gods of Egypt I will execute judgments"—I and not a messenger; "I the Eternal"—I and no other.

"With a strong hand"—this refers to the cattle plague, as it is said in the Bible; "Behold, the hand of the Eternal will be against the cattle that is in the field, against the horses, the donkeys, the camels, the oxen and the sheep, a very grievous plague" (Ex. 9:3).

"And with an outstretched arm"—this refers to the sword, as the Bible states: "His sword drawn in his hand, outstretched over Jerusalem" (1 Chron. 21:16).

"And with great terror"—this refers to the revelation of God to Israel, as it is said: Has any god ever tried to go and remove one nation from the midst of another nation, with trials, with signs and with wonders, and with battle, and with strong hand and outstretched arm, and with great terrors, as all that the Eternal your God did for you in Egypt before your eyes?" (Deut. 4:34).

"And with signs"—this refers to the rod of Moses, as it is said: "And you, Moses, shall take in your hand this rod with which you shall do the signs" (Ex. 4:17).

"And wonders"—this refers to the plague of blood, as is written in Scripture: "I will put wonders in heaven and on earth: Blood, Fire, Pillars of smoke" (Joel 3:3).

Another interpretation is as follows:

"With a strong hand"—refers to two plagues; "with an outstretched arm"—two; "with great terror"—two; "With signs"—two; and "with wonders" refers to two plagues. Thus we have the ten plagues that the Holy One, blessed be He, brought upon the Egyptians in Egypt; and they are as follows:

1. Blood, 2. Frogs, 3. Vermin, 4. Beasts, 5. Cattle disease, 6. Boils, 7. Hail, 8. Locusts, 9. Darkness, 10. Slaying of the first-born.

13.3.6 Mishnah Bikkurim 3:1–6:
The Ceremony of the First Fruits in the Temple[79]

The bringing of the first fruits was a beautiful procession which was intended to show the joy of Israel at being blessed with God's produce. The Mishnah describes the manner in which this ritual was celebrated in Second Temple times.

᠊᠊᠊ ᠊᠊᠊

3:1 How do we set apart the first fruits? When a man goes down to his field and sees a ripe fig or a ripe cluster of grapes or a ripe pomegranate, he ties reed-grass around it and says, "These are first fruits."

Rabbi Simeon says: "Even so, he again declares them 'first fruits' after they are plucked from the soil."

2 How do they bring up the first fruits to Jerusalem? All the smaller towns which belong to the *ma'amad*[80] gather in the town of the *ma'amad* and spend the night in the open square of the town, and they do not go into the houses. Early in the morning, the appointed man said: "Arise, let us go up to Zion to the Lord our God" (Jer. 31:6).

3 Those who were near [Jerusalem] would bring fresh figs and grapes, and those who were far away would bring dried figs and raisins. Before them walks the ox, its horns overlaid with gold and an olive wreath on its head. The flute would be played before them until they approached Jerusalem. When they approached Jerusalem, they sent messengers before them and they decorated their first fruits. The grandees, the chiefs, and treasurers of the Temple would go forth to meet them. They would go forth according to the honor due to those who were coming in. And all the craftsmen in Jerusalem would rise before them and greet them, saying, "Brothers, men of such-and-such a place, welcome!"

4 The flute would be played before them until they reached the Temple Mount. When they reached the Temple Mount even King Agrippa[81] would take his basket on his shoulder and enter until he reached the Temple court. When they reached the Temple court the Levites sang the song, "I will extol you, O Lord, for You have lifted me up, and have not let my enemies triumph over me" (Ps. 30:2).

---

79. Trans. S. Berrin.

80. A division of popular representatives appointed to accompany the daily sacrifices with prayer, coming from the same town as the priests serving during that week.

81. Probably a reference to Agrippa I.

5 The pigeons which were [hung] upon the baskets were [sacrificed] as burnt-offerings, and the people gave the priests that which [they carried] in their hands.

6 While the basket was still on his shoulder, he would recite [the passage of Deut. 26:3–10] from "I acknowledge this day before the Lord your God" until he finished the passage. Rabbi Judah says: "until he would reach the words, 'A wandering Aramean was my father' (Deut. 26:5). When he reached the words "A wandering Aramean," he took the basket down from his shoulder and held it by its rims. The priest put his hand under it and waved it. Then the man would recite [the words] from, "A wandering Aramean" until he finished the passage. Then he would place the basket beside the altar, bow down, and leave.

13.3.7 Mishnah Sukkah 1:1–11:
The Building of a Sukkah[82]

The holiday of Sukkot (Tabernacles) is celebrated by living in booths for seven days, commemorating the booths Jews are said to have lived in after the Exodus from Egypt. The sukkah (booth) must be built according to specific regulations designed to ensure that it is a frail, temporary structure.

ॐ

1:1 A sukkah which is more than twenty cubits high[83] is unfit, [but] Rabbi Judah permits it. If it is less than ten handbreadths high, or does not have three sides, or if its unshaded area exceeds its shaded area, it is unfit. An old sukkah: the House of Shammai declares it unfit, but the House of Hillel validates it. And what is an "old sukkah"? Any one which he made thirty days before the festival. But if it was made for the sake of the festival, even from the beginning of the year,[84] it is valid.

2 One who builds his sukkah under a tree, it is as though he built it inside a house. If one sukkah is [built] on top of another, the upper one is valid but the lower one is unfit. Rabbi Judah says: "If there are no occupants in the upper one, the lower one is valid. . . ."

4 If he suspended a grapevine or a gourd vine, or ivy over it and spread sekhakh[85] upon them, it is unfit. But if the sekhakh exceeds them or if he cut them, the sukkah is valid. This is the general rule: whatever is subject

---

82. Trans. S. Berrin.
83. Approximately 30 feet.
84. That is, even if it were made right after the conclusion of the festival a year earlier.
85. "Covering," the roof of leaves, grass, or boards.

to defilement[86] or does not grow from the ground may not be used as *sekhakh*; whatever is not subject to defilement and grows from the ground may be used as *sekhakh*.

5 Bundles of straw, or bundles of wood, or bundles of sprouts may not be used as *sekhakh*. But all of these, if they are untied, are valid, and all of these are valid for the walls [of the sukkah].

6 Boards may be used for *sekhakh*, according to Rabbi Judah. But Rabbi Meir forbids [them]. If one puts a board four handbreadths wide over the sukkah it is valid, provided that he does not sleep under it. . . .

9 One who suspends the walls from above downward, if the height [of the space] is three handbreadths higher than the ground, the sukkah is unfit. If [he extends them] from below upwards, and they measure ten handbreadths high from the ground [even if they do not reach the roofing], it is valid. Rabbi Yose says: "Just as from below upwards the height must be ten handbreadths, so from the top downwards there must be ten handbreadths." If the roofing is three handbreadths away from the walls, the sukkah is unfit.

11 One who makes his sukkah like a hut ("v-shaped"), or props it up against a wall, Rabbi Eliezer declares it unfit since it has no roof, but the Sages declare it fit. A large reed-mat which was made for lying upon is subject to defilement and may not be used for *sekhakh*. [If it was made] for roofing, it may be used and is not subject to defilement.

Rabbi Eliezer says: "It is all the same whether it is large or small. If it was made for lying upon it is subject to defilement and may not be used for *sekhakh*. [If it was made] for *sekhakh*, it may be used for *sekhakh* and is not subject to defilement."

13.3.8 Mishnah Sukkah 3:1–7: Lulav and Etrog[87]

Also associated with the Sukkot festival is the taking of the lulav (palm frond along with myrtle and willow leaves) and etrog (Citrus medica: a yellow citrus fruit). Detailed laws prescribe the specific qualifications for these "four species." Many homiletical explanations for this ritual extend its significance beyond its origins in asking God for rain and a successful harvest.

---

86. Foods, as well as manufactured vessels, even of natural materials, are susceptible to ritual defilement. They may not be used for *sekhakh*.

87. Trans. S. Berrin.

ֵֶ

3:1 A stolen or withered palm-branch is unfit. If it came from an *asherah*[88] or from a condemned city,[89] it is unfit. If its tip was broken off or if its leaves were split, it is unfit; if its leaves were spread apart, it is valid. Rabbi Judah says: "It may be tied up at the top." The thorn-palms of the Iron Mount[90] are valid. A palm-branch three handbreadths long, which is long enough to shake, is valid.

2 A stolen or withered myrtle-branch is unfit. If it came from an *asherah* or from a condemned city, it is unfit. If its tip was broken off or if its leaves were split, or if its berries exceed its leaves, it is unfit. But if one removed a number of its berries, it is fit, but one may not remove them on the festival day.

3 A stolen or withered willow-branch is unfit. If it came from an *asherah* or from a condemned city, it is unfit. If its tip was broken off or if its leaves were split, or if it was a mountain-willow, it is unfit. If it was shrivelled, or had lost some of its leaves, or had grown in a field [and not near a body of water], it is fit.

4 Rabbi Ishmael says: "[The commandment consists of taking] three myrtle-branches, two willow branches, one palm-branch, and one citron, even if two [of the myrtle-branches] have their tips broken off and one does not."

Rabbi Tarfon says: ". . . even if all of the three have their tips broken off."

Rabbi Akiva says: "Just as there is one palm-branch and one citron, so too there is one myrtle-branch and one willow-branch."

5 A stolen or withered citron is unfit. If it came from an *asherah* or from a condemned city, it is unfit. If it was of *orlah*[91] it is unfit. If it was of impure *terumah*,[92] it is unfit. If it was of pure *terumah*, he should not take it, but if he took it, it is fit. If it was *demai*,[93] the House of Shammai declares it unfit, but the House of Hillel declared it fit. If it was of the sec-

---

88. A tree devoted to idolatry.

89. A city condemned to destruction as a result of its idolatrous worship (Deut. 13:13–19).

90. Mentioned in Josephus (*War* IV, 454) among the mountains that are located to the north of Moab, opposite Jericho.

91. Fruit grown in the first three years of a tree's fruit-bearing.

92. The priests' portion.

93. Produce about which there is a doubt as to whether it has been properly tithed.

ond tithe,[94] it should not be taken [even] in Jerusalem, but if it was taken, it is valid.

6 If lichens arose on most of [the citron], or if its tip[95] was gone, or if it was peeled, or split, or had a hole, and was missing something, it is unfit. If lichens arose on a minority of [the citron], or if its stem was gone, or had a hole and was not missing anything, it is fit. A black citron is unfit. A [citron] which is green like a leek, Rabbi Meir declares it fit, and Rabbi Judah declares it unfit.

7 The minimum size for a citron, Rabbi Meir says: "the size of a walnut." Rabbi Judah says: "the size of an egg." The maximum size is such that two can be held in one hand, according to Rabbi Judah. Rabbi Yose says: "even so that one can be held in two hands."

13.3.9 Mishnah Sukkah 5:1–4: The Water Drawing Ceremony[96]

During the time that the Temple still stood in Jerusalem, the Water Drawing Ceremony held on the second night of Sukkot was a highlight of the festival. While the lulav and etrog rituals were continued after the destruction, this ceremony was only remembered.

৵

5:1 . . . They said: "Whoever did not see the joy of the Water Drawing Ceremony has not seen joy in his life."

2 At the end of the first festival-day of Sukkot, they went down to the Women's Court,[97] where they had made a great preparation. There were golden candlesticks there with four golden bowls at the top and four ladders to each candlestick, and four young priests had in their hands jars of oil holding 120 *logs*[98] which they poured into all the bowls.

3 They made wicks from the worn-out pants and belts of the priests and lit [the lamps] with them, and there was not a courtyard in Jerusalem which was not lit by the light of the Water Drawing Ceremony.

4 Hasidim (pietists) and men of good deeds danced before them with burning torches in their hands, singing songs and praises before them. The Levites played harps, lyres, cymbals, trumpets, and innumerable musical

---

94. Produce to be brought to Jerusalem and eaten there.

95. Most *etrogim* have a protuberance at the tip (the opposite end from the stem). If removed, it renders the *etrog* unfit.

96. Trans. S. Berrin.

97. Of the Jerusalem Temple.

98. About 15 gallons. A *log* is approximately 1/3 of a quart.

instruments on the fifteen steps leading down from the Israelites' Court to the Women's Court, corresponding to the fifteen "Songs of Ascents" in the Psalms.[99] The Levites stood upon them with their musical instruments and sang songs. Two priests stood at the upper gate which leads down from the Israelites' Court to the Women's Court with two trumpets in their hands. When the rooster crowed,[100] they sounded a blast, a tremolo,[101] and a blast. . . . When they reached the gate that leads out to the east, they turned their faces to the west and said, "When our fathers were in this place, [they turned with] 'their backs toward the Temple of the Lord and their faces toward the east, and they bowed to the sun toward the east' (Ezek. 8:16), but we—our eyes are turned to God." Rabbi Judah says: "They used to repeat the words, 'We are God's, and our eyes are turned to God.'"

13.3.10 Babylonian Talmud Shabbat 21b: The Significance of Hanukkah[102]

The holiday of Hanukah, celebrating the Jewish victory over the Seleucids and the rededication of the Temple in 164 B.C.E., was observed by the lighting of lamps, symbolizing the relighting of the Temple menorah. The Babylonian Talmud explained the significance of the festival and detailed its observance.

࿄

Our Rabbis taught: "The commandment of Hanukkah is [to light] one candle for a man and his household. Those who are more exacting—one candle for each and every person. And those who are the most exacting—the House of Shammai say: 'On the first day one should light eight; from there on, he reduces [the number of candles] as the holiday progresses.' But the House of Hillel say: 'On the first day one should light one; and from there on, he should add as Hanukkah continues.'"

Ulla says: "Two amoraic sages argued about this in the west (the Land of Israel), R. Yose bar Avin and Yose bar Zevida. One says: 'The reason of the House of Shammai is [that the number of lights] corresponds to the days that are still to come. The reason of the House of Hillel is [that the number of lights] corresponds to the days that have already passed.' And one says: 'The reason for the House of Shammai is that [the decreasing

---

99. Psalms 120–34.
100. Early in the morning, indicating that the new day had begun.
101. A quivering musical sound.
102. Trans. S. Berrin

lights] correspond to the bullocks of the festival (of Sukkot) [which decrease day by day],[103] and the reason of the House of Hillel is "We increase in holiness, and we do not decrease." "

Our Rabbis taught: "It is a commandment to place the Hanukkah light at the entrance to one's house outside. If he lives in an upper chamber (second storey), he should place it in the window closest to the public thoroughfare. But in a time of danger[104] he should place it on his table, and that will be sufficient." Said Rava: "It is required that there be an additional lamp, the light of which may be used.[105] But if there is a fire (in the fireplace), it is not necessary. But if he is a distinguished man, even if there is a fire, an additional lamp is still required."

What is [the significance of the holiday of] Hanukkah? Our Rabbis taught: "[From] the twenty-fifth day of Kislev are the days of Hanukkah, which are eight, on which eulogies and fasting are forbidden."[106] When the Greeks[107] entered the Sanctuary, they defiled all the oil in the Sanctuary. But when the Hasmonean House grew mighty and defeated them, they searched and could find but a single cruse of oil which was sealed with the seal of the high priest. And in it there was sufficient [oil] for but a single day. A miracle occurred, and they lit [the menorah] from it for eight days. The next year they established them and made them festival days with *Hallel*[108] and thanksgiving.[109]

13.3.11 *'Al ha-Nissim*: Additional Prayer for Hanukkah[110]

'Al ha-Nissim, inserted in the Amidah and the Grace after Meals on all eight days of Hanukkah, is only preserved in medieval texts. Yet its concentration on the military victory—not on the miracle of the burning of the oil for eight days—testifies to its antiquity.

---

103. According to Num. 29:12–31 where the number of bullocks starts with thirteen and decreases every day.

104. A time of persecution during which the holiday of Hanukkah might be outlawed.

105. It is forbidden to make use of the Hanukkah lights for any purpose other than for publicizing the miracle of Hanukkah. Hence, an additional lamp is lit along with the Hanukkah lights so as to provide light which may be used for other purposes. It later became customary to use that additional light to kindle the Hanukkah lights.

106. The Talmud quotes the *Megillat Ta'anit* (Scroll of Fasts) and then continues by explaining it.

107. The Seleucid Syrians, termed "Greeks" since they were successors to the empire of Alexander the Great.

108. A designated group of joyful psalms (Psalms 113–18) inserted into the daily prayers on special occasions such as festivals.

109. Fulfilled by the recitation of the *'Al ha-Nissim* prayer.

110. Trans. P. Birnbaum, *Daily Prayer Book* (New York: Hebrew Publishing Co., 1949), pp. 92–3.

❦

We thank thee for the miracles, for the redemption, for the mighty deeds and triumphs, and for the battles which thou didst perform for our fathers in those days, at this season. . . .

In the days of the Hasmonean, Mattathias ben Yoḥanan, the High Priest, and his sons, when a wicked Hellenic government rose up against thy people Israel to make them forget thy Torah and transgress the laws of thy will. Thou in thy great mercy didst stand by them in the time of their distress. Thou didst champion their cause, defend their rights and avenge their wrong; thou didst deliver the strong into the hands of the weak, the many into the hands of the few, the impure into the hands of the pure, the wicked into the hands of the righteous, and the arrogant into the hands of the students of the Torah. Thou didst make a great and holy name for thyself in thy world, and for they people Israel thou didst perform a great deliverance unto this day. Thereupon thy children entered the shrine of thy house, cleansed thy Temple, purified thy sanctuary, kindled lights in thy holy courts, and designated these eight days of Hanukkah for giving thanks and praise to thy great name.

13.3.12 Mishnah Megillah 1:1–2: The Holiday of Purim[111]

The book of Esther indicated that the Jews overcame their enemies on the fourteenth of Adar in most places, but in the Persian capital of Susa, they were victorious only on the fifteenth. Accordingly, the Scroll of Esther (Megillah) is read on the fourteenth and fifteenth and sometimes, in talmudic times, even on the eleventh, twelfth or thirteenth.

❦

1:1 The Scroll [of Esther] is read on the eleventh, twelfth, thirteenth, fourteenth, or fifteenth [day of Adar], never earlier and never later. Cities which were surrounded by a wall from the days of Joshua the son of Nun read it on the fifteenth. Villages and large towns read it on the fourteenth, but villages read it earlier on a day of assembly.[112]

2 How is it [that the above dates are implemented]? If the fourteenth fell on a Monday, villages and large towns read [the Scroll of Esther] on that day, and walled cities on the following day. If it fell on a Tuesday or a

111. Trans. S. Berrin.
112. Monday or Thursday, when the courts were in session.

Wednesday, villages read it earlier on the day of assembly (Monday the 13th), large towns on the day itself, and walled cities on the following day. If it fell on a Thursday, villages and large towns read it on that day, and walled cities on the following day. If it fell on a Friday, villages read it earlier on the day of assembly (Thursday the 13th), large towns and walled cities on the day itself. If it fell on the Sabbath, villages and large towns read it earlier on the day of assembly (Thursday the 12th), and walled cities on the following day. If it fell on the day after the Sabbath (Sunday), villages read it earlier on the day of assembly (Thursday the 11th), large towns on the day itself, and walled cities on the following day.

13.3.13 Mishnah Megillah 2:1–2:
The Reading of the Scroll of Esther[113]

The book of Esther must be read exactly, in order, with intention and from a scroll.

৯৩

2:1 One who reads the Scroll [of Esther] out of order has not fulfilled his obligation. If he "read" it by heart, or if he read it in Aramaic or in any other language [which he does not understand], he has not fulfilled his obligation. But it may be read in a foreign language to those who speak the foreign language. One who speaks a foreign language who heard it in [Hebrew read from a scroll written in] Assyrian script[114] has fulfilled his obligation.

2 One who read it at intervals or while dozing off has fulfilled his obligation. If he was copying it, expounding it, or correcting [a copy of] it, if he directed his heart to fulfill the obligation], he has fulfilled his obligation. If not, he has not fulfilled his obligation. . . .

13.3.14 Mishnah Ta'anit 4:6–7:
Days of National Mourning[115]

The Mishnah fixes the days on which the tragedies which befell the Jewish people were to be commemorated, the Seventeenth of Tammuz and the Ninth of Av. Each of these days commemorates a series of occasions connected primarily with the destruction of the First and Second Temples.

---

113. Trans. S. Berrin.
114. The square Aramaic script used after the Persian period for the writing of Jewish scrolls.
115. Trans. S. Berrin.

꘏

4:6 Five things happened to our fathers on the Seventeenth of Tammuz and five on the Ninth of Av. On the Seventeenth of Tammuz: the tablets [of the Ten Commandments] were broken,[116] the daily offering ceased,[117] the city [walls of Jerusalem] were breached, Apostomus[118] burned the Torah, and he set up an image in the sanctuary. On the Ninth of Av: it was decreed that our fathers would not enter the Land of Israel,[119] the Temple was destroyed the first and second time,[120] Betar was captured,[121] and the City [of Jerusalem] was ploughed up. When Av comes in, we minimize gladness.

7 In the week in which the Ninth of Av falls, hair-cutting and clothes-washing are prohibited, but they are permitted on Thursday in honor of the Sabbath. On the eve of the Ninth of Av one may not eat two cooked dishes, eat meat, or drink wine. Rabban Simeon ben Gamliel says: "One must simply make some change." Rabbi Judah requires turning over one's bed,[122] but the Sages do not agree with him.

13.4 THE SANCTIFIED TABLE

13.4.1 Leviticus 11:
Permitted and Forbidden Animals[123]

The Torah sets forth the regulations regarding which animals are permitted to be eaten and which are not. This aspect of the laws of kashrut has remained effectively unchanged throughout history.

꘏

11:1 The Lord spoke to Moses and Aaron, saying to them: Speak to the Israelite people thus:

These are the creatures that you may eat from among all the land animals: 3 any animal that has true hoofs, with clefts through the hoofs and that chews the cud—such you may eat. 4 The following, however, of

---

116. By Moses after the incident of the Golden Calf (Ex. 32:19).

117. Most probably a reference to the destruction of the First Temple.

118. Apostomus cannot be identified with certainty.

119. After the negative report of the spies sent by Moses (Num. 14:1–25).

120. The First Temple in 586 B.C.E. and the Second Temple in 70 C.E.

121. At the end of the Bar Kokhba rebellion (135 C.E.).

122. So as to sleep uncomfortably as a sign of mourning.

123. Trans. from *Tanakh: The Holy Scriptures* (Philadelphia: Jewish Publication Society, 1985).

those that either chew the cud or have true hoofs, you shall not eat: the camel—although it chews the cud, it has no true hoofs: it is unclean for you; 5 the daman[124]—althoughs it chew the cud, it has no true hoofs: it is unclean for you; 6 the hare—although it chews the cud, it has no true hoofs: it is unclean for you; 7 and the swine—although it has true hoofs, with the hoofs cleft right through, it does not chew the cud: it is unclean for you. 8 You shall not eat of their flesh or touch their carcasses; they are unclean for you.

9 These you may eat of all that live in water: anything in water, whether in the seas or in the streams, that has fins and scales—these you may eat. 10 But anything in the seas or in the streams that has no fins and scales, among all the swarming things of the water and among all the other living creatures that are in the water—they are an abomination for you 11 and an abomination for you they shall remain: you shall not eat of their flesh and you shall abominate their carcasses. 12 Everything in water that has no fins and scales shall be an abomination for you.

13 The following you shall abominate among the birds—they shall not be eaten, they are an abomination: the eagle, the vulture, and the black vulture; 14 the kite, falcons of every variety; 15 all varieties of raven; 16 the ostrich, the nighthawk, the sea gull; hawks of every variety; 17 the little owl, the cormorant, and the great owl; 18 the white owl, the pelican, and the bustard; 19 the stork; herons of every variety; the hoopoe, and the bat.

20 All winged swarming things that walk on all fours shall be an abomination for you. 21 But these you may eat among all the winged swarming things that walk on all fours: all that have, above their feet, jointed legs to leap with on the ground—22 of these you may eat the following: locusts of every variety; all varieties of bald locust; crickets of every variety; and all varieties of grasshopper. 23 But all other winged swarming things that have four legs shall be an abomination for you.[125]

24 And the following shall make you unclean—whoever touches their carcasses shall be unclean until evening, 25 and whoever carries the carcasses of any of them shall wash his clothes and be unclean until evening—26 every animal that has true hoofs but without clefts through the hoofs, or that does not chew the cud. They are unclean for you; who-

---

124. Assyrian hyrax, a small mammal.
125. Due to a loss of the tradition regarding the identity of these animals, Rabbinic law forbade the eating of all creeping things.

ever touches them shall be unclean. 27 Also all animals that walk on paws, among those that walk on all fours, are unclean to you; whoever touches their carcasses shall be unclean until evening. 28 And anyone who carries their carcasses shall wash his clothes and remain unclean until evening. They are unclean for you.

29 The following shall be unclean for you among the things that swarm on the earth: the mole, the mouse, and great lizards of every variety; 30 the gecko, the land crocodile, the lizard, the sand lizard, and the chameleon. 31 Those are for you the unclean among all the swarming things; whoever touches them when they are dead shall be unclean until evening. . . .

41 All the things that swarm upon the earth are an abomination; they shall not be eaten. 42 You shall not eat, among all things that swarm upon the earth, anything that crawls on its belly, or anything that walks on all fours, or anything that has many legs; for they are an abomination. 43 You shall not draw an abomination upon yourselves through anything that swarms; you shall not make yourselves unclean herewith and thus become unclean. 44 For I the Lord am your God: you shall sanctify yourselves and be holy, for I am holy. You shall not make yourselves unclean through any swarming thing that moves upon the earth. 45 For I the Lord am He who brought you up from the land of Egypt to be your God: you shall be holy, for I am holy.

46 These are the instructions concerning animals, birds, all living creatures that move in water, and all creatures that swarm on earth, 47 for distinguishing between the unclean and the clean, between the living things that may be eaten and the living things that may not be eaten.

13.4.2 Mishnah Ḥullin 1:1–2: Laws of Ritual Slaughter[126]

The laws of Kosher slaughter must be performed by or under the supervision of a competent person. The knife must be smooth so as to spare the animal pain.

ೈಲ

1:1 All may slaughter and what they slaughter is valid, except a deaf-mute, an imbecile, and a minor, lest they incorrectly slaughter. But if any of these slaughtered in the presence of others, what they slaughtered is

---

126. Trans. S. Berrin.

valid. Whatever is slaughtered by Gentiles is carrion,[127] and it transmits impurity by being carried.[128] One who slaughtered at night, and in the same way a blind man who slaughtered, what he slaughtered is fit. One who slaughtered on the Sabbath or on the Day of Atonement, although he is liable for his life, what he slaughtered is fit.

2 One who slaughtered with a hand sickle, flint or reed, what he slaughtered is fit. All may slaughter at any time and with any implement except a scythe, a saw, teeth, or fingernails, since these choke [the animal by mangling the windpipe rather than cutting it]. One who slaughtered with a scythe, drawing the blade backwards, the House of Shammai declares it unfit, but the House of Hillel declares it fit. If the teeth [of the scythe] are filed down, then it is like a knife.

13.4.3 Mishnah Ḥullin 8:1–4: Separation of Meat and Milk[129]

The Mishnah also specifies the exact requirements in the separation of milk and meat as understood to be prohibited by the Torah.

ʂ۶

8:1 No meat may be cooked in milk, except the meat of fish and locusts.[130] No meat may be served on the table with cheese except the meat of fish and locusts. One who vowed to abstain from meat may eat the meat of fish and locusts. Fowl may be served at the table together with cheese, but may not be eaten with it. This is according to the School of Shammai. But the House of Hillel say: it may not be served or eaten with it.[131] Rabbi Yose said: This is one of the lenient rulings of the House of Shammai, and one of the strict rulings of the House of Hillel. What kind of table did they refer to? A table at which people eat. But on a table upon which food is only set out one may put one beside the other without concern.

2 One may tie up meat and cheese in the same cloth so long as they do not touch each other. Rabban Simeon ben Gamliel said: "Two inn-

---

127. It is considered like an animal that had died a natural death and therefore is not kosher.

128. Cf. Lev. 11:40.

129. Trans. S. Berrin.

130. Only the meat of animals and fowl (the latter by Rabbinic ordinance) must be separated from milk.

131. This was the ruling adapted by the Talmud as law.

guests [who are strangers] may eat at the same table, one meat and one cheese, without concern."[132]

3 If a drop of milk fell upon a piece [of meat cooking in a pot] and there was enough to give flavor to that piece, it is forbidden. If one stirred the pot and there was enough to give flavor to the [whole] pot, it is forbidden. One should cut open the udder and empty out the milk, but if he has not cut it open, he has not transgressed. He should cut open the heart and empty out the blood, but if he has not cut it open, he has not transgressed. If one served fowl and cheese on the table together, he has not transgressed [a negative commandment].[133]

4 It is prohibited to cook or derive any benefit from the meat of a clean (kosher) animal with the milk of a clean animal. It is permitted to cook or derive benefit from the meat of a clean animal with the milk of an unclean animal or the meat of an unclean animal with the milk of a clean animal.[134] Rabbi Akiva says: "Wild animals and birds are not [prohibited] by the Torah, for it is written three times, 'You shall not seethe a kid in its mother's milk' (Exod. 23:19; 34:26; Deut. 14:21), excluding wild animals, birds, and unclean animals [from this prohibition]."[135]

Rabbi Yose the Galilean says: "It is said, 'You shall not eat carrion' (Deut.14:21), and it is said, 'You shall not seethe a kid in its mother's milk.' Whatever is forbidden under the law of carrion, it is forbidden to seethe in milk. One might think that a bird, which is forbidden under the law of carrion, is forbidden to be seethed in milk. Thus, the verse says, 'in its mother's milk' a bird is excluded since it has no mother's milk."[136]

13.5 MARRIAGE AND THE FAMILY

13.5.1 Mishnah Ta'anit 4:8: Choosing a Spouse[137]

In Second Temple times, perhaps as a survival of pre-Israelite practice, there was a sort of "Sadie Hawkins Day," in which young men and women would choose their mates. The Mishnah emphasizes that marriage symbolizes the union of God and Israel while reminding young people of the correct criteria for choosing a spouse and building a family.

---

132. Since they are strangers there is no concern that they may share their food, thus eating milk and meat together.

133. But it was prohibited by Rabbinic ordinance.

134. Despite the fact that such a mixture may not be eaten.

135. The prohibition of eating these animals with milk would therefore be Rabbinic.

136. Nonetheless, the Rabbis ruled that it was forbidden to eat fowl with milk because of the similarity of fowl to meat.

137. Trans. S. Berrin.

ॐ

Rabban Simeon ben Gamliel said: "There were no better days for Israel than the Fifteenth of Av and the Day of Atonement, for on those days the young women of Jerusalem used to go out in borrowed white garments, so as not to embarrass whoever did not have any. All the garments required immersion.[138] And the young women would go out and dance in the vineyards. What would they say? 'Young man, lift up your eyes and see, what do you choose for yourself? Do not set your eyes toward beauty, [but] set your eyes toward family.' 'Grace is deceptive, beauty is vanity'" (Prov. 31:30). And it says, "Praise her for the fruit of her hand, and let her works praise her at the gates" (Prov. 31:31). And thus it says, "Daughters of Zion, go forth and see King Solomon,[139] wearing the crown that his mother gave him on his wedding day, on the day of the rejoicing of his heart" (Song 3:11). "On the day of his wedding": this refers to the Giving of the Torah. "The day of the rejoicing of his heart": this refers to the building of the Temple, may it be rebuilt speedily in our days, Amen!

13.5.2 Mishnah Qiddushin 1:1: The Law of Marriage[140]

Marriage was described in terms of a financial arrangement long after Jewish marriage had become an act of free will by husband and wife. The Rabbis debated how significant a sum must be used to effect the symbolic acquisition of the bride by the groom. For the House of Hillel, whose ruling was followed, even a minimal, symbolic sum sufficed.

ॐ

1:1 By three means is a woman acquired [in marriage], and by two means she "acquires herself." She is acquired by money, by contract, or by intercourse. "By money": The House of Shammai say: "by a *denar*[141] or by that which is worth a *denar*." The House of Hillel say: "by a *perutah* or that which is worth a *perutah*." How much is a *perutah*? An eighth of an Italian *issar*. And she acquires herself by a bill of divorce or by the death of her husband. The widow of a deceased brother is acquired [by the living

---

138. In order not to single out those who were ritually impure and would have to immerse their garments, all the women would have to immerse their garments. This was in keeping with the general character of the occasion which sought to ensure equality for those who participated.

139. Taken here symbolically to represent God.

140. Trans. S. Berrin.

141. 1 *denar* = 192 *perutot*.

brother] by intercourse,[142] and she acquires herself [143] by *ḥaliẓah*,[144] or by the death of her deceased husband's brother.

13.5.3 Babylonian Talmud Ketubot 8a: The Marriage Benedictions[145]

The benedictions ordained by Rabbinic tradition for the marriage celebration, recited both at the wedding and throughout the week following, express the notion that marriage reflects the ideal state of the Garden of Eden and of the messianic era.

☙

1 Blessed are You Lord, our God, King of the universe, Who creates the fruit of the vine.

2 Blessed are You Lord, our God, King of the universe, Who has created everything for His glory.

3 Blessed are You Lord, our God, King of the universe, Creator of humanity.

4 Blessed are You Lord, our God, King of the universe, Who has created man in His image, in the image of the likeness of His form, and prepared for him from himself an eternal building.[146] Blessed are You, Lord, Creator of Man.

5 Bring intense joy and exultation to the Barren One (Zion) through the gathering of her children to her midst in joy. Blessed are You, Lord, who causes Zion to rejoice in her children.

6 Gladden greatly the beloved lovers, as You gladdened Your creation in the Garden of Eden in ancient times. Blessed are You, Lord, who gladdens the groom and the bride.

7 Blessed are You, Lord our God, King of the universe, who created joy and gladness, groom and bride, delight, singing, dance, happiness, love, companionship, peace and friendship. Speedily, O Lord our God, may there be heard in the cities of Judah and in the streets of Jerusalem, the sound of joy and the sound of gladness, the voice of the groom and the voice of the bride, the sound of the celebrating of grooms from their

---

142. In the case of levirate marriage (Deut. 25:5–6).

143. That is, exits the marriage.

144. A ritual which cancels the obligation of a man to marry the wife of his deceased brother (Deut. 25:7–11).

145. Trans. S. Berrin.

146. That is, woman from man's rib (Gen. 2:21–24).

wedding canopies, and of young men from their feasting and singing. Blessed are You, Lord, who gladdens the groom and the bride.

13.5.4 Babatha's *Ketubah*: An Early Marriage Contract[147]

This is one of the earliest ketubot known to us. The purpose of the ketubah (marriage contract) is to protect the wife by providing a guaranteed financial settlement (the ketubah payment) in the event that the marriage ends by the death of the husband or divorce. The ketubah contains the following elements: date and place of its writing, names of the groom and bride, the marriage proposal, the promise to give the bride her due, the mandatory ketubah clauses or "court stipulations," the statement that the document will be replaced, and the statement by the groom that he accepts all the above provisions.

🙠

RECTO:
On the [thi]rd of Adar in the consulship of . . . [that you will be] my wife [according to the la]w of Moses and the "Judaeans" and I will [feed you] and [clothe] you and I will bring you (into my house) by means of your *ketubah* and I owe you the sum of four hundred *denarii* which equal one hundred tetradrachms whichever you wish "to take and to . . ." from . . . together with the due amount of your food, and your clothes, and your bed(?), provision fitting for a free woman . . . the sum of four hundred *denarii* which equal one hundred tetradrachms whichever you wish "to take and to [. . . from] . . . together with the due amount of your food, and your bed(?), and your clothes, as a free woman.

And if you are taken captive, I will redeem you, from my house and from my estate, and I will take you back as my wife, and I owe you your *ketubah* money . . . [and if I go to my eternal home before you, male children which you will have by me will inherit your *ketubah* money, beyond their share with their brothers,] female [child]ren shall dwell and be provided for from my house and [from my estate un]til the time when they will be [mar]ried. And if I go to my eternal h[ome] before you, you w[il]l [d]well in my house and be provided for from my house and from my estate [until] the time that my heirs wish to give you your *ketubah* money. And whenever you tell me [I will exchange this document as is

---

147. Trans. Y. Yadin, J. C. Greenfield, A. Yardeni, "Babatha's *Ketubba*," *Israel Exploration Journal* 44 (1994), pp. 79–84. This papyrus document was discovered in 1961 by the expedition led by Yigael Yadin to the Cave of the Letters in Naḥal Ḥever in the Judean Desert.

proper]. . . . . [And I Yehudah son of El'azar Khthousion], I [acce]pt [all that] is written [above].

VERSO:
. . . for Babatha daughter of Shim'on due from
Yehudah son of El'azar
signatures
[Yehudah son of El'azar for himse]lf wrote it
Baba[ta daughter of] Shim['on] for herself
fragment of name witness
Toma son of Shim'on wi[tn]ess

13.5.5 Papyrus Yadin 18:
Jewish Marriage Contract in Greek[148]

Some Jews, even in the tannaitic period, still made use of non-Jewish legal instruments. This marriage contract, from the Bar Kokhba caves, was executed in Hellenistic style. Note that the two contracting parties are not the bride and groom but the groom and the bride's father.

ॐ

In the consulship of Publius Metilius Nepos for the 2nd time and Marcus Annius Libo on the nones of April, and by the compute of the new province of Arabia[149] year twenty-third on the fifteenth month Xandikos,[150] in Maoza, Zoara district,[151] Judah son of Eleazar also known as Khthusion, gave over Shelamzion, his very own daughter, a virgin, to Judah surnamed Cimber son of Ananias son of Somalas, both of the village of En-gedi in Judea residing here, for Shelamzion to be a wedded wife to Judah Cimber for the partnership of marriage according to the laws, she bringing to him on account of bridal gift feminine adornment in silver and gold and clothing appraised by mutual agreement, as they both say, to be worth two hundred *denarii* of silver, which appraised value the bridegroom Judah called Cimber acknowledged that he has received from her by hand forthwith from Judah her father and that he owes to the said Shelamzion his wife together with another three hundred *denarii* which he

---

148. Trans. N. Lewis, *The Documents from the Bar Kokhba Period in the Cave of Letters: Greek Papyri* (Jerusalem: Israel Exploration Society, The Hebrew University, The Shrine of the Book, 1989), pp. 80–81. Blank lines below indicate breaks in the manuscript that cannot be restored.

149. The Roman province of Arabia was inaugurated in 106 C.E.

150. April 5, 128.

151. At the south end of the Dead Sea.

promised to give to her in addition to the sum of her aforesaid bridal gift, all accounted toward her dowry, pursuant to his undertaking of feeding and clothing both her and the children to come in accordance with Greek custom upon the said Judah Cimber's good faith and peril and [the security of] all his possessions, both those which he now possesses in his said home village and here and all those which he may in addition validly acquire everywhere, in whatever manner his wife Shelamzion may choose, or whoever acts through her or for her may choose, to carry out the execution. Judah called Cimber shall redeem this contract for his wife Shelamzion, whenever she may demand it of him, in silver secured in due form, at his own expense interposing no objection. If not, he shall pay to her all the aforestated *denarii* twofold, she having the right of execution, both from Judah Cimber her husband and upon the possessions validly his, in whatever manner Shelamzion or whoever acts through her or for her may choose to carry out the execution. In good faith the formal question was asked and it was acknowledged in reply that this is thus rightly done.

[2nd hand, Aramaic][152] Yehudah son of Elazar Khthousion: I have given my daughter Shelamzion, a virgin, in marriage to Yehudah Cimber son of Ḥananiah son of Somala, according to what is written above. Yehudah wrote it.

[3rd hand, Aramaic] Yehudah Cimber son of Ḥananiah son of Somala: I acknowledge the debt of silver *denarii* five hundred, the dowry of Shelamzion my wife, according to what they wrote above. Yehudah wrote it.

[1st hand] I, Theenas son of Simon, *librarius*, wrote [this].
on the back, individual signatures
Yehudah son of Eleazar wrote it.
Yehudah son of Ḥananiah [wrote it].
Of_____son of _____, the hand?
Shim'on son of _____, witness
Eliezer son of Ḥilqiah, witness
Yohsef son of Ḥananiah, witness
Wanah son of _____, for himself.

---

152. Aramaic subscriptions were used since these Jews apparently could not write Greek.

13.5.6 Mishnah Gittin 1, 3, 9: The Law of Divorce[153]

The halakhah required that divorce documents be written for the specific woman and that it be certain that this was the case before the writ would be honored. Divorces had to be complete and fixed, severing all legal relationships between the parties.

፨

1:1 One who brought a bill of divorce from beyond the sea[154] must say, "It was written in my presence and signed [by the witnesses] in my presence."

Rabban Gamliel says: "even if he brought it from Rekem or Ḥeger."[155]

Rabbi Eliezer says: "even from Kefar Luddim to Lod."[156]

But the Sages say: "Only one who brings [a divorce document] from a city beyond the sea need say, 'It was written in my presence and signed in my presence.' One who brings it from one province to another within a country beyond the sea, must say, 'It was written in my presence and signed in my presence.'" Rabban Simeon ben Gamliel says: "even from one jurisdiction to another jurisdiction [within a province]."

3:1 Any bill of divorce which was not written specifically for the particular woman is not valid. How is this [that a bill of divorce could have the correct data if not written for a particular woman]? If a man was passing through the market-place and heard the scribes reading [a sample bill of divorce in order to instruct their students]: "So-and-so is divorcing so-and-so of such-and-such a place" and he said, "that is my name and that is the name of my wife," that is not a valid document for divorcing [his wife]. Furthermore, if he had had [a bill of divorce] written to divorce his wife but changed his mind, if a man of his city found him and said, "My name is like yours and my wife's name is like your wife's name," it is not a valid document for [the second man] to divorce [his wife]. Furthermore, if he had two wives of like names and he had had [a bill of divorce] written to divorce the elder, he may not divorce the younger one with it. Moreover, if he said to the scribe, "Write it so that I may divorce with it whomever I wish," it is not a valid document for divorcing [anyone].

9:1 One who divorced his wife and said to her, "You are free to marry any man but so-and-so," Rabbi Eliezer permits it but the Sages forbid it. What should he do? He should take [the bill of divorce] from her and give

---

153. Trans. S. Berrin.
154. Usually understood as any city outside the Land of Israel.
155. Places on the eastern boundaries of the Land of Israel.
156. A very short distance.

it to her again and say, "Behold you are free to marry any man." However, if he had written [the exception] in the document, even if he went
back and erased it, it is not valid.

13.5.7 Murabba'at Aramaic Papyrus (Mur 19 ar): Writ of Divorce[157]

*Among the documents brought to the caves on the shore of the Dead Sea
during Bar Kokhba revolt was this divorce document, prepared in accord with
tannaitic practice. The couple had lived at Masada.*

RECTO:
On the first of Marḥeshvan, the year six,[158] at Masada: I divorce and
repudiate of my own free will today, I Joseph, son of Naqsan, from [ ]h,
living at Masada, you, my wife, Miriam, daughter of Jonathan, [fro]m
Ḥanablata, living at Masada, who have been up to this (time) my wife, so
that you are free on your part to go and become a wife of any Jewish man
that you please. And n[ow] you have from me a bill of repudiation and a
writ of divorce. Now I give (back) [the dow]ry, and (for) all ruined and
damaged goods and . . . [I reimbur]se you. So let it be determined and
paid fourfold. And at (any) ti[me] that you say to me, I shall replace for
you the document, as long as I am alive.

VERSO:
Joseph, son of Naq[san], for himsel[f].
Eliezer, [son] of Malka, witness.
Joseph, son of Malka, witness.
Eleazar, son of Ḥanana, witness.

13.6 RITUAL PURITY AND IMPURITY

13.6.1 Mishnah Niddah 2:4, 6: Some Laws of Purity[159]

*Talmudic law continued the biblical regulations of menstrual impurity.
Here the Mishnah discusses the requirement to insure purity before and after*

---

157. Trans. J. A. Fitzmeyer and D. J. Harrington, *A Manual of Palestinian Aramaic Texts*
(Rome: Biblical Institute Press, 1978), pp. 139, 141.
158. This document has been dated to either the sixth year of Provincia Arabia, 111
C.E., or to the sixth year of the Great Revolt, 71/2 C.E.
159. Trans. A. Oded.

sexual relations, as well as the nature of the blood which renders a woman impure.

✿

2:4 All women are [considered] in a legal state of purity to their husbands.[160] When the husbands return [home] from traveling, their wives are [considered] in a legal state of purity. The House of Shammai say: she needs to check herself with two cloths for each time they have relations,[161] or examine it [each time] under a candle. The House of Hillel say: It is sufficient for her to use two cloths for the whole night [and examine it in the morning].

6 There are five [colors] of blood which render a woman impure: red, black, [the color of] a bright colored crocus, the [color of a puddle of] water on [red] earth, and [the color of red] wine mixed with water. The House of Shammai say: even [the color of] water that contained fenugreek[162] and [the color of] water that contained roasted meat, but the House of Hillel say that she is pure.[163] And yellow [blood]: Akaviah the son of Mehalalel [declares her] impure and the Sages [declare her] pure. Rabbi Meir says: "If it does not render impure because of the stain [of menstrual blood], it renders impure because of liquids."[164] Rabbi Yose says: "In neither way does it render impure."

13.6.2 Mishnah Niddah 4:1–2:
The Laws of Purity and Jewish Sectarians[165]

The Samaritans and the Sadducees practiced ritual purity laws at variance with those of Rabbinic halakhah. Accordingly, in Temple times, they rendered objects they sat on impure. After the destruction of the Temple, however, the laws pertaining to secondary forms of ritual purity fell into disuse.

✿

4:1 The daughters of the Samaritans [are considered] menstrually impure from their cribs. And the Samaritans render impure the bottom

---

160. Assuming she was pure when he left.
161. Before and after.
162. A red-leafed plant which was used for medicinal purposes.
163. Referring to the last two cases which the House of Shammai say render a woman impure.
164. It makes food susceptible to impurity.
165. Trans. A. Oded.

seat like the top,[166] because they have relations with menstrually impure women,[167] and because they sit for any kind of blood.[168] But one is not obligated for entering the Temple [with garments they have rendered impure], and we do not burn the *terumah* [with which their impure clothing has been in contact] because their impurity is uncertain.

2 The daughters of Sadducees, when they are accustomed to follow in the ways of their fathers, they are considered like the Samaritan women. If they separated in order to go in the way of the Jews, they are considered like the Jews. Rabbi Yose says: "They are always considered like Jews unless they diverge to follow the manners of their fathers [the Sadducees]."

13.6.3 Mishnah Miqva'ot 2:2–4, 8:1: The Fitness of a Ritual Pool[169]

A mikveh is an artificial pool designed to gather and hold water for ritual purification. This passage deals with the requirements for such a pool.

🦎

2:2 If a mikveh[170] is measured and found to be lacking [the necessary amount of water]; all pure food that was prepared based on immersion in it,[171] whether [the mikveh is located] in [a] private or public [domain], is retroactively considered impure. Which things does this [principle] concern? Severe impurity. But more lenient impurity,[172] as [for example, if one] ate impure food, or drank impure drinks, or if his head and most of his body were submerged in drawn water,[173] or if three *logs* of drawn water fell on his head, and if he went down to immerse himself: if he is

---

166. Even if ten cushions are piled one on top of the other, and the Samaritan is on the top one, all those below are also equally impure as that on which he is lying. Even the lowest cushion renders food and drink impure by contact.

167. Since the Samaritan women are considered perpetually impure because they do not follow the Rabbinic interpretation of the purity laws.

168. Because they are overly strict and consider all colored liquids to be impure blood, they begin their period of impurity too early, therefore concluding it too soon after their menstrual cycle.

169. Trans. A. Oded

170. Ritual immersion pool.

171. During Temple times, pure food had to be prepared by someone who was ritually pure. If that person had become impure for any reason, immersion in a valid mikveh was one part of the purification process.

172. A category of ritual impurity decreed by the Sages.

173. Water for the mikveh must be from either rainfall or a naturally running stream. Drawn water may not be used, except to supplement a mikveh already containing 40 *se'ah* of natural water.

uncertain whether he immersed or not, or if he [certainly] immersed but is uncertain whether [the mikveh] contained forty *se'ah*[174] [of water] or not; or if there were two mikva'ot and one had forty *se'ah* and the other did not, and he immersed himself in one of them, but does not know in which one he was immersed, he[175] is considered pure. Rabbi Yose [says that he is] impure, because Rabbi Yose says: anything that is of impure status, is always unfit until it is certain that it has become pure. But [when there is] uncertainty regarding whether something has become impure and [therefore] can render impure—it is considered pure.

3 [What is the case of] possibly drawn water that was declared pure by the Sages: if it is uncertain if [drawn water] fell in or if it did not fall [into the mikveh]; even if [drawn water] did fall [into the mikveh], if it is uncertain whether [the mikveh] has forty *se'ah* or not; two mikva'ot, one that contains forty *se'ah* and one that does not, if [drawn water] fell into one of them but he does not know into which of them [the water] fell: it is presumed pure because he has something to rely on [to assume it to be pure]. If both were less than forty *se'ah* and [drawn water] fell into one of them, and he does not know into which it fell, it is presumed impure, because he does not have something to rely on [to assume it to be pure].

4 Rabbi Eliezer says: "A quarter *log*[176] of drawn water in the beginning[177] disqualifies the mikveh, [as do] three *logim* [of drawn water] on top [of the pure water].[178] The Sages say: "Whether it is in the beginning or at the end, the [maximum] amount [of drawn water allowed is] three *logim*."

8:1 The Land of Israel is pure and its mikva'ot are [considered] pure.[179] The mikva'ot of the nations that are outside the Land of Israel are considered fit for [immersion of] those who have had a seminal emission,[180] even if the [water] was filled up using a swipe,[181] since in the Land of Israel, outside the entrance [to the] cities, they are considered valid [for immersion] even for menstrually impure women. Inside the entrance [to the cities], they are valid for those who have had a seminal emission, and unfit for all [other] impure [people]. Rabbi Eliezer says: "Those that are near the city and the road are considered impure because of the laundry [water that may be spilled] there, and those that are far [from the city] are pure."

---

174. The required amount of water, equal to about 88 gallons at least.
175. Literally, "his doubtful case."
176. A quarter *log* is equal in bulk to an egg and a half, about 4 oz.
177. Before there was any water in the pool.
178. After the pool has natural water, but before it has the required volume of 40 *se'ah*.
179. They are considered to be fit for immersion.
180. A lower level of impurity, not required by the Torah.
181. A lever and bucket device used to draw water from a well.

13.6.4 Mishnah Yadayim 1:1–4: Hand Washing[182]

*The washing of the hands was an important part of Rabbinic purity law,
especially after the destruction of the Temple. The hands were washed at rising
in the morning and before eating, in imitation of the priestly ritual for eating
their sacred portions (terumah). The Rabbis specified exact requirements for
the method of hand washing and the vessel from which the water was to be
poured. The Mishnah here reflects a setting in which Temple purity regulations were still observed.*

ṣ̌

1:1 [To render the hand clean][183] a quarter *log* or more [of water] must
be poured over the hands [to suffice] for one person or even for two; a
half *log* or more [suffices] for three persons or for four; one *log* or more
[suffices] for five or for ten or for a hundred. Rabbi Yose says: "Provided
that for the last among them there remains not less than a quarter *log*."
More [water] may be added to the second [water that is poured over the
hands], but more may not be added to the first.[184]

2 The water may be poured over the hands out of any vessel, even from
vessels made from cattle-dung or vessels of stone or vessels of [unbaked]
clay. It may not be poured over the hands out of the side of [broken] vessels or out of the flanks of a ladling-jar[185] or out of the plug of a jar, nor
may a man pour it over his fellow's hands out of his cupped hands, for
they may not draw the water or mix the ashes or sprinkle the sin-offering
water,[186] or pour [water] over the hands, except by means of a vessel; and
only vessels that have a tightly stopped-up cover afford protection [against

---

182. Trans. H. Danby, *The Mishnah* (London: Oxford University Press, 1958), pp. 778–
9.

183. The hands, in their ordinary condition, were assumed to suffer second-grade
uncleanness; thus, unless they are washed with the intention of rendering them ritually
pure, they convey third-grade uncleanness to food that is heave-offering, making it invalid.

184. The law required the hands to have a double rinsing. On the first rinsing, the
entire hand had to be covered by the water. If there was not enough to reach the wrist, a
fresh quarter *log*'s supply had to be used. However, the law is more lenient about the second rinsing. For the second rinsing, if the remaining water was not enough to reach the
wrist, more water may be poured on the part of the hand not covered until the entire hand
has been covered by water.

185. The large earthenware bucket used to draw water out of a well.

186. If persons or utensils contracted uncleanness from coming in contact with a dead
body or having been present in a "tent" (that is, any building) along with a dead person,
they may be purified by the sprinkling of the ashes of the sin-offering. This offering was
prepared by burning a red heifer, collecting its ashes, and mixing them with water (Numbers 19).

uncleanness in a "tent" wherein lies a corpse]; and only vessels afford protection against [uncleanness present in] earthenware vessels.[187]

3 If water was [so polluted that it was], unfit for cattle to drink, if it was in vessels, it is invalid [for the washing of hands], but if it was on the ground, it is valid. If ink, gum,[188] or copperas[189] fell therein and its color was changed, it becomes invalid. If a man did any act of work therewith, or if he soaked his bread therein, it becomes invalid. Simeon of Teman says: "If it was his intention to soak it in other water but it fell in this water, the water remains valid."

4 If he rinsed vessels therein or if he scrubbed measures[190] therein, it becomes invalid. If he rinsed therein vessels that had been already rinsed or that were new, it remains valid. Rabbi Yose declares it invalid if the vessels were new.

13.7 LIFE CYCLE

13.7.1 Mishnah Shabbat 18–19: From Birth to Circumcision[191]

In the context of Sabbath law, a number of issues pertaining to children, birth, and circumcision are discussed. Circumcision was a central rite connected with Jewish identity in the ancient world. Its status as a positive commandment meant that it overrode the Sabbath prohibitions.

꽃

18:2 . . . Calves and young donkeys may be pulled along in the public domain [on the Sabbath]. A woman may pull her child along. Rabbi Judah said: "When [is this the case]? When the child lifts up one [leg] and puts down the other; if he only drags [his legs], it is forbidden."

3 It is forbidden to deliver cattle of their offspring on the festival-day, but it is permitted to assist [the newborn animal]. But it is permitted to deliver a woman of her baby on the Sabbath and to summon a midwife from one place to another, and to violate the Sabbath for the mother's sake and to tie up the umbilical cord. Rabbi Yose says: "It is also permitted to cut it. And all that is necessary for circumcision is permitted on the Sabbath."

---

187. Liquid in an open jar may contract impurity of the dead if it is present in a tent with a dead body, and an earthenware jar is more susceptible to impurity than a glass or stone vessel.

188. The resin of a tree.

189. Sulfate of iron.

190. Measuring utensils.

191. Trans. S. Berrin.

19:5 A baby boy is circumcised on the eighth, ninth, tenth, eleventh, or twelfth [day after his birth], but never earlier or later. How is this? According to the usual way, [it is done] on the eighth day. If he was born at twilight,[192] he is circumcised on the ninth day.[193] If [he was born] at twilight on the eve of the Sabbath, he is circumcised on the tenth day. If a festival-day falls after [that] Sabbath, he is circumcised on the eleventh day. If the two festival-days of the New Year [fall after that Sabbath], he is circumcised on the twelfth day. A sick baby is not circumcised until he becomes well.

13.7.2 Mishnah Avot 5:21: Stages of Life[194]

The Rabbis set forth the stages of life of a male Jew. They recommended that schooling begin at an early age, and that marriage take place before the pursuit of a career or the assumption of authority.

༈

5:21 He[195] used to say: At five years old [one is fit] for the [study of] Scripture, at ten years for [the study of] the Mishnah, at thirteen for [the fulfilling of] the commandments, at fifteen for the Talmud, at eighteen for the bride-chamber, at twenty for pursuing [a calling], at thirty for authority, at forty for discernment, at fifty for counsel, at sixty to be an elder, at seventy for gray hairs, at eighty for special strength,[196] at ninety for bowed back, and at a hundred a man is as one that has [already] died and passed away and ceased from the world.

13.8 STUDY IN THE SERVICE OF GOD

13.8.1 *Qinyan Torah*: The Acquisition of the Torah[197]

Often associated with the Ethics of the Fathers and presented as the sixth chapter of Mishnah Avot is the collection of sayings regarding the study of Torah called Qinyan Torah. In this text we learn how Torah study was understood by the Rabbis to mold the personality of the sage and his relationship to God.

---

192. When there is a doubt over whether it is part of the previous day or the next.

193. It is permitted to set aside the Sabbath regulations only to circumcise a boy on what is definitely his eighth day.

194. Trans. Danby, *The Mishnah*, p. 458.

195. Scholars are in doubt as to whom to attribute this quotation.

196. Ps. 90:10.

197. Trans. Danby, *The Mishnah*, pp. 458–61.

🕊

[These things] have the Sages taught in the language of the Mishnah. Blessed is he that chose them and their Mishnah![198]

1 Rabbi Meir said: "He who occupies himself in the study of the Law for its own sake merits many things, and, still more, he is deserving of the whole world. He is called friend, beloved [of God], lover of God, lover of mankind; and it clothes him with humility and reverence and fits him to become righteous, saintly, upright, and faithful; and it keeps him far from sin and brings him near to virtue, and from him men enjoy counsel and sound knowledge, understanding and might, for it is written, "Counsel is mind and sound knowledge, I am understanding, I have might" (Prov. 8:14).[199] And it gives him kingship and dominion and discernment in judgment; to him are revealed the secrets of the Law, and he is made like a never-failing spring and like a river that flows ever more mightily; and he becomes modest, longsuffering, and forgiving of insult; and it magnifies him and exalts him above all things."

2 Rabbi Joshua ben Levi said: "Every day a divine voice goes forth from Mount Horeb,[200] proclaiming and saying, 'Woe to mankind for their contempt of the Law!' For he who does not occupy himself in the study of the Law is called 'reprobate'. . . . And it is written, 'And the tables[201] were the work of God, and the writing was the writing of God, engraved (*harut*) upon the tables' (Ex. 32:16). Read not *harut* (engraved) but *herut* (freedom), for you find no free man except him who occupies himself in the study of the Law; and he who occupies himself in the study of the Law shall be exalted, for it is written, 'From Mattanah to Nahaliel, and from Nahaliel to Bamot'" (Num. 21:19).[202]

3 He who learns from his fellow a single chapter or a single halakhah or a single verse or a single expression or even a single letter, must pay him honor, for so we find it with David, king of Israel, who learned only two things from Ahithophel,[203] but called him his teacher, his companion,

---

198. This introductory statement makes clear that what follows is a series of *baraitot*, statements attributed to the tannaitic period. It is phrased as a benediction formula recited upon the study of the teachings of the Rabbinic sages.

199. Wisdom, identified by the Rabbis with Torah, is the speaker in this biblical passage.

200. An alternate name for Mt. Sinai.

201. The tablets on which the Ten Commandments were inscribed.

202. The three place-names are understood literally: Mattanah, "a gift;" Nahaliel, "God has led me;" Bamot, "(to) high places."

203. One of David's advisors who was known for his wisdom. Ahithophel supported Absalom's revolt against David's authority.

and his familiar friend; for it is written, "But was it you, a man my equal, my companion and my familiar friend?" (Ps. 55:13).[204] And is there not here an inference from the less to the greater?—if David king of Israel, who learned but two things from Ahithophel, called him his "companion," and his "familiar friend," how much more then must he who learns from his fellow a single chapter or a single halakhah or a single verse or a single expression or even a single letter pay him honor! And "honor" is nothing else than "the Law," for it is written, "The wise shall inherit honor" (Prov. 3:35) and "The perfect shall inherit good" (Prov. 28:10); and "good" is nothing else than "the Law," for it is written, "For I give you good doctrine; forsake not my Law" (Prov. 4:2). . . .

9 Rabbi Yose ben Kisma said: "I was once walking by the way and a man met me and greeted me and I returned his greeting.

"He said to me, 'Rabbi, from what place are you?'

"I answered, 'I come from a great city of Sages and scribes.'

"He said to me, 'If you will dwell with us in our place, I will give you a thousand thousand[205] golden *dinars* and precious stones and pearls.'

"I answered, 'If you gave me all the silver and gold and precious stones and pearls in the world, I would not dwell except in a place of [knowledge of] the Law.'"

And thus it is written in the book of Psalms by David, king of Israel, "The Law of your mouth is better to me than thousands of gold and silver" (Ps. 119:72). Moreover, at the time of a man's departure, neither silver nor gold nor precious stones nor pearls go with him, but only [his knowledge of] the Law and good works; for it is written, "When you walk, it[206] shall lead you; when you sleep, it shall watch over you; and when you awake, it shall talk with you" (Prov. 6:22). "When you walk, it shall lead you"—in this world; "when you sleep, it shall watch over you"—in the grave; "and when you awake, it shall talk with you"—in the world to come. And it says, "The silver is mine, and the gold is mine, says the Lord of hosts" (Hag. 2:8).

---

204. Ps. 55:13 is understood here to be a psalm by King David referring to Ahithophel.
205. One million.
206. Referring to wisdom which is understood here as equivalent to Torah.

13.9 THE MYSTIC WAY

13.9.1 Mishnah Ḥagigah 2:1:
Teaching the Secrets of the Torah[207]

The Mishnah outlaws the public teaching of esoteric religious traditions regarding creation and the divine chariot or throne. The traditions alluded to were part of a corpus of teachings tracing their origins to Second Temple period sources and continuing to develop alongside and in relation to Rabbinic aggadot on the same subjects.

🕊️

The forbidden sexual relations may not be expounded before three [or more] people, nor the account of creation[208] before two, nor the Chariot (Maʻaseh ha-Merkavah)[209] before one, unless he is a Sage who understands by his own knowledge. Whoever speculates about four things, it would have been better for him if he had not come into this world: what is above, what is below, what was before, and what will be afterwards. Whoever is not sensitive to the honor of his Creator, it would have been better for him if he had not come into this world.

13.9.2 Jerusalem Talmud Ḥagigah 2:1 (77a):
Merkavah Speculation[210]

Talmudic tradition alludes to Rabbis who experienced mystical visions of the Maʻaseh ha-Merkavah, the divine throne. From the descriptions in these texts, it appears that these visions are to be understood in light of the Hekhalot mystical texts collected in the early Middle Ages but including a core of traditions which may date back to the amoraic period. Precursors of such notions have even been found in Second Temple texts, including the Dead Sea Scrolls. Some Rabbis, we can conclude, understood the biblical descriptions of God and His retinue as the basis for a continuing tradition of mystical revelation.

---

207. Trans. S. Berrin.
208. Genesis 1.
209. Ezekiel 1.
210. Trans. D. J. Halperin, *The Merkabah in Rabbinic Literature* (American Oriental Series, 62; New Haven: American Oriental Society, 1980), pp. 108–9.

෴

There is a story concerning Rabban Yoḥanan ben Zakkai that he was going on the way, riding the ass; and Rabbi Eleazar ben Arakh was walking after him.

He said to him, "Rabbi, teach me one segment of Ma'aseh ha-Merkavah."[211]

He said to him, "Did not the sages teach, 'Nor the Merkavah, unless he is a scholar, understanding on his own?'"

He said to him, "Rabbi, give me permission to speak a word before you."

He said to him, "Speak."

When Rabbi Eleazar ben Arakh opened his discourse concerning Ma'aseh ha-Merkavah, Rabban Yoḥanan ben Zakkai descended from the ass. He said, "It is not fitting that I should hear the Glory of my Creator while I am mounted on the ass. They went and sat beneath a tree. And fire descended from heaven and surrounded them. And the ministering angels were leaping before them, like a wedding party rejoicing before a bridegroom.

One angel answered from the midst of the fire and said, "In accordance with your words, Eleazar ben Arakh, so is Ma'aseh ha-Merkavah!"[212]

Thereupon all the trees opened their mouths and uttered song: "Then all the trees of the forest shall shout with joy" (Ps. 96:12).

When Rabbi Eleazar ben Arakh finished [his discourse] concerning Ma'aseh ha-Merkavah, Rabban Yoḥanan ben Zakkai arose, and kissed him on his head, and said: "Blessed be the Lord, the God of Abraham, Isaac, and Jacob, who gave to Abraham our father a wise son, who knows to expound the Glory of our Father in Heaven. You have those who expound properly but do not practice properly, those who practice properly but do not expound properly; Eleazar ben Arakh expounds properly and practices properly. Happy are you, Abraham our father, that Eleazar ben Arakh emerged from your loins!"

And, when Rabbi Joseph Ha-Kohen and Rabbi Simeon ben Nathanel heard, they also opened discourse concerning Ma'aseh ha-Merkavah.

They said, "It was a summer day; and the earth shook, and the rainbow was seen in the cloud. And a heavenly voice went forth and said to them: The place is cleared for you, and the couch is spread for you! You and your disciples are designated for the third set.[213]

---

211. The account of the divine Chariot in Ezekiel 1.
212. You have correctly expounded this difficult topic.
213. You are among those who merit a vision of the divine Presence.

13.9.3 Jerusalem Talmud Ḥagigah 2:1 (77a–77c): Four Who Entered the Pardes[214]

The following aggadic narrative demonstrates the reasons for the Rabbinic hesitation to teach esoteric traditions. After Elisha ben Abuyah becomes an apostate, his student Rabbi Meir continues to respect his immense learning while feeling the pain of his loss to the Rabbinic community of sages.

𝕊

Four entered the Pardes:[215] One peeked and died; one peeked and was harmed (went crazy); one peeked and cut the shoots;[216] one entered in peace and left in peace.

Ben Azzai peeked and was harmed. Concerning him the verse says, "If you found honey, eat what you need [(and no more) lest you get sick and throw it up]" (Prov. 25:16).

Ben Zoma peeked and died. Concerning him the verse says, "Precious in the eyes of God is the death of his pious ones" (Ps. 116:15).

Aḥer (Other) peeked and cut the shoots. Who is Aḥer? Elisha ben Abuyah who used to "kill" Torah scholars. They say that when Elisha would encounter a student who excelled in Torah, he would "kill" him.[217] Moreover, when he would enter the academy and see children before their teacher, he would ask, "Why are they sitting here? The profession of this one is a builder, the profession of this one is a carpenter, the profession of this one is a hunter, the profession of this one is a tailor." When they heard this they abandoned [their studies] and left [the academy]. Concerning him the verse says, "Do not let your mouth bring guilt on your flesh" (Eccl. 5:5), for he spoiled the works of that same man (i.e., himself).

Also, in the time of the persecution,[218] they made the Jews carry burdens [on the Sabbath] and they tried to carry them two at a time, because "two who perform a single labor [are exempt]."[219] [Elisha] said, "Make them carry singly." They carried singly, but attempted to place the objects

---

214. Trans. A. Oded.

215. Pardes, a cognate of English "paradise," is an orchard or garden in old Persian. Here it refers to mystical speculation.

216. Became a heretic.

217. By discouraging him from Torah study and encouraging him to pursue an alternative career.

218. The Hadrianic Persecution at the time of the Bar Kokhba Revolt (132–5 C.E.).

219. From the Torah's prohibition.

in a *karmelit*,[220] in order to avoid moving [objects] from the private domain to the public domain. [Elisha] said, "Make them carry flasks."[221] They went and carried flasks.

Rabbi Akiva entered in peace and left in peace. Concerning him the verse says, "Draw me, and after you we will run" (Song 1:4). Rabbi Meir was sitting and expounding in the academy of Tiberias. Elisha his teacher passed by riding a horse on the Sabbath.

[The students] came and said to him, "Your teacher is outside." He stopped teaching and went out to him.

[Elisha] said, "What did you expound today?"

[Rabbi Meir] replied, "And God blessed the end [of Job's life more than the beginning]" (Job 42:12).

[Elisha] said, "How did you begin?"

[Rabbi Meir] replied, "'The Lord restored Job's fortunes, and gave him twice the possessions he had before' (ibid.); God doubled his possessions."

[Elisha] said, "Woe to those who are lost and not found! Your teacher Akiva would not have expounded thus, but rather, 'And God blessed the end of Job's life more than the beginning,' on account of the commandments and good deeds that he had performed in the beginning."

[Elisha] said to him, "What else did you expound?"

[Rabbi Meir] replied, "The end of a matter is better than its beginning" (Eccl. 7:8).

[Elisha] said, "How did you begin?"

[Rabbi Meir] replied, "Like a man who had children when he was young and they died, but when he was old [he had children and] they lived, this is 'the end of a matter is better than its beginning.' Like a man who did business in his youth and lost [his money], but in his old age he prospered, this is 'the end of a matter is better than its beginning.' Like a man who learned Torah in this youth and forgot it, but in his old age he remembered it, this is 'the end of a matter is better than its beginning.'"

[Elisha] replied, "Woe to those who are lost and not found! Your teacher Akiva would not have expounded thus, but rather 'the end of a matter is better than its beginning' when it is good from the beginning. And mine is a case in point. Abuyah, my father, was among the great men of Jerusalem. When the day of my circumcision arrived, he invited all the great men of Jerusalem and set them in one house, and Rabbi Elea-

---

220. An area which is neither a public nor fully private domain, to or from which carrying on the Sabbath is only a Rabbinic prohibition.

221. Flasks could not be set to rest in the *karmelit* and had to be carried directly from domain to domain, resulting in violation of the Torah's prohibition.

zar and Rabbi Joshua in another house. [While the guests] were eating, drinking, singing, clapping, and dancing, Rabbi Eleazar said to Rabbi Joshua, 'While they do their thing, let's do ours.'

"They sat down and learned Torah, and from Torah to Prophets, and from Prophets to Writings. A fire descended from heaven and enveloped them.

"Abuyah said to them, 'My masters! Did you come here to burn my house down on me?'

"They said to him, 'Heaven forbid! We were sitting and reviewing words of Torah, and from Torah to Prophets and from Prophets to Writings, and the words were as joyous as when they were given at Sinai, and the flames licked them up, like [the flames] licked them up at Sinai. And the main feature of their giving at Sinai was with fire [as the Scripture states], "And the mountain burned up to the midst of the heavens" (Deut. 4:11).'

"My father Abuyah said to them, 'My masters, if this is the power of Torah, and if my son survives, then I will dedicate him to Torah.' Since his intentions were not for the sake of heaven, his desire was not fulfilled in that same man.'"[222]

[Elisha] said to him, "What else did you expound?"

[Rabbi Meir] replied, "Gold and crystal can not be compared with it (God's wisdom)" (Job 28:17).

[Elisha] said, "How did you begin?"

[Rabbi Meir] replied, "Words of Torah are as difficult to acquire as vessels of gold, and as easy to lose as crystal vessels. And just as vessels of gold and vessels of crystal can be made whole again after they are broken, likewise a Torah scholar who forgot what he learned can go back and learn it again as in the beginning."

[Elisha] said, "Enough, Meir! This is the Sabbath limit."[223]

[Meir] said to him, "How do you know?"

[Elisha] answered, "From the steps of my horse I counted two thousand cubits."

[Meir] said to him, "All this wisdom is in you, and yet you do not return?"

[Elisha] said to him, "I cannot."

[Meir] said to him, "Why?"

---

222. He was convinced of the power of Torah only because of the burning fire he saw, not because of an intrinsic commitment to its truth.

223. Two thousand cubits, and it is forbidden to walk any further beyond the outside of the settled area on the Sabbath.

[Elisha] said to him, "One time I was riding my horse by the Holy of Holies on Yom Kippur which fell upon the Sabbath, and I heard a heavenly voice come out from the Holy of Holies, and it said, 'Return children, except for Elisha ben Abuyah who knew my power and rebelled against me.'"

And why did all this happen to him?

Once he was sitting and learning in the Ginnosar Valley[224] and he saw a man climb a palm tree and take the mother bird and her young, and he went down from there in peace. The next day he saw another man climb a palm tree, shoo away the mother and take the young, and when he went down from there, a snake bit him and he died. Scripture states, "Send away the mother and the young you may take for yourself, in order that it may go well with you and your life be lengthened" (Deut. 22:7). [He said to himself:] Where is the good of this man? Where is the long life of this man? He did not know that Rabbi Jacob had previously explained that "in order that it may go well with you" refers to the world to come that is all good, and "may your life be lengthened" refers to the future (end of days) that is all long.

And there is one who says that it occurred when he saw the tongue of Rabbi Judah the Baker[225] in the mouth of a dog, dripping blood. He said, "This is Torah and this is the reward? This is the tongue that used to give forth Torah perfectly! This is the tongue that was occupied with Torah all its life? This is Torah and this is the reward? It seems as though there is no granting of reward and there is no resurrection of the dead!"

There are those that say that when his mother was pregnant with him, she used to pass pagan temples and smell the sacrifices. And the smell permeated her body like the poison of a snake.

Years later Elisha fell ill. They came and said to Rabbi Meir, "Your teacher is ill." He went to visit him and found him ill.

[Rabbi Meir] said, "Will you not repent?"

[Elisha] replied, "If I repent, will it be accepted?"

[Rabbi Meir] said, "Does not Scripture state, 'You turn men back to dust?' (Ps. 90:3) Until the destruction of the soul they are accepted." At that moment Elisha wept, passed on and died.

Rabbi Meir was happy in heart and said, "It seems my teacher died in repentance."

When they buried him, a fire came down from heaven and burnt his grave. They came and said to Rabbi Meir, "Your teacher's grave is burn-

---

224. Near the shore of Lake Tiberias.
225. Who was tortured and killed by the Romans in the Hadrianic Persecutions.

ing." He went out wishing to visit [the grave] and found it burning. What did he do? He removed his cloak and spread it over [the grave]. He said, 'Rest this evening; then in the morning, if he will redeem you, good! Let him redeem you. But if he does not desire to redeem you, I will redeem you, by God!' (Ruth 3:13) 'rest,' in this world that is similar to night, then in the morning, this is the world to come that is all morning. 'If he will redeem you, good! Let him redeem you,' this refers to God, who is good, as is written regarding Him: 'God is good to all, and is merciful to all his creations' (Ps. 145:9), 'and if he does not desire to redeem you, I will redeem you, by God!'" (Ruth 3:13). And [the fire] was extinguished.

They said to Rabbi Meir, "If they say to you in the world to come, 'Whom would you rather visit, your father or your teacher,' [whom would you choose?]"

He replied, "I would approach my teacher first, and after that my father."

They said to him, "Will they listen to you?"

He replied, "Did we not learn, 'We save the Torah covers with the Torah, the tefillin case with the tefillin?' They will save Elisha the Other (Aḥer) by the merit of his Torah."

Years later, the daughters [of Elisha] went to ask for alms from Rabbi [Judah the Prince]. Rabbi decreed and said, "May no one show him mercy, may none pity his orphans" (Ps 109:2).

They said to him, "Our teacher, do not look at his deeds, look at his Torah."

At that moment, Rabbi wept and decreed that they be supported. He said, "If this one, who labored in Torah not for the sake of heaven—see what he raised,[226] one who labored in Torah for the sake of heaven, how much more so!"

13.9.4 Babylonian Talmud Shabbat 33b: Rabbi Simeon bar Yoḥai and the Cave[227]

Later Jewish mystical tradition saw the tanna Simeon bar Yoḥai as a major figure in the development of Jewish mysticism, even identifying him as author of the Zohar, a great medieval compilation of hidden Jewish lore. In this selection, we hear of the years he spent in a cave where he was later said to have acquired his esoteric knowledge. This narrative is typical of a number of stories in Rabbinic literature which cast sages as having extraordinary powers so that those who sin against them are miraculously destroyed.

226. The eminent disciple, Rabbi Meir.
227. Trans. A. Oded.

§

Rabbi Judah, Rabbi Yose, and Rabbi Simeon [bar Yoḥai] were sitting. And Judah ben Gerim was sitting near them. Rabbi Judah began and said, "How great are the deeds of this [Roman] nation! They made markets; they made bathhouses; they made bridges."

Rabbi Yose was silent. Rabbi Simeon bar Yoḥai answered and said, "What they made, they made for themselves. They made markets so they could set prostitutes there, bathhouses so they could enjoy themselves, bridges to collect a toll." Judah ben Gerim went and repeated their words which were heard by authorities.

[The authorities] said, "Judah who elevated will be elevated, Yose who was silent will be exiled to Sepphoris, and Simeon who disgraced will be killed."[228]

He [Rabbi Simeon] and his son went and hid in the house of study. Every day his wife brought him bread and a jug of water, and they ate.

When the decree was harshened, he said to his son, "Women have a weak constitution; perhaps they will torture her and she will reveal us." They went and hid in a cave. A miracle occurred and a carob tree and a well of water were created for them. They used to remove [their clothing] and sit up to their necks in sand. All day they used to commit traditions to memory, and at the time of prayer they dressed, covered and prayed. And then they took off their clothes so that they would not wear out.

They lived in the cave for twelve years. Elijah came and stood at the opening of the cave. He said, "Who will tell the son of Yoḥai that Caesar is dead and his decree was canceled?"

They went out. They saw people plowing and planting. He [Rabbi Simeon] said, "They are forsaking eternal life[229] and occupying themselves with temporal life."[230] Every place they cast their eyes was immediately burned.

A heavenly voice came out and said, "Did you come out to destroy my world? Return to your cave!" They returned and lived in the cave for twelve months. They said, "The sentence of the wicked in Gehinom is twelve months." A heavenly voice came forth [and said,] "Get out of your cave."

---

228. Here the section written in tannaitic Hebrew ends, and there begins a later Aramaic narrative.

229. The study of Torah.

230. Earning a living.

They went out. Everything that Rabbi Eliezer destroyed, Rabbi Simeon repaired. Rabbi Simeon said, "My son, I and you are enough for the world!"[231]

When the Sabbath was about to start they saw an old man carrying two bundles of myrtle, running at twilight. They said to him, "Why do you need these?"

[He said to them,] "In honor of the Sabbath."

They said to him, "And isn't one enough for you?"

He said to them, "One is for 'remember' (Ex. 20:8), and one is for 'keep'" (Deut. 5:12).

He said [to his son], "See how the commandments are beloved by Israel!" Their minds were at ease.

His son-in-law, Rabbi Pinḥas ben Yair, heard and went out to meet him. He took him into a bathhouse. When he was treating his flesh, he saw that there were cracks in his skin. He started crying and his tears flowed and caused him pain. He said to him, "Woe to me that I saw you thus!"

He said to him, "Blessed are you that you saw me thus, because had you not seen me thus, you would not have found me thus [learned].[232] In the beginning, when Rabbi Simeon bar Yoḥai asked one question, Rabbi Pinḥas ben Yair would give twelve answers. In the end, when Rabbi Pinḥas ben Yair would ask a question, Rabbi Simeon bar Yoḥai would give twenty-four answers.

[Rabbi Simeon bar Yoḥai] said, "Since a miracle occurred,[233] let me go repair something."[234] As it says: ". . . and Jacob arrived whole [to the city of Shechem]" (Gen. 33:18). Rav says, "Whole in his body, whole in his money, and whole in his Torah."

". . . and he found favor in the city." Rav says, "he established coins for them." And Samuel says, "he established markets for them." Rabbi Yoḥanan says, "He established bathhouses for them."

He said, "Is there something that needs repair?"

---

231. It is sufficient for the world that we have studied the Torah and thus sustained it in the time of persecution.

232. Had I not suffered in the cave, I would not have been able to study during the time of the persecution.

233. In gratefulness for my survival.

234. Let me undertake actions to help others.

They said to him, "There is a plot of land where there is a question of uncleanliness and it disturbs the priests to go around it."[235]

He said, "Is there a person who knows that there is pure [land] there?"

A certain old man said to him, "Here ben Zakkai pulled out lupines for the priestly portion."[236] He also did as he did:[237] wherever [the ground] was hard, he declared it pure, wherever it was loose, he marked it.[238]

The old man said, "Bar Yohai [alone] purified the cemetery!"[239]

He said to him, "If you had not been with us, or if you had been with us and had not agreed with us, you spoke well. But since you were with us and did agree with us, they will say, 'Prostitutes beautify one another, don't scholars do the same?' "[240] [Rabbi Simeon bar Yohai] put his eye on him, and [the old man] died.

He went out into the street and saw Judah ben Gerim. He said, "This one is still in the world?"[241] He put his eyes on him and turned him into a pile of bones.

13.9.5 *Ma'aseh Merkavah*: A Mystical Prayer[242]

Ma'aseh Merkavah is an early Jewish mystical text which emphasizes the liturgical aspect of the mystical quest to ascend through the seven heavens and stand before God on His throne. This and other similar texts were redacted in the early Middle Ages and are based on late talmudic traditions. The prayer preserved in this text shows the extent to which Jewish liturgy is clearly related to—even dependent on—the Merkavah mystical tradition.

꽃

Rabbi Ishmael said: I asked of Rabbi Akiba the prayer that one recites when he ascends to the Merkavah, and I asked of him the praise of

---

235. Priests are forbidden from contracting impurity of the dead and had to take an inconvenient, circuitous route to avoid becoming impure.

236. Yohanan ben Zakkai was a priest, so this proved that part of the field had been pure.

237. Like Yohanan ben Zakkai, he picked lupines, a type of legume.

238. Where the ground was hard, he was sure no grave lay beneath. Where it was soft, it was possible that there was a grave.

239. Excluding himself, as if he had not participated.

240. Simeon bar Yohai objected that if even prostitutes could cooperate with one another, so could Rabbis!

241. He is alive despite having repeated conversations which should have been private and having thus caused the persecution of the Jews.

242. Trans. M. D. Swartz, *Mystical Prayer in Ancient Judaism* (Tübingen: J. C. B. Mohr, 1992), pp. 222–4.

RWZYY, Lord, God of Israel—who knows what it is? He said to me:
[There must be] purity and holiness in his heart, and he says a prayer;

Be praised forever.
At the Throne of Glory You dwell,
in the Chambers on high, and the exalted Hekhal.[243]
For you have revealed the secrets and the deepest of secrets,
and the hidden things, and the most hidden things
to Moses, and Moses taught them to Israel
So that they can engage in Torah with them, and increase study with them.

Rabbi Akiba said: When I ascended and gazed at the Power (Gevurah),[244] I saw all the creatures that are in all the paths of heaven, those whose lengths are above and widths are below, and those whose widths are above and whose lengths are below.

Rabbi Ishmael said: How do the ministering angels stand on them? He said to me: like a bridge laid over a river that everyone passes over; so is a bridge laid from the beginning of the entrance to its end; and the ministering angels go around on it and recite song before TRQYLYY YHWH God of Israel. . . .

And this is the prayer:
'El RWZYY YWY God of Israel:
Blessed are you, God, great in power.
Who is like you in heaven or on earth
Holy in heaven and holy on earth?
He is a holy King, He is a great King,
He is a magnificent King over all the Merkavah.
You stretched out the heavens and established Your Throne,
and Your great name is adorned at Your Throne of Glory.
You spread out the earth;
You founded in it a seat for your footstool,
Your glory fills the world
Your name is great and mighty in all power,
and there is no limit to your understanding.
You know the mysteries of the world
and oversee wisdom and hidden ways.
Who is like You, who searches hearts
and examines the innermost parts
and understands thoughts?
There is nothing concealed from You; and nothing hidden from Your sight.

---

243. Literally "palace," referring to the seven palaces surrounding the divine throne.
244. The divine presence, termed "Shekhinah" in Rabbinic texts.

All life and death, blessings and curses, good and evil, are in Your hand;
and Your name is mighty in heaven and earth,
of great strength in heaven and earth,
blessed in heaven and earth,
honored in heaven and earth,
merciful in heaven and earth,
holy in heaven and holy on earth,
Power is the remembrance of Your name
forever and ever, to the end of all generations.

Rabbi Akiba said: Who can contemplate the seven Hekhalot, and gaze at the highest heavens, and see the inner chambers, and say, "I have seen the chambers of YH?" In the first Hekhal there stand four thousand myriads of Merkavot of fire, and forty thousand myriads of flames of fire go in among them. In the second Hekhal there stand one hundred thousand myriads of Merkavot of fire, and forty thousand myriads of flames of fire go in among them. In the third Hekhal there stand two hundred thousand myriads of Merkavot of fire, and one hundred thousand myriads of flames of fire go in among them. In the fourth Hekhal there stand one thousand of thousands of thousands of myriads of Merkavot of fire, and two thousand myriads of flames of fire go in among them. In the fifth Hekhal there stand four thousands of thousands of myriads of Merkavot of fire, and two thousand myriads of flames of fire go in among them. In the sixth Hekhal there stand a thousand thousands of thousands of myriads of Merkavot of fire, and two thousand thousands of myriads of flames of fire go in among them. In the seventh Hekhal there stand one hundred thousands of thousands of myriads of Merkavot of fire, and two thousand thousands of myriads of flames of fire go in among them.

13.9.6 Ḥorvat Kanaf Amulet: Incantation against Fever and Pain[245]

This Aramaic inscription, written on a copper sheet incised with a pointed instrument, was found at Ḥorvat Kanaf in the Golan, about 3 1/2 km. from the northeastern shore of the Sea of Galilee. It dates to the late 6th or early 7th century C.E. It indicates the extent to which magical practices and amulets had penetrated the Jewish communities of the Land of Israel into late antiquity.

---

245. J. Naveh and S. Shaked, *Amulets and Magic Bowls: Aramaic Incantations of Late Antiquity* (Jerusalem: Magnes Press, the Hebrew University; Leiden: E. J. Brill, 1985), p. 51.

౸

A song of praise to the King of the Worlds Yah, Yah, Yah, Yahish of the Worlds, I-am-who-I-am,[246] the King who speaks with distinct mystery to every bad and evil-doing spirit, that you should not cause pain to Rabbi Eleazar the son of Esther, the servant of the God of Heaven. Ḥzq and G'r, Shrd and Prt, Trgyn, 'Std and Bqth, Slslyrh', Qllqm, Yqyps, Suriel, Raphael, Abiel, Anael, Nahariel, Nagdiel, Aphaphel and Ananel Ms Ps Yqrndrys Yahu Krmsys the great god Thth Ghgh Tfhth Mrmr Psps Y-H-W-H, sanctity.

In every place where this amulet will be seen, you (the evil spirit) should not detain Eleazar the son of Esther. And if you detain him, you will be cast immediately into a burning fiery furnace.[247]

Blessed are you our Lord, the Healer of all (people on) earth, send healing (and) cure to Eleazar, Bwbryt, Tbryt, Bsht'rwt, the angels that are [appointed] over fever and shivering, cure Ele[azar] by a holy command!

13.9.7 Aramaic Magic Bowl: The Expulsion of Lilith[248]

Babylonian Jews also practiced a variety of magical practices as part of their popular religion. A common practice was the burial in various rooms of the house of a clay bowl inscribed inside with magical incantations, usually under a threshold. In this example, we see the common practice of granting magical divorce to demons to expel them from the house and protect its inhabitants.

౸

Overturned are the curses upon Burzin the daughter of the Smiter, upon Prince Bagdina, the king of the devil(s) and the great ruler of the liliths. I adjure you, Lilith Ḥablas, the granddaughter of Lilith Zarnai who dwells on the threshold of the house of Meḥishai the daughter of Dodai, smiter and burner of boys and girls, male and female foetuses (?). I adjure you that you be struck in the membrane of your heart, and with the spear of Qatros the mighty. Lo, I have written (a divorce) for you and lo, I have expelled you, as demons write divorces for their wives and furthermore, (they) do not return. Take your divorce, receive your oath, flee, take flight, and go forth from the house and from the back of Meḥishai the daughter of Dodai. In the name of Rt Mḥs Mḥs, the Ineffable Name from the six days of Creation. Hallelujah for Your Name! Hallelujah for Your King-

---

246. Ex. 3:14.

247. Dan. 3:6.

248. Trans. C. D. Isbell, *Corpus of the Aramaic Incantation Bowls* (Missoula, MT: Society of Biblical Literature, Scholars Press, 1975) Bowl 22, p. 69.

dom! Sbyrt Sbyrt Ywdg' Ywdb' Shtbyrt Sbyrt Ywdg' Ywdb' Sbyrt Shb-
yrt Ywdg' Ywdb' I have acted for your name. Amen.

13.9.8 Aramaic Magic Bowl:
For Protection of the Family[249]

*In this magic bowl we see how the bowls were used to protect all members of
the family from a wide variety of forces which would bring about misfortune
and disease.*

ॐ

Salvation from the heavens for Dadbeh the son of 'Asmanduk and for
Sharqoi the daughter of Dada, his wife, and for their sons and their
daughters and their house and their possessions, that they may have sons,
that they may live and be established and be protected from demons, from
devils, from bands (of spirits), from satans, from curses, from liliths, and
from monsters which appear to them. I adjure you, O angel which comes
down from heaven—as it is kneaded in the shape of a horn on which
honey is poured—the angel which does the will of his lord and which
walks upon the steps of his lord, Sa'u, even the one praised in heaven,
Sa'u, and his praise is in the earth, Semu.

They are filled with glory who endu[re] and remain pure from the
days of eternity. Their feet do not appear in the dances for the entire
world. They sit, they stand in their place, they blow like the blast, they
flash like the lightning. These will frustrate and ban all familiars, counter-
charms, necklace-charms, curses, invocations, knockings, rites, words,
demons, devils, bands (of spirits), liliths, idols, monsters, and everything
bad, that they may depart and go away from Dadbeh the son of
'Asmanduk and from Sharqoi the daughter of Dada, his wife and from
Ḥoniq and from Yasmin and from Kufitai and from Mahduk and from
Abraham and from Pannoi and from Shili, the children of Sharqoi, and
from their house, from their possessions, and from all their dwelling in
which they dwell, from this day and forever, In the name of Y-H-W-H of
hosts. Amen, Amen. Selah. May Y-H-W-H guard you from all evil, may
He guard your life.[250]

[The exterior reads:] For the inner room of the hall.[251]

---

249. Isbell, bowl 23, pp. 71–2.
250. Ps. 121:7.
251. Indicating where the bowl is to be buried.

14

Epilogue: The Hegemony of the Babylonian Talmud

By the time the talmudic period drew to a close, a variety of historical events had led to the ascendancy of the Babylonian Rabbis to leadership over those areas which came under Moslem control after 638 C.E. Babylonian Jewry almost in its entirety came under the sway of the Rabbinic sages whose authority was backed up by the exilarchate, even though there continued to be tensions between this civil institution and the Rabbinic class.

Both of the major Rabbinic academies were now located in Baghdad, the seat of the Islamic caliphate, which controlled much of the Jewish world. As a result, Babylonian Rabbis, under the leadership of the geonim, were successful in spreading their teachings throughout the far-flung reaches of Jewish settlement. By the time the gaonate entered into decline at the end of the first millennium C.E., the Babylonian Talmud had been fully established as the norm for Jewish practice.

Some sense of the nature and function of the Babylonian academies in the early Middle Ages can be gained from the account of Nathan ha-Bavli (text 14.1.1), which refers specifically to the *kallah* months in which large numbers of Babylonian students assembled at the geonic academies. The pomp and circumstance which surrounded the investiture of an exilarch are described by him as well (text 14.1.2). This text testifies also to the complex modus vivendi reached between the exilarch and the sages who, to a great extent, derived their power indirectly from the exilarch's official recognition by the Islamic rulers.

Several accounts exist tracing the succession of the Babylonian geonim. Abraham ibn Daud's *Sefer ha-Qabbalah* (text 14.1.3) is distinguished for its sense of historical development and for its detailed and, for the most part accurate, historical narrative. This text allows us to trace the continuity of geonic tradition and teaching, on the one hand, and, on the other hand, to highlight some of the major developments in the process of the solidification of talmudic Judaism in the early Middle Ages. This text deals almost exclusively with the bearers of talmudic learning, pausing only briefly to discuss efforts in other areas of Jewish intellectual development.

There is no question but that a full picture of this period must go way beyond talmudic studies to include developments in biblical studies, Hebrew language and linguistics, and Jewish philosophy and mysticism. Certainly, in some of these areas, the new Islamic environment, with its own attraction to aspects of the Greek philosophical tradition, played a major role. Nonetheless, in these other fields of Jewish learning, it was the continuity of talmudic tradition which paved the way for the immense creativity and expansion of intellectual horizons which Judaism manifested in medieval and modern times.

14.1.1 Nathan ha-Bavli: The Babylonian Academy[1]

Nathan ha-Bavli (the Babylonian) was a tenth century chronicler who probably lived in Baghdad. His writings are preserved only in fragments. He describes the conduct of the affairs of the Babylonian academies in his own day. While much of what he describes developed afterwards, aspects of these patterns had their origin in the talmudic period. He emphasizes the hierarchy based on respect for knowledge and authority which the scholars maintained. This text concerns those who participated in the Kallah study session in the months of Elul, at the end of the summer, and Adar in the winter, but who studied in their home locations during the rest of the year.

---

1. Trans. D. M. Goodblatt, *Rabbinic Instruction in Sasanian Babylonia* (Leiden: E. J. Brill, 1975), pp. 161–2.

And they gather together and come from everywhere in the *kallah* month, which is the month of Elul in the summer and Adar in the winter. And during the five months [since the previous *kallah*] each one of the disciples had been diligently studying at home the tractate announced to them by the *rosh yeshivah*[2] when they left him. In Adar he would say, "We will study tractate such-and-such in Elul." Likewise, in Elul he would announce to them, "We will study tractate such-and-such in Adar." And they all come and sit before the *rosh hayyeshivot* in Adar and Elul, and the *rosh yeshivah* supervises their study and tests them.

And this is the order in which they sit. The *rosh yeshivah* stands[3] at the head, and before him are ten men (comprising) what is called the "first row," all facing the *rosh yeshivah*. Of the ten who sit before him, seven of them are *rashe kallot*[4] and three are *haverim*.[5] They are called *rashe kallot* because each one of them is in charge of ten members of the Sanhedrin, and they are the ones called *allufim*.[6]

And this was the custom when one of the *rashe kallot* died. If he had a son who could take his place, the son inherits his father's place and sits in it, even if he were young. And likewise the *haverim* when one of them dies. If his son could take his place he sits in it, and no one can pass over his colleague. However, if the son cannot take his father's place but is worthy of sitting in one of the seven rows, he sits in it. And if he is not worthy to sit with them, he sits with the *bene rav*[7] and with the rest of the disciples who number 2400.

And the seventy (comprising) the Sanhedrin are the seven rows. The first row sits as we mentioned. In back of them are (another) ten (and so on) until (there are) seven rows, all of them facing the *rosh yeshivah*. All the disciples sit behind them without any fixed place. But in the seven rows each one has a fixed place, and no one sits in the place of his colleague. Even if one of the members of the seven rows was greater in wisdom than another, he may not be seated in the latter's place—for he did not inherit it from his father. However, they do increase his stipend because of his wisdom.

---

2. Head of the academy.
3. Some texts have "sits."
4. Heads of assemblies.
5. Literally "colleagues," but designating scholars.
6. Chiefs.
7. The students, literally, "sons of the teacher."

When the *rosh yeshivah* wants to test them in their studies, they all meet with him during the four Sabbaths of Adar.[8] He sits and the first row recite before him while the remaining rows listen in silence. When they reach a section requiring comment, they discuss it among themselves while the *rosh yeshivah* listens and considers their words. Then he reads and they are silent, for they know that he has already discerned the matter of their disagreement. When he finishes reading, he expounds the tractate which they studied during the winter, each one at home,[9] and in the process he explains what the disciples had disagreed over. Sometimes he asks them the interpretation of laws. They defer to one another and then to the *rosh yeshivah*, asking him the answer. And no one can speak to him until he gives permission. And (then) each one of them speaks according to his wisdom. And he expatiates on the interpretation of each law until everything is clear to them. When everything is fully clarified, one of the first row arises and publicly lectures on it until everyone understands. And all who see him standing know that he stands only to clarify the *baraita* which supports the tradition. The rest of the disciples closely examine it and carefully explain it. Thus they did all month long.

On the fourth Sabbath[10] the whole Sanhedrin and all the disciples are called, and the *rosh yeshivah* examines each one of them and interrogates them till he discerns who are the more accomplished students. When he notices one whose learning is deficient, he is harsh towards him, diminishes his stipend, rebukes him, indicates those areas in which he is deficient, and warns him that if he repeats his poor performance once more, his stipend will be completely cut off. Therefore, they would sharpen their wits and diligently apply themselves so that they would not make any mistakes before him regarding a matter of law.

None of the rows leaves him till he announces the tractate which each one should study at home. He does not have to inform the rest of the disciples, rather each one studies whatever tractate he wishes.

14.1.2 Nathan ha–Bavli: The Installation of an Exilarch[11]

Because of the lateness of this account, dating as it does to the Islamic era in which the exilarchate had developed considerably, it cannot provide a reliable picture of the exilarch in the talmudic era. Nevertheless, Nathan ha-Bavli

---

8. February/March.

9. This procedure assumes the existence already of written texts of the Talmud.

10. Of the *kallah* month.

11. Trans. B. Halper, *Post-Biblical Hebrew Literature, an Anthology* (Philadelphia: Jewish Publication Society, 1921), vol. 2, pp. 64–8.

gives us a sense of the glory of the exilarch in the Islamic age and of how Jewish self-government served as a unifying factor for Jews under the Caliphs.

༷

When the community agreed to appoint an exilarch, the two heads of the academies, with their pupils, the heads of the community, and the elders assembled in the house of a prominent man in Babylon, one of the great men of the generation, as, for instance, Netira,[12] or a similar man. That man in whose house the meeting took place was honored thereby, and it was regarded as a mark of distinction; his esteem was enhanced when the great men and the elders assembled in his house.

On Thursday they assembled in the synagogue, blessed the exilarch, and placed their hands on him. They blew the horn, that all the people, small and great, might hear. When the people heard the proclamation, every member of the community sent him a present, according to his power and means. All the heads of the community and the wealthy members sent him magnificent clothes and beautiful ornaments, vessels of silver and vessels of gold, each man according to his ability. The exilarch prepared a banquet on Thursday and on Friday, giving all kinds of food, and all kinds of drinks, and all kinds of dainties, as, for instance, different kinds of sweetmeats.

When he arose on Sabbath morning to go to the synagogue, many of the prominent men of the community met him to go with him to the synagogue. At the synagogue a wooden pulpit had been prepared for him on the previous day, the length of which was seven cubits, and the breadth of which was three cubits.[13] They spread over it magnificent coverings of silk, blue, purple, and scarlet, so that it was entirely covered, and nothing was seen of it. Under the pulpit there entered distinguished youths, with melodious and harmonious voices, who were well-versed in the prayers and all that appertains thereto.

The exilarch was concealed in a certain place together with the heads of the academies, and the youths stood under the pulpit. No man sat there. The precentor of the synagogue would begin the prayer, "Blessed be He who spoke,"[14] and the youths, after every sentence of that prayer, would respond: "Blessed be He." When he chanted the Psalm of the Sabbath Day (Psalm 92), they responded after him: "It is good to give thanks

---

12. A wealthy Baghdad businessman, who died in 916, and who was a major figure in the politics of the Babylonian Jewish community.

13. About 10½ x 4½ feet.

14. The benediction before the preliminary psalms (*Pesuqe de-Zimra*).

unto the Lord" (Ps. 92:2). All the people together read the "Verses of Song," (Ps. 145–150) until they finished them.

The precentor then arose, and began the prayer "The breath of all living,"[15] and the youths responded after him: "Shall bless Thy name"; he chanted a phrase, and they responded after him, until they reached the Qedushah,[16] which was said by the congregation with a low voice, and by the youths with a loud voice. Then the youths remained silent, and the precentor alone completed the prayer up to "He redeemed Israel."[17]

All the people then stood up to say the Eighteen Benedictions.[18] When the preceptor, repeating these Benedictions, reached the "Qedushah," the youths responded after him with a loud voice: "The Holy God." When he had completed the prayer, all the congregation sat down. When all the people were seated, the exilarch came out from the place where he was concealed. Seeing him come out, all the people stood up, until he sat down on the pulpit, which had been made for him. Then the head of the Academy of Sura came out after him, and after exchanging courtesies with the exilarch, sat down on the pulpit. Then the head of the Academy of Pumbeditha came out, and he, too, made a bow, and sat down at his left.[19]

During all this time the people stood upon their feet, until these three were properly seated: the exilarch sat in the middle, the head of the Academy of Sura at his right, and the head of the Academy of Pumbeditha at his left, empty places being left between the heads of the academies and the exilarch. Upon his place, over his head, above the pulpit, they spread a magnificent covering, fastened with cords of fine linen and purple.

Then the precentor put his head under the exilarch's canopy in front of the pulpit, and with blessings that had been prepared for him on the preceding days he blessed him with a low voice, so that they should be heard only by those who sat around the pulpit, and by the youths who were under it. When he blessed him, the youths responded after him with a loud voice; "Amen!" All the people were silent until he had finished his blessings.

---

15. The benediction after the preliminary psalms.

16. This refers to the *Qedushah de-Yozer*, the recitation of God's sanctification in the blessing preceding the Shema. See text 13.2.2.

17. The benediction of the reading of the Shema, recited immediately before saying the Amidah (text 13.2.4).

18. The Sabbath Amidah.

19. Both of these talmudic academies were by this time located in Baghdad, the seat of the exilarch.

Then the exilarch would begin to expound matters pertaining to the biblical portion of that day, or would give permission to the head of the academy of Sura to deliver the exposition, and the head of the academy of Sura would give permission to the head of the academy of Pumbeditha. They would thus show deference to one another, until the head of the academy of Sura began to expound. The interpreter[20] stood near him, and repeated his words to the people. He expounded with awe, closing his eyes, and wrapping himself up with his tallit, so that his forehead was covered.

While he was expounding, there was not in the congregation one that opened his mouth, or chirped, or uttered a sound. If he became aware that anyone spoke, he would open his eyes, and fear and terror would fall upon the congregation. When he finished his exposition, he would begin with a question, saying: "Verily, you need to learn. . . ." And an old man who was wise, understanding, and experienced would stand up, and make a response on the subject and sit down. Then the precentor stood up, and recited the Qaddish.[21] When he reached the words, "during your life and in your days," he would say: "During the life of our prince the exilarch, and during your life, and during the life of all the house of Israel."

When he had finished the Qaddish, he would bless the exilarch, and then the heads of the academies. Having finished the blessing, he would stand up and say: "Such and such a sum was contributed by such-and-such a city and its villages"; and he mentioned all the cities which sent contributions for the academy, and blessed them. Afterwards he blessed the men who busied themselves in order that the contributions should reach the academies. Then he would take out the Book of the Law,[22] and call up a priest, and a Levite after him.

While all the people were standing, the precentor of the synagogue would bring down the Book of the Law to the exilarch, who took it in his hands, stood up, and read in it. The heads of the academies stood up with him, and the head of the academy of Sura translated it to him.[23] Then he would give back the Book of the Law to the precentor, who returned it to the Ark. When the precentor reached the Ark, he sat down in his place, and then all the men sat down in their places. After the

---

20. Actually an announcer who relayed the exposition in a loud voice to the audience.

21. A prayer of sanctification of God which signals transition from one part of the service to another.

22. The Torah scroll.

23. It was customary to translate the Torah reading into Aramaic which was the vernacular, and this was done by the head of the academy in Sura.

exilarch, the instructors read in the Book of the Law, and they were followed by the pupils of the heads of the academies; but the heads of the academies themselves did not read on that day, because someone else preceded them.[24]

When the Maftir[25] read the last portion, a prominent and wealthy man stood near him, and translated it. This was a mark of distinction and honor for that man. When he finished reading, the precentor again blessed the exilarch by the Book of the Law, and all the readers who were experienced and well-versed in the prayers stood round the Ark, and said: "Amen!" Afterwards he blessed the two heads of the academies, and returned the Book of the Law to its place. They then prayed the additional prayer,[26] and left the synagogue.

14.1.3 *Sefer ha-Qabbalah* VI: The Succession of Geonim[27]

Abraham ibn Daud, writing in the twelfth century, traced the history of the geonim from the end of the talmudic period through the last gaon, Rav Hai. This account emphasizes the continuity of the geonic tradition while at the same time testifying to the internal and external reasons for the decline of centralized Rabbinic authority. This decline led to the growth of local centers of Jewish learning throughout the world.

℘

The first generation of the heads of the academy of Pumbeditha: Rav Ḥinena of Nehar Peqod served as head of the academy for eight years until 4457[28] [696/7 C.E.]. His successor was Rav Hilai ha-Levi, who served as head of the academy for eighteen years and passed away in 4475 [714/15 C.E.].

The second generation: Rav Jacob of Nehar Peqod served as head of the academy for eighteen years and passed away in 4493 [732/3 C.E.]. His successor, Rav Samuel—a descendant of Amemar, the colleague of Rav Ashi—served as head [of the academy] for eighteen years and passed away in 4511 [750/1 C.E.]. These were of Pumbeditha.

---

24. Once the exilarch had been called up, the heads of the academies (geonim) could no longer be called.

25. The man called up to the last portion of the Torah reading who then read the prophetic portion (haftarah).

26. Known as the Musaf service, recited on Sabbaths and festivals.

27. Trans. G. D. Cohen, *A Critical Edition with a Translation and Notes of The Book of Tradition (Sefer ha-Qabbalah) by Abraham ibn Daud* (Philadelphia: Jewish Publication Society of America, 1967), pp. 46–62.

28. These numbers are according to the "year of creation," *anno mundi*.

During the terms of these four heads of the academy, the following served as heads of the academy of Mata Meḥasya:[29] Rav Huna bar Joseph [began to serve] in 4449 [688/9 C.E.]. His successor was Rav Ḥiyya of Messena. The latter was succeeded by Mar Yanqa, who is the same as Raba bar Natronai and who became head [of the academy] in 4479 [718/19 C.E.]. His successor was Rav Judah Gaon. He was succeeded by Rav Joseph [who died] in 4499 [738/9 C.E.]. He was succeeded by Rav Samuel bar Mari [who died] in 4508 [747/8 C.E.]. In the days of this Rav Samuel there lived Rav Simeon Qayyara, who, however, was not appointed gaon. He composed *Halakhot Gedolot*[30] in 1052 of the Seleucid Era, which is equivalent to 4501 [740/1 C.E.] or the third year of the term of Rav Samuel bar Mari and the eighth year of the term of Rav Samuel the descendant of Amemar. He cited traditions "in the name of Kohen-Ẓedeq." However, we have no knowledge of a gaon of his days by the name of Kohen-Ẓedeq. It may, therefore, be that this Kohen-Ẓedeq, who had been his master, was a scholar who had not been appointed [gaon]. After Rav Samuel bar Mari there was a great scholar [by the name of] Rav Aḥa of Shabḥah, who composed his *She'iltot* on all the commandments specified in the Torah.[31] This book, which has survived to this day, was examined and scrutinized by all who lived after him; we have heard that to this day not a single error has been detected in it.

Nevertheless, this Rav Aḥa was not appointed gaon because of the hostility of the exilarch of his generation toward him. Instead, he appointed Rav Aḥa's secretary, whose name was Rav Natronai. Incensed at this, Rav Aḥa went off from Babylonia to Palestine where he passed away. Rav Natronai served as head [of the academy] for thirteen years until 4521 [760/1 C.E.]. These eight heads of the academy in Mata Meḥasya served during the terms of the four heads of the academy of Pumbeditha.

The third generation of geonim in Pumbeditha: After the passing of Rav Samuel in 4511 [750/1 C.E.], Rav Mari ha-Kohen of Nehar Peqod served as head in Pumbeditha for eight years and passed away in 4519 [758/9 C.E.]. He was succeeded by Rav Ada [who served] for half a year and passed away in the very same year. He was succeeded by Rav Yehudai [who served] for three years and a half and passed away in 4523 [762/3

---

29. Mata Meḥasya in southern Babylonia was the location of the academy of Sura. Originally, they were separate places, but they came to be identified as one, probably as the result of their close proximity.

30. A code of Jewish law.

31. A work of exposition of the weekly Torah portions which quotes extensively from the Babylonian Talmud, the Midrashim and other traditions.

C.E.]. He composed *Halakhot Pesuqot*,[32] which he compiled from *Hala-khot Gedolot*. He was blind.

In his days there lived Anan and his son Saul, may the name of the wicked rot. Although this Anan was a descendant of the house of David and, at first, a scholar as well, some blemish was detected in him, and he was, accordingly, not appointed gaon; nor was he vouchsafed divine assistance to become exilarch. Because of the sordid envy in his heart, he revolted and set out to seduce the Jews away from the tradition of the sages, which the latter had taken over from the prophets—[all of them] trustworthy witnesses reporting in the name of trustworthy witnesses,[33] as we have set forth in this book. Thus he became an elder who rebels against the decision of the court "in disregarding"[34] the judges. He composed books, set up disciples, and fabricated "statutes that were not good, and ordinances whereby they should not live" (Ezek. 20:25). Alas, after the destruction of the Temple the heretics had dwindled until Anan came and gave them strength. . . .[35]

Following that,[36] Rav Kohen-Zedeq Gaon bar Isomai Gaon was appointed [and he served] for ten years and a half. He was succeeded by Rav Sar-Shalom bar Rav Boaz [who served] for ten years. His successor was Rav Natronai Gaon bar Rav Hilai Gaon bar Rav Mari [who served] for five years. He was succeeded by Rav Amram bar Sheshna [who served] for eighteen years.[37] He sent an order of the liturgy to Spain.[38]

After that, there was no scholar in Mata Mehasya worthy of appointment. However, David ben Zakkai the exilarch chose a certain weaver whose name was Rav Yom-Tov and appointed him.

---

32. A code of Jewish law.

33. Passing on the oral law accurately and faithfully.

34. Cf. Deut. 17:12.

35. This is an explanation of the founding of the Karaite movement, described here as based on personal bitterness on the part of Anan who was not appointed to his desired post. The Karaites believed in the literal meaning of the biblical text and not in the oral law or traditional interpretation. They therefore rejected the Talmud. Nonetheless, their customs reflected their own innovations. Anan's most famous opponent was Rav Saadiah Gaon (al-Fayyumi). In fact, Karaism resulted from the amalgamation of age-old sectarian traditions with opposition to the hegemony of the Babylonian Talmud, primarily in Babylonia's eastern provinces.

36. Following a hiatus in the gaonate of Sura for two years. Ibn Daud is here listing geonim of Mata Mehasya who served in the period of 825–881.

37. Died ca. 875. By 858 he was certainly serving as gaon, a title he seems to have had already in the days of his predecessor.

38. This is the first mention of a written compilation of Jewish prayers. This collection reflected the prayer service as it was developed by the Babylonian amoraim with considerable additions stemming from the geonic period.

Subsequently, he sent word to Egypt and brought Rav Saadiah al-Fayyumi[39] from there. Accordingly, he became head of the academy in Mata Meḥasya [and served] for two years. After that, a great quarrel and dispute broke out between him and David ben Zakkai the Prince; for these exilarchs were not men of integrity, but [actually] used to purchase their authority from the kings like publicans. Once, David ben Zakkai was involved in a litigation in which he obtained a favorable judgment by improper means. He then sent it to Rav Saadiah to countersign, but the latter refused. He then sent it a second time through his son Zakkai in order to coerce Rav Saadiah into signing. The former said to him: "If you do not countersign, I will strike your head with a shoe." At once all of the members of the academy became infuriated and, arising to a man, struck the son of the Prince considerably with their shoes. So, he went to his father in utter disgrace. His father then invoked the support of the government[40] and that of a large faction of the community. Rav Saadiah [found support] in another faction of the community, and they appointed Josiah ben Zakkai as exilarch in place of his brother David. After that, David gained the upper hand with the help of the government and deposed his brother Josiah. He then sought to put Rav Saadiah to death, and Rav Saadiah went into hiding for approximately seven years. While in seclusion he composed all of his books. Now Rav Saadiah was of the nobility of [the tribe of] Judah, of the descendants of Shelah the son of Judah, and of the seed of Rav Ḥanina ben Dosa. [Then] David ben Zakkai appointed Rav Joseph bar Rav Jacob bar Rav Mordecai. Subsequently, however, David the Prince and Rav Saadiah made peace; nevertheless, Rav Joseph was not removed nor Rav Saadiah reinstated to the gaonate.

Rav Joseph served as gaon for fourteen years. After that David ben Zakkai died. And after him Rav Saadiah passed away in 4702 [941/2 C.E.], when he was about fifty years of age,[41] of black bile,[42] after having composed any number of worthwhile books and having accomplished great good for Israel. He wrote refutations of the heretics[43] and of those who denied the [authority of the] Torah. One of the latter was Ḥiwi al-Kalbi,[44] who fabricated a scripture out of his own mind. Rav Saadiah testified that he saw teachers of children giving instruction from it—both in

---

39. Known as Saadia Gaon (882–942) from the Fayyum, the Nile Delta region in Egypt.

40. The Islamic Caliphate.

41. Actually, he was 60 years old.

42. Usually taken to mean the disease of melancholia, but it may refer to some other degenerative disease.

43. The Karaites.

the form of books and of tablets—to [their] pupils, until Rav Saadiah succeeded in overcoming them. Now the rest of the acts of Rav Saadiah and the goodness which he had shown unto Israel, behold, they are written in *Sefer ha-Galuy*[45] and in the epistle which his son Rav Dosa wrote to Rav Ḥisdai the Nasi bar Rav Isaac, may he rest in glory. After the passing of Rav Saadiah the academy of Mata Meḥasya declined steadily, and Rav Joseph finally emigrated to the city of al-Baẓra and died there.

The sixth generation [of geonim] in Pumbeditha: After Rav Hai bar Rav David, Rav Qimoi bar Rav Aḥunai became head [of the academy] in 4650 [889/90 C.E.] for eight years and a half; and he passed away in 4659 [898/9 C.E.]. He was succeeded by Rav Judah bar Rav Samuel, the grandfather of Rav Sherira, who passed away in 4671 [910/11 C.E.]....

Then Rav Ḥananiah, the father of Rav Sherira, became head [of the academy] for five years and a half, and he passed away in 4701 [940/1 C.E.].... After the passing of Rav Ḥananiah, Rav Aaron ha-Kohen ben Sarjada [became head of the academy].... He passed away in 4720 [959/60 C.E.]. He was succeeded by Rav Nehemiah [who served] for eight years.

He was succeeded by Rav Sherira [in 967/8 C.E.], who lived a very long life, in fact for about one hundred years.[46] When he saw that his life was prolonged and that his son, Rav Hai, was worthy of being head of the academy, he stepped down in favor of his son. The latter was Rav Hai Gaon bar Rav Sherira Gaon. He spread Torah abroad throughout Jewry more than all of the other geonim, and by his light walked those who sought the Torah from east and west. After living for ninety-nine years, he passed away on the eve of the last day of Passover in the year 1349 of the Seleucid Era, which is equivalent to 4798 [1037/8 C.E.]. Of the geonim before him there was none like him, and he was the last of the geonim. He was of the house of David, of the royal line, of the descendants of Zerubbabel the son of Shealtiel and of the princes and exilarchs who came after him. I have seen his seal affixed to documents which he issued, and a lion was engraved in it just as there had been on the pennant of the camp of Judah and on the pennants of the kings of Judah.

---

44. A skeptic who raised objections to the Bible in the second half of the ninth century. "Kalbi" is probably an error from "Balki," meaning that he came from Balk in Khorasan, Persia. His work survives only in quotations by his opponents.

45. A work by Saadiah surviving only in fragments.

46. He lived from ca. 906 to 1006 C.E.

However, ever since the beginning of Muslim rule, the exilarchs did not exercise their authority fittingly. In fact, they used to buy their position with large sums of money, like publicans, and were worthless shepherds. Consequently, his ancestors did not wish to become exilarchs, and they turned to the gaonate instead. He was [also] descended from Rabbah bar Abbuha.[47] Some lawless Jews denounced Rav Sherira and Rav Hai, and the king of Babylonia[48] imprisoned them, confiscated all of their possessions and left them no source of support whatever. However, Rav Sherira did manage to get some aid, although he was at the time approximately one hundred years old, and they were not deposed from the gaonate. Rav Sherira became gaon in 4728 [967/8 C.E.] and Rav Hai in 4758 [997/8 C.E.], their combined gaonate lasting seventy years: Rav Sherira's for thirty and Rav Hai's for forty. The latter's generation is the eighth generation of the gaonate.

In his days the head of the academy in Mata Mehasya was Rav Samuel ha-Kohen ben Hofni, Rav Hai's father in-law. He, too, composed many books. He passed away during Rav Hai's term, four years before the death of Rav Hai. However, the members of Rav Hai's academy appointed Hezekiah the Exilarch, the grandson of David ben Zakkai, to the see of Rav Hai, of blessed memory. He served for a term of two years. Then informers denounced him to the king, and the latter imprisoned him, put him in chains, tortured him grievously and left him no survivors. His two sons fled to Spain to Rav Joseph ha-Levi the Nagid ben Rav Samuel the Nagid, who had great affection for Hezekiah the Exilarch and head of the academy. They remained there with him until the time of the massacre in Granada, when the Nagid was killed. One of the sons of Hezekiah then fled to the land of Saragossa where he married and had children. Afterwards, his descendants migrated to Christian Spain. One of them was Rav Hiyya ben al-Daudi, who passed away in Castile in 4914 [1153/4 C.E.]. After him there did not remain in Spain a single person known to be of the house of David.

After Hezekiah the Exilarch and head of the academy, there were no more academies or geonim.[49]

---

47. A talmudic sage.

48. The Muslim caliph.

49. In fact, the gaonate continued beyond this time, but the geonim were no longer recognized beyond Iraq. The decentralized local Rabbinate now took over its functions in providing for the future development of Jewish law.

Bibliography

Beyer, K., *Die aramäischen Texte vom Toten Meer, Erganzungsband* (Göttingen: Vandenhoeck & Ruprecht, 1994)

Birnbaum, P., *Daily Prayer Book* (New York: Hebrew Publishing Company, 1949).

Bokser, B., L. H. Schiffman, *Yerushalmi Pesaḥim* (The Talmud of the Land of Israel: A Preliminary Translation and Explanation, vol. 13; Chicago Studies in the History of Judaism; Chicago: University of Chicago Press, 1994).

Braude, W. G., I. J. Kapstein, *Pesikta de-Rab Kahana, Rav Kahana's Compilation of Discourses for Sabbaths and Festal Days* (Philadelphia: Jewish Publication Society, 1975).

Cary, E., *Dio's Roman History VIII* (Loeb Classical Library 176; Cambridge, MA: Harvard University Press; London: William Heinemann, 1925).

Charlesworth, J. H., ed., *The Old Testament Pseudepigrapha* (2 vols.; Garden City, NY: Doubleday, 1983–5).

Cohen, G. D., *A Critical Edition with a Translation and Notes of The Book of Tradition (Sefer ha-Qabbalah) by Abraham ibn Daud* (Philadelphia: Jewish Publication Society of America, 1967).

Colson, F. H., *Philo VIII* (Loeb Classical Library 341; Cambridge, MA: Harvard; London: William Heinemann, 1939).

———, *Philo IX* (Loeb Classical Library 363; Cambridge, MA: Harvard; London: William Heinemann, 1941).

Conybeare, F., "Antiochus Strategos' Account of the Sack of Jerusalem in A.D. 614," *English Historical Review* 25 (1910), pp. 506-13.

763

Dewing, H. B., *Procopius VI: The Anecdota or Secret History* (Loeb Classical Library 290; Cambridge, MA: Harvard University Press; London: William Heinemann, 1935).

Dewing, H. B., with the collaboration of G. Downey, *Procopius VII: Buildings* (Loeb Classical Library 343; Cambridge, MA: Harvard University Press; London: William Heinemann, 1940).

Epstein, I., ed., *The Babylonian Talmud* (35 volumes; London: Soncino Press, 1935-52).

Falls, T. B., *Writings of St. Justin Martyr* (Washington, DC: The Catholic University Press of America, 1948).

Feldman, L. H., "Diaspora Synagogues," in *Sacred Realm*, ed. S. Fine (Oxford: Oxford University Press; New York: Yeshiva University Museum, 1996).

Feldman, L. H., and M. Reinhold, ed., *Jewish Life and Thought among Greeks and Romans* (Minneapolis: Fortress Press, 1996).

Fitzmyer, J. and D. J. Harrington, *A Manual of Palestinian Aramaic Texts* (Biblica et Orientalia 34; Rome: Biblical Institute Press, 1978).

Frey, J.-B., *Corpus Inscriptionum Iudicarum* II (Rome: Pontificio Instituo di Archeologia Cristiana, 1952).

García Martínez, F., *The Dead Sea Scrolls Translated* (trans. W. G. E. Watson; New York; Leiden: E. J. Brill, 1994).

Geller, B. H., *The Fourth-Century Jewish "Revolt" During the Reign of Gallus: Archaeological and Literary Evidence and Background Issues* (unpublished).

Glatzer, N. N., *The Passover Haggadah* (New York: Schocken Books, 1953).

Goldberg, N., *The Passover Haggadah* (Hoboken, NJ: Ktav, 1973).

Goodblatt, D. M., *Rabbinic Instruction in Sasanian Babylonia* (Leiden: E. J. Brill, 1975).

Grafman, R., "The Rehob Inscription: A Translation," in *Ancient Synagogues Revealed*, ed. L. I. Levine (Jerusalem: Israel Exploration Society, 1981), pp. 152-3.

Green, W. M., *Saint Augustine: The City of God Against the Pagans,* vol. 2 (Loeb Classical Library 412; Cambridge, MA: Harvard University Press; London: William Heinemann, 1963).

Halper, B., *Post-Biblical Hebrew Literature, An Anthology* (Philadelphia: Jewish Publication Society, 1921).

Heinemann, J. with J. J. Petuchowski, *Literature of the Synagogue* (New York: Behrman, 1975).

Hoffleit, H. B., *Plutarch's Moralia VIII* (Loeb Classical Library 424; Cambridge, MA: Harvard University Press; London: William Heinemann, 1969).

Horbury, W. and D. Noy, *Jewish Inscriptions of Graeco-Roman Egypt* (Cambridge: Cambridge University Press, 1992).

Horovitz, H. S. and I. A. Rabin, *Mekhilta' de-Rabbi Ishmael* (Jerusalem: Bamberger & Wahrmann, 1960).

Isaac, E., "1 Enoch," in *The Old Testament Pseudepigrapha*, ed. J. H. Charlesworth (Garden City, NY: Doubleday, 1983) I, pp. 5–89.

Isbell, C. D., *Corpus of the Aramaic Incantation Bowls* (Society of Biblical Literature Dissertation Series 17; Missoula, MT: Scholars Press, 1975).

Jones, W. H. S., *Pausanius I: Description of Greece* (Loeb Classical Library 93; Cambridge, MA: Harvard University Press; London: William Heinemann, 1918).

Kee, H. C., "Testaments of the Twelve Patriarchs," in *The Old Testament Pseudepigrapha*, ed. J. H. Charlesworth (Garden City, NY: Doubleday, 1983) I, pp. 775–828.

Lake, K., *Eusebius: The Ecclesiastical History*, vol. 1 (Loeb Classical Library 153; Cambridge, MA: Harvard University Press; London: William Heinemann, 1926).

Lauterbach, J. Z., *Mekhilta de-Rabbi Ishmael* (JPS Library of Jewish Classics; Philadelphia: Jewish Publication Society, 1976).

Lehrman, S. M., *Midrash Rabbah* (London: Soncino Press, 1977).

Leon, H. J., *The Jews of Ancient Rome*, updated edition, with appendix by C. Osiek (Peabody, MA: Hendrickson, 1995).

Levine, L. I., "The Inscription in the `En-Gedi Synagogue," in *Ancient Synagogues Revealed*, ed. L. I. Levine (Jerusalem: Israel Exploration Society, 1981), pp. 140–45.

———, *The Rabbinic Class of Roman Palestine in Late Antiquity* (Jerusalem: Yad Izhak ben-Zvi; New York: Jewish Theological Seminary of America, 1989).

Lewis, N., *The Documents from the Bar Kokhba Period in the Cave of Letters: Greek Papyri* (Jerusalem: Israel Exploration Society, The Hebrew University, The Shrine of the Book, 1989).

Lewy, H., et al., *Three Jewish Philosophers* (New York: Harper & Row, 1965).

Lieberman, S., *Tosefta, Nashim* 2 (New York: Jewish Theological Seminary of America, 1973).

———, *Midrash Devarim Rabbah* (Jerusalem: Wahrmann, 1964/5).

Linder, A., *The Jews in Roman Imperial Legislation* (Detroit: Wayne State University; Jerusalem: Israel Academy of Sciences and Humanities, 1987).

Montgomery, J. A., *Aramaic Incantation Texts from Nippur* (Philadelphia: The University Museum, 1913).

Moore, C. H., *Tacitus III: Histories 4–5 and Annals 1–3* (Loeb Classical Library 249; Cambridge, MA: Harvard University Press; London: William Heinemann, 1931).

Naveh, J. *'Al Pesipas va-'Even* (Jerusalem: Israel Exploration Society, 1977/8).

———, and S. Shaked, *Amulets and Magic Bowls: Aramaic Incantations of Late Antiquity* (Jerusalem: Magnes Press, the Hebrew University; Leiden: E. J. Brill, 1985).

Neusner, J., *Aphrahat and Judaism* (Leiden: E. J. Brill, 1971).

———, *From Politics to Piety: The Emergence of Pharisaic Judaism* (Englewood Cliffs, NJ: Prentice-Hall, 1973).

———, *A History of the Jews in Babylonia*, vols. 1, 4 (Leiden: E. J. Brill, 1969).

———, *The Tosefta* (New York: Ktav, 1977–80).

Peters, F., *Jerusalem* (Princeton: Princeton University Press, 1985).

Pharr, C., *The Theodosian Code and Novels, and the Sirmondian Constitutions: a Translation with Commentary, Glossary, and Bibliography* (New York: Greenwood Press, 1969; reprint of Princeton University Press, 1952).

Porten, B. *The Elephantine Papyri in English* (Leiden; New York: E. J. Brill, 1996).

———, and A. Yardeni, *Textbook of Aramaic Documents from Ancient Egypt* (Jerusalem: The Hebrew University, Department of the History of the Jewish People, Texts and Studies for Students, 1986).

Preisigke, F., F. Bilabel, and E. Kiessling, ed., *Sammelbuch griechischer Urkunden aus Agypten* 5 (Heidelberg and Weisbaden, 1934–55).

Pritz, R. A., *Nazarene Jewish Christianity* (Leiden: E. J. Brill; Jerusalem: Magnes Press, 1988).

Rabinowich, N. D., *The Iggeres of Rav Sherira Gaon* (Jerusalem: Moznaim, 1988).

Rackham, H., *Pliny: Natural History*, vol. 2 (Loeb Classical Library 352; Cambridge, MA; London: William Heinemann, 1942).

Ramsey, G. G., *Juvenal and Persius* (Loeb Classical Library 91; Cambridge, MA; London: William Heinemann, 1940).

Ratner, B., ed., *Midrash Seder 'Olam* (New York: Talmudical Research Institute, 1966).

————, *Revised Standard Version Apocrypha* (New York: National Council of Churches, 1957).

————, *Revised Standard Version of the Bible* (New York: National Council of Churches, 1971).

Rolfe, J. C., *Suetonius*, vol. 2 (Loeb Classical Library 38; Cambridge, MA: Harvard University Press; London: William Heinemann, 1914).

Rosenthal, E. S., and Lieberman, S., *Yerushalmi Neziqin* (Jerusalem: Israel Academy of Sciences and Humanities, 1983).

Schechter, S., "Genizah Specimens," *JQR* O.S. 10 (1898), pp. 656-8.

Schiffman, L. H., *Who Was A Jew? Rabbinic Perspectives on the Jewish Christian Schism* (Hoboken, NJ: Ktav, 1985).

————, "The Conversion of Izates and Monobazus II in Bereshith Rabbah," *Josephus, Judaism, and Christianity*, ed. L. Feldman and G. Hata (Detroit: Wayne State University Press, 1987).

————, *Reclaiming the Dead Sea Scrolls* (Philadelphia: Jewish Publication Society, 1994).

Shutt, R. J. H., "Letter of Aristeas," in *The Old Testament Pseudepigrapha*, ed. J. H. Charlesworth (Garden City, NY: Doubleday, 1985) II, pp .7-34.

Stern, M., ed. *Greek Authors on Jews and Judaism* (Jerusalem: The Israel Academy of Sciences and Humanities, 1980).

Swartz, M. D., *Mystical Prayer in Ancient Judaism* (Tübingen: J. C. B. Mohr, 1992).

————, *Tanakh: A New Translation of the Holy Scriptures* (Philadelphia: The Jewish Publication Society, 1985).

Tcherikover, V. A. with A. Fuks, *Corpus Papyrorum Judaicarum* (Cambridge, MA: For Magnes Press, Hebrew University by Harvard University Press, 1957).

Thackeray, H. St. J., with R. Marcus, A. Wikgren, and L H. Feldman, *Josephus: in Nine Volumes* (Loeb Classical Library; Cambridge, MA: Harvard University Press; London: William Heinemann, 1976-79).

Theodor, J., and Albeck, Ch., *Midrash Bereshit Rabba* (3 vols.; Jerusalem: Wahrmann Books, 1965).

Townsend, J. T., *Midrash Tanhuma* (Hoboken, NJ: Ktav, 1989).

Walford, E., *The Ecclesiastical History of Sozomen* (London: Henry G. Bohn, 1855).

Weissbach, F. H., *Die Keilschriften der Achmeniden* (Vorderasiatische Bibliothek 3; Leipzig: J. C. Hinrichs, 1911).

Whiston, W. *The Works of Josephus: Complete and Unabridged*, new updated edition (Peabody, MA: Hendrickson Publishers, 1987).

Whitby, M. and M. Whitby, *Chronicon Paschale, 284-628 AD* (Liverpool: Liverpool University Press, 1989).

Wintermute, O. S., "Jubilees," in *The Old Testament Pseudepigrapha*, ed. J. H. Charlesworth (Garden City, NY: Doubleday, 1985) II, pp. 35-142.

Wright, W. C., *The Works of the Emperor Julian,* vol. 3 (Loeb Classical Library 157; Cambridge, MA: Harvard University Press; London: William Heinemann, 1923).

Yadin, Y., *Bar-Kokhba: The Rediscovery of the Legendary Hero of the Last Jewish Revolt against Imperial Rome* (London: Weidenfeld & Nicholson, 1971).

———, J. C. Greenfield, A. Yardeni, "Babatha's *Ketubba,*" *Israel Exploration Journal* 44 (1994), pp. 79-84.

Yonge, C. D., *The Works of Philo* (Peabody, MA: Hendrickson, 1993).

Zundel, H., *Midrash Tanhuma* (Tel Aviv: Pardes, no date).

Index of Sources